MW00574885

LAW'S RELATIONS

Law's Relations

A RELATIONAL THEORY OF SELF, AUTONOMY, AND LAW

Jennifer Nedelsky

OXFORD
UNIVERSITY PRESS

OXFORD
UNIVERSITY PRESS

Oxford University Press, Inc., publishes works that furthers
Oxford University's objective of excellence
in research, scholarship, and education.

Oxford   New York
Auckland   Cape Town   Dar es Salaam   Hong Kong   Karachi
Kuala Lumpur   Madrid   Melbourne   Mexico City   Nairobi
New Delhi   Shanghai   Taipei   Toronto

With offices in
Argentina   Austria   Brazil   Chile   Czech Republic   France   Greece
Guatemala   Hungary   Italy   Japan   Poland   Portugal   Singapore
South Korea   Switzerland   Thailand   Turkey   Ukraine   Vietnam

Copyright © 2011 by Oxford University Press

Published by Oxford University Press, Inc.
198 Madison Avenue, New York, New York 10016

www.oup.com

Oxford is a registered trademark of Oxford University Press.

All rights reserved. No part of this publication may be reproduced,
stored in a retrieval system, or transmitted, in any form or by any means,
electronic, mechanical, photocopying, recording, or otherwise,
without the prior permission of Oxford University Press.

Library of Congress Cataloging-in-Publication Data
Nedelsky, Jennifer.
    Law's relations : a relational theory of self, autonomy, and law / Jennifer Nedelsky.
        p.   cm.
    Includes bibliographical references and index.
    ISBN 978-0-19-514796-4 (alk. paper)
 1. Law—Psychological aspects.   2. Interpersonal relations.   3. Autonomy (Psychology)   I. Title.
    K346.N434 2011
    340'.19—dc22   2011002751

1 3 5 7 9 8 6 4 2

Printed in the United States of America
on acid-free paper

For Joe, Michael, and Daniel—the heart of my relations.

Table of Contents

Acknowledgments

THIS BOOK HAS been made possible by many things. Some of them are specific, personal, material. Those I gratefully acknowledge below. Others are more general. One of these general enabling factors was the rise of feminist theory as a significant form of scholarship in law and political science (as well as other disciplines). As I discuss in chapter 1, this book would not have been possible without the wider context of feminist scholarship and activism, and the transformations they continue to foster in the form and content of academic research. I have always been conscious of the importance of feminism for my work and grateful for the feminist scholars I saw as my interlocutors and as a central part of my audience. (Even as I was also conscious that the wonderful expansion of feminist scholarship over the long years I have been working on this book has meant that I have only directly engaged with a fraction of it.) I had, by contrast, much less of a sense of the growing importance of relational theory. I now find it in every field I encounter. It is there in theology, in biology, in physics, in psychology, and, of course, in ecology (see chapter 1, section II.D.iv and chapter 7 for some examples). When I first began this book, I was barely aware of these resonances in other fields. I was only looking to other variants of legal and political theory. Nevertheless, I am certain that this increasing prevalence of relational theory has helped welcome this book into the world. I now see *Law's Relations* as part of this larger constellation of relational approaches without which my aspirations for this book would not be possible.

This book has been a very long time in the making. I have, therefore, accumulated even more than the usual debts for support and assistance. Indeed, I think it is inevitable that I will fail to mention some of the people who offered helpful comments, inquiries, and research assistance over the years. Nevertheless, it is a pleasure to be able to thank some of those who have been particularly important.

Let me begin with an event that was crucial in the last stages of writing this book. Mayo Moran, dean of the Faculty of Law at the University of Toronto, had over the years inquired whether there was anything she could do to help to bring the book to fruition. In 2008 I took her up on her offer and asked her to provide financial support for a day-long workshop on my manuscript. She generously agreed. Even more generously, seven colleagues took time out their busy schedules to read and comment on chapters and attend the workshop. Rebecca Johnson of the University of Victoria Faculty of Law introduced me to the wonders of Skype, which enabled her and her colleagues, Hester Lessard and Maneesha Deckha, to participate long distance. My University of Toronto colleagues Kerry Rittich and Karen Knop also each took on responsibility for a chapter. My longtime friend and colleague Jane (Jenny) Mansbridge traveled from Harvard to participate, as did Frank Michelman. Jenny also gave wonderful summary remarks and offered still more in follow-up e-mail exchanges. In addition to these chapter "presenters," many of my colleagues and graduate students from both law and political science attended and contributed to excellent conversations. I felt proud that the graduate students had been able to see such a fine example of supportive, collegial critique and exchange. The workshop was further facilitated by my excellent research assistants, Jess Eisen and Iffat Sajjad, who took detailed notes, allowing me to reflect on (and discuss with them) the many ideas that arose in the conversation. The workshop was a great experience for me, and it significantly shaped the final outcome of the book. I am very grateful to all who participated.

I owe a further debt to Frank Michelman, who was an advisor and supporter for my first book as well. It was nice to have that sense of continuity at the workshop. The further debt is with respect to the "genealogy" of the book's title. I first thought of the title *Law's Relations* as a kind of successor to Frank's "Law's Republic," a title that provoked a reminder of Ronald Dworkin's *Law's Empire*.

The University of Toronto workshop was in May 2008. Fortunately for me, Brenna Bhandar invited me to spend several days as a visiting scholar at Kent Law School in the U.K. The following fall, therefore, I had the benefit of engaging with a very different set of questions about my manuscript. These conversations were crucial in reminding me that I had become somewhat preoccupied with trying to answer the critiques of egalitarian liberals, even though I was equally interested in reaching my fellow critics of liberalism. I am very grateful for the thoughtful engagement with my work offered by colleagues at Kent. And I am also grateful for the lovely hospitality offered by Toni Williams and Iain Ramsay who put me up during my stay. While in the U.K., I also had the opportunity to give a seminar at the Gender Institute of the London School of Economics, organized by Anne Phillips. Nicola Lacey offered excellent comments, one of her many helpful encounters with my work. I found the conversation in that seminar both interesting and helpful.

There have also been other venues in which I received particularly helpful comments. I presented drafts of what became chapter 6, "Reconceiving Rights and Constitutionalism," at the Law and Public Affairs Program at Princeton University in 2007 and at the University of Toronto Centre for Ethics in 2010. In 2003 I had the opportunity to have excellent discussions of draft chapters as a visitor to the University of Victoria colloquium on Legal, Political and Social Theory. Also in 2003, Ronalda Murphy offered her home and hospitality for a discussion of what became chapter 4. Her colleagues from Dalhousie University—Susan Sherwin, Jennifer Llewellyn, Jocelyn Downie, Dianne Poither—took the time to offer helpful comments on the draft. In 2002 I had an important set of conversations with Martha Minow, Molly Shanley, Traci Levi, and the audience at a round-table on "Can Relational Rights Answer the Critiques of Liberal Rights?" at the American Political Science Association annual meeting.

In addition to these more formal exchanges, friends, colleagues, and graduate students have taken the time to give me comments on drafts and/or talk with me about the project. I would particularly like to thank Kathryn Abrams, Amaya Alvez, Larissa Atkinson, Lisa Austin, Dan Avnon, Ryan Balot, Shelley Burtt, Joseph Carens, Kimberly Carter, Geneviève Cartier, Mitzi Cowell, Carys Craig, Yasmin Dawood, Michael Fakhri, Jane Flax, Donna Freireich, Andrew Green, Roger Hutchinson, Sonia Lawrence, Robert Leckey, Audrey Macklin, Martha Minow, Ronalda Murphy, Zoran Oklopcic, Tobold Rollo, Sean Rehaag, Sara Ruddick, Cameron Sabadoz, David Schneiderman, Martha Shaffer, Molly Shanley, Joe Singer, Simon Stern, Leslie Thiele, Mary Tomlinson, James Tully, and Iris Young. Rod Macdonald generously provided help on legal pluralism, which, in the end, I was only barely able to incorporate. I also have to single out Pamela Shime, who repeatedly, and at crucial junctures, gave me just the kind of detailed critique and encouragement that I needed. I am, again, very grateful to all of them.

I have also been extremely fortunate in the research assistants I have had. For several years Mary Liston, now a colleague at the University of British Columbia, provided not only excellent research assistance but valuable editorial help as well. Amy Smeltzer provided creative help for several months, Candice Telfer provided excellent assistance when I was revising a version of chapter 6, and Molly Leonard tracked down additional sources for me. Iffat Sajjad not only provided bibliographic help but also participated in many discussions of the manuscript after the workshop. Jennifer Simpson saw the manuscript through endless rounds of footnote searches and editorial amendments and saw to it that it was finally sent off to the publisher. She did her excellent work with dedication, care, and good cheer. Janani Shanmuganathan also helped track down sources in those final weeks. Finally, I have had the incredible good fortune to have Jess Eisen working with me on the manuscript during the months after the workshop and then turning out to be available at every further crucial juncture. She has consistently provided excellent research, meticulous editing, and substantive critique. Her final read through of the manuscript not only ensured that all details were attended to but also identified important points I needed to develop. And she helped me put the finishing touches on the copyediting. Having her keen mind part of this process has made this a better book.

As always, responsibility for any remaining errors rests with me.

Of course, having such fine research assistants takes money, and writing takes time. I am grateful for the financial support that made both possible. I received a Connaught Research Fellowship in the Social Sciences in 2000, an SSHRC Standard Research Grant for 2000–2003, and the Bora Laskin National Fellowship in Human Rights Research for 2000–2001. Despite the fact that I was quite sick during those years, the support was important for my work on this book. I also received small, but vitally important, grants from the Wright Foundation and the Faculty of Law Internal Grant funding. I would not have been able to finish the book without this support.

While the long process of writing this book was far more a labor of love than the tortured process of finishing my first book, there were still barriers to overcome before I could finally finish it. In the early stages, Kristi Magraw was important in helping me to work those through. And I must thank Ann Yeoman for (among other things) helping me to finally write with sustained focus and joy—as well reminding me to keep the importance of the work in perspective.

Last, but actually first and foremost, I am deeply grateful to my husband, Joe Carens, for his love, support, and forbearance. It is a sad thing that books so often seem to require an expression of gratitude to loved ones who put up with undivided attention being focused on a manuscript. In a better world, structured to support the relationships that really matter the most, this wouldn't happen. But it does, and it did in this case. So I offer my love and my gratitude, and my hopes that it won't happen again next time.

LAW'S RELATIONS

Introduction

Relationships are central to people's lives—to who we are, to the capacities we are able to develop, to what we value, what we suffer, and what we are able to enjoy.[1] This book makes that relational dimension of human experience central to the concepts and institutions by which we organize our collective lives.

The self, autonomy, and law form a constellation of ideas, practices, and institutions. In the prevailing Anglo–American version, human beings are seen as essentially separate from one another. Relationships exist, of course, but they are not treated as constitutive. I want to reconstruct this constellation so that relationships become central to each part of it. The individual self is, then, constituted in an ongoing, dynamic way by the relationships through which each person interacts with others. The values that people experience as central to their selfhood, to the possibility of their flourishing, are made possible through relationships. Autonomy, for example, comes into being (or is harmed) through relationships with parents, teachers, and employers. And law, including rights, is one of the chief mechanisms (both rhetorical and institutional) for shaping the relationships that foster or undermine values such as autonomy.

At one level, what I am advocating is just a shift in emphasis that moves relationship from the periphery to the center of legal and political thought and practice. But, at another level, I think this shift amounts to a gestalt-like change in how people see the world, in daily habits of thought as well as political theory and jurisprudence. My aim is, thus, simultaneously grandiose and humble: to shift habits of thought so that people

3

routinely attend to the relations of interconnection that shape human experience, create problems, and constitute solutions. My aspiration is a relational habit of thought in everyday conversation, in scholarship, in policy making, and in legal interpretation.

My focus here is the intersection in law of concepts of self, autonomy, and rights. Law is a powerful means of structuring human relations, and it also an important way in which concepts like self and autonomy take shape in the world. Law is itself also in constant relation with other social norms and frameworks of thought. Thus, a deep shift in relational habits of thought will have to exceed the context of law. But law can both reveal the importance of such a transformation and participate in it.

While I aim at transformation, this is not a utopian project. The relational approach can be used right now. My argument (in chapters 1 and 6) is that rights *do* structure relationships, not that they are currently failing to, but should do so. Right now, for example, property rights create relationships of power, allowing homeowners to exclude the homeless, factory owners to claim the products their employees have made, and nontraditional families to resist intrusions of disapproving neighbors. A relational analysis provides a better framework for identifying what is really at stake in difficult cases and for making judgments about the competing interpretations of rights involved. I offer a variety of examples of what such a relational analysis looks like. I also make arguments about why engaging in this form of analysis is workable and does not exceed existing judicial authority.

Another way of describing the transformation I am aiming at traces a linear connection from self to autonomy to rights and law. While, as I will explain shortly, this linear connection can be misleading, it can also provide a useful shorthand for the project. In chapter 1, I explain each of these terms in detail. Here I provide the shorthand.

In the schematic version, we move from relational self, to relational conceptions of values (autonomy in particular), to a relational approach to rights and law. The self is relational because human beings become who they are—their identities, their capacities, their desires—through the relationships in which they participate. These include intimate relationships with parents and lovers, more distant relationships with teachers and employers, and social structural relationships, such as gender, economic relations, and forms of governmental power.

When we see the self as constituted by relations, then the core values of human life have to be understood in ways that take account of this centrality of relationship. The role of relationship for autonomy, for example, is clearest in the parent–child context. Everyone can picture how relationships with parents can harm or encourage a child's autonomy. My claim is that constructive relationships are necessary for autonomy to flourish throughout one's life. Teachers can be authoritarian or they can invite critical thought. Employers can encourage the participation of their employees in structuring the forms and demands of work or they can focus on discipline and compliance. Governments can set up forms of social assistance that are intrusive and humiliating or systems through which recipients are given the tools and resources to make choices among good options about how to live. Optimal systems could also enhance autonomy by inviting recipients to participate in the formulation and implementation of qualifications for entitlement. All of these relations enhance or undermine people's autonomy. Autonomy cannot, therefore, be understood as independence from others; autonomy is a capacity made possible by constructive relationship.

And since the prevailing Anglo–American conception of law and rights rests so heavily on underlying conceptions of self and autonomy, there must be corresponding changes in the understanding of law and rights. Law makes assumptions about the sort of independence and responsibility that characterize mature human beings, and people are entitled to rights such as freedom of expression and association because they need them to be autonomous beings. So if rights are based on such a faulty conception of autonomy as independence, they are not likely to do a good job of facilitating the relationships that actually foster autonomy.

In general, the rights the relational self is entitled to will need to be relational rather than individualistic conceptions. Both law and rights will then be understood in terms of the relations they structure—and how those relations can foster core values, such as autonomy. In sum, a relational self requires relational conceptions of values, which then require appropriate forms of law and rights built around those conceptions.

This sort of linear schema provides a neat summary. But it is also misleading because self, autonomy, and rights and law are each tied to each other—as a set of ideas, beliefs, practices and institutions. The prevailing liberal conception of the self *is* an autonomous self with rights. And individual(istic) rights are what an autonomous self (or rational agent) is entitled to. Law (in its ideal liberal form) protects equal, autonomous, rights-bearing selves from harm by each other and by the state. There is thus not a linear ordering beginning with self and ending in law. A shift in any of these concepts (and practices) would entail a shift in all of them. This book aims to advance such a shift by focusing on each dimension and on their interactions.

My point throughout is that law needs an alternative conceptual framework to do its work optimally, and new concepts need to be given life in the law.

II. THEORETICAL FRAMEWORK AND AUDIENCE

This book is intended to extend a wide variety of ongoing conversations. It is aimed at the diverse group of my fellow feminists and at the many different people who work within a relational framework. It aims to engage fellow critics of liberalism, who share many of my concerns,[2] as well egalitarian liberals, who share many of my aspirations. The book is also aimed at lawyers, judges, and activists who engage daily with the puzzles of rights and are interested in a framework that can capture what they see as most vitally at stake in their work. It is also intended to reach the general public, especially those interested in a formal articulation of their sense of the importance of relationships to their lives and values.

A variety of challenges arise from trying to speak simultaneously to such diverse audiences. Let me begin with a few words about my relation to feminism and then turn to liberalism, first critics then adherents. I then address my fellow relational thinkers and the wider reading public. Lawyers are included in all of these categories.

This project, which began many years ago, would not have been possible without the emergence of feminist scholarship. That diverse scholarship helped to create the intellectual and institutional space (e.g., publication, teaching) for a project like this. In particular, during the time I have been working on this book, relational feminism has become a thriving form of scholarship.[3] That is a part of the ongoing conversation that is especially important to me. The collective project of articulating a full alternative to traditional liberalism is a large one, undertaken in many different forms. The liberal tradition has had hundreds of years to refine its framework. Relational feminism is a relative newcomer. My aim is to help advance the ongoing project of developing a persuasive and workable alternative that can sustain shared values, such as equality and autonomy, while transforming their meaning to be consistent with the relational nature of life.

In chapter 1, I take up the question of whether the relational approach this book presents is a feminist project. I have puzzled over this question for many years, since people have often asked me. I have concluded that it extends beyond feminism, even though I could not have written it but for my feminism and the presence of feminist scholarship. Most of my examples focus on harms suffered by women. My objectives, both conceptual and practical, are shared by many feminists. My fellow feminists are a crucial part of my audience, but they are not all of it. I see my project as useful to scholars, activists, and lawyers whose primary concerns are other than women and gender.

For my fellow critics of traditional liberalism (a large and diverse group), I want to address what may seem an undue focus on meeting the concerns of liberals. To these critics, my topic itself may seem too close to the main preoccupations of liberalism. In chapter 1, I take up this latter concern. I talk about why I focus on autonomy, a central liberal value, and why I engage with law and rights, arguably the institutional tools of the liberal state. Here I want to comment on my efforts to meet what I see as the likely concerns of egalitarian (and thus partially sympathetic) liberals.

One fellow critic of liberal legalism, Katherine O'Donovan, closes an article with this question: is ours "a rhetorical, ironical, strategy of pointing out law's antinomies, and of challenging law's contingencies Or are we engaged in an institutional project of finding a new language and new concepts in which to express our subjectivities and through which to enact laws?"[4] When I read this, I thought, "yes," the second is what I am doing. But O'Donovan herself immediately suggests that she is wary about such a project. She says that "in posing this question in binary form, it is my intention to undermine it.... To create spaces for freedom to be and become without the rigidities of the past is surely sufficient. If the utopian moment [opened by deconstruction] is a moment of definition, and therefore prescription for others, then the very rigidities we are endeavoring to escape may be reimposed."[5]

I think my approach is about as open as any framework can be. It invites widespread participation and ongoing judgment and reflection about all its terms. But it does prescribe: rights, self, and autonomy should be framed in relational terms. And it does reject individualistic approaches that treat relations as peripheral rather than central and constitutive. It makes claims about how to think about the human self and its capacities and about how best to think about fostering those capacities through law. In short it *is* "an institutional project of finding a new language and new concepts in which to express our subjectivities and through which to enact laws."[6]

The question of why I run the risks of prescription is related to why I try to meet the concerns of liberalism. I see the relational approach as immediately useable in existing legal systems, and I want it used there. I believe judges can and should use it to make decisions and articulate what they are doing in relational terms. I believe egalitarian projects will be better advanced in relational terms. I want those who work within liberal frameworks to see this and to experiment more with relational analysis, even as they recognize the ways it will ultimately require them to shift their presumptions.

The individualism of traditional liberalism remains a powerful part of the dominant framework of thought. It is that dominance I want to shift, so I need to speak to it. I identify what values I share with liberals, and why I think these values can be better advanced through a relational approach. When invoking shared values, like autonomy, I argue that my approach transforms rather than threatens them because the transformation actually advances what is really at their core.

In short, I want to persuade liberals that my approach yields better protection of the real value of autonomy and critics that the transformation is deep enough to transcend the individualistic limitations of traditional liberalism.

Some of the misapprehensions I try to dispel are concerns that critics of liberalism share (in different form) with liberals. The use of state power is such a shared concern.[7] In my view, it is a real issue, and so I make a point of arguing that the relational approach I advocate need not increase the scope of state power.

Many critics of liberal individualism also share my view that a sense of the inherent value of each individual must be part of a good alternative to traditional liberalism. Part of my point (like those of other critics) is that traditional liberal individualism is not the only, or the best, way to articulate and implement care and respect for individuals. For me, this shared purpose is best pursued through attention to the relations that constitute those individuals and that make their values real for them. In insisting that my approach does not abandon concern for individuals, I thus engage with the concerns of both liberals and many of their critics.

Of course, by trying to embrace within my readership both critics of liberalism and egalitarian liberals, I risk satisfying neither. Nevertheless, I turn now to what I imagine as my partially sympathetic, but skeptical, liberal audience. (I envision this audience as including legal scholars and practitioners as well as political theorists.)

I think the skepticism takes two somewhat contradictory forms. The first is that there is really nothing new or necessary about the relational approach I propose because egalitarian liberals have already taken account of the need to pay attention to social context and to the social nature of human beings. The second is that there is a dangerous erosion of protection for the individual in this relational approach. The second I take up in various places in the book, including chapter 1, where I offer my own account of respect for the individual. The first I address here.

First, in order to claim that making relationship central to legal and political analysis can make a difference, I do not need to claim that no liberal theorists have taken important steps in this direction. Such a claim would be false.[8] I do, however, say that liberal individualism is still the dominant mode of thought. One of the easiest ways to see this is through the role "independence" plays in liberal theory. (This dimension of liberal individualism is, of course, particularly salient to this project because of my rejection of independence as a good shorthand for autonomy.) Many other scholars have already taken up this point, so here I primarily point to their work.

In chapter 1, I note Alasdair MacIntyre's discussion of the prevalence of assumptions about human independence in political theory. Eva Feder Kittay offers a careful argument about how Rawls's "original position" excludes not only those dependent on others but also those with primary caretaking obligations for dependent others. Martha Nussbaum picks up Kittay's argument in her own exploration of the problems posed by the inclusion of people with severe mental impairments for Rawls's social contract theory. Nussbaum contrasts the Rawlsian contractarian starting point of those who are "free, equal, and independent" with her capabilities approach, which includes the ideas of people's "fundamental sociability and of people's ends as including shared ends."[9] (Nussbaum is careful to note that Rawls's doctrine of reciprocity takes account of the Aristotelian idea of the good of a human being as both social and political. But she argues that his social contract framework prevents him from extending it to the difficult cases of severe disability.[10]) I think Nussbaum herself, despite her insightful Aristotelianism, sometimes shifts into a more individualistic framework[11] (perhaps when she is in her more Rawslian rights mode).

I would add that Rawl's doctrine of reciprocity is a fairly limited and formal engagement with the inherently relational meaning of equality itself. For Rawls, justice requires that human beings recognize each other as free and equal persons with whom they must cooperate on shared terms of fairness. This recognition takes the fact that human beings live together as a starting point and stipulates that equality must be part of the recognition. But in my terms (as I explain in chapter 1), this is closer to an effort to engage with the fact of human plurality than a deep engagement with the relational dimension of human lives. Rawls's concept of reciprocity remains a highly formal form of equal relations.[12]

Of course, Rawls is also rightly famous for paying attention to some dimensions of the conditions for equality, which, in my terms, means attending to the actual relations of equality. One could say that is the heart of what the "original position" was intended to offer, and by defining the "basic structure" of society as the proper subject of justice, he invited a reflection on the most important structures of relations and the role law plays in shaping them.[13]

More broadly, all egalitarian liberals are concerned with the conditions for equality.[14] Indeed, *all* liberals subscribe to equality and thus must have some stance on the requirements of human relations of equality. My claim is that the relational approach presented here offers a deeper, more fruitful way of attending to the important details of those relations than that taken up even by many egalitarian liberals.

Most egalitarian liberals do pay attention to the complex consequences of economic inequality. This means that they turn their attention at some level to the significance of social relations for such issues as self-esteem and capacity for political participation. But that does not mean that they consistently make relationship central or that they do not slip back into assumptions about people as independent, rational agents. Most thoughtful egalitarian liberals display some combination of attention to social context and social relations, on the one hand, and individualism intended to protect individual rights, on the other hand. It is not my task here (though some might wish it had been) to parse these combinations in particular theorists. I think that it is enough to say that tensions remain that should be shifted in the direction of a more consistently relational approach. This is true at the level of legal interpretation as well as political theory.

What matters to me is not the consequences of the failures of particular theorists to use a consistently relational approach (even though that would be one way of showing why it matters). What matters to me is constructively engaging their interest so that they will try relational analysis more often, more deeply, and more consistently to see if it yields helpful results—which, of course, I believe it will.

I would say something similar about the particular project of advocating a relational conception of autonomy: it is not new,[15] but neither is it deeply integrated into popular culture, political theory, or law. Marilyn Friedman argues in one of her own essays on relational autonomy that, "although the language of autonomy in popular culture might still suggest asocial atomistic images of the self-made man, academic philosophers now seldom share this view…many contemporary philosophers of autonomy…gravitate toward relational or intersubjective accounts of autonomy."[16] As with the recognition of the social context of equality, I think that, broadly speaking, the attention to intersubjectivity and social context for autonomy coexists with a still powerful individualism within academic political theory and philosophy. My project is to advance a shift in presumptions about the self and its core values so that a relational perspective becomes a routine part of theorizing about justice, equality, dignity, security, or autonomy. I think the tensions between a long-standing individualism and attempts to acknowledge social context will continue until some of the core puzzles of relational autonomy are resolved[17]—and until people are satisfied that a relational approach will not threaten what have long been thought of as the rights of individuals.

In addition, as I noted at the outset, my aspirations include a shift in popular culture as well as the institutionalization of shared understandings in law. The partial recognition of the social dimensions of human beings (and thus of their core values) that one can see in many contemporary theorists has not accomplished the kind of deep integration of the relational approach that I am aiming at in theory, everyday language, or law.

Finally, for friendly liberal theorists, I offer a brief engagement with some of their terms. This book does not propose or rest on what Rawls would call a comprehensive theory of the good; it is not a picture of ideal relations. It is premised on equality and argues for the importance of the ability of all to participate in the creation of the norms that govern them, but it does not offer a model of either equality or participation—though it offers examples of what will advance both.[18] I am not offering a theory of justice, though the implication of my arguments is that justice debates are best structured around a relational inquiry.

As I note in the conclusion, I think this relational approach disrupts conventional categories like rights versus "the good" or welfare or the public good. This book engages with the concept (and institutionalization) of rights in a way that is intended both to shift their meaning (to how they structure relationships in order to implement core values) and to be useable in existing structures. It is thus in conversation with liberal theorists and lawyers about concepts that are central to them—even as it tries to shift the meaning of those concepts.

My hoped-for audience also includes those who have long seen things in relational terms but have not yet found an adequate language for articulating this perspective. One of the purposes of political theory, in my mind, is to help people formulate a language for how they see the world. When people's frameworks do not fit with the dominant one, they can be rendered inarticulate. Indeed, they can be made to feel stupid, perhaps especially in formal settings, such as university classrooms or workplace meetings. When someone then works out the details of a framework similar to one they hold intuitively, works through its puzzles and how it fits and doesn't fit with the dominant framework, this work can contribute to a language in which they can participate in collective deliberation—whether in a coffee shop, a classroom, or a courtroom.

I also envision my audience as including those who have experience with traditions of relational thinking. I hope that the relational framework I present for Anglo–American law can serve as a kind of bridge of connection to other systems (of thought and law) that are based on, or have deeply integrated, a relational approach. I particularly have in mind North American aboriginal traditions,[19] and I think something similar would apply to some African traditions.[20] For example, traditions with long experience of conceptualizing and implementing autonomy in a relational way will have a lot to offer to the project of working through the puzzles of relational autonomy. And I hope that my argument about the possibility of using the relational approach in existing liberal legal systems will make it easier for those working within those systems to see the potential contributions of aboriginal legal traditions. This should also facilitate the possibility of the two systems working together, which is important in North America (and probably elsewhere). This book does not take up that cross-tradition conversation but intends to invite and facilitate it.

Finally, I cannot meet the broadest of my aspirations for this book unless it is read by the ordinary reading public. This poses a challenge to readers and to me as author. I have tried to write in an accessible style at the same time that I try to attend to the questions I think my fellow scholars will have. I hope nonspecialists will persevere through (or skip over) some of the intricacies of scholarly and legal debate.

Because I am trying to speak simultaneously to lawyers, judges, legal scholars, *and* the engaged, nonacademic public, I often refer to legal issues about which the ordinary reader may know little. I have included endnotes, some of them extensive, so that those without legal training can follow the details of the argument if they wish. Sometimes I have also included detailed notes so that those *with* legal training can pursue the matter more deeply than seems appropriate for the mixed audience of the main text.

The reading public that I have in mind for the book includes students. Having been reminded that students often get assigned particular chapters rather than the entire book, I have allowed for a bit of repetition between chapters where a previous point is important for the argument.

III. AUDIENCES I HOPE FOR BUT HAVE NOT ADDRESSED

There are additional audiences I have had in mind, and hope to engage, but have barely addressed in the text. The first of these are queer theorists, to whom I would note that much of my discussion of gender is organized around the relations between men and women. But I try to keep in mind that these relations are not all of what constitutes and expresses the meaning of gender and sexuality. My discussion of the relation of violence to masculinity and the many puzzles of reconstructing gender and sexuality (addressed in chapter 8) goes beyond a focus on male–female relations. I hope queer theorists find resonances with my approach and that a fuller conversation between us will develop.

Comparativists and those who work within the civil law tradition will notice that I have kept almost all of my examples to those arising in common law contexts, and most of them are drawn from North America. I have done this so that I can be as familiar as possible with the examples I use. It is Anglo–American liberalism that I have in mind when I speak about traditional liberalism. My claims about how the relational approach can work are addressed to an Anglo–American audience.

Nevertheless, I think that this relational approach should work in very similar ways in civil law contexts. I think the basic structure of rights structuring relationships which in turn foster core values should translate easily—even though the legal institutions, legal concepts, and conventions about legal argument are different. The nature of the objections and resistance from positivist scholarship and jurisprudence also will be different.

All these differences are significant enough that though I am optimistic about the trans-lation, I have not actually attempted it here.

While I restrict my claims to the North American context, I think the relational approach has a particular value for comparative work. It avoids prescriptions to others about the particular forms that law or relations should take. It invites the idea that different contexts will require different relational structures to foster the same values, such as autonomy or dignity.

I also hope my audience includes environmentalists. Within the mainstream of North American culture, they may be the people who have most cultivated a relational approach to their projects. The very concept of ecology is relational. It is about fundamental inter-dependence. So it is important to acknowledge at the outset that this book does not address this most basic interdependence, our relationship to the earth.

Environmentalist Thomas Berry suggests at the end of *The Dream of the Earth* that an understanding of the human–earth relationship must be prior to any understanding (or at least the best understanding) of human–human relations.[21] I think there is something to that, and thus one might say that this book has started in the wrong place. But he also argues that what is most important is a complete reorientation in how we see the world and our place in it. The dominant myths, institutions, and academic disciplines currently fail to provide the necessary respectful, relational perspective. I like to think that my argument here is a step in the direction of such a reorientation. Even though its focus is on relations among human beings, it invites the kind of relational thinking that will pro-mote a respectful relation to earth and her many life-forms. (I briefly address the issues of human relations with nonhuman entities at the end of chapter 3.)

Finally, a note on language and audience. In many places in the text I have avoided the use of the term "we" in order not to make presumptions about what I and my diverse audiences share with one another. But in some contexts, I find the alternatives, "people," "they," or "one," rather distancing. These terms tacitly invite the reader to imagine that I am talking to and about *other* people. Thus sometimes when I particularly want the reader to imagine him- or herself as part of the proposal or claim I make, I use the term "we," despite the risk of presumption.

IV. CHAPTER SUMMARIES

Each chapter offers a different set of examples, a different angle of vision on what it means to bring a relational approach to bear on both concrete and conceptual problems. Collectively, the chapters also aim to acknowledge and grapple with the difficulties that a shift to a relational framework might entail.

Let me begin with an overview of the connections between the chapters. Chapter 1 offers an introduction to the key terms of the book: relational self, relational autonomy, and a relational approach to law and rights. In setting out this framework, it also provides the reader with tools for thinking through what is most difficult or troubling about the approach.

Chapter 2 then develops the concept of the relational self in the context of explaining—and rejecting—boundary as a dominant metaphor for both self and law. Chapter 3 connects the relational self to a relational conception of autonomy and shows its importance for the modern administrative state. Chapter 4 begins with an objection to the entire project: why isn't the traditional abstracted notion of the "rational agent" adequate for *law*. In answering this question, I present a multidimensional self—embodied, affective, relational, and particular in each dimension—and show its importance for law and rights. I also argue that autonomy is best understood as part of "the capacity for creative interaction," and I elaborate how these conceptions fit with my understanding of equality. Chapter 5 treats violence against women as a systemic failure of the liberal state. In the context of this failure, I take up the challenge that this issue of violence seems to cry out for boundary language. I show the importance of a relational rather than bounded conception of self even in this difficult context, and I show how it helps to overcome the limitations of the traditional liberal approach to self, law, and rights. Chapter 6 develops the relational approach to rights and presents a corresponding change to the way constitutionalism is understood. Chapter 7 returns to the issue of autonomy and argues that "control" (like independence) is not a helpful way to understand autonomy. Here I also return to the question of responsibility touched on in previous chapters. Chapter 8 offers more detailed examples of what it means to analyze a problem (violence against women) in relational terms and to propose restructuring relations to reduce this violence. Here I confront the kind of disagreement over core values a relational approach must work with.

A. Chapter 1

Chapter 1 introduces the framework for the entire book. It explains each of the key terms and identifies what I see as the major puzzles and problems this relational approach can give rise to. It thus equips the reader to work through the detailed arguments and examples of subsequent chapters with the big questions—and the structure of my answers—in mind. It also gives readers a sufficient framework to pick and choose which chapters they want to read first (although there are some advantages to reading them in order). Readers of the first chapter may also choose to skip my engagement with puzzles arising from academic debates they may not be interested in.

This chapter explains why I have chosen to focus on autonomy and law/rights: because I think the value of autonomy matters and law should be the concern of everyone. This argument is also, in part, a response to challenges that these are the preoccupations of liberal theorists, which ought not to be reinforced by people (like me) who are trying to shift the individualistic premises of liberal theory.

I also explain how my approach aims at transforming a traditionally individualistic conception of the self into a relational one without subsuming the individual into the collective. I argue that the relational approach is actually the best way to respect the unique value of all individuals.

B. *Chapter 2*

Chapter 2, "Law, Boundaries, and the Bounded Self," is about the centrality of the boundary metaphor in the conceptual structure of Anglo–American law and its relation to an underlying conception of the "bounded self." I argue for a new image of the self and a corresponding conception of the relation between the collective and the individual— for which boundary is not an apt metaphor. This chapter explores the rejection of boundary and points toward an alternative language for the self, autonomy, and the rights that are to protect them.

The chapter begins with an account of the development of the conception of rights as limits (boundaries) in the early development of American constitutionalism. I then discuss the pervasiveness of the boundary metaphor not only in law but in other domains as well. I argue that the boundary metaphor consistently misdirects attention away from the relationships actually necessary to achieve the values at stake.

I then turn to the issue of alternatives, beginning with the question of whether there is something essentially "bounded" about human beings that sustains the image of the bounded self and its need to have these boundaries protected. I argue that there is not and turn to a set of images of the deeply interconnected, relational self. These alternatives invite us to reimagine the rhetoric of law and freedom.

C. *Chapter 3*

Chapter 3, "Reconceiving Autonomy," elaborates my understanding of a relational conception of autonomy. In particular, it argues against the idea of independence as a core dimension of autonomy and explains why a relational conception of autonomy is especially well suited to the problems of the modern welfare and regulatory state. I look at the complex relation between people's beliefs about what makes one autonomous and their experience of autonomy. Considering these subjective dimensions of autonomy highlights the difficulties in effecting a deep transformation of a central cultural value.

Beginning with American examples, I turn to administrative law, the branch of law that mediates between administrative agencies (such as welfare bureaucracies) and those subject to their decisions. Legal attention to fair procedure can provide insights into how to structure bureaucratic power so that it enhances rather than undermines the autonomy of those who interact with it—for example, by ensuring that the voices of the most dependent are heard by decision makers. I then look at various limitations to these legal solutions and at some of the most promising developments in Canadian administrative law.

At the close of the chapter, I return to the issues of welfare to look at the factors that make it difficult to restructure dependency relations so that they foster autonomy. I argue that both power disparities and entrenched beliefs about subordinate status can pose serious obstacles. I conclude, however, that it is the very inevitability of some power disparities that makes it essential to structure power relations so that they can foster rather than undermine autonomy.

D. Chapter 4

I begin Chapter 4, "The Multidimensional Self and the Capacity for Creative Interaction," with the claim that the "self" and its capacity for autonomy, agency, or creation are inherently elusive phenomena. This chapter is a further engagement with alternative language for these phenomena. I offer the "multidimensional self" as a way of reflecting on a creative self and take up the challenge of why this multidimensional self serves law better than does the traditional "rational agent." Here I also expand the relational focus of the previous chapters to develop a picture of the self as also particular, embodied and affective,[22] that is, capable of emotion or affect in ways centrally related to the capacity for reason and autonomy. In rejecting the argument that the "rational agent" is the appropriate subject of law and rights, I show the failures of this dominant conception in terms of the underlying notions of both rationality and agency.

Since my project in this chapter is directly taking up the challenge that law does not need these alternative conceptions, I offer a detailed example of how they can help. Here I return to my earlier relational focus to present an extended example of how relational conceptions of the self and autonomy help with the troubled issue of assigning legal responsibility to women who kill a battering partner who has threatened to kill them. I then address the larger question of how a relational approach complicates the problem of responsibility.

I also look at how equality should be understood in light of the multidimensional self and autonomy as part of the capacity for creation. I then respond to another challenge: that notions of rights based on the traditional conception of the self serve their purposes well. Here I return to the dimension of embodiment and show ways that a fully embodied self serves as a better subject of rights.

Finally, I add a "coda" on the ways my arguments in this chapter have participated in drawing an exclusionary boundary: including human beings and excluding all other life forms in the chapter's engagement with equality, law, and rights. I offer a sketch of how I think a relational approach can contribute to the necessary reflections on wise and respectful relations with all of the earth (and, indeed, the universe).

E. Chapter 5

Chapter 5, "Violence against Women: Challenges to the Liberal State and Relational Feminism," opens with the claim that the liberal state has failed to protect women and children from violence. If we take this failure seriously, then we must rethink the role of the liberal state and the conception of rights optimal for making good on liberalism's most basic aspirations. This claim forms the core of my argument that the relational approach provides a better way of understanding the problem of violence and of assessing solutions than the traditional liberal, boundary-based conceptions of rights.

Yet there is no issue that more powerfully evokes the need for legally protected boundaries than violence. Thus violence against women poses a challenge not only to liberalism but also to my project of replacing boundaries with relationship as the central organizing concept for rights. I take up this challenge to the relational approach in the context of the liberal state's failure on its own terms. This challenge also allows me to further address one of the key anxieties that I think my approach provokes: this sort of relational analysis will lead to a vast expansion of the scope of the state.

I build my argument around Judith Shklar's defense of liberalism as the "only system devoted to the project of lessening [cruelty]."[23] Shklar's evocation of the horrors of the fear of cruelty serves as an indictment of societies in which women live in fear. Focusing on rape, I explore the limitations of boundary language to capture the horror of rape; I then argue that the cycle of fear and domination can only be broken by transforming relations between men and women— which means that such transformation must be a legitimate project of the state.

Shklar's central purpose is, however, to limit the scope of the state, which she sees as the most dangerous source of cruelty. I use an analogy to Robert Cover's analysis of how violence was integral to racial subordination in the American South to show why rethinking the role of the state is essential to dismantling hierarchies that are embedded in the culture and sustained by "private" violence. In the end, a relational analysis reveals that, in the case of sexual assault, appropriate changes in the law only appear to be an expansion of the scope of the state. In fact, what is involved is a recognition of the way law currently structures relations between men and women and how that structuring can be altered to reduce violence and improve equality.

F. Chapter 6

Chapter 6, "Reconceiving Rights and Constitutionalism," offers a framework for bringing a relational approach to rights. It also presents a view of constitutionalism as a dialogue of democratic accountability in which rights do not serve as trumps. I present rights as a form of collective choice, different from the collective choices of legislatures but collective choices nonetheless. I argue that these changes in the conceptions of rights and constitutionalism allow for the necessary recognition of the contingent and contested nature of legal rights. I also argue that this recognition need not undermine the capacity of rights to serve as standards for the legitimacy of governmental action. That legitimacy will be assessed through a "dialogue of democratic accountability."

I show how this approach to rights solves or mitigates some of the most persistent critiques of rights. And the "dialogue of democratic accountability" model avoids the kind of democratic critiques that the American model of rights as trumps generates.

I provide examples of how a relational approach can help guide debates over which rights should be constitutionalized as well as the interpretation of existing constitutional rights. I present the purpose of constitutional rights as structuring relations of equality not only between citizen and state but also among citizens. Finally, I offer a model of protecting social and economic rights that is consistent with my picture of constitutionalism as a dialogue of democratic accountability. This model encourages a relational approach and highlights the limits of the dominant, court-centered understanding of rights and constitutionalism.

G. *Chapter 7*

In chapter 7, "Relinquishing Control: Autonomy, The Bodymind, and the Psyche," I return to reflections on the nature of autonomy. In chapter 3 I argued that we should reject the common identification of autonomy with independence. Here I make a similar argument about autonomy and control. Seeking control is not a path to autonomy, and control is not a component of autonomy. This is important because control is not a respectful stance toward others with a capacity for autonomy. Indeed, the link between autonomy and control (and independence) is also a link to domination: the illusion of control and independence can be sustained only through domination.

I use the fact of our embodied nature and the puzzles of the mind–body relationship to examine the puzzles of a capacity for autonomy whose actuality depends on relationships beyond one's control. Rethinking the connection between autonomy and control disrupts the autonomy-control-responsibility nexus that is central to law. This chapter anticipates the discussion in chapter 8 of whether law can deal with the nuance and contingency of a relational approach to autonomy and its implications for a similarly contingent approach to responsibility.

To better understand both why it is important to disentangle autonomy from control and why it will be difficult to do so, I turn to a psychoanalytic account of the role of control and domination in the prevailing conception of autonomy. Here we also encounter the link between an optimal conception of autonomy and the capacity to engage with difference in a way that advances equality.

Finally, I return to our embodied nature to reflect on the grain of truth in the conventional associations of control and independence with autonomy. I also suggest that a focus on the body offers paths out of the difficulties of conventional understandings and practices.

H. *Chapter 8*

Chapter 8 offers detailed examples of the project of "Restructuring Relations." The heart of my argument has been that values like equality or autonomy are made possible by structures of relationship. Thus transformative projects such as feminism involve restructuring relations. This chapter turns to a variety of scholars, each of whom provides an example of what it means to bring a relational analysis to bear on the problem of violence against women. It also takes up some of the most important challenges to projects of restructuring relations though law.

The first challenge is the question of whether advocating the use of law to restructure relations involves an increase in state power (thus returning to the issue in chapter 5). I show again that it does not, that we can now see that this is rarely a useful question, and that what matters is that the relational approach leads to clarity about existing uses of state power. The next issue is the degree of contestation to be expected around the "values" law is to advance by restructuring. I highlight the ways that reducing violence against women involves changes in the meaning of gender, which inevitably touches on issues of sexuality. This "tricky, risky" area allows us to see the depth of conflict over the values law should be promoting. The third issue is the degree of uncertainty about the kinds of relations that will advance those values and the kind of law that will foster those relations. (These issues follow the steps of relational analysis that I spell out in chapter 6)

I conclude that the values that my approach invokes will inevitably be contested and that the judgments about what will advance them will be inevitably tentative or speculative. But I argue that judges are de facto making choices among competing values now. A relational approach would make those choices more apparent. Similarly, judges make judgments about the effects of their legal interpretations. A relational approach will generate a higher degree of self-consciousness about all these judgments and, thus, improve their quality.

In sum, this long chapter provides more examples of what a relational analysis contributes and what the major challenges are for advancing core values through legal restructuring of relations. In offering my answers to those challenges, I also make the case that this approach is immediately usable in existing legal systems.

1

My Relational Framework: Terms, Puzzles, and Purpose

All political and legal theorists, and every institution of law and government, recognize that human beings live together. But a relational approach to human life is something more than the recognition of this fact. In my version of a relational approach (feminists have generated many), the human subjects of law and government are not best thought of as freestanding individuals who need protection from one another. People's interactions with one another matter not simply because their interests may collide. In my view, each individual is in basic ways constituted by networks of relationships of which they are a part—networks that range from intimate relations with parents, friends, or lovers to relations between student and teacher, welfare recipient and caseworker, citizen and state, to being participants in a global economy, migrants in a world of gross economic inequality, inhabitants of a world shaped by global warming.

What does it mean to be constituted by relationships rather than just living among others? The most familiar example of people being fundamentally shaped by relationship is the idea that children are shaped by their families, often their parents in particular. People routinely accept the idea that cruel, neglectful, or abusive parents are likely to harm the development of their children's capacities—both intellectual abilities and social, emotional abilities to form constructive relationships. Conversely, parents who provide material security and manage to be loving and encouraging, who provide just the right (shifting) balance of support and independence, are widely thought to provide their children with lasting gifts that become central to their personalities. Both the child and the future adult are recognized to be profoundly shaped by the kinds of relationships they had with their parents.

This widespread recognition of the constitutive nature of relationships somehow seems to disappear for people over the age of twenty-one. It is as though once people are "formed," once they emerge as "rational agents," relationships are things they simply have or choose. As we will see more fully in the next section on autonomy, the idea of adults as autonomous actors seems in tension with, even to contradict, the idea that people continue to be profoundly shaped by relationships. Indeed, I think some will find the relational approach off-putting because it seems both infantilizing and feminizing: it treats mature adults as the relationally dependent creatures we know children to be and grants the kind of importance to relationship associated with women. In fact, however, it is not hard to think of formative adult relationships.

Teachers and mentors are common examples. Relations with fellow students in university and professional schools are another. Indeed, people sometimes choose a university or law school because of its relational norms: they think they will thrive best in an atmosphere of high-level competition, or mutual support and cooperative exploration, or relations characterized by diversity or homogeneity. Neighborhood relations may shape the kinds of employment opportunities young adults are able to envision and access. Relational norms at a workplace—hierarchy, arbitrary authority, cooperation, autonomy, trust, consultation, prejudice—may shape how one sees the world. And all of these relations, and their formative effects, are often affected by larger structures of economic relations, such as high unemployment and the power of employers to fire at will. Many people will see their personal relations with friends and intimate partners as formative. These relations, in turn, will be shaped by wider patterns of relationship, such as heterosexual norms, gender norms, and gendered division of caretaking work. Many people can see how these relational patterns have shaped the persons they have become.

A. Nested Relations

In the brief sketch above, I have linked personal relations with wider relational patterns. In my approach, the significance of relationship always refers to both. To see this more clearly, let me return to examples of the constitutive relationships of childhood to set them in their wider context.

In many parts of the world, a girl child will be greeted at birth with disappointment. She will get less to eat, less protein, and less education than her brothers. She may be married very young, have little choice about her husband, and run a much greater risk of violence in her marital home than will her brothers.[1] In this context, the significance of gender relations in her society in constituting the adult she becomes seems clear. The formative relations of parent and child, among siblings, and between husband and wife are all shaped by the wider societal, cultural relations of which they are a part.

Of course, something similar operates in North America; it is just not as obvious. Children are shaped by their parents' relation to gender roles (what they articulate, what they model, what they believe unconsciously) and by gender relations in parents' communities, such as extended family, neighborhood and religious communities. Is the sexuality of girls seen as dangerous, to be controlled by parents, teachers, neighbors? Is rule breaking more tolerated from boys than girls? Are boys called on in class more than girls? What kind of scope for adult choice are girls exposed to? Is marrying and staying home to care for children presented as the best path for women, or are girls told that all options are open to them?[2] A girl's chances of experiencing the trauma of sexual assault or having a close friend with that experience are much higher than those of her brothers. The experience, and even the sense of its ever present threat, are likely to affect her sense of basic security and trust. These are all ways that the wider structure of gender relations may shape the person she becomes.

The lives of boys are, of course, also shaped by wider structures of relations, including gender and class relations. The boys of one neighborhood may come to see the available paths in life as defined by skilled trades. Boys in another neighborhood may see these same trades as not at all an acceptable career choice. The narrowing of their choices may take a very different form: only high-paying professional jobs would count as a successful form of adulthood. Both sets of boys may be unable to see staying home with young children as an acceptable choice.

Once people begin to make a habit of relational thinking, of seeing how both personal relationships and personal choices are inevitably shaped by wider relationships, they can see how these relationships intersect with institutions, such as family law (which defines marriage and stipulates spousal and parental obligations), a market economy, the presence or absence of state-supported child care, the presence or absence of a "family wage" (and thus norms of one or both parents in the paid labor force). These national (or regional) institutions, in turn, interact with global markets and institutions, such as the World Bank, as well as with relations of economic and political power generated over centuries. For example, impoverished countries export their women to perform the care work (sex work, child care, and housework) for those in wealthy countries.[3] Many children in both sending and receiving countries receive much of their care from women who are not their mothers. And, as we are increasingly coming to acknowledge, all of these levels of relationship are affected by—and have affected—still larger patterns, such as global warming (for example, severe weather patterns causing migration, disruption of families, and increased conflict over natural resources).

As the last sentence suggests, this relational habit of reflection will reveal that the impact is never unidirectional. Every member of a family affects family relations even as those relations shape her. For example, heterosexual marriage relations in North America are shaped by long-standing norms of gender roles. Individuals, nevertheless, have the power to shift or to reinforce those norms. Self-consciousness about both the power of norms and the possibility of affecting them can make a difference to the individual, to the particular relationship, and to the wider set of norms. Carolyn McLeod, for example, reflects on how individual behavior can reinforce or disrupt patterns of relationships: "how am I structuring my relationship with my husband by routinely cooking dinner because I feel as though that is my wifely responsibility, even though I consciously reject such a view?"[4]

Every family shaped by cultural and legal norms has the ability to affect and shift those norms. Thus each family organized around a equal division of caretaking labor offers not only to their children, but to their children's friends, to neighbors and colleagues a concrete example of an alternative and thus challenges the tacit notion that it is natural or appropriate for women to do the majority of care work, even if she is also working outside the home. Communities (such as church or school communities) who encourage such equal division of labor both support particular families trying to live according to that model and provide further challenges to the prevailing norms. And families can encourage their communities to take on this supportive role. When entire countries provide decent maternity leave policies or well-funded collective child care, they shape the families within them and provide models for others. In short, every level is both shaped by and shapes those it intersects with. All human beings are both constituted by, and contribute to, changing or reinforcing the intersecting relationships of which they are a part.

And, as suggested above, the earth itself is both condition and effect of these relationships. Once attention is drawn to what kinds of relationships generate a given problem, and what is shaping those relationships, it will become clear that the human institutions and norms I offer as examples above are themselves conditioned by the availability of natural resources as well as the way humans have constructed control over those resources and the way humans understand their entitlement to them.

B. Harm and Interconnection

Another way of understanding what I mean by relational selves is to see the fundamental interconnectedness among human beings. (Again, I think this interconnectedness extends to earth and her many life forms, but here I am focusing on human interconnectedness.) A path into seeing this interconnectedness is thinking about what harms or benefits each of us. Of course, the question of what harms others has been central to law and political theory (perhaps most famously in John Stuart Mill): people are free to do what affects only them, but their liberty will be constrained by harm to others.[5] Most of these notions of harm, however, as well as "commonsense" understandings, are much too limited by presumptions of individualism.

Again, children offer the clearest examples of the way harm is often as much a function of relationship as it is of direct individual injury. It is widely recognized that children are harmed by witnessing violence in their homes, even if that violence is not inflicted directly on them.[6] Less dramatically, many people recognize that children are affected by constant stress, anger, and tension between their parents, even if it is not manifested in physical violence. It is hard to develop a basic sense of security and trust under those conditions. I think something similar happens to all of us when we are surrounded by violence and suffering. I am not talking here about the acute conditions of, say, living in a refugee camp or a war zone. Those traumas are widely recognized (again, particularly for children). I have in mind the routine violence and suffering of affluent North American cities.

Young women are raised with a sense of the ever present threat of sexual violence. Habits of what a woman does with her drink in a bar, even the rules about what customers may do with their drinks, casually incorporate the idea that men may put "knock-out" drugs in her drink for the purposes of sexual assault.[7] "Normal" rules for women's behavior—don't be the last to leave a house party hosted by a male, don't walk alone on isolated streets at night, ask the bus driver to stop closer to your home than the regular stop (a service proudly advertised by the Toronto Transit Commission)—all reflect a norm of male violence. Normal, responsible behavior for men—offering to walk women home at night or waiting to see if they are safely in their door when dropping them off by car—also reflects these norms of violence. Both young men and women grow up learning that male violence against women is to be expected. (Here I am not counting what children learn who grow up witnessing male violence against their mothers.)

Learning that one belongs to categories of predator or prey, even if this knowledge is never fully acknowledged, even if one tells oneself that he or she will be an exception, is to learn that one lives in a society in which regular violence against women is tolerated, is normal enough to be routinely expected and guarded against. The harms of this collective tolerance do not only affect the women who are actually assaulted or the men who commit the violence. Women learn that men are both the source of the threat and the means of protection. They need a man to guard against other men (very often literally "Other" men, the dark strangers who are the mythical source of the threat—thus perpetuating the violence of racism as well). Men learn that they will be feared as a threat, valued as protector, and that violence will be tolerated should they be so inclined. They also learn that if they resist norms of masculinity they put themselves at risk of shifting into the category of prey. (Norms of masculinity include violence, toughness in response to violence, tolerance of violence, and enjoyment of violence in entertainment media.[8]) At the very least, these are not gender roles and relations that bode well for mutual respect or for a sense of security and trust. It is hard to believe that anyone growing up in urban North America (probably anywhere in North America, but I focus on what I know best[9]) has not been deeply shaped—and harmed—by this background culture of violence.

Homelessness is another form of suffering and often violence that urban North Americans have become accustomed to. What does it do to us to walk around a homeless person on the street once a week or once a day? How does it affect us to routinely see such vivid examples of a lack of collective care, of the failure of multiple social institutions? At some level we must confront the question of how it can happen in a rich society that people are cold and begging on city streets. When we see a lineup of homeless people seeking shelter in a church on a cold winter night it must generate at least an unconscious sense that if something goes badly wrong for someone there may be only the most limited kind of help available: shelter for one night, if there is a space. We live with a knowledge of vulnerability to disaster and of callousness, of indifference to suffering that character-izes the community we live in. Or perhaps there is a knowledge that, for some, there is no community, only an indifferent collectivity. How can this not be frightening at some level (even if we tell ourselves it could never happen to us or anyone we care about)?

I remember the first time I encountered a homeless person. It was 1978, and I lived in Halifax, Nova Scotia. I was visiting Philadelphia for a job interview in the political sci-ence department at the University of Pennsylvania. I was crossing a busy street with the chair of the department on our way to an appointment. In the middle of the street, right in front of me, a manhole cover opened, and a man climbed out of it. I stopped in shock. The chair hurried me on, saying casually that the man lived down there. He seemed to think that no further explanation or comment was necessary. I can still remember the shock of seeing the man emerge and of what seemed to be the chair's casual disregard. Now I think about how I am *not* shocked when I routinely encounter homeless people in Toronto. Now I, too, take homelessness near my home for granted. Even if it distresses me, it no longer shocks me. And maybe when I am in a hurry, as the chair was, I, too, scarcely notice it.

But I am not under any illusion that it does not harm me to participate in such harm. Even if I am not always conscious of it, I know that there is a direct relationship between my legally protected right to exclude even a cold and hungry person from my home and that person being on the street. If she and I did not both assume my right to exclude, she would not be out in the cold. As is often the case with property rights, there is no need for me to call the police, to make manifest the way my property is backed by the power of the state, for me to exercise the power my property provides. My right to exclude creates an asymmetrical relation of power and advantage between me and the homeless person, and it creates a relation of responsibility—in this case an absence of (legal) responsibility on my part for her immediate well-being. I can hurry by secure in the knowledge that I have violated no rights of hers and thus remain under an illusion that my entitlements are in no way responsible for her predicament.

This illusion can provide the protection that most illusions do. It can permit me to avoid thinking about the problem.[10] But like any painful matter that we push away from our consciousness, it affects us anyway. We live with a sense of shame, vulnerability, and insecurity, with a sense of being enmeshed in some kind of failed set of social institutions and relations. People may tell themselves stories about whose failure this is, even attribute it to the individual failures of the thousands of homeless, to try to insulate themselves from both responsibility and vulnerability. But I do not believe that such stories can actu-ally keep at bay either the shame or the insecurity of participating in this collective failure of responsibility. These feelings may, however, take the form of contempt or fear of the homeless or anger at those who want to make them confront the problem or just an inchoate anxiety and insecurity.

I think that habits of individualistic thought make the illusions easier to sustain. Conversely, I think habits of relational thought will make it easier to see the interconnection and thus to accept the urgency of stopping the harm that causes such acute suffering to many and harm to all who live in the societies that tolerate it.

I use these examples of harm because I think they point to the difference between the fundamental interconnectedness of human beings (the relational approach) and the more conventional notion that because humans live in company with others their actions often affect others, or even that risks to some may spill over to others. Consider the famous quotation:

> First they came for the Communists, but I was not a Communist—so I said nothing. Then, they came for the Social Democrats, but I was not a Social Democrat—so I did nothing. Then came the trade unionists, but I was not a trade unionist. And then they came for the Jews, but I was not a Jew—so I did little. Then when they came for me, there was no one left who could stand up for me.[11]

One might interpret this quotation as saying that no one's rights are secure while the rights of some are trampled. On this interpretation, I am at risk if the laws do not protect everyone because I can never know when the violence or oppression might be directed at me. This view might reflect recognition of the importance of a collective sense of justice, security, and rights for all as necessary to avoid vulnerability for anyone. Or similarly, it could reflect the view that the habits of domination and violence can always be turned on different groups or individuals as it suits the advantage of the dominant.

Consider the difference between that interpretation and the idea that even if they never came for me it would harm me to live in a society that tolerated or condoned the abuse of others. I see this meaning as captured in the saying that "No one is free while anyone is in chains."[12] The first interpretation is consistent with the relational approach I am advocating. It is, however, less fully relational than saying that I cannot live in peace in a society characterized by violence and oppression, even if I am in the dominant group and thus at very little risk.

The harm, on my account, is not potential, but actual when the lives of others are violated.

A counterstory offers a different way of seeing this same issue of interconnection. In chapter 3, I discuss the example of Sweden's policy of generous support for a quadriplegic law student, enabling her to study without calling on basic care from her family. Seeing the publicly funded care this student received reassures every member of the society that if they or their family members should have an accident that rendered them incapacitated, or if they should bear a child with such physical limitations, collective care would be forthcoming. Again, the benefit is not just potential, but actual, in the sense of the security of living in a compassionate and responsible society.

In these stories the nature of the potential and actual harm varies. In the Swedish story and the stories of homelessness, the security and insecurity arise in part because people can imagine the possibility of finding themselves in such circumstances (even if consciously they do not). Thus, the actual harm—of fear, insecurity, knowledge of collective failure of care and responsibility—is shaped by the potential harm. Something similar is true for women who have not been sexually assaulted. But the actual harm exceeds this. Witnessing violence is harmful. We know this about children. Sometimes we recognize it for adults in the context of post-traumatic stress disorder (PTSD). But, collectively, we seem to imagine that people can inure themselves to the violence that is routine in their society. People get used to living around loud noise so that they don't hear it anymore, but that doesn't mean their ears are not damaged. Being surrounded by violence and the threat of violence damages people.[13]

The intrinsic harm of harm to others is important because in many cases our societies permit harm to "others," whom members of the dominant group have no potential of becoming. That is part of the function of harm organized by categories such as gender, race, or ethnicity. In these cases, the actual harm to the dominant group can come in multiple forms: the harm of being witness to violence, the harm of knowing one's community permits this violence (even if one will not be vulnerable to that form of violence), the harm of being the "innocent bystander" who does nothing to stop the violence, and the harm of being a perpetrator of the violence or one who reaps its benefits. (See chapter 8.) If one expands the term "violence" to include the domination inherent in racism, most people in privileged positions find themselves suffering a least some form of these harms. Men are harmed in similar ways in relation to violence against women. In addition, being cast in the symbiotic roles of predator and protector poses a huge barrier to relations of equality—thus denying men as well as women the benefits of such relationships.

This analysis of the kinds of harm that follow from human interconnection arises from a view that relations of equality are not simply a formal legal entitlement, but what human well-being requires. This means that relations of domination and violence are intrinsically harmful to the dominator as well as to the subordinate/victim. I have tried to do a bit more than assume this by pointing to some of the dimensions of the harm, without actually trying to prove it. It is one of the many ways in which my argument presumes a commitment to equality.[14] But part of the point is that the relational implications of a commitment to equality require an expanded view of harm.

Finally, one more example of the way relationships shape who we are: whether people are healthy or not turns out to depend significantly not just on whether they are rich or poor, but on "relative deprivation—where one lies in the local hierarchy, a notion that applies not simply to finances but also to power and independence at work, levels of social participation, education, and early life experiences." Studies of British civil servants revealed that while none of them were poor, "the least well off had mortality rates nearly eight times as high as the wealthiest. More important, there was a significant gap between each step in the hierarchy. In other words, "the problem is in not confined to the high risk at the bottom." "Control over life," said [Sir Michael Marmot, director of the Whitehall I and II studies of the health of British civil servants] "and opportunities to participate fully in society are powerful determinants of health." And health is a powerful factor in how people experience themselves.[15]

I close this section with another articulation of the meaning of relational selves (which anticipates my discussion of relational autonomy). In the following quote, Anna Yeatman links the issues of participation and disability while explaining their wider significance for selfhood (my term) and individuation. This quote also points to the fact that this relational approach does not stand in opposition to the importance of individuality; it is an account of what makes it possible.

> No one can participate in the conduct of their life except as they are invited by relevant others to so participate. Put differently, this is the proposition that being and becoming an individual depends not just on the desire and capacity of a person to be so individualized. It depends also on the skills and willingness of others to respond to this person in ways that enable him or her to have a say in what happens in his or her life. The dependence of individual participation, of an individual getting to be and become an individual, on specific forms of social assistance is . . . perforce emphasized in disability led conceptions of participation. . . . To become an effective individual in one's social world means that an individual is invited to be his or her own person. . . . Autonomous individuality is possible only to the extent that the social world of individuals is mediated by their participation. Persons are invited to be/become individuals by being invited to participate in the conduct of their lives.[16]

C. Dependence, Interdependence, Independence

Human dependence on others, and the collective interdependence that follows, are central features of my version of a relational conception of human selves. Many feminist theorists, particularly care theorists, emphasize the basic fact of human dependence. And increasingly other theorists have taken up their arguments that a true recognition of this fact changes how one does political theory.[17] There are, however, different understandings of the nature of this dependence. I want to begin by distinguishing my own understanding or emphasis from the common focus on infancy, sickness, disability, and old age. Alasdair MacIntyre, for example, is one of those theorists who takes up the feminist challenge to pay attention to dependency:[18]

> We human beings are vulnerable to many kinds of affliction and most of us are at some time afflicted by serious ills. How we cope is only in small part up to us. It is most often to others that we owe our survival, let alone our flourishing, as we encounter bodily illness and injury, inadequate nutrition, mental defect and disturbance, and human aggression and neglect. This dependence on others is most obvious in early childhood and in old age. But between these first and last stages

our lives are characteristically marked by longer and shorter periods of injury, illness or other disablement and some among us are disabled for their entire lives.

These two related sets of facts [our vulnerability and our dependence on particular others] are so evidently of singular importance that it might seem that no account of the human condition … could avoid giving them a central place. Yet the history of moral philosophy suggests otherwise. From Plato to Moore and since there are usually, with some rare exceptions, only passing references to human vulnerability and affliction and to the connections between them and our dependence on others. Some of the facts of human limitations and of our consequent need of cooperation with others are more generally acknowledged, but for the most part only then to be put on one side.[19]

I agree with all of this, but I think it understates the nature of our dependence and interdependence. They are not episodic, but a constant part of the human condition. For most adult human beings, for example, language is a central part of who they are. Language is a social phenomenon. Not only is language acquisition in childhood dependent on having others around from whom to learn it, but the function of language—communication with others—means that it shifts and evolves in social relations. We are dependent on our social world for language and not just in childhood. Hannah Arendt makes the further persuasive argument that some of our cognitive faculties, including both thinking and judging, require the presence of others (even though on her account thinking is done by oneself).[20] Borrowing from Kant, she argues that judging requires our ability to take the perspectives of others. Without others, and our ability to communicate with them, there would be no capacity for judgment. Thus while I note later that attention to embodiment highlights our dependency on others, it is not just our material needs that render us dependent on others.

It is, therefore, not just when our physical capacities are diminished that we need others. We are dependent on others for the social world that enables us to develop all of our core capacities—for love, for play, for reason, for creativity, for autonomy, among others. We are usually dependent on particular others and always dependent on the webs of relations of which we are a part. Our fundamentally social, relational nature—and thus our dependency—cannot be set to one side when we think of any of the core puzzles of law or politics, such as justice, mutual obligation, or the good life.

My point here is to identify dependency as a core dimension of the relational self rather than to spell out the implications of this recognition. Nevertheless, I think a brief indication of some of those implications may help to make clear both the meaning and the significance of human dependence and interdependence. When one takes dependence seriously one must also take care seriously. The failure of both the tradition of Western political thought and Western political institutions to do either has meant that the responsibilities, burdens, and benefits of caretaking have been distributed grossly unequally. It is important to remember here my point above that not just human physical needs require care, but also the development and nurture of the less tangible capacities, such as love or autonomy. And, again, (as we shall see more fully with respect to autonomy) these needs are not restricted to children.

In the Western tradition, care work has been devalued, as have the people who provide it. Eva Kittay offers a compelling argument that just social relations require care for caregivers so that they do not suffer great disadvantage by taking up this responsibility—without which neither individual humans nor their societies could flourish or, indeed, survive. We cannot begin to imagine what just relations would look like unless we build in the point of view of those who take on the well-being of others as well as their own as primary goals. (Unlike what is suggested by the original position in Rawl's *Theory of Justice*.[21]) In a related argument, Kathryn Abrams argues that to provide security for those whose primary work is the care work of the home "requires...a society that values interdependence as well as autonomy."[22] (As we will see, I would rephrase this as the need for a society that recognizes interdependence as a fact of life, recognizes the care work that entails, and sees both as inextricable from autonomy.) Nancy Fraser specifically takes up the gendered structure of care work but also embeds it in a wider set of justice and democracy concerns. She effectively argues that only when care work is equally shared by men and women can the basic values of justice and democracy be realized.[23]

I would add here that no amount of care or compensation for caregivers can redress the loss that both men and the community face as long as caregiving is overwhelmingly done by women. Men lose both the joy and the knowledge that comes from the intimacy of caregiving. For the community, this loss is disastrous when policy making is also divided along gender lines. As long as one set of people does the caregiving and another the policy making, the policy makers will be ignorant of key dimensions of human life.[24] They will not have the knowledge or experience to govern well—or, reflecting on MacIntyre's comments above, to write political theory well. (Taking on responsibility for caretaking does not, of course, require one to have children of one's own.[25])

There are, of course, many puzzles about the nature of human dependence and interdependence. Some of them I will explore more fully in the chapters of this book. (Because independence is so often used as synonym for autonomy, I will return to this issue in the section on relational autonomy as well as later in the book.) But I will note one puzzle in advance, even though it becomes clearest in the context of autonomy, I would describe this puzzle as "are we not also fundamentally separate and distinct from one another?"[26] I think this question arises from a concern that this notion of relational, dependent selves will end up erasing such distinctions. There will be no space left for our individuality.

Martha Nussbaum provides an example of this sort of insistence on separate individuality in *Women and Human Development*:

> It has been claimed by Veena Das that even this very intuitive idea that each person has her own dignity and that questions of well-being should be considered one by one, rather than in the aggregate, is a western intrusion. Indian women are simply

unable to form the concept of their personal well-being as distinct from the well-being of family members. If Das simply means that Indian women frequently judge sacrifice for the family to be a good thing, and frequently subordinate their own well-being to the well-being of others, it is plausible enough, but hardly an objection to the type of political focus on the individual that I have recommended; there is no incompatibility between the idea that politics should treat each person as an end and the idea that some people may choose to make sacrifices for others. If, however, Das really means to say that Indian women cannot distinguish their own hunger from the hunger of a child or a husband, cannot really distinguish their own body and its health from someone else's body and its health, then she does not have a leg to stand on.[27]

To me this captures a kind of inability to see the nature of relational selves as consistent with what actually matters about individuality. Of course women can distinguish between their hunger and their children's. But it can be equally true that a mother is in pain when her children are hungry, that she cannot feel happy or satisfied when her children are hungry or in pain. This is not a question of self-sacrifice. Even in the absence of great deprivation, many parents recognize that their own well-being is tied up with that of their children. Many parents experience the sense of their lives unraveling when something goes seriously wrong for their child. Their well-being is not fully separable, even though the parent knows he or she is a distinct self. That distinctness coexists with a profound interdependence, the nature of which shifts as children grow up.

Of course, it is also true that this deeply relational conception of the self is consistent with what Nussbaum really cares about: individual dignity and the idea that "questions of well-being should be considered one by one, rather than in the aggregate."[28] My point here is that Nussbaum insists on a kind of separateness in order to maintain the worth and dignity of the individual. I think this is unwise and unnecessary, despite the many instances in which women's well-being has been subordinated to the welfare of others. The relational self can claim dignity as well as autonomy, which will include her own judgment about what constitutes her well-being. In the end, my claim is that what matters to individuals, and what matters about individuality, are best understood and fostered in relational terms.

D. What I Do Not Mean by Relational Selves
i. Not Just Intimate Relations, but Nested Structures of Relations

I hope that it is clear from the examples I have offered above that when I refer to relationships, I do not just mean intimate relationships. I risk repetition here because the term "relationship" is so often assumed to refer only to personal relationships, such as family or friends.

Intimate relations, such as spousal relationships, are shaped by societal structures of relationship such as those formally shaped by family law as well as powerful informal norms of gender roles. These structures will be shaped by patterns of economic relationships, such as employers' preference for hiring men in high-paying jobs, expectations that authority should be exercised by men over women, and governmental policies that ensure the availability of (overwhelmingly female) child care workers from abroad who will accept low pay. The availability of such workers arises from long-standing relations of global economic inequality. Each set of relations is nested in the next, and all interact with each other. Relational selves shape and are shaped by all interactions.

ii. Constitutive but Not Determining

Perhaps the most important thing that I do not mean by relational selves is that people are determined by their relationships. That would, of course, be an odd position for a feminist to take. Feminists have long objected to women being defined by their relationships as wives or mothers. In my view relationships are constitutive, yet not determinative. The very concept of relational autonomy presupposes that autonomy is possible for relational selves; and if that is so, then relationships cannot *determine* who a person is or what she does or becomes. Otherwise there would be no true autonomy.

Part of the modern sense of self, which I embrace even as I try to shift its dominant conceptualization, is that human beings have a significant ability to make themselves who they are. The language I use is the capacity for creative interaction (developed in chapter 3), with the emphasis on interaction with others as well as the capacity for genuine creativity. This capacity has many similarities with Hannah Arendt's concept of "the human ability to act—to start new and unprecedented processes whose outcome remains unclear and unpredictable."[29] For Arendt, it is the very "human capacity for freedom, which, by producing the web of human relationships, seems to entangle its producer to such an extent that he appears more the victim and the sufferer than the author and doer of what he has done."[30] While this entanglement means the inevitability of unpredictability of the consequences of human action, it does not preclude the possibility of freedom. Arendt warns, however, that we must not confuse freedom with sovereignty, a kind of mastery and control that is impossible given the reality of human plurality: life among others who also have the capacity for freedom.

At the beginning of *The Human Condition*, Arendt offers statements that capture what I mean by the nondeterministic centrality of relationship: "Men are conditioned beings because everything they come in contact with turns immediately into a condition of their existence.... On the other hand, the conditions of human existence—life itself, natality and mortality, plurality, and the earth—can never 'explain' what we are or answer the question of who we are for the simple reason that they never condition us absolutely."[31]

I will return to this question of nondeterministic relationship, but for now I will close this subsection with another, quite different, articulation of the ways humans are constituted by relationship, in ways that simultaneously enable a power of constituting their (relational) environment. (One might say that Arendt's comment on entanglement pointed to the other half of that circle: the way that the power of constituting creates that which is constitutive of us.) As Steven Winter puts it:

> Situatedness is...a way of describing the epistemological ecology in which we are simultaneously constituting and constituted. We are *constituting* because meaning arises in the imaginative interaction of the human being with the environment. We are *constituted* because the situated quality of human existence means that both the physical and social environment with which we interact is already formed by the actions of those who have preceded us.[32]

iii. Relationships Are Not Necessarily Benign

My claim that relationships are constitutive of who people are and become does not, of course, mean that all relationships are good. Part of the point of a relational approach is to understand what kinds of relationships foster—and which undermine—core values, such as autonomy, dignity, or security. (The next step is to examine what kinds of laws and norms help structure constructive relationships and which have helped generate the problems people are trying to solve.) My version of the relational project (and all other versions that I know of) is intrinsically evaluative and aimed at transformation. It is not, therefore (as people sometimes wrongly say of care theory[33]), about *maintaining* existing relationships.

One of the contributions of feminism to relational theory is that it is particularly unlikely to make the mistake of romanticizing community or relationship. Feminists know all too well the destructive power of bad structures of relationship—such as the gendered division of caring labor. It is because relationships are not as such benign that it is important to understand how relationships are structured (by law for example) and how those structures foster or impede the values (like equality or autonomy) that people care about. Part of the reason relational autonomy is so important is that it is part of what enables people to extricate themselves from bad relationships as well as to transform the structures that shaped those relationships.

iv. *People* are Relational

When I say that human selves should be understood as relational, I do *not* mean that really it is women who are relational. Whatever differences—whether culturally induced or shaped by such physical experiences as pregnancy and nursing—that may currently exist between men and women in how they experience relationship, these differences do not distinguish men and women in what I mean by relational selves.[34] Men and women are, of course, shaped differently when societies' structures of relationship are highly gendered. And, as suggested above, it may be that the profound relational experiences of pregnancy and nursing shape men, women, and baby boys and girls differently. (At this point in our history, I think it is close to impossible to distinguish between such physical–relational experiences and the ways they are culturally mediated.) But the point remains that relationships are equally constitutive of males and females.

v. Relational Privacy

To insist on the centrality of relationships in human lives is not to deny the value of privacy or solitude. Both of those values require structures of relationships that support them—that allow people the opportunities to retreat from others in various ways.[35]

vi. No Supremacy of the Collective

To say that relationships are fundamental to who and how human beings are is not to say that the collective powers (of government or community) that shape those relationships should take primacy over individual values. The values that matter to individuals, such as freedom and autonomy, cannot exist without supporting relationships. Collectives should, therefore, make their decisions in light of the ways their laws or norms will structure relationships that will foster such values. Of course, individual rights and values can conflict with one another and with collective goods, such as sustaining the environment. Some values are best thought of as both individual and collective values and, thus, as public goods. For example, this is true of the environment and of free speech.[36] Freedom, too—while of course a value for individuals—is best understood as "relations of freedom," as Linda Zerilli puts it.[37]

Governments will often have to face difficult choices between conflicting values. My point here is that to recognize the significance of community relationships or the inevitable power of collectives is not to give them moral primacy or a legitimacy independent of *how* they use their power to structure relationships. In chapter 6 I offer a relational conception of rights and an understanding of constitutionalism that uses rights as standards of legitimacy for collective decisions. In this model, however, rights do not function as "trumps,"[38] but are enforced through a dialogue of democratic accountability. I return, in chapter 8 and the conclusion, to the anxieties about collective power that I think my relational approach may give rise to.

vii. Embodied, Affective *and* Relational Selves

By focusing on the relational dimension of human beings, I do not mean to suggest that that is the only, or the most, important dimension of us or even the one most in need of additional attention. In chapter 3 I talk about the fully human self as embodied, affective, and relational. An optimal conception of human selves would integrate all three. Off and on throughout the book I make reference to the importance of affect as a dimension of cognition as well as to the importance of bonds of affection, and I make reference to the significance of humans as embodied beings. But my focus is on the relational dimension, and these others aspects are not as fully integrated as I think would be optimal. My main justification is the amount of time it has taken me to work out the relational implications for selves, autonomy, and law. But I want to be clear (as I argue in chapter 3) that affect is central to the cognitive processes than enable autonomy (as well as directly necessary for other core values) and that a good relational approach to law will always see human beings as fully embodied and as beings shaped by affect as well as what is called reason (which I see as inseparable from affect).

I see a close link between the failures to take dependency and care seriously and the traditional "subject" of legal and political thought who is abstracted away from his embodied state. If a sense of ourselves as embodied were always central to thinking about how to structure our lives together, I do not think that physical caretaking could be treated with the disdain that it is. Similarly, I see a link between the disembodied subject and one of the most fundamental and neglected relationships, that of human beings to earth and to the other beings who inhabit it with us. Again, if we truly saw ourselves as integrated "bodyminds,"[39] I don't think we could stand in the relation to the material world that characterizes most of North American society. In an optimal relational approach, our place in the ecology of earth would be recognized as a relationship that shapes and is shaped by all others. (In chapter 3, I discuss why I use the language of a fully *human* self, when I think that our relationships with animals and the earth are so fundamental.)

E. How I Mean What I Mean by the Relational Self: Historicism and Truth Claims

During the many years of work on this book I have often wondered and been asked about the kind of truth claims I am making when I refer to the *fact* of human dependence (a language that MacIntyre uses, too[40]) or assert that human beings are constituted by relationships. I now see a way to frame these claims in their own historical context, to situate them in a relational ecology of constituting and constitutive meaning (in Steven Winter's terms[41]).

Let me begin with what I think of as the relatively easy issue of the truth of human dependence. Of course, the kind of care that people believe that children need, and the length of time people are treated as children, has varied across time and culture. And there are differences in norms and practices around the kind of care the elderly, the disabled, or the very ill receive. These differences will affect people's experience of dependency. Nevertheless, I think that at the material level of physical need (infancy, disability, sickness, and old age) that MacIntyre focuses on, human dependence is as justifiably phrased in the language of truth as the claim that plants need sun and water to grow. I think something similar is true of the claim about the social nature of language.

The claims for the importance of constructive relations for the nurturing of capacities for love, for autonomy, for creativity are more complex but not less compelling. If these capacities are central to one's conception of human selves, then the ways human beings are dependent on others is also more complex but no less fundamental. The kind of claims of dependence that I make are thus a combination of what I see as simple truth claims (infants are dependent on the care of others) and claims that many human values and capacities require relationships that nurture and develop them. As I am about to discuss, human understanding of and attachment to those values is historically contingent. And exactly what kinds of relationships are thought to nurture the values of any given society will also vary. But I think that the idea that values such as love, creativity, autonomy, and security require human relationship can be treated as a truth claim. Human dependence on others follows.

I turn now to the more complex matter of my claims about human selves as relational. As I was in the final stages of writing and editing, Nicola Lacey wisely and generously gave me a copy of her brilliant book, *Women, Crime, and Character*, which made clear to me the importance of historicizing my presentation of relational selves. Using eighteenth-century English novels and a wealth of secondary sources, Lacey presents a compelling picture of a transformation from "an early confidence about reliance on external markers of status to a world in which credibility, identity and responsibility gradually came to be seen as residing in the mysterious interior world of human being."[42] She links this changing conception of self, identity, and the ways of knowing or recognizing this self, to changing conceptions of legal responsibility (which makes her argument especially relevant to mine here):

> In the pre-*ancien regime* world of fixed status, and in the *ancien regime* world of espoused identity, there is little reason for the legal system or any other system of judgment, to look behind appearances, even if the institutional mechanisms for doing so had existed. Only with the modern idea of selfhood as residing in an inner depth would an investigation of the psychological interior [such as subjective intent] become important to the legitimation of practices of judgment such as criminal law.[43]

As Lacey presents it, neither the development of the conception of self nor the development of the criminal law's focus on subjectivity were simple or linear. Similarly, the place of individual agency or autonomy in the conception of self, the significance of social status or context, and the interaction of environment, education in particular, and the development of the unique self do not offer a simple story of linear progression toward either individual autonomy or versions of social determinism. Lacey shows with great nuance that both agency and determinism can take different and overlapping forms. What is clear in her presentation is that conceptions of the self are historically contingent and that they are connected in complex, dynamic ways with equally historically contingent understanding of law and legal responsibility.

From this perspective, one can see conceptions of the relational self as part of this modern unfolding.

In some ways my focus on autonomy participates in the vision of self-defining interiority as the core of what is human, the ground and purpose of the liberal commitment to freedom. At the same time, I urge a return to attention to relationality as constitutive of self (though not as determinative, nor simply chosen, nor assumed). One might say that I am trying to claim the best of both worlds, to propose a kind of synthesis. I embrace the notion of the unique, infinite value of each individual, and the value of interiority, and the value of the ability of individuals to shape their own lives. But I reject the liberal variants of these values that fail to see the central role relation plays in each of them. I claim that, at this historical juncture, one can best understand and promote those values if one conceptualizes them in relational terms and makes judgments about optimal institutions from a relational perspective. For example, as I noted above, freedom is best understood as relations of freedom, and these relations are not simply in service of protecting the individual or promoting the interior value of autonomy. Relations of freedom are a source of joy, creativity, expression, and fulfillment, which people enjoy in connection with one another. Relational freedom and relational autonomy are mutually supporting. (I return later to how law can foster such support.)

Put slightly differently, my conception of relational self and relational law is very specifically historically situated. It is offered in response to what I see as the still dominant individualistic conception of self—whose early development Lacey traces. So, in part, my advocacy of a relational approach to law and self is a call for another in a long series of shifts in dominant conceptions. One might say that I am trying to highlight and endorse a shift that is present in many forms but not widely accepted in the realm of law and rights—nor I think in prevailing "commonsense" ideas about self and rights.

Part of what Lacey helps us see is that deep transformations in cultural understandings of self must take institutional form. She refers to "the social and cultural institutions within which ideas of selfhood are played out, and which are needed to stabilize and coordinate them and indeed to make them livable."[44] Similarly, I see my conceptual and institutional objectives in reciprocal relation to each other: I am trying to articulate and promote a conception of selfhood which will help law better accomplish its objectives of securing core values, such as dignity and equality; I am advocating a relational approach to law which will help articulate and reinforce a conception of the self that will foster optimal relations among people and the planet they live on.

The modest, and probably best, form of my claims is, then, that a shift to a more relational approach will be an improvement over the still dominant individualism. This sort of comparative claim invites a form of judgment of which human beings are capable. Most people recognize the capacity to assess whether one thing is preferable to another— whatever one's views about the human capacity to ascertain truth and however inevitably complex and speculative it must be to make a comparative assessment about how to understand human selfhood.

I have now explicitly inserted historical context into my claims, and I want this context to be read into all similar claims that I make. (After all, the claim that "the human self is relationally constituted" can easily be read as shorthand for the claim that "at this historical juncture the best conceptual framework for understanding the human self is a relational one.") But what difference do I think it makes to acknowledge the role of history in shaping both the concepts I object to and those I propose in their place? Is it more than a gesture of language into an otherwise a-historical set of arguments? Am I actually making underlying truth claims of a universal, timeless nature about human selves (and their implications for concepts like autonomy and institutions like law)? Readers will notice that the book does contain language that has the ring of universal truth claims.

There is (at least) one way in which there is a truth-like quality to my view of the relational approach. As I suggested at the outset, I think the call for historicist argument is itself a relational claim. It is a claim that the very way we think, the conceptual frameworks we use, the values and institutions we presume are the product of the complex of intimate, social, and institutional (and natural–environmental) relations of which we are a part. And these relations, in turn, are always part of structures of power that position people differently in relation to them. As a result, the way one assumes, sees, uses, or challenges conceptual and institutional frameworks depends in part on one's location within these power structures.

The claims above might be characterized as truth claims of universal situatedness. The particularities of the relations, including power relations, will vary, but at least some degree of their salience for human experience—including experience of selfhood and attachment to values like autonomy—will not. I think most historicist claims take this form (as do most postcolonial claims.) To the extent that this is true, I can make claims about the relational nature of selves in ways that sound like universal truth claims (and which I often think of in such terms) and, at the same time, can be consistent with the basic insights of historicist argument.

While I ask my historicist-minded readers to "read-in" my acknowledgment of historical context, the (to some disturbing) truth-like sound of some of my language comes, I admit, from my sense that we *do* live in a complex web of interconnection, and that in many contexts the language of relationship best captures (the fact of) that interconnection. Thus while I can comfortably acknowledge the inevitability of the historical context of the conceptual framework I try to develop and the language I draw on, and I can settle for an argument that the relational approach is better than the dominant alternative, there is something close to a cosmology[45] of interconnection that shapes how I see the world. I think that making an awareness of the interconnection central to human projects ranging from science to religion, from philosophy to politics, from psychology to law is (at this historical juncture) crucial to improving the quality of life (for all) on the planet and sustaining its possibility for human beings.

Another truth-like quality of some of my language is the suggestion of a logic that requires a relational approach to values and to law, if they are to be true to the reality of a relational self. As I noted in the introduction, this invocation of linear logic can provide a helpful shorthand. But the relation among these concepts is best understood as the sort of articulation of idea, common sense, and institution that Lacey spells out. She shows us this "articulation" in her portrayal of the relationship between the changing conception of self, revealed in novels, and the emerging "subjectivity" of criminal responsibility—in both theory and institutional practice. In my argument, some of the pieces of the "articulation" among my terms are the following claims: the misguided individualism of the conception of self is paralleled in an equally misguided conception of autonomy as independence; in the modern, bureaucratic welfare state, the idea of autonomy as independence does not help us understand the best way to protect autonomy in the face of state power; we need a relational approach to law to achieve the values law is widely held to sustain. Thus, a relational approach to law and autonomy is one of the ways of making a relational self "livable," because of the inevitability of inter-connection between ideas, values, and institutions—an interconnection which, indeed, is part of what we mean by "law."

In the Anglo-American tradition, conceptions of self, autonomy, and rights are mutually constitutive. By offering a shift in the conception of each, and by linking these shifts to legal theory and practice, I advance a new "articulation" in the context of law, of the language of rights, and in the political theory of selfhood. But my aspiration is that a relational way of thinking about self, about core values like autonomy, about law and rights, becomes part of common sense, the everyday understanding of ordinary people. It is then that the articulation will really take hold.

A historicist context does not remove the aspiration for transformation (or indeed a quest for the truth); it makes the context of the aspiration or quest more comprehensible.

F. Conclusion

Human beings are in a constant process of becoming, in interaction with the many layers of relationship in which they are embedded. What matters here is fully integrating the centrality of relationship into the sense of "self" that underlies mainstream thinking about legal and political institutions. What too often happens is that examples such as those I have sketched are seen as a kind of commonsense matter of sociological influence, which somehow remains distinct from the core of the separate, autonomous self who is the proper subject of law and politics. These social dimensions can then be hived off from ideas, such as basic rights, and the institutions that will protect them. I want to show the importance of making them central and integral—for rights, for law, for basic inquiries of legal and political theory.

II. RELATIONAL AUTONOMY
A. Introduction and Examples

Several chapters of this book are devoted to developing what I mean by relational autonomy. But there is a set of clarifications and puzzles that I think will provide a helpful framework for those more detailed explorations. This section of the introduction sets out that framework.

Before launching into the framework, I thought it would be helpful to offer a few brief examples of what I mean by my central claim that autonomy is made possible by constructive relationship (or undermined by destructive relationship). These examples also give a further sense of the nested relations I discuss above. They also point toward issues I develop more fully in later sections. And, finally, the examples are intended to give a sense of why a relational conception of autonomy matters, particularly in the modern bureaucratic/welfare state.

Of course, as we saw in the previous section, the easiest examples are the importance of constructive relationship for the development of autonomy in childhood. But my claim is that autonomy requires constructive relationship throughout a person's life. Autonomy can thrive or wither in adults depending on the structures of relationship they are embedded in. Even relations of dependence and hierarchies of power can be structured in ways that foster rather than undermine autonomy. (Of course, the classic example of childhood reveals that possibility, but the links to adult institutional structures are not often made.) So I begin with adult examples of dependence and power.

A single mother on social assistance is clearly in a relationship of dependence on the state. And despite contemporary rhetoric of empowerment,[46] most such relationships are structured in ways that undermine rather than enhance the autonomy of welfare recipients. Lack of information about eligibility rules, a stance of suspicion from the bureaucracy, invasions of privacy, arbitrary or incomprehensible suspension or reduction of payments keep recipients insecure, off balance, unable to plan ahead, anxious, and uncertain.[47] The payments permit them (barely) to survive, but the way they receive these payments is corrosive of their autonomy.

Some might say (and judges have said[48]) that their autonomy is compromised by the very fact of their dependency. (This, as we will see later, is one of the practical problems of equating autonomy with independence.) On this view, there is no point in trying to figure out how to structure recipients' relations with the state (via the bureaucracy) in ways that would foster their autonomy. Individual autonomy is protected by keeping the state (and others) out of one's affairs. That's what rights and the law do. But they cannot do so here because a welfare recipient has already invited the state in when she asked for social assistance. She is dependent and necessarily subject to a power hierarchy. No one should be surprised that such relations do not promote autonomy.

Consider now another kind of position of dependence on the state: tenured professors at public universities. We too are dependent on the state for our income. But in our case, vast creative resources have been expended to structure that basic dependence in a way that maximizes our autonomy. In the case of professors, people think that their autonomy is important to the kind of work they do. (And of course, professors enjoy a kind of status that welfare recipients do not.) The institution of tenure insulates them from the inevitable hierarchies of power at the university and in the university's relation to the state.

The funding structure of the university, in turn, is designed to minimize the vulnerability of the institution and individual faculty members to the kind of politics or caprice that could compromise faculty's autonomy. Tenured professors work within relations of dependence and hierarchy, but their autonomy is incredibly well protected.[49]

The problem then, is not the fact of dependence on the state, or even the presence of hierarchy; it is how that dependence and hierarchy are structured. In the professor's case, elaborate precautions have been put in place through law, through internal university norms and procedures. No such care and effort is in evidence in the laws, rules, and internal bureaucratic norms that structure the relations between those who receive social assistance and those who administer it.[50] (In chapter 2, I discuss the kind of improvements that law and policy could make.)

Another example is the classroom, with its (almost) inevitable hierarchy of power between student and teacher. That power relation can be exercised in ways that enhance or undermine the autonomy of students, including their capacity for autonomous thinking. Classes can be structured so that students are expected to memorize material from lectures and texts and to parrot back professors' views on exams. Class discussion can encourage respectful disagreement among students and with the professor or it can be characterized by harsh criticism or failure to take alternative views seriously. Professors can engage in tacit collaboration with other students' dismissal of questions or comments that bring in new perspectives or they can reinforce the importance of attending to new perspectives. Again, the power hierarchy (and the students' dependence on the professor for grades) remains. The question is whether it is structured to create relations conducive to autonomy.

When I was visiting Japan in the 1990s I was struck by another example of how nested structures of relations affect autonomy. As in many countries, fairly early in their education (around age eleven) Japanese children had to compete in exams that would determine the future path of their education and employment. I was at a children's rights conference, and there was much talk about the pressures that parents brought to bear on their children with respect to school performance. I realized that the structure of the education system was such that it encouraged parents to control their children's behavior rather than encouraging the development of their autonomy. Parents could reasonably think that no ten year old could really understand the long-term significance of the upcoming exam. A responsible parent might well decide that it would be a dangerous indulgence to encourage autonomous choice about studying. The kinds of autonomy promoted by parent–child relationships here are shaped by the larger structures of competition, and early (largely irreversible) decisions about the path of education. By contrast, Ontario, Canada, has no such early streaming exams[51] (although other less direct forms of streaming do take place). Moreover, children who do poorly in high school, and even drop out, will have a chance later to apply to university as mature students with different admissions criteria. This structure of keeping educational options open can allow parents to be less anxious and controlling. The price for fostering their children's autonomy will not seem so high.

These are a few examples of how relations enable or undermine autonomy. They are also examples of why it matters to think about autonomy in relational terms: it can help us structure relations, even in circumstances of dependence and hierarchy, in ways that make autonomy available to all. In the modern state, most people find themselves dependent on bureaucratic decision making. Understanding how to structure such dependence is essential to the protection of autonomy.

The idea of relational autonomy is not, however, self-evident (even though I think it is compelling once people understand it). I think that the relational conception of autonomy cannot really take hold in people's imaginations when it is blocked by a set of (often unexamined) frameworks and presuppositions that are deep in Anglo-American culture. In this section, I try to articulate what I think these blocks are and dispel them. And I try to articulate the value I see in autonomy, as distinct from the form that value takes in much legal and political theory and in everyday understanding. My objective is to enable people to make sense of a conception of autonomy that will resonate with many of their values and intuitions—even as I try to dislodge the powerful image of autonomy as independence that is so much part of the Anglo-American picture of desirable adulthood. I have tried to limit my engagement with the philosophical debates around autonomy to those issues that I think are crucial either to expressing my sense of the meaning and value of autonomy or to removing the barriers to grasping and affirming it.

B. Why Autonomy

The first point I want to make is that the relational approach I develop here can be applied to any value, not just to autonomy. All core values, such as security, dignity, equality, liberty, freedom of speech, are made possible by (or undermined by) structures of relationships. In some cases, such as equality and perhaps dignity, it makes sense to say that the value is itself a relationship. I think it is clear that equality consists in equal relationships, even if there are important disagreements about *which* relationships—economic, social, political, legal— are necessary for what people mean by equality as a core value.[52] For some, only the relationship between citizen and state need be characterized by equality. For others, that equality is only possible if there are high levels of economic equality among people. Somewhat less directly one could say that to experience dignity is to be treated by others in ways consistent with dignity, to experience relations of dignity. Free speech is a different kind of example of the kind of relations necessary for people to enjoy the value. In section III I talk about Joseph Raz's treatment of free speech as a public good.[53] On this account, individuals can only enjoy the right of free speech when there is a public culture of free speech, when the patterns of relations among people protect and respect free expression. In chapters 3 and 5 I offer examples of violence against women in the context of the kinds of structures of relations that are inconsistent with basic physical security for women.

Thus, in part, my development of a relational approach to autonomy is meant to model the way any value can be examined from a relational perspective. (I return to this issue in section III) The question then arises, why focus on autonomy? The most obvious form of that question is why choose a value that is practically synonymous with the liberal, individualistic approach I want to supplant or at least shift? The purpose of this subsection is to answer that question.

The first answer (though perhaps not the most important one) is that it is precisely the individualism of the traditional conception of autonomy that renders it particularly in need of a relational reconception and that makes it a compelling challenge to a relational approach.[54] A student once reported to me that a colleague had described the concept of relational autonomy as an oxymoron. If I can show the usefulness (at the level of theory, legal interpretation, and "common sense") of a relational approach for a concept so heavily identified with individual independence, perhaps its usefulness for other values will be clearer still.[55]

The second answer is that autonomy is not just central to Anglo-American legal and political thought. It has a kind of iconic value in the culture: everyone should aspire to be independent and in control of his life, and those who are admirable are. But this form of autonomy is distorted in ways that virtually guarantee the inequality of its enjoyment and that undermine everyone's ability to understand what would promote it. Consider Margaret Urban Walker's description of the "autonomous individual…entrenched in the values of the middle class:"

> The image of the fit, energetic, and productive individual who sets himself a course of progressive achievement within the boundaries of society's rules and institutions, and whose orderly life testifies to his self-discipline and individual effort, remains an icon of our culture. This picture of autonomy, rather than abstract ideals of acting out of one's own interests and preferences or acting on principles that one can rationally endorse, is really our central cultural ideal. It is a picture of autonomy as energetic self-superintendence with a consistent track record over a lifetime to show for it. It is instructive to notice how this more robust picture of physical vitality, reliable performance, and cumulative achievement—an individual's life as a career—recurs in the late twentieth century both in studies of aging and in contemporary ethics.[56]

In the twenty-first century, I think there has been some significant erosion to the "Protestant ethic" quality of this description in favor of a picture of an economic actor who is not just rational, but crafty at promoting his interests, without much emphasis on self-discipline or society's rules. Nevertheless, I think Walker captures something important. She also adds that this view of the model autonomous self "eclipses our dependence on others and vulnerability to each other, and it overshadows our life-defining connections to and responsibilities for each other."[57]

Walker notes the way this model excludes many. First, it poses problems for people as they age. "The ill fit between norms of autonomous, self-reliant, and self-interested agency and social reality is evident in the situation of aging persons who are vulnerable and dependent and those who are responsible for their care."[58] Even without acute dependency, when life is a career, it seems to end with retirement. And she points out that "autonomy has been defined concretely in ways at odds with the social demands for appropriately feminine behavior in women." Her picture is, of course, also connected to the issues of dependence I discussed in the previous section: "values of interdependence and attentiveness to need are…associated with people of lower status: women, the working or lower classes, and people of color. Independence and executive control are linked to higher social status."[59]

Walker also argues that the dominant conception of autonomy has been "elaborated in ways that reflect middle-class expectations of stability and control."[60] These expectations have been significantly disrupted in the early twenty-first century by the changes in the structure of employment. Few of the once secure, prestigious jobs, such as banker or lawyer, now provide the kind of security that was common a generation ago. Many people now face the need to change jobs many times, and many men face the kind of part-time jobs with no benefits that once characterized women's employment.[61] The acute anxiety that this disruption has caused is probably linked not just to economic insecurity as such, but to the threat to people's self-conception as the autonomous individual that has been the model for successful adulthood.

I would recast her emphasis on the unequal ability of different groups of people to enjoy this picture of autonomy. I would say (and I think she would agree) that what is unequal is the ability to sustain this illusion of autonomy, in particular the illusion of autonomy as independence. (I develop this point about illusion in chapter 2.) But, of course, this inequality matters when the illusion is an important part of what allows people (more often men) to feel competent, successful, and in control of their lives. When this is the image of the proper, adult member of society, those excluded from it will suffer. When such a misguided image of autonomy is a central marker of full, competent adulthood, both equality and the actual value of autonomy call out for a reconception that can embrace dependency—including the dependence on constructive relations with others to achieve and sustain autonomy.

Of course, not all feminists or other critics of liberal individualism want to reclaim the value of autonomy. Walker's characterization is helpful again. She speaks of relational feminists, theorists of care, communitarians, and historicists as "resistant" to "autonomy as the dominant ideal of self. They claim that autonomy is, at best, a restricted or partial expression of human moral agency and, at worst, an impoverishing aim for it. Autonomy cannot encompass the realities of human interdependence and community, or explain the concrete conditions of responsibility, the commitments, and the attachments to others that move us to action."[62]

But I think that feminism, and indeed all other emancipatory projects I know of, cannot do without an adequate conception of autonomy. It is too central to our aspirations not to let others define our lives, constrain our opportunities, or exclude us from the power to shape collective norms. In the above passage, Walker tacitly accepts the liberal definition of autonomy as independence in describing this "resistance" to autonomy as a positive value. I argue that we cannot afford to cede the meaning of autonomy to the liberal tradition and that we should redefine rather than resist the term.

One way of seeing the importance of autonomy to feminism, in particular, is to note that feminism is rife with conflicts which are in essence debates over what real autonomy calls for: is prostitution a choice of work that should be respected, or is it inherent violence that can never be properly understood as an autonomous choice? Is contractual pregnancy (sometimes called surrogate motherhood) a free exercise of control over one's own body, or is it essentially exploitation, undermining proper respect for both women and children?[63] Should the decision about whether to carry a pregnancy to term be governed by the mother's autonomy only? Even cosmetic questions become puzzles of autonomy for women, such as breast augmentation surgery or less weighty matters of makeup, high-heels, or shaving one's legs. Are these expressions of oppressive social norms or of autonomous choice? Can one autonomously choose compliance with coercive norms?[64]

Another way I think of the power of autonomy as a cultural norm is the role it plays in fiction. Women's coming-of-age stories are often about a young woman overcoming the constraints of a tradition she has been born into.[65] (I return to this example in my discussion of the puzzle of determinism.) Such stories are circulated in the nonfiction context as well.[66] Whether we define ourselves as feminists or not, I think women respond to these stories with admiration and see them as an affirmation of the human possibility of transcending limitations, including those of family, culture, and even religion (usually the religion of "others"). These pictures of people remaking identities, making their lives "their own," have a powerful hold on the North American imagination.[67]

Of course, another reason for taking on autonomy is its centrality in Anglo-American legal and political thought. The liberal tradition assigned great value to autonomy, articulated that value, and skewed our understanding of it. This dominant conception is (with some variation in its form) so deeply integrated into presumptions about the value of human selves and the (legal) rights such selves should have—or inherently do have (moral rights)—that the distortions of that conception will play themselves out throughout our legal and political systems.

I think these are all good reasons for making autonomy my chief exemplar of how to reconceptualize a core value in relational terms. But, even though I have not yet tried to explain the way in which *I* value autonomy or what I think my reconceptualization contributes, an anxiety arises. When viewed through the historicist lens I discussed in the previous section, one might say that what this all adds up to is that my project simply mirrors the centrality of autonomy in the constellation of cultural, philosophical, legal, and political norms that govern the early-twenty-first century Anglo-American world.

I can easily accept that the particular attachment I have to autonomy, and the attachment I presume in most of my readers (even feminists who reject the term), is a historical, cultural product. I think most people raised in the West cannot but embrace some version of the value of making and implementing choices about how they live, even as they may recognize the contingency of what they see as choices, what they experience as good reasons for making them, as well as the more obvious practical constraints of implementing such choices. I see the idea that people should make their own lives and selves as the product of historical context. I see this idea, which prevails in the West, as extraordinarily demanding, a source of tremendous stress, embedded in huge disparities of resources for enacting this idea and virtually irresistible (as both demand and lure) for those raised to it. I think this is true, in different ways, both for those in relative positions of privilege and for those who are taught to imbibe the idea that their absence of privilege is somehow an individual or class failure to achieve autonomy and reap its benefits. (The idea of the failed culture of the American urban black underclass or of aboriginal peoples in Canada offers a collective rather than individual account of failure but failure nonetheless.)

Since most of us raised in the West have this value, it is best to understand it (and its prevailing illusions) relationally and to see where it arises in law. This is so in part because such inquiry will make it easier to see what is actually valuable and how this value may be made practically available to all.

I think this is a worthwhile project even though I can also imagine a desirable constellation of values in which autonomy is just one, balanced among others like harmony, compassion, attentiveness, responsibility, intimacy, and respect for tradition—each of which might be in tension with autonomy. (This is a list deliberately distinct from the liberal rights that are intertwined with, and yet might also compete with, autonomy.) My project here does not treat autonomy as "truly" the highest of human values. I treat autonomy as a powerful existing value, and I claim that we can best understand the core of that value in relational terms. I do not see my project as imagining a new value that I will call autonomy. Nor, despite my language of "distortion" and "illusion," do I believe that I know a timeless truth about the "true" core of the existing value.

I do claim that parts of the dominant picture of autonomy as independence are not really human possibilities and that the aspiration to achieve them (to experience their illusion) can only come at the cost of subordinating the others who do the (unacknowledged) work made necessary by dependence. The kind of autonomy that *is* possible is made possible by constructive relationship working together with individual effort and attention—enabled, in turn, by constructive relationship.

C. What I Mean by Autonomy and Why I Care

I see autonomy as the core of a capacity to engage in the ongoing, interactive creation of our selves—our relational selves, our selves that are constituted, yet not determined, by the web of nested relations within which we live. We have the capacity to interact creatively, that is, in an undetermined way, with all the relationships that shape us—and thus to reshape, re-create, both the relationships and ourselves. The idea that such acts arise from the actor rather than being determined by something else is captured by the notion of autonomy. (Of course there are a host of puzzles contained in this claim, some of which I will turn to shortly.) The value of the capacity for creative interaction is at the heart of why I care about autonomy, so I introduce the idea here (and develop it in chapter 3). In chapter 2 I also refer to autonomy as finding one's own law. Almost all versions of autonomy have some component of what is "one's own," and in this section (and again later) I will discuss what "one's own" means in a relational context.[68]

I share the widely held belief in the capacity for autonomy and its value. But I do so in a way that not does not embrace a picture of a sovereign self that can simply be presumed to be autonomous. I *do* presuppose a capacity for autonomy. I do so on the basis of evidence, but not irrefutable evidence, and experience, but not with the assumption that experience is always reliable. (See my discussion of the illusion of autonomy in chapter 2.) I focus on what enables this capacity to develop, to thrive, to manifest in autonomous behavior and the experience of autonomy.

I think the best language to capture this focus is "relations of autonomy."[69] I prefer this language to "conditions" for autonomy because I think the language of relations of autonomy highlights the dynamic, interactive quality of autonomy—in contrast to a picture of it as a strictly internal state of mind that comes into being when certain—separable—conditions are in place. The functioning of the capacity for autonomy is highly fluid; it varies across time and spheres of our lives. Autonomy exists on a continuum. As we act (usually partially) autonomously, we are always in interaction with the relationships (intimate and social–structural) that enable our autonomy. Relations are then constitutive of autonomy rather than conditions for it.

Because we are always dependent on others for the possibility of autonomy, it follows that autonomy cannot mean independence (chapter 2). I also reject another commonplace synonym for autonomy: control (chapter 7). Even thoughtful theorists invoke that language. For example, Grace Clement has written, "While no one can escape his or her socialization, it is obvious that some people are more autonomous—i.e., in control of their lives—than others."[70] While I don't disagree with the observation I think she is making, the language of control misdirects our attention. Our lives involve other people, and control is not a respectful relation to other autonomous beings (including children).

The effort at control almost always involves some form of domination. While feeling "out of control" probably reflects a capacity for autonomy that is not thriving (at that time or in that sphere), control itself is a poor way to express the aspiration to enhanced autonomy.[71] And control is an illusion with respect to the world in general (and, indeed, arguably a disrespectful relation to earth and other life-forms). The challenge is to foster autonomy in a world we cannot control.

i. The Capacity for Creative Interaction

As I use the terms, "autonomy," is a key component of the "capacity for creative interaction." These terms are not synonymous because this creative capacity involves more than autonomy. Creative interaction also requires capacities for attention, for receptivity,[72] and for responsiveness (and perhaps more). These dimensions help remind us that since creative interaction involves *interacting* one must be able to attend, receive, and respond to what one is interacting with. Otherwise the full potential for creativity will not be achieved. But that potential also requires the possibility of *new* engagement, breaking or transforming received patterns, giving rise to and acting on one's own distinctive perceptions, insights, and forms of engagement. This is the dimension of creative interaction captured by the idea of autonomy. (This description is drawn from chapter 3.)

I think there is something obvious and observable about the human[73] capacity for creation and its component of autonomy. Stories from history, folklore, and literature abound with examples of people breaking old patterns of relation, of new inventions, of creating art, agriculture, tools, families, and empires. Everyday experience reveals small examples of innovation, rebellion, and transformation. But I think there is also something ineffable or mysterious about this capacity. In discussing the human capacity for action and the "fact of natality," Hannah Arendt uses the language of "miracle." She refers to

the faculty of interrupting [the inexorable path from life to death], and beginning something new, a faculty which is inherent in action like an ever present reminder that men, though they must die, are not born in order to die but in order to begin.... Thus action, seen from the viewpoint of the automatic processes which seem to determine the course of the world, looks like a miracle. In the language of natural science, it is the "infinite improbability" which occurs regularly.[74]

D. W. Winnicott offers additional language to capture the value of this ordinary miracle of creating the new. He uses the term "creative apperception," a kind of creative engagement with the world. He says, "It is in playing and only in playing that the child or the adult is able to be creative and use the whole personality, and it is only in being creative that the individual discovers the self."[75] "It is creative apperception more than anything else that makes the individual feel that life is worth living. Contrasted with this is a relationship to external reality which is one of compliance, the world and its details being recognized but only as something to be fitted in with or demanding adaptation."[76] "Creativity involves the individual in spontaneous action."[77] Madeline Davis and David Wallbridge, commentators on Winnicott, say that "the self discovery that Winnicott describes as taking place in the potential space [where play takes place, an intermediate area of inner and outer reality[78]] is the same thing as the realization of individual potential, including the potential to evolve new forms in which potential can be realized."[79]

This, of course, is very close to the claim I opened this section with: human beings have the capacity to interact creatively with all the relationships that shape us—and thus to reshape, re-create, both the relationships and ourselves. Finally, one further invocation of the capacity for the new: "The world is continually 'woven into the texture of imagination' so that new patterns of imaging emerge and a man is able to be truly original"[80]—including altering the environment, institutions, and mores.

I use the language of the capacity for creative interaction to simultaneously emphasize that creativity always takes place in relation to what exists and that the creativity exceeds, transforms, generates something new out of what exists. I think this must be close to what Winnicott means by intermediate space—the inner capacity for the new interacting with the constellation of relations that enabled that capacity. Some such capacity seems to me to be essential to individual thriving and joy as well as to the ability of communities to avoid stagnation. Life changes around us all the time, so if we don't want to get stuck in old patterns no longer optimal for shifting realities; we need a creative capacity of interaction. Sometimes that capacity will be exercised to induce a shift, which will then call on the creative capacity of others to respond to it.

The positive dimension of the Western attachment to autonomy has to do with this capacity to undertake, to envision something new, to do something surprising, to shift the terms of relations, of how things have always been done—whether through an idea, an invention, art, a garden, rearing a child, modeling a different way of relating to others, or collaborating to change an institution. All of that requires a capacity not to be bound by existing patterns of thought, institutions, or relationships. It requires a capacity to go beyond habit, beyond the expected, the conventional, at least in small ways to be imaginative and innovative, to shift things slightly to create a moment of joy or so that they suit one better, or improve things for others.

It is important not to read the above as invoking a human capacity for greatness or genius (which is sometimes attributed to Arendt). I think what is often seen as greatness *does* come from this creative capacity, both the greatness of Michelangelo and the greatness of Caesar, for example. (Creativity, after all, does not only produce the good. I intended to gesture toward this in my earlier inclusion of empire in my list of creations.) For my purposes, however, it is the ordinariness of the capacity for creativity that matters most. Think, for example, of the child's joy in creating a tower of blocks. Neither the joy nor the creativity lies in there never having been a tower before. The newness, the originality lies in her vision, her experimentation, her desire, her developing skill. Other examples abound: children's daily capacity to create new games, a new, attractive arrangement of furniture in a room, designing a garden or even just buying one plant and finding the right place for it. I think humor is another example. The funny juxtaposition of stories or words is an act of creation, as is the capacity to suddenly see oneself from a new angle and laugh at oneself. I think there is an important link to love. Love can foster the attentiveness and responsiveness that allows one to see new things. (See, for example, Evelyn Fox Keller's discussion of Barbara McClintock's love of her corn plants, giving her a new perspective on genetic mutation.[81]) And creative interaction can nurture love, shift an old pattern of relating between intimate partners that then allows for deeper connection.

All of these small abilities that make life dynamic and joyful, as well as generate the resilience to respond to extreme deprivation, involve creativity. Sometimes this capacity for creativity will bring forth something brand new, an important shift in how things had been before. That potential is part of why the capacity is so important, but it is not the essence of creativity. The spontaneity, the imagination of the new comes from within the actor (enabled by her relational web). It is this capacity that I think the Western concept of autonomy points toward. And I think it is of great value, despite the ugly caricature of it in the iconic independent, self-made man.

ii. Creating Oneself, What Is One's Own?

Having just disparaged the idea of the self-made man, I turn now to the ways in which the capacity for creative interaction includes the capacity to create oneself (throughout one's life, in interaction with others). Some people express the centrality of our *relational* selves in ways that cast doubt on this capacity. For example, as Emily Jackson writes, "None of us chooses some of the crucial determinants of our values and beliefs, such as parents, nationality, education, religion, etc. But the fact that we cannot choose *who we are* does not necessarily mean that we should not be allowed to choose *what we do*."[82] I do not choose to express the significance of our relations in this way. For many people the ongoing task of constructing, recognizing, becoming conscious of themselves—in some ways shifting who they are—is part of the project of autonomy. And part of the attraction of the language of creative interaction is that it can encompass the ability to interact creatively with all those "crucial determinants" in ways that not only shift who we are, but those "determinants" themselves.

Of course, at the heart of such disagreements over expression is the idea of determination itself. In the previous section I presented the relational self as constituted, but never determined, by her complex web of relations. I will return to this issue in the next section because I think it is at the core of the puzzle about the possibility of relational autonomy. Here I will outline some of the main components of my understanding of autonomy. One might see it as the framework I use for thinking about how anything—choice, desire, value—can be called "one's own," when, for a relational self, nothing can ever be "only" one's own. The processes by which we make something our own are always enabled by the relations of which we are a part, and the resources we use in this process—ideas, frameworks, values—always come to us from the creations of others. Just as neither fact denies the possibility of the genuine creativity of our unique interaction with these sources, neither fact denies the significance of the experience of making or claiming something as one's own—or the value of using that language in a duly relational way.[83]

In chapter 3 I talk about "finding one's own law" as a useful (and literal) understanding of autonomy. The word "finding" captures the importance of discernment in the exercise of the capacity for autonomy, and "law" points to the importance of commitments to oneself. Like most theorists, I do not think that autonomy can reduced to choice or doing what one wants to. The question always arises whether the choice or desire is itself autonomous.[84] The idea of finding one's own law suggests the discernment of the form, in the broadest sense, which choices should take. It is a discernment of the kinds of commitments to oneself that will foster different components of the capacity for creative interaction. Such commitments could include habits of introspection, mediation, consultation with wise others, efforts to take the perspectives of others into account in exercising judgment, learning to tune into one's body to access that distinct kind of knowledge, learning from dreams, attending to what gives one joy and following that joy, encouraging playfulness and humor. It could also include commitments to core values, but generally such values will be sufficiently general that ongoing discernment will be required to know what it means to live in accordance with them. The practices noted above are of the kind that can enable the ongoing discernment and renewed examination of the values.

This list above is meant to suggest that the kind of self-reflection that I think is essential to autonomy is not necessarily of an intellectual kind. Many philosophers' accounts of such self-reflection strike me as excessively intellectual and thus not only ill-suited to many people, but also premised on far too narrow an understanding of what enables wisdom or discernment. In addition, while there are obvious limits to "gut feelings" (they can be conditioned responses never subjected to reflection), bodily responses can be a guide to autonomy. Some form of discernment is necessary, but it need not always take the form of prolonged "rational" reflection.

As the list perhaps also suggests, I think that self-consciousness is a component of autonomy (chapter 7). Again, I think this can take many forms, and many kinds of practices can promote it. But some ongoing, if not constant, effort to know oneself is necessary. At the same time, I do not envision a fixed, "true" self that can be uncovered. The creation of oneself is a lifelong process. What enables autonomy are processes and dynamic, constructive relations that enable those processes. Neither the self nor autonomy is static; it is never simply arrived at or achieved. So a protected, bounded sphere cannot be an optimal metaphor for the enhancement of either. The long-standing association in the liberal tradition between private property and autonomy[85] is replaced in my approach by dynamic processes and interactive relations. As Hester Lessard put it to me, the spatial metaphor is replaced by a temporal one.[86] Becoming oneself, becoming autonomous are processes of value. The central questions are the kinds of relationships within which these processes thrive.

D. Puzzles of Relational Autonomy

While I hope I have presented a persuasive outline of my understanding of the relational self and relational autonomy (to be fleshed out in subsequent chapters), I know from my experience of teaching theories of relational autonomy[87] that students find something deeply puzzling, indeed elusive about the idea of relational autonomy. I believe that this sense of puzzlement comes from two sets of beliefs that are widely, and deeply, held in the Anglo-American world. I have already sketched the first belief. It is the idea of autonomy as independence. But what I have not stressed so far is that that independence is understood in opposition to the community (or the collective or the state), which poses a constant threat to it. In the liberal tradition, part of the function of law is to contain that threat—by bounding off a sphere of individual autonomy into which no one, including the state, can intrude. Bounding the power of the state by individual rights is a central project of Anglo-American liberalism. The second set of beliefs is a sort of pseudoscientific view of the world as characterized by determinism, to which I will return in the next subsection. But I will begin by trying to capture the opposition between the individual and the collective—whether in the form of family, community, or most commonly the state—that has been central to Anglo-American understandings of autonomy. (As I discuss in chapter 3, it takes its starkest, but nevertheless characteristic, form in the United States.) I think this deep sense of opposition is one of the barriers to "grasping" the idea of relational autonomy.

i. Autonomy and the Opposition between Individual and Collective

Let me begin with stories. North American literature is replete with moving tales of people who transcend their origins, who chart new territory. And this is perhaps particularly true for feminist fiction (whether the authors would so self-describe or not). Women need to be able to escape or transform their traditional roles. The heroines of fantasy novels often draw on the strengths of their traditions—their knowledge of herb lore, their healing skills, their love of the land, the strength of their bonds to family—and use them to transform the scope of their role. Sometimes they become models for others' understanding of the limitations of those roles, of the full capacities women have.

In these stories of heroic efforts at transcending and/or transforming the traditions one is born to, we see reinforced a sense of an opposition between individual and community and the crucial role of autonomy in enabling the individual to rise above the constraints of community. And as I have just noted, this heroic story is one that resonates powerfully for women who chafe at still prevailing gender norms and stereotypes.

There is something true in these stories. Creativity in both the individual and the community require the capacity to resist and transform existing patterns. Without that ability, societies and individuals would stagnate. Part of what we cherish in the human capacity for innovation, for artistic creation, for new forms of social relations, for perceiving and overcoming long-standing harmful patterns is the ability of individuals not to be determined by their history or the prevailing norms and practices of their communities. We observe and honor the capacity to bring forth the new, to create, to transform, to resist.

Of course, this capacity does not always seem oppositional. We see the nonoppositional form in children's invented games, in poetry, or the invention of new medicines. But often the urge for transformation or creation arises out of some constraint posed by the old patterns. The new form emerges out of a struggle against the old. In the stories, we cheer the emergence of a greater freedom, a wider scope, or a fuller, deeper form of life than the old bounds allowed. Usually the heroine needs not only vision (of new possibilities) but also courage to break existing rules, disappoint the expectations of others.

The law has its own version of these stories. The individual's autonomy is protected against the collective through such rights as freedom of speech and conscience, freedom of assembly, and a right to privacy. The collective poses a threat through invasive and coercive laws, and constitutional rights shield individuals from this threat. The media reinforces this story of threat and protection through tales of "others" who lack this legal protection and are forced to wear burkas or are sent to prison for expressing opinions the government sees as hostile. Without adequate protection, the individual becomes subservient to the collective—often, but not always, through the power of the state. (Another popular story these days is of women's compliance enforced by family members, most notoriously by honor killings.)

In these stories, then, autonomy stands in opposition to the collective. And our commonplace synonym for autonomy, independence, reflects this sense. One is autonomous when one is free of the constraints of others—whether one's family, community, or state.

This is a powerful picture. It is also a distorted picture, even though it takes part of its strength from the element of truth I pointed to above—the importance of the possibility of resistance and transformation. A relational conception of autonomy runs up against this picture. A given story that shows how relationship enables autonomy might be persuasive. But a claim that autonomy itself is inseparable from relationship can seem a contradiction in terms. If it is autonomy that enables one to resist, overcome, or transcend relationship, how can autonomy rely on relationship? If the community is the ever present threat to autonomy, how can its relations be the source of autonomy? If autonomy depends on relationship, doesn't that mean that one's inner autonomy depends on something external, the very external thing one might need autonomy to resist? For some, an understanding of autonomy that routinely depends on something outside oneself would be a contradiction in terms. And in my version of relational autonomy this problem is particularly acute because I claim that autonomy requires constructive relationship throughout one's life, not just as a child when one is first developing the capacity.

As long as the dominant picture of autonomy in opposition to the collective prevails, a relational approach becomes relegated to exceptions, such as childhood or someone's particular experience of, say, an exceptional teacher. As a general concept it becomes an unproductive paradox or an unsolvable puzzle. The questions that arise out of the oppositional framework can never be satisfactorily answered. The framework of the question needs to be changed. (One might say that it is the project of the book to change that framework.) It is not that a better framework makes the puzzles, both theoretical and practical, simply disappear. But they are reconstituted in a way that makes them productive rather than illogical or simply frustrating. The contradiction in terms does disappear when the meaning of the terms changes.

ii. Presumptions of Determinism

I return now to the issue of presumptions of determinism and the ways constitutive relations become confused with deterministic conditioning. (I do not mean here a systematic philosophical determinism but what I take to be deterministic habits of thought.) Conflation of social conditioning and determinism pits autonomy (understood as independence from the collective) against the inevitability of social conditioning.

There is obviously a tension between social conditioning and autonomy. If people are really the sum of their social conditioning, there is no place for autonomy. By emphasizing the social relations that are themselves necessary for autonomy, relational autonomy seems to exacerbate the tension. And, of course, if autonomy is understood as independence from the collective, and social conditioning is understood deterministically, autonomy and social conditioning must be incompatible. Relational autonomy becomes an oxymoron.

On a deterministic model, all human acts, if fully understood, would be revealed to be caused, that is determined, by something (though perhaps on a chemical/biological model the something might not be external; the cause might be internal to the brain of the actor). But despite the (reasonable) popular belief in social conditioning, I do not think my students (or most North Americans) accept a fully deterministic account of human beings. They believe in something like autonomy, and they find a relational account of human selves plausible. But they find the concept of relational autonomy hard to hold in their minds.

So I am going to turn now to restatements of the puzzlement that I observe and suggestions about ways to resolve it. This matters not just because "relational autonomy" will otherwise remain a paradox or an oxymoron, but also because, as we will see shortly, actual problems of autonomy in the modern state cannot be solved by a model of autonomy as independence in opposition to the collective. Habits of determinist thought hold this model in place.

The puzzles about autonomy and the relational nature of human beings are not simply theoretical. They take many practical everyday forms, which (as I noted earlier) generate conflicts over policy. For example, should we understand battered women as trapped by their relationships, constrained by "steel fences in their minds," such that they no longer have real autonomy?[88] (I discuss this example in chapter 4.) Then perhaps we can understand why they stay in these abusive relationships: they feel they do not have a choice. And perhaps we can even understand the extreme, seemingly desperate, actions they take of killing their abusive partners. Or does this sort of "understanding," this focus on context and relationship, do a disservice to women in abusive relationships? Does it wrongly deny their autonomy? Is it both truer and better for these women to say, as a student of mine did, "You can always leave. There is always a choice to leave." (She did, at age fourteen.)

This story offers a stark choice between a "relational" approach that treats the constraints of relationship as determinative of behavior (thus eliminating autonomy), on the one hand, and, on the other hand, a bald assertion of the ever present possibility of choice that threatens to be unforgiving and judgmental about "bad choices" and even naive about constraints of both psychological damage and unavailability of resources, such as shelters and financial support.

My students feel torn and divided among themselves—some on the side of autonomy and some on the side of social context. Sometimes they bounce back and forth between competing intuitions about the existence of autonomy and the determinism of social conditioning.

What is wrong with this stark choice? How can a relational approach avoid it, avoid both a determinism that denies autonomy and a naive assumption of autonomy that ignores its conditions? How can a commitment to autonomy take a form to which relationship is central rather than peripheral? By treating relationships not just as objects about which autonomous choices can be made, but as what makes such choices possible.

iii. The Possibility of Relational Autonomy: Reframing the Relation between Individual and Community

There are two distinct (though related) puzzles that relational autonomy gives rise to in the face of a tradition that has inchoate presumptions about determinism and that sets individual autonomy in opposition to community (and other forms of relations people are embedded in):

1. How can people actually *be* autonomous if they are dependent on relations with others for their autonomy?
2. How can people *know* when they are autonomous? When they are constituted by relationship, it seems impossible to know what is truly "their own" and not the result of the norms or desires of others.

I will postpone my discussion of the second question until later in this chapter.

It may be that a disbelief in the possibility of relational autonomy is actually the core of the resistance to the idea of relational selves. I think that for many it is the idea of human autonomy that holds back the threat of determinism, that allows people to see human beings as distinctly above the determinism of the natural world. Individual autonomy, on this view, makes people more than the sum of conditioning. Autonomy is what enables people to sort, choose, reject, embrace, and transform the many factors that might otherwise merely condition us. (I agree with that part.) But then, when autonomy itself is said to have external, relational sources, it looks like it cannot possibly do its job of transcendence. It must be imagined as somehow separate, radically distinct, from all those relations, beliefs, and values that need to be sorted through. There must be some kind of core of the self (a kind of unmoved mover[89]) that can stand against all the external forces.

But one does not need to be caught in this framework. Not all societies construct either the individual or the capacity for autonomy in opposition to the collective.[90] When human individuality is seen as naturally and necessarily arising out of community, there can be a greater valuing of both community and autonomy. Neither needs to be vigilantly on guard against the other.

If one has a picture of human flourishing, including individuation, arising out constitutive relations that allow human capacities to develop (throughout life), there is nothing mysterious about the capacity for creation developing—like all other capacities—in constant interaction with layers of social relations. If one abandons the radical disjuncture between child development and the continuing development of human capacities, the relational approach no longer seems so contradictory. It is in part the picture of the mature adult as suddenly fully independent (and autonomous) that requires this radical disjuncture.

Relations (at all levels) are then not just the "conditions" under which a freestanding self emerges. It is the very nature of human selves to be in interaction with others. In important ways, they do not exist apart from these relations. (People can, nevertheless, withdraw from most relations temporarily and can decide not to continue to develop others. Even rejected relations, however, remain a part of oneself if they have been important.) People's capacities for language, for memory, for conscience[91] all continually develop in interaction with others.

From this perspective, it is no more mysterious or paradoxical to say that an individual's capacity for autonomy is made possible by, is constituted by, her relations than it is to say that the language she has acquired is made possible (not just in childhood but throughout her life) through her interaction with others. Autonomy is a mode of interacting with others. Relations, including those with collectives of all sorts, become not just potential threats to autonomy but its source. (In chapter 3 I address the enduring question of threat.)

A different, in some ways more familiar way of reframing the puzzle of relational autonomy is to remember that although the liberal tradition set individual autonomy in opposition to the collective, it also has its own versions of bounded structures of relations enabling freedom. Rights set bounds to my freedom in order to enable yours, and vice versa. I give up my untrammeled and precarious freedom within the state of nature in order to secure a more limited freedom. People structure their interactions with one another around limitations in order to make secure freedom possible. On the American version of constitutionalism, the government itself, which on these stories is largely responsible for securing freedom by enforcing these bounds, is also bounded by constitutional rights. The scope of the power of the state is limited by the constitutional rights of citizens. And thus the relations between citizen and state, as well as citizen and citizen, are shaped by constitutional norms, such as equality.

These are all examples that, one might say, have their own paradox: it is the bounded quality of the relations that enables freedom. (The eighteenth-century insistence on the value of liberty, not license, was intended to diffuse that paradox.) Thus to the extent that one sees the puzzle of relational autonomy as the question of how a given structure of relations can generate creativity itself, the puzzle is no different from the familiar idea that freedom requires certain bounds.

Indeed, one might say that relational autonomy is more capacious than this bounded freedom because the relations that enable it are always themselves a possible subject of transformative interaction—in ways that may further enhance (or undermine) autonomy.

And the relational approach that I suggest is more capacious in another way. The American liberal tradition in particular is quite focused on freedom as enabled by limits and boundaries defined by rights: limits on both individual actions, bounded by the rights of others, and limits on the collective action of the state, bounded by constitutional rights. But, as I have suggested, the capacity for creative interaction will be fostered—and manifested—by a great variety of human values and capacities. I have already mentioned harmony, attentiveness, and receptiveness. These involve an opening out to others, not a closing in within boundaries. In a similar way, the expansive nature of play, humor, and joy also both enables and enacts creative interaction.

iv. Transforming Reflexive Determinism

I return now to the second set of beliefs which, in interaction with the opposition between individual and collective, "mis-frame" the problem of autonomy: determinism. Over the course of many conversations about relational autonomy, I have come to think that the issue of determinism interferes in three, often convoluted, ways which I try to distinguish here. First, people have a kind of reflexive habit of moving from the importance of social relations to social conditioning to deterministic social conditioning. The real puzzles of exactly what it means to be constituted by one's relationships (which I think are closer to the question of how one can *know* when one is acting autonomously) become transformed into assumptions about the determinism of relationships. The second "step" is that the relational approach is rejected because most people don't actually believe that human beings' lives are determined. Why not? Because, as I just outlined, autonomy is supposed to lift humans above determinism; this then means that autonomy cannot be relational (i.e., deterministic) because it couldn't then be real autonomy and do its job of rescuing humans from determinism. This sense of the contradiction in terms of relational autonomy is not just that individuality must be protected from (not rooted in) relations of community.

I think it reflects a third, deeper sense that genuine creativity cannot itself be caused or conditioned. (If the capacity for creation is seen as generated by something external to it, that capacity must be denied by determinism; it cannot be genuinely creative.) A true creator must be, like some images of God, an unmoved mover. If humans have this capacity, it must be freestanding, we must just be born with it; it cannot be enmeshed in, dependent upon relations with others.

Put baldly like that, I think many people will both recognize this last intuition and see that it is wrong. The fact that a capacity for creative interaction can emerge out of particular conditions doesn't mean there is not actual creative capacity. Of course, committed determinists would say there never is real creativity (in my terms, the undetermined brings forth the new), and there is no real autonomy. But I am not trying to persuade such people, since they would have no interest in autonomy or the practical steps of making it available to people (unless they thought the illusion of autonomy served some purpose).

For many who are not systematic determinists but have deterministic habits of thought, I think a different framework for understanding the nature and possibility of genuine creation may help make sense of relational autonomy. I think such a framework is available from contemporary scientists who look at the conditions of creation in the natural world. In a completely different context, they allow us to make sense of the idea that creation has conditions that do not, of course, determine exactly the form the creative capacity will take but nevertheless are what enable the capacity itself. And these conditions are, essentially, certain kinds of relationships. Examples include genetic mutation, the development of new social behavior in primates responding to changes in conditions, and the capacity of single-cell amoebas to transform into multicellular organisms under conditions of food scarcity.[92] Seeing the relational conditions for creation in the natural world helps shift the deterministic habit of thought that is (tacitly) skeptical of any real (undetermined) creation and that, at the same time, denies the character of real creation to anything that has enabling conditions. Once this habit of thought is shifted, it is easier to see that real autonomy can have relational conditions.[93]

Finally, I remind the reader that I said that I think there is something inherently illusive or mysterious about the capacity for creation and autonomy. I stand by that, but I also believe that sometimes the sense of mystery arises out of the false frame of determinism. Remember that Arendt says that "action, seen from the viewpoint of the automatic processes which *seem to* determine the world, looks like a miracle"[94] (my emphasis). The apparent contradiction between true autonomy and autonomy that relies on relationship arises from a failure to see that all moments of creation emerge out of the constellation of conditions that give rise to the capacity for creative interaction with one's environment.[95] Human beings are, then, not an exception, but a part of the capacity for creative interaction that characterizes all life-forms. Human autonomy, while it may be distinctive (in ways the capacity for creative interaction is not), does not have to do the job of warding off determinism by lifting humans above all other life-forms. This is so even if humans have a wider scope for creativity than other living beings. Life is characterized by a capacity for creative interaction, and certain structures of relations bring that capacity to fruition.

v. Judgment, Autonomy, and the Limits of What We Can Know

I return now to my postponed question: if dependence on relations with others is built into the relational conception of autonomy, how can one ever *know* if one is autonomous? While I think the puzzles I have addressed above (variants on relational autonomy as a contradiction in terms) are based on misunderstandings, I think the puzzle of how we can know is a real one. Nevertheless, the problem of *being* autonomous in a socially conditioned world is closely intertwined with the question of knowing whether one is acting autonomously. How is it possible to choose which of the myriad of influences in one's life to make "one's own"? How is it possible to know that such choices, inevitably influenced by the very subjects of choice, are autonomously made? What enables one to reject some influences and embrace others? The idea that it is possible to make such determinations is, I think, the essence of autonomy. The language of creative interaction with these influencing factors invokes their given-ness, their enduring role in our lives, and the possibility of rejecting, embracing, and transforming them through our creative abilities.

An apparently more clear-cut alternative to this approach is a stipulation of freestanding, autonomous selves who can take an objective, evaluative stance on all that surrounds them because nothing can become part of them without their will. Such a picture is, at the least, incompatible with formative child development and the role of language in thought. That is, the picture is incompatible without a further story of freestanding cognitive tools unshaped by childhood or cultural experience with which one can objectively evaluate the influences (conscious and unconscious) of one's childhood and culture. Of course, some versions of reason do look like that. But that picture requires such a radical separation between people's cognitive abilities and everything else in their lives (perhaps most obviously language) that I find it implausible. It "solves" the problem of how one can objectively know a choice as autonomous, by an implausible picture of how people know things.

For the relational self, I think the path through the puzzle is not knowledge or certainty, but judgment. I draw here on my work on Hannah Arendt's theory of judgment.[96] I cannot reproduce the details of the theory here, but I can highlight the points that matter most for the puzzles of relational autonomy. First, in my terms, Arendt's theory of judgment (building on Kant's) is itself relational. (Indeed, I have argued elsewhere that some of the puzzles of Arendt's theory are resolved when one understands autonomy in relational terms.[97]) Judgment requires taking into account the perspectives of others in forming one's own judgment. It is a cognitive ability that is only possible in a social context. Second, one exercises judgment about matters which are neither simply a matter of personal preference nor matters about which one can prove truth claims. In Kant's view, beauty (as opposed to liking) was such a matter.

As I see it, when one tries to act autonomously, to decide which of the values one has grown up with to make "one's own," one must exercise judgment. There can be no proven truth to the matter, but neither does it make sense to call such decisions mere matters of personal preference. One cannot be autonomous without doing the work of exercising judgment about how one engages with the inevitably conditioned desires, interests, or aspirations one has. Similarly, when one reflects on one's decisions, or a path of life one has chosen, trying to discern whether the choice was an autonomous one requires judgment.

One can learn to exercise judgment well, to use the perspectives of others to become conscious of one's presuppositions and biases. For Arendt, to exercise judgment *is* to exercise it autonomously. As we use the perspectives of others to liberate ourselves from our private idiosyncrasies, we become free to make valid judgments. Indeed, I see a reciprocal relation between judgment and autonomy. Each requires the other, and experience with one enhances the other: as we exercise judgment about the values we want to embrace, we become more fully autonomous; as we become more autonomous, our capacity for judgment increases.[98]

But no matter how good our judgment is, it cannot yield provable truths or even certain knowledge. Arendt says we can claim validity for our judgments but that is not a claim of certainty or provability. Judgment is required in the exercise of autonomy, and this concept of judgment helps us see the limits of the kind of knowledge that discernment of autonomy can afford. That we can never know with certainty that our decisions were autonomously made follows from the role of judgment in both the decision and the reflection on it. It is in the nature of the kind of cognition available to us about such matters. Judgment is always open to further reflection. The uncertainty is not a failure of a relational conception of autonomy. It flows from our nature as conditioned but not determined beings with cognitive abilities to make judgments about matters that are neither about mere preference nor about truth.

The longing for certainty, and for theories that purport to offer it, seems powerful. Perhaps this is especially so with respect to what we call "our own." But all that we can do is understand what fosters our capacity for judgment and the reciprocal capacity for autonomy. We can then do both the personal work, such as expanding our capacity for judgment through engaging with the perspectives of others, and the institutional work of structuring relations to foster these capacities for all.

vi. The Internal and the External
a. Is Autonomy an Internal Process or an External Standard, Neither, or Both?
There are debates in the theories of autonomy about whether an action should be understood as autonomous if one has gone through an appropriate set of reflections about it (often called a procedural approach), or whether the question must be answered by evaluating the actual choice made. For example, can a choice (such as prostitution) be declared to be incompatible with autonomy, regardless of the nature of the chooser's reflections? (This is often referred to as a substantive approach.[99]) I think these formulations assume a sharper line between what is internal and what is external to people's minds than I think makes sense for my approach.

Of course, if autonomy is fundamentally a matter of relations of autonomy among people, then it cannot be a strictly internal matter. At the same time, in my discussion of judgment above and my earlier discussion of finding one's own law, I invoke the need for self-consciousness, for reflecting on the perspectives of others, for tuning into one's body to see what knowledge is available from that source—among other forms of personal reflection. These can be reasonably seen as internal processes, even though I see them as enabled by constructive relations. And here, too, these relations are often themselves part of the exercise of reflection: conversations with friends, teachers, or therapists can be an integral part of the necessary reflection. They are not just "conditions" for the real, separate, internal processes of autonomy.

In addition, I think one should be very cautious and humble about one's judgments about what could constitute a "substantively" autonomous choice. Many spiritual traditions involve obedience or acceptance of a highly structured set of rules of behavior while within the domain of the spiritual teaching. I take the underlying idea to be that obedience to one with more extensive spiritual knowledge or experience (or to the rules and practices that such experience has generated) can free one from illusion, obsession, false values, and other interferences with what the Buddhists call true freedom. I think this is entirely plausible in some contexts.

Many things that people may experience as "their own," such as consumerist desires or concern with professional status, may come to be seen by them as limitations to their autonomy. Various forms of discipline, including obedience, could foster such recognition. So sometimes what might appear to some as a decision antithetical to autonomy, such as joining a convent with a vow of obedience, may reasonably be experienced as autonomy enhancing by the initiate. In other cases, the suspect set of relations (of say hierarchy and obedience) may advance other values, such as peace, harmony, discernment, and spiritual attunement. Unless one is willing to stipulate autonomy as always the highest value (which I am not), there must be space for respecting as autonomous a choice to foster other values (perhaps ones that contribute to other dimensions of the capacity for creative interaction) even if there is some cost to autonomy. This is not to say that there could not be extreme examples involving coercion and harm, which preclude revising one's decision, that are truly incompatible with autonomy. But in my view, one should not treat autonomy as always the highest value, nor be quick to judge the kinds of highly structured relations that may actually foster autonomy.

b. Freedom and Autonomy

Many theorists make a distinction between freedom and autonomy, and often that distinction places more emphasis on the *external* dimensions of freedom and on the *internal* dimensions of autonomy. This is true even of theorists like Nancy Hirschmann, who insist on both the internal and external dimensions of freedom:

> the idea of social construction challenges the possibility of an essential "inside," which seems so vital to autonomy theory, and demands that determinations of freedom must consider internality and externality together. [Diana] Meyers notes that "Since one must exercise control over one's life to be autonomous, autonomy is something that a person accomplishes, not something that happens

to persons." But freedom is precisely a combination of self-creation and what happens to you, the internal as well as the external, the combination of and dynamic between the two."[100]

Of course, my view of autonomy does not posit an essential (unconstructed) inner self, nor subscribe to the idea of autonomy as control. And Hirschmann's description of the dynamic nature of the internal and the external dimensions of freedom is close to my own with respect to autonomy. Nevertheless, I think she offers a helpful contrast between what she calls autonomy and what she calls freedom. This is clearest in the context of the question that both autonomy and freedom theorists are rightly concerned about: deciding for someone else what's good for them or what they really want.

> Granting that second-guessing must be rejected by a feminist theory of freedom because it is antithetical to women's agency and self-determination does not mean that the interrogation of desire—which is what often *leads to* second-guessing— should itself be avoided. On the contrary, it is vitally important to freedom that critical questioning about desire, about who we are and what we want, be constantly engaged. The issue is where we draw the line in the process of asking questions and coming up with answers. Feminist freedom says that others can and indeed should, ask me questions. But only I can come up with the answers, nobody else can answer those questions for me. Autonomy theorists, for instance, as well as positive-liberty theorists like Rousseau, tend to provide external standards for what answers are legitimately autonomous—or in the case of "procedural" autonomists like Meyers and Dworkin, what standards the answers must meet. Freedom, however, cannot really involve itself with the answers. Indeed, it does not even require that you come up with any reasoned answers at all; you can say, "I don't really know, I just want to do it" and still be considered free, even if your decision fails the autonomy test.[101]

While I have already said that I think one must be very wary about applying the sorts of tests that Hirschmann ascribes to autonomy theorists, I think she is pointing to something interesting here in the example of refusal to give, or indeed have, reasons for one's choices. What I see in the example is the idea that people can "choose" to use their freedom in a weakly autonomous manner. I think there are probably individual temperamental preferences that play some role. People who feel themselves well suited to conventional expectations may not feel called to do the work of exercising and developing autonomy. Hirschmann makes the additional important point that finding one group of people who seem consistently to develop more autonomy capacities than another group should signal a potential problem of inequality to be investigated.

In the discussion above I argued that judgment is required for autonomy, and I have often argued in class that the phrase "*exercising* judgment" is an apt one because one needs to exert oneself in the exercise. Not everyone who has the freedom to do so will exert herself to exercise autonomy. I think this is related to Arendt's view that most people do not ordinarily "think," in the sense of exercising a critical perspective on conventional views.[102] But it is also important to remember the point I made earlier, that this "work" can take many forms of attention to what one is doing. They need not all look like the philosophers' intellectual form of critical reflection. I think even the way one engages with the perspectives of others in the exercise of judgment can take different forms.

It is useful to remember here, too, that judgment is in part required because not everything that is internal is either arrived at autonomously or conducive to autonomy. Indeed, some of what is internal, such as fears, anxieties, and even a sense of duty, can interfere with the exercise of judgment. Accepting the usefulness of an internal dimension of autonomy does not, for my approach, involve an essential self that simply needs to be uncovered. That would be inconsistent with the relational picture I have drawn.

Richard Flathman offers another way to see the value of the distinction—again even though freedom and autonomy are very close in his usage. I agree with what I take to be his point that people are likely to enjoy their freedom more and be better able to use it to resist incursions on it if they have developed their autonomy.[103] He closes his book with a moving statement about (what I take to be) those who use their freedom autonomously. It is very close to what I mean by the self-creation that is part of the capacity for creative interaction discussed in chapter 3:

> Whether admirable or otherwise, their feelings and thoughts, and hence their actions, differ from and are commonly at variance with those around them. As with creative artists, they engender new feelings in their fellow human beings and they give the latter things to think about and thoughts to think about them that would not have entered their minds. Having resisted and partly freed themselves from the received, the conventional, and the authoritative, they are themselves free in a distinctive sense and their feeling, thinking, and acting sometimes enlarges and enhances the freedom of others. As with great works of art, the works of art, namely themselves, that they create are gifts to humankind that are beyond all price.[104]

All of this discussion raises the question of what the distinction between freedom and autonomy means for how one tries to structure relations. Much of what constitutes "relations of freedom" will also constitute "relations of autonomy." When we stand in relations to others that permit, foster, and express freedom, those same relations are likely to permit, foster, and express autonomy—especially if one's conception of freedom has an internal element to it.

I think, however, that the argument above implies that something additional is necessary for autonomy. One can exercise freedom simply by choosing; to choose autonomously takes some kind of conscious work. So the relations that foster autonomy must not only enable but also encourage that work. So, for example, one could imagine two high schools in similar background contexts of freedom (liberal democracies), one of which encouraged and rewarded students to think critically, to try to form "their own" views by exercising an Arendtian kind of judgment, and another that focused on rote learning and deference to authority. The former school would be fostering relations of autonomy. In the "Closing Reflections" to this book, I return to the question of the relations of freedom.

In chapter 4, I make another, related distinction between agency and autonomy. I use Susan Sherwin's distinction, describing agency as the making of a choice and autonomy as self-governance. She argues that we need a relational conception of autonomy in order to "distinguish genuinely autonomous behavior from acts of merely rational agency."[105]

Finally, I think this is a useful place to warn against a misunderstanding I have encountered. I agree with Hirschman that in many contexts it makes sense to think of freedom as a requirement for autonomy. Nevertheless, it is a mistake to assume that those whose freedom is highly constrained have no autonomy. Indeed, even those who seem embedded in relations that undermine autonomy should not be taken to have none. (I was distressed to find this conclusion drawn by law students who heard me lecture on the relational approach: they argued that an aboriginal woman with a long-standing substance abuse problem could be compelled into treatment since she was situated in such oppressive relations that she had no autonomy anyway.)

There are two issues here. The first has to do with the resilience some people display in their capacity to develop their autonomy despite very adverse conditions. I think that if one explored the details of their relations, it is likely that one could see some dimension of these relations that nurtured that resilience. But one can never know for certain whether individuals have the resources to develop their autonomy despite structures of relations that seem antithetical to it. Thus conclusions that no one can have autonomy under such conditions can be dangerous. Put in the terms of this section, evaluations of external relations ought not to be used to form conclusions about the internal state of autonomy of any given individual.

The other question touches directly on the issue of the "internality" of autonomy: the extent to which individuals can sustain a capacity for autonomy they have developed even when they are later surrounded by destructive relations. Nelson Mandela's actions while in prison seem to be an example. Another variant of the question is the example of a person who withdraws from human relations as much as possible, such as the meditative hermit in the cave or (less realistically) the person stranded on the desert island. I do not think that my relational approach requires the conclusion that they can have no autonomy because they are no longer in relationships that foster it. Of course, I think it matters that in many of the actual stories of hermits in retreat, they are not really outside supportive human relationships because people bring them food. They know there is a community that values what they are doing enough to do the work of supplying food to them. (Mandela was also not completely without contact with supportive relations.)

Equally important, I think it makes sense to say that the capacities for autonomy that a person has developed throughout her life will not simply desert her when she is alone or in a hostile environment. That would be a very weak form of autonomy. At the same time, I think it does follow from my relational approach that prolonged exposure to autonomy-undermining relationships, and the absence of sustaining relationships, will erode autonomy. Whether in all cases the details of some previous relationships will account for the variation in individuals' endurance, I am not certain. There may be individual variation in the capacity to develop and sustain autonomy.

Let me conclude these reflections on the internal and external dimensions of autonomy with a quote from Judith Butler that nicely captures my sense of their relation: "One can only determine 'one's own' sense of gender to the extent that social norms exist that support and enable that act of claiming gender for oneself. One is dependent on this 'outside' to lay claim to what is one's own. The self must, in this way, be dispossessed in sociality in order to take possession of itself."[106] The idea of "one's own" continues to make sense in my relational approach, but only if one is attentive to what makes claiming it possible.

E. Conclusion

In closing this section, I want to return to my opening examples of people, such as the single mother on social assistance, who stand in relations of dependence and hierarchy with respect to the state. As I said, a relational approach to autonomy can be extremely important to thinking about how to structure such relations so that they foster autonomy rather than undermine it. Here I want to highlight the broader problem for which I also think the relational approach is helpful: hierarchies of power are as inevitable as human dependence (chapter 3). While it is vitally important to work toward eliminating unnecessary hierarchies (so that core values are genuinely available to all), even the best, most egalitarian societies will still have hierarchies of power as well as the inequalities that flow from the unequal distribution of human talents and strengths. The relations between students and teachers, for example, will be characterized by the inequality of knowledge inherent in the relation, and in most cases there will be an inequality of power involved in the importance of the teacher's evaluation of the student's knowledge and ability. But teachers can be prevented (or allowed) to augment that power through the use of physical punishment, and they can be constrained (if never completely prevented) from such abuses as susceptibility to bribes or arbitrary favoring of some students over others. When students can bring complaints for impartial adjudication, the structure of power relations shifts.

A relational approach directs our attention to such structuring of power relations. People should no more give up on autonomy in the face of hierarchy than in the face of dependence. A relational approach to both autonomy and law helps to figure out what constructive forms of power relations would look like.

Finally, I want to make explicit what has been implicit so far: my approach presupposes a commitment to equality. It does not to try answer all the questions of exactly what equality should look like, but it starts from the assumption that, ideally, relations of autonomy should be equally available to all. I treat relations of equality as a basic presupposition of the rule of law, of democracy, and of aspirations to core values, such as autonomy. Relations of domination are antithetical to all such values and aspirations. Another way of describing my point above would be that a relational approach helps us figure out ways to ensure that the inevitable hierarchies of power (and the advantages of unequal strengths and talents) do not become relations of domination.

While it is possible to value autonomy as independence and to approve of high levels of social and economic inequality (one often sees this combination in the United States), a commitment to equality and relational autonomy are mutually reinforcing. A culture that values autonomy *and* understands autonomy in relational terms will be better equipped to treat everyone with respect. People will be better able to see themselves with respect (which in turn enhances autonomy). For example, those who experience themselves as dependent (because of old age, sickness, or economic need) can still experience themselves as autonomous adults deserving of respect. And those who find themselves at some times and spheres of their lives at the lower end of a hierarchical relationship need not feel humiliated, inadequate, or otherwise unable to claim respect as equal members of society.

* * *

Most of the brief examples I have used of the relationships that foster or undermine autonomy have not been cast in terms of rights or the law. This is appropriate because many of the most important relationships, such as with family, religious communities, or teachers, are in their daily workings quite removed from the law. But as my discussion of nested relations hinted at, the law very often lies behind, beneath, or around these more personal relations, shaping them in important ways. This is a central part of why it is important to turn to law and rights even though I never mean to suggest that they are always the best way to enhance the capacity for creative interaction. While law and the language of rights are sometimes crude tools, we ignore them at our peril since they are at work in far more ways than many people imagine.

III. A RELATIONAL APPROACH TO LAW AND RIGHTS
A. Introduction

The core of my claim about a relational approach to law and rights is twofold:

1. Questions of rights (and law more generally) are best analyzed in terms of how they structure relations. Doing so can make a difference in how people understand the issues at stake and the kinds of judgment they exercise.
2. What rights and law actually *do*, right now, is structure relations, which, in turn, promote or undermine core values, such as autonomy. This is why a relational approach can, and should be (and sometimes is) used in current legal systems.

While a relational approach may, in the long run, invite changes in legal systems, it need not await any such change.

Let me begin then with some brief examples of how rights and law structure relations and how those relations in turn enhance or undermine core values. (There are, of course, more extended examples through out the book.) We can start with the example I used in section II on autonomy, the single mother on social assistance. Many welfare regimes create relations of domination and subordination between recipients and their caseworkers. For example, the ability of welfare workers to withhold information about eligibility puts recipients in a subordinate position. Effective rights of access to information would shift those power relations and enhance their ability to exercise autonomous judgment. Policies that encourage neighbors to report abuses of the welfare system ("snitch hotlines" as they were called in Ontario during the Harris regime in the 1990s) generate relations of disrespect and suspicion toward welfare recipients. Such relations undermine equality and are destructive of self-esteem, which some see as important for autonomy.[107] (Such policies probably also generate relations of disrespect and suspicion on the part of recipients toward the welfare bureaucracy and perhaps the state more generally. Such relations undermine responsible citizenship. I would say something similar about welfare rates and rules that virtually require recipients to break the rules in order to feed their children.) Laws that do not carefully limit the power of officials to conduct an unannounced home visit create relations of subordination and insecurity. One welfare recipient during the Harris regime described her experience with the welfare bureaucracy as "walking on egg-shells," never knowing when or why a blow might fall. This was the same language women used to describe their relationships with abusive partners.[108]

Interpreting recipients' rights to privacy, liberty, and security as requiring strict limitations on such visits, shifts the relations between recipients and the welfare officials but also more generally between recipients and other members of society. When recipients of social assistance enjoy the same rights as others, they stand on more equal footing with everyone—not just in relation to the state. So not only is the particular value, say, of privacy, enhanced by an interpretation of rights that does not subject recipients to the caprice, disrespect, or suspicion of caseworkers; the value of equality is enhanced as well. An especially thoughtful examination of such issues can be found in Judge Laskin's opinion in the Ontario case *Falkiner*.[109] One issue in that case was the definition of spouse in the regulations under the *Family Benefits Act*. It had functioned to presume that people living together were "spouses" providing financial support of the kind that must be counted for assessing eligibility. He noted that this presumption prevented recipients (who were disproportionately single women) from being able to "try on" relationships as other people are able to do and forced them into financial dependence they did not want.[110] He found this to be an unacceptable violation of their dignity.[111] Another example of the way the law can structure relations to enhance the autonomy of welfare recipients is a right to participate in a hearing before benefits are cut off. This could shift the relation between recipient and welfare bureaucracy from one of powerless supplicant to (optimally) a co-participant in shaping the meaning of the relevant rules. (See chapter 3.)

The problems in cases like *Falkiner*[112] arise because the existing law (or practice) has structured relations in ways that undermine core values, such as autonomy and privacy. Debates then ensue that often are about competing values, such as the state's interest in avoiding exploitation of the welfare system. The best analyses will look at how well the impugned law and the relations of insecurity and inequality that it generates achieve that end and how significantly such relations undermine core values, such as privacy, equality and autonomy. The structure of the legal analysis that follows will depend on the context. (For example, the structure of the analysis is different in the United States and Canada and would be different still in Germany.[113]) At the policy level, the most helpful suggestions will be about how to structure the relations (of dependence) between recipients and welfare bureaucracy in ways that both address legitimate state objectives and enhance the autonomy and well-being that is supposed to be the objective of the welfare system.

To take a different example, one can see that laws governing landlord–tenant relations have shifted the structures of those relations over the years. Tenants once had few protections against invasions of privacy and landlords' decisions to evict tenants. There was a clear hierarchy of power in the relationship that left tenants subject to the caprice and shifting interests of landlords and even to their enjoyment of domination or harassment. One can, of course, tell this story in a language of rights that does not invoke the language of relationships: tenants now have more rights, better protection of privacy, more security. Landlords, arguably, have less freedom to do as they will with their property and less security (it's harder to evict nonpaying tenants). But particularly from the side of tenants, I think the language of the shifting of relationships best captures both the previous harms and the significance of the expansion of their legal rights. A relationship of asymmetrical and highly unconstrained power (even a "private" or "nonstate" contractual relationship about property), in a sphere that closely touches values of privacy, intimate relations, and autonomy, is likely to be inimical to those values.

A very different kind of example, the change to no-fault divorce law, shows the far-reaching relational consequences of law. I often try to avoid family law examples because their relational significance can seem too obvious. But I think this example is useful exactly because its significance goes beyond any particular relationship. It shows the links between law, relationship, and social meaning as well as core values.

In a public conversation I had with my Catholic colleague Guilio Silano[114] (we both agreed it would not be a "debate") on the subject of gay marriage, he made an exceptionally interesting comment. He said that he thought that gay marriage was a very small threat to the institution of marriage compared to the changes in the law of divorce that rendered divorce legally easy in Canada. He said that the ease of divorce and its commonness have made it impossible for people now getting married to understand marriage as meaning "'til death do us part." The legal change had transformed the meaning of a social, legal, and religious institution. Particular couples, and even religious communities, cannot create for themselves the meaning they want marriage to have. The relationships that are now constituted by marriage are different from those when large numbers of people believed that marriage was a lifelong commitment—and saw that belief mirrored back to them in the law, reinforced in both meaning and consequences. The change in the law meant a change in the kind of relationship marriage *is*. Of course, it is an open question how much of this change was itself the cause of the law and how much the law advanced change that had already taken place. But I took Professor Silano to say that the change in the law made an important difference, which I think is likely. Some of the competing values at stake are equality, autonomy, freedom, security, responsibility, and the capacity for commitment. (Of course, our legal and policy vocabulary are not as well equipped to articulate the relational impact on commitment or even responsibility as they are to advocate the importance of equality, autonomy, or freedom.)

I am not, of course, making an argument against this legal change. I am offering it as an example of a law that restructured relations in ways that affected core values. Also engaged, as in all questions of the law of marriage, is the extent to which it is appropriate for the state to reinforce or reward certain kinds of intimate relations over others. Skills in thinking about how relationships foster such values as autonomy, equality, or security— or responsibility and commitment—would aid reflection on this important question.

Sometimes judges are self-conscious about the significance of the relational context of an issue. For example, there are cases in which husbands have wanted to use the family home as security for a loan.[115] Normally, the wife will have to agree to this in order for the husband to secure the loan. Legal cases arise when the wife has signed, some business deal has gone bad, the loan cannot be repaid, and the family is faced with losing their house. Some version of a claim of undue influence is then made to say that she did not freely consent to the loan (so the home is not available to make good on the debt). These cases are sometimes seen as part of a family of cases in which a relationship itself may give rise to undue influence:

> The law has long recognized the need to prevent abuse of influence in these "relationship" cases despite the absence of evidence of overt acts of persuasive conduct. The types of relationship, such as parent and child, in which this principle falls to be applied cannot be listed exhaustively. Relationships are infinitely various…the question is whether one party has reposed sufficient trust and confidence in the other, rather than whether the relationship between the parties belongs to a particular type.… For example, the relations of banker and customer will not normally meet this criterion, but exceptionally it may.[116]

The nature of the relationship poses the problem. But then there is a question of what the law should do about it. One set of solutions, such as requiring independent legal advice for the wife, could be seen as trying to shift the terms of the relationship in the particular context of the loan application. (Some think this requirement can be complied with in such a superficial manner as to not shift the relationship at all.) But part of what makes this example interesting is that there is an ongoing debate over what kind of legal requirement would actually promote the wife's autonomy, equality, and security (recognizing possible conflicts among these). Some suggest that normally the respectful, equality-promoting stance of the law should be to assume (absent some specific evidence) that women who sign such forms do so of their own free will. To assume otherwise and routinely require special protective measures will not actually enhance women's equality or autonomy. It keeps them in a kind of subordinate relationship requiring protection. Others insist that given the common reality of the potential for undue influence in these circumstances, for the law to fail to provide protection will sustain relations of unequal power which will put women (and their children) at risk.

This is, then, one of many examples where shared judgments about the values at stake—say, equality, autonomy, security—and about the importance of the relational context yield different judgments about how the law ought to shape relations so as to best promote the value in question.

Finally, I offer one more invocation of the significance of law for the structuring of relations, in this case those that foster or undermine equality. This comes from John Borrows, in the context of the relationship between Indigenous law and Canadian law:

> Law in North America does not just orient our relationships to one another on a horizontal axis. It does much more than merely mediate individual's actions on an even plane. Law also has a vertical orientation that builds relationships hierarchically and thereby forges how we interact with one another.[117]

B. *Why Law and Rights*

Despite what I hope are intriguing examples of how law structures relationships that are central to core values, such as autonomy and equality, my choice to focus on law and rights requires some comment. I begin with the issue of law.

i. Law and the State

There are a variety of objections to looking to law as a means of achieving greater freedom or a better distribution of power and the goods of this world. The core of the objections is the identification of law with the state and, for some, with the liberal tradition. Most of the arguments are based on some version of the claim that since the state is controlled by the powerful (often, particularly, the economically powerful), there is little hope that the state will act to more equitably redistribute power, goods, and advantage. The discourse versions of the argument focus on the ways in which those in power (in control of state institutions, including the law) see the world through the very lenses the critics seek to shift (often variants of liberal individualism). To invoke law is to reinforce the significance and legitimacy of the dominant framework.

There is an important scholarly debate about the capacity of courts to act on the basis of principles, such as equality, rather than merely the interests of the powerful.[118] While I will not engage with that debate directly, I think it is simplistic to envision the law as simply the tool of the powerful: it could not be as effective in sustaining the legitimacy of existing structures of power if it advanced only the interests of the powerful. History points to law as both serving their interests and acting to improve equality in ways that do not simply reinforce existing power structures. I think the discourse argument is, in some ways, more powerful. But then, as we will see, my objective is to shift the nature of legal discourse.

Both these arguments, nevertheless, point to important cautions about what one can hope for from law. And I share the concern that feminists and other equality seekers have turned too habitually to the state to solve their problems.[119] Indeed, I think one of the major challenges to contemporary equality projects is to turn their attention away from the state. Too often, a correct conclusion that there is matter of collective responsibility, say for the care and education of children, is assumed to mean that the only solution is for the state to assume and directly implement that responsibility.[120] Often, as in the case of child care, the state should have a role. But what is needed is a great deal more imagination about the ways of structuring relations of responsibility.

This is an important contribution the law can make. It can restructure relations of power and responsibility *without* necessarily giving the state the power to implement the practice in question. For example, Ronald Davis makes an excellent argument for using the law to give workers who have contributed to pension funds direct control over the use of those funds.[121] The law currently gives that power to managers of these funds with very little control in the hands of the workers. A change in the law could shift that control and very substantially shift an important structure of power. The shift in power from one group to another is done by the law, but it does not result in increased power for the state. It does not result in a new state regulatory agency. This is the sort of imaginative use of the law to restructure relations (here enhancing both equality and autonomy) that I hope the relational approach will encourage. (Of course, the question remains whether the existing structure of power will prevent such a change.)

My point here is that law is an important focus not just because one might want to look to the law to intervene, but also because the law already is present in so many contexts that matter to the possibility of the equal enjoyment of the values a society (ostensibly) treats as basic human entitlements. As I will discuss in chapters 5 and 8, most of the kinds of legal changes feminists advocate are not calling for an *increased* role of law and the state but a *different* role. Law is *currently* structuring relations in ways that undermine women's equality, and a change in the law could structure more equal relations between men and women.

It is important to be clear about when a proposal calls for increased state power. People of all political views should note such calls with attention, even if ultimately with approval. Part of the advantage of a relational approach is that it can identify particularly clearly when the issue at stake calls for existing law to be changed to structure relations *differently* and when it is a call for law where it did not exist before and, thus, an increase in the exercise of state power.

Throughout the book I point out when a call for legal intervention is really a call for a different rather than an increased use of law. I do this partly because I think, as I just said, that clarity on this issue is important. I also do it because I think there is widespread concern about the scope and nature of state power. I thus emphasize the point that the relational approach does not necessarily lead to an increase in state power. But this emphasis can be misleading.

My approach does not presuppose that the existing level power of state power in any given context is optimal. The use of a relational analysis will not predetermine whether a problem is best solved by an increase, decrease, or redirection of state power. Sometimes a relational analysis will call for the withdrawal of state power, as in the decriminalization of sex between same-sex partners. Sometimes it will call for new exercises of state power, such as legal prohibitions against sexual harassment—although preexisting laws of assault and norms of abuse of authority would, if enforced, have prevented a great deal of harassment. In many instances, a relational analysis will reveal how existing law is contributing to a problem and how it could be shifted to promote rather than undermine relations conducive to the value at stake, such as dignity or autonomy.

Another reason for directing the relational approach to law is related to the above issue of state power. When for a long time the law has either explicitly or tacitly provided impunity for certain kinds of (normally illegal) behavior, and then it removes that impunity, it often appears that the scope and power of the state has increased. Those now subject to its constraints object strenuously, often denouncing an inappropriate role for the state. The continuing evolution of law and policy with respect to intimate partner violence (wife assault being its most common form) is an example. The law once explicitly allowed husbands to physically chastise their wives, limited by the now infamous "rule of thumb" (referring to the thickness of the rod allowed for beating). This explicit impunity from the laws of assault was replaced by the implicit impunity allowed by the sanctity of the privacy of the home and intimate relations.[122] This deference to privacy still prevails in many norms and practices, including those of state actors, such as police and judges.[123] But both formal law and legal practice have significantly shifted so that men now are arrested for assaulting their female partners. Sexual harassment is another form of abusive (sometimes assaultive) behavior that was long tolerated, even condoned, as not a serious issue. The new attention to it in many workplaces, encouraged by legal change (and fear of lawsuits), is often treated as intrusive, inappropriate, and foolish. In Canada, the feminist campaign of "no means no" (with respect to sexual touching) is backed by a change in the law of sexual assault that requires the accused to show that he took "reasonable steps" to ascertain consent. The belief that when a woman said "no" she really meant "yes" will no longer be treated as a reasonable ground for believing there was consent.[124]

All of these issues often give rise to a sense that the law has become unreasonably intrusive, interfering in relationships that would be perfectly fine, or at least better, without it. In each case I think it helps to see that the earlier patterns of relationship were shaped by impunity for assault, created by both formal law and legal practices. That impunity has been significantly (though by no means wholly) withdrawn, causing resentment against what is characterized as new and inappropriate interference. A relational analysis reveals what is really at stake; it invites a more accurate reflection on the role of the state.

There is yet another related advantage of bringing a relational approach to law. It is often the case that when it is understood how problems, like intimate partner violence, are generated by relational structures in which law plays a role, *less state involvement* will be necessary to fix the problem at its source than is needed after the violence has occurred. (See chapter 8.)

For all these reasons, even those wary of turning to law and the state for solutions, may see that a relational approach to law offers a better framework for assessing the nature of state action: it highlights the way law participates in creating the problem; can identify ways of shifting the problem by making changes in the way existing law structures relations; and can make it clearer when a solution actually calls for additional state action. It can also highlight the way many "interventions" are in fact the removal of unjustified impunity for actions to which the state would otherwise react.

Another way of putting these points is that a relational approach turns our attention to the ways law inevitably structures relations, in ways that, in turn, affect core values and who can enjoy them. It is thus not so much a choice to *use* law as a means of seeing how law is currently being used and its consequences. In addition, in many practical instances, such as women who need social assistance, women who face deportation, or women facing custody battles, there is no choice but to engage the law. A relational framework helps people see all the ways in which law shapes important relationships (through layers of nested relationships) so that these ways may be evaluated.

Law is an important way power is exercised, shaped, and justified. And relations structured by law often serve to hide power and to hide the role of the state in that power. For example, the power that flows from the ownership of private property is often seen as simply self-evident entitlement—the right to exclude others, even homeless others— rather than an exercise of power. And the fact that the state lies behind that power is also often invisible. The role of the law in constructing the basic terms of "the market" (property and contract) is also often invisible, allowing "the market" to be presented as a "non-state" alternative to state regulation. A relational approach makes the role of law and the state in structuring relations of power clearer.

Law is important both because of its practical effects in the world and the way it participates in giving meaning to collective values. Law is, thus, an important way in which abstract notions such as justice, equality, and dignity are given practical meaning. And the language of the law reinforces, gives authority to, the conceptual frameworks for articulating core values. A relational approach to law engages with it at both the practical and conceptual levels.

For example, consider this description of the workings of law (the context is protection for women in battering relationships): "One of the discursive powers of law is that it recasts social dynamics as characteristics of individuals."[125] (So, for example, the problem is a man's anger management, not economic inequality between men and women and the failure of the state to protect.) Part of the contribution of a relational approach is to resist individualistic characterization, to urge a consistently relational analysis that will reveal the relevant social dynamics. (See the discussion of battering in chapter 4.)

One important dimension of autonomy is the ability to participate in the shaping of norms and institutions that affect one's life. Law is an important source of norms, an important way in which values are framed and given effect. If ordinary people are to exercise their freedom in shaping powerful norms and values, they need some understanding of the role law plays. By bringing a relational approach to law, I hope to facilitate that understanding and ability to engage. (See chapter 6.)

Finally, let me offer some clarifications and a return to an opening caveat. When I refer to law above, I am not distinguishing between law that is generated through legislative processes and that which arises out of court decisions, such as the common law.[126] (In some legal theories, the modes of analysis ought to be very different in the two contexts.) Legal pluralists might object that my discussion above implies that the state is the only source of the law. They argue that there are many sources of normative orders within society that ought properly to be understood as law. While I share their interest in different normative orders, my focus here *is* on state law. One of the issues that my arguments brush up against without fully engaging is the ways in which state law intersects with other normative orders. As I will discuss in the conclusion, I think my relational approach has implications for shared norms of responsibility beyond those enacted in state-based law.

ii. Why Rights

In chapter 6 I offer a set of objections to the language of rights and my arguments about how a relational conception of rights can overcome them. The core of the argument is that the individualism of liberal rights is significantly transformed through a relational approach. The most important argument for why I focus on rights is that I think the language of rights has become a worldwide phenomenon. People use "rights" to identify serious harms, to make claims from and against governments, to make claims for international intervention and assistance. The battle over the use of the term has been decisively won in its favor. I argue, therefore, that the best thing to do is to engage with the meaning of rights, to shift it in a relational direction. The language of rights has huge rhetorical power, and the institutions of rights, such as constitutional bills of rights, are, again, a worldwide phenomenon.[127]

I will just note here that it seems possible to me that an optimal framework for both moral and legal rights (I am focusing on legal rights) would be combined with an equal engagement with the idea of responsibility. Although it is commonly recognized that responsibilities flow from rights, I think it makes a difference whether the starting point for one's understanding of entitlement and obligation is rights or responsibilities. Joseph Singer makes a compelling argument for the ways obligation is entailed in a relational approach to law and rights.[128] I will not pursue the issue further here. Whatever the optimal role for responsibility in a society's understanding of both individual and collective entitlements and obligation, a relational conception of rights will be of benefit.

The last response to objections I will make here is to the argument that rights are state-focused. Casting political arguments in the language of rights thus often misdirects political energy toward the state, the courts in particular. I think this is correct. It is often the case that there are other, better ways for restructuring relations than bringing in the state. And the strategy of turning to courts generally has the serious problem of shifting control of the political agenda to lawyers. Nevertheless, for the reasons given above, it is important to extend as much as possible the understanding of the role legal rights do play in the creation of the problems to be addressed. A relational approach offers a framework for such an understanding.

C. A Relational Approach to Rights

What I mean by a relational approach to rights is elaborated in chapter 6, and some of its challenges are discussed in chapter 8. Here I just want to sketch what I mean and note some of the problems my approach raises.

Rights structure relations of power, trust, responsibility, and care. This is as true of property and contract rights as it is of rights created under family law. All claims of rights involve interpretations and contestation. My argument is that these inevitable debates are best carried on in the following relational terms. First, one should ask how existing laws and rights have helped to construct the problem being addressed. What patterns and structures of relations have shaped it, and how has law helped shape those relations? The next questions are what values are at stake in the problem and what kinds of relations promote such values. In particular, what kind of shift in the existing relations would enhance rather than undermine the values at stake? There may, of course, be more than one value at stake, and they may compete with one another. For example, the relations that enhance the freedom and autonomy of the renter may decrease the security and freedom of the landlord. What interpretation or change in the existing law would help restructure the relations in the ways that would promote a given value?

As can be seen in my phrasing of the questions above, I make a distinction between rights and values. I treat rights as rhetorical and institutional means for implementing core values, such as security, liberty, autonomy, and equality. I prefer this language to simply defining such core values as rights. Usually when people do this they mean these values are moral rights. But I am focusing on legal rights, and I want to emphasize that it is a certain kind of choice to describe a value as a legal right and to construct institutions for implementing that right. Not all values lend themselves to the language of rights. Harmony, for example, an important value for some societies and individuals, does not seem to me to be well captured or implemented through rights.

I also think that debates over how a particular right should be interpreted—for example, freedom of speech with respect to hate speech—should be structured around questions of which interpretation will promote the underlying, possibly competing, values. The distinction between rights and values allows such a structuring. The distinction also makes possible a claim that there are universal values, such as dignity and autonomy, but that different cultures choose to foster them in different ways. Some choose the language and institutions of rights; others do not. (Many Canadian Indigenous traditions, for example, do not.) It also seems likely that particular forms of legal rights, say the forms of property rights familiar in advanced capitalist societies, promote certain kinds of autonomy. But those same forms of rights would not be well suited to foster the kinds of autonomy valued by some aboriginal traditions. In fact, this is actually a contested issue—some arguing for a greater range of private property rights to be made available to those living on collectively held reserves and others arguing against it. The distinction between rights and values makes it easier to see when the dispute is about what should be treated as a core value and when it is about the best means for promoting that value.

This distinction leaves open the question of where core values come from. As I just suggested, it is consistent with claims about universal values. But it is also well suited to historicist arguments about the shifting ways in which cultures understand their core values as well as in their choices to implement them via rights. For the purposes of most of my discussions, I refer to the core values of a society—leaving open how one would ascertain what they are. For many purposes, one can use values designated as constitutional rights as an expression of their status as core values. I do not think I have to resolve the question of the source of societal values in order to make an argument for the usefulness of the relational approach to rights that I propose.

Autonomy seems to me an example of a widely shared value, though one that is given different weight and priority in different societies. I think it is most helpful not to designate it as a right as such—as indeed most constitutions do not. This is because of its strong internal dimension and the role of individual work to develop it. Of course, as my previous discussion made clear (I hope), autonomy is only possible in the context of relations of autonomy. And law, rights, and the state bear a large responsibility for constituting those relations. Thus it is very often the case, as in the welfare examples, that what is wrong with the way law is structuring relations is that they undermine autonomy. And, conversely, it is often important to ask how relations can be shifted so that they foster autonomy and what role law can play in this. Fortunately, autonomy is so closely linked to liberty and freedom, and so widely recognized as a core value in society, that it is generally possible to invoke autonomy as a relevant value in legal argument.

Of course, since I argue that rights *do*, in fact, structure relations, it is not surprising that many other theories of rights will engage with this fact. I am not going to try to offer a survey of how my approach compares to that of others. But I will offer a few points of contrast.

First, sometimes I use the phrase "relational rights" to describe my approach to rights. I do not mean only rights involving particular relationships, such as that between parents and children. (I will return later to Mary Shanley's advocacy of a right to a parent–child relationship, which she refers to as a relational right.) A great part of what the law does, and what rights do, is structure relations among strangers. Contract law, which governs the rules by which people can make binding contracts with one another, and the remedies available to them for breach of contract, are examples. As I note in chapter 6, those rules can structure relations of trust. If the presumed rule of contractual relations is caveat emptor (buyer beware), the relations of trust will be different from those arising from a rule holding that if I reasonably rely on something you say, you can be held responsible for (some of) the consequences of your statement not being reliable. To attend to the way law structures relationships is not to deny the importance of relationships among strangers. Patricia Williams makes a compelling case for the importance of "arms-length" relations of respect, especially for racialized people who have long been denied such respect.[129]

Of course, many contracts are formed between people who have ongoing business relationships with one another. Stewart Macaulay's[130] famous work on relational contract showed how the importance of maintaining those relations often outweighed the formal legal rules of contract in decisions about how to go forward when the original agreement could not be carried out. This argument is different from mine though in no way inconsistent with it. He was pointing out how legal entitlements alone do not structure relationships. The mutual value of sustaining an ongoing relationship made people willing to forgo strict legal entitlements that would have disrupted the relationship.

I mentioned earlier Joseph Raz's argument that free speech is a public good. In my terms, the right of free speech creates relations that make the enjoyment of the right possible. He argues that this is true of many rights, such as freedom of contract, freedom of marriage, and freedom of occupation. Again, in my terms, these rights structure relations in ways that affect everyone, not just those who make direct use of them. (He draws interesting conclusions with respect to the relation between rights and the common good, which I will not go into here.[131]) His arguments about the public, collective significance of rights fit well with my relational analysis, though they are not identical.

Raz also offers a description of a common understanding of the relational character of rights that serves well to identify what I *do not* mean by a relational approach to rights:

The contemporary orthodoxy has a simple explanation of the relational character of rights. According to it rights are essentially confrontational. To assert a right is, as we know, to assert that the right-holder's interest is sufficient reason to hold another subject to a duty. The duty's purpose is to protect the interest of the rights-holder. The protection of that interest is its *raison d'être*. The person subject to the duty is encumbered in the interest of the right-holder. Their relationship need not be adversarial in fact. One may be, for example, the child of the other, who very much wants to help his parent in the prescribed way. But the relationship is confrontational in principle. The duty does not depend on any harmony of interests between the right-holder and the persons subject to the duty.[132]

Raz's use of the language of right, interest, and duty are familiar from Wesley Newcomb Hohfeld's famous discussion of how these concepts correspond to one another. I see my approach as distinct from Hohfeld's.[133] Hohfeld's focus is conceptual: the reciprocal relations between the concepts of rights and duties. I am trying to draw attention to the ways rights structure human relations. (I see Raz as sharing an interest in this focus.)

I close this introduction to a relational approach to rights with a reassurance that I elaborate on in chapter 6. There is nothing to suggest that any of the basic rights familiar in Western democracies would disappear in a relational approach. I do argue that it is best not to treat property as a *constitutional* right, as the *Canadian Charter of Rights and Freedoms* does not. And I highlight, as I have done here, the inevitability of contestation over the practical meaning of core values, such as equality or freedom of speech. Even apparently simple prohibitions (Congress shall make no law . . . abridging the freedom of speech[134]) or guarantees (Everyone has the right to life, liberty, and security of the person[135]) require interpretation and thus are amenable to a relational approach. A relational approach would shift the mode of analysis used in those contestations, yielding better understanding of the core issues, more apt arguments, and, sometimes, different results from a more traditionally individualistic approach. But in part because, as noted above, the relational approach does not entail a subordination of the individual to the collective, there will not be any less protection for individual rights (I, of course, think there will be better protection for the values underlying rights) nor any tendency to abandon basic rights.[136] In chapter 6 and again in chapter 8 I address the questions of whether a relational approach to rights can "work" in practice.

IV. THE RELATIONAL APPROACH: CLOSING CLARIFICATIONS
A. Method or Substance?
i. The Value of Relational Methodology

In his book *Contextual Subjects,* Robert Leckey calls for a clarification of whether the relational approach that I (and others) advocate is merely a methodology or whether it is based on substantive normative claims.[137] I take up that call here to clarify several points.

At times I disagree with his characterization of my arguments, but that only shows the need for this clarification: if as careful and thoughtful a reader as Leckey has misinterpreted my arguments, they warrant further clarification.

The distinction he draws is between a methodological call to attend to relational context, on the one hand, and, on the other hand, claims for normative standards that grow out of a commitment to relational autonomy in particular and to the value of other "thick relationships."[138] Let me begin by agreeing that there is a distinction between the methodology I advocate and the normative commitments that flow from my relational approach. I turn first to the methodological side.

I think there is value to the relational methodology as such. The set of questions I advocate above for analyzing rights debates are an example of the relational methodology I envision. The most general form of it would be the importance of attending to the ways in which law structures relationships, which, in turn, enhance or undermine core values. My claim is that such an analysis will clarify what is really at stake in any given conflict or debate and will allow a clearer assessment of the best steps to take. My claim is not that disagreements will disappear as the result of such an analysis (see chapter 8). On the contrary, often the purpose of a relational analysis is to clarify the nature of substantive disagreements: is the disagreement about the means (say, which interpretation of a right) that will best promote a shared end (say, a value like equality)? Or is it a disagreement about the relative weight of competing values, such as security and autonomy? Or the disagreement could turn on different underlying views about human beings, about what is of greatest value to them and the role of relationships in giving effect to those values. I will return to an example of such a disagreement shortly. Of course, sometimes, once the nature of the disagreement is sorted out, people can move forward more easily, say, on why they differ over the best means of achieving a shared value. But often what I think will happen is not agreement, but a more productive discussion about what is actually the source of the disagreement.

Another advantage of a relational methodology is that it often cuts through arguments based on superficial, almost grammatical, parallels between two actually (relationally) dissimilar cases. An example is the argument that if control over a woman's own body underlies the belief that the law should not constrain women's decision to have an abortion, then people holding that belief must also be in favor of contract pregnancy (or the unfortunate term "surrogate motherhood"): allowing (perhaps enforcing) contracts to carry and give birth to a child who is then to be turned over to the woman who commissioned the pregnancy. This is presented as a matter of logical consistency because both issues involve "controlling one's own body." Without detailing the analysis here,[139] the way relations between parents and children, and between men and women, as well as norms of respect for life, are likely to be shaped by treating the decision to terminate a pregnancy as resting with the pregnant woman will be very different from the relational impact of laws that treat pregnancy as outside the purview of legal contract.

Of course, both kinds of laws (or their absence) will also shape relations in ways that affect women's autonomy. But consider the relational difference. In one case, there is the constraint of the inability to use the law to enable the buying and selling of women's reproductive capacities. In the other, there is the vastly greater autonomy impairment of taking the decision about termination of a pregnancy out of the hands of the pregnant woman. (For example, who will now stand in relations of power with respect to her at this crucial junction in her life?) I do not suggest that I have spelled out the argument here. It is in the nature of relational arguments that they require a great deal of detailed understanding of the issue and the context. That is why it is rarely the case that the relational "answer" to a problem is obvious or can be given off the top of one's head. I mean here only to indicate the way a relational analysis can be useful in cutting through spurious, but all too common, arguments that take the form of these linguistic parallels. What I am suggesting is still a matter of methodology rather than substantive normative commitment, although, of course, at some point normative substance must enter in to assess the different relational impact of these two cases.

Leckey also suggests that (what he sees as) a failure to commit to the substantive dimensions of my relational approach "misleadingly suggests that relational theorists…are neutrally concerned with identifying and enhancing whatever relationships happen to exist."[140] I have tried earlier in this introduction to make clear that my version of a relational self is not about protecting or enhancing the status quo of relationships. The context for Leckey's comment is my discussion in chapter 4 of nineteenth-century cases in which courts admitted defenses from husbands who had discovered their wives having affairs and then, much later, killed the paramour. (The context in that chapter was a relational analysis of defenses for women who killed their battering partners.) I raised this as an example of how disturbing values and stereotypes *can*[141] play a role in a relational analysis. The relevant relational dimension was the judges' invocation of the need to uphold marriage and the authority of husbands, coming at a time of transition around both legal and societal norms of marriage. I stand by my description of these cases as involving a reflection on how interpreting the law one way rather than another (allowing a certain kind of defense) would affect relations—here between husbands and wives as well as their relations to others.

It matters to me that a relational analysis can be used even when I do not share the values that the analyst (here a judge) wants to promote. Otherwise it cannot serve the purpose of revealing where disagreement lies. In an open democratic society, the range of disagreement over even core values is such that it would be far too limiting to say that the relational approach can only be used by those who share my understanding of autonomy. (I discuss some of these disagreements and their significance for my approach in chapter 8.)

For example, I think a relational analysis could illuminate the points of dispute between libertarians, who emphasize the importance of private property and a minimal state for liberty, and egalitarians who advocate redistributive measures to control economic inequality in order to achieve liberty (and other values) for all. Libertarians could be invited to spell out how they see private property working to create relations of liberty. And they could be reminded that private property and contract are legal structures enabled by state power, about which there are inevitable choices of the form they should take. In thinking about such choices (say attention to unequal bargaining power in contract or the environmental dimensions of the old common law idea of prohibiting the use of property that interferes with the "quiet enjoyment" of others' property), libertarians might see that they do want the legal regime to structure relations in some ways rather than others and be pressed to see if liberty is always the only or ultimate value. Egalitarians might be persuaded of many of the liberty-enhancing functions of private property and agree that redistribution should be organized in a way that minimizes interference with the relations of liberty enabled by private property. They might be persuaded that "private ordering" via property and contract also structure relations and that sometimes these will be better tools than direct state intervention via regulation. In the end, both libertarians and egalitarians may come to a better understanding of the concrete ways (particular structures of relations) in which their primary value is incompatible with the competing value of the other. They may also recognize contexts in which this incompatibility can be avoided. This seems more fruitful than the mutual disdain which arises when the disagreement is assumed to be about the relative value of liberty or equality.

The debate around gay marriage offers another example. One way of framing the debate is the claim by advocates that making the legal institution of marriage available to same-sex couples is essential for equality. The availability of another institutional construct, such as civil partnership, cannot do the job because the exclusion itself is a badge of inferiority that must structure unequal relations. I think putting the argument in these terms may make it clear that some of the opponents do not want to use the law to promote *social relations* of equality. Their conception of the basic legal equality of all members of society does not encompass this kind of social equality. They do not want this "lifestyle" to be treated as acceptable, as one among many family forms (such as children living with grandparents). Their moral disapprobation is a ground for refusing social equality, even though they may say they are in favor of nondiscrimination in spheres like employment and government benefits.

The relational approach then asks whether social relations of inequality and exclusion can be consistent with full equal status as political and economic members of society. Are these relations necessarily so interdependent that structures of inequality in one will inevitably affect the other? Opponents might, however, point out that the factual claim that *only* inclusion in marriage can structure relations of equality may prove to be erroneous. It may turn out that, at least in Britain, the availability of civil partnership— commonly referred to as marriage in everyday usage—will succeed in generating the same level of social equality as gay marriage in Canada. Disagreements over the relation between law and morality (and the inevitable problem of whose morality) are likely to emerge. A greater clarity about the kinds of equality that opponents actually have in mind also is likely. Perhaps most importantly, what is often made as a statement of principle, "equality demands gay marriage," will be revealed as a contestable factual claim about how gay marriage and alternatives like civil partnership structure relations of equality.

Of course, context matters here. In Britain there was very little public debate about the introduction of civil partnership. In Canada and the United States there has been very vocal opposition to gay marriage. It may be that in the face of such public opposition the exclusion has indeed become a badge of inferiority such that only inclusion in the institution of marriage can structure relations of equality.

ii. Context

Leckey offers another terminological clarification: the distinction between a relational approach and a contextual approach. In his terms, "context is larger than the set of personal relationships."[142] I, however, (as spelled out in section I) use the term "relationship" also to refer to structural and institutional relations. For example, I think it is helpful to see that property relations are relations: relations of power and potentially relations of responsibility. Seeing the multiple layers of relationships in which we are embedded as sets of nested relationships, which interact with each other, seems more helpful to me than reserving the language of relationship for personal relationships. Our personal relationships are always shaped by the larger structures of relationship of gender norms, family law, economic relationships, etc.

It is true that "a focus on relationship automatically turns our attention to context."[143] And when people advocate a contextual approach it often involves a kind of relational analysis.[144] But I do not think that what is called a contextual approach in law invariably asks the questions of how law structures relationships. If it does not, then it is not the same as what I mean by a relational approach.

Leckey further says that "a 'contextual' approach appears more open than a 'relational' one to different normative presuppositions and conclusions. A contextual approach can be appropriate for analyzing structural and institutional relations; the normative commitment to promoting relational autonomy cannot be."[145] Of course, part of our disagreement here is a question of a preference of terms—in the way that I argued above for why I prefer the language of relation even for institutional relations. But part also is the extent to which my version of a relational approach can have both methodological and substantive dimensions, which are separable from one another. It seems what Leckey is suggesting is that the best way to get such a separation is to call one relational and insist that the substantive dimension is inseparable from it, and to call another contextual and separate out the normative from that one. My preference is to clarify the nature of my substantive, normative commitments, but also to insist that the relational method can be used by others with different commitments.

I think that my version of a nested relational approach can be used for analyzing structural and institutional relations. (That is what I try to do in several chapters.) I also think that it is often helpful to do this analysis with an explicit attention to the value of relational autonomy. In many cases there will be wide agreement on the relevance of the value of autonomy. And then a relational analysis can make clear why, say, the existing practices or law are structuring relations in a way that undermines autonomy. Such analysis can then also help people to see how alternative practices, or laws, or interpretations of rights could shift those relations in a way to better promote and protect autonomy. Thus explicit normative commitments are often helpful in issues of institutional relations, and the language of a relational analysis also is appropriate.

iii. Normative Commitments

Now let me clarify the substantive normative commitments that I bring to my version of a relational approach. First, as I said in the section on autonomy, I do *not* see autonomy as the only or even the central value of my relational approach. I do value autonomy, for the reasons I laid out in my discussion of the capacity for creative interaction. In many contemporary legal disputes and debates over rights and policy, autonomy is a relevant value. But the relational approach I envision can be used for other values as well. And while I value the capacity for creative interaction very highly, and see autonomy as a key component of it, it is not obvious to me that there could not be a good society that gave similar weight to harmony and to the respect for elders and that sets a lower priority on autonomy—even understood relationally. I do not think I know what constellation of values would best promote the creative capacity, certainly not for every culture. It is true that it is hard for me to envision a good society which did not treat autonomy as a value at all. But that is far from saying that it is the top priority in my relative ranking of values or that its priority is built into my relational analysis. It is, in the examples in this book, very often the value I am exploring, but other values could be used as well.

Equality is a normative commitment that underlies all my arguments. I increasingly think that dignity will be even more useful than equality when it comes to thinking about wise relations with the earth and her many dimensions, including other life-forms. But I do not see either equality or dignity as *generated* by my relational approach. I take them as widely shared values (and ones I am committed to) to which a relational approach can helpfully be applied in concrete situations. My argument is not about the relational meaning of equality as such,[146] but over and over again it is about how to make a value like autonomy actually equally available to all.

There are other values that I think *are* generated by a relational conception of selves. Recognizing the inherently dependent and interdependent nature of human existence draws one's attention to the importance of care. Many care theorists construct arguments about why care—both giving and receiving it—should be treated as a central value.[147] I share that objective, and I think it follows from my view of relational selves. Once care is recognized as a core value, it follows that societies should be organized so that those who provide care are not disadvantaged and that they are not relegated to the bottom of hierarchies of relationships.[148] Some theorists, such as Mary Shanley, argue for the need to treat certain relationships, such as the parent–child relationship, as a core value. Shanley shows the ways in which existing laws violate such relationships in routine ways. (She gives examples of foster care, contact between incarcerated parents and their children, and immigration—and argues that in each area the state has an obligation far beyond what is currently acknowledged to help parents to establish and maintain a parent–child relationship.) She raises the question of whether the best way of claiming the status of core value for parent–child relationships is to invoke the language of rights.[149] These are all questions of the kind of values that a relational approach itself brings to light and makes claims for.

In sum, then, what are my core substantive normative commitments in this project? I share the commitment to recognition of the value of care, of the need to construct just relations with caregivers, and of the need for more explicit recognition and protection of the value of intimate relations. These commitments flow from the relational approach, though they are not my primary subject here. My commitment to equality does not flow from the relational approach as such. It serves as a presumption from which the relational approach works—though I offer an argument in chapter 3 for my take on equality rather than treating it literally as a presumption. I explain why I see autonomy as a value (in addition to explaining the need to reconstruct the dominant understanding of autonomy). I do not try to deduce the value of autonomy from the relational nature of selves, but I do try to explain why it should be understood in relational terms. One might say, however, that autonomy only makes sense as a concern for relational selves. Creatures whose values, desires, and beliefs are either completely determined by others or are completely impervious to influence from others have no need for autonomy. Neither do solitary creatures.

I also insist that other core values in addition to autonomy are fostered by nested, interacting layers of relationships. And that law very often shapes these relationships. I use the example of autonomy, but I advocate relational analyses of law and other values, such as security and dignity.

Not only the meanings of core values but also what should count as a core value and what should be its relative weight, both in general and in particular cases, will always be contested in a democratic society. This is why, as I said above, it is important that the methodological side of my relational approach can be used by those who disagree with me substantively—so that our disagreements can be more productively explored. In this sense, I do not see my substantive commitments as *defining* my relational approach.

Let me also return to my claim that structural and institutional analyses *should* be carried out in terms of a normative commitment to autonomy. This is such a central value in Anglo-American societies, and law so often fails to structure autonomy enhancing relationships, that this combination of methodology and normative commitment is entirely appropriate for contemporary legal and policy analysis. The project of this book is very much about helping people to think about autonomy in a relational way and to see how this contributes to an understanding of the many concrete ways in which people's autonomy is affected by the law. I think the underlying normative commitment to equality is similarly entirely appropriate for a relational approach to law in contemporary Anglo-American societies. A relational approach should also help clarify the nature of the disagreements among people about what "equality" should mean in practice.

B. Feminism

The question of my substantive commitments makes this a good place to discuss the role of feminism in this project. Leckey boldly says that my relational theory is "much more than a focus or an inquiry. It is a feminist political project."[150] That is true in some ways, but I also think my relational theory is more than a feminist project. It extends beyond feminism in ways that make it methodologically available to those whose relational stance is not primarily feminist.

First, as I noted in the introduction, this entire project is deeply grounded in feminism. I developed my relational theory of the self in the context of ongoing intellectual exchange about feminism. I do not think I could have worked out these arguments without a vibrant feminist theory and practice around me. But it is also true that the first piece of this project that I wrote, "Reconceiving Autonomy" (now revised as chapter 2), was inspired by my reflections on administrative law. My focus was, as I noted above, on the need to protect the autonomy of those already within the sphere of state power, those who were dependent on the state. And I thought that relational autonomy was the best conceptual framework for accomplishing that. Perhaps it mattered that the primary example was a welfare recipient, the majority of whom are women.

As the reader will see, almost all my elaborated examples involve women. And gender is a constant concern. As I just noted, I see a commitment to care as arising from my relational approach, and the people who do most of the care work are women. Justice for caregivers and a full valuing of care would have a dramatic impact on women's well-being and their ability to actually exercise the rights their societies proclaim as the entitlement of all. But it is also the case that a recognition of the inherent dependence of human beings on one another and the need for care goes beyond the question of women's equality. MacIntyre's engagement with these issues (noted in the first section of this chapter), for example, is not a feminist argument as such (though he acknowledges that he draws heavily on the feminist theorists who developed the arguments about care and dependence).

Feminism today involves intersectionality: gender is shaped by racialization, class hierarchy, and religious norms, among other things. Nevertheless, I do not think it is useful to try to redefine feminism as including all equality projects. I also think feminist concerns go beyond a simple starting point that men always have the advantage over women (as Janet Halley defines feminism[151]). When one places significant value on intimate relationships for the quality of one's life, a relational analysis of the comparative advantage of men and women in North America is not likely to yield a simple advantage for the men—despite their greater economic and political power and the consequences deriving from it. This is not to deny that the gendered division of labor both at home and in the workplace is destructive or the unequal opportunities and pay scale unjust. Merely that the harm our gender norms do to both men and women does not always leave women worse off. One of the greatest harms is with respect to violence. Violence is gendered but not always in ways that simply privilege males—despite the shocking prevalence of sexual assault and intimate partner violence. (See chapter 8.)

A relational analysis of the consequences of the gendered division of household labor will show that women are unlikely ever to enjoy full equality while this division of labor holds as a widespread organizing norm of society. But the relational implications of the gendered division of labor exceed the inequality between men and women. Other values of justice and democracy are involved.[152] And I think one of the most compelling arguments is, as I noted earlier, that leaving policy making in the hands of those who have virtually no experience of care work means asking people to govern who do not have the necessary knowledge or life experience to govern well.

These are all examples of the ways in which my commitments to feminism both involve gender issues that are not just about male–female equality and which constantly spill over into areas that are not simply feminist as such.

This point is made even more clearly by the range of topics that I think urgently need relational analysis. Earlier I gave examples of pension funds, contract, and the obligations of property holders. Freedom of speech and the law of copyright are other examples that have benefited from the kind of relational analysis I propose here.[153] In the volume following this one I will offer still more examples, some of which will be feminist in content and some not.

I claim that all matters of justice will benefit from relational analysis. All areas of law will be clearer through this lens. From this perspective, defining my relational theory as a feminist project seems too narrow. Even though it is also true that virtually every area of law has gender implications, and no theory of justice can be adequate that does not make gender and care central to it, I think it is unhelpful to call all relational analyses—of the kind I recommend—feminist. While everything in this book is shaped by my feminist commitments, I want the method used by those whose primary concerns are other than feminist.

Would I extend this even to those who are antifeminist, or, for that matter, homophobic or racist? I think my claim for the advantages of clarity extends even this far. I argued in the example of gay marriage that the contestable presumptions and consequences stand out more clearly via a relational analysis. I will pursue that a bit further here. For those who say they want to end discrimination against homosexuals but oppose same-sex marriage, I think it would help to be clear about whether one of their objectives is to reinforce norms about the moral unacceptablity of same-sex relationships. Spelling out those norms in terms of relational practice—who would be invited to one's home for dinner, who would be welcome in contexts of workplace socializing, whose children would be welcome to play with one's child, who one would choose as a close business associate, whom one would be able to refuse to hire as a receptionist or private school teacher, or whom one would want to be able to exclude from renting a room in one's house—will make it clearer whether the relational impact they hope for by preventing gay marriage is consistent with their own or others' understanding of equality. In the case of "antifeminism" or advocacy of traditional roles for women, the question will arise whether private relations of hierarchy in the home can be fully consistent with full political and economic equality.

Similarly, if women are expected to take responsibility for child rearing and household caretaking (whether they also work outside the home or not), will these "private" relations interfere with their capacity to stand in relations of equality in the "public" realm of politics and economy? As I said above, it is not that I expect that such relational questioning will yield agreement. But I think it will often reveal whether the differences are about claims of natural difference (say between men and women), about the compatibility of inequality in private spheres with full legal and political equality, or about the value and nature of equality.

I conclude by saying that *my* relational project is feminist. But my relational theory is not bounded by feminist concerns.

C. Relation to Liberalism

It once mattered to me to sharply distinguish my relational approach from liberalism. I still think there is an important difference between making a relational analysis central to one's framework of analysis and treating human beings as fundamentally independent rational agents. (See chapter 3.) I can now see, however, that I share with most of Anglo-American liberalism a belief in the infinite and equal worth of every individual. The commitment to equality that underlies liberal theory (however contested its precise form) underlies my approach as well.[154] So does the sense that the distinctness of each individual matters, and the value of each individual should never be subsumed under some aggregate—whether family, community, or nation. But I think that understanding how to honor and nurture each individual is best done through a relational approach. It is relationships that enable individuals to flourish and develop the capacities that liberalism has long highlighted—reason, autonomy, liberty—as well as the capacities for love, play, and emotion that make life valuable and that have not received the same attention in the liberal tradition. Relationship must therefore be central rather than peripheral to legal and political thought and to the workings of the institutions that structure relations.

I think a relational approach makes it more likely that the formal commitment to equality will become a reality in ways that it has not been in either the origins of liberalism or its contemporary practices. While I share the commitment to the inherent value of every individual, I think the individualism of the liberal tradition impedes practices and habits of thought that can give effect to that equal value.

Of course, critiques of liberal individualism have been around for quite a while, and they have had some impact. Many of the most important contemporary liberal theorists include some acknowledgment of the centrality of culture, or of social context to the well-being and development of individuals.[155] Nevertheless, I think the attention to relationship often remains peripheral. Relationship is a subject of attention in particular contexts, but is not treated as constitutive. It can be ignored for many purposes. Cognitive capacities, such as reason, are still often presumed rather than seen as requiring relational support. (And reason is also still often treated as sharply distinct from emotion.)

In the context of law, conscious attention to the relational dimension of the problem at hand is sporadic. And systematic reflection on how different interpretations will affect the structures of relations, and thus the values in question, is rare. Presumptions about the liberal individual and corresponding conceptions of rights hold a powerful sway.

In neither the theoretical nor the judicial context do I claim that no one ever uses what is, in effect, a relational approach. Nor do I try to prove that a more conventionally individualistic approach can never shed light on important values or protect important rights. Rather, for the part of my audience that is drawn to, or used to, an individualist framework, my purpose is to highlight the importance of a relational approach for most of the theoretical projects they care about as well as its usefulness for the kind of legal analysis in which most judges and lawyers are engaged.

D. Relation to the Ethic of Care

It seems necessary to comment briefly on how I see my project in relation to the ethic of care, in part because my work on autonomy has been mischaracterized in these terms.[156] I admire the work of Carol Gilligan, who introduced the term as a form of reasoning distinct from what she called the ethic of justice. The ethic of care focuses on the particular rather than the abstract principle and attends to context and to relationships in particular. Identifying this form of moral reasoning—as genuine reasoning—was an important contribution. And it is obvious why people would see similarities in our approaches. However, I do not see my work as creating a moral theory, which is the case for most theorists who work within the care framework. And, as I stated above, my primary interest is the role of relationship, institutional as well as personal, in enabling core values. Thus, relationship in my terms is not exclusively, or even primarily, about personal relationship.

I have already noted that I think it is misleading to say that for Gilligan the ethic of care was concerned with maintaining existing relationships. Nevertheless, some care theorists seem to take that view.[157] In any case, my own project is not focused on maintaining existing relationships, but evaluating them—particularly with respect to whether they support or undermine core values, such as autonomy. My project aims at evaluation and transformation. (There is a subtler version of the concern which focuses on avoiding any coercive disruption of existing relations, even discriminatory ones.[158] This touches on the issue of the kind of Burkean deference to tradition that might be due to long-standing structures of relations. I address this concern in "Closing Reflections.")

I also admire Joan Tronto's work and that of others whose project is to think through what it would take (theoretically and practically) to make care a core value (to use my terms). My arguments support such a project (as I have indicated above), but it is not the central argument of this book. Some people try to advance this project by using the language of a right to give and receive care.[159] This points to the fact that the field of "the ethic of care" is, happily, now wide enough that there is huge variation within it. Other care theorists treat rights as part of the ethic of justice and thus as distinct from an ethic of care. Of course, part of my project is to think of rights in relational terms, so they are within rather than outside of my relational framework.

Finally, I want to comment on a particularly intriguing formulation of the ethic of care: "The crucial ontological presumptions of human rights thinking [ethic of rights] is that ethical value resides within the individual human being. In contrast to this, care thinking puts value not on any characteristic located within the human being but on a particular kind of relation between human beings, one in which care and dependence are a primary feature."[160] While not all care theorists would subscribe to this position, I think it (tacitly) poses an interesting question of how my relational approach fits with this claim.

I think that most descriptions of the kinds of harm people are subject to (from which rights are supposed to protect them) will involve a relational dimension. Even the idea of torture expresses a relation between victim and assailant, not just a degree of pain. Most expressions of what one values in human life will include a relational dimension. And sometimes it is helpful to bring to consciousness the relational dimension of a right said to inhere in human beings, such as property or freedom of speech. Of course, these are all reasons why I think a relational approach to rights and to understanding human selves and values is desirable.

Nevertheless, as I noted in my comments on liberalism above, I think the idea of unique and immeasurable value of each individual remains helpful. This is related to my view that a formal notion of inherent equality is a necessary part of my relational approach (which I explain in chapter 4). Indeed, I think there is a unique and immeasurable value to each living thing (and possibly to things the English language classifies as inanimate, like rocks). (I discuss this, and its tensions with human equality claims, at the end of chapter 4). I see the critical quote above as pointing to a kind of gestalt shift between a focus on an individual and a focus on the relations enabling that individual to be who she or he is. Sometimes one focus is more helpful than the other. I have been emphasizing the relational focus because it is neglected in Anglo-American culture. And I do not think that only a focus on the individual can capture uniqueness: one's distinct location in a relation web provides a relational articulation of individual uniqueness. In the end, I think the idea of value inhering in individual entities—human and nonhuman—is an important component of articulating what wise relations among them would look like.

V. CONCLUSION

This opening chapter has sketched the relational framework elaborated in the book with the aim of anticipating some of the questions and concerns that I think are likely to arise. The following chapters work out the arguments in much more detail and with more detailed examples. In the conclusion to the book I return to what I see as the major challenges that my version of the relational approach gives rise to. Here, I will just anticipate those points.

There are two issues that my approach to rights and law gives rise to, which I elaborate in chapter 8 and in "Closing Reflections." The first is the question of predictability and contingency. The question of which structure of relations will best foster a given value involves prediction. And prediction is always limited by contingency as well as imperfect knowledge. The same is true about arguments that interpreting a right one way rather than another will have a certain relational impact. I do not think such arguments can be avoided. Shifting the language to claims of inherent rights which admit of no consequentialist argument will not help. If (as I argue) rights can only be given effect through human relationships (which are structured by those rights), one is back in the same position. One still has to figure out how to give those rights effect through the particular wording, interpretation, or implementation of law. And one must have some sense of what such wording, interpretation, or implementation will actually mean in the lives of people. This is just what my relational approach claims to do. In the conclusion, I turn to what to do about the inevitability of contingency and unpredictability.

The second question is whether the relational approach itself can help sort out the priority that should be given to core values. I have argued that these values, particularly what they should mean in practice, will always be contested. And in many cases, values will compete with one another. I return to the question of whether the relational approach—in either its methodological or substantive form—can help resolve these inevitable conflicts.

With the details of my argument available to the reader, I will return to the question of the relation between the individual and the collective implied in my approach. In particular, I will argue again that my approach entails no subordination of individual to collective. Chapter 8 takes up one variant of this issue: I argue in detail that my approach does not, in itself, involve an expansion of state power. The relational approach offers, rather, a way of evaluating what forms of state power could optimally structure relations to foster values like liberty and security. In "Closing Reflections," I acknowledge that a widespread embrace of a relational approach would give rise to a shift in norms of individual and collective responsibility. I address the question of whether such a shift would entail a reduction of individual freedom or autonomy or a greater weight toward collective well-being at the possible cost of the scope of individual choice.

Finally, it is important to remember that virtually all my examples are taken from Canada and the United States and that the theoretical and legal conventions that I am trying to shift are those of the Anglo-American world. In the conclusion, I briefly address the question of the applicability of my argument beyond this context.

2

Law, Boundaries, and the Bounded Self

I. INTRODUCTION

Law, like all conceptual systems, relies on metaphor.[1] An optimal language of law requires metaphors that highlight rather than hide the relationships that law fosters and reflects. This chapter explores the centrality of the term "boundary" in the metaphoric structure of Anglo-American law and its relation to an underlying conception of the "bounded self." I argue for a new image of the self and a corresponding conception of the relation between the collective and the individual—for which boundary is not an apt metaphor. This chapter explores the rejection of boundary and points toward an alternative language for the self, autonomy, and the rights that are to protect them.

Within the Anglo-American liberal tradition, one of the most important functions of rights—both rhetorical and institutional—has been to define the legitimate scope of the state. American constitutionalism articulates and institutionalizes this function in a particularly stark way. While the particulars of the American form of liberal constitutionalism are not found in all constitutional democracies, the American approach reveals especially clearly the assumptions that underlie not only constitutionalism but also the wider legal systems (such as the common law) premised on liberalism. I argue here that the limits to legitimate state power central to liberal legalism are built on a particular picture of the bounded self: rights serve to mark and protect the bounded self and, thus, the legitimate scope of the state. But neither the "bounded self" nor the "boundaries of state power" are optimal concepts for articulating and protecting core values, such as autonomy or equality.

In the American tradition of constitutionalism, property has served as a powerful symbol of rights as limits to government. This notion of "rights" functioning as "limits" to "government" involves a complex set of abstractions and metaphoric links that nevertheless is taken as common sense by most Americans. Perhaps the clearest form of that common sense is "Government can't take what's mine" or the more elegant "A man's home is his castle." These phrases convey an image of property as a source of security, the sacredness of which acts as a barrier even to the power of the state. The enduring power of this image reflects (among other things) the original importance of property in shaping the American conception of rights as limits to the legitimate scope of the state.

This conception is, in turn, a part of a deeper phenomenon: the focus on boundaries as the means of comprehending and securing the basic values of freedom or autonomy. The importance of property in American constitutionalism both reflects and exacerbates the problems of boundary as a central metaphor in the legal rhetoric of freedom.

In an earlier book, *Private Property and the Limits of American Constitutionalism*, I argue that in the early development of the American Constitution property served as the defining instance of the notion of rights as limits and that this notion is an attempt to address the inevitable tension between the individual and the collective.[2] I concluded that the attempt is deeply flawed and that the problems go beyond the particular limitations of the focus on property. In the end, an optimal vision of constitutionalism requires something more than the replacement of property with other rights that can serve as boundaries.

Drawing on my earlier work, I start (section II) by discussing the American Constitution as an instance of the ways boundary has been central to the American conceptual and institutional framework and give an account of how the U.S. Constitution came to have the boundary-like structure that it does and the role property played in the emergence of that structure. I offer a critical appraisal of the lasting consequences of the original focus on property that is within the conventions of constitutional discourse. (Those not interested in this history of American constitutionalism can skip to the last paragraph before section III.)

My argument leads, however, to the claim that the particular limitations of the focus on property are themselves reflective of the deeper problems that made property an attractive focus in the first place: a picture of human beings that envisions their freedom and security in terms of bounded spheres. I then begin to explore why boundary is destructive as a central metaphor for addressing the real problems of human autonomy. At this point, I go beyond the particularity (and peculiarities) of American constitutionalism to address an issue at the heart of liberal legalism: the relation between the bounded self and the bounded state. In section III, I look at the power and problems of the boundary metaphor. Then (in section IV) I consider the challenge posed by the use of the boundary metaphor in other discourses that are far removed from the traditions of legalism and that I trusted and respected. I look at examples of these other invocations of boundary and the possibility of envisioning boundaries not as the rigid walls of property, but as fluid, shifting, and permeable. But I conclude that the boundary metaphor still provides the wrong focus for exploring the best possibilities of human autonomy.

The centrality of the boundary metaphor in the language of law hides rather than illuminates the ways law and rights structure relationships. Thus, in section V, I consider the emergence of new mythic structures, new visions and metaphors that may provide alternative frameworks for law, rights, and conceptions of the self.

II. UNEQUAL PROPERTY AND THE RISE OF RIGHTS AS LIMITS (BOUNDARIES) IN AMERICAN CONSTITUTIONALISM

One of the ways of understanding both the power and the perversity of American constitutionalism is to examine its origins. In my earlier work I discussed the importance of property in the design of the Constitution of 1787 and the subsequent rise of judicial review. Here I will just give the core of my argument, particularly my claims about the distortions that the focus on property both expressed and gave rise to.

During the 1780s the newly independent confederation of states seemed to pose problems for which the revolutionary conceptions of politics were inadequate. The new governments had solved the problem of "no taxation without representation," but many men of property felt that their rights were still not secure. During the Revolution they had proclaimed that a state that takes an individual's property without consent "destroys the distinction between liberty and slavery."[3] By the 1780s that consent was thought to have been ensured through representation, but the new representative governments were themselves threatening property. The depreciating currency and debtor relief laws promulgated by virtually every state were widely seen as violations of property rights— and thus illegitimate even though passed by duly elected representatives. For many of the great statesmen of the time, the threats these laws posed came to be understood as part of a more general problem. Their important (and now trite) insight was that democracy[4] solves some problems of tyranny but creates its own: the tyranny of the majority.[5]

The forms of representation that the colonists had demanded to secure the rights of Englishmen turned out to threaten those very rights. Property in particular turned out to be just as vulnerable to debtor relief measures in the republic as it had been to unjust taxation under the monarchy. Indeed, many thought this would always be so: property would be inherently vulnerable in a republic because the many would always be poor and the few rich; what would prevent the many from using their numerical power in the legislature to take the property from the few?

The problem of designing a republican government that could provide security for property was a central one for the Federalists, whose views prevailed at the Constitutional Convention of 1787. It was an immediate problem that had to be solved if the republic was to survive, and, for the most thoughtful Framers, it became the defining instance of the larger problem of securing rights against the threat of majority oppression.[6] Ironically, it is because this original preoccupation with property was not limited to a crass concern with protecting the interests of the rich that it has had such a lasting and destructive legacy. Originally invoked as the defining instance of the larger problem of securing justice and liberty in a republic, property indeed came to define the terms of that problem for at least one hundred and fifty years.[7]

There were many complex consequences of this original focus on property. To begin with, the problem of property arose for the Framers because their conception of it was inseparably tied to inequality. The link to inequality was liberty. Property was important for the exercise of liberty, and liberty required the free exercise of property rights; this free exercise would inevitably lead, in turn, to an unequal distribution of property. Property thus posed a problem for popular government because this inequality required protection; those with property had to be protected from those who had less or none. Without security, property lost its value. And the threat to security was inevitable, for (the Framers presumed) it was in the very nature of a productive system of private property that many, perhaps most, would have none.[8] It was this inequality, which the Framers both feared and accepted as natural, that skewed their conception of republican government.

The republic the Framers envisioned required the security of a right to which the majority posed a constant and inevitable threat. Defense against such a threat was a problem quite different from that arising from the general insight that in a republic the majority may oppress the minority. It is one thing to say that everyone's rights are vulnerable to the possibility of majority oppression. It is another to say that an essential ingredient of the republic is the protection of rights that the majority will never fully enjoy, will always want more of, and will therefore always want to encroach upon. The vulnerability of property bred a fear of and, perhaps, contempt for the propertyless, those with less or no property, who were expected to be the vast bulk of the people. With this fear came an urgent sense of the need to contain the people's threatening power.

Given the historical context, one can understand both the focus on property and the insistence that it stood for broader issues and deeper values. The Framers who focused on property were not crass materialists of either the self-interested or philosophical variety; they were not devoted to property for its own sake. Their preoccupation with property had its origins in the connections they presumed between property and other basic human goods, in particular, liberty and security. Property came to be not merely a link to those basic values but also the symbolic focal point for the effort to make republican government compatible with both liberty and security.

Property was a powerful symbol of these goals because it could both crystallize complex aspirations and problems and provide a practical focus for dealing with them. Property was an effective symbol in part because it was not *merely* a symbol but also a concrete means of having control over one's life, of expressing oneself, and of protecting oneself from the power of others, individual or collective. In addition, the need for security in order for property to serve those purposes expressed the important link between security and liberty: although the two values are not the same, and can be in tension with one another, some level of security is necessary for liberty to have meaning.

Property effectively captures this link between liberty and security in that it literally loses its meaning without security. Property *means* that which is recognized to be ours and that cannot be easily taken from us—hence the connection between property and what are seen as the sources of its security: law and government. Of course, all rights require collective definition to function as entitlements the state will enforce and respect. But the very meaning of property entails collective recognition of entitlement and sufficient enforcement for security. This need for collective definition and defense makes property peculiarly vulnerable to collective power—at the same time that one of the basic purposes of property is to provide a shield for the individual against the intrusions of the collective. Property defines what the society, or its representative the state, cannot touch (in the ordinary course of things). It defines a sphere in which the property owner can act largely unconstrained by collective demands and prohibitions. But the definition and protection of that sphere must reside with the collective itself.

Property thus captures the essence of the problem of self-limiting government. But a focus on property also provides a distorted image of the problem.

Property (at least as the Framers understood it) must distort because it makes inequality rather than liberty, or individual autonomy, the central problem of government. (Note that what follows is not an argument that there must be equality of property. It is an argument about what happens when property, conceived of as inherently unequal, becomes the central symbol for the protection of individual rights.) The Federalists presumed that the threat that inequality posed to property captured the inevitable threat that democracy posed to individual freedom and security. But the Federalists were wrong: not all rights, all components of liberty, must be enjoyed with the stark inequality the Federalists envisioned with respect to property. Perhaps even property need not be enjoyed unequally, but the Framers' conception of property had inequality—and thus fear, anger, and resentment—built into it. The centrality of inequality skewed the Federalists' comprehension of the basic problem of republican government. They failed to see that protecting the rights of the propertied few against the demands of the many is not the same as protecting individuals from the ever present possibility of collective oppression. The cost of the Framers' insight is that they cast the general problem in the terms of the particular—and both popular and legal thinking have continued to be shaped by that framework.

The tension between the individual and the collective does not inevitably involve inequality, power, and domination in the way that protection of unequal property does. In accepting vast economic inequality as a given, and the contours of property rights as obvious, the Framers were in fact focusing on protecting the few from the many, not the individual from the collective of which he or she is a part.[9]

The Framers' focus on property turned attention away from the real problem: the need for an ongoing collective formulation of individual rights in a political culture that respects both democratic decision making and individual freedom and that recognizes the need to sustain the inevitable tension between them. The Framers recognized this tension, but they were preoccupied with one dimension of it: insulating property from democratic decision making. Rights became things to be protected, not values to be collectively defined. The most thoughtful Framers transformed a widespread fear about threats to property into a sophisticated analysis of the inherent problem of majority oppression. But in so doing they also transformed this general problem into a question of how to contain the power of the people.

The 1787 Constitution did indeed "insulate" property rather than set up rigid boundaries to protect it.[10] Its solution was a carefully structured system of institutions that would minimize the threat of the future propertyless majority in large part by minimizing their political efficacy. This undermining of democracy was justified in part by an articulation of competing categories of civil and political rights. Civil rights, with property as the leading example, were the true ends of government; political rights were merely means. It was therefore no sacrifice of basic principle to tailor the means to the end. But this conceptual hierarchy remained institutionally fluid in the Constitution of 1787; there was no clear answer to how the priority of civil over political rights was to be enforced. There were few formal declarations of rights as limits to the power of the federal government.[11] Rather, the Constitution the Framers wrote protected civil rights in more subtle ways by channeling the power of the people in order to minimize their threat to property and civil rights generally.

By 1800 this channeling seemed insufficient to contain the threats posed by Jeffersonian democracy. With the rise of judicial review the conceptual hierarchy of civil over political rights hardened into an institutional one: the judiciary wielded the power to strike down the outcomes of the democratic process in the name of constitutionally protected rights. Those rights were proclaimed as clear boundaries to the legitimate power of the state, boundaries to be defined and defended by the judiciary.[12]

We are now coming to my central point. The vision of constitutionalism sketched above—the tension between democracy and individual rights, the hierarchical distinction between civil and political rights, the notion of rights as boundaries—not only has the dark underpinning of inequality but also rests on a flawed conception of the individual, a conception captured, amplified, and entrenched by its association with property. The boundaries central to American constitutionalism are those necessary to protect a bounded or "separative" self: the boundaries around selves form the boundaries to state power.[13] Now, the boundedness of selves may seem to be a self-evident truth, but I think it is a wrongheaded and destructive way of conceiving of the human creatures for whom law and government are created.

III. THE POWER AND PROBLEMS OF THE BOUNDARY METAPHOR

Much of American constitutional protection can be understood as a (misguided) attempt to protect individual autonomy. The primary content of this underlying conception of autonomy is protection from the intrusion of the collective. The autonomy the American system is designed to protect can be achieved by erecting a wall of rights around the individual. Property provided an ideal symbol for this vision of autonomy, for it could both literally and figuratively provide the necessary walls. The perverse quality of this conception is clearest when taken to its extreme: the most perfectly autonomous man is the most perfectly isolated.

The image of rights as boundaries defining the sphere within which human autonomy (or freedom or privacy) resides is an American commonplace (even if those particular words are not).[14] Certainly within Anglo-American legal theory that image is routine. These images abound, for example, in Charles Reich's classic "new property" article in which he tries to expand the traditional meaning of property to cover government largess:

> The institution called property guards the troubled boundary between individual man and the state.... Property draws a circle around the activities of each private individual or organization. Within that circle, the owner has a greater degree of freedom than without. Outside, he must justify or explain his actions, and show his authority. Within, he is master, and the state must explain and justify any interference.[15]

Reich wants to redefine property so that it can continue to define protective spheres but ones that are appropriate for a regulatory state.

Boundary images have a powerful hold even over those who have a sense of their limitations. Laurence Tribe, for example, argues against relying solely on sphere-like conceptions of human autonomy: "Meaningful freedom cannot be protected simply by placing identified realms of thought or spheres of action beyond the reach of government.... The very idea of articulating constitutional constraints and obligations is threatened with incoherence by the same interdependence that has made liberal individualism of Mill's variety inadequate to the contemporary task of building doctrine."[16] Nevertheless, in order to capture the enduring importance of personhood and of protecting it from governmental coercion, Tribe turns to the sphere metaphor even as he tries to suggest the difficulties of defining it: "The tight interdependence of persons in advanced industrial and post-industrial societies precludes any attempt to define the protected sphere in terms of conduct that is wholly self-regarding or needs that are wholly personal."[17] And he soon moves to repeated references to the "invasion" of personhood.[18]

Not surprisingly, the image of bounded space is invoked particularly often in discussions of privacy. For example, Robert Post writes that the tort of intrusion "guards against the penetration of private space." Post's image explicitly draws on boundary metaphors found in nonlegal discourse, for example Georg Simmel's image of "the ideal sphere [that] lies around every human being" and that "cannot be penetrated, unless the personality value of the individual is thereby destroyed." Post then makes use of Erving Goffman's metaphor of the "territories of the self": "We indicate respect for a person by acknowledging his territory; conversely, we invite intimacy by waiving our claims to a territory and allowing others to draw close."[19]

The examples from Post suggest far more than the success of American constitutional images; they suggest that the image of protective boundaries as essential to the integrity and autonomy of the self is deep and pervasive in Western culture. Must my challenge to the rhetoric of boundaries then extend beyond the peculiarities of the property-based boundary forms of American constitutionalism? Yes—at the least because, as I noted earlier, I do not advocate simply removing the perversions of the original focus on property by replacing it with other rights to serve as boundaries and, more broadly still, because the boundaries of American legal discourse effectively capture a wider (and deeper) phenomenon. So I must pose my question more broadly: what is wrong with boundary imagery?

I start by focusing on autonomy because it (like privacy) is an aspect of the individual self for which both law and other discourses routinely invoke boundary. As I said in chapter 1, I see individual autonomy as a fluid capacity, not a static human characteristic to be posited as a presupposition of legal or political theory. This capacity must be continually developed; it can flourish or become moribund throughout one's life. What is essential to the development of autonomy is not protection against intrusion, but constructive relationship. The central question then for inquiries into autonomy (legal or otherwise) is how to structure relationships so that they foster rather than undermine autonomy.

The boundary metaphor does not direct our attention to this question. Instead it invites us to imagine that the self to be protected is, in some crucial sense, insular and that what is most important to the preservation of such a self is drawing boundaries around it that will protect it from invasion (or at least that that is the most crucial thing the law can do).

I should make clear before proceeding further that all metaphors inevitably distort or shape our perceptions in the sense that they hide some dimensions of the phenomenon they refer to and highlight others. And it is, further, not an option simply to avoid metaphors. I accept George Lakoff and Mark Johnson's view that all our thinking is metaphoric in structure.[20] There is in that sense nothing peculiar or perverse about the recourse to metaphor to explore the issue of autonomy. The problem arises exactly because metaphors are so important in shaping how people experience the world. (For example, Lakoff and Johnson open their book with a compelling picture of how the dominant metaphor of war structures people's experience of what argument is and how they ought to engage in it.)

It is therefore crucial that the reigning metaphor for autonomy and other basic aspects of selfhood be one that directs our attention in the most fruitful way. For example, the image of the child developing autonomy teaches us not to see dependence as antithetical to autonomy. That image is, of course, very different from that of a man securely ensconced on his property, the boundaries of which are well guarded against intrusion.[21]

There are practical virtues to better imagery. As we will see more fully in the next chapter, if we understand autonomy as made possible by relationship rather than by exclusion, we can better understand the distinctive problem of autonomy in the modern state. Our central problem today is not maintaining a sphere into which the state cannot penetrate,[22] but fostering autonomy where people are already within the ambit of state control or responsibility. More broadly, we change our whole conception of the relation between the individual and the collective when we see that the collective is a source of autonomy as well as a threat to it. We would no longer take "a boundary guarded by property" or "invasion" as suitable metaphors to guide us in designing the legal structures to optimize that relationship.

IV. BOUNDARY LANGUAGE OUTSIDE THE LAW

I turn now to some examples of boundary language outside the realm of law. I begin with an example within feminism that reveals the perversity of conceiving of selfhood and autonomy in boundary terms. Andrea Dworkin has written a powerful and disturbing indictment of the meaning of sexual intercourse in our society, which, as she interprets it, is inseparable from domination. What is striking, and important for my purposes here, is that her analysis assumes the understanding of humanness as boundedness. Since that boundedness is either nonexistent or routinely violated in women, they are seen as less than human. Here are examples of her vision:

> In the experience of intercourse, she loses the capacity for integrity because her body—the basis of privacy and freedom in the material world for all human beings—is entered and occupied; the boundaries of her physical body are— neutrally speaking—violated.[23]
>
> A human being has a body that is inviolate; and when it is violated, it is abused. A woman has a body that is penetrated in intercourse: permeable, its corporeal solidness a lie. The discourse of male truth—literature, science, philosophy, pornography—calls that penetration violation. . . . She, a human being, is supposed to have a privacy that is absolute; except that she, a woman, has a hole between her legs that men can, must, do enter. . . . That slit which means entry into her—intercourse—appears to be the key to women's lower human status. By definition, as the God who does not exist made her, she is intended to have a lesser privacy, a lesser integrity of the body, a lesser sense of self, since her body can be physically occupied and in the occupation taken over.[24]

Dworkin vacillates in her argument between suggesting that intercourse *must* have this meaning because of its essential nature as invasion and suggesting that in our society this is the inevitable *social construction* of the meaning of intercourse. I think the social construction version is compelling (though I do not accept the claim of inevitability). It also shows us the deep perversity of making boundedness the central metaphor for humanness. When boundary is the routine metaphor for integrity, privacy, or the conditions of autonomy, it is indeed not surprising that intercourse "has in it, as part of it, violation of boundaries, taking over, occupation, destruction of privacy."[25] It is not enough to meet the force of Dworkin's images with the conventional argument that it is only nonconsensual boundary crossing that constitutes violation. Of course, she has reasons why we should doubt that intercourse is ever fully consensual (because of the pervasiveness of different forms of coercion). But her point goes deeper than that.

Consensual invasion is an odd concept, and if boundary is central to our conception of self, it will not be surprising that intercourse comes to be seen and experienced as invasion or violation, even if consented to. When boundary is central and intercourse is violation, women come to be seen and experienced as something less than fully human. (And of course women's boundaries seem indistinct in other ways: they blur with nature, with their children, their families, their lovers. Their contours do not seem hard, clearly defined or well protected.)

This is perhaps why there is so much popular psychology literature about women's need to protect, claim respect for, or shore up their boundaries.[26] Most of what is meant in these contexts is that women need to be able to pay attention to their own needs and not "lose themselves" in attending to the needs of others. They need to be able to discern when requests of them (including requests for physical and emotional intimacy) are reasonable and whether they really want to grant those requests. And they need to be able to claim respectful, attentive engagement from others. All of this seems appropriate to me. But boundary is not a metaphor that directs attention to the self-awareness and respect that is really at the heart of structuring the positive relations aimed at by this boundary language. This language is in keeping with dominant conceptions of selfhood and thus may be seen to protect that selfhood. But in my view it does not serve that purpose well. The focus on barrier and boundary will not invite the optimal reflection on relationship.

Because boundary is such a poor metaphor for the relations at stake, I do not think it is wise to advise women to shore up their boundaries (as opposed to a genuine sense of self, which often *does* need strengthening). Nor should they, at least in the long run, try to find ways to draw circles of protection around themselves that are the same as men's. And my point is not that the boundary metaphor is apt for men but destructive for women. Rather, it is misleading about the nature of human selfhood and thus about the institutions and concepts that will foster the flourishing of that selfhood.[27]

I have a similar comment with respect to Dworkin's use of boundary language. I use Dworkin's views on intercourse as a troubling indicator of the problems of boundary metaphors for selfhood. But I do not mean to suggest that the physical nature of intercourse—that an intimate part of one body is taken (or pushed) inside an intimate part of another—has nothing to do with the experience.[28] I think the physical fact of bodily interconnection has a great deal to do with the deep intimacy of intercourse and with the profound violence of rape. And I think it is related to the continuum of experience women have of intercourse: unease or distress when they consent with ambivalence or without desire as well as joy in lovemaking and horror in rape. (Consent to sexual intercourse may be an adequate standard for law; it is a sad minimum for personal relationships.) My point is that the physical boundary crossing takes place in all these forms of intercourse. It is the nature of the relationship at the time of intercourse that determines the pleasure, satisfaction, or harm. It is the relationship, not the physical boundary crossing, that defines the experience as a joy, a violation, or something in between.[29]

I think the most likely objection to my rejection of boundary (at least from those sympathetic to the social dimensions of selfhood) is that the function of boundaries *is* to structure relationships, indeed to structure them in ways that "enable an autonomous self to emerge."[30] It is, of course, true that our conceptions of boundaries, including legal ones, do structure our relationships. But do they do a good job of it? And does the focus on boundary in fact help us understand what those relationships are or should be? Relationships structured around boundaries have not been optimal, and, equally important, the boundary metaphor consistently inhibits our capacity to focus on the relationships it is in fact structuring. I will turn later to an inquiry into privacy and property to explore the distortions boundary language brings. But first I want to examine the sources of my own doubts about rejecting boundary.

As I was finishing my book on property, I began to notice the frequency of boundary metaphors. In particular, I realized that two quite different sorts of literature I was engaged with gave great weight to boundaries. The first was child-development literature. The form in which that use of the metaphor is familiar to everyone is "children need limits" or "it's important to set clear boundaries for children." In fact the metaphor recurs repeatedly in related forms, such as this: "My [sexual feelings for a parent] are all right. There is nothing wrong with me for having them. My parents will help me keep them within bounds."[31] These metaphors sound so familiar that they seem to be obviously "right." They are related to another spatial metaphor: the idea of creating a "safe space" in which the child can develop. This is, I think, closely related to the idea underlying the bounded sphere of rights for the adult. If, therefore, the boundary metaphors ring true in the context of children, should that at least relax my suspicion of the metaphors' capacity to capture the conditions for adult selfhood?

Although child-development literature might at first seem to be well removed from legal discourse (and thus a sort of "independent" validation of boundary metaphors), it not surprisingly reflects the dominant modes of thought in our society. Much of this literature is aimed at helping parents raise their children so that they will fit in well, an enterprise that requires being attuned to (even if not theoretically conscious of) prevailing values and modes of thinking. For example, Dorothy Corkille Briggs's book *Your Child's Self-Esteem* (1975) neatly presents in the space of six pages the connection between private property, the notion of autonomy, and the self conceived of as essentially separate.[32] First, the author explains that "only by *practicing* separateness can the child capture the feeling of autonomy"; indeed, the "Terrible Twos" would be better labeled "The Age of Separateness."[33] She then proceeds to offer some helpful suggestions about how to aid this emerging selfhood by respecting the child's efforts at autonomy. But along with these suggestions are those based on her view that "separateness means possession":

> Possession is one device the young child uses to hammer out autonomy. Consequently, ownership takes on special meaning to the toddler set. To them, separateness *means* the right to possess.
>
> Just as babbling comes before talking, so owning comes before sharing. *To fully share, a person must FIRST fully possess.* None of us can share what we don't have. And the little child needs time to get the feel of ownership thoroughly worked into his experience before he can let go.[34]

Now I trust that the culturally specific, not to say ideological, quality of this picture is clear. The author's concept of sharing is largess. It is the situation in which one who has control of an object chooses to let another interact with it. It is of course tautologically true that one cannot learn this form of sharing unless one first learns about ownership. And there is indeed a very complex set of ideas the child needs to incorporate—first, that some things are "his" and that that means he can do virtually whatever he wants with them regardless of other people's feelings, needs, or preferences; then, that he may wish to respond to their feelings by "sharing," and indeed it would be "good" if he did, but it is up to him. Exercising that power of control and choice not only over objects, but over other people, is treated as an important part of autonomy.

These implicit lessons about property, power, and relationship are no doubt important in our society, and they are closely related to a notion of selfhood as separateness. But surely this is also an odd (though by no means idiosyncratic) notion of "sharing": we can only "share" by largess those things that are our "own," that is, not truly shared. Suppose, by contrast, that the basic task were to communicate to a child that much of her environment is such that several people (and other creatures) have need of it and claims on it— that it is "shared." Here her selfhood would not be hammered out in possession but developed in the context of the norms of reciprocal connection. We would end up with a different picture of sharing and of the self who shares.

It is possible that early ownership and the power to dispense largess are essential to the separateness so widely identified with autonomy. But this striking link alerts me to the presence of the same ideological framework and metaphoric structure as those we find in the apparently different contexts of law and political theory. The boundary metaphors are not independent similarities, but the result of the same conception of selfhood, autonomy, and property.

What I am still left with is the powerful intuitive appeal of these metaphors in the context of children. Perhaps their persuasiveness there should make one more open to the underlying ideology even after having recognized it as such. (Of course this is actually a common form of argument: children are said to be inherently possessive, and thus it follows that a regime of private property is natural and desirable.) To proceed with this inquiry, one needs to go "behind" the boundary metaphor, to unpack what it stands for. The question then is whether the notion of boundary focuses one's attention on what really matters. But I will defer this exploration until we consider another example of the use of boundary.

If some of the child-development literature seems to share an ideological framework with legal discourse, my next example is a self-conscious and radical rejection of that framework. Starhawk is a feminist author who uses the tradition of witchcraft to explore issues of "magic, sex, and politics," as one of her books is subtitled.[35] She offers an alternative framework for thinking about political action and personal psychological transformation. But even here, at this deliberate remove from conventional thought, I find the invocation of boundaries.[36] The metaphor arises (as before) in an effort to describe "safe space." Starhawk offers ideas for what makes groups sufficiently safe either for planning radical political action, exploring the powers of magic, or personal transformation. Of course the space here is not around individuals, but groups, and it is in large part for the purpose of bonding together in solidarity. But boundary remains an important metaphor:

> Somewhere a line of demarcation must exist, dividing the group from what is not the group. In Witchcraft, one of our magical tools, the *athame*, the knife, is used to make divisions. With it we draw the magic circle, which divides ritual space and time from ordinary space and time. A group, too, needs a circle around it to define it.

The *athame* is a powerful tool: it is double-edged to remind us that any separation cuts both ways. Boundaries contain our power so that it can deepen and intensify, and they may keep out what could threaten or disrupt our group. But boundaries may also exclude those who might benefit us or bring us power. A boundary is always, in essence, somewhat arbitrary and false: an island of separation carved out of the rippling whole.

Nevertheless, we cannot trust unless we feel safe from intrusion. Each member of a group needs to have some control over who comes in. Each group needs some sense of focus and purpose, which necessarily excludes other possibilities. A group needs a shape and an edge, a skin. Like skin, a boundary both separates and interacts with the world, keeping some things out, letting others in. Boundaries can be thick or thin, solid or permeable, fixed or elastic. But a group with no boundaries is not a safe place to be.[37]

Starhawk clearly distinguishes her vision of selfhood from the "set-apartness" she sees as a widespread and dangerous delusion. And she distinguishes the safety in solidarity she advocates from the perverse and doomed effort to defend ourselves "behind the barriers we erect, like the walls of ancient citadels, to guard us from the world."[38] Yet she also draws parallels between her invocation of boundary and the more conventional usages:

> Every member of a household needs areas of physical and emotional privacy that are respected by others. . . . We all also need some physical place that is ours alone to control; if not a room, then a corner, a desk, a special altar spot. We can give a young child a special box, saying, "This is yours, to keep whatever you want in it. I will never open it or look in it unless you tell me I can."[39]

Starhawk is of course right that the concept of boundary conveys a clear image. And it is crucial that we have compelling images for our most important values and concepts. So we must ask again whether the boundary metaphor is helpful when Starhawk uses it, and, if so, why would we exclude its power from the important and difficult problem of mediating the relationship between the individual and the collective?

(It is worth noting that Starhawk herself seems willing to use boundary for this purpose: "In reality, what laws and rules do best is to impose limits on hierarchical power. . . . The Bill of Rights, for example, is an instrument designed not to control the people, but to control the government. It outlines what laws Congress shall *not* make."[40] Starhawk is literally right about the history of the Bill of Rights but not about the general purpose of judicial review or the uses to which the Bill of Rights has been put. "The people" often want to use the government to effect some action they think is important, and the Bill of Rights serves as the limit to what they can do (for example, campaign finance laws overturned in the name of freedom of speech). Starhawk is missing the basic insight behind the Constitution: in a democracy we cannot simply think of the government in opposition to the people. Despite all the distortions of economic power, in some ways the people are the government, and it is the people and their propensity for injustice that the Framers of 1787 wanted to limit. The boundary problems here are as complex as in the personal and group relationships Starhawk understands so well.

One of the general problems with the boundary metaphor, like all metaphors that are so deeply established that they appear natural and obvious, is that it obscures the questions it was intended to answer; it closes down rather than invites inquiry. But in Starhawk's case the necessary unpacking is easy because (in keeping with her philosophy) she is forthright about the objectives and values she has in mind. What then are boundaries supposed to accomplish? We can combine this inquiry with the one I postponed earlier: what is really at issue in the search for "safe space" for a group to work or a child to develop in? The answers are similar. Both require a sense of trust and security; an ability to count on protection; some kind of comprehension of expectations, consequences, practices, or of the rules governing situations; realistic confidence that promises will be kept. It is said that a clear sense of boundaries aids all of these things. But what are these "things"? They are experiences the subjects in question must have to develop well, and they point to the sorts of relationships that generate those experiences. Let us look a little more closely at one issue of boundary language in the context of children to see whether the notion of boundary helps us focus on the experiences and relationships that, in fact, constitute "safe space."

Parents are supposed to provide boundaries so a child knows that if she does something really bad or dangerous her parents will stop her. She can use her energies freely and expansively, knowing that her parents will step in if necessary. And it is very plausible that if the parents fail to provide this sense of boundary, the child will feel unsafe and may set up her own internal, often rigid and unnecessarily confining boundaries to protect her from the risk of doing something "really" bad.

Now I am very sympathetic with this notion of the need for a child to have confidence in her parents' attention, reliability, good judgment, concern, and capacity to act—in short all those attributes and affects necessary for the parents to stop the child from doing anything really dangerous or harmful. I also think it is very important that parents be able to communicate effectively about what sorts of behavior they consider unacceptable and to be clear and consistent about what they treat as falling into that category (what is known as setting *clear* boundaries). But I doubt whether the admonition to set clear boundaries attunes the parents to the experiences the child needs to have or to the quality of the relationship that will bring them about. Surely the injunction will often be heard to be essentially a requirement for rules rather than an invitation to think about what the child (or parent) is experiencing and why.

Of course part of the function of effective metaphors is that they provide a useful shorthand for complicated patterns of relationship. By invoking the metaphor people do not have to think everything through from scratch. There may be some circumstances in which the shorthand of boundary, even if translated as "make clear, consistent rules," is as much as one can hope to get a parent to listen to. Nevertheless, the images the concept of boundary invites do not seem to me optimal, even as a shorthand. They focus the mind on barriers, rules, and separateness, perhaps even oppositional separateness. They do not direct attention to the nature of the relationship between the parent and the child, and that, not rules or their clarity, is the essence of what provides the child with "safe space," the sense of confidence and security to explore and develop.[41]

In addition, boundary imagery teaches both parents and children that security lies in walls. The image of bounded space as essential to autonomy reinforces the image of bounded selves. And, of course, the boundary rules of possession send far less subtle (if no less complex) messages about power, about who is entitled to it (those with property), what its entitlements are (you may ignore the wishes of others), and that its essence is to be wielded by some over others. The child learns that his world is to be "mastered" and that this mastery includes learning to wield or bow to the power of property in appropriate ways. Boundaries structure relationships, but they do not help us to understand or evaluate those structures, and often the structures are undesirable.

Is that true even for Starhawk's uses of boundary? Of course, she avoids the use of the word *property*, but her example of "safe space" is part of her discussion of establishing boundaries, and the sort of control she describes is what some people mean by property and what everybody agrees is a component of property. The concept of space as Starhawk uses it is a way of organizing patterns of respect and expressing the capacity for commitment. When given the special box, the child learns that her parent respects her need to be able to hide things, to control who sees them and when. And she learns about one of the great features of human relationship, the capacity to make and receive promises. The box is a good vehicle for these forms of communication, particularly if promise and respect rather than ownership are the central messages about the box. The box seems to work as a focal point for defining rather than denying relationship. It takes its basic meaning from the promise of the parent to the child, which is quite different from the message "this is yours," meaning the child's will takes priority, or "this is your little sphere in which you may exercise power over others."

In the group dynamic the same basic issues arise, with one exception. Here it is important not simply that everyone knows what the expectations are but also that they know they share in determining them. Part of Starhawk's use of boundaries is to insist that everyone should know where the power lies in the group, who counts as a member (who is "in"), and who determines membership. For her, exploring the issue of boundary brings these questions into focus.[42] This is the opposite of asserting the presence of a boundary whose quality of givenness closes down inquiry (like "That's mine!").[43] But the most important dimension of establishing group boundaries seems to be mutual commitment, the capacity to bind oneself and others in joint action and restrictions on action. Here we find a close parallel with the issue of constitutional limits on democratic decision making. The essential problem is the same: How can the group meaningfully bind itself with respect to its future actions? And, in a sense, the puzzle is the same: How is it that one decision can control future decisions? What sets the initial "boundary-setting" decision apart? How do we know which things belong in which decision-making category? In constitutional politics we can recognize this as the basic problem of self-limiting government.

Although it has been the very essence of American constitutionalism, the invocation of boundary language here does not help, but hinder. At least in the constitutional context, treating rights as boundaries has given them a reified quality that does not direct our attention to the ongoing process of determining those boundaries. We see the rights, the boundaries, as things, not as a particular set of decisions that stands in a special relation to other decisions, thus inviting ongoing inquiry into the nature of that decision making. (I take up these issues in chapter 6.)

Starhawk tries to avoid this reification by acknowledging the artificial, even "false," quality of boundaries and by insisting that boundaries need not have the wall-like quality that we (with our property-oriented vision) ordinarily assume. She insists that boundaries can be "thick or thin, solid or permeable, fixed or elastic."[44] And most importantly, she reminds us that boundaries are not just barriers that separate but also points of connection and contact. The human skin is perhaps the most compelling alternative to the wall image of boundaries: it is permeable, slowly and constantly changing while keeping its basic contours, and a source of sensitive connection to the rest of the world.

V. BOUNDARY LANGUAGE FOR LAW AND RIGHTS

Will such new images of boundary help? Yes, to the extent that they focus the mind on connection and patterns of relationship. But in the traditional legal spheres we are still better off without them. The imagery associated with boundary is too well established, too wall-like, too closely tied to a separative self. People have thought of the problems of the self and the collective in boundary-like terms for so long that they invite no new modes of inquiry; boundaries are barriers to understanding reality.

In constitutional discourse, troubling problems of the meaning of democracy and the process of defining basic values masquerade as boundary issues. This is the converse of what Starhawk observes: "conflicts in groups often develop about boundaries, and generally masquerade as something else."[45] In law the concept of boundary has become more of a mask than a lens.

One of the things the language of boundaries masks is power. We can see that most clearly by returning to our starting point of property. Property is conceived in boundary terms and continues to be seen as an important source of autonomy. In North America, virtually everyone is familiar with the notions that property gives owners control, property allows people to express themselves by shaping the space around them, property provides privacy and security, owning a house gives a sense and impression of stability. And in almost every case it seems as though the physical contours of the property are essential to these desirable experiences. But, of course, property really is a set of legal rules and norms that structure power and relationships. The boundaries the law defines and enforces are a means of wielding power, of shielding power, and of shielding from power. The rules of property tell us who has to ask whom for what and how much power or powerlessness they will have in their request. As Robert L. Hale explained a long time ago, the power to exclude that our legal structure of property gives us is the starting point of all contracting, all negotiation over use of, access to, and exchange of property and labor.[46]

The focus on the naturally bounded, thing-like quality of "property" obscures the fact that the power people derive from it in no way inheres in the object but is allocated to them by the state. The power to exclude exists because it is backed by the power of the state, and all the other dimensions of property and its relation to autonomy and security flow from that power. The boundary metaphor permits us to indulge in focusing on the experiences we can have in, on, and with our property (whose value I do not deny) and ignore the patterns of relationship shaped by the power to exclude. Private property permits us to flaunt power at the same time that we deny its state-created nature.[47] And that denial has of course sustained the distorted quality of the prevailing discussions of the "free market" versus state "interference" via regulation. A discourse of property that always kept at its center the relationships structured by property backed by the power of the state could not sustain the myth of the free market as radically distinct from state power.[48]

Our focus on boundary turns our attention away from relationship and thus away from the true sources and consequences of the patterns of power that property constitutes.

It should now be clear that my objection to the language of invasion and intrusion in the boundary metaphors in Reich, Tribe, and Post (as discussed in section II above) is not that there can never be forms of invasion of person or property that do violence to autonomy. Laws against unreasonable search and seizure,[49] for example, provide security that is important for autonomy as well as privacy. And the respect among family members that create private times and spaces would, if breached, cause a cruel sense of violation and invasion. The routine absence of such relations of respect would be destructive of autonomy. Thus, as is always the case in these matters, it is not that the common language of invasion, intrusion, or boundary is unrelated to or intrinsically inappropriate for the deep issues of autonomy. It is that the centrality of the boundary metaphor misdirects our attention away from relationship and toward the barriers around a bounded self.

Both property and privacy raise similar issues. They entail relationships of respect. Of course, when people treat bounded spheres as indices of personhood, respecting those boundaries constitutes respecting persons. The question here, as always, is whether the focus on boundaries is the best way for people to understand the sorts of relationships they want to foster. Privacy is so closely associated with boundary imagery that I expect a suggestion to abandon boundary will be heard as a rejection of the concept of privacy itself. That is not my intention.

The concept of privacy captures, illusively, important values, such as people's capacity to decide for themselves some of the ways they will or will not enter into relationship with others. Privacy touches on the importance of the capacity for temporary withdrawal from interaction with others, for seclusion. I think people can best foster the range of values underlying privacy by focusing directly on the expressions and patterns of relationship that foster those values rather than on "respecting boundaries."[50] As with "boundaries" for children, the metaphor may be said to be a shorthand for the relational values at issue. But I doubt that it helps people to think about them creatively and constructively. It presumes answers to questions that we should not take as given.

Consider, for example, some of the ways the term "privacy" is used and the puzzles claims of privacy give rise to. Should an adolescent's backpack be protected against being searched by school authorities? This question can be posed in boundary-like terms: the backpack is a private space. But as soon as it comes to the question of the circumstances under which that privacy could be invaded for the purposes of school security, the boundary metaphor only restates the question; it does not guide us to answers. The answers will have to come from an understanding of why that privacy matters, say, to the self-expression, self-development, and autonomy of the youth.[51] One can see the backpack as a little, movable "home" that provides security, comfort, and a place where a youth can keep things he feels an intimate connection with. Will relations of (potentially capricious) power with respect to access to the backpack impede these values? Do even security concerns have to take the form of power structured around notions like probable cause? My use of the word "home" might be said to conjure up the respect associated with property and thus boundary. But my point is to make the link between the values associated with "home" and the kinds of relations necessary to sustain them. The boundary-like quality of "home" is a way of expressing those relations through a tangible symbol. But that symbol is only helpful if it does not obscure the relations that give effect to the underlying values.

The concept of privacy is invoked also with respect to control over images or information about a person. The kinds of information (text, visual, auditory) that we share with others express and define the relations we have with them. People share some things with intimate friends and lovers, others with more casual acquaintances, and others with particular strangers (people with whom they are in a business transaction), and others still with the world at large (phone numbers in a phone book). Control over how information is circulated allows people to ensure that the desired correspondence between information and relation is maintained. When information that is part of an intimate relationship is distributed to the world at large, people experience it as a violation. It could be a personal betrayal of trust. Or it could be that strangers can now claim a kind of relationship of intimacy that is an intrusion because it is a forced, nonconsensual intimacy. Of course, norms about what is shared with whom are in rapid transition due to the growing popularity of Internet social networking sites like Facebook. New kinds of relationships are being formed based around new kinds of information sharing. The nature of threats to privacy via information circulation also has changed. In all of these cases, the metaphor of boundary is far less helpful than direct exploration of the relational dimension of how the circulation of information matters to people.

People also seek "privacy" as a context for sexual and emotional intimacy. They may signal their desire for privacy by creating a physical boundary, a locked door. But, of course, what matters about the privacy cannot be captured just by a locked door. Listening by the door would also be an intrusion on the intimacy. Asking questions could be a disturbing intrusion. If one partner talks to another person about the experience without permission, the nature of the intimate relation changes and the relationship may be harmed. Again, one can recognize the symbolic importance of the locked door to mark a bounded zone of privacy, but it is not the crossing of that physical boundary that captures the disruption of relationship in these examples. The language of boundary can be stretched to describe these transgressions, but it does not help to articulate what is wrong and why it matters. It is more helpful to think of these "violations" as failures to respect the intimacy of the relationship and the ways in which that intimacy is shaped and expressed by keeping the exchange (physical or emotional) between the people wanting to experience that intimacy.

Finally, consider the question of whether it should be legal to covertly install cameras in a home to record what the nanny is doing while the employer is out of the house. There are many issues at stake here, such as what counts as a relation with one's nanny that manifests the minimal legal requirements of basic respect, on the one hand, and anxiety about the well-being of one's children, on the other hand. I do not see either as well captured by boundary language.[52]

As I said earlier, boundaries do structure relationships. But they often structure them badly, in part because boundary imagery masks the existence of relationships and their centrality to concepts like property and privacy. When the dominant metaphors turn our attention away from relationships, we cannot give either the relationships or the legal concepts that mask (and structure) them the critical scrutiny they require.

VI. ALTERNATIVES TO THE BOUNDED SELF

Having pointed to the problems the boundary metaphor raises, I must come finally to the most basic question: can we do without it? Is there not something *essentially* bounded about us that makes us routinely invoke boundary metaphors to describe those things we experience as basic to our selfhood—like property, privacy, and protection against the power of others, individually and collectively? I think not. What is true is that the dominant notion of selfhood is that of the "separative self," and we take that notion so much for granted that our boundedness seems natural and essential.

For example, Lakoff and Johnson make a startling claim in their discussion of the body as a source of imagery and metaphor. Despite their recognition of cultural diversity, of the way in which some metaphors "are so natural and so pervasive in our thought that they are usually taken as self-evident, direct descriptions of mental phenomena," they treat the experience of the body as a "container" to be exactly such a self-evident, direct description of "our" experience of the body. They assert that "we are physical beings, bounded and set off from the rest of the world by the surface of our skins."[53] While this may, indeed, sound self-evident, Catherine Keller offers a very different picture: "Our skin does not separate—it connects us to the world through a wondrous network of sensory awareness. . . . Through my senses I go into the world, and the world comes into me. It is precisely in embodiment that the many are becoming one and the outer becoming inner."[54] Lakoff and Johnson tell us that "we experience the rest of the world as outside of us."[55] But as Susan Griffin reminds us, "For the part of the mind that is dark to us in this culture, that is sleeping in us, that we name 'unconscious,' is the knowledge that we are inseparable from all other beings in the universe. Intimations of this have reached us."[56] Lakoff and Johnson say, "Each of us is a container, with a bounding surface and an in-out orientation."[57] But for Alfred North Whitehead, "Each actual entity is a locus for the universe."[58]

Lakoff and Johnson's bold assertion of "our" experience reminds me of a conversation I once had with a student in class. I asked the class why they thought legal and political theory continued to take the separate individual as its starting point when we had such good information about (at least) the social dimension of language and knowledge. A student answered that he thought it was because when we look inside ourselves it is our singularity that most immediately and powerfully strikes us. I was at the time eight months pregnant. I certainly did not experience myself as essentially singular. When I first wrote the article this chapter draws upon, my first child was two and I still did not think that singularity could capture my sense of my essence (although Michael was only part of the reason for that). I think the intense bond to young children may be one of the sharpest experiences of connection, of nonsingularity. But a deep sense of interconnection that is in tension with a primary experience of bounded singularity can come from many sources.

As Lakoff makes clear in his later work, it is important for Johnson's theory that the experience of the body as container is a kind of primal experience, unmediated by concepts. This bodily experience then forms the basis for the metaphoric structure of such concepts as boundary and in-out.[59] Johnson's basic idea of looking at the connections between our concepts and our experience of the body is surely an excellent one. But there is a great deal in feminist literature that should make us wary of any assertion that our experiences of our bodies are unmediated through culture and language and thus concept and metaphor.[60] "The body as container" seems a perfect example of the metaphoric structuring of our experience of the body, as in Dworkin's reflections on the bounded body. (It seems worth noting as well that many of our boundary metaphors do not, as I noted above, have a very "skin-like" quality to them. On the contrary, it often seems that we conceive the boundaries to our selves to be like walls: nonporous, hard, clear, and defendable against invasion.)

I do not mean to deny that most people in North America experience themselves as individuals with natural and essential boundaries to their physical selves. It seems plausible to me that people in all cultures have some such sense of physical, bounded, distinctness. This is of a piece with my sense that the unique individuality (experienced as embodied) of each person is essential to an optimal conception of self. My point here (and throughout) is that in North America, our language, conceptual framework, metaphors, and institutions serve to emphasize the individual boundedness and are extremely poor at capturing the equally important interconnection. Our bounded bodies could not function as living beings without the constant exchange of oxygen and carbon dioxide, not just through the nose and mouth but also through the very boundary itself: the skin. People could experience themselves as both bounded by their skin and essentially interconnected by it. But the currently powerful boundary metaphors do not facilitate such experience.

Boundary metaphors are certainly ubiquitous (as Lakoff and Johnson suggest) and have a deep coherence with the basic values of our culture. But there are better ways of understanding this phenomenon than positing "the body as container" as an unmediated experience.[61]

Keller, for example, offers a sweeping, brilliant exposition of Western culture and the centrality in it of sexism and the "separative self." The conception of the self that she sets out to question has remarkable resonances with both Johnson's purportedly immediate experience of the body and the model of child development I discussed earlier:

> To be a self, must I be something separate and apart? How else could I be myself: Myth and religion, philosophy and psychology center our civilization on the assumption that an individual is a discrete being: I am cleanly divided from the surrounding world of persons and places; I remain essentially the same self from moment to moment. Common sense identifies separateness with the freedom we cherish in the name of "independence" and "autonomy." The assumption that selfhood requires separation is even rooted in language. The Latin for "self," *se*, meaning "on one's own," yields with *parare* ("to prepare") the verb "to separate." For our culture it is separation which prepares the way for selfhood.[62]

In Keller's view we cannot fully understand the genesis or power of this vision of selfhood unless we see its connection with sexism: "Separation and sexism have functioned together as the most fundamental self-shaping assumptions of our culture."[63] And until we recognize their interdependence, "the old world view will retain the momentum of unconsciousness."[64] I find this complex interdependence particularly resistant to condensation, so I can offer only glimpses of her basic insights. She says, "Fear of merger and self-dispersion motivates all insistence on separate selfhood. But let me suggest that in such fear of self-loss lurks a profound fear of women."[65] She opens her introductory chapter with a revealing quote from C. S. Lewis that suggests a further link to the issues this essay began with, the need to protect the individual from the threat of the collective: "In the hive and the anthill we see fully realized the two things that some of us most dread for our own species—the dominance of the female and the dominance of the collective."[66]

Over the course of several chapters, she draws a connection between the fear of women, the fear of the collective, and the fear of the "oceanic feeling," of "an indissoluble bond, of being one with the external world," which is associated with the mother.[67] In Freudian psychology, she tells us, "this indissoluble bondedness would then belong to the vestiges of earliest childhood, lingering only as an abnormal and regressive infantilism."[68] But it is this very bondedness that Griffin suggests is the fundamental truth of the world, even though it is "dark to us in this culture." And despite the fear and condemnation, "intimations of this [truth] have reached us."[69]

Keller merges mythology and psychology with philosophy—drawing on Whitehead in particular—to provide an alternative image of selfhood, true to these "intimations." She tries both to explain the fierce resistance to such an alternative—"Creative connectivity then appears as chaos and confinement, as an undifferentiated heap, a constrictive—maternally monstrous—mix of matters"[70]—and to take seriously what "differentiation in relation" or integrity without oneness might mean.[71] She draws on Williams James's "streams of self" and Whitehead's immanence to envision a self that is "an event, a process, and no fixed substance, no substantive."[72]

In the course of constructing an alternative, Keller helps us understand the relation between the separative self and the problems of power and domination—and the ways those problems are in turn linked to the boundaries of constitutionalism, property, and privacy. Here her views link well with those of Dorothy Dinnerstein and Jessica Benjamin: the separative self is on an endless and doomed search for security, a security that seems possible only through power and domination.[73] Thus, the sought-after walls of protection (like property) are those that entail domination. Keller focuses on control, a classic virtue associated with property:

> The separative ego as we have characterized it—as self-objectifying and other-exclusive—cannot separate its strategies of self-perpetuation from its drive to control. In its emphasis upon self-control, being "on top of things," it is simultaneously keeping the influent others under control as well. Domination is its best defense, and retreat its familiar back-up plan. And these defensive strategies inadvertently confirm the truth of internal relations: that the world gets inside us, gets under our skin, does not keep a respectful distance.
>
> Control is the age-old alternative to connection. The denial of internal relations issues in external manipulation.[74]

These links between the separative self, control, and domination offer a new perspective on the distortions of inequality that the focus on property brought to American constitutionalism. The way the Framers' sense of the need to control the threat of the people distorted the democratic institutions they designed no longer looks like an anomaly born of a particular historical preoccupation with property. Rather, property appears as a logical preoccupation for separative selves, providing the sought-after illusion of security through power, domination, and isolation. And property can crystallize the fears of loss of control, of intrusion, and of the threat of impending chaos if things are not under control. An emerging democracy stirs up (not entirely unwarranted) fears of the collective (and, in 1787, repeated references to the need for a strong, *manly* republic untainted by feminine vices).[75]

Property focuses these fears in ways that are paradigmatic of the efforts of separative selves to protect themselves through boundaries: the protection of those boundaries is inevitably tied to fear and domination and to the inequalities of power necessary for security through domination. The protections the Framers sought from property (and for property) were inseparable from domination. But from this perspective, the inequality and fear of the people that shaped American constitutionalism is not anomalous, but characteristic of the protection of boundaries sought by separative selves.

American constitutionalism has the power it does in part because its metaphoric structure resonates so powerfully with the fears and (elusive because illusory) goals of the separative self. And the fact that one can find the boundary metaphor and its distortions not only in the discourse of law, but everywhere, reflects both the metaphoric coherence of the dominant North American culture and the centrality of the separative self to the culture and the coherence.

Keller's exploration of the power and pervasiveness of the separative self helps us understand our culture, including constitutionalism (which she does not address). But her purpose is not acceptance or accommodation, but transformation. If we accept Keller's accounts of the depth of the separative self in mythology, philosophy, and psychology (as well as law), we know we need more than a good theory to change things. In this case I am not thinking of political action (which is of course required), but of new symbols, myths, and metaphors to replace the old.

In contemplating this daunting task, I was tremendously encouraged by Estella Lauter's *Women as Mythmakers: Poetry and Visual Art by Twentieth-Century Women*.[76] Lauter persuades me that she sees in art the makings of a new mythology. She recognizes, of course, that the potential for myth that she sees in the work of these individual women will only become genuine myth if it continues to resonate and be echoed again and again. But she thinks the germs are there, the flashes of individual genius that can capture an emerging spirit and give it focus and power. Those of us inclined to foster an alternative to the deeply entrenched "separative self" will need such images not only to sustain and inspire us, but also to make a credible case that alternatives are actually possible. We will need a new vocabulary, new metaphors to invoke if we are not to be sucked back into the forms we are resisting even as we argue against them.

Recall the claim that started my inquiry here: we need new ways of conceiving of the relation between the individual and the collective for which boundary is not an apt metaphor. Let me give you a sample of what Lauter offers:

> Over and over again this "chordal" analysis of common images and themes leads us back to a view of relationships with the world in which the customary boundaries are not preserved. Inside is barely distinguished from outside, and the distinction matters only momentarily. What matters is the How of energy from one realm to another, so that life is sustained.... The images (or bundles including images, stories, themes, ideas) that are repeated in the separate lines of myth I treat here *include* antinomies rather than mediating them.[77]

Boundary mediates. Our new conception will focus on the complexities of the interpenetration of individual and collective. Boundaries and mediation imply a separation and opposition that does not capture the complex, fertile, and tension-laden interconnection between self and others that a transformed constitutionalism must respond to. Lauter helps us see that the necessary forms of reconception are possible by providing examples of boundary-dissolving metaphors.[78] And, equally important, she tries to meet the fears that Keller has warned us will be stirred up by any effort to transcend the boundaries crucial to the separative self. Writing on Griffin's poem "Matter," Lauter finds it to be

> a ritual gesture, an incantation, above all an image of an idea of self that is incandescent or evanescent. "I have no boundary," the speaker says, and with these words she undoes centuries of mythology.... The "center," the self that is defined by its categorical differences from others, does not hold, as Yeats predicted it would not. But "things" do not fall apart, nor does the human being relinquish consciousness. We merely participate in reality differently—as one among equals.[79]

We can approach the vast task of reimagining the rhetoric of law and freedom with this inspired reassurance in mind.

VII. CONCLUSION

There is something profoundly and I think irreducibly mysterious about the combination of individuality and "enmeshedness," integrity and integration that constitutes the human being. Western culture has constructed a multitude of myths and metaphors to capture the extraordinary capacity for human action, for initiation, for the creation of something genuinely new out of all the multiplicity that has shaped and constituted the actor up to that moment of action. The notions "human will," "agency," "autonomy," and "freedom" each insist that not even the fullest account of that multiplicity can ever account for or determine the moment of action. And the structures of philosophy and law built around these notions insist further that this extraordinary capacity is to be cherished and protected.[80] American mythology (the pioneer, the yeoman farmer, the rugged individual, the self-made man) and the institutions and rhetoric of American constitutional law (which also have a kind of mythic status) have done an impressive job of capturing a particular vision of this dimension of humanness. But the very separateness thought essential to this dimension distorts our understanding by splitting it off from, and setting it up in opposition to, the integration, interpenetration, and unity that are also part of our humanness and without which the capacity for creative action would not exist.

We have seen this oppositional splitting off take the form of the fear of the collective. In the American context the fear was originally focused around the protection of property, the symbol for separative freedom, power, and control, ever vulnerable to invasion by the many. The Constitution was designed to ward off that threat, and although the protection of minority rights has sometimes taken more benign forms, it usually carries a tone of contempt and fear of the many. One can be concerned, for example, about the tone many liberals in the northern United States use in speaking about southern "bigots," even if one has nothing but revulsion for the inherent violence of racism. People need to become attuned to the distortion of the values they care most deeply about. For example, it is important to see how a separative vision of freedom of speech can blind people to the ways in which the speech of some silences the voices of others by virtue of the patterns of power and dominance entailed in the protected speech.[81] An exclusive focus on containing the threat of the collective cannot capture the genuine values of "freedom of speech." The nature of the collective itself and the relationships it sustains will determine the kind of freedom of speech its members enjoy.[82]

The boundaries so central to American law are the boundaries that feel desperately necessary to the separative self to keep the threatening others at bay—the impossibility of that task only fueling the desperation. When I say the task is impossible, I do not mean to imply that the boundaries do nothing. They do protect people from certain kinds of threats. But equally (or more) important, boundary-setting rights protect people from the seemingly overwhelming responsibility that would flow from a recognition of unity. This is, I think, a frightening form of the "oceanic feeling," intimations of which have reached us. I think (most) people in North America fear being "invaded," "taken over," not just by threats but also by demands—the overpowering demands of those in pain and hunger all around us. We wall ourselves off from the cries—genuinely do not hear them most of the time, even though we "know" they are there—by telling ourselves that we are "within our rights," that rights define our obligations as well as our entitlements, and that as long as we have violated no one's rights, we are doing nothing wrong in our daily nonresponsiveness. The separative self, clinging to the rights that affirm its separateness, can deny the interconnection that would implicate it in the surrounding pain.

That particular form of freedom would, I think, be radically transformed if we were to come to see ourselves as "inseparable from all other beings in the universe." The fear of such a transformation is old, deep, and not completely unfounded. I think we see it lurking under the Framers' assertions of the illegitimacy of redistributing property as well as in modern attacks on the welfare state—which have been given fresh vigor in the American health care debate.[83] Throughout American history, anxieties about redistributive legislation have been accompanied by cries of "where will it all end?" If such a redistribution (in the form of paper money or a progressive income tax or workers' compensation or socialized medicine) is permitted, what boundaries can we count on? Won't the demands of the collective become insatiable, finally devouring us and the orderly society that keeps chaos and the collective at bay? Lauter acknowledges some grounds for these fears: "The female envisioned (or hoped-for) is one of vastly increased responsibility."[84] And that responsibility will not be fully compatible with the scope of privileged freedom that rights have carved out for some—including most of the readers of these words.[85]

As we develop the new myths and metaphors that truly combine rather than mediate antinomies, we will have to find new ways of comprehending and responding to our responsibilities.[86] And of course we cannot do so by accepting law as the realm of boundaries, leaving the rest (in good Kantian fashion) to individual morality or compassion. That division makes sense only for the separative self. We will need new ways of deciding which responsibilities are best handled collectively and whether and how the state should take up such responsibility. And we will need new ways of capturing the mystery of human creativity, the undetermined capacity for human action.

The puzzle of a nonsubmerged selfhood amid connective responsibility cannot be solved by walls of rights. We need to take our traditional concepts, like property, and ask what patterns of relationship among people and the material world we want, what patterns seem true to both integrity and integration. Those questions do not necessarily preclude a concept of property, but they imply a focus not on limits, but on forms of interaction and responsibility for their consequences.

Here I would offer a closing qualifier for those deeply wedded to boundary language. My claim is not that boundary could never be a helpful metaphor for the self or for legal practices designed to protect and promote core values. My claim is that in current North American (and probably Western) culture, boundary distorts understanding and reinforces weaknesses in the culture's capacity to recognize and reflect on the importance of relationship. Given this historical context, I urge at least an experiment: pick a problem or a value to which boundary seems especially important and try to articulate it without invoking boundary (or easy synonyms like "limit"). See if the exercise does not yield a richer understanding of what is at stake. My students have found this useful with respect to violence against women, the problem I turn to in chapter 5.

In rejecting the categories of the past, we should never underestimate the task. The American Constitution is only a particularly vivid modern form of an age-old effort to use the concept of boundary to mediate, to "grasp," to "bring under control" the illusive mysteries of human freedom and connection. Without the boundary metaphor, the structure of legal conceptions of freedom disintegrates. But some of that disintegration is already under way. At least in the academic legal community there is no consensus on the basic meaning of law or of the values it is supposed to protect. New metaphors are a genuine option because they are in fact emerging. We are in a period of flux when our presuppositions are in doubt. It is therefore possible to exercise some deliberate choice about the frame of reference through which we see the world. We can try to transform our own language, push it in the direction of the barely articulated "intimations" that have reached us. Disintegration entails promise. If we can let go of our walls of rights, the reintegration is likely to be far fuller and more promising.

3

Reconceiving Autonomy

A. Introduction and Overview

Feminists are developing a new conception of autonomy.[1] The still prevailing conception stands at the core of liberal theory and carries with it the individualism characteristic of Anglo-American liberalism.[2] This traditional conception cannot meet the aspirations of feminist theory.[3] The basic value of autonomy is, however, central to feminism. Feminist theory must retain the value while rejecting the traditional incarnation.

My central argument here is that autonomy is not to be equated with independence. Autonomy is made possible by constructive relationships—including intimate, cultural, institutional, national, global, and ecological forms of relationship—all of which interact.

Such a relational conception of autonomy is particularly apt for the bureaucratic state, with its welfare and regulatory regimes. The central problem in the modern administrative state is no longer the traditional liberal objective of protecting individual autonomy by keeping the state at bay. The problem is how to protect and enhance the autonomy of those who are *within* the (many) spheres of state power, from welfare to public education to securities regulation. The objective is not to achieve a mythic independence, but to structure relations so that they foster autonomy.

In this chapter, feminist theory provides the impetus for the reconceptualization of autonomy, and administrative law points to the institutional reforms that can make relational autonomy a reality in the modern state.

Feminism is not, of course, alone in its rejection of liberal individualism. The individualistic premises of liberal theory (and their inadequacies) continue to be an important subject of debate in contemporary political and legal theory.[4] Feminism offers us a particularly promising avenue for advancing this debate not because it provides a fully articulated alternative to liberal theory, but because feminist concerns so effectively capture the problems such an alternative must address.

Feminism (including my own) sometimes appears equivocal in its stance toward liberalism because it simultaneously demands a respect for women's individual selfhood and rejects the language and assumptions of individual rights that have been Anglo-American culture's primary means of expressing and enforcing respect for selfhood. This apparent equivocation is not the result of superficiality or ambivalent indecision. On the contrary, it reflects the difficulties inherent in building a theory (and practice) that adequately reflects both the social and the individual nature of human beings. Feminist perspectives and demands can guide the inquiry: they point to dangers, define aspirations, and indicate the contours of an approach that transcends the limitations of traditional liberal theory while fostering its underlying values. This chapter is part of that process: an inquiry into the meaning of autonomy guided by both feminist objectives and the challenges of the administrative state.

A relational conception of autonomy turns our attention to the kinds of relations that undermine or enhance autonomy, and the forces that structure those relations—from institutional design to gendered division of labor to beliefs about entitlement. Examining institutional practices (and the law that shapes them) can, in turn, shed light on what fosters autonomy and thus on both the practical and theoretical contours of this value. Autonomy, in this approach, is not a static presumption about human nature, but a capacity whose realization is ever shifting. Thus property, traditionally both symbol and requirement for autonomy as independence, is replaced with an attention to the inherently fluid and contingent dynamics of process and relationship. The focus I propose emphasizes the fluid over the fixed, temporal over spatial metaphors. The puzzle of finding a symbol as powerful as property remains.

The chapter proceeds as follows: I begin (section I) with the need for a new conception of autonomy and the ways in which feminism is particularly well suited to working through the inherent difficulties of a relational approach to autonomy. I show how this relational approach is, in turn, especially useful in understanding the distinctive problems of autonomy in the bureaucratic state. I then turn (section II) to the insights available from the treatment of property and autonomy in the American political tradition. Among other things, that tradition points to the relation between people's beliefs about autonomy and their subjective experience of it. Section III examines the ways in which subjective experience is an essential but sometimes misleading dimension of autonomy. Attending to this dimension alerts us to some of the difficulties in effecting a deep transformation of a central cultural value. Section IV turns to the insights available from modern administrative law—the chief legal mechanism for mediating between governmental agencies and those subject to their decisions. Here I look at the potential and limits of due process as a means of fostering autonomy. I also return to the limits of conceptions of rights and autonomy premised on the idea of maintaining a boundary between state and individual. This section closes with a discussion of recent developments in Canadian administrative law, which focuses on participation by the subjects of administrative decision making. The following section V outlines the complex relationship between participation, democracy, and autonomy.

The penultimate section VII returns to the earlier example of welfare (section VI) to look at the factors that make it difficult to restructure dependency relations so that they foster autonomy. I conclude that both power disparities and entrenched beliefs about subordinate status can pose serious obstacles. In the case of welfare, I argue that a universal entitlement system is the best way of restructuring relations between the state and those in need of social assistance. More generally, I argue that it is the very inevitability of some power disparities that make it essential to structure them so that they can foster rather than undermine autonomy.

To concede all spheres of human relations characterized by either dependence or power imbalance to be incompatible with autonomy would be to accept that huge numbers of people are to be deprived of one of the core values of North American societies. Transforming that value into a relational conception of autonomy directs our attention to the crucial task of rethinking our core concepts and restructuring the institutions that implement them.

B. Liberal Theory, Feminist Tensions, and the Relational Approach to Autonomy
i. Self-Determination and Social Construction

The notion of autonomy goes to the heart of liberalism and of the ambivalent relation many feminists have with liberalism. The now familiar critique by feminists and communitarians is that traditional liberalism took atomistic individuals as the basic units of political and legal theory and thus failed to recognize the inherently social nature of human beings.[5] Part of the critique is directed at the liberal vision of human beings as self-made and self-making men (my choice of noun is, of course, deliberate). The critics rightly insist that, of course, people are not simply self-made. We come into being in a social context that is literally constitutive of us. Some of the most essential characteristics of human beings, such as the use of language and the conceptual framework through which we see the world, are not made by, but given to, us (or developed in us) through our interactions with others. Until the social, relational dimension of humanness becomes central rather than peripheral to legal and political theory, efforts to modify traditional liberalism will fail to provide an adequate framework for envisioning optimal institutions or optimal concepts for understanding human potential and the barriers to realizing it.

The image of humans as self-determining creatures nevertheless remains one of the most powerful dimensions of liberal thought.[6] For most people raised in liberal societies, the deep attachment to freedom takes its meaning and value from the presupposition of humans' self-creating nature. That is freedom's deepest purpose: the institutions of freedom are for enabling that capacity (as well as for protection against violence). No one among the feminists or communitarians is prepared to abandon freedom as a value, nor, therefore, can any of us abandon the notion of a human capacity for creation in the shaping of one's life and self. (The reverse is also true: commitment to this creation entails a commitment to freedom.)

Indeed, feminists are centrally concerned with freeing women to shape their own lives, to define who they (each) are, rather than accepting the definition given by others (men and male-dominated society, in particular). Feminists therefore need a language of freedom and autonomy with which to express the value underlying this concern. But that language must also be true to the equally important feminist precept that any good theorizing will start with people in their social contexts. And the notion of social context must take seriously its constitutive quality; social context cannot mean merely that individuals will, of course, encounter one another.

This difference is nicely captured by a comment I once heard from an (otherwise thoughtful) liberal theorist. He was dismissing, with exasperation, the critique that liberal theory fails to take seriously the social nature of human beings. "Of course it recognizes their social nature," he said. "Liberal theory is all about the proper rules governing the interaction among people, so of course it recognizes their social nature." This observation misses the point. Drawing boundaries around the sphere of individual rights to protect those individuals from the intrusions of others (individuals or the state) takes for granted the existence and interaction of independent (potentially threatening) others. Such an assumption, however, has little in common with the claim that every person is in significant part constituted by her interactions with others. The fact of social encounters entails no more than a plurality of individuals whose nature need owe nothing to relations with others. Since these separate individuals can harm or benefit one another, their encounters need to be mediated and controlled by rules (many enforced via law by the state). But that is quite different from saying that their "selves," their identities, their capacities are not comprehensible in isolation from their relationships. On a relational view, the persons whose rights and well-being are at stake are constituted by their relationships such that it is only in the context of those relationships that one can understand how to foster their capacities, define and protect their rights, or promote their well-being. This is a very different starting point from simple plurality of independent beings whose inherent rights and obligations mediate their encounters with each other.

The problem, of course, is how to combine the claim of the constitutiveness of social relations with genuine scope for the value of autonomy.[7] If autonomy is defined as innate freedom or self-determination, independent of all social context, then it has no true social component and is not consistent with a relational conception of the self. Yet if, in the effort to insist on the centrality of social relations, "constitutive" comes to be defined in ways that amount to the self being *determined* by its relationships, then genuine autonomy becomes impossible. This problem is common to all social theorists who take the constitutiveness of social relations seriously but is particularly acute for feminists. This is true both because of feminists' troubled relation with traditional liberalism and because defining women in terms of their relationships is part of what feminists have tried to overcome.

Traditional liberalism has played an important role in defining the relevant questions (and the appropriate forms of answers) in ways that are inhospitable to feminist concerns. For centuries, a particular conception of the rational agent defined away issues of familial relations, of dependency, of the body, of affect that were central to many women's experience and to the possibility of their full equality and autonomy. Yet in North America, liberalism has been the source of the standard language of freedom and self-determination. The values feminists cherish come embedded in a theory that has little scope for the core of so much feminist knowledge: the centrality of relationships in constituting the self.

That knowledge has its own ironies: women know this centrality through experience, but the experience has often been an oppressive one. One of the oldest feminist arguments is that women are not seen and defined as themselves, but in their relations to others. The argument is posed at the philosophical level of Simone de Beauvoir's classic claim that men constitute women as "Other"[8] (a perverse form of "relationship") and in the mundane, but no less important, form of objections to being defined as someone's wife or mother.

We need a language of self-creation that avoids the blind literalness of the liberal concept of self-determination.[9] We can engage in creative interaction with the relations that shape us, but we cannot simply determine who we are. We need concepts that incorporate women's experience of embeddedness in relations, both the importance of this embeddedness and the oppressiveness of its current social forms.[10]

Indeed, it is because feminists recognize that social relations provide both the potential for oppression and the nurture necessary for autonomy that feminism is a particularly hopeful source for a new conception of autonomy. In rejecting the individualism of traditional liberalism, feminists are particularly unlikely to romanticize "community" or relationships as such.[11] Social relations that undermine rather than foster women's autonomy are all too common a reality throughout the world. And while that reality makes the traditional liberal concepts of autonomy and rights look to some like the best available solution, for many feminists only an approach that makes central the relational nature of the self can be true to their aspirations and their understanding of the kinds of solutions that are likely to make a deep difference.

The purpose of focusing on the centrality of relationships is not to valorize relationships as such, nor to assume that existing relationships deserve preservation. On the contrary, it is exactly to distinguish between those structures of relationship that foster autonomy and those that undermine it. It is only when such attention to relationship replaces the mere stipulation of autonomy as a human characteristic that the concept of autonomy can guide the transformation of destructive relationships into those that foster autonomy for all. It is because I think this is a real possibility that I think it is worth trying to reconceptualize the term autonomy.

ii. Finding One's Own Law

It is worth noting that there are theorists who share my general theoretical approach and objectives but reject the term autonomy as a vehicle for achieving these objectives. For some, the word "autonomy" is so closely tied to the liberal tradition that it is treated as symbolizing the very individualism from which I am trying to reclaim it.[12] The phrase "autonomous individuals" is sometimes used with derision, to express the absurdity of conceiving of individuals in isolation from one another. But even among critics of traditional liberalism, one also hears the word used with approbation, usually in the context of the problem of achieving true autonomy (as opposed to mere stipulation or an individualistic conception of independence). Despite my respect for those who bravely reject the term and invent alternatives,[13] my strategy is to advocate a reconceptualization of the term. In part, I do so because the underlying value is so crucial to feminism (and other egalitarian projects of transformation) that I think the term must be reclaimed. In addition, I think the word itself carries with it the complexity of the issue. The literal meaning of the word is to be "governed by one's own law."[14] To become autonomous is to come to be able to find and live in accordance with one's own law.

I speak of "becoming" autonomous because I think it is not a quality one can simply posit about human beings. People must develop and sustain the capacity for finding their own law, and the task is to understand what structures of power, patterns of relationship, and personal practices foster that capacity. I use the word "find" to suggest that we do not make or even exactly choose our own law. The idea of "finding" one's law[15] is true to the belief that even what is truly one's own law takes particular forms that are shaped by the society in which one lives and the relationships that are a part of one's life. "Finding" also permits an openness to the idea that one's own law is revealed by spiritual sources, that our capacity to find a law within us comes from our spiritual nature.[16] From both perspectives, the law is one's own in the deepest sense, but not made by the individual; the individual develops it but in connection with others; it is not simply chosen, as if from an unlimited market place of options, but recognized, developed and affirmed. "One's own law" connotes values, limits, order, even commands just as the more conventional use of the term "law" does. But these values and demands come from within each person rather than being imposed from without.

The idea that there are commands that one recognizes as one's own, requirements that constrain one's life but come from the meaning or purpose of that life, captures the basic connection between law and freedom[17]—which is perhaps the essence of the concept of autonomy. The necessary social dimension of the vision I am sketching has two components. The first is the claim that the capacity to find one's own law can develop only in the context of relations that nurture this capacity. The second is that the "content" of one's own law is comprehensible only with reference to shared social norms, values, and concepts. Our conception of the content is, for example, mediated through language, itself a social phenomenon.[18] To be autonomous is to find one's own law and live in accordance with it. This is a lifelong process, the individual dimensions of which are embedded in a social context.

This concept thus has inherent tensions between the idea of autonomy as both originating with oneself and being conditioned and shaped by one's social context. Those tensions are the tensions of feminism, as of all theories that take seriously both individual freedom and social embeddedness. The word "autonomy" is thus a suitable vehicle for achieving feminist objectives. It is capable of carrying the full dimensions of feminist values and perspectives. And sticking with the word, working toward a reconception, has the further virtue of rescuing not only a term but also a basic value, from the confines of traditional liberalism.

iii. Understanding and Overcoming Pathology

There are many ways of trying to articulate a new value or, as in the case of autonomy, to help that value emerge from the process of transforming an old one. Here I want to focus on a particular dimension of the current conception of autonomy that stands in the way of the necessary transformation: the dichotomy between autonomy and the collective.

This dichotomy is part of Anglo-American liberalism, but it is, once again, particularly starkly revealed in the tradition of law and political thought in the United States. One of the clearest forms it takes is the idea that individual autonomy is to be achieved by erecting a wall of rights between the individual and those around him. Property (as we saw in the previous chapter) is, not surprisingly, the central symbol for this vision of autonomy, for it can both literally and figuratively provide the necessary walls. The logic of this is that the most perfectly autonomous man is thus the most perfectly isolated.[19] The perverse quality of this implicit ideal is, I trust, obvious. This vision of the autonomous individual as one securely isolated from his threatening fellows seems to me to be a pathology that has profoundly affected Western societies for several centuries.[20]

If we ask ourselves what actually enables people to be autonomous, the answer is not isolation, but relationships—with parents, teachers, friends, loved ones—that provide the support and guidance necessary for the development and experience of autonomy. I think, therefore, that the most promising model, symbol, or metaphor for autonomy is not property, but child rearing. There we have encapsulated the emergence of autonomy through relationship with others. We see that relatedness, even dependency, is not, as the Anglo-American theoretical tradition teaches, the antithesis of autonomy, but a literal precondition of autonomy and that interdependence is a constant component of autonomy. This model of what actually sustains autonomy is, appropriately, the opposite of the isolated, distancing symbol of property. We may, in fact, learn as much about the nature of autonomy by thinking about child rearing than by the sort of inquiry into law and bureaucracy that I undertake here. But there are advantages to avoiding the problems of extrapolating from intimate relationships to large-scale ones. And some of the relationships that either foster or undermine autonomy are not of an intimate variety but, rather, are part of the more formal structures of authority (which include employment relations as well as the officially "public" sphere I deal with here).[21]

C. *Bureaucracy, Collectivity, and Autonomy*

The American administrative state threatens individual autonomy because it threatens to transform people[22] into objects of bureaucratic decision making—dependent, passive, helpless before the power of the collective. This threat is not peculiar to American forms of bureaucracy.[23] Whenever a democratic society assumes collective responsibility for individual welfare, it faces the task of implementing this responsibility in ways that foster rather than undermine individuals' sense of their own competence, control, and integrity. The traditional Anglo-American conception of autonomy impedes this task and thus limits the understanding of the problem and the potential for its solution. The tradition of American political thought sets individual autonomy in opposition to collective power.[24] This opposition continues to distort perceptions.

The characteristic problem of autonomy in the modern state is not, as the Anglo-American tradition suggests, to shield individuals from the collective, to set up legal barriers around the individual which the state cannot cross; the problem is to ensure the autonomy of individuals when they are within the legitimate sphere of collective power. The task is to render autonomy compatible with the interdependence that collective power (properly used) expresses.

The problem of interdependence, individual autonomy, and collective power takes its characteristic modern form in the relations between administrative bodies and those subject to their decisions.[25] For many people, their most direct encounter with state power is as recipients of state services (such as public education, health care, pensions, and employment insurance) and subjects of regulation (licenses, health and safety regulation, zoning, securities regulations). The nature of people's interactions with bureaucratic decision making may be as important as the nature of legislative policy making[26] in determining whether people are autonomous members of a democratic society or dependent objects of collective control. (The same issue arises in interactions with decision making within corporations, but I will not be addressing that context here.)

The traditional focus on protecting the individual from the collective does not provide optimal tools for dealing with the distinctive challenges of the administrative state. It has provided a distorted image of the problem of autonomy and of alternative visions of society. The prevailing conception of autonomy sets alternatives in the context of a false choice: when autonomy is identified with individual independence and security from collective power, the choice is posed between admitting collective control and preserving autonomy in any given realm of life. It is as though the degree of collective responsibility for, say, people's material needs must result in a corresponding decrease in the autonomy of those receiving the benefits. Such a dichotomy between autonomy and collective power forecloses a whole range of social arrangements—at least to anyone who values autonomy.

A classic example of a choice premised on this dichotomy is the claim that a free press is possible only if newspapers are privately owned. This claim rests on a notion of what the law can and cannot do that is unfounded. It assumes, first, that the law can protect property against collective power and that this protection will provide the necessary insulation and foundation for freedom of expression. At the same time, the claim assumes that the law cannot provide comparable *direct* protection of this freedom by legal limits on the power of the state to control expression. The implicit conclusion is that if there were public rather than private ownership of the press, those wishing to express their views would require the (virtually uncontrollable) "permission" of the state. The state would directly control expression.

This conclusion is based on a plausible assessment of the ways in which property, as opposed to other legal rights, has been protected and respected. But the conclusion goes far beyond a historical comparison. It evades the constraints posed by economic power to a private profit-making press. It denies the possibility of structuring relations between people and a public press, their corresponding rights and powers, in a way compatible with freedom of expression. But we need no more assume that the relationship would take the form of "asking permission" to use the press than we assume the necessity of asking permission to use public schools, parks, or water. There is nothing in the nature of the legal protections themselves (as I shall return to later) nor in our experience of public resources, including public broadcasting corporations, to justify the stark dichotomy between freedom founded on private property and tyranny produced by collective control.[27]

State control of resources always poses problems, but modern legal systems, including the American, have found ways of distinguishing control from caprice, of rendering dependence upon state services (imperfectly) compatible with freedom and autonomy. Were the dichotomy between state power and autonomy exhaustive and inevitable, we would be forced either to give up on autonomy in large spheres of our lives or to advocate a vast limitation on state power—which would be incompatible both with modern economic and political realities and with aspirations for a more responsible and equitable society. This choice is not necessary.

Despair about individual freedom in the face of collective power reflects a poverty of imagination about the possibilities for protection and control.

Belief in the false choice between autonomy and collective power is the product of a powerful tradition of political thought. Paradoxically, the tradition (mis)shapes the perception of the problem while pointing in the direction of solutions. The American legal tradition, for example, suggests possibilities of protection and control. To see both the problem and the possibilities more clearly, we need first to examine the tradition.

II. AUTONOMY AND PROPERTY IN THE AMERICAN TRADITION
A. Boundaries and Dichotomies

The American political tradition has virtually identified freedom and autonomy with the private sphere and posed them in opposition to the public sphere of state power.[28] (Here, again, the American tradition provides a particularly stark version of characteristics shared in the broader Anglo-American tradition of legal and political thought.) The idea of a boundary between these spheres, a line dividing individual autonomy from the legitimate scope of state power, has been central to the American conceptions of freedom and limited government. As we have seen, the notion of a boundary took shape in the early development of the American Constitution, and it was property that was the focal point for this idea. While parts of this story are well known, they bear a retelling (and reformulation) here as the framework for the prevailing conception of autonomy.

The revolutionary slogan "no taxation without representation" posed consent as the basis for legitimacy. It asserted not that private property could never be taken by the state, but that such taking was legitimate only if consented to by the governed. This idea also took the form of claims that a government that could take property without consent was tyrannous and reduced men to slaves.[29] These claims reflected the sense that the major threat to freedom and autonomy was the inability to have some say in the decisions that affected important aspects of one's life. But this emphasis on consent shifted with the grim realization that consent alone was no guarantee against injustice or tyranny.[30]

In the 1780s, duly elected state legislatures passed a variety of debtor relief laws, which were widely viewed as violations of property rights and as evidence of the intrinsic vulnerability of property rights (and, more generally, minority rights) under popular government. The concern turned to making popular government compatible with the security of individual rights and to asserting as a matter of political principle that consent was not a sufficient basis for legitimacy. "Rules of justice"[31] and the concept of basic rights formed independent standards against which to measure the legitimacy of democratic outcomes. The need to inculcate these independent standards, and the particular preoccupation with protecting property against tyranny by the majority, led to a differentiation between civil and political rights and a clear hierarchical relation between them. Political rights were merely means to the true end of government: the security of civil rights. (The term civil rights should not be confused with current usages, which often include political rights, as in the American civil rights movement. The eighteenth-century Americans, such as James Madison, who articulated the hierarchy of civil over political rights meant rights that today might be called private rights, such as property and personal security.[32]) The security of civil rights, as well as the principle of consent, required some form of representative government. But for the Federalists[33]—whose views triumphed in the writing of the Constitution and in the dominant tradition of American political thought—the focus of concern was not on designing means for men to have an active share in their own governance but, rather, on designing means to achieve republican government while containing, controlling, and minimizing the threat of popular political power. There is virtually nothing in Federalist thought that treats political participation as an important component of individual autonomy, as a dimension of self-determination with intrinsic (as opposed to instrumental) value.[34]

The Federalists drew on a tradition (Locke, for example) which emphasized rights as the object of legitimate government and hence the limit to it. But in the context of the American fear of *popular* tyranny, the conception of rights as limiting values hardened into opposed categories of state versus individual and public versus private. Individual autonomy was conceived of as protected by a bounded sphere—defined primarily by property—into which the state could not enter. The sphere of rights, freedom, and autonomy was private. And the means of assuring those rights, that autonomy, was to keep the public realm distant, separate, at bay. The people (in a highly mediated, carefully structured system of government) would control the public realm: collective decisions would be made according to democratic principles. But every effort was made to minimize the chances of those decisions encroaching on the private sphere. The idea of a boundary to the legitimate scope of the public realm then crystallized in judicial review. Courts would determine when the government exceeded its legitimate power. And, as in the earlier conception of divided spheres, property was the central issue around which the idea of judicially enforceable boundaries developed.[35]

There was, finally, another dimension to the parallel divisions between state and individual, public and private: the opposition between politics and market. This dichotomy was part of the conceptual framework which placed freedom and autonomy on the side of the "individual," "private," and "market" and placed coercion on the side of the "state," "public," and "politics." The coercive power of the collective was manifested in legislation. The rights of individuals (private rights), by contrast, were given order, protection and scope through the common law, which permitted market transactions—ostensibly without the coercive intervention of the state, without the purposive, collective decision making of the legislature.[36] Free, private, individual (trans)actions stood in defensive opposition to coercive control by collective (public, legislative) power.[37]

We now have a picture of a legal and political ideology which identified autonomy with a private sphere defined and bounded by property. This was the conceptual framework that prevailed (despite major deviations from it in practice) until 1937[38] and that continues to haunt and shape both theory and practice in the United States.

Three things need to be said about this picture of law, state, and autonomy. The first (which in its full dimensions is beyond the scope of this chapter) is that the dichotomous categories of liberal theory have always been illusory. Second (and only apparently in contrast), these categories and constellations of beliefs, and their related concepts of the rule of law and the sanctity of property, could not have had such power and endurance if they were based only on illusion. If I am right that their meaning was not what it purported to be, then our task is to discover the insights which lay behind them. Third, whatever the insights of the tradition, its basic components of property and boundary are no longer adequate to the contemporary problems of autonomy (as I will outline in section C). I shall begin with the illusions, turn to the particular inadequacy of property, and then note the insights this misleading tradition nevertheless provides.

B. Illusions

The dichotomies of state–individual, public–private, politics–market, legislation–common law were always illusory. The central part of the illusion was the association of freedom with the second term of each dichotomy and coercion with the first. It is not simply that things have changed so much that the categories no longer make sense. Rather, from the beginning the dichotomies served to mask the role of state power in the market, the common law, the ostensibly private realm.[39]

To take a central example, property rights are defined by the legal system.[40] The security they provide rests on the power of the state to punish those who trespass on those rights—and on the widespread acceptance of property rights as legitimate. The power and independence that individuals derive from property rests on the rules the legal system has set up to define what constitutes legitimate and enforceable transactions, what goods can be demanded on the basis of what sorts of claims. Property takes its power and importance in large part from "the market"—which is itself defined by the legal system. "The market" in modern states is not a freestanding, natural phenomenon[41] but, rather, consists of rules defined by law and backed by the power of the state.[42]

Only a radical difference between common law and legislation (such as Friedrich Hayek eloquently, but in the end unpersuasively, defends[43]) can maintain the claim to the essential privateness and freedom of property and the market. Hayek argues that the common law is neutral, nonpurposive, and the articulation of spontaneously arising custom. It is "the law of freedom" because it merely provides the framework for the exercise of freedom. Legislation, by contrast, is aimed at the achievement of some collective purpose and must by its nature be coercive.[44] But the actual workings of the common law have not been Hayekian.[45] They have not had the essential lack of purposiveness he claims. The common law has been informed and shaped by particular conceptions of fairness, freedom, and progress. The "neutral" rules of the game correspond to a particular vision of the good society, one that gives advantages to some players over others in systematic, if not perfectly predictable, ways. (This is so even in the absence of class bias or blindness on the part of judges. Such bias or blindness, in particular the inability to see things from the perspectives of others from different (usually less advantaged) backgrounds from themselves, adds another dimension to systemic disadvantage generated by the law.)[46] And today much of the common law has been codified so that the sharp distinction between common law and legislation is still more difficult to maintain—though it is also true that the judicial interpretation of codified dimensions of, say, contract, still follow common law norms.

I have embarked on this argument about property, the market, and the common law to show that the long-prevailing conception of autonomy was embedded in a set of categories and oppositions that were in basic ways illusory. And to the extent that the contrasts are illusory, the choices they point to are false.

Property is the creature of the state. To replace property as the symbol and source of autonomy may redefine the relations between people and the state. But the choice to do so is not a choice between private and free, on the one hand, and collective and coercive, on the other hand. Private property has at times enabled coercion and domination; collective power—in forms such as collective bargaining legislation, antidiscrimination legislation, and public education and health care throughout the Western world—has often enhanced freedom. Because reality has never corresponded to these neat oppositional categories, there is no need to choose between them. Freeing ourselves from misleading categories and false choices opens the possibility for individual autonomy in the context of collectivity.

C. Contemporary Inadequacies

While the dichotomies of liberal theory have always been illusory, there is a particular inadequacy to the role played by property today. In the United States, private property was for 150 years the central and defining instance of the boundary between governmental authority and individual autonomy. Property can, however, no longer serve this function because it has lost its original political significance.

Property no longer provides people with the basis for independence and autonomy in the eighteenth-century sense. For the farmer who tilled his[47] own land or the craftsman who owned his tools, property was a real source of independence. However much they depended on good weather or customers, their property gave them a control over their livelihood, and hence their independence, which was significantly different from that of modern wage earners, salaried professionals, or stockholders. The dependence of wage earners on their employers is obvious. But even stockholders, who own their shares, have little control over the source of their income. Their income, like that of most professionals, embeds them in a network of relationships characterized by interdependence rather than independence. And the kinds of relations that characterized small-scale production for local markets are very different from large-scale production for distant markets so that even those who farm their own land or own factories are now generally embedded in complex relations of interdependence with employees, banks, and a multilayered system of product distribution and marketing. Thus, the percentage of Americans for whom property provides the traditional independence of the yeoman farmer is now so small that the idea of property as the basis for autonomy has lost most of its original meaning.[48] In addition, property itself is now subject to regulation to such an extent that it cannot serve symbolically or substantively as the boundary between individual rights and governmental power.[49]

More importantly, the very idea of an inviolable sphere can no longer be the central issue of autonomy in the modern state.[50] As more and more issues are seen to involve collective as well as individual responsibility, there will be fewer and fewer spheres of activity in which the state is not involved. As the reality of interdependence shapes the scope of collective action and control, people will increasingly be subject to governmental authority to license, regulate, and distribute benefits and burdens. The model for autonomy must be constructive relationship, not isolation. The task is to make the interdependence of people and state conducive to, rather than destructive of, autonomy.

We have some reason to be optimistic about finding the means of doing so. The old dichotomies prove to be misleading. There are examples of states, such as Canada, taking responsibility for providing decent health care for all, not just the wealthy who can afford it.[51] And this example shows not only significant success of state power promoting equality with respect to a basic good, but also a system that, overall, affords greater autonomy to both patients and doctors than the current organization of most of the privately run systems of the United States.[52] This is one of the clearest examples that autonomy need not be a casualty of state power. And, as the final section of this chapter will suggest, contemporary administrative law offers glimpses of how to structure state power so that it produces relationships that enhance rather than undermine autonomy. But in reconceiving autonomy, in reconstituting its sources and protections, we should also try to uncover the insights that have sustained the traditional framework for so long.

D. Lessons for Reconceiving Autonomy: The Individual–Collective Dichotomy and the Lessons from Property

There are, of course, explanations other than wisdom for the endurance of ideology. Those in power usually have considerable resources for fostering beliefs that sustain the status quo. But it seems likely that when particular conceptions have endured for centuries in both the popular imagination and theoretical writings, they can provide insights into the problems they address. It is not possible here to unpack everything embedded in the tradition I have outlined. But we can examine some of the directions the tradition points to, some of the problems it alerts us to, in the effort to reconceive autonomy.

The first is that while the stark opposition between autonomy and collectivity presumed in the American tradition is misleading, that opposition points to something important. There is a real and enduring tension between the individual and the collective, and any good political system will recognize it. The problem with the Anglo-American tradition is that this tension so predominates that there is only a limited view of the nonoppositional aspects of the relation and of the social dimension of human beings.

There is thus a twofold objective in reconceiving autonomy: (1) to recognize that the irreducible tension between the individual and the collective makes choices or trade-offs necessary and (2), at the same time, to move beyond a conception of human beings which sees them exclusively as separate individuals and focuses on the threat of the community.

The collective is not simply a potential threat to individuals; it is constitutive of them and, thus, a source of their autonomy as well as a danger to it.[53] For some purposes it makes sense to talk about the separate constructs of "the individual" and "the community." Those constructs are, however, misleading[54] if they obscure the fact that people do not exist in isolation, but in social and political relations. People develop their values, predispositions, interests, and autonomy—indeed, their identity—in large part out of these relations. As I noted earlier, the very way one experiences and perceives the world, for example, is shaped by the social constructions of language.

The task, then, is to think of autonomy in terms of the forms of human interactions in which it will develop and flourish.[55] And the starting point of this inquiry must be an attention both to the individuality of human beings and to their essentially social nature. Both are necessary for the reciprocal process of asking what kinds of social relations foster autonomy and developing a better understanding of the nature of autonomy.

Ultimately, the objective is to find the optimal relation between individual and collective and, more particularly, to understand the core of human autonomy and the forms and scope of collective activity that will foster it. We can take from the tradition a recognition that the new forms of autonomy within collectivity will involve choices, even trade-offs. But knowing the limitations of our current conceptions should lend us confidence that to choose new forms of autonomy is to reconstitute, not abandon, it.

The tradition also provides a way of understanding the kinds of institutions that promote and protect autonomy. An understanding of the powerful associations between property, security, and autonomy is likely to provide a clearer sense of the nature of autonomy and the requirements for it. This is so despite the fact that the preoccupation with private property never actually led to autonomy for all and despite the project of arriving at a new understanding of autonomy. I should add here that I am not opposed to a material basis for autonomy; I am opposed to a system that generates vast inequality.

The rhetorical, even mythical power of the identification of property with freedom goes beyond the literal power and advantages of property under liberal capitalism. And the experience of the rights of property as qualitatively different from, and more secure than, other legal rights cannot be accounted for by the legal history of property rights. Property rights have in fact been subject to a great deal of state interference and to redefinition that amounted to destruction.[56] As I argued earlier, there is nothing intrinsic about legal rights of property which make them a more promising basis for freedom than other legal rights. Property rights, like all legal rights, take their formal meaning from definitions and guarantees provided by the state. The security that property provides rests, on an institutional level, on the state's power to protect what it defines as property.

And the forms and means of defining and protecting property are, at root, indistinguishable from those of other legal rights.

What then accounts for the enduring associations between property and autonomy? Two striking and distinguishing characteristics of property are its concreteness and the relative unobtrusiveness of the state power which lies behind it.[57] The concreteness of property makes it an effective symbol. It is easy for people to see the relationship between owning property and autonomy, and it seems (deceptively) easy to know what property is and when it is violated. And most people do not think of their ownership of property as in any way involving the state; it is simply theirs. It is not granted to them by the state or administered by the state. Most property rights can be exercised most of the time without the obvious intervention of the state. The fact that property rights only have meaning when backed by the power of the state[58] seems an abstraction that students have a hard time grasping, many sophisticated theorists ignore entirely, and the general population has no idea about. The role of the state is unobtrusive to the point of being invisible to many.[59]

If concreteness and state unobtrusiveness are the characteristics that make the association of property with freedom so compelling, we should be alerted to the probable limitations of any alternative source, symbol, or protector of autonomy that lacks them. Due process, for example—which I will be discussing shortly—is, by comparison with property, abstract rather than concrete and clearly requires official action.

III. THE SUBJECTIVE DIMENSION OF AUTONOMY

Reflections on the tradition lead to another dimension of autonomy that we need to understand to give effect to an optimal conception of autonomy: the complex relation between autonomy and the feeling or subjective experience of being autonomous. People may feel a strong connection between, say, home ownership and autonomy (in ways that need to be attended to in order to understand what promotes autonomy) and yet be attached to an illusion about the separateness of property from the state and thus about their own independence.[60] The tradition points to complex connections between *beliefs* about autonomy and independence and *feelings* of independence interpreted as autonomy. And both are connected with institutional structures.

To transform a deeply held conception of autonomy, it is important to understand the subjective dimension of it. If people are to accept a relational conception of autonomy, those currently in privileged positions will have to give up illusions of independence and of autonomy as flowing from that independence. To know how to transform institutions so that they actually foster autonomy, it will be helpful to know how the people subject to those institutions experience them. It is important to know what fosters the experience of autonomy. Neither conceptual nor institutional transformation will take hold unless there is a corresponding transformation in the subjective experience of autonomy.

Such a transformation challenges the existing structure of privilege. A reconception of autonomy that rejects the link with independence threatens the hierarchy of who is autonomous. While there is a connection between power, powerlessness and autonomy (which I will consider in the last section), degrees of autonomy do not simply map onto the distribution of economic power and privilege. A relational approach to autonomy points to the ubiquitous structures of dependence and interdependence that characterize everyone's lives. It thus denies most conventional claims to independence. It denies that autonomy is fundamentally about independence, and so it challenges the claim to autonomy by those who base it on their (usually illusory) independence. The result is that it challenges people's beliefs about themselves as autonomous, a highly valued component of relative power and privilege. (As we will see, I do not think that beliefs about being autonomous are the same as the experience of autonomy, but I treat both as part of the subjective component.)

The points above suggest the tensions between the different subjective dimensions of autonomy. I would break it down as follows: (1) some subjective experience of autonomy is necessary in order to be autonomous; (2) people's subjective experience with institutions is an important guide to what fosters or undermines autonomy; (3) people's subjective sense is not alone a reliable guide because they can have an illusion of autonomy; and (4) belief in one's autonomy is a highly valued component of power and privilege. One can assume challenges to it will be resisted. All of these points matter to understanding the nature of autonomy, the institutions that can foster it, and what it will take to bring about change.

A. Feelings of Autonomy and Self-Consciousness

To say that the feeling of autonomy is a component of being autonomous is not to say that there is anything self-evident about the feeling.[61] Indeed, just as we need to develop a new conception of autonomy, probably most of us need to learn what real autonomy feels like. For many, their actual experiences of autonomy—those rare moments when they feel they are following an inner direction rather than merely responding to the pushes and pulls of their environment—are so fleeting that it is often difficult to know or remember what it is like to live by one's own law. (It is a useful exercise to think about when it is that one has felt most autonomous and why.) North American society offers misleading images of autonomy (such as economic power and consumption choice) and thus misleading notions of the kinds of experiences and states that should be interpreted as autonomous. We not only learn, as I noted above, notions of autonomy that link autonomy to the power to keep others at bay; we are also taught that money is power and power is freedom—freedom from others and power over them, not the power to discern and to follow one's own law.

Another common idea links autonomy to a kind of control or capacity to effectively manipulate ones environment. On this view, autonomous people are those who are confident that their actions will generate predicted and desired results as opposed to those who feel powerless to control their lives, who feel buffeted about by forces beyond their control.[62] The feelings of powerlessness and helplessness are not conducive to autonomy, but it does not follow that those who feel in control in this way are autonomous. Many people learn to "play the game" effectively, to do what is wanted of them, and to confidently predict and reap the rewards handed out for compliance. This counts as success and generates the feeling of control, confidence, and efficacy. It is not autonomy. Playing someone else's game well is not the same as defining the path of one's own life.

Despite these complexities, it is difficult to imagine someone being autonomous without some subjective experience of it. To be autonomous, a person must have some sense of her power to shape and direct her own life. While one may fail to correctly assess the scope of one's freedom, I think one cannot be autonomous and not know it. It is often the case that people actually have more freedom and more options available to them than they think. For example, people often feel constrained by expectations they have internalized so that they cannot see the full range of options actually available to them. These expectations can be familial, for example, the sorts of employment that are considered suitable; or cultural, for instance, the importance of marriage and child rearing for a woman. In these examples, people will feel much less free than one might say that they "are" in the sense that there is a much wider range of options available to them than they can see. "All" they need to do is recognize that the source of constraint is largely internal.[63]

I think it is fairly common to have at least some small experience of realizing that what one felt one had to do was not really the constraint that one had made it out to be. One discovers that one has more freedom than one thought. But I don't think one can say something comparable about autonomy because the internal, subjective dimension of autonomy is central. One does not realize that one is more autonomous than one thought, though one may become more autonomous by recognizing the way one's actions have been governed by values that are not really one's own.

I think this is the case in part because I see self-consciousness as an element of autonomy. For example, I don't think it makes sense to say that one unconsciously lives in accordance with one's own law, at least over the long run. One might unconsciously resist external demands and expectations in ways that are in accord with one's own values, but that is still at quite a remove from full autonomy. Self-consciousness is an aid to autonomy as well as a component of it. Self-consciousness assists in recognizing when one is allowing one's life to be driven by fear, or anxiety, or values that are not really one's own. Self-consciousness is important because, as with fear or anxiety, one can experience constraints that are self-imposed rather than externally imposed, which nevertheless interfere with one's autonomy. (Of course, these self-imposed constraints have their origin in relations with others. The self I am discussing is the relational self, not the atomistic individual.)

I am not suggesting that one must achieve perfect self-consciousness in order to be autonomous. I think there is a continuum of self-consciousness, as there is a continuum of autonomy—and they may not be the same. In addition, people do not simply arrive at a fixed level of autonomy; one's autonomy varies across time and spheres of one's life. Autonomous action can be erratic, episodic—perhaps particularly when there is not a high degree of self-consciousness. Thus such intermittent autonomy will be more common than deep levels of self-consciousness. (And, as I say in chapter 1, the sort of self-reflection necessary for autonomy need not take the form of intellectual, reasoned deliberation.)

B. Sources of Subjective Experience of Autonomy

There are probably other subjective states, such as self-esteem and determination, that also are linked to the capacity to exercise one's autonomy.[64] I do not intend to explore them here, though a full picture of autonomy would need to do so. What matters to my argument here is that there are subjective components of autonomy and conditions for its exercise and that institutional arrangements affect these components and conditions. Thus while there are personal practices that may develop self-consciousness (such as meditation and psychotherapy), it is not just a matter of individual responsibility or a concern of psychology. Those designing or evaluating institutions that claim to foster autonomy, such as social assistance bureaucracies, need to find out how those who have to deal with them experience their interactions.

If there are consistent stories of feeling humiliated and helpless, something is seriously wrong. It is unlikely in the extreme that such institutions are fostering the autonomy of those dependent on them.[65] The importance of the subjective dimension to autonomy is just one of the reasons that the subjects of bureaucratic decision making should be part of the policy-making process.

Autonomy involves a complex interplay between (individual and collective) beliefs about autonomy, subjective experiences, structures of relationship, and the institutions that shape and interact with all of these. I will return, for example, to the destructive influence of conceptions of autonomy that see the collective (usually the state) as primarily a threat to autonomy. My point here is that it is important to study how institutions generate subjective experiences that are conducive to or undermine autonomy. It is often easier to find examples of bureaucratic structures that generate feelings of powerlessness, inadequacy, and humiliation—which undermine autonomy. In section VII, I will briefly discuss some of the features of welfare systems that recipients report to have these effects. I will note a study of different ways of implementing a system of parental involvement in the assessment of the special educational needs of their children. I compare the effect on the parents' autonomy, including some of the subjective dimensions, such as feeling competent, effective, and able to participate meaningfully in decisions that affect their lives.

Attending to the subjective dimensions of autonomy also helps to avoid an unduly simplistic way of looking at relational autonomy. The key point is that constructive relationships make it possible for autonomy to develop and thrive, and thus it is important to understand how institutions and ideas affect the relevant relationships. But that does not mean that people who live within oppressive relationships of domination, and even abuse, are devoid of autonomy. People's lives are composed of complex layers of relationship, and it is rare that all of them are destructive. Literature abounds with stories of people's capacity for autonomy in the face of overwhelming odds—often with the help of some important relationship. As we will see in chapter 4, some of the problems surrounding women who kill their abusive partners arise out the difficulties in recognizing them as autonomous actors. Part of the contemporary challenge of analyzing how oppressive relationships work is to accurately describe the destructive consequences of, say, unequal gender relations or systemic racism without characterizing the disadvantaged groups as victims devoid of agency or autonomy. In fact, I think it is very difficult to completely destroy autonomy. People are resilient, relationships are multiple and complex, and people are able to call upon inner resources developed in other contexts when they are faced with terrible external constraints and dangers. Ultimately, the purpose of a relational approach is to understand all the different dimensions of human relationships—including their interaction with ideas, institutions and personal practices—that foster autonomy. It is not to yield simplistic conclusions that people in destructive relationships—whether intimate, institutional, or cultural—must be without autonomy.

C. The Challenge of Evaluation and Transformation

Finally, recognizing the subjective element of autonomy is important because the very fact that autonomy is in part a feeling may make people particularly resistant to changes in its form. The institutions, social practices, and relations that foster the feeling of autonomy may vary considerably across cultures and over time within a culture.[66] Different conceptions of autonomy, different beliefs about what it is, may affect what is experienced as autonomy. Bruno Bettelheim, for example, suggests that the ancient nomads, as they watched society shifting to agriculture, may have responded with anxiety and contempt as they saw their fellows give up "for greater economic ease and security, a relative freedom to roam."[67] In this instance, Bettelheim is willing to make a tacit judgment that the new settled life was not, in fact, a diminished one. But he does suggest that actual accommodations had to be made. Because, as I argued above, trade-offs are probably inevitable, hostility to new approaches to autonomy may be based on real perceptions of loss. Perhaps it is even likely that the new approach will draw the contempt Bettelheim mentions. Perhaps all alternatives to what has been perceived as the essence of freedom are likely to be denigrated. The protections of minimum wage and maximum hours were decried as dangerous infringements not only on freedom of contract, but also on freedom more generally. Claims that economic equality is a precondition of autonomy are sometimes dismissed by libertarians as mere envy or greed. It seems likely to me that some will see relational autonomy as abandoning real autonomy for "greater economic ease and security."

It is in this context that I want to return to my earlier claim that while one cannot be autonomous without some feeling of autonomy, one can feel autonomous and not be so. One of the powerful markers of privilege in North American culture is a sense of being independent and autonomous. Autonomy is one of the highest values of the culture and the dominant conception of it links it closely with independence. Those in relative positions of power learn to see themselves as autonomous, which means learning to be blind to their multiple forms of dependence and interdependence. This can take the form of the "self-made man" blind to the infrastructure of society and the market that have made his economic ventures possible. Another form is the ordinary worker who decries those who live off the largess of others, dependent on welfare handouts, unconscious of his own dependence on publicly funded schools, highways, employment insurance, health and safety regulations. Or the corporate executive who attributes his success to his intelligence, hard work and ambition, blind to the facilitating role of class, race, and gender privilege as well as a system of laws that constructs not only his power but the very existence of the corporation as well. All of them may ignore the ways their lives are made possible by the unpaid labor and attention of their wives.

To say that these positions of relative power and privilege do not constitute independence, but are the result of uncompensated reliance on the work of others (in the case of female partners) or a structure of dependence (some of which distributes benefits on unjust grounds of gender, class and racializing practices), is to challenge not just the legitimacy of their status, which they experience as superior to others. It is to challenge a core dimension of their sense of themselves, as autonomous. Of course, this is because their conception of autonomy is one of independence. Without that link, the insistence on the fact that they, like everyone else, are part of a web of interdependent relationships, would not feel like a challenge to their autonomy and thus an attack on their self-worth. In fact, the people in the relations of unacknowledged dependence that I pointed to in my examples might or might not be autonomous. What my analysis challenges is the confidence that because one is independent one is autonomous. People who falsely believe they are independent, and falsely believe that their independence means that they are autonomous, are likely to feel autonomous without being so.

Attention to the subjective dimension of autonomy thus reveals that adopting the sort of relational approach to autonomy that I am advocating here involves a deep transformation. A full acceptance of one's dependence and interdependence on the part of people who have always thought of themselves as independent involves a deep change in their sense of themselves. Like all deep transformations (such as gender equality or the end of racialization), it entails not "just" a redistribution of resources and advantages—as the call to restructure institutions in ways that foster autonomy for all does—but a change in how people see themselves—their values, their successes, what they take pride in. I think the combination of the challenge to the distribution of privilege and the challenge to people's sense of self (such as their pride in being independent) is likely to elicit considerable resistance. It is important to pay attention to the multiple ways in which transformations may be threatening.[68]

Acknowledging the complexities of understanding, comparing, and evaluating feelings of autonomy, it is still useful to look to actual practices that seem to have fostered this feeling, or at least have been associated with the concept. Past practices, however deficient, may provide important clues to new sources of autonomy and to the problems they are likely to entail. And present practices offer concrete examples of the efforts to reconcile autonomy with collective control. Let us turn therefore to what modern legal practices have to offer us.

IV. THE INSIGHTS OF ADMINISTRATIVE LAW

I begin again with American law. I look at the way, in 1970, the U.S. Supreme Court case *Goldberg v. Kelly*[69] offered important insights about how, even in contexts of extreme dependence (welfare), the law can provide for forms of participation that work to enhance rather than undermine autonomy. Then, in section B, I look at practical limitations to such requirements for participation: examples of the ease with which they can be circumvented and what it takes for legal requirements to actually enhance autonomy. In section C, I turn to conceptual failures of the American approach and then, in section D, to hopeful signs in the development of Canadian administrative law.

A. The Potential of Procedure

My objective in this section is to look at the development of the law governing the procedures of administrative agencies as indicative of the kinds of values and practices needed to make autonomy more viable in a bureaucratic state.[70] I shall start with an early contribution of American law and then identify some of its problems—problems that reflect the errors this tradition invites and the difficulty of avoiding them.

Administrative law mediates between governmental agencies and those subject to their decisions. It defines the rights and obligations of both parties, and it has shown impressive—if flawed—attention to the problem of making dependence upon bureaucratic decision making compatible with autonomy. One of the important contributions of administrative law has been to articulate the ways in which the subjects of this decision making should be allowed to be active participants in the process. In the United States this move toward requiring participation took place through constitutional challenges and is sometimes characterized as the "due process explosion" (followed by retrenchment) signaled by *Goldberg*,[71] in which the Court adopted the idea that welfare payments were the kind of benefit—a form of "new property"[72]—that could not be taken away without due process. Specifically, the Court held that a welfare recipient was entitled to a hearing *before* benefits were terminated.

The Court stressed the fact that welfare recipients were dependent on government for their basic necessities and that this made the provision of a pretermination hearing particularly important. This case seems to be an instance of an effort to provide some degree of effective participation to those in the most dependent relation to the government. The opportunity to be heard by those deciding one's fate, to participate in the decision at least to the point of telling one's side of the story, presumably means not only that the administrators will have a better basis for determining what the law provides in a given case, but also that the recipients will experience their relations to the agency in a different way. The right to a hearing declares their views to be significant, their contribution to be relevant. In principle, a hearing designates recipients as part of the process of collective decision making rather than as passive, external objects of judgment. Inclusion in the process offers the potential for providing subjects of bureaucratic power with some voice in the decisions as well as a sense of dignity, competence, and power. A hearing could of course be a sham or be perceived to be so even if it was not. But the possibility of failure or perversion of the process leaves its potential contribution to autonomy unchanged.

This case, in particular the (shifting) trend it started, is of interest because it suggests something important about the possibility of achieving autonomy within a context of dependence. Dependence is a reality, and will be a reality in any society based on collective responsibility for the material well-being of some or all of its members. The problem is to avoid making autonomy a casualty of such collective responsibility. *Goldberg* suggested that there are forms of participation in administrative decisions which may prevent their subjects from becoming passive objects. The relationship can be shaped by the nature of the decision making and the subject's role in it. The nature of the relation to the agency to which he or she is subject need not be wholly dictated by the substance of the agency's power, for example, to grant or withhold basic necessities. This enormous power and corresponding dependency will affect, but need not destroy, the person's autonomy.

Many of the contributions of contemporary administrative law are of this order: provisions for participation in one form or another. In fact, the particular line of cases that *Goldberg* led to turned out (perhaps predictably) not to expand on this insight, but to restrict it. (I return to this retrenchment briefly in section C.) But, my purpose here is not to analyze the line of cases through which the rights to hearings have been elaborated and restricted but, rather, to suggest that the cases reveal something important about the possibility of autonomy in the modern state and the requirements for it.

The components of autonomy to which these legal developments seem responsive are dignity, competence, and comprehension as well as defense against arbitrariness. However mixed the cases, they provide some hope that there are ways of structuring bureaucratic decision making so that the relations between individuals and the state foster rather than undermine these values.

It is worth noting that, in welfare cases, the harms to dignity and to autonomy often overlap (as in the case of intrusive surveillance), and, as we just saw above, the shift in structures of relations that can enhance autonomy also enhance dignity. I think this is in part because being treated in a degrading and demeaning way undermines one's ability to act autonomously—to be able to see situations clearly, make good judgments, and feel competent to act. Nevertheless, I see dignity and autonomy as separate values. The kinds of relations that express dignity include respect and recognition of one's inherent value as an equal. Such relations also foster autonomy. But, to use my earlier phrase, the ability to find and follow one's own law is something distinct. Dignity is not necessarily about perception, competence, judgment and capacity to act. Not all the relations that express dignity will foster these abilities. Administrative law can and should also ensure that those subject to bureaucratic decision making are treated with dignity.[73] But my focus here is on autonomy.

B. The Limits of Due Process

Of course, legal rules alone will not determine whether bureaucratic encounters actually promote autonomy. Joel Handler offers an account of the failures of a federal law (*Education for All Handicapped Children Act*, P.L. 94–142), which seemed designed to ensure optimal conditions for interaction between parents of disabled (or differently abled) children and the officials who would determine the children's placement.[74] The law had all the ingredients one might want: its required ongoing participation by the parents in the decision making, flexibility, individual tailoring of programs, hearings, and full rights of appeal. But stipulating these requirements did not make them a reality. In particular, it did not mean that parents actually took an active part, that they were listened to, or that they felt as though they were actors in the decision making rather than (indirect) objects of it.[75] The schools had strong incentives of time and money not to have the parents actively involved, and they had been successful in complying with the formal requirements of the law while, at the same time, undermining its purposes.

Handler's message was not, however, that bureaucratic encounters cannot be structured so that clients could be genuinely autonomous actors; it was merely that formal law alone cannot achieve this end. Indeed, he provided a detailed example[76] of the schools in Madison, Wisconsin, which seemed to have achieved genuine participation, and to have done so with similar (only this time actually realized) means: participation, information, and flexibility as well as formal rights of appeal. Among the many factors that accounted for the difference, the most important seems to have been that the relevant personnel in the Madison schools actually wanted parental participation; they thought it was necessary for the special education programs to work effectively. Given this goal, they were able to design the process of decision making to encourage participation and to make it meaningful. For example, parents participated in the earliest stages of assessing the child's needs and planning a program rather than being called in merely to consent to a diagnosis and plan already formulated (as was generally the case in the other systems). The teachers saw the parents' information and judgment about the child as valuable and thus treated them as actual partners in the decision making. By contrast, in other systems studied, parents who raised questions were treated as "trouble makers."[77] Handler thought it was particularly important that in Madison, conflict between the parents and the schools was not deflected, suppressed, or avoided, but treated as part of a constructive process through which a better decision could be reached.

The Madison schools also recognized that even with their positive attitude toward the parents and their acceptance of conflict, there was a power imbalance of resources and information that had to be addressed if the parents were to be able to take part effectively. "Parent advocates" were made available to try to redress the imbalance. In Massachusetts, by contrast, in the meetings at which the parents were presented with plans (made in their absence), the parents "were outnumbered, they were strangers confronting a group of people who had struck a bargain between them, and the discussion was often in technical jargon with the subtle implication that the child or the parent or both were at fault."[78] In Madison, information in clear, ordinary language was provided. The decision-making process was ongoing and open-ended, with room for readjustment. In most other school districts what was supposed to be an ongoing process of consultation was usually collapsed into one or two meetings.

In short, "the conclusion of virtually all the research is that whereas P.L. 94–142 seems to have resulted in more parental *contact* with the school authorities, there has not been much change in parental *involvement* in the actual decision-making process."[79] Throughout the Madison approach, there is a recognition that the parents are in a continuing relationship with the school. The objective is not simply to arrive at a decision to which the parents will not object, but to sustain a relationship such that the necessary ongoing decisions can be collectively made in the best interests of the child (which in turn are recognized to involve relations with the parents and with the school and relations between the school and the parents).

The parents' own testimony is the most compelling evidence that the system in Madison was "working," that the parents were not subordinated objects of bureaucratic decision making, but partners in a relationship that fostered their dignity, efficacy, comprehension, and competence and that protected them from arbitrary power. The parents were dependent on the schools, but their relationship was nevertheless characterized by autonomy. The dependence was not removed; it was transformed. The autonomy was thus, of course, not based on independence, on the capacity to make decisions without being subject to anyone else's preferences, judgments, or choices (the sort of autonomy Reich associates with property[80]). It was autonomy within relationship. And for some parents, the autonomy fostered in the relationship with the school seems to have made them feel more generally competent and secure in their ability to understand and help make decisions about their children.[81]

There are also cautionary dimensions to the Madison story. First, Handler notes that Madison has a long history of popular participation that may have made possible both the inception and the success of this experiment. But while that means that one should not be overly sanguine about simply transporting the model elsewhere, it also suggests that patterns of social and political interaction can foster autonomous relationships. It further invites us to inquire into the details of the institutional and social practices that have fostered this participatory culture.

A little more troubling is the suggestion that participation actually dropped off once parents developed a high level of trust in the school. A successful relationship seemed to make parents feel that they need not work to sustain it. This is, of course, easily understandable. With all the competing pressures on one's time, why not delegate time-consuming decision making to those one trusts? (And of course genuine participation is very time consuming. Handler suggests that is one of the reasons most school districts comply with the legal requirements for parental participation in a perfunctory way.) In Madison, it was the school officials who complained about the parents' lack of participation.

Of course it is an old problem that genuine power sharing and democracy are time consuming. One would need to know more about the Madison story to say whether the parents' stepping back from active involvement necessarily undermined the autonomy fostered by the original relationship. It may be that the Madison parents were exercising their autonomy to make a reasonable choice of delegation—a choice that has nothing in common with forced acquiescence in the presumed superior authority of school officials. Perhaps it is enough if the parents continue to feel able to understand and evaluate what is happening with their child and able to become involved whenever it seems necessary to them. Their sense of a *capacity* to participate may be what is crucial rather than participation itself. Unfortunately, it may also be that while the parents' autonomy remains intact, the child's education suffers when participation drops off.

There are other problems (e.g., the question of whether the "parent advocates" are actually used and what their role should be) and quibbles (Handler's language of negotiation and bargaining does not capture my image of an optimal relationship, and even the parental statements he likes best have hints that the primary decision makers are the school professionals).[82] But overall, Handler's argument shows both that legal requirements of participation can foster autonomy and that legal requirements alone are insufficient. [83]

C. *Conceptual Failures of Liberal Rights*

These developments in the law governing administrative agencies grew out of the best in the American liberal tradition: its emphasis on the protection of individuals from the power of the state. But this same tradition has also been the source of problems with the judicial response to conflicts between individuals and the bureaucracies upon which they are dependent. It is hardly surprising that a tradition that has conceived of the relationship between the individual and the collective primarily in terms of the threat of the latter does not provide an adequate basis for defining individual rights in the context of affirmative responsibilities of the state. The dichotomy between individual rights and state power has meant that the courts have particular trouble in cases which require them both to accept the state's intrusion into previously private spheres and to develop a useful framework of individual rights that will enhance autonomy in the context of dependence.

Another U.S. Supreme Court case, *Wyman v. James*,[84] dramatically illustrates the justices' inability to analyze rights in the context of dependence. The Court held that a social worker did not need a warrant for a "home visit" to a woman receiving Aid for Families with Dependent Children. Justice Blackmun's underlying argument for the majority was essentially this: in accepting the state's offer of responsibility for the welfare of her child, Mrs. James had declared her home life to be the state's business. She could not then turn around and stand on the traditional rights of individuals against state intrusion. In dissent, Justice Douglas made an impassioned argument against the state's capacity to "buy up" rights when it distributes largesse and convincingly argued that if Mrs. James were a businessman objecting to administrative searches, she would win.[85] But Douglas showed virtually no acknowledgement of the ways in which traditional rights may have to be reconceived as the state takes on responsibilities that transform its relations to the individual. Neither approach seems to recognize that the task is to think creatively about the protections of autonomy given the realities of overlapping spheres of public and private interest. Neither a denial of rights nor a denial of realities can solve the problem.

Even when courts do try to protect individual rights in the face of collective power, they tend to use a private-rights model to define and justify the rights in question. Thus *Goldberg* used the concept of "new property" to explain why welfare recipients are entitled to pretermination hearings. The choice of property is understandable but particularly unfortunate.

As subsequent developments[86] have shown, characterizing dependents' rights as property invites a focus on entitlement that misses the point and facilitates retrenchment. Property also carries with it a powerful tradition of inequality that should not be incorporated into new conceptions of autonomy.[87] But the problem with the concept of new property is more general. It is a mistake to tie protections for peoples' autonomy to particular substantive rights. The objective is to protect the autonomy of all in their interactions with government. The appropriate forms of those interactions may vary depending on the kind of interest involved. But the entitlement to autonomy, and to bureaucratic encounters conducive to autonomy, should not depend upon or be deduced from the particular interest at stake. What is at issue here is autonomy and democratic membership in society, which are not relevant only to particular rights.[88]

And for reasons suggested in my discussion of *Wyman*, the use of a private-rights model may only lead to the abandonment of any judicial protection. Jerry Mashaw's similar argument about private law and public law models suggests that the evident inappropriateness of private law models for such state undertakings as welfare may lead courts to cede complete authority to legislatures to define the terms on which benefits are granted or withdrawn.[89]

D. *The Limits and Potential of Due Process as a Path to Participation*

While the line of American cases following *Goldberg* failed to develop the potential for structuring people's relations with bureaucracy in ways that enhance their autonomy, the Canadian development of administrative law helps us see further into both the potential and limitations of due process—or procedural fairness—as a path to such restructuring. In the important case *Singh v. Minister of Employment and Immigration*,[90] the Supreme Court of Canada recognized the ways in which those claiming refugee status in Canada are dependent for their lives and liberty on the decisions of the Immigration Appeal Board. In the cases appealed, the claimants had not been allowed an oral hearing at any stage of the proceedings or been given reasons for the denial of their claims. Given the serious nature of the consequences for such claimants, the Court held that nothing short of a full oral hearing would meet the requirements of "fundamental justice."[91]

In *Cardinal v. Director of Kent Institution*,[92] the Court also responded to another form of extreme dependence on official decision making, that of prisoners. The court held that given the serious consequences of decisions about whether to subject prisoners to "administrative segregation" (something the prisoners referred to as solitary confinement, though prison officials denied the appropriateness of the term), the prisoner had the right to tell his side of the story.[93] Indeed Justice LeDain pointed to the apparent close-mindedness of the prison director and said that the director "had a duty to hear and consider what the appellants had to say."[94] He concluded that, "the right to a fair hearing must be regarded as an independent unqualified right which finds its essential justification in the sense of procedural justice which any person affected by an administrative decision is entitled to have."[95]

In perhaps the most important recent case, *Baker v. Canada*,[96] the Court addressed the rights of a noncitizen with Canadian-born children with respect to a deportation order.[97] Baker had asked to be allowed to stay in Canada on humanitarian and compassionate grounds of both her health and her children. The Court took up Baker's argument "that she was accorded insufficient participatory rights" and that there was a duty on the decision maker to give reasons. This case was important for many reasons, which I won't touch on here and which advance the cause of attention to the autonomy of those who are dependent on bureaucratic decision making.[98] But it also shows an important limit to what one can expect from judicial oversight of procedure. Consider this statement, which sets the framework for the analysis:

The purpose of the participatory rights contained within the duty of procedural fairness is to ensure that administrative decisions are made using a fair and open procedure, appropriate to the decision being made and in statutory, institutional, and social context, with an opportunity for those affected by the decisions to put forward their views and evidence fully and have them considered by the decision-maker.[99]

This is a very judicial model of fairness, of the purpose of participation. The purpose is to ensure good, transparent procedure so that the adjudicator can provide—and be seen to provide—a fair, informed decision, which will in turn be communicated, via reasons, in ways the subject of the decision can understand and respond to. But even with the importance of reasons and the opportunity to be heard initially and to respond, this is not really a model of participation as conversation. The model is the courtroom where the judge stands above and beyond the litigants and listens to them impartially. This part of the model seems to remain in effect even when the procedures are much less formal than those of a courtroom.

This model has been important in allowing administrative law to point to the ways in which bureaucratic encounters can be structured in different ways—ways that can enhance or undermine the autonomy of those subject to the decisions. But to transform their status from recipients of a fair decision to active participants in those decisions requires something more.

There are two other problems with this judicial picture of participation. The first is that when "being heard" means a hearing, and hearings are envisioned from a judicial perspective, they tend to involve lawyers and complicated procedures. This is so despite the judges' regular invocation of the need for flexibility and informality depending on the context. The result has been that in some key areas when courts have ordered the protection of hearings, critics have pointed to vast expense and delays. In the context of American welfare, critics have argued that the large amounts of money spent on hearings following *Goldberg* would have been much better spent directly on those in need.

The second problem is that the kind of protection that administrative law has brought often has an after-the-fact quality to it. Even a requirement for a *pretermination* hearing in a welfare case does not fundamentally restructure the ongoing relations between caseworker and recipient. Of course, the purpose of the judicial intervention is to structure how particular crucial decisions are made—termination of benefits, denial of refugee status, deportation orders, "administrative segregation" orders—not to try to make welfare agencies, immigration offices or prisons actually conducive to the autonomy of their "clients." But that is, in the end, *my* interest, and the question is the ways in which administrative law points us in the direction of accomplishing that end.[100]

Of course, sometimes just the possibility of judicial oversight can shift the relations of power in ways that offer people—in prisons or subject to deportation decisions—a greater measure of autonomy in their interactions with those whose decisions are so crucial to their lives. And perhaps a decision like *Baker* can provide directions toward the kind of stance decision makers should take toward those dependent on them. *Baker* says that immigration decisions "demand sensitivity and understanding by those making them. They require a recognition of diversity, an understanding of others, and an openness to difference."[101]

A true openness to difference is an invitation to a relationship that would respect and foster the autonomy of those seeking decisions about their immigration status. Like all of the best of administrative law, it points in the direction of what would be required for true autonomy-enhancing relations within bureaucracy, without actually being able to accomplish it.

I close this section with an optimistic view of administrative law as carrying the seeds of just such a transformation. Geneviève Cartier develops a conception of the discretion that is inherent in administrative decisions, which she calls "discretion as dialogue" (as opposed to discretion as power), and of the corresponding judicial oversight that can constrain discretion to be exercised according to this model. She argues that her conception best accounts for existing administrative law (or perhaps accounts for the best of existing administrative law) as well as articulating the principles that should continue to guide its development in the direction that she argues is most consistent with the underlying values of democracy and autonomy.[102] Her conception does two things:

> First, it conditions the validity of any exercise of discretionary power on the participation of the individual in the determination of the norms that will govern her situation. Second, by mandating that the outcome of the decision-making process be responsive to the dialogue that took place, to the statutory framework and to the public interest, discretion as dialogue favours public accountability.[103]

Thus, she explicitly transcends the judicial framework of participation I noted above. Participation means more than a chance to convey the particularities of one's situation; it means participation in determining the norms that will govern the decision. By taking these norms as always involving discretion and thus interpretation and evolution, she transforms the client or petitioner from one seeking an impartial application of norms to an active participant in the necessary evolution of those norms. And she recognizes that the mere requirement of fair procedure will not itself result in such dialogue: "meaningful communication would need to be established between the parties involved, thus requiring substance be added to procedure."[104] That is, it will not be enough to follow a participatory procedure if the substance of the decision ignores that participation. Again, she is explicit in her view that this approach transforms the bureaucratic relationship: "This first aspect of discretion as dialogue established that the very 'relation' that develops between the individual and the state is two-way. It indicates, in other words, that the individual is not passively subjected to the state."[105]

As I interpret Cartier, she is suggesting that decision makers think about what their client/petitioner says as they do the inevitable work of interpreting the norms to apply to the case. For example, petitioner's argument that, as was the case in *Baker*, the welfare of her children must be considered in the decision about her deportation should weigh in as the hearing officer tries to decide how to interpret the scope of humanitarian and compassionate grounds and how they apply in this case. Often the shifts in the interpretation of the norms and guidelines will be subtle. The point is that since that interpretation is never fixed, the hearing officer should be talking to the petitioner with the objective of understanding her perspective on the meaning of the norms—since that is an essential component of the question of their application to her case. (There is, of course, another layer to the problem of participation here: is it the petitioner or her lawyer who is framing and making the argument?) The relationship between petitioner and decision maker shifts if they are actually in dialogue about the meaning of the norms, as opposed to one party being the (relatively passive) recipient of the (fair and informed) decision of the other. There is a difference between listening to the petitioner in order to be sufficiently well informed of the "facts" to fairly apply the rules, on the one hand, and recognizing the petitioner as a participant in the interpretation of those rules, on the other hand.[106]

This is an imaginative and inspiring picture of the way judicial oversight of administrative decision making could work toward just the kind of deep transformation that I suggested above was beyond the scope of administrative law and in tension with much of its tradition. And since it is crucial to have administrative law mediating—and thus shaping—the relations between people and the state, one must hope that it will develop along the lines she suggests. But it is a very demanding picture of these relations. Dialogue, she says, is "'co-operation in a shared endeavor.' It is 'the process of two people coming to understand each other. A dialogue entails a common bond, mutual respect, a genuine listening, an openness to test our own opinions.'"[107] This is, obviously a lot to ask of the overworked caseworker in a welfare office.[108] It is even a lot to ask of officials at immigration hearings.

An optimal administrative law such as that Cartier outlines would be an important guide to an optimal relationship but could work only if there were both the political will and the institutional creativity to develop the conditions in which such a relationship could actually function. Much of that creativity will need to come from outside the legal arena. Administrative law, particularly interpreted as Cartier does, can guide political actors, including popular action groups, to work toward the kind of deep transformation that could actually structure relations between clients and frontline bureaucrats so that genuine autonomy-enhancing dialogue was possible.

V. PARTICIPATION, DEMOCRACY, AND AUTONOMY

Cartier's inspiring picture highlights the centrality of participation in the administrative law model of structuring bureaucratic relations so that they foster both autonomy and democracy. Clients' participation not only protects their rights (the traditional judicial focus); it also gives them an active and central role in the ongoing process of norm creation. At the level of rights to autonomy, for example, clients' participation is designed to foster their sense of efficacy, comprehension, dignity, and capacity to shape their lives. And their participatory role as clients of the bureaucratic state becomes an important forum in which they exercise their democratic autonomy as equal members of society.

Given the centrality of participation as the key to this picture of autonomy in bureaucratic encounters, it is important to clarify the distinctions (as well as overlaps) among autonomy, democracy, and participation. The key point is that despite the centrality of participation to giving effect to autonomy, autonomy is a distinct value that can be threatened by democratic decision making. A focus on fostering autonomy through procedural protections that try to ensure appropriate participation (arising out of the insights from administrative law) might lead to a failure to recognize that autonomy is not simply a matter of participating in procedures; it is a substantive value that requires attention and protection.[109]

This problem is particularly acute if the issue of participation at the bureaucratic level becomes blurred with the question of democratic participation at the legislative level.[110] If autonomy comes to be seen exclusively in terms of participation, one might make the mistake of thinking that if democratic participation (at the legislative level) is optimal, the value of autonomy will be secured. Democracy and autonomy are then collapsed into a single value. This is a serious mistake on two distinct counts: (1) it misunderstands the need to protect autonomy from democratic decision making (such as the authorization of intrusive and constraining surveillance of welfare recipients) and (2) it fails to see that, in the modern state, people must be able to exercise their autonomy not only in their role as voters but also in their diverse roles as participants in bureaucratic decision making.

The second point follows directly from the section above. Even if people are optimally active, informed, and involved in the formulation of legislative policy, the translation of policy into bureaucratic decision making can threaten the autonomy of those dependent upon it. The question of how to structure autonomy-enhancing relations in interactions with bureaucracies[111] remains. Put differently, participation at the legislative level must be matched by structures of bureaucratic relations that render their subjects active participants in the creation and implementation of the norms of bureaucratic decision making.

Because bureaucracies are sites of norm creation, of a kind of lawmaking, they require their own forms of participation. And only with full participation at this level is it likely that the entire pattern of interaction—the daily practices of prisons and immigration and welfare offices—will respect and foster the autonomy of those whose lives they affect. Optimal forms of participation in the bureaucracy are an expression of autonomy as well as essential to protect it. Even ideal participation at the legislative level is no substitute. In the modern state, both autonomy and democracy require bureaucratic relations of mutual respect, attention, and understanding as the context for participation.

The issue in the first point is that autonomy must sometimes be protected *from* democracy. The collapsing of autonomy and democracy (or participation) reflects a misunderstanding of constitutionalism and, more broadly, of the kind of political system that can foster both collective goods and individual rights. As we have seen, in the American tradition, property was once the core of a tension between democratic values of popular rule and liberal values of individual rights as limits on state power.[112] Property neither can nor should continue to serve this role. But the tension itself is the core of constitutionalism, which captures the irreducible tension between the individual and the collective that any good society must recognize and find ways of dealing with. The need to protect autonomy from democracy is one form of this tension. The recognition of the social nature of individuals does not dispel this tension.

Autonomy should be contrasted with democratic values in the following related senses: (1) democracy is not itself sufficient to ensure autonomy; (2) autonomy is a substantive value which can be threatened by democratic outcomes, even though the democratic process is itself a necessary component of autonomy; (3) the outcomes of democratic processes should be held accountable to a standard of respect for the autonomy of all.

The perfection of democracy thus cannot alone assure protection of autonomy. Democracy is crucial to protect rights, including autonomy, but democratic majorities can decide to trample the rights of individuals and minorities. What is required is an understanding of the nature of autonomy and of the practices that foster it so that people can hold their democratic institutions accountable; they need to be able to ask (institutionally) whether the actions or institutions proposed in their collective decision making are consistent with the autonomy of all. Such questions must be posed both to the democratic outcomes of legislative decision making and to bureaucratic practices. For example, legislation that sets up structures of surveillance of welfare recipients' intimate relations may be intrinsically incompatible with the clients' autonomy as well as with their dignity. Bureaucratic practices should be scrutinized to ensure that they do not deny clients basic respect, unreasonably constrain their choices, or treat them in ways that makes them less able to understand what is happening to them, less able to participate effectively in the decisions affecting their lives, less able to define and pursue their own goals—in short, in ways that undermine their autonomy.

As we have seen in the bureaucratic context, it may be that if such failings are found, increased participation will be an important remedy. But there is no simple equation between opportunities to participate and autonomy. Clients may need information or support. Or the outlook of the official (e.g., seeing parents as time-consuming sources of trouble rather than as participants valued for their information and judgment[113]) may be the source of the problem. Or it may be that the interaction, such as intrusive home visits, is inherently incompatible with the autonomy of the client and can be justified only under exceptional circumstances (e.g., the sort of probable cause needed for a warrant). Patterns of intrusive questioning and surveillance may be evidence that the relationship between client and authority must be restructured if it is to foster the client's autonomy.

Optimal democratic participation at both legislative and bureaucratic levels constitutes excellent protection against abuse of power and violations of rights. But even together they are not sufficient. There must be additional mechanisms for holding decision makers accountable to core values. There must, for example, be mechanisms to encourage and facilitate the posing of questions about institutional compatibility with autonomy. But, such an inquiry is only possible if we have a concept of autonomy that is distinct from the democratic processes that may threaten it. In other words, there must be means of measuring the content of collective decisions against the (separate and substantive) value of autonomy. This method would include appropriate institutions, language, and habits of inquiry through which members of society and representatives of some kind (including judges) could check whether the laws, rules, or patterns of official behavior were consistent with the value of autonomy.

My insistence on the potential tension between democracy and autonomy, as a form of the ever present potential for tension between the individual and the collective, raises the question of whether I have ended up reinstating the very dichotomies I set out to overcome with a relational approach to autonomy. I said earlier that the collective is a source of autonomy (through constructive relations) as well as a threat to it. The weakness of traditional liberalism was to focus exclusively on the threat. But to simply reverse that emphasis would also be a mistake. The collective—via democratic decision making—*is* a potential threat to autonomy (and other core values) as well as a source of these values.[114] The recognition of the inherently social nature of human beings does not negate the possibility of democratic abuse. Majorities are still capable of fear, short-sightedness, and unjust self-interest, even when we recognize that they are made up of socially constructed human beings.

But I am not proposing simply to reinstate traditional forms of individual rights as limits to collective power, as I will discuss more fully in chapter 6. In addition, the value of autonomy to which democratic decision making would be held accountable would be a relational conception of autonomy. The autonomy I am talking about does remain an individual value, a value that takes its meaning from the recognition of (and respect for) the inherent individuality of each person. But it takes its meaning no less from the recognition that individuality cannot be conceived of in isolation from the social context in which that individuality comes into being. The value of autonomy is inseparable from the relations that make it possible; there will thus be a social component built into the meaning of autonomy. Institutions will be held accountable for structuring relations in ways that foster rather than undermine autonomy.

In sum, then, participation at both legislative and bureaucratic levels is necessary to protect autonomy and is an expression and component of it. But ensuring democratic participation alone is not sufficient. Democratic decision making always carries the potential to threaten core values, including autonomy. Autonomy is an independent value that cannot be reduced to—or derived from—democratic decision making, because autonomy is of value for reasons other than participating in democratic decision making. Autonomy is therefore a substantive value to which democratic decision making should be held accountable. But neither the means of holding institutions accountable, nor the conception of the values that are the standard, need take the form of American liberal constitutionalism.

The recognition of the social nature of human beings does not alter the need for accountability, but it may help us envision mechanisms other than judicial review. And with a relational conception of autonomy as one of the standards, the inquiry will be directed to how relations can be structured to foster autonomy and other values. In chapter 6 I will return to the links between a relational conception of rights (which give effect to core values) and an alternative conception of constitutionalism as "a dialogue of democratic accountability."

VI. THE PROBLEM OF POWER AND THE POWER OF IDEAS

The possibility of structuring relations of dependence so that they are autonomy-enhancing is, of course, my central claim in this chapter. I have so far been emphasizing the importance of recognizing this possibility and thinking creatively about how law can assist in it.[115] But it is also the case that there are factors that make the necessary restructuring of relations very difficult. Indeed, my opening example of welfare regimes in North America is, sadly, characterized by such factors. This section reflects on how to take these factors into account—both in the specific context of welfare and more generally.

Let me begin with a summary. My main point above has been that autonomy is made possible by constructive relationship, not by independence. Dependence and interdependence are inherent parts of human life. They need, however, to be structured so that they foster autonomy. This is also true of dependence on the state, a ubiquitous feature of modern life. Structuring client–state relations so that they foster rather than undermine autonomy is crucial and possible. Administrative law is a key mechanism for mediating relations between bureaucrats and recipients of their decisions, and it provides insights into how to structure relations that are optimal for both autonomy and democracy.

It is however, crucial that the restructuring be deep, not just at the level of a review of several layers of earlier decision making. If one looks at the complaints and recommendations of people on welfare, few of them have anything to do with hearings.[116] It is the daily interactions of clients and frontline workers and the internal structures of institutions that most directly shape the relations of dependence of clients. If the values of autonomy and participation in norm creation guided all the structures of bureaucratic institutions, they would meet many of the concerns of welfare recipients—though not necessarily the most basic one, the inadequacy of the funds they receive. In many cases, the funds are insufficient to secure the range of meaningful choices necessary for optimal autonomy.[117] (Although if recipients were really listened to at the policy stage of determining "norms" of support, they might be able to effect such a change.)

In addition, while courts can provide guiding insights, they cannot accomplish the necessary transformations. The key issues of protection and expression of autonomy and participation in norm creation must be taken up at the political level of legislative and bureaucratic policy making. The greater the participation of clients in norm creation, the greater the hope for deep transformation. But none of that can happen without the political will to move in that direction and the resources to make it possible. Courts can sometimes provide an impetus to change and an effective articulation of core values, but administrative law can ultimately be a guide only.

All this is to affirm the basic claims of this chapter about the nature of autonomy and the possibility of making state–client relations consistent with it, with the caveat that the process must involve not just the courts, but the entire political system—which itself would ideally change as the process of norm creation changes.

There are, however, two kinds of problems that cannot be fully addressed at the level of structuring bureaucratic relations: what I am calling the problem of power and the power of ideas or preconceptions. The issue of "welfare" involves both of these—great disparities in power and stigmatizing beliefs—such that it will be extremely difficult to transform in ways that, in principle, it could be.

Vast imbalances of power have long been recognized as making mutually respectful, autonomy-enhancing relations difficult. Yet some power imbalances and the dependency they involve are inevitable: parent–child, teacher–student, doctor–patient. And part of my point has been that one must not assume such relationships to be incompatible with autonomy. Indeed, both the parent–child and teacher–student relationships might be thought of as models of power disparity one of whose purposes is the development of autonomy. It all depends on the nature of the relationship, whether the power is used to enhance or undermine autonomy. One might say that one of the purposes of modern medical ethics is to render the power of doctors compatible with patient autonomy. And I have argued that one should look at the inevitable power imbalance and dependence involved in client–state relations in a similar way. All these relationships need to be structured to enhance autonomy.

There are, however, some forms of power imbalance that combine with beliefs about inferiority and stances of denigration to make autonomy-enhancing relations virtually impossible. The residential schools aboriginal children were forced to attend throughout North America are an example. The Law Commission of Canada sees these schools as instances of "total institutions" in which abuse is predictable.[118] Vulnerable populations dependent on people with virtually unchecked power cannot have their autonomy protected without radical transformation of the institutions. The very structure of these institutions is incompatible with the autonomy and democratic rights of those subject to them.

Welfare regimes in North America are not "total institutions." But these regimes routinely exacerbate the power imbalance of poverty that they are, in principle, meant to redress. If one looks at the experiences of welfare recipients in most North American contexts, they consistently report feeling humiliated, being denied access to the information that would allow them to understand their entitlements, being subject to arbitrary decisions and unexplained changes in the payments they receive, being subject to surveillance and invasions of privacy that constrain their autonomy and are an affront to their dignity. The "work fare" they are increasingly compelled to participate in rarely helps equip them for good, long-term jobs. Single mothers are left scrambling to find suitable care for their children. And the levels of support they receive are such that they are unable to afford adequate housing, food, and resources that allow their children to participate fully in school activities—thus extending the humiliation and constraint to the children and making it still worse for their mothers.[119]

The retrenchments in welfare provisions in the 1990s made all of this worse. But the long history of welfare in the Anglo-American world presents a consistently dismal picture.[120] There has always been a stigma attached to welfare, and the institutions designed to dispense it have never been characterized by respect for recipients. The centuries-old suspicion of the poor as undeserving has been kept alive by the project of dividing the poor into "deserving" and "undeserving" categories. Although these terms are no longer in vogue, variations of these categories have justified the intense surveillance that has characterized North American welfare systems as well as the demeaning character of so many caseworker–client interactions. The idea that state-funded welfare should only go to the "deserving" is so deeply entrenched that it is hard to imagine a welfare system operating without it. And the mechanisms of surveillance as a means of sorting out the undeserving has an almost equally commonsense status. Degrees of intrusiveness vary from one system to another and depend somewhat on the political party in power. The Ontario Court of Appeal declared one particularly invasive set of practices to be contrary to the *Canadian Charter of Rights and Freedoms*.[121] Nevertheless, despite these variations and fluctuations, intrusive and stigmatizing surveillance has long been a characteristic of welfare systems.

In sum, the overall picture is such that it is very difficult to believe that these systems are actually designed to promote the autonomy of the recipients. The problem is not just with contemporary politics but also with a system that has a long history of deeply embedded suspicion and disrespect. Trying to restructure relations within existing welfare regimes would involve battling both politics and history. However insightful a relational analysis into the structures that would foster autonomy, it will be of little use if those who control the institutions are not actually interested in autonomy for the recipients.

One way out of this long history is a system of universal entitlement, such as a guaranteed annual income (GAI) for everyone over age sixteen (whose benefits would be recovered from the well off through taxation). Only a system that does not use any means testing to determine who can claim it can shift these long-standing patterns. While a GAI would face resistance to providing for the "undeserving," it would have the political benefit of vastly reducing a huge and expensive bureaucracy. It would dramatically shift the forms of dependence on the state in ways that would circumvent the destructive aspects of the current welfare systems. By making the entitlement universal, the demeaning and invasive sorting out of the deserving would be eliminated, as would the humiliating caseworker–client relationships. There would still be the need for some state-funded services for the "hard-to-serve" populations[122] and perhaps assistance in finding employment or housing. But their clear purpose would be to assist rather than detect fraud or otherwise "cut the welfare rolls." The chance for autonomy-enhancing relations would therefore be greatly increased. And the scope of these services would not replace the huge existing bureaucracy.

Of course, even the restructuring provided by a universal program would not immediately address the most important and pervasive complaint of welfare recipients: inadequate resources. Almost certainly, in order to get a guaranteed annual income in place it would initially have to come in at something like the low levels of welfare assistance. But as it was removed from the centuries-old stigma associated with welfare, I think there is a reasonable hope that it would climb to a more reasonable level. It is likely that a much wider range of people would find that they knew someone who had benefited in important ways from this income.

The case of welfare thus reveals both the importance and the difficulty of restructuring relations of dependency. Such restructuring is urgent because the current systems are so damaging to the autonomy (and dignity) of recipients. It is also especially difficult because people (disproportionately women) who need this assistance are among the least powerful people in society. They are both particularly at risk of abusive practices and are the least able to organize to advocate for change. As we have seen, not all forms of dependency are characterized by this kind of power imbalance. (Remember my example in chapter 1 about university professors.) When such power imbalance is combined with long-standing ideas about poverty, fault, and who is "deserving," the resulting system is particularly difficult to reform incrementally. It is not that, in principle, existing systems could not be restructured to better foster autonomy. It is that in this historical and political context, it will be extremely difficult to do.

Of course, as long as these systems exist, efforts should be made to minimize the ways they undermine autonomy. (One might say something similar about prisons.[123]) And a relational analysis can guide those efforts. But I think a system of universal entitlement, like a GAI, is a more promising way to significantly restructure relations between those in need of social assistance and the state (and society generally).

The question that arises from my view about the difficulty of restructuring current welfare systems is how optimistic one should remain about restructuring in other arenas of bureaucratic dependency. I say the problem with welfare is the combination of power disparity and denigration of poverty. But how common is some such combination, and how much of a problem is power disparity alone?

My basic point stands that dependency itself can be rendered compatible with autonomy. For example, critics of the demeaning character of welfare agencies have long pointed out that other forms of dependency on the state, such as state retirement funds (e.g., Canada Pension Plan or Social Security in the United States) are not so characterized. But at least one study suggests that those seeking disability support have similar complaints.[124] Students in my classes report humiliating experiences applying for student loans. It would be interesting to do a study correlating degrees of powerlessness of the clients with their experience of the bureaucracy as humiliating, withholding relevant information, suspicious—in short not characterized by respectful fostering of their autonomy, much less their actual participation in norm creation. (There are also, of course, power disparities in the other direction: huge pharmaceutical companies facing regulation by overworked bureaucrats.) One would want to examine the role such companies have in making the policies that affect them and the kinds of hearings they are granted.

Perhaps most troubling for my project are destructive relationships that arise even in dependency contexts that seem free of the worst features of the welfare system. For example, I have heard disturbing anecdotal reports by students with experience volunteering in a legal clinic for female victims of violence. Here law students, presumably motivated by their desire to help and some understanding of the plight of their clients, find themselves handling heavy caseloads and succumbing to irritation, impatience, and condescension in dealing with clients. The hierarchy of status, education, and knowledge, combined with the stress of overwork created subtly demeaning relations when clients, overcome with their emotional distress, proved unable to fill out simple forms competently or otherwise follow instructions.[125]

The inevitability of power disparities makes the project I am describing both essential and difficult. There are many forms of power hierarchies in addition to stark disparities of income and resources. Some are unavoidable, like hierarchies of knowledge between lawyer and client, teacher and student, doctor and patient. Yet these hierarchies can be exacerbated by hierarchies of status and income or mitigated by structures that foster mutual respect. The question is how to mitigate rather than exacerbate the hierarchy. At the same time, it is important to recognize that mitigation will always be an uphill battle.

Unnecessary power disparities must, therefore, be resisted as inimical to autonomy and democracy. The power disparities of poverty are particularly destructive because they undermine these values in every sphere of life: political, social and educational as well as economic.

In sum, figuring out how to structure autonomy-enhancing dependence on the state is crucial and possible. Imagining that it can be fully accomplished without addressing underlying power disparities is naive.

Welfare systems, "total institutions," and anecdotes about the legal clinic teach a wariness about the kinds of conditions—power disparities and patterns of subordination—that make it difficult or ultimately impossible ("total institutions") to restructure relationships so that they enhance rather than undermine autonomy. The pervasiveness of these conditions, and their combination, is sobering. But I do not conclude that one can abandon the project of trying to render dependence consistent with autonomy. Rather, I conclude that the kind of restructuring I have been discussing must ultimately be part of, and would support and feed into, a wider political transformation.

In the meantime, attending to the relational nature of autonomy and the possibility of improving existing bureaucratic relations to foster autonomy will continue to provide insight into what makes autonomy flourish.

VII. CONCLUSION

This inquiry has been prompted more by an interest in future possibilities than by hopes for the true fostering of autonomy under current Anglo-American legal systems. Forms of bureaucratic decision making—however participatory, respectful, or otherwise optimal—cannot change basic power relations and structures of inequality.[126] These, more than anything, determine the potential for autonomy for everyone—because subordination and powerlessness inevitably undermine autonomy. But even in a quite imperfect society, experiments with forms of collective (often bureaucratic) power and with the relations between those implementing it and those dependent upon it can give us insight into what optimal forms and relations would look like. For example, a small-scale pilot project of social assistance designed around the now substantial literature on a relational approach to public care would be of tremendous value.[127] What I have tried to do is suggest a framework that can both guide such projects and be used to help extract what is useful out of current experiments—since I believe that a new conception of autonomy is not likely to spring full-blown from theory.

I see the development of such a conception as essential for working out alternatives to the present Anglo-American systems. The alternatives which seem compelling to me all involve a far greater role for collective (though not necessarily state) power and responsibility than the current systems. Those who aspire to such alternatives must be able to persuade themselves as well as their critics that such changes need not diminish, though they will certainly change, autonomy. More importantly, we must have language that adequately captures the tradition's highest goals, in terms that reflect both the individual and the social dimensions of human beings. That language will take some time to be fully developed, but in the meantime we cannot cede to liberal convention a monopoly on the value of autonomy.

Feminist theory provides us with a relational conception of the self that respects both the individual and social nature of human beings. Relational feminism is not romantic about community or relationship, but it sees the great creative capacity of human beings as always interacting in relationship with others. Conceiving of autonomy as relational both yields a theoretical language that can capture the heart of that value and directs our attention to the institutional structures that can inform the articulation of the value and point to the need for transformation.

4

The Multidimensional Self and the Capacity for Creative Interaction

I. INTRODUCTION
A. Statement of Purpose

The "self" and its capacity for autonomy, agency,[1] or creation are inherently elusive phenomena. This chapter offers the multidimensional self as a way of reflecting on a creative self and takes up the challenge of why this multidimensional self serves law better than the traditional "rational agent" does.

Here I expand the relational focus of the previous chapters to a picture of the self as also embodied and affective,[2] that is, capable of emotion or affect in ways centrally related to the capacity for reason and autonomy. In each of these dimensions there is also an essential particularity. Each person is uniquely situated within the web of relations, and her embodiment and affect give her a distinct particularity that is key to her own experience of herself and to how others interact with her.

My argument here is designed to answer a challenge to this entire project: why do rights and the law need a conception of the self as particular, relational, embodied and affective? Even if the self is most fully understood in these terms, the challenge would go, why isn't the far more limited, deliberately abstracted model of the individual(istic) rational agent better suited to the realm of law and rights? Don't the practical requirements of law—the need for predictability, for stability, for ease and consistency of judicial application—call for a relatively simple, formal picture of the person? The abstracted rights bearer, one might say, is just such a formal picture: the rational agent whose intrinsic rationality and agency entitle him to rights.

My argument is that the prevailing stripped down image of the "rational agent" of both law and political theory is unnecessarily and destructively narrow. In particular, it neglects or obscures the affective, embodied, and relational nature of human self-hood. And the abstractness obscures the particularity. An optimal language for legal and political discourse would direct our attention to these dimensions of our humanness.

This chapter also offers another angle on why this book focuses so much on autonomy. First, within the Anglo-American legal tradition, autonomy is a key mediating concept between rights and the underlying conceptions of the self. Autonomy will therefore be central to any project of examining and transforming the ways a misconception of the self is connected to the understanding of law and rights. Second, autonomy is, in my own terms, a key component of a core human value: the capacity for creative interaction.

B. *Choosing Language*

The language we use for the self and for autonomy is a kind of metaphor for something that cannot be fully captured. And metaphors inevitably direct our attention to some things and obscure others.[3] Nevertheless, some metaphors, some conceptual structures, direct out attention more fruitfully than others. The choice of language for the self and its autonomy is important both theoretically and practically. It is tied to the understanding of rights and to the kinds of social context that are attended to in debates about rights. And, as we shall see in the example of women accused of murdering their battering partners, dominant frameworks of thought have real consequences for people's lives.

A distorted picture of the self is likely to generate a distorted understanding of autonomy, and a system of rights designed to promote and protect that vision of self and autonomy is unlikely to optimally foster and protect human capacities, needs and entitlements. In addition, rights discourse is so important in many societies that it is not plausible that an impoverished picture of the self underlying rights will not spill over to more general collective misunderstandings.

Here, I shall argue that the best language for autonomy is not independence, self-determination, or control[4]—despite their common associations with autonomy. The language I propose is autonomy as part of the capacity for creative interaction—which includes the capacity for self-creation. I will show how this approach makes the embodied, affective, and relational nature of human beings central rather than peripheral. We shall also see that attention to the particularity of these dimensions leads to attention to difference in ways that can foster equality.

Finally, though I am focusing on the concepts underlying rights discourse, I am not only concerned about conceptual change. On the contrary, one of the virtues of my understanding of the multidimensional self is that it immediately directs our attention to the conditions that make values like autonomy possible. Autonomy stops being a theoretical presupposition and becomes an object of substantive inquiry.

C. Structure of the Chapter

I begin (section II) with an answer to the challenge that a conception of the self as the abstracted "rational agent" is appropriate for law and for rights in particular. I argue that this dominant conception is faulty in its assumptions about both rationality and agency. I look first at rationality and argue for the need to make the embodied, affective dimension of human beings central to an understanding of human cognitive capacities. I then turn to autonomy, the dimension of agency that is most crucial for law and rights: the rational agent is an agent capable of autonomous action. I continue the argument (from previous chapters) that the dominant conception of autonomy needs to be replaced. Section III explains the idea of autonomy as part of the human capacity for creative interaction, a conception I see as suited to the multidimensional self. In section IV, I return my focus to the relational component of this conception of the self and to the links between autonomy and responsibility in law. I offer an extended discussion of cases of "battered women" accused of murdering their battering partner. The example shows both the advantages of a using a relational approach to autonomy and the challenges it poses for assigning legal responsibility. Section V looks at the question of whether the multidimensional self and the capacity for creative interaction can "ground" equality in the way that the traditional "rational agent" has done. In section VI, I return to another challenge: that the most important function of rights is to protect people against the worst forms of harm and that, for that purpose, the traditional conception is adequate and, indeed, preferable for its clarity. In my response, I offer examples of the significance of embodiment for rights.

II. THE RATIONAL AGENT AND ITS LIMITATIONS

Let me begin with the counterargument to my advocacy of the multidimensional self: Of course the "rational agent" is a stripped-down conception of the self. The self that underpins contemporary liberal legalism is intentionally abstracted to capture the essence of "rights holders." As such it is perfectly suited to its task, even if other domains of inquiry—such as psychology, literary narrative, theology, or even epistemology—may wish to explore and invoke a fuller, richer conception of humanity. Even if human beings are most fully described in their particularity and as embodied, affective, and relational, why are these dimensions crucial to law and political theory and to conceptions of rights in particular?

A. The Puzzle of Equality and the Abstracted Self

I begin my answer with the claim that the core (benign or defensible[5]) purpose of a highly abstracted conception of the self is equality. Any society committed to equality must find a way of conceptualizing the vast array of human particularity—with its manifest differences of strength, health, intelligence, talents, aptitudes, temperaments, and abilities—in a way that gives effect to a belief in the inherently equal value of all human beings. That is, there must be a way of expressing a belief in a core or fundamental equality of human beings despite the obvious inequalities of their abilities, characteristics, and even virtues. Philosophers often use the term "equal moral worth" to capture this idea (meaning of inherently equal value, not equally moral in the sense of equally virtuous). I will use both "equal moral worth" and "inherent equality" to distinguish this fundamental equality from the (sometimes natural) inequalities of capacity as well as from practical inequalities in social relations.

If inherent equality is to translate into concrete legal and political rights, it may seem that people need a way to see each other not in terms of the obvious multitude of differences among them, but as equal rights bearers, and in that sense identical to and interchangeable with one another. If, for example, law professors want to use examples of the liability "A" incurs to "B," they must have the confidence that such shorthand will make sense—that is, for the purposes of legal rights, people can reasonably be depicted as the interchangeable units of "A" and "B." If people could only know their mutual rights and obligations if they knew the full details of the context of their lives and relationship to one another, it would hardly seem that we were talking about something that could be recognized as a legal right.[6] The abstracted self thus captures the core equality and identity of people as rights bearers.

The problem is that to achieve this equal interchangeability, liberal legalism has stripped away crucial dimensions of human beings. These dimensions are necessary to optimally conceptualize the rights that can best protect people and allow them to thrive. The language of rights is a vehicle also for articulating and institutionalizing core values of a society. Neither objective can be optimally pursued if the stripped-down picture of the individual is actually misleading in ways directly related to those values, such as the nature of autonomy and the conditions under which it can flourish.

The trick is to find a way of capturing the core belief in the inherent equality of all people without distorting the picture of humanity in order to articulate the equality. In the end, two different components are needed for an adequate framework for rights. The first is a purely formal claim of equality that serves as an underlying principle and a standard of justification for all claims of equal but different treatment: can they be persuasively justified as consistent with equal moral worth?[7] In its purely formal quality, the claim makes no substantive claims; it asserts nothing about the actual characteristics of human beings. This purely formal claim is a necessary starting point, despite its substantive emptiness.

I should add as a point of clarification that taking formal equal moral worth as a starting point does not mean taking what has come to be called "formal equality" as a starting point. I believe that coherent, effective arguments for equality cannot do without a claim of equal moral worth that is formal, that is not empirically substantive, in its nature. But the practical meaning of equality will always have to be determined with the kind of attention to context that "formal equality" often rejects. While claims for differential access to rights or opportunities must be defended as consistent with equal moral worth, the assessment of that consistency will always be made with attention to context. The requirement to defend this consistency does not therefore mean that there is some presumption in favor of formal equality.

The starting point of formal equal moral worth is, thus, necessary, but not sufficient. The second component is attention both to actual human characteristics and to particular contexts in order to know what it would take to give effect to equal moral worth, to actually treat every person as inherently equal.

I think a central part of the problem in the tradition of liberal legalism has been the move to an intermediate step: the assertion of rational agency as that which constitutes our identity as equals and thus forms the basis for our claims as rights bearers. Perhaps historically and philosophically, there was an unease with the way in which a purely formal claim of equal moral worth seemed a mere article of faith, something which by its nature could not be demonstrated or disproved. Perhaps some more substantive claim about *why* people are inherently equal to one another and deserving of rights seemed required—especially once the grounding in the soul became unavailable in legal and political discourse. At least since Kant, rational agency has been offered as this ground, with the further alleged virtue of providing a means for deducing the rights to which rational agents are entitled.

The treatment of rational agency as the core of equality and the foundation for rights claims has caused problems precisely because it is not a purely formal claim; it asserts certain properties as the ones relevant to rights while denying the significance of others. In particular, as many feminists have argued, it denies the relevance of our embodied nature, of emotion or affect and the differences and individual particularities that both our bodies and our feelings make manifest.[8] The problem lies both with the conception of reason, as radically disconnected from the body and affect, and with the conception of agency or autonomy.

I do not propose to rehearse all the arguments that have been made about the limitations of the abstracted, stripped-down individual that is the presumed subject of liberal legalism.[9] Rather I will note the issues that seem particularly important for my affirmative claim that an optimal approach to rights requires a full picture of the embodied creative beings that humans are. Let me begin with the image of the rational agent as the disembodied reasoner.

B. The Rational Agent as Disembodied

Of course, when I say that the dominant conception of rights presupposes an image of the rational agent as disembodied, it does not mean that the concept of rights literally cannot take account of bodies. From ordinary tort law to international human rights prohibitions against torture, the need to protect people's bodies from harm is one of the things legal rights are concerned with. The claim, common in feminist critiques of liberalism, is that the image of the subject in legal and political theory is one stripped of its bodily nature. The "A"s and "B"s of law school examples have none of the characteristic ways bodies are experienced and interpreted as part of identity: no gender, no race, no particular physical strengths and weaknesses. The nature of a subject's body is a specific detail that might have to be brought in for a particular purpose. But the core subject of the dominant legal and political theory is the rational agent—whose rationality and agency alone are what really matter, what entitle him or her to rights. And neither rationality nor agency is conceptualized as integrally connected to the body or to affect.[10] Later I will discuss the work of a neurologist who argues that we cannot understand human reasoning and judgment without understanding the role of affect and the body. Here let me note some of the ways in which this image of the disembodied rational agent can be found in what I take to be notions about the body that are commonplace for most able-bodied people.[11]

I think the demands of the body are very often experienced as an affront to autonomy. In my own case, I find it particularly distressing when it seems that my body's chemistry or hormonal changes affect my state of mind, my mood, my clarity of thought. Similarly, stories of environmental pollution causing depression, irritability, or the inability to concentrate seem particularly frightening to me. In both cases, I think the distress arises from the sense that something very close to who I think I am, how I experience myself as an agent in the world, could be controlled, or at least significantly influenced by, something "else," something not essentially "me." In the case of the environmental pollution it may seem clearer that the cause is really something external, something heteronymous (to use philosophers' language), interfering with my autonomous control of my self, my state of mind. But in both cases it actually is the relation of the body to states of mind that is at stake.

The tacit image of rational agency as disembodied casts the body as something other than self, something heteronymous. When people experience sickness, injury, or fatigue as an interference with their capacity to live as they want to, the body becomes a threat to the constancy of reason and agency, which the tradition treats as the core of our humanness. The "otherness" of the body is both a cause of such experience and is reinforced by it.

Our bodies pose a tacit threat to the dominant image of autonomy as independence, as being unilaterally in control of our lives. It is in part our embodiment that makes us inevitably and obviously dependent on others.[12] In sickness and death we are forced to recognize both our need for others and our ultimate lack of control. I think it is this dependency and inherent lack of control that, in North American culture, breeds a fear, distaste, and hostility to all things bodily. The visions of freedom from necessity, the ultimate image of autonomy, falter in the face of the sick or dying body.

Recognizing the ways in which the body is routinely seen and experienced as an interference (with "its" fatigue or illness), a threat, or an affront to autonomy helps to make sense of the way in which dominant conceptions of self and agency are disembodied, even though, at another level, no one denies that people have bodies and that particular areas of rights are directed to protecting those bodies.

Similarly, no one denies that people have feelings. But the affective component of ourselves is treated not only as sharply distinct from reason but also, in a sense, as heteronymous. When affect is treated as distinct from cognition, feelings become a sort of raw data of nature, to be controlled by reason. When reason fails to control emotion, then we are not in control of ourselves; we are not acting autonomously.

C. Incorporating the Body and Affect into the Reason of the Rational Agent

There are many ways of addressing what is wrong with this image of the rational, disembodied agent. I will return later to the ways in which it has served to exclude women and other subordinated groups who are associated with affect and the body. Here I want to point to a particular way of seeing this image as entailing a misunderstanding of reason, which, in turn, distorts the understanding of autonomy. Since the value of autonomy is so central to rights, and the rational agent is treated as the subject of rights, if we misunderstand the nature of reason and autonomy, it is unlikely that we will be able to develop an adequate conception of rights.

Many feminist philosophers have written on the ways in which affect is part of reason.[13] A very different kind of research supports the feminist challenge to the reason/emotion split. In *Descartes' Error* (1994), neurologist Antonio Damasio offers a fascinating theory of how emotions are an essential part of reasoning.[14]

Much of Damasio's research is based on patients with severe but highly particular brain damage. These subjects retained their intelligence, memory, and perceptual abilities but seemed completely unable to exercise the judgment necessary either to plan for their future or to interact socially in ways that respected the feelings of those around them. Through a series of experiments and studies of case histories of such patients, Damasio concludes that the damaged area of the brain is one that processes information about somatic (bodily) states, especially those associated with emotion. The patients showed a startling flatness of affect in relating past events of (what would ordinarily be) a highly emotional nature. And though they displayed normal skin-conductance responses (like those elicited in lie-detector tests) to immediate stimuli that startle (e.g., an unexpected sound or glare of light), they showed none of the normal responses when shown pictures of scary, horrific, or disturbing events.[15] Later they could describe the pictures precisely, and even identify the kinds of emotions associated with such events, but they seemed not to feel the emotion. Damasio describes one patient who commented in a debriefing session that although he knew that the content of the pictures ought to be disturbing, he himself was not disturbed. Damasio concludes that

the patient was telling us, quite plainly, that his flesh no longer responded to these themes as it once had. That somehow, *to know does not necessarily mean to feel*, even when you realize that what you know ought to make you feel in a specific way but fails to do so.[16]

Damasio's theory (in compressed terms) is that effective reasoning requires what he calls "somatic markers." Somatic markers are emotional responses that (for the most part) we have learned, through experience, to associate with certain images. In deciding what to do in a given circumstance, one imagines a certain action and associates it with an outcome, which, in turn, triggers an emotional reaction. "When the bad outcome connected with a given response option comes into mind, however fleetingly, you experience an unpleasant gut feeling."[17] The crucial function of these markers is to help sort through the otherwise overwhelming array of possible actions. "Somatic markers do not deliberate for us. They assist the deliberation by highlighting some options (either dangerous or favorable), and eliminating them rapidly from subsequent consideration."[18] Patients whose brains do not allow them to use somatic markers fail to learn from bad experiences and become lost in the details of even routine decision making.

Damasio comments that "in the end, if purely rational calculation is how your mind normally operates, you might choose incorrectly and live to regret your error, or simply give up trying, in frustration." In one of the great lines in the book, he relates his findings to the image of reasoning that I have been discussing: "What the experience with patients...suggests is that the cool strategy advocated by Kant, among others, has far more to do with the way patients with prefrontal [brain] damage go about deciding than with how normals usually operate."[19]

Interestingly, Damasio also links the cognitive failures that arise from the inability to use the information provided by affect to a loss of autonomy. He describes patients who must rely on their unaided, and otherwise unimpaired, intellect as having lost their free will.[20]

Of course, Damasio acknowledges that there are ways in which emotions can get in the way of good reasoning. But this should not lead us to conclude that good or optimal reasoning can do without emotion. Effective reason requires a partnership between "so-called cognitive processes and processes usually called 'emotional.'"[21] And this partnership requires a responsiveness to the reasoner's body states.

Damasio's work has intriguing implications for the feminist project of making the body an integral part of our conception of the self rather than a source of contingency, particularity, and difference—to be set aside when identifying the human essence that founds the contemporary commitment to equality and rights. After all, if the core capacities for reason and autonomous decision making cannot be well understood without their connection to affect and the body, it hardly seems appropriate that our conception of the self should exclude or ignore these components.

Once we bring in the body, we must confront difference. The justification for leaving the body aside was to find some core commonality that was truly universal, unvaried and free of contingency. If law, political theory, and institutional design fully incorporated a sense of human beings as embodied, it would be much harder to ignore bodily differences such as sex, age, and mental and physical abilities. But attention to these differences is vital; they are too integral to human identities and experiences to be treated as peripheral to the core issues of justice, equality, dignity, or harmony. Whatever valid forms of universal rights may emerge, they must be based on a fully embodied picture of human beings, with all the claims upon attention to difference that that will bring.

In a previously published article, I discuss the ways in which understanding the role of affect in judgment directs our attention to the need to educate our affective responses as well as to transcend them through reflection.[22] I comment there on the implications this has for legal education and argue that diversity throughout the legal profession is essential if we are to hope for optimal capacities for judgment in our judges—because this diversity will facilitate both the education of affect and the judges' capacity for reflective transcendence. This argument is, or course, linked to my claim here that the conception of rights must be based on a full conception of humanness rather than the abstraction of rational agency.

If the very nature of reason entails a basic connection to the body and to affect, then an image of the rational agent that leaves out these dimensions must be inadequate. This is particularly clear when we see the links between reason, affect, and the body in reason's capacity to facilitate autonomy, to allow people to formulate life plans and act in accordance with their values and goals. We will not be able to think intelligently about what fosters this key capacity if we misunderstand its nature. And if rights are to be conceptual and institutional means of fostering and protecting autonomy, then they must not be based on misunderstandings of this capacity. And, at an instrumental level, if the judges to whom we entrust the ongoing definition and enforcement of rights misunderstand the role of affect in judgment, they will not be able to do an optimal job.

I have not tried here to present a full account of what a conception of reason integrally connected to the body and affect would look like, but to insist that we must have one as part of the picture of the human being who is entitled to rights—and therefore that such a picture is appropriate for law and other discourses about rights. Thus the rationality of the "rational agent" must be understood in embodied and affective terms. I now turn to the conception of agency or autonomy that is implicit in the "rational agent" and argue that we must reconceptualize autonomy as well as reason.

III. AUTONOMY AS PART OF CREATIVE INTERACTION

Originally, I planned to treat the "capacity for creative interaction" as the best descriptor or synonym for autonomy. But I now think that autonomy is just one component of the capacity. Creative interaction also requires the capacity for attention, for receptivity[23] and responsiveness (and more). These dimensions help remind us that since creative interaction involves *interacting*, one must be able to attend, receive, and respond to what one is interacting with. Otherwise the full potential for creativity will not be achieved. But that potential also requires the possibility of *new* engagement, breaking or transforming received patterns, giving rise to and acting on one's own distinctive perceptions, insights, and forms of engagement. This is the dimension of creative interaction captured by the idea of autonomy.

What I am really offering is an alternative metaphor for examining autonomy, and, as we have seen, metaphors are important in shaping how we see problems and their solutions.[24]

In the previous chapter I addressed one of the most common metaphors (indeed often synonym) for autonomy: independence. I argued that thinking of autonomy as independence distorts our understanding of what actually makes autonomy possible, namely, constructive relationships. Of course, "independence" captures something about what we value in autonomy; it suggests that one can make one's life choices for oneself, free of the constraint or control that dependence on another can bring. The problem is that this vision of freedom misses the reality that the capacity for autonomy can only develop and thrive when fostered by constructive relationships, such as those with parents, teachers, friends, and agents of the state. As we have seen, this is not simply a matter of child development. The capacity for autonomy can wither or thrive through one's life, and those who value autonomy must not simply posit it as a human characteristic but also inquire into the conditions for its flourishing. And we can only understand those conditions when we understand how relationships shape the development of our core capacities in ways that make interdependence a basic fact of life—throughout our lives.

As a result, our understanding of rights, and the institutional mechanisms for implementing them, must be conceived with this core relational nature of humans in mind.

Just as I contrasted relational autonomy to independence, here I want to contrast the idea of creative interaction with the common phrase "self-determination." In particular I suggest that it is more helpful to refer to an ongoing capacity for interactive "self-creation" than to "self-determination."[25] Once again, it is not that "self-determination" has nothing to do with autonomy. Rather, I think the shift in emphasis from self-determination to interactive self-creation offers a more helpful way of thinking about a wide variety of problems posed by the realities of our interdependence. At the heart of many contemporary debates is the question of how to conceptualize selfhood or autonomy such that it acknowledges both the ways in which we are profoundly shaped by, indeed significantly constituted by, the relationships of which we are a part (whether personal, cultural, national, or global) and at the same time captures the way in which we genuinely are autonomous beings who are not *determined* by these relationships.

The problem with the term "self-determination" (and many conceptions of autonomy that deny or ignore its relational nature) is that it presumes or implies that the nature of our "selves" is entirely a matter of our choice. And, conversely, a common objection to "communitarian" thought is that it so overstates the constitutive nature of human embeddedness in community, that it leaves no room for choice, for genuine autonomy. For both theoretical and practical reasons we need a fully adequate way of understanding how people come to be who they are.

We need something better than the routine bifurcation between a "sociological" common sense about the ways in which people are shaped by their social contexts, on the one hand, and, on the other hand, a presumption that choice and autonomy are the primary dimensions of self-hood relevant to law. Whether for purposes of conceptualizing groups and cultural rights in constitution making or for the broad theoretical purposes I pose here, an integrated understanding of self and autonomy is needed.

Let me offer an example of a debate within feminist theory that I think turns on these issues. This debate is a compelling example of the passionate sense that it matters deeply whether we find an optimal way of capturing both the realities of the relationships, including power relations, that shape our lives and the equally real, but elusive, capacity to interact with these forces in a genuinely creative and, thus, autonomous way. In the exchange between Seyla Benhabib and Judith Butler in *Feminist Contentions: A Philosophical Exchange*[26] one can see the way in which each sees the other's theoretical approach as threatening a conception of agency that is defensible philosophically and that can empower women politically. This is clearest in their discussions of women's historiography.

Benhabib refers to a "clash between the social history from below paradigm...the task of which is to illuminate the gender, class, and race struggles through which power is negotiated, subverted, as well as resisted by the so-called 'victims' of history, and the paradigm of historiography, influenced by Foucault's work, in which the emphasis is on the 'construction' of the agency of victims through mechanisms of social and discursive control from the top."[27] Butler replies that the issue is "how one accounts for the agency that exists....In one view agency is an attribute of persons, presupposed as prior to power and language, inferred from the structure of the self; in the second, agency is the effect of discursive conditions which do not for that reason control its use; it is not a transcendental category, but a contingent and fragile possibility opened in the midst of constituting relations....[the point] is to ascertain what constitutes agency within the very relations of power that constitute women as active beings."[28]

I think that part of what fueled the historiography debate was the sense on one side that if the focus is all on the "constitutive" power wielded from the top, that the genuine agency, the creative, sometimes heroic efforts of those on the bottom, is erased in their presentation as victims. The point of finally giving women their proper place in history was not to present them as passive victims. But for the other side, if the constitutive context of power relations is not given appropriate attention, then at best we will fail to understand the true magnitude of women's achievements in, say, acts of resistance, and, at worst, we will hold them inappropriately responsible for a failure to do more. And, most importantly, we will fail to understand the dynamics of how autonomous agency, genuine creative interaction with constitutive structures of power, is possible.

I think this drama of constructing agency in the face of unequal power relations is played out over and over again—and often with the same passions engaged, since women's power, autonomy, victimization, and "responsibility" in the face of circumstances beyond their control are at stake. As we will see, the contemporary debates over the "battered women's syndrome" are concrete legal examples of these same issues.[29]

A similar dilemma emerges for all groups trying to overcome oppression and its consequences. Some of those consequences play themselves out in individual behavior, such as violence, substance abuse, and crime. How should such behavior be understood? How can individual responsibility be fostered in a way that fully recognizes the wider structures of power relations and distribution of privilege? As Melissa Harris-Lacewell put it, should one focus on the "bad behavior" (to figure out how to stop it) or on the pattern of privilege that governs the consequences (as well as, in part, the causes) of the behavior? She says she opts for the focus on privilege because the bad behavior is a necessary,[30] but not sufficient, condition for such consequences as incarceration. She notes, for example, that bad behavior, for example, alcohol abuse, dropping out of school, and sexual promiscuity, can lead to the presidency (a reference to President George W. Bush) or to prison, depending on where one is positioned in structures of privilege.[31]

John Borrows grapples with similar issues with respect to aboriginal peoples in Canada.[32] In a compelling narrative he suggests that individual choice is crucial in the development of people's lives. But in assigning responsibility, both legal and moral, one wants to be cognizant of the fact that the choices often take place in extremely difficult contexts—which are not the responsibility of the chooser. How does one respect and promote both individual and community agency while acknowledging the power and constraints of the larger context? (He offers a telling juxtaposition between "Indian agency" and the destructive role of the federal "Indian agents."[33]) Perhaps a relational approach, building on Susan Sherwin's distinction,[34] suggests that true autonomous agency is possible only when the inequalities of power and opportunity have been addressed. And yet, one cannot postpone either fostering or assigning responsibility until that point is reached.

The problem of understanding individual autonomy and responsibility in the context of oppressive power relations (which, as Sarah Hoagland reminds us, is the norm rather than the exception[35]) is a matter of both strategic political action and reflection on the language, the concepts that can facilitate both understanding and action. I think the concept of autonomy as part of a capacity for creative interaction offers a path for working through both the theoretical and practical debates. At the theoretical level, the context of creative interaction highlights both the genuinely creative and inevitably interactive dimensions of all our exercises of autonomy. It thus directs our attention to the constraining as well as enabling dimensions of circumstance without underplaying the core capacity for creation.

In hundreds of ways we are presented with dimensions of our world and our selves that we did not "choose." And what we are presented with—whether the personalities and child-rearing practices of our parents, or our citizenship (or absence thereof), or how our gender and race is constructed in the society in which we were raised—makes a huge difference to the person each of us becomes. At the same time, people interact with, and thus may shift and shape all the dimensions of their lives.

I think the idea of a capacity for creative interaction can help us reflect on these basic issues of autonomy and responsibility. I mean to use the term "creative" in a strong sense: human beings have the capacity to create something new, something that (in this particular form) did not exist before, that was not simply determined by what preceded it, that could not have come into being but for the act of creation, the exercise of autonomy that transformed what had previously existed into something new.

But this genuine creative capacity is itself shaped in both form and scope by the kinds of relationships that foster or impede it. And, of course, we neither choose nor control many of these relationships—though we always retain the capacity to interact with, and thereby change (or reinforce), them.

Thus I intend a language that is true both to the miraculous (and ordinary) human capacity for creation and to its inherently relational and thus contingent qualities. Conceptualized in these terms, as part of the capacity for creative interaction, autonomy is shaped by the structures of relations, including power relations with which any individual interacts, but it cannot be reduced to or deduced from those relations. I *do* end up asserting an underlying innate capacity, but the form it takes is not "presupposed as prior to power and language." Similarly, one might say that the human capacity for creative interaction (of which autonomy is a part) is "inferred from the structure of the self" in the sense that I claim that a central part of what we mean by a human self is a self with such a capacity—a capacity which, however, manifests in a wide variety of forms.

The form it takes varies across many factors: stage of life, such as infancy, adolescence or senility; structures of power relations, such as slavery, incarceration, hierarchies of gender, class, and racialization; personal relations, such as abusive or nurturing parents, teachers, or spouses. In relation to each such factor, individuals will develop their capacities in different ways and in different ways in different times and spheres of their lives. The form, though not the root capacity, is a "contingent and fragile possibility opened in the midst of constituting relations." Or perhaps I should say that the root capacity itself is not contingent, but its nature is a possibility that is both fragile and tenacious. Finally, the root capacity for creative interaction is not a transcendental category, but a phenomenon that can be observed, in varying degrees, in all life-forms.[36]

Just as the "capacity for creative interaction" seems a more helpful framework than self-determination, it also stands in contrast to the common association of autonomy with control (as will be shown more fully in chapter 7). Despite the popularity and allure of the idea of "being in control of one's life," no one ever is. Nor should we be. Much of our lives is formed by interaction with other autonomous beings, and control is not a respectful stance toward them. (A nontrivial benefit of my approach to autonomy might be to erode the deadly "management" culture of control that pervades much of North America.)

Of course, as with the term "self-determination," I recognize that there is something to the aspiration to "be in control of one's life" and that the sense of "things being out of control" is a common way of experiencing periods when one is not functioning autonomously. Clearly if someone else is in control of one's life, one cannot be autonomous. (Hence the common struggle between teenagers and their parents.) And if the daily course of one's life seems to be an ongoing struggle to respond to one external demand after the other, one's autonomy is probably not thriving.[37] But the language of control is a poor guide to establishing the kinds of relations that could actually foster autonomy for everyone.[38]

The same issues apply to self-creation, the ongoing creative interaction with oneself—a process Catherine Keller calls "selving."[39] Indeed, "creative-selving" might be a better term than self-creation because of its focus on process and because it does not inadvertently imply that we can create ourselves out of whole cloth, in whatever way we wish. (But even as I type my spell check program reminds me that "selving" is not yet a recognized word.) And in any case, the potential hubristic danger of the term "self-creation" seems matched on the positive side by its expression of the extraordinary nature of this human ability.

As with everything else, our ongoing creative interaction with our selves is shaped by a great many factors that are not of our choosing, that we cannot control, and for which we are not responsible. What matters is understanding the conditions that foster or undermine that creative capacity. As I said earlier, autonomy—a key component of our actual capacity for creative interaction—is not simply a characteristic that can be posited about human beings. It cannot simply be a presupposition of theory or (as we shall see) of law. Rather it poses a problem: How can the underlying root capacity be optimally developed? What social, legal, and political structures allow it to flourish? What forms of language, what kinds of conceptual tools, help us explore this problem?

So far I have argued that the concept of creative interaction can capture both the astonishing human capacity for genuine creation and the complex ways in which that capacity is always interacting with forces beyond its control. As such it avoids what Seyla Benhabib refers to as the Promethean self that privileges mastery[40] while not denying the central importance of autonomy.

It is also important to see this capacity as both extraordinary and, in its daily reality, very ordinary. In chapter 1, I offer ordinary examples of creation: playing, a child building a tower of blocks, making a garden, making a joke. I think Audre Lorde helps to capture what I mean by this capacity in her discussion of the erotic. In so doing she also highlights, as I have not so far, the affective or feeling dimension of autonomous creativity:

> Another important way in which the erotic connection functions is the open and fearless underlining of my capacity for joy. In the way my body stretches to music and opens into response, hearkening to its deepest rhythms, so every level upon

which I sense also opens to the erotically satisfying experience, *whether it is dancing, building a bookcase, writing a poem, examining an idea.*[41]

Lorde thus emphasizes the ordinary, everyday things that can be truly creative, that can fill us with the joy of the erotic. At the same time, she insists on the demanding quality of the erotic, of living what I would call a truly autonomously creative life: "that deep and irreplaceable knowledge of my capacity for joy comes to demand from all my life that it be lived within the knowledge that such satisfaction is possible."[42]

I think Lorde is right to point to this quality of a life lived creatively. But it is equally important to me (and I think to her) that neither heroism nor genius is entailed in living out the capacity for creative interaction (though courage is often called for). As I have said, autonomy is experienced on a continuum, and it varies across times and spheres of our lives. It is both a routine possibility and an inspiring ideal.

Before closing this section, let me note two further advantages of the language of creative interaction. First, it invites inquiry into interaction with one's body as part of the process of self-creation (as Lorde so eloquently expresses). This sort of attention to the body allows a recognition that the body itself is a source of knowledge for this process. Reflecting on the limitations of the body, and what it means to optimally interact with those limitations, has the potential to reveal the importance of a sympathetic response to limitations on autonomy. This lesson is important since compassion in the face of limitations itself fosters autonomy.[43] More generally, as I argued in discussing Damasio's understanding of reason, it is important that the concept of autonomy embraces an image of the embodied self, or we will not be able to adequately explore what fosters reason and autonomy.

The second advantage I want to highlight is that an approach to autonomy as part of the capacity for creative interaction of relational, embodied selves is well suited to the central problem of difference. This issue is best understood by contrasting my conception of autonomy with the traditional rational agency. By excising the body and affect from the essence of the rights-bearing self, the multiplicity of differences among people is removed as well.[44] Conversely, when the conceptions of reason and autonomy have the body and affect integrated into them, the differences that both make manifest become central. The realities of differences in abilities and in emotional states—as well as the relational differences of power and status—are no longer presumed to be marginal to the issues of equal rights; they appear as integral to the full particularity of the subject of those rights.

Conceptions of the core capacities—such as reason and autonomy—that affirm difference are crucial because figuring out the appropriate role of difference in conceptualizing and promoting equality is one of the central challenges everywhere that people take rights seriously. To note just a few examples, one sees these challenges in the disputes over affirmative action in North America, in the interpretations of gender equality in Lebanon, and in South Africa, where the postapartheid government must grapple with the tensions that arise from its multiple commitments to equality, to cultural rights, to discerning and respecting customary law, to redressing the wrongs of apartheid and nonracialism.[45]

I turn now to narrow the focus from the meaning and advantages of the concept of the capacity for creative interaction to the particular advantages to law in the relational dimension of the multidimensional self. The narrowing of focus will allow a greater degree of detail. I use the issue of responsibility discussed above in the context of the complex problem of assigning legal responsibility. I discuss an extended example of a legal problem to show in detail how bringing a relational approach to autonomy both improves and complicates legal analysis of responsibility.

IV. RELATIONAL AUTONOMY AND RESPONSIBILITY: CONTRIBUTIONS TO LAW

A relational conception complicates the concept of autonomy. And this leads to complications in the conception of responsibility as well. Just as the relational approach offers better conceptual tools for understanding and fostering autonomy, it also offers a better way of thinking about difficult problems of how to assign responsibility. But it does make the analysis more complex and places new demands on institutions, such as the judiciary, that are accustomed to relying on conventional liberal understandings of autonomy and responsibility. In this section I will use the legal issue of women who kill their battering partners to show the ways in which the dominant conception of autonomy has hindered the capacity of the legal system to adequately respond to this issue. It also shows the promise and challenges of using a relational approach.

As we have seen, people's actual capacities for autonomy will vary enormously both across individuals and within a given person across time and across different spheres of one's life. Autonomy is thus not a given on the basis of which we can (appropriately) assign responsibility for action. Moreover, autonomy is not something that has an on/off quality: either a person has it and is responsible or doesn't have it (e.g., she is insane) and isn't responsible. Autonomy will be experienced on a continuum. Thus it is important to inquire carefully, not only prospectively into what will foster autonomy but also retrospectively into the kind of autonomy, say, a particular accused woman had and why. The difficult reality for everyone is that we cannot control all the circumstances that foster or undermine our creative capacities, even though we have a responsibility to optimize them.[46]

To those sympathetic to a relational approach this picture of autonomy as contingent, shifting, and variable may look self-evident. But when we turn to the law, we can see a logic behind treating autonomy as a presumption, something to be ordinarily assumed as a characteristic of human actors. It might appear that the law has to assume autonomy, because it is necessary for all forms of legal responsibility.[47] When a legal system is based on a conception of the person as a rational agent who can be held responsible for his actions, then justice and legitimacy seem to require a link between autonomy and responsibility. This is so for the obvious reason that no just system of law would hold people accountable for actions that were not really "their own."[48] (I elaborate on the philosophical and legal complexities underlying common law approaches to autonomy and responsibility in note 53 of this chapter.) But, again for obvious reasons, the common law does not require that judges or juries inquire into all the nuances of what it might mean for an action to be "one's own." Autonomy is presumed unless quite limited exceptions are met.

While legal analysis often uses the term "agency," I think it is fair to say that it is actually autonomy and not just agency that the law usually presumes for the purposes of assigning responsibility. (Remember Sherwin's distinction between agency [the making of a choice] and autonomy [self-governance].[49]) The case of someone actually moving the actor's limbs for her would be a case where there is not even agency. Of course, that is the clearest case for no responsibility, but it is rare. The defense by reason of insanity is a claim that there was no autonomy—the capacity for self-governance was so impaired that there can be no responsibility. The complex issues of duress and provocation also speak to the issue of autonomy—the agent has made choices, exercised agency, but the choices are seen as so constrained that they are not fully autonomous. For provocation, for example, the test traditionally has been words or actions that would cause an ordinary person to lose control such that she or he cannot properly be understood as acting autonomously. They are under the control of the heat of passion or anger (a heat of passion no "normal" person could resist) and thus not fully responsible for their actions.[50]

An example outside criminal law is constructive dismissal, where the agency is clear— the actor has quit her job—but the claim is that the action was effectively forced, not autonomously chosen.[51] One can also see employment regulation, such as minimum wage and maximum hours, as a judgment that, absent such legislation, the unequal bargaining power of employers will in many cases yield contracts in which the employees exercise agency but not genuine autonomy. The law should thus not allow people to bind themselves to contracts (to which the law would then hold them responsible) when effective coercion prevents autonomous action. Or put the other way around, the law should not allow people to use the (legally backed) freedom to contract to extract agreements that are not autonomously given. (Indeed one might say that the debates over all such "paternalistic" legislation are about what really promotes autonomy: choice in the face of unequal bargaining power or mandatory constraints on the terms of the bargain.[52])

In sum, then, the law recognizes exceptions to and constraints on autonomy, but unless one can show that one falls within one of the exceptions, autonomy will be assumed for the purposes of assigning responsibility. If there is to be a more nuanced, contingent, and spectrum-like quality to autonomy based on a relational approach, the law will be faced with a vastly more complicated question of assigning responsibility.[53]

A. The Example of Women Who Kill Their Battering Partners

If the issue of legal responsibility reveals a kind of logic to the presumption of autonomy, it also reveals the problems with both assuming autonomy and trying to apply a more nuanced, relational approach. The contemporary problem of the kinds of responsibility that should be assigned to "battered women" who kill their batterers is a compelling example of both problems. Most defendants in these cases are women who have been in long-standing relationships characterized by physical and psychological abuse by their male partners. The cases usually arise when the partner threatens to kill the woman and she decides she has to kill him before he kills her. In many of these cases, she is able to kill her partner because he is asleep or otherwise unaware of her attack. Thus part of what makes the cases difficult to fit within ordinary self-defense claims is that she does not kill him at the exact moment he is threatening her, but at a time (shortly thereafter) when she has the opportunity to do so relatively safely. This pattern does not fit the legal definition of insanity,[54] and, as already noted, provocation is not a full defense, but a mitigating factor.[55]

Feminist defense lawyers have spent many years trying to assist lawyers, judges, and juries to analyze these cases in ways that will allow a fair trial for the accused women. As Elizabeth Schneider so clearly states, she and other advocates working in this area have never tried to create a "battered woman defense" that would simply apply to any woman who kills her batterer. The particular facts of each case are crucial. What they have tried to do is to overcome some of the conceptual barriers to understanding the cases that exist in both the popular understanding and in the minds of legal professionals. One of those barriers is the presumption of the rational agent and an on/off conception of autonomy. This general conception is exacerbated by long-standing stereotypes about women's autonomy. Thus, as Schneider puts it, there is a victim/agent dichotomy that must be overcome in order for courts to assess fairly the situations these women are in. These women are neither simply agents nor victims; they are both.

Feminist lawyers have, often successfully, worked to have expert testimony admitted about the kind of abuse the accused has suffered and the kinds of damage such long-term abuse can cause. The patterns of damage that have been recognized have often been called the battered women's syndrome. It is characterized by learned helplessness, a feeling of being trapped in the relationship, low self-esteem, and great dependence on the battering partner. This syndrome is said to help account for why women who are in abusive relationships do not leave them. This, in turn, is important so that judges and juries do not discount the stories of abuse as unbelievable—on the assumption that if the abuse had been as bad as she claimed, she would have left.

While it seems to be the case that this expert testimony has made a difference in courts' capacities to understand why a woman might stay in an abusive relationship, the danger has been that the accused woman then comes to be seen simply as a victim. Her agency disappears, even if the facts are that she had made prior efforts to leave and had employed many strategies to protect herself and her children. The passive, helpless victim is a stereotype available for casting the woman as not responsible for her situation or for her actions. Indeed, there are interesting arguments that even the psychological experts who testify in court end up drawing on these stereotypes.[56] Thus the stereotypes and the on/off conception of autonomy collude to provide an apparent solution to the problem of assigning responsibility to a woman in a desperate situation.

But there are a variety of problems with this seeming solution. First, as noted above, it is often factually inaccurate and demeaning to the accused woman. Second, it helps the law perpetuate stereotypes that do not advance the real project of providing equally fair trials to all men and women. And, third, it is often unavailable to women who do not seem to fit the stereotype. Women who have been physically aggressive; women subject to countervailing stereotypes, like some women of color; or women who just don't come across as helpless victims may be unfairly found guilty of murder because they don't fit the categories that judges and juries have come to understand as battered women's syndrome.[57]

In addition, the depiction of the accused woman as so damaged as to not be an agent runs at cross-purposes to the actual structure of the legal argument for self-defense on a murder charge. Although the exact terms of the defense vary by jurisdiction, the basic structure is the same. It is very clear in the *Canadian Criminal Code*.[58] There must have been an illegal assault on the accused (which can include a threat). The accused must have had a reasonable belief that the batterer posed a threat to life or serious bodily harm *and* that she had to use deadly force in order to protect herself from those threats, that there were no other options. Demonstrating the reasonableness of her beliefs and actions is in tension with depicting her as immobilized by learned helplessness. I think that some of the confusion, or unpersuasiveness, of what are seen as being some of the best opinions on these cases comes from this tension.

What is needed is a nuanced, relational conception of autonomy that can make sense of a picture of a woman whose capacity for autonomy has indeed been seriously damaged by an abusive relationship but who is nonetheless capable of reasonable judgments about the nature of the threat she faces and the options she has to protect herself. And, as we shall see, what is needed is a relational approach that looks at not just how personal relationships shape autonomy but also how societal institutions, practices, and beliefs structure relationships in ways that can both damage the capacity for autonomy and call for violent self-defense.

As I read the cases and commentary, it seems to me that the best opinions are characterized by two steps. First, they take seriously the abuse the woman has suffered and the harm it has done to her, and they also make it clear that the fact of her staying in the relationship is not to be seen as evidence against the seriousness of her abuse or of her being viewed as at fault for finding herself in this life-threatening situation. This part of the opinion often seems an appropriate discussion of the ways in which abusive relationships can be destructive of the capacity for autonomy. Second, the courts accept the argument that the woman had acquired a kind of expertise over her long experience with violence and threats at the hands of her partner. Based on this experience, she was able to make a reasonable judgment about the seriousness of the threat. Thus, to this point in the argument, they are at least tacitly acknowledging both impaired autonomy and a capacity for the kind of reasonableness the law requires for self-defense.

I think the problem arises for judges (and probably for most people hearing about these cases) with the reasonableness of killing the batterer during a moment of relative safety—when he was asleep in some of the best known American cases and with a gun-shot to the back of the head as he was leaving the room in *R. v. Lavallee*,[59] the leading Canadian case. It is clear that the legal standard is reasonableness of belief that lethal action was necessary to protect herself. But in *Lavallee*, as we shall see shortly, sometimes the argument is one of reasonableness, and sometimes it slides into a claim of impairment of autonomy. And I think some of the feminist legal commentary blurs these issues as well. This raises the question of how best to think about the kind of responsibility to assign in these cases—remembering, of course, that each case will turn on its particular facts.

What is the underlying reason for thinking that in many cases it is not appropriate to impose criminal sanctions on a woman who takes advantage of a moment of safety to kill her battering partner who has threatened her life? Is it because her autonomy and perhaps her judgment is so impaired that she cannot see the alternatives—leaving the scene, calling the police, going to live someplace else? Is it that at that moment it looks to her, given her long experience of abuse, that the only way to save her life is to kill, even though others without that experience might see alternatives? These seem to me to be arguments that she is not responsible because she did not have the kind of autonomous judgment upon which one can base criminal responsibility. She may well retain partial autonomy, a capacity to protect herself, but not the kind necessary for criminal sanctions. This is an *impairment* argument, even if does not portray the woman simply as a helpless victim.

An alternative account is a true reasonableness argument. The argument would be that on the facts of the case she made a reasonable assessment that if she didn't take advantage of this opportunity to kill her partner he would come after her and kill her. In many cases, there is past evidence of her partner coming after her, sometimes even after she has moved a long distance away. Often beatings follow. In addition to the evidence of a particular pattern within the relationship, there is more general evidence of what has been called "separation assault." The danger of serious injury or death is greatest when the woman is about to leave her batterer.[60]

Both the particular and the general evidence suggest an inability of the police or anyone else to protect the woman against violent assault. Thus if she has correctly (or reasonably) assessed the seriousness of the death threat, then it is reasonable for her to believe that the only way to save her life is to take advantage of the opportunity to kill him. Some of the commentators making this argument point out that (at least in many jurisdictions) self-defense does not require one to leave one's home in order to avoid the threat posed by an illegal intruder.[61] In the case of a woman in a battering relationship, she would often have to leave not just her house but also her province or state. And in many cases there is evidence that even that would not be sufficient. She would have to go into hiding—without the aid of something like a witness protection program. Is that a reasonable alternative? Would it be possible at all if she had children? Are women in this situation being held to standard of reasonableness that is more demanding than that required of others?

On the other hand, as a general matter, the law does not allow one to kill in self-defense on the basis of future risk assessment. Even if one has good reason to believe that another may intend to carry out a threat to his life at some future time, ordinarily that is not grounds for shooting him in the back of the head as he leaves. Why? Presumably because the legal system is structured to require people to seek the help of police rather than to undertake their own protection by killing. The problem, of course, is that in the case of women in battering relationships, the police and others have already failed, usually over many years, to protect her from violence. She has excellent grounds, both particular and general, to believe they will fail again if she misses this opportunity to protect herself.

So how do judges handle this problem? In *Lavallee*, the Supreme Court of Canada explicitly said that the threat does not have to be immanent in the case of a woman accused of killing her battering partner. This was reaffirmed in *R. v. Malott* and follows a variety of feminist arguments that one has to use an expanded time frame to understand the nature of the threat from a battering partner.[62] How do judges explain why they allow what looks like a kind of future risk assessment, why they don't require the woman to seize any alternative to killing? (Of course there are many American cases where judges *do* in effect say that fleeing was the reasonable alternative.) Martha Mahoney offers a succinct distinction between the two different kinds of accounts I noted above: "Learned helplessness is in essence a theory of deficiency at perceiving exit. Separation assault confirms the difficulties of exit."[63] I think both commentators and judges often blur impairment (or deficiency) and true reasonableness (in assessing objective danger).

I reproduce below an extended excerpt from Justice Wilson's judgment in *Lavallee*. In many ways this is an exemplary judgment that makes a strong case for the reasonableness approach and shows a fine sense of the broader social context. But the part on the reasonableness of the accused's perception of her options illustrates, I think, the shifting terms of the argument I have just noted: sometimes it is a true reasonableness argument, and sometimes it is about the impairment of autonomous judgment.

> The same psychological factors that account for a woman's inability to leave a battering relationship may also help to explain why she did not attempt to escape at the moment she perceived her life to be in danger. The following extract from Dr. Shane's testimony on direct examination elucidates this point:
>
> Q. Now, we understand from the evidence that on this night she went—I think you've already described it in your evidence—and hid in the closet?

A. Yes.

Q. Can you tell the jury why she, for instance, would stay in that house if she had this fear? Why wouldn't she so [*sic*] someplace else? Why would she have to hide in the closet in the same house?

A. Well, I think this is a reflection of what I've been talking about, this ongoing psychological process, her own psychology and the relationship, that she felt trapped. There was no out for her, this learned helplessness, if you will, the fact that she felt paralyzed, she felt tyrannized. She felt, although there were obviously no steel fences around, keeping her in, there were steel fences in her mind which created for her an incredible barrier psychologically that prevented her from moving out. Although she had attempted on occasion, she came back in a magnetic sort of a way. And she felt also that she couldn't expect anything more. Not only this learned helplessness about being beaten, beaten, where her motivation is taken away, but her whole sense of herself. She felt this victim mentality, this concentration camp mentality if you will, where she could not see herself be in any other situation except being tyrannized, punished and crucified physically and psychologically.

I emphasize at this juncture that it is not for the jury to pass judgment on the fact that an accused battered woman stayed in the relationship. Still less is it entitled to conclude that she forfeited her right to self-defence for having done so. I would also point out that traditional self-defence doctrine does not require a person to retreat from her home instead of defending herself: *R. v. Antley* (1963), 42 C.R. 384 (Ont. C.A.). A man's home may be his castle but it is also the woman's home even if it seems to her more like a prison in the circumstances.

If, after hearing the evidence (including the expert testimony), the jury is satisfied that the accused had a reasonable apprehension of death or grievous bodily harm and felt incapable of escape, it must ask itself what the "reasonable person" would do in such a situation. The situation of the battered woman as described by Dr. Shane strikes me as somewhat analogous to that of a hostage. If the captor tells her that he will kill her in three days time, is it potentially reasonable for her to seize an opportunity presented on the first day to kill the captor or must she wait until he makes the attempt on the third day? I think the question the jury must ask itself is whether, given the history, circumstances and perceptions of the appellant, her belief that she could not preserve herself from being killed by Rust that night except by killing him first was reasonable. To the extent that expert evidence can assist the jury in making that determination, I would find such testimony to be both relevant and necessary.

Thus we see a clear "impairment" argument from the expert witness followed immediately by the hostage analogy, which seems to be making a reasonableness argument. The hostage analogy does serve to show the complexities of "immanent" danger and why it should not be understood as "immediate" in the context of "battered women." But I find it troubling as a way of accounting for why the accused saw no alternative but to seize the moment and kill. The problem for the hostage is not that if she escapes no one will help her if the hostage takers try to track her down. The problem for the hostage is that she is alone with an armed assailant and the ordinary observer can understand why she should seize a moment to attack her captor. In *Lavallee* there were other people in the house. Lavallee and her common law spouse Kevin Rust had hosted a party at their home that night, and several of the guests were still in the house at the time of the shooting. Earlier in the evening, she told one of the party guests, Herb, that she was in danger of being beaten by Rust; on a separate occasion that evening, she hid behind another friend, Norman Kolish, after Rust had chased her out of the house. Lavallee later recounted to the police: "He said 'wait till everybody leaves, you'll get it then' and he said something to the effect of 'either you kill me or I'll get you' that was what it was. He kind of smiled and then he turned around. I shot him."[64]

Is the suggestion that she felt as trapped as a hostage and thus could see no alternative? If so, was the experience of feeling trapped due to "learned helplessness" or the result of a reasonable assessment of the objective reality of the absence of reliable help? Could it be that the phenomenon identified as "learned helplessness" comes into being only after a long-standing absence of reliable protection against violence?[65] Perhaps it is not just that the personal relation with the batterer "teaches" learned helplessness but also that the structure of social relations—including family, neighbors, police, social workers—fails to protect.

The Canadian Supreme Court has made it clear that in assessing the reasonableness of the accused person's belief (in the threat and that the only option was lethal force) judges and juries should consider what was reasonable from *her* perspective, given her experiences. I am persuaded that this is a good thing in that it fosters the capacities of judges and juries to understand the situation these accused women were in and thus to assess the reasonableness of their actions. It allows judges to make reference to the wider context that might limit a woman's ability to leave an abusive relationship As Justice L'Heureux-Dubé explains in her and Justice McLachlin's concurring judgment in *Malott*, "a judge and jury should be made to appreciate that a battered woman's experiences are both individualized, based on her own history and relationships, as well as shared with other women, within the context of a society and a legal system which has historically undervalued women's experiences."[66] But I think it is also part of what leads to an odd blurring of arguments about incapacity and reasonableness at the very same time that it fails to direct attention to the relation between impaired autonomy and the objective failure of society to provide basic protection against violence.[67]

The focus on the woman's perspective also allows Canadian judges to stop short of saying that battered women often find themselves in situations where the only objectively reasonable way to protect their lives against a future threat is to kill. The reason this future threat has to be treated differently from most future threats is because of a systematic failure to protect these women against violence by all the institutions whose job it is to do so. Thus the hostage analogy seems to help explain why sometimes a future threat requires immediate defensive action (the key hurdle for many judges and juries). But I doubt whether it actually directs our attention to why this is so: systematic societal failure to protect.

Mahoney, however, thinks that the analogy is useful because it can serve to emphasize how coercive force holds battered women in the relationships, making exit unavailable not only in the past but also in the face of an impending death threat (which is the link Wilson was making). I think this link is often not made as clearly as it could be, either in the commentary or the cases. And sometimes not in the expert testimony. That the woman's autonomy has been impaired by the relationship slides into a picture of a woman so victimized that she cannot see the alternatives either to the relationship or to violent self-defense. This is not surprising since this picture is supported not only by the agent/victim dichotomy (as Schneider calls it, or, the on/off conception of autonomy as a presumed human characteristic) but also by the radical challenge of recognizing the extent of the failure of institutions from police[68] to family to prevent the violence.

Mahoney comments that "the persuasive power of the hostage analogy depends on the recognition that the woman in the abusive relationship is not free to leave. At issue is our understanding of the woman's functional autonomy."[69] In the discussion that follows this claim, her focus is concentrated almost exclusively on the realities of external threats and the failure of protection. So, for Mahoney, "functional autonomy" is not primarily about "steel fences in her mind," but external realities.

It would seem that a full understanding of the impact of battering on a woman's autonomy requires attention both to deep psychological impairment—feelings of worthlessness, dependence on the batterer, difficulty in seeing a way out, a profound sense of helplessness—*and* the sorts of coercive force that, absent societal protection, even a fairly conventional understanding of autonomy would see as a serious constraint. It is the "absent societal protection" that I think is the sticking point and why only a broad relational approach that looks at patterns of belief, practices, and structures of institutions can fully make sense of the impact of battering on autonomy.

As I have said, an approach to autonomy that looks to both the influence of personal relationships and societal structures is necessary to understanding the harm that battering does to autonomy and thus to determining the kind of responsibility that should be assigned to women who have killed their batterers. But in at least two different ways, a relational approach poses a major challenge. Initially, I thought that most "battered women" cases were about impaired autonomy and that the reason the discussion of the reasonableness of the self-defense lacked clarity was that judges were ill-equipped to articulate conceptions of partial autonomy—as opposed to an on/off conception.[70] I now think, though, that in most of the leading cases the problem lies in the unwillingness to directly confront the external reality, the institutional failure that makes the woman's actions reasonable. That is a different kind of challenge.

There is thus a kind of irony to the way a relational understanding of autonomy is necessary to an appropriate assignment of responsibility in these cases. Once the nature of the threat and the lack of protection are recognized, the constraints on the woman's autonomous action are easily cognizable within the conventional understandings of autonomy. The objective threat to her life is external, and though the ongoing failure of protection has led to impaired autonomy, the assessment of her options to save her life is reasonable because of the *external* constraints on her actions. And yet these constraints are not easy to see, as is obvious from many judicial opinions. Even when the constraint is an ever present threat of physical violence, backed by the repeated use of violence, which has escalated to a death threat, it is not easily seen as an objective coercive constraint because the key to the power of the coercion lies not in individual action, but in social structures that fail to protect. Thus while physical violence can easily be recognized as an interference with conventional autonomy, the sustained violence, threat, and failure of protection can be fully understood only in relational—both personal and social structural—terms. Once understood, the implications for criminal responsibility are (depending on the facts, of course) relatively straightforward. If there is no reasonable alternative to save her life, she must be seen to have killed in self-defense.

The exception to prohibiting killing on the basis of future risk assessment is justifiable because of society's consistent, long-standing structural failure to provide protection against violence, both in her particular case and in the case of battered women generally. This is, however, such a radical—and frightening—challenge that people are lured back to the "victim" solution, which fits not only stereotypes of women but also the on/off approach to autonomy.

The external threat and lack of protection are always constraints in any issue involving battered women. But in some cases, it may be that it is more the psychological damage that will account for the woman's actions; that is, it is the feeling of being trapped, the "steel fences in her mind," that make her see no alternative—rather than her reasonable assessment of the danger she faces from her partner. Perhaps this still counts as "reasonable from her perspective." But in the long run, I think cases such as these are best treated as cases where the degree of the impairment of autonomy should determine the degree of responsibility. Although I have not looked closely at the issue, I think that cases involving battered women's responsibility to protect their children also pose difficult problems. It seems likely that in many cases a fair assignment of responsibility would require attention both to the external realities—of threat, violence, failure of protection, financial constraints, lack of support, such as housing—and to the impairment of her autonomy caused by the combination of her relationship to the batterer and these societal failures.

Taking impaired (as well as constrained) autonomy seriously would, however, force judges to articulate a conception of autonomy and responsibility that has the shifting contingent quality I discussed earlier. It is easy to see why judges would want to avoid this sort of explicit analysis. As I noted earlier, once one takes a relational approach to autonomy, one sees that people's actual capacity for autonomy varies across a wide continuum. I think very few people could be described as fully autonomous most of the time. How nuanced should the law's understanding be? I have already said that the common law requires autonomy for responsibility and so ordinarily presumes autonomy. If it is not to be presumed, how close an inquiry should it make, or under what circumstances should it not presume? I have not tried to provide full answers to these questions. But the Supreme Court of Canada's approach (however imperfect) to assigning legal responsibility to women who kill their battering partners gives cause for optimism about an evolving capacity to conceptualize both responsibility and autonomy in relational terms.

B. Implications of Relational Analysis for Law

The relational approach offers explicit tools for analyzing the contingent nature of autonomy and thus for inquiring into the actual degree of autonomy an accused was able to exercise. To say that judges should ultimately engage in such an inquiry does not mean that they would have to take up the task "from scratch," unaided and afresh in each case. As with all complex legal concepts, like "reasonableness" or "intention," leading cases on autonomy would come to be identified as capturing key dimensions of the problem and articulating subcategories and concepts that help sort out the nuances. For example, key cases might characterize common points along the continuum of autonomy to serve as examples of benchmarks judges could use. "Battered women's syndrome" might become just one among many terms used to capture common forms of partial autonomy. And cases that offer a full recognition of the reasonableness of a battered women's self-defense could provide an important example of how individual responsibility is sometimes shaped by choices constrained by social failure. Of course, as with "intention" or "duty of care," these cases and categories would not dispense with the need for judges to attend to the particulars of each case and exercise judgment in assessing the kind of autonomy to attribute and thus the kind of responsibility to assign.

Thus I do not mean to imply that an explicit relational analysis makes these cases easy. The assessment of the facts will often be difficult. And there remains the underlying question of what kind of responsibility, if any, one thinks women who are battered have to extricate themselves from these destructive relationships. Part of the point here is that legal and personal responsibility need not be identical (as they often are not). As I said at the beginning of this section, people have a responsibility to try to optimize their response to the circumstances that affect their capacities for autonomy, even though they often cannot control those circumstances. In the case of battered women, I would suggest that there is a personal responsibility to try to leave or transform destructive relationships, but the exercise of that responsibility is so complex and so dependent on circumstances and support beyond the control of the individual woman that the law should not (as Canadian law does not) try to assign any fault for being in a battering relationship.

Battering is a social phenomenon (otherwise the courts would not have been able to recognize a battered women's *syndrome*) that has been sustained by patterns of behavior by police, prosecutors, judges, neighbors, friends, and family, which together constitute a long-standing failure to protect women from intimate partner violence (and, indeed,

violence generally). It is possible for women to become enmeshed in abusive relationships
only because of a wide set of institutions, behaviors, and beliefs that are beyond the control of any individual woman. The attention to the social structure of relationships keeps
this larger framework in view and thus helps to make clear why, for *legal* purposes, there
can be no individual responsibility for being in a battering relationship.

In the interest of full disclosure, I should note that there are some troubling historical
examples of judges venturing into what one might call a relational approach to vary the
presumptions of autonomy. They have often not served women's interests well. Of course,
notoriously, married women were once thought not to have the kind of autonomy
necessary to enter into contracts and hold property. Their relationships with their husbands essentially extinguished their legal autonomy in many areas. But there are also less
obvious examples.

Until quite recently, in many common law jurisdictions men who walked in on their
wives having sex with a lover could kill the lover and/or wife with legal impunity.[71] This
was treated as a classic example of losing control in the heat of the moment, though it also
had strong residue of an honor component. But Hendrik Hartog has documented an
interesting variant of that doctrine in the mid-nineteenth-century United States in cases in
which there was a long gap in time between a husband finding out about an affair and
deliberately killing his wife's lover.[72] The judges were explicit that given the changing norms
and increased freedom for women, the doctrine should accommodate this time gap in
order to protect the sanctity of the home and the honor and authority of husbands.

In these cases, the judges saw a need to provide what we might call a contextual or
relational account of autonomy. The husband's autonomy and thus responsibility could
be assessed only by taking into account both the circumstances of his own relations to his
wife and the man he murdered and the broader social circumstances that required legal
immunity for revenge on "seducers." In constructing the extension of the defense, judges
created what might be seen as an exculpatory impairment of the husband's autonomy—
he was driven to do what any decent, responsible husband would do—and a corresponding
denial of the wife's autonomous choice to engage in the affair in order to emphasize the
nefarious role of the seducer preying upon the wife. It seems as though, as with the excul-
pation of the battered wife, the situation here is an inchoate mix of impaired autonomy
and what was seen, in the context, as rational behavior.

The reasons for such a mix may best be understood in historical context. Hartog's
nineteenth-century innovation may be a kind of hybrid of our modern autonomy based
notions of responsibility and an older conception of justification. Nicola Lacey argues
that

> long standing defenses which would today be interpreted in largely psychological
> terms, and which even abut on mental incapacity defenses, had a very different
> meaning in their original context. The classic example here ... is that of provocation,
> which in early modern criminal law constituted not an excuse based on loss of

self-control but a partial justification of homicide, which was rooted in a distinctively gendered system of honour.[73]

Cynthia Lee shows that in some places in the United States such honor-based justifications lasted well into the twentieth century: "A husband's observation of his wife in the act of adultery was thought to be such a grievous injury and affront to the husband that several states, including Georgia, Texas, Utah, and New Mexico deemed the husband's killing of an adulterous wife or her lover a justifiable homicide—not a crime at all."[74] Thus here, too, provocation of the wronged husband was sometimes understood as loss of control in the heat of passion (impaired autonomy)[75] and sometimes as justification—a context in which a rational agent could reasonably act to kill.

Ought this sort of story make one wary of invitations to judges to move beyond a simple presumption or denial of autonomy? Once they move beyond the on/off framework, are they likely to import stereotypes into what is supposed to be nuance? As we have seen, this has been part of the history of the battered woman defense, and it was part of what might be called the wronged husband defense.[76] Are these reasons why one would think that the path to a more egalitarian law, that is, to a law that lives up to its own equality norms,[77] is to see the legal subject not as the multidimensional self, but as the abstracted, disembodied, rational agent I have been criticizing?[78] Would the move to a recognition of the multidimensional self and the relational nature of autonomy just invite greater latitude for judges and thus more room for stereotypes and prejudice?

First one needs to recognize that the norm of the rational agent has not prevented the active role of stereotypes in the law.[79] Indeed, the concept of reasonableness itself has been a vehicle for stereotypes, such as different standards of care for the "reasonable boy" and the "reasonable girl."[80] But would a more vigorous adherence to the traditional concept of the rational agent work better than an avowed departure? Whenever judges are called upon to be self-conscious about the kinds of contextual factors that influence their judgment, some people worry that this will free them from constraints that, however poorly they work, are better than an open invitation to let personal values and ideologies guide their judgments. There is something to this position. When long-standing norms of judgment shift, an opening always results, and not everything that goes through it will advance the goals of a just and fair legal system. Certainly, the invocation of "social context" or a relational approach cannot itself guarantee outcomes that advance equality.

My view remains, however, that self-consciousness about what is entailed in optimal decision making is, in the long run, desirable. In the case of autonomy, judges will do a better job of developing just law if they are able to take a more nuanced view of the capacities of those who appear before them. And that nuance will be assisted by understanding the relational (as well as embodied and affective) dimensions of the legal subjects before them. In the absence of such nuance, they cannot assign responsibility in a just and coherent way. For example, as we saw in the cases of women killing their battering partners, an understanding of the scope of her autonomy and of the reasonableness of her decision to kill requires an understanding of her relationships, both personal and social–structural. Sometimes, when there are known dangers of stereotypes influencing judgment, legislation can direct and structure the discretion that judges exercise.[81] It is possible, for example, that legislation would be the best way to handle the issue of the self-defense for women who kill their batterers.

In the meantime, one can applaud the Supreme Court of Canada's tacit recognition of relational autonomy in these cases as well as an imperfect recognition of the reasonableness of battered women's acts of self-defense. They went beyond an on/off approach to autonomy by recognizing both impaired autonomy and a capacity for rational assessment of threat and options for self-defense. Both Wilson and L'Heureux-Dubé point to the broader structures of social relations that enable battering to both constrain and impair women's autonomy—even though they are not fully explicit about how societal failure to protect can make killing in the face of future threat "reasonable." And, finally, in *Malott*, L'Heureux-Dubé explicitly addresses the need to avoid stereotypes in the analysis of these cases. The Supreme Court of Canada takes important steps toward assigning responsibility on the basis of a relational approach to autonomy, and, in my view, these cases and the issue more generally show both the advantages of a relational approach for addressing difficult issues of legal responsibility and the scope of the challenges posed by such an approach.

V. EQUALITY AND THE MULTIDIMENSIONAL SELF

I return now to the full dimensions of the self—particular, embodied, affective, and relational—and to the conceptual problem I posed earlier in the chapter: on what is the idea of inherent equality based? Can the multidimensional self and its capacity for creative interaction replace rational agency as the ground for equality?

Let me begin with my earlier claim that we need both formal equality and attention to context and particularity in order to implement rights equally. I argued that the problem with rational agency was that it was somewhere in between the purely formal and the substantive context: it was treated as an abstraction that rendered it universal, but it made substantive claims about what was relevant to being a bearer of rights. Historically, the asserted universal abstraction in fact had a particular substance to it that was associated with middle- and upper-class white men. Not only did the concept of rational agency exclude the body and affect, but the political and legal systems premised on that concept excluded those people associated with the rejected dimensions of humanness. Thus, at different times, the working class, women, and racialized people have been treated as so characterized by uncontrolled passions, or limited intellect, or dependency—and thus lacking in autonomous rational agency—that they cannot be treated as equal responsible members of society entitled to the same civil and political rights as white men of property.

Of course, one response to this allegation is that the mistake was only to fail to give women and other subordinated groups the status of disembodied rational agents. If we now apply that concept to the previously excluded groups, so the argument goes, there is no need to change the concept. I think the limitations of that answer must now be clear. First, there is the issue that when obvious dimensions of humanness are excluded from the paradigm of the legal–political subject, they must go somewhere else—as indeed historically they have in their attribution to subordinated groups.

Second, the problems could not be overcome even if it were possible to imagine a kind of bifurcation in which all people were thought of as traditional rational agents for the purposes of, say, public deliberation and as embodied, emotional human beings when in intimate relations in the privacy of the home. Not only does the question arise of how rights are to be constructed differently in the two realms, but the fundamental objection of my arguments above cannot be met in this way. If all of our basic capacities for forming our life plans and adopting values, the kinds of capacities that rational agency was intended to capture, cannot be adequately understood without a full understanding of our relational, embodied, emotional and interactively creative nature, then no amount of "inclusion" in traditional rational agency will provide an adequate framework for rights or law.

The question remains, can my conception of the creative self avoid the problems caused by universalistic claims for rational agency? Earlier I argued that substantive claims for rational agency did damage by departing from the pure formality of the claim of equal moral worth. The nature of their substance became the grounds for exclusion. The concept of autonomy as part of creative interaction (inherently relational and embodied) is substantive. It makes empirical rather than purely formal claims about human capacities. Can it serve the grounding function traditionally assigned to rational agency—without the exclusion? In other words, does it make sense to say that people are equal and entitled to rights *because* they all have the capacity for creative interaction? It is true that this capacity does not have the same kind of exclusionary quality as traditional rational agency because creative interaction offers a fuller picture of the core human capacities. There are not obvious dimensions of humanness, such as emotion and embodiedness, that are pushed to the periphery. Nevertheless, I have come to the conclusion that some of the same problems would still arise.

For years the claim of rational agency as the foundation for claims to human dignity, respect, and rights seemed implausible to me because there are so many human beings who are not rational agents: babies, the insane, those who are senile. And yet there is no question[82] that they are entitled to basic claims of equal moral worth, even if we differentiate between the civil and political rights they can claim. The explanation that babies have the potential for rational agency or that the senile have some kind of residual claim because they were once rational agents seemed completely unpersuasive if rational agency was supposed to be the ground for rights claims. If rational agency is truly the *basis* for equal moral worth, then those who do not have it lose their equal status. The capacity for creative interaction is broader and more flexible. Certainly even newborns have it, and any state of impaired capacity allows for some form of creative interaction.

Nevertheless, there are variations within the actual capacities for creation as well as within the role of autonomy in those capacities that arise not only with age and infirmity but also with the conditions of people's lives. It is a basic part of my conception of autonomy that it is not static, that it requires constructive relationships, and that throughout one's life it can wither or thrive depending both on the kinds of initiatives one takes and on the conditions one finds oneself in. Given this variation, my conception of autonomy cannot be the core grounding of claims for rights: the core claim of equal moral worth does not vary; autonomy does. Autonomy as part of creative interaction is an improvement over traditional rational agency in many ways. But both are substantive, empirical concepts whose variation among human beings means that neither can ground a universal claim of equality.

For this reason I have come to the conclusion that there is no substitute for a purely formal claim of equal moral worth of all human beings. It should be treated as a kind of starting point, an article of faith, for which one might advance arguments but which is not really subject to proof since it is not ultimately an empirical claim about any actual characteristics of human beings.[83] Despite its purely formal quality, I see a belief in, a commitment to, the inherent equality of all human beings as a necessary (but not sufficient) condition for creating relations of equality and for using rights claims to do so. As long as claims of inherent equality are contested, the battle must be for recognition of equality in those terms.[84]

Once equal moral worth is acknowledged, however, it is essential to move to an understanding of actual human capacities and the conditions under which they can develop. To know what it would take to actually treat someone equally, one needs not only an optimal conception of the human self but also knowledge of the specific characteristics and circumstances of the person—the dimension of the particular. That is, one must start with equal moral worth and then move to attend to specifics and context, where one will encounter the complexities of difference.

How difference is acknowledged and attended to will vary in different circumstances. Where the acceptance of equal moral worth is in doubt or is fragile, it may be that both legal and political rhetoric must emphasize this universal form of equality. For example, the insistence on nonracialism[85] and suspicion of the North American rhetoric of difference held by many in South Africa is surely the result of their recent emergence from the long era of apartheid. But in their attempts to ensure both gender equality and respect for cultural tradition, the Constitutional Court has had to grapple with the problems of when attention to different circumstances requires different measures to ensure equality.[86]

Of course, one of the problems is that those who effectively deny equal moral worth often do so in the name of salient difference. They may say they accept some basic equality but also that it does not translate into equal civil or political rights because of some relevant difference. I do not claim that any of my proposals—neither my (relational, affective, embodied) concept of autonomy as part of the capacity for creative interaction nor the two-step approach, from formal equal moral worth to specific, substantive context—can simply solve this problem. Rather I claim that both will help sort out these inevitable conflicts. The purpose of the substantively empty, formal claim of equal moral worth is to serve as a standard, a check, a challenge. It generates useful questions: Can a differential in rights really be reconciled with inherent equality? Is the situation that is being defended in fact consistent with conditions that respect and foster the development of autonomy? Posing these questions also provides an opening to the possibility that there is more than one way, say, to meet the requirements of gender equality. As long as conversation about equal moral worth is possible, one need not leap to the conclusion that every form of gender role differentiation is incompatible with equality—though, almost by definition, gender roles pose a limit to autonomy.[87] When used with openness, respect, and humility, the formal concept of equal moral worth allows the development of shared standards to which justifications of difference can be held at the same time that it fosters an openness to diverse interpretations of equality and other rights.[88]

It is thus the embrace of the formal claim of equality and the attention to the context of social relations that, together, are necessary for an optimal approach to core human values, such as equality and autonomy. My approach to the multidimensional self brings us both.

VI. RIGHTS AND THE MULTIDIMENSIONAL SELF

At the outset I raised the question of why rights in particular need a fully adequate picture of the human subject. I want to close with a response to a defense of more traditional approaches to rights followed by an argument about how attention to embodiment matters to rights.

One might argue that the most important function of rights is to protect people against the worst forms of harm and that, for that purpose, the traditional conception is adequate and, indeed, preferable, since it doesn't muddy the waters with a seemingly endless array of conditions and issues that might affect something as amorphous as a capacity for creative interaction. One of the important functions of rights is rhetorical, to articulate wrongs in the strongest possible terms, which can command the attention of others. At one level, standard legal concepts of bodily integrity and prohibitions, such as those against torture, do serve the purpose of identifying basic harms. At another level, the capacity of a legal and political system to recognize violations of rights does not lie only with the adequacy of legal concepts, such as of assault. We have seen this in the history of legal and political response to egregious bodily harm done to women by their husbands. The same issue of "privately" perpetrated harm continues to arise in the issue of what kinds of dangers are recognized for the purpose of refugee status.

Everything turns on what enables those in power to *see* bodily harm and interpret it as a violation of a right. For these crucial purposes a full and relational conception of the self will help.[89] When the conception of the self directs our attention to the relations in which it is embedded and the degree to which they foster such key values as autonomy, security, and bodily integrity, then the salience of "private" relations becomes obvious. Of course, one should not underestimate the power of willful blindness to harms done to subordinate groups. But a conceptual framework that always directs our attention to context, to the structures of relation that form the conditions for the realization of rights, is less likely to allow any set of social relations to fall beyond the purview of scrutiny for rights violations.

Similarly, there are issues of persuasion and complex problems of interpretation in different cultural settings. If the invocation of rights is to serve its rhetorical, political purpose of getting people to stop their abuses, the nature of the claim of right must be heard to show some sensitivity to the context. To discern the difference, for example, between child labor as part of a family enterprise that interferes with but does not preclude education, on the one hand, and indentured servitude, on the other hand, it will help to have a framework of rights analysis that is well suited to examining the structures of relationship that foster or undermine basic values like autonomy. In general, the puzzles or seeming dilemmas of debates surrounding human rights versus respect for cultural autonomy are best explored in relational terms that see human beings as embodied, endowed with affect, and capable of creative interaction.

I turn now to a final focus on the embodied dimension of the multidimensional self and what it brings to our understanding of rights. First I want to suggest that one of the virtues of making embodiment central to the image of the human subject of rights is that it might generate a different stance toward physical caretaking. The disdain with which virtually all aspects of physical caretaking are held in North America is part of the general disregard of the body. Not only would the full integration of embodiment into the legal subject help to shift this general destructive stance; it would also help in attending to a wide variety of public policy issues. For example, I think attending to the kinds of relationships that foster autonomy and dignity for the embodied self would lead to a recognition of the irreplaceable connection created by physical caretaking. Not only nursing infants, but the connection that comes from changing their diapers and spoon-feeding a sick loved one are examples. The importance of a loving touch for all those requiring physical care is another example. This kind of recognition would shape how one thought about such issues as the length of maternity leave, flexibility for nursing working mothers, or leave for the care of sick family members or even friends. Decisions about whether such policies should be legal entitlements or left to the discretion of the employer would be shaped by one's sense of the relation such caretaking had to autonomy and dignity, of the person in need of care as well as the one doing the caretaking.

The issue of physical caretaking also links back to the relational dimension of autonomy and its rejection of independence as the essence of autonomy. With a relational conception that focuses attention on the inevitability of both interdependence and dependence, those who find themselves dependent on the physical care of others are more likely to be able to see themselves as autonomous beings entitled to equality and dignity. Similarly they are more likely to be seen and treated by others as people whose autonomy and preferences are to be respected.

I also want to note here that simply calling for attention to embodiment can be risky unless it works to transform our collective image of the legal or political subject. Even the term "embodiment" can serve to reinforce a mind–body dichotomy, with the body seen as a "container" for the mind. (In chapter 7 I use the term "bodymind" in order to avoid this dichotomy.) In addition, attention to embodiment only in particular instances can be counterproductive.

The places where people are inclined to attend to the body are just where the status of equality is in question—for example, the now commonplace feminist observation that women are seen as bodies and, thus, not the rational agents who are the true subjects of rights. As I noted earlier, people of color and the laboring classes have historically also been reduced to this status of body. I think something similar may happen with the disabled: the disabled *person* becomes an impaired *body* and invisible as a human subject of rights. It is as though when the body does come to the foreground of attention the subject status recedes. Thus given the dominant norm of the disembodied rational agent, calling attention to embodiment in a context like rights for the disabled will be most effective when it consciously challenges this norm.

I think we see a different form of distorted attention to the body in the realm of human rights violations. When we think of victims of human rights violations, the examples that draw headlines are of extreme bodily harm. The classic images of subjects of rights violations are not the women whose poverty and daily struggle for food for themselves and their children constrain their lives, but the people whose bodies are so emaciated that they make dramatic subjects of photographs. Victims are best seen as dramatically violated bodies. Routine impairment of autonomy that arises from the unmet bodily needs of poverty fits neither the model of the rational agent nor the victim of rights abuses. It falls from view.

So there is a sort of bizarre attention to the body in the context of rights violations, and it is connected to a simplistic engagement with the issue of rights. Here the violated body is recognized as a subject of rights, but the bodily violation comes to define the subject. The voyeuristic fascination with egregious bodily harm does not actually facilitate an engagement with the full dimensions of the people who are harmed and the context of those harms. There is an apparent simplicity: when the harm is dramatically bodily, it appears as an obvious rights violation, which can then simply be "stopped." More obviously complex issues like poverty (despite is bodily consequences) seem not as clearly to entail rights violations—in part because it is obvious that ending it will not be simple.[90] Egregious bodily harm offers the illusion of a simplicity about rights violations—their nature, their cause, their transformation.

How would a thoroughly embodied conception of the human self help with all this? If the imagined subject of law and rights always had a body, one would immediately start asking about which details of the body are relevant to the issue at hand. If such inquiries were routine, the obvious presence of embodiment—say in the pregnant woman or the disabled person—would not stand out as exception to the rational agent who is the normally imagined rights holder. Routine attention to embodiment might also help reveal the tacit presumptions of maleness in the "standard" legal subject. If the human subject of law were always seen as embodied, these subjects would be seen as encountering one another not as abstracted rational agents with conflicting wills, but as three-dimensional humans embodying bodily needs and desires characterized by interdependence as well as difference in their particularity. A routine engagement with embodiment could shift the pattern I described above of the subject status receding as the body comes to the foreground.

Such a routine engagement might also shift the preoccupation with egregious bodily harm as paradigmatic of rights violations. The complex harms of poverty would be more easily recognized. When attending to the embodied subject, one can see the way routine nutritional deprivation has links to security versus anxiety, to autonomy versus constraint, to good versus impaired judgment about one's choices and the means of exercising them. In this example, the embodied subject is also then a subject whose affect, such as chronic anxiety, is linked to bodily need, to cognitive capacity, and to the structural relations that generate the poverty. For the multidimensional self, the rights violations of poverty stand out.

The embodied subject thus offers an alternative to the rational agent as the subject of rights, one that combines the universal and the particular in just the way necessary for my two-stage approach to equality (to which I will turn in a moment). We can see embodiment as a part of a universal commonality, a part of the equality all humans share with one another but one that immediately turns our attention to particularity, difference, and context. All humans have bodies, and each of these bodies is unique. Earlier I emphasized that attention to embodiment highlights difference in a way that requires it to be central rather than peripheral to law and rights. Here we see the same claim turned the other way: our differently particular bodies are a universal we share. But this is a universal that calls attention to difference. It is not the universal of Kantian reason, identical not only among humans but even among angels or any other rational beings.[91] Thus as Anna Grear has put it, "The human rights subject might emerge from such a perspective as fully embodied—embracing what is most particular and what is most universal about us in one powerful trope."[92]

One could say something similar about the affective and relational dimensions of humanness: they are, in their shifting ways, unique to each of us as well as a universally shared dimension of our humanness.

Let me close with one final example of the way the embodied, affective, and relational self can shift our understanding of rights. At a conference on rights, I raised the question of the costs of removing the impediments that are often the source of the disabilities suffered by those with differently abled bodies. Maria Grahn-Farley offered the compelling story of a former fellow law student in Sweden who was quadriplegic. The student was entitled to four attendants who, on a rotational basis, cared for her twenty-four hours a day so that she was able to attend law school and did not have to rely on her family for care. Professor Grahn-Farley noted that studies showed that the cost to taxpayers of such provisions was very small. (Presumably because there are relatively few such cases.) But more importantly, she articulated the relational implications of such collective responsibility for bodily needs. Seeing the care this student receives reassures her fellow citizens that if they or their family members should have an accident that renders them incapacitated, or should they bear a child with such physical limitations, collective care would be forthcoming.

It is difficult to calculate the way such confidence would shape one's sense of security, one's sense of whether the world is a safe and caring place in which to venture forth with one's life plans. The contribution of this understanding of the rights of the disabled is not just to the disabled who are no longer relegated to the margins of society—and often to poverty and poor health. This kind of equality reduces fear and anxiety (however unconscious most of the time) for everyone, enhancing relations of autonomy, security, and dignity for everyone in the society. Calculations of costs and benefits for individual rational agents would probably miss this contribution. By contrast, the multidimensional self draws our attention to: how our core values are shaped by and manifested in relationships; how our bodies are connected to such feelings as security; and how those feelings, in turn, are connected to our capacities for judgment and autonomy. This is a better framework for thinking about rights.

Finally, let me just note two further examples of rights issues that a fuller conception of the human subject would help us understand. The much-debated issues of citizenship and the rights and duties of membership are issues where claims of universal equality meet the special demands of the bonds that hold societies together. I do not suggest that the image of the subject I have outlined here would offer any simple solutions. But were all the deliberations on the issues based on an ongoing inquiry into how structures of relationships shape human capacities, including those we closely associate with rights, such as autonomy, I think we would be better equipped to reflect on these hard questions. If conventional rights analysis remains distant from this approach, there will always be a kind of disjuncture between rights discourse and political or sociological arguments about social cohesion.

Another example is the issue of the constitutional status of social and economic rights. I just want to suggest that the stance toward these issues might be different if the subject people had in mind really were embodied. The material conditions that make the exercise of rights possible may seem more central when the essence of the rights holder is not disembodied rationality.

VII. CONCLUSION

In sum, then, the full dimensions of the self—including particularity, embodiment, the role of affect in cognitive capacities, and the ways in which relationships constitute selves and enable capacities—are necessary for identifying and institutionalizing the rights people are entitled to. These dimensions of selfhood cannot simply be relegated to other spheres of inquiry, because we cannot optimally understand what fosters core values, such as autonomy, without understanding the role of body, affect, and relationship in the development of human capacities. If rights are to effectively articulate these values and serve to promote and protect them, our legal and political institutions must be designed with multidimensional selves in mind, in all their diverse particularity. Thus, the traditionally abstracted, disembodied rational agent should no longer be the model of the legal and political subject.

Reason will remain an important dimension of humanness, but it will no longer be seen in opposition to affect. The human capacity for reason will be seen as integrally connected to the body and to affect. Reason continues to play an important role in people's capacity to choose their values and to live in accordance with them. But this capacity for autonomy will be seen not as a matter of independence or control, but as part of the wider capacity for creative interaction, including self-creation. This capacity will be understood as inseparable from the relations that enable and sustain it—even as those relations are themselves the subjects of creative interaction.

When the law uses this wider, relational conception of autonomy, it can better assess the kinds of responsibility that should be assigned. Opening the conceptions of both autonomy and responsibility to variability and contingency poses formidable challenges to legal reasoning. But these challenges can be accommodated within the common law's vast capacity to develop complex, general concepts from the particularities of cases. The reward for taking on these challenges is a greater capacity to live up to the legal ideals of equality and justice.

The idea of the multidimensional self that I have laid out in this chapter rejects the abstraction of the rational agent. It does not, however, reject the need for a purely formal commitment to human equality. On the contrary, by acknowledging the need for a two-step approach to equality—a commitment to inherent (formal) equality together with an inquiry into the specific, substantive context necessary to give reality to that equality—this approach avoids grounding equality in any empirical, and thus necessarily variable, human characteristic.

The result, I claim, is a conception of autonomy and the multidimensional self that will aid in the analysis of the many complex and highly contested debates around rights that characterize the contemporary legal and political world.

CODA

There is a boundary-like exclusion in the argument above about equality. The "capacity for creative interaction" is, of course, not something unique to human beings. Everything living has it. Since I have not based my claim to inherent *human* equality on this capacity, the problem is not a literal inconsistency. But I have offered no justification so far for (tacitly) excluding animals (and other life-forms) by drawing a line around human beings as the subjects of my inquiry.

Such a boundary is not really compatible with a relational mode of thinking. Below I sketch the framework of what I see as an optimal approach, give some sense of the perspective a relational approach offers, and then an account of why I nevertheless accept a linguistic compromise: I use the language of inherent equality with respect to humans (to guide human-human relations) and the language of incalculable, intrinsic worth for other entities as a starting point for the project of figuring out what would constitute respectful and responsible relations with the wide array of other entities with which we share the earth, and the universe.

A fully adequate framework for analysis of moral, political and legal issues will do (at least) two things: (1) it will articulate and foster the basic equality of all human beings and (2), at the same time, express and foster a respect and concern for the vast diversity of other life-forms (indeed all other forms of matter and energy). This is a challenging task because the traditional ways of articulating human equality have expressly or indirectly drawn a circle around humanity, excluding the nonhuman from equal ethical concern. One can see this directly in the many arguments that treat what is distinctive about humans as the basis for entitlement to rights and to respect and concern from others. Even when that argument is not explicitly articulated, the almost ubiquitous focus in the liberal tradition on rational agency as the ground of entitlement and respect is a tacit exclusion of nonhuman animals and, of course, of other entities with whom we share the planet (and the universe).[93]

Sometimes there is an acknowledgment of the moral significance of the pain and suffering of animals, but they are largely treated as objects without claims of their own. And even those concerned about animal rights are often willing to ignore the possibility that entities that the English language labels inanimate may have claims[94] upon us. The language of stewardship sometimes found in Christian environmentalism often calls for human responsibilities to care for the earth but without trying to ground them in such claims. (The writings of aboriginal scholars are an important exception. Although they generally use the language of responsibility, there is usually a strong sense that the animals and the earth have a claim upon the humans to live up to that responsibility.[95]) It may be that the language of responsibility is better suited to these issues than it is to the language of rights or claims of entitlement. Still, it is striking that the protection of human values sounds in the language of claims of entitlement that (in principle) *must* be met, while human relations with the nonhuman call forth mere exhortations to responsibility.

Part of the puzzle of integrating equality for all humans with respect and concern for all other entities is that equality denies hierarchy while it is exactly hierarchy that has defined the relations between humans and other life-forms. To virtually anyone schooled in Western political thought, it is self-evident that if one were interested enough to ask about the proper relations between humanity and our fellow creatures, the answer would not be equality. No one (in this tradition) seriously thinks that the life of a mosquito has equal moral worth with that of even the most cognitively limited human being—whether infant, senile, insane or comatose.

When I first started thinking about the ways in which my arguments for the intrinsic, purely formal, equal moral worth of human beings ended up replicating the traditional exclusionary circle around humans, I found this puzzle of hierarchy insurmountable. I could only frame the question of inclusion as a question of how to rank order those included. At some point, I remembered Carol Gilligan's analysis of the differences between eleven-year-old Jake and Amy's response to Kohlberg's problem of whether Heinz should steal the drug his wife needed to live, which he couldn't afford to buy.[96] Jake had a neat calculation of hierarchy: the right to life ranks higher than the right to property so it's all right to steal the drug. Amy, to the increasing frustration of her interviewer, kept trying to think about how the relationships might be shifted through dialogue and contact so that the dilemma would be transformed rather than "solved." (If the druggist met the people, understood the problem, he might give them the drug.) Like Jake, I kept puzzling over the rank order of hierarchy. (Even though I could also see that this could not yield a solution to the puzzle of wise relations.)

Finally, inspired by Amy, I realized that the contribution of my relational approach to this problem of inclusion could not come from figuring out a rank ordering among different life-forms. Amy kept trying to tell her interviewer that he was asking the wrong question (while, with increasing impatience, he kept trying to get her to answer it). The most important ethical question is not how to choose between two bad options, but how to change the situation (often by restructuring the relations) so that those are no longer the only options. If the question is how one is to rank order different life-forms to create a hierarchy of their claims to moral consideration, which can be used to solve moral dilemmas of bad options, the relational approach does not have much to offer. One *could* try to rank order different entities' capacities for creative interaction. Or order them by the kinds of bonds humans can form with them. But I don't think that would tell us much or not much that we couldn't already know from conventional approaches based on the degree to which other entities are similar to humans—whether in ability to experience pain, cognitive abilities, or social relations.[97]

The relational approach would ask how human actions are currently structuring patterns of relations among the diverse entities of our world and where these can be easily identified as harmful. Perhaps often the first step would be to try to reduce our impact in those areas. The project would be to try to discern how human action could have as positive (or as minimal) an impact as possible while fostering wise relations between humans (both individuals and in the aggregate) and the other entities, broadly conceived. Similarly, one would ask how these relations are setting up what people currently experience as difficult choices (such as cheap food through cruel and perhaps environmentally unsustainable factory farming of animals). It is a large task to understand what all the relevant values should be and what will foster them. This book will not do that work.

Nevertheless, I want to frame my inquiries into an intrahuman relational approach by insisting, as I said, that relations with the other entities in our environment are equally important. The most obvious reason why this is so is a human-centric understanding of the nature of our relations with our environment: if we don't understand those relations, we will destroy our environment rendering it unable to support human life and taking a very large number of other life-forms with us. Yet even with this limited starting point, it seems at least possible to me that the process of discernment of wise relations with our environment will be inadequate if it is driven entirely by instrumental reasoning, that is, by asking only the question what is good for humans. Even if that is all one cared about, I think it is likely that a full understanding and good judgment (about difficult choices) will best be fostered by a sense of care, concern, and respect for the nonhuman entities with which we live. Insight into the complex web of interdependence that characterizes human interaction with our environment (as with each other) will be fostered by the kind of attentiveness and responsiveness that comes from care and respect, and is much less likely to be yielded by objective, instrumental reasoning that treats the rest of the world (universe) as objects to serve the needs and pleasures of humans. (We are already littering space with our trash, so earth is not a sufficient framework.)

Another human-centric, but still important argument is that I think the violence and suffering of slaughterhouses harms all of us, just as ignoring the violence and suffering in prisons does or the pain and hunger of the homeless (as I argued in chapter 1). When people know that suffering but pretend not to, they repress pain, foster ignorance, and construct their lives around illusion. Everyone who eats meat produced in factory farms is complicit, and yet most people pretend they are not routinely sustaining an unjustifiably violent practice. In this sense, I think human beings cannot stand in wise relations with each other or with themselves when they tacitly support factory farming or the current prison practices.

I believe that when we live surrounded by violence, we do violence to ourselves. When we engage in routine consumption practices that are unsustainable, we tacitly deny the equality of our descendents as well as those who suffer malnutrition in the (removed) face of opulence.

The relationships that urgently need restructuring include relationships with animals and the vast variety of entities with which we share the planet (and the universe). I do not think there can be optimal human–human relationships—that foster and manifest such core human values as equality, dignity, security, harmony, or autonomy—in the context of violent disregard for our relations with the nonhuman world.

Habits of relational thinking cannot be adequately fostered if they are practiced within unacknowledged and unjustified boundaries of exclusion.[98] Many people now believe that the universal equality claims of the Enlightenment had a more than coincidental relationship with the exclusion and domination practiced through colonization as well as through the subordination of women, people of color, and the laboring classes at home. Even in recent times, as eminent an egalitarian as John Rawls could casually exclude the physically and mentally disabled from the core puzzles of a just society.[99] In similar ways, habits of exclusionary thinking that bracket animals and the earth from questions of the kinds of relationships societies should foster will undermine the very project of a relational approach.

How, then, can I justify the language of equality exclusively for humans?[100] One answer that I do not find acceptable is that the current failure of achieving real equal rights for all humans is so pressing that the question of animals (and other entities) should be set aside until the human problems are redressed. This form of exclusion by postponement is all too familiar. (As recently as 1992, upon hearing that I had been invited to South Africa for a conference on gender, a left-wing friend of mine said, "Surely South Africa has more important things to deal with right now than gender." That 50 percent of the important others he had in mind were women was either invisible or irrelevant.)

My answer is a kind of linguistic compromise, justified in part by the way the language of equality is understood. As I see it, there would be two ways of avoiding the exclusion. First, I could use the language of inherent equality for all entities (not just humans). Second, I could use a language of incalculable, inherent value for each entity (including humans).

I think that to say that there is an inherent equality among humans and all other entities would be confusing. People might think that I am certain (which I am not) that it must always be morally wrong for humans to eat animals. People might think equality must mean that there can be no justification for a human killing a mosquito. The language of equality does not seem a good way to communicate my sense that the relational approach obliges us to try to figure out what *would be* relations of respect and responsibility with the other entities in our world. I think that obligation is in part captured by saying that all entities have an intrinsic and incalculable value.

I also think that it would be awkward and confusing to use an unfamiliar and contested language across human and nonhuman beings by giving up the language of equality in human contexts. The work that I have ascribed to my formal claim of inherent equality among humans would be hard to accomplish with the language of intrinsic value—leaving out the term "equality." It is much easier to get at what I have in mind by saying that gendered practices, for example, must be able to meet the test of consistency with inherent equality than to cast that test as consistency with inherent worth. This is so even though equality does not mean that sameness and some kinds of different treatment (affirmative action, efforts to accommodate nursing mothers) *will* meet the test of inherent equality.

I think the "work" that a formal claim of inherent, incalculable value does for other entities is that human well-being cannot simply be used as an automatic trump. To explore what respectful, responsible relations consist in cannot be answered simply by saying that a given practice has significant benefit to humans. As with the formal claim of human equality, the difficult judgments about what respect means in practice will have to be worked out in detailed context.

Western political and legal thought is in its infancy in doing this work and in figuring out what an optimal conceptual framework for it would be. I think it is possible that "dignity" may prove to be a concept that can bridge the gulf I just noted between language for intrahuman relations and language for human relations with other entities.[101] It might ultimately allow for the consistency test I currently base on the language of equality. But, at this juncture in Anglo-American history, I think equality carries a force in the direction of wise relations among humans that intrinsic worth cannot. Despite the deep disagreement about what equality should mean in practice, there is a high level of consensus that all human beings are inherently equal. This consensus supplies some leverage in instances of manifest failure, such as child poverty.

There is virtually no consensus about the obligation even to figure out what human responsibilities are to nonhuman entities. It is my hope that relational habits of thinking will move people in the direction of taking up that responsibility. My linguistic compromise of restricting my claim of equality to humans may run the risk of impeding that move. But I think the language of human equality is too important to the intrahuman project of this book. When I actually take up the wider task my relational approach entails, I hope to do better than a compromise.

Women will not be free from violence until they achieve equality with men, and equality cannot be achieved until violence and the threat of violence are eliminated from women's lives.
"VIOLENCE AGAINST WOMEN," Health Canada

Gender-based violence is perhaps the most wide-spread and socially tolerated of human rights violations. It both reflects and reinforces inequities between men and women and compromises the health, dignity, security and autonomy of its victims.
UNITED NATIONS POPULATION FUND (2005)[1]

5

Violence against Women: Challenges to the Liberal State and Relational Feminism

I. INTRODUCTION

One of the uncontested objectives of a liberal regime is the protection of its citizens from violence.[2] Yet the liberal state has failed in this basic task with respect to women and children.[3] If we take this failure seriously, we must rethink the role of the liberal state and the conception of rights optimal for making good on liberalism's most basic aspirations. This rethinking flows from my central claim that violence against women[4] cannot be prevented until the relations between men and women are transformed—which means that transformation of these social and intimate relations must be an objective of the liberal state. A conception of rights that routinely directs our attention to structures of relationships is better suited to facilitate that transformation than one, like the traditional liberal conception, aimed at the protection of boundaries.[5] Yet there is no issue that more powerfully evokes the need for legally protected boundaries than violence.

Thus violence against women poses a challenge not only to liberalism but also to my project of replacing boundaries with relationship as the central organizing concept for rights.[6] My purpose is to take up this challenge to the relational approach in the context of the liberal state's failure on its own terms. I conclude that even in the realm of violence against women, a relational approach best reveals the nature of the problem and potential solutions. This challenge also allows me to further address one of the key anxieties that I think my approach provokes: this sort of relational analysis will lead to a vast expansion of the scope of the state. I will show that in the case of violence against women, no such expansion follows. And we will see why this is also likely to be the case in other areas.

I begin by outlining the genesis of this chapter: my effort to meet the most compelling challenges I think my work on relational feminism has encountered. I then turn to a section on background sources which illuminate my core claim that a relational approach is the optimal way of understanding issues of violence. The heart of my argument takes as its starting point Judith Shklar's fascinating defense of liberalism as the "only system devoted to the project of lessening [cruelty]."[7] Shklar's powerful evocation of the horrors of the fear of cruelty serves as an indictment of societies in which women live in fear. Focusing on rape, I explore the limitations of boundary language to capture the horror of rape and then argue that the cycle of fear and domination can be broken only by transforming relations between men and women.

Shklar's central purpose is, however, to limit the scope of the state, which she sees as the most dangerous source of cruelty. To take on this project of transformation seems to transcend the limits of the state that Shklar advocates. And Shklar is not alone. Most accounts of liberalism (not merely libertarian ones) would see taking on the kind of transformation I have in mind as dangerously enlarging the appropriate scope of the state with vague, open-ended and inevitably contested objectives, thus inviting both intrusion and expanded state power to which no clear limits could be drawn. I use an analogy to Robert Cover's analysis of how violence was integral to racial subordination in the American South to show why rethinking the role of the state is essential to dismantling hierarchies that are embedded in the culture and sustained by "private" violence.[8] In the end, a relational analysis reveals that in the case of sexual assault, what is at stake only appears to be an expansion of the scope of the state. In fact, what is involved is a recognition of the way law currently structures relations between men and women and how that structuring can be changed to reduce violence and improve equality.

II. GENESIS

This chapter reflects my attempt to deal with a worry that I kept pushing aside while working on my project of reconceptualizing various concepts basic to liberalism, such as autonomy and rights. The core of my concern was whether there was something myopically utopian about my effort to use relational feminism to develop new conceptions of rights, law, autonomy, and constitutionalism. These new conceptions were inspired in part by aspirations toward radically different forms of relations among people in which violence and domination do not disappear but play a far less central role in the structure of society.

I take these aspirations to be grounded in an understanding of human beings that is realistic. Indeed, part of my purpose here is to make clear that my conception of human selfhood as constituted by relationship has nothing warm, mushy, or romantic about it. Feminists above all know that the web of relationships in which we exist is not necessarily benign.[9] Nevertheless, I know that I am consistently drawn to the side of feminism that explores the exciting possibilities of transformation rather than the grim realities of people's lives. So I thought it appropriate that I confront some of these realities as a kind of test of my approach. If my reconceptualizations are actually to be useful, something other than a sort of inspirational literature, then they must be able to cope with what is most horrible as well as what is most beautiful and promising about human existence.[10]

More specifically, I want to try to answer a set of critics' questions—some from actual external critics and some from my own voices of unease. The questions that began this project arose primarily in response to my arguments that we should abandon "boundary" as the dominant metaphor in law and to my argument that we should reconceptualize rights in terms of the relationships (of power, trust, responsibility) that rights in fact structure. (I elaborate this reconceptualization in the following chapter.) The questions fall into two groups:

1. Given the violence to which women are subject, don't we need more, stronger boundaries? Isn't the appropriate strategic focus to claim the protection of boundaries, of bodily integrity in particular, which men claim? This question comes most powerfully from students who work in areas of violence against women, such as sexual harassment and sexual assault. The underlying issue is whether my approach can protect us from the truly dark and dangerous forces that manifest themselves in the daily lives of millions of women.

2. Will not the magnitude of responsibility implicit in my approach be overwhelming personally, psychologically, and socially? Will it not end up erasing the divisions of rights, boundaries, and limits that have made freedom and security possible? Doesn't it invite vast intrusion at a collective level such that the scope of the state will be dangerously expanded?

I think these problems are serious. And if they cannot be resolved, then I would have to abandon my project. Nevertheless, I think they must be posed in the context of another question: from what have the traditional forms (both conceptions and institutions) of liberal rights *not* been able to protect us? As I already noted, I have in mind the pervasive and systemic violence against women and the abuse of children,[11] which are now widely recognized as extremely common. Of course, the problem is not that the rights to bodily integrity and security are not recognized by the liberal state. On the contrary, the problem is that despite the primacy accorded these rights in principle, they are not in practice protected for women and children. The challenge then is to understand how prevailing conceptions of rights and the scope of the liberal state have participated in this failure and how an alternative might help.

The violence against women and children is so widespread that it cannot properly be understood simply as a matter of individual pathology or criminality or wickedness. It is a characteristic of our society, and, at least in the case of violence against women, we have a general idea of how it serves to keep a structure of power in place.[12] I will suggest that these evils are best dealt with through the sorts of relational reconceptions I propose. Most importantly, I claim that the very features of my approach that generate the critics' questions are those that make it well suited for tackling these dramatic failures of our current regime of rights.

III. RELATIONAL REFLECTIONS ON VIOLENCE

I want to begin with the sources I used to help me think about this daunting topic. I will start with those I refer to least in the main body of the chapter, for they in particular form a kind of background context for my approach, a way of seeing the relational nature of the violence I address. Susan Griffin's *A Chorus of Stones* is subtitled "The Private Life of War."[13] It is a complex interweaving of stories and reflections ranging from the secrets of her own family, and the silences and disconnection they bred, to Werner von Braun's development of rockets, to Heinrich Himmler's preoccupation with secrets and the sadistic child-rearing practices advocated by a leading child psychologist in the Germany of Himmler's youth. Griffin tells terrifying stories of Hiroshima and the suppression of a report on the safety of nuclear power plants and of the very ordinary lives of those who work in a nuclear weapons plant and the everyday events that led a particular woman to participate in the suppression of the report. Griffin gives us a sense of the anguish of a brutal murderer and of a survivor of the Holocaust. We see patterns of links between individuals' psyches, their families, and their history writ large and small. Griffin manages to convey a vision of the connections between the large-scale horrors of war and the private, often secret, pain of all of us who live in this culture of domination and destruction. This vision is both compelling and illusive.

Griffin does not try to offer neat theoretical synopses of these interconnections which could serve as a framework for my discussion. Her vision serves to remind me of the scope and variety of the violence in our culture, the complexity of its sources, and the means by which it is sustained and perpetuated. Two points matter particularly for my argument here. The first is that though I focus here on conceptions of rights, I am, of course, under no illusion that liberal rights are the essential source of the problem or that simply a better conception of rights will solve it. The second point is that the particular evils I have in mind here are part of a larger pattern. Part of that pattern can crudely be described as patriarchy, in which domination, not just of women by men, is a central dynamic. Now, of course, patriarchy precedes liberal rights and exists in nonliberal regimes. Nevertheless, part of the project is to see how a particular vision of rights fits with a particular conception of the self—which is in turn connected to a long tradition of patriarchy (the demonstration of this last connection is beyond the scope of this book).[14]

It is important to see that we need not make exaggerated claims about the importance of rights in order to draw connections between the forms of conventional liberal rights and the violence they fail to prevent and the larger culture of which both the rights and the violence are an integral part. And this attention to interconnection need not deny that liberal rights regimes have succeeded in protecting many of their people from important forms of violence, brutality, and fear.

Part of the purpose of keeping in mind the broader picture of the culture in which this violence is embedded is to guide the reconceptualization of rights by the broader aspirations for change (while remembering that rights *alone* cannot be the engine for such change). The law will always respond to and reflect the culture as well as have the capacity to shift relations within it.

The violence men perpetrate against women (and, I think, against children as well) must be understood in the context of the destructive gender roles that are central to our psyches.[15] More generally, the violence and pain that are so much a part of our ostensibly safe, civilized North American world must be understood in terms of collective, systemic psychological patterns that take a unique form for each individual yet are comprehensible only in these broader terms.[16] The healing required needs to take place on both the individual and the societal level. If the basic mechanisms of protection, rights, are to be reconceptualized in order to lessen the violence, to be part of a restructuring of the relations between men and women, it should be with the guidance of the most thoughtful approaches we have to the destructive patterns built into gender.

The single most illuminating author I have encountered on these subjects is Marion Woodman, a Jungian analyst who has written widely on the nature of the masculine and the feminine in both men and women.[17] I want to describe two ways in which her approach informs mine.[18] First, Woodman's perspective provides a context for reflecting on violence against women which avoids presenting women as helpless victims and men as the agents of evil. Her focus is on the dynamics *between* men and women (and between the masculine and feminine in each) that generate the violence and destruction.[19] Even in the case of rape, our concern must be with restructuring relations, not simply "stopping men"—not because it sounds less condemnatory and threatening, but because men *cannot* be stopped unless relations change.

Second, Woodman helps us see that a simple shift in power between men and women, taking the form of giving women an equal share of the kind of power men hold, will never solve the problem of violence and destruction endemic to North American society. The violence is too much a part of the nature of that power. As Woodman tells us, "What [the twentieth] century has brought to light by acting it out in the most public and explicit ways is the psychological condition of the raped woman. Indeed, the raped woman has in some sense replaced the crucified Christ as the most powerful and meaningful of icons."[20] The feminine (whether in men or women)—with its different approach to power and relationship—is itself a target of violence, and that violence pervades the culture.[21] Robert Johnson, another Jungian, adds to this perspective in his exceptionally illuminating insights into the way the thrill of violence replaces something missing at the core of Western culture.[22] A far broader transformation than an equalizing of conventional power (or a more equal enforcement of existing rights) is required to achieve the minimum aspirations of a liberal society:

to enable its members to live free of fear, at least sufficiently so for the purposes of liberty, and, on many accounts, for the wider purpose of well-being or human flourishing.[23]

Nel Noddings, a relational feminist theorist, offers an approach to the problem of evil that I see as another perspective on the importance of a relational approach. Her book *Women and Evil* (1989) is an attempt to describe a "morality of evil," a "carefully thought out plan by which to manage the evil in ourselves, in others, and in whatever deities we posit."[24] Although her book is not written from a Jungian perspective, she borrows this notion of a morality of evil and draws heavily on the Jungian concepts of "shadow" and "projection."[25] Her starting presumption is that there is evil in all of us and that one of the basic problems in the dominant approach to evil is that it treats evil as "out there," something other than ourselves. This dangerous mistake is usually part of a projection of our own evil (individual and cultural) onto others. And it is now widely recognized that women—from Pandora to the seductive Eve to the "witches" of Europe and Salem—have been an important target of such projection. This projection is especially visible today in the need to control the dangerous sexuality of women found in all forms of religious fundamentalism.[26] When we consider the special problems of violence against women, it is helpful to remember that when women carry the projection of evil, they also bear the brunt of evil actions—and that evil will appear justifiable.

Noddings develops a phenomenology of evil from the standpoint of women's experience. She says that "three great categories of evil" emerge: "pain, separation, and helplessness."[27] For my purposes, her identification of separation as a condition as well as a category of evil is particularly important. In the evil of separation, often the issue is the failure of compassion and what stands in the way of this ordinary and essential human response. Part of what sustains the human capacity to inflict suffering is the move to abstraction, the transformation of a suffering person into an "other," into a category such as "black," prisoner, or enemy.[28] It is easy to feel separate from a category and thus to avoid feelings of compassion that might be aroused by the sufferings of a person like oneself.

I think that part of what permits people to engage in unimaginable cruelty is that they see the objects of their violence as something radically other than themselves, something less than fully human. It is this otherness that allows me to comprehend the stories of the violence individual whites inflicted on individual blacks in apartheid South Africa or in the United States, not just during slavery or the heyday of the Ku Klux Klan, but on the streets and in prison cells today. (The violence a brutalized population inflicts on itself involves, perhaps, a variant of this explanation: perpetrators of such violence experience both themselves and their victims as dehumanized.[29])

I want to suggest that the conception of rights as relationship can mitigate the dangerous capacity to treat people as categories or as removed "others" while the conventional language of rights as boundaries fosters people's inclination to project evil onto others, imagining that secure fences and sanctions can keep evil away.

Of course, what makes the experience of otherness possible is extremely complex. The prevailing conception of rights is surely just one piece of the puzzle.[30] As we saw in chapter 4, "The Multidimensional Self," the very purpose of the abstraction of rights is to render them applicable to all people regardless of their multiplicity of particular differences. Yet the form this abstraction has taken, and the modes of thinking associated with it, may foster the capacity for distancing ourselves from others that encourages cruelty. I think this is particularly true of what Noddings calls "cultural evil,"[31] such as poverty, racism, and war.

For example, our conception of rights insulates us from the pain of the poverty around us and permits us to let this cruelty continue.[32] As we pass a homeless woman on the street (whether we give her money or not), we can dispel our unease with the "knowledge" that her condition is not our fault, that we have not violated her rights. We remain comfortably unconscious that our property rights in our homes permit us to exclude her. Our sense of rights as individual entitlements permits us to avoid thinking about the connection between her plight and the system of property rights, which is a source of privilege for us[33] and misery for her. But if we focus on the relationships that our rights structure, we will see the connection between our power to exclude and the homeless person's plight. We might still decide to maintain that right of exclusion, but the decision would be made in full consciousness of the pattern of relationships (of power and privilege) it helps to shape. And I think we are likely to experience our responsibilities differently as we recognize that our "private rights" always have social consequences.[34]

From Noddings's perspective, I think even this phrase "social consequences" sounds rather abstract. What matters is a relational habit of thinking not just in rights discourse, of course, but also in the range of ways she outlines in her idea of "pedagogy for the oppressor" and in chapter 9: "Educating for a Morality of Evil." What matters, not only at the level of policy making and formal adjudication but also in our individual encounters with specific human beings, is that our conception of rights turns our attention to the relationships of which we are a part rather than permit us to be blind to them.

The distancing of rights language is not, of course, the same as seeing others as less than human. But I think there is a family of capacities for not seeing the human reality of suffering before us, a group of mechanisms for cutting off compassion and responsiveness that are related. The capacity to see another person only as a category operates at an individual level to foster moral evil. It is not the same as seeing someone as subhuman, but it has a dehumanizing quality, and it shares the features of abstraction and distancing of conventional rights language. Habits of relational thinking seem an antidote to this cluster of human tendencies.

This antidote may be least effective in combating a radical sense of otherness, for just as the "others" would not be seen as rights bearers in a system of universal rights, they could be seen as outside of the network of relationships to which attention is due. But despite this possibility, I think a relational approach to rights, in the context of a broader respect for relational thinking, discourages the distancing of abstraction and thus encourages the attention to the particular human realities before us. This attention seems to me likely to erode the capacity to use such categories as race and gender to blind us to the full humanness of our fellow beings. It may indeed be the *combination* of a culture of rights with its claims of universal moral equality *and* the transformations of thinking of rights as relationship that holds out the best possibility of undermining the age-old propensity to see some as "others" not deserving of fully human treatment. (Of course this is a variant of my argument in chapter 4, "The Multidimensional Self," that an optimal conception of rights and self requires both a purely formal commitment to inherent equality and a contextual attention to the particular.)

Now let me turn more briefly to the no less important issue of "projection." I am persuaded by Noddings (and the Jungian approach she draws on) that one of the chief problems with the way Western culture has traditionally treated evil is to project it onto others. I see the dominant metaphor of rights as boundaries as linked to this pattern of projection. As we saw in chapter 2, the boundaries so central to American law are the boundaries that feel desperately necessary to the separative self to keep the threatening others at bay—a task whose impossibility only fuels the desperation. The separative self, trying to escape from the frightening reality of interconnection, is on an endless and doomed search for security, a security that seems possible only in power and domination. The anxiety of the separative self is thus a combination of the projection onto others of what seems dark, dangerous, and unacceptable within oneself and the (related) sense that the security hoped for from walling off others is in a constant state of failure. That failure is inevitable because of the fact of human interconnection and is exacerbated by the real threats domination provokes. The conceptual structure of rights as boundaries thus both sustains and is driven by a separative self characterized by projection. The traditional rights that are supposed to protect people from evil are themselves shaped by the basic problem of projecting evil outward.

Noddings argues that we should ask "what is wrong with the vast majority of us? The answer...is that we do not understand or accept our own disposition toward evil and that we lack a morality of evil...there is a continuum of susceptibility to the evil within, but no one is immune. Evil is neither entirely out-there nor entirely in-here; it is an interactive phenomenon that requires acceptance, understanding and steady control rather than great attempts to overcome it once and for all."[35] When we move away from the dominant metaphor of rights as boundaries toward a conception of rights as relationship, we will be better equipped to use rights to understand that interactive phenomenon and to exert the steady control that has always been claimed as a virtue of liberalism.[36]

Finally, it is important to see the compatibility between my focus on the dangers of projection and my earlier invocation of patriarchy as a source of violence. I do see a pattern of relations and thinking that one can describe with the shorthand of "patriarchy" as intricately connected to both the evils I am concerned with and the limitations of the traditional modes of dealing with violence. But that does not mean that I make the mistake of projecting all evil onto men or even onto the abstraction "patriarchy." As I noted earlier, the inquiry into gender must be an inquiry into the dynamic of interaction between men and women. It is only to the extent that the concept of patriarchy helps us to understand these patterns of relations and modes of thought that it is useful. Finally, I hope that my discussion of Noddings makes clear that while I think it is possible to have a culture where domination is less central and pervasive, I do not succumb to fantasies that evil can be eradicated. I subscribe to Noddings's advocacy of understanding the nature of evil and to the need for the steady exercise of self-conscious judgment. I think that my conception of rights will foster both.

IV. "LIBERALISM OF FEAR" AND ITS FAILURES
A. Shklar's "Liberalism of Fear"

In the early stages of thinking about this chapter, I read George Kateb's obituary for Judith Shklar. He referred to her defense of constitutionalism as "the system that tends to lessen cruelty because it is the only system devoted to the project of lessening it."[37] This was just the sort of claim on liberalism's[38] behalf that I thought I should take on in order to explore my concerns about violence and relational feminism as well as my belief that ultimately a relational approach will do a better job than conventional liberalism. Cruelty is not all there is to violence, but it is a good starting place. And indeed I found Shklar's *Ordinary Vices*[39] and her essay "The Liberalism of Fear"[40] extremely helpful but not quite in the oppositional sense I had anticipated. I agree with Shklar's view that we should "put cruelty first," both in our ordering of vices and as a primary political concern. And I find this a form of universalism that I accept:

> The liberalism of fear in fact does not rest on a theory of moral pluralism. It does not, to be sure, offer a *summum bonum* toward which all political agents should strive, but it certainly does begin with a *summum malum*, which all of us know and would avoid if only we could. The evil is cruelty and the fear it inspires, and the very fear of fear itself. To that extent the liberalism of fear makes a universal and especially a cosmopolitan claim, as it historically has always done.[41]

I want to begin with her extraordinary evocation of the horror of fear and cruelty and the urgency of making security against them a true priority. I can think of no better introduction to my indictment of the liberal state's failures with regard to women and children.

While "putting cruelty first" is Shklar's recurring theme, her real preoccupation seems to be with fear and the way the two are linked. Let me provide a sampling of her claims: "In Montesquieu's eyes, fear is so terrible, so physiologically and psychologically damaging, that it cannot be redeemed by consequences."[42]

> When one puts [cruelty] first one responds, as Montaigne did, to the acknowledgment that one fears nothing more than fear. The fear of fear does not require any further justification, because it is irreducible. It can be both the beginning and the end of political institutions such as rights. The first right is to be protected against

this fear of cruelty. People have rights as a shield against this greatest of public vices. This is the evil, the threat to be avoided at all costs. Justice itself is only a web of legal arrangements required to keep cruelty in check.[43]

It is really fear that is the bedrock: "It is an undifferentiated evil in which all lesser vices and faults have their origin.... Cruelty comes first, then lying and treachery. All, every single one, are the children of fear.... One can be afraid of fear because fear is the ultimately evil moral condition."[44]

Of course, Shklar makes no exaggerated claims that liberal societies have eradicated fear or cruelty, only that they can and will always do better than any other form of government. But even with this qualification, Shklar's articulation of the evil of fear cries out for the response that in North America women's lives, virtually all women's lives, are shaped by fear, as are those of many, many children. On Shklar's own terms, liberal North American society[45] fails dramatically.[46]

What I have in mind is the incidence and impact of violence against women and children, particularly rape and child abuse. In the case of rape, it is not just the shattering consequences for the staggering numbers of women raped each year but also the fear of rape that pervades and controls the lives of women, even those whose privilege otherwise provides them with great security. I will focus here on these violent forms of terror, but the picture ought to be completed by the evils of poverty—pain, separation, helplessness, and fear—which virtually all societies inflict disproportionately on women and children.[47]

B. Cruelty, Fear, and Systemic Violence against Women and Children

Rape and child abuse are traumas. But we must now face the contradictory, and thus unassimilable, fact that these traumas are routine. As Judith Herman explains:

> In 1980, when post-traumatic stress disorder was first included in the diagnostic manual, the American Psychiatric Association described traumatic events as "outside the range of usual human experience." Sadly, this definition has proved to be inaccurate. Rape, battery, and other forms of sexual and domestic violence are so common a part of women's lives that they can hardly be described as outside the range of ordinary experience.... Traumatic events are extraordinary, not because they occur rarely, but rather because they overwhelm the ordinary human adaptations to life.[48]

Herman also gives us a political context for making sense of what seems unimaginable:

> Only after 1980, when the efforts of combat veterans had legitimated the concept of post-traumatic stress disorder, did it become clear that the psychological syndrome

seen in survivors of rape, domestic battery, and incest was essentially the same as the syndrome seen in the survivors of war. The implications of this insight are as horrifying in the present as they were a century ago: the subordinate condition of women is maintained and enforced by the hidden violence of men. There is a war between the sexes. Rape victims, battered women, and sexually abused children are its casualties.[49]

The impact of trauma corresponds closely to both Shklar's and Noddings's discussions of evil. Trauma shatters the victim's sense of safety and security in the world. Not only is the trauma itself characterized by extreme terror and utter helplessness, but the experience lives on. "Being psychologically overwhelmed, the sensation of being 'reduced to nothing'...is such a hideous feeling that the victim seeks never to experience the sensation again." Fear of further fear, "fear of fear itself," cannot only immobilize victims at the time of the trauma; it also may come to dominate their lives.[50] "The very 'threat of annihilation' that defined the traumatic moment may pursue the survivor long after the danger has passed. No wonder that Freud found, in the traumatic neurosis, signs of a 'daemonic force at work.' The terror, rage, and hatred of the traumatic moment live on in the dialectic of trauma."[51]

Those exposed to the primal evil of trauma have surely not been provided with the basic security from fear and cruelty that should be the first principle of Shklar's liberal regime. But can we say that the prevalence of this trauma is such that it is a fundamental failure? Is it something other than the inability of any regime to ensure that all its members are law-abiding?

Clearly Herman sees the fear and violence as systemic.[52] So do Susan Brownmiller and Catherine MacKinnon, indeed every feminist I know of who has studied the subject. There is, of course, disagreement over the numbers. Getting accurate statistics is difficult since almost everyone agrees that most rapes are not reported and that child abuse and intimate partner violence pose their own reporting problems.[53] The estimates from large-scale (telephone interview) victimization studies in the United States range between 12.65 percent and 18 percent of women who have been raped during their lifetimes.[54] The most detailed information on sexual assault in Canada is available from the 1993 national Violence against Women Survey (VAWS).[55] At that time, 39 percent of Canadian adult women reported having had at least one experience of sexual assault since the age of sixteen. (The definition of sexual assault in this survey included violent sexual attacks and unwanted sexual touching, both of which are consistent with *Canadian Criminal Code* definitions of sexual assault.[56] This is, of course, a broader definition than rape.)[57]

One can get another perspective on the scope of the problem from a 1993 study based on in-depth interviews with women from the metropolitan Toronto area.[58] The findings were that 98 percent of the women interviewed had experienced some form of sexual violation.[59] Of course this number was so high because the study covered a wide range of sexual abuse, from obscene phone calls to sexual assault. While it is important to distinguish between forms of abuse (as of course the report did), I think its shocking cumulative statistic is important.

There will always be debates over the numbers, but they are consistently large enough to reveal a profound problem. Given the devastation of the trauma, are we not dealing with a problem that is a fundamental challenge to the state's commitment to protecting its members from violence? And when we add together rape, intimate partner violence, and child abuse, do we not have a problem that must be treated as systemic?[60]

I want to turn to the issue of fear, beginning with a personal example of the significance of the more minor forms of assaultive behavior. In 1992, an envelope on the door to my women's studies office was defaced with antifeminist obscenities. I was surprised to find how upset I was. In fact, I was scared. I came to realize in a new way that such obscenities, like jokes about violence against women, and the strong norms against interrupting a class or social occasion to object to any of the routine forms of trivializing violence against women, are all part of a pervasive pattern of reminders to women that we are always at risk of violence and that the violence is tolerated, condoned, and not taken seriously. It does not take a direct threat to keep the fear alive. My sense of vulnerability as a woman and as a publicly identified feminist, and my urge for male protection, reminded me of the social control that fear achieves, in a way far more compelling than my long-standing theoretical views on the subject.

The wide range of sexual violations to which women are subject are of a piece. They serve to remind us of our subordinate status and that this status is maintained by violence and fear. The sense that violence against women somehow doesn't really matter (its shocking prevalence is tolerated and even joked about) sustains the idea that women are not equally worthy of protection, not really equal members of society.[61] Similarly, the sense that a woman needs a man for protection (and for a status worthy of protection) adds to the power violence has to maintain women's subordination. Of course, the threat of violence also directly constrains women's freedom—in ways contrary to the picture of the autonomous person competent adults are supposed to be.

Even if they do not they think of themselves as afraid, most women routinely organize their lives around the effort to avoid sexual assault, whether this takes the form of not walking alone at night, avoiding certain locations, or never putting one's drink down at a bar for fear of its being drugged.[62] Of course, most young women know they are particularly vulnerable and devote more effort to this project than do older women. In many circumstances—such as living in affluent neighborhoods and being able to afford cabs—(older) women can become so efficient at organizing their lives around the background fear that it indeed recedes into the background. Nevertheless, the fear is affecting their lives, and it can be propelled into the foreground in a moment, from the stranger on a deserted subway platform to a suspect touch in a crowded room or sexualized attention from a man in a position of power. The fear can be managed, but it shapes the vast majority of women's lives.

The intensity and the level of awareness of the fear varies enormously across different women, depending on where they live; whether they live alone; their temperament; whether they have additional vulnerabilities, such as a disability or being the kind of woman that others (including police) think are less deserving of protection, such as prostitutes, alcoholics, or women of color or aboriginal women. And the nature of the fear varies across different times and stages of a woman's life. But virtually no woman lives free of fear of male assault, whether from strangers, acquaintances, "dates," family members (especially for young girls), or intimate partners.[63] The practical questions are about the degrees of constraint and the modes of defense for coping with the unavoidable reality of fear.[64]

Let us say that you are persuaded that fear shapes women's lives and even that that fear is an important part of what keeps women in a subordinate position. There is still the question of whether this is the sort of fear Shklar had in mind and whether its impact and pervasiveness amounts to the indictment I claim. When Shklar describes cruelty and fear as the *summum malum* of liberalism, she goes on to ask "what is meant by cruelty here?": "It is the deliberate infliction of physical, and secondarily emotional, pain upon a weaker person or group by stronger ones in order to achieve some end, tangible or intangible, of the latter." I think there is no question that rape qualifies. And that it is perpetrated regularly (a sexual assault is committed every two minutes in the United States[65]) by members of the group that holds most positions of public power against a less powerful group makes it compelling evidence of something seriously wrong.[66]

But the question is still whether this failure goes to the heart of the object of Shklar's liberalism. (I will turn later to the question of whether the failure is of the sort that a more thorough application of liberal principles can cure.) She goes on to say that "public cruelty is not an occasional personal inclination. It is made possible by differences in public power." Bracketing for a moment the issue of publicness, this description still fits rape. But is rape *public* cruelty? "[Public cruelty] is almost always built into the system of coercion upon which all governments have to rely to fulfill their essential functions." This is not the minimum fear and coercion inherent in any system of law. "The fear [that 'liberalism of fear'] wants to prevent is that which is created by arbitrary, unexpected, unnecessary, and unlicensed acts of force and by habitual and pervasive acts of cruelty and torture performed by military, paramilitary, and police agents in any regime.... Systematic fear is the condition that makes freedom impossible and it is aroused by the expectation of institutionalized cruelty as by nothing else."[67]

We now have a manifest divergence from the practice of rape. Although public officials do use their power to rape, the systematic fear that pervades the lives of North American women is fear of rape by private citizens, not public officials.[68] But it is this very divergence that points to a limitation in Shklar's vision (a limitation I take to be characteristic of many defenders of traditional liberalism) of what it would take to implement the basic principle of protecting people from fear and cruelty. Exploring this limitation will also take us a step toward the broader question of whether the sorts of issues with which I am concerned are beyond the proper scope of law. To address this issue of public versus private violence, I want to draw an analogy to a brilliant argument by Robert Cover about the expansion of the judicial role that was entailed in overturning the apartheid (his term) of the American South.

C. The Problem of "Private" but Systemic Violence

Cover argues that blacks were not able to use competitive democratic politics to protect themselves, as other minorities had done, "because of white terror and the failure of the will to control it":

> Whether in a one, two or three-party system, the probable losers, who perceived an alliance with Blacks as the road to victory and power, confronted a powerful temptation to cheat on the White bargain. Precisely because that tension was present, racist domination required that the politics of the region be violent and extreme. In a more civilized context the bargain would not have been kept, as it has not been since 1965. Thus terror has always been part of Southern regional politics.[69]

What matters for the analogy with women is not the particulars of the structure of politics, but the ways in which terror, largely privately perpetrated, was an essential part of a social and political system in which one group was kept subordinate.[70] The "close fit between private terror, public discrimination, and political exclusion"[71] distinguishes the treatment of blacks from other minorities. But it has a powerful resonance with the complex mechanisms by which women (a majority, who have had the vote for some time) are kept in their place. Again, it is not the specifics that matter, but the broader issue of the "resonance of society and politics" that "accounted in part for the peculiar intransigence of the state action problem."[72] Cover charts the process by which the U.S. Supreme Court came to see that it could not dismantle apartheid while respecting the traditional boundaries of judicial intervention, defined by state action. In 1935, the Court was still refusing "to pierce the state-action barrier that was the formal embodiment of a distinction between state and society—a distinction that was meaningless when custom and terror could be expected to enforce what the state could not."[73]

If we are to stop the violence against women we will have to think differently about the task of law and the state. The violence-based subordination of women is so deeply embedded in the fabric of our society that it cannot be captured by the conventional picture of what the liberal state is to protect us from. Like the violence of the American south, it is neither simply individual criminal violence nor state perpetrated.

Let me offer you one more analogy from Cover to bear in mind when thinking about Shklar's description of the "unlicensed acts of force" and official acts of "cruelty and torture" at which the liberalism of fear is aimed. In 1944, Gunnar Myrdal was asked whether the south was fascist. He answered no.

"The South entirely lacks the centralized organization of a fascist state.... The Democratic party is the very opposite of a state party in a modern fascist sense. It has no conscious political ideology, no tight regional or state organization and no centralized and efficient bureaucracy."

This, then, is the paradox suggested to me by these Myrdal observations. Southern Apartheid was in large part a creation of fragmented, weak administration, of local autonomy and politics.[74]

An intricate system of oppression, sustained by terror, sanctioned by officials (though often not technically by the law), did not require either conscious ideology or state organization. The same is true for the complexities of women's subordination and the role of terror in sustaining it. And as was the case with southern apartheid, it cannot be overcome without crossing conventional boundaries—and risking genuine values. In the case of the south, the question was will "the real political values inherent in local autonomy survive the penetration of national norms in the interest of destroying Apartheid?"[75] In the case of violence against women, individual liberty (primarily for men) and the traditional privacy of the home and of sexual relations are potentially threatened by the transformation of patterns of violence. The value of privacy provides both the opportunity for violence and the justification for noninterference, just as the local autonomy of the south did.

The role of privacy is particularly clear with respect to the widespread violence against women by their male intimate partners.[76] But something similar is at work in the resistance to changing the patterns that give rise to acquaintance rape and to the long continuum of male imposition of unwanted sexual talk and touch, emotional coercion, bribery and threats in employment contexts, and physical force to gain access to sex. Trying to change or regulate sexual encounters is often seen as inappropriate intrusion into a private domain of intimacy—despite the fact that what often characterizes the encounters in question is not intimacy, but coercion.

The problem of violence against women cannot be solved in terms of the conventional boundaries of state and society. This violence, like the apartheid of the south, cannot be seen as "isolated instances of impropriety or as transitory hysteria. Against hysterical politics it is necessary to offer protection, make amends, award compensation, but not to remake the political structure."[77] In responding to the demands to dismantle apartheid, the Court in effect rewrote the Constitution by transforming the scope of judicial review so that it could respond to the "private" perpetration of discrimination.[78]

Similarly, the fear and violence to which women are subjected must be overcome if the aspirations of the liberalism of fear are to be honored—even if in doing so we must challenge the very purpose of articulating those aspirations, the maintenance of the boundaries to the liberal state.

D. Rape and Boundaries

To reflect further on the inadequacy of boundary language and the advantages of understanding rights in relational terms for dealing with violence against women, let me return to one of the critics' questions: isn't rape quintessentially about boundary violation, and don't women desperately need better protection for the boundaries of their persons? Isn't this of all places where we need to claim the same kind of boundary protection men get?

Let me begin with the question whether the metaphor of boundary violation captures the essence of the horror of rape. Let us start with Judith Herman's description of trauma:

> Traumatic events violate the autonomy of the person at the level of basic bodily integrity. The body is invaded, injured, defiled. Control over bodily functions is often lost; in the folklore of combat and rape, this loss of control is often recounted as the most humiliating aspect of the trauma. Furthermore, at the moment of trauma, almost by definition, the individual's point of view counts for nothing. In rape, for example, the purpose of the attack is precisely to demonstrate contempt for the victim's autonomy and dignity.[79]

Moreover, "helplessness constitutes the essential insult of trauma."[80] (Remember that Noddings lists helplessness as one of the basic forms and conditions of evil.) In rape, as in all trauma, the victim's sense of self is shattered.[81]

As I noted in chapter 2, where boundary is a basic metaphor for the integrity of the self, it is not surprising that rape is described as a violation of boundaries. The self, after all, has been deliberately violated. However much the physical invasion, the violent claim of intimate contact, is part of the horror, I think the language of boundary crossing misdirects our attention. It is worth remembering that rape laws used to require penetration for the assault to count as rape. But in the lobbying for reform it was widely argued that this was a standard from a male perspective that did not correspond to the women's experience of the horror.[82]

What Herman emphasizes is the radical disconnection entailed in trauma and the need for reconnection for recovery. Traumatic events "shatter the construction of the self that is formed and sustained in relation to others."[83] They "destroy the belief that one can *be oneself* in relation to others."[84] "The restoration of a positive view of the self [after rape] includes…a renewed sense of autonomy within connection."[85] Part of the horror of rape in our society is that the reconnection is often so difficult. In most instances of rape, the offender is known to the victim. "To escape the rapist, the victim may have to withdraw from some part of her social world," and her "feelings of fear, distrust, and isolation may be compounded by the incomprehension or frank hostility of those to whom she turns for help."[86] Part of the reconnection is "the restitution of a sense of a meaningful world."[87]

But for this it is essential that the victim be able to share her story with others. This is often particularly hard for victims of rape—and not just in the notorious situations of trials.

> Returning veterans may be frustrated by their families' naive and unrealistic views of combat, but at least they enjoy the recognition that they have been to war. Rape victims, by and large, do not. Many acts that women experience as terrorizing violations may not be regarded as such, even by those closest to them. Survivors are thus placed in the situation where they must choose between expressing their own point of view and remaining in connection with others.[88]

But both the expression and the connection are essential to their recovery. Susan Brison notes that "psychologists writing about trauma stress that one has to tell one's trauma narrative to an empathic *other* in order for the telling to be therapeutic."[89] Although Brison argues that it may be helpful to tell stories to "*imagined* others" (through, for example, journal writing), her emphasis on narrative as a means of reconnecting with others is clear:

> Working through, or remastering, traumatic memory (in the case of human-inflicted trauma) involves a shift from being the object or medium of someone else's (the perpetrator's) speech (or other expressive behavior) to being the subject of one's own. The act of bearing witness to the trauma facilitates this shift, not only by transforming traumatic memory into a narrative that can be worked into the survivor's sense of self and view of the world, but also by reintegrating the survivor into a community, reestablishing connections essential to selfhood.[90]

If this understanding of rape as a shattering of self-in-connection reinforces my objection to boundary language, what is the alternative to relying on boundaries? There are several different, interconnected, levels to this question. I want to start with brief reflections on what it would take to stop rape, mention the kind of language that should replace boundary, and indicate the sort of shifts in the law that would move in the right direction. In the process, we will get some sense of the contributions of a shift to thinking of rights in relational terms. And we will see why adequate protection for women cannot be achieved simply by enforcing for them the same rights as men—as if such enforcement would have no serious consequences for the rights and privileges of men.

Let me begin with the issue of fear.[91] To achieve freedom from fear for all, we would have to end men's domination of women.[92] And to end that domination, we must eliminate the fear that keeps it in place. This apparent circularity means that we must work on both at the same time. Beginning to lessen the fear will shift the relations of power, and no mechanism for trying to lessen the fear that does not shift the power will work.[93] In terms of stopping rape in particular, it is necessary to end not only the domination of women by men but also the primacy of domination in general, the role of violence in our culture, and its association with masculinity. Catherine MacKinnon makes compelling arguments that dominance itself is eroticized in our culture.[94] Thus we are talking not only about achieving equality between men and women but also about transforming their experience of sexuality, their understanding of what it means to be a man or a woman. Now I am not, of course, saying that law or a reconception of rights can achieve all this. But we must not back off too quickly, assuming that the project must be beyond the scope of law and intrinsically dangerous for any state to embark on. As I have tried to argue, to abandon the project would be to abandon the basic aspirations of liberalism—even if the project requires a rethinking of the scope of the liberal state.

Since what is required to end violence against women is, ultimately, a transformation of the relations between men and women, we need language that directs our attention to these relations and laws that shift them. Few of the basic protections adult women need can be captured adequately by simple prohibitions. Most of the words and touching that can be threatening, frightening, demeaning, and assaultive in one context can be welcome in another. That is the inherent problem in rape as well as sexual harassment. Simple prohibitions are a problem because coercion is often not simple.

The essence of rape is coercive, unwanted intercourse or attempted intercourse. What makes it rape is not penetration of body parts or (in even more old-fashioned terms) a breaking of the hymen, or other physical boundary violation. It is not even the presence of (additional) violence. What makes rape so radically violent is that it is coerced intimate contact. Many rape victims feel angry at commonly made distinctions between "violent" and "nonviolent" rapes.[95] Rape is intrinsically violent, and it may or may not be accompanied by other forms of assault. Again, it used to be common in North America that a woman who accused a man of rape had to show violent physical resistance on her part; it wasn't really rape if she had not physically tried to fight him off. (This was the case even at the time that police were advising women that the safest thing to do was not to resist. A new twist on this is women, fearful of life-threatening HIV infection, bargaining with a rapist, his use of a condom in exchange for her nonresistance—and this bargaining being used to cast doubt on the absence of consent.[96]) To make further clear that it is not (additional) physical violence as such that constitutes rape, some women enjoy engaging in sex with physical violence. This violent, consensual sex is not rape. In sum, rape is not essentially about physical boundary crossing; it is about relations of coercion leading to unwanted sex.[97]

I think a better language than simple prohibition or "respect for boundaries" is that men have an obligation to make a respectful effort to determine whether and what kind of touch (or contact) is desired.[98] In addition, they need to maintain a continued alertness to this desire rather than treat the relation as an on/off one in which once permission (which actually implies acquiescence rather than desire) is acquired no further attention to desire is necessary.[99] Of course, calling for respectful attention to desire is addressing the vastly more common form of sexual assault, that among people who know each other, rather than stranger rape.

V. AN EXAMPLE OF TRANSFORMATION THROUGH LAW: THE CANADIAN LAW OF SEXUAL ASSAULT

Now lest anyone think such an approach is hopelessly inappropriate to law, let me briefly discuss the changes to Canada's law of sexual assault, introduced in 1992. The preamble to the act introducing these changes stated that "the Parliament of Canada is gravely concerned about the incidence of sexual violence and abuse in Canadian society, in particular, the prevalence of sexual assault against women and children." Parliament "recognizes the unique character of the offence of sexual assault and how sexual assault and, more particularly, the fear of sexual assault affects the lives of the people of Canada."[100] Finally, the preamble declared Parliament's wish "to encourage the reporting of incidents of sexual violence or abuse and to provide for the prosecution of offenders within a framework of laws that are consistent with the principles of fundamental justice and that are fair to complainants as well as to accused persons." This preamble is in part an attempt to anticipate constitutional challenges to these changes to the *Canadian Criminal Code* as a violation of the rights of the accused. But it is also broadly important in its assertion that standards of fairness must be applied to the complainant as well the accused and that a good law encourages reporting. (Compare Herman's indictment of American law: "The legal system is designed to protect men from the superior power of the state [as Shklar says it should be] but not to protect women or children from the superior power of men. It therefore provides strong guarantees for the rights of the accused but essentially no guarantees for the rights of the victim.[101])

In terms of the substantive content of these changes, the redefinition of the meaning of consent has great potential for changing long-standing patterns of power and (ir)responsibility. Women routinely have found themselves in the position of willingly engaging in socializing and even sexual contact and then being told that if the man then forces her to have intercourse that either "she asked for it" or that it is plausible that he believed she consented. Section 273.2 addresses this problem directly: no consent is obtained where "the complainant, having consented to engage in sexual activity, expresses, by words or conduct, a lack of agreement to continue to engage in the activity."[102] Of course, even this leaves open the question of the man's responsibility to pay attention to what the woman is communicating.

The central role of intent, of *mens rea* in the criminal law, has long been used to insist that the only option in the law of sexual assault is a subjective standard of intent. The argument goes that the man's perspective, his understanding (or lack of it) of the situation, has to be privileged over the woman's experience of violent harm because the requirement of subjective intent has been at the heart of the common law tradition of criminal law. To hold someone criminally accountable for an act he did not "intend" would violate his basic rights.

The problem long recognized by feminists is that, as I noted above, this approach must give priority to the man's perspective over the woman's. (Remember Herman's statement that "at the moment of trauma, almost by definition, the individual's point of view counts for nothing."[103] It is no wonder that many women experience a rape trial as a second rape.) The problem is particularly acute since in sexual assault men and women often experience the encounter completely differently, even if they agree on a "factual" description of what took place. The law is then faced with an exceptionally difficult situation. Even if everyone is telling the truth, judges will routinely be faced with wildly different accounts of what happened.[104]

The way consent is defined will inevitably shape whose story the law validates and thus whom the law protects. There does not seem to be a "neutral" solution to the problem. Clinging to the common law tradition of intent is obviously one-sided in its impact—an impact with respect to one of the most horrific forms of violence against women. When one adds to that the recognition that the prevalence of violence against women—and the fear of violence—maintain their subordination in society, thus preventing the possibility of genuine equality, acquiescence in the consequences of the traditional meaning of *mens rea* seems unconscionable.

The alternative has always seemed to me to hold men to a standard of reasonable care in determining whether a woman has consented to sexual contact. This could work toward equalizing power relations between men and women instead of entrenching the patterns of inequality (sustained by violence) as the privileging of the man's perspective does. The Canadian law of sexual assault is an important step in this direction.

The *Criminal Code* stipulates that "It is not a defense...that the accused believed that the complainant consented to the activity that forms the subject-matter of the charge, where (a) the accused's belief arose from the accused's (i) self-induced intoxication, or (ii) reckless or wilful blindness; or (b) *the accused did not take reasonable steps, in the circumstances known to the accused at the time, to ascertain that the complainant was consenting.*"[105] This standard of reasonableness holds out the possibility that the law will impose a new kind of responsibility on men to make some effort to find out if a woman consents to sex. Unexamined stereotypes of "no means yes" will presumably no longer provide a defense, even if the accused had managed to so insulate himself from public education on the subject that he actually believed it, in general and in a particular case.[106] With sympathetic interpretation, the net effect will be to significantly change the degree of impunity with which men inflict violence against women—which in turn would shift the overall relations of power between men and women. (Of course, this change in the law requires attentiveness to consent, not to desire. It seems likely that while young men and women should be educated to attend to the mutuality of desire, the most law can do is require attentiveness to consent.)

Once we are confronted by the inevitability of the legal system's favoring one perspective over another, and thus of providing better protection for one of the parties than the other, then an analysis in terms of how the law affects the relations of power gives us a reasoned means for deciding what to do. Assuming a recognition of the systemic subordination of women[107] and a commitment to equality, it is clear that a commitment to the traditional meaning of *mens rea* in this context is a commitment to inequality. The relational analysis leads us here, as always, out of sterile quandaries about neutrality or the intricacies of conventional legal categories. And, of course, to do so is by no means to simply disregard the rights of the accused. It is to recognize the consequences of those rights as they have been traditionally understood and to see the incompatibility of those consequences with equality.

The amendments to the *Criminal Code* discussed above brought forth a flurry of attacks.[108] The central charge, that they abandoned the neutrality that is essential to the rule of law, is typical of opposition to new laws designed to promote equality. In the case of the change to the Canadian law of sexual assault, the argument was that to require compliance with an objective standard of reasonableness—rather than rely on the traditional requirement of subjective intent—was to single out sexual assault as an exception to the norms of the common law. *Mens rea* (subjective intent) had traditionally been a component of a common law crime and remained a component of virtually all crimes (with the exception of some absolute liability offences[109]). The argument went that to treat sexual assault as an exception in this way violates the principles of neutrality: one group, female alleged victims of sexual assault, gain a benefit, and another group, men who are accused, suffer a detriment, because it is now easier to prove (or convict for) certain kinds of crimes normally committed by men against women. Since the law should be neutral with respect to all parties, this looks like bias, like building in advantages to one group over another.

What is typical of this argument about neutrality is its reliance on a kind of grammatical logic, with no attention to context, to the relational meaning and consequences of the law.[110] The grammatical logic is that if *mens rea* is a requirement for criminal law and an exception is made (with a differential impact between groups), there is a prima facia case that neutrality has been violated. I call this grammatical logic because it looks only to a superficial parallel in the structure of the law: if *mens rea* is required in one form of law, neutrality must require its presence in all instances of that form. The terms of criminal law must be the same.

Sometimes the argument has a next step that engages context and impact in a simplistic way. This step is necessary to distinguish the offending changes to the law of sexual assault from other laws that do not require *mens rea*, such as drunk driving and narcotics laws. Here the argument goes that those laws do not target a particular group, whereas the law of sexual assault can be seen to have a differential effect on men and women[111] (since overwhelmingly the accused are men; the victims, women). This engagement with context and impact is simplistic because it does not inquire into the differential impact of the *previous* law—the way it insulated men from responsibility for violence and thus sustained patterns of inequality of power and respect between men and women.

A relational approach always directs attention to context and consequences. In asking how a law structures relationships it directs attention to the difference context makes, to how the law affects different people in different circumstances. As a result, it shows that laws are rarely neutral in the sense of having the same significance and impact on everyone regardless of circumstance. For example, a law of contract that takes *caveat emptor* (buyer beware) as its norm has a different impact on buyer and seller, and while some people are both, many are not. It also has a differential impact on well-educated or informed buyers than on those without the resources to acquire the necessary information. When the law shifts to protect people who have relied on what the seller says, the power relations between consumers and sellers are shifted. The rule of law cannot actually require neutrality of impact between groups because it would so regularly be breached.[112]

The relational approach both helps identify what the differential impact is and offers a framework of analysis for bringing the law into greater conformity to one of our legal system's core values, equality. Looking closely at how the law structures relations of power, trust, responsibility, and privilege makes it easier to see how the law might change to shift those relations in the direction of equality. To do so is to recognize that the law will not be neutral, in the sense of undifferentiated in its impact on different groups. But a law promoting such a shift will be truer to the values of equality and the rule of law than one that has the superficial "grammatical" parity of the same legal terms for all groups but with differential consequences that sustain inequality.

Finally, it is worth noting an ironic shift in the affect usually invoked when "subjectivity" is associated with feminism. I have repeatedly heard the argument that the law requires objectivity, and thus that the subjectivity inherent in many feminist reconceptions of reasoning, of fairness, of adjudication is unsuitable for the legal system as we know it. But when we turn to the criminal law, where a subjective standard has long been the norm, suggesting an "objective" standard of reasonableness is equated with the collapse of civil liberties.[113]

However unreasonable this conclusion, it does point to the reality that men's rights were changed. As is often the case, it did not turn out to be possible to protect women simply by taking rights traditionally enjoyed by men and making them available to women too. For the law to protect the security and equality of women, new responsibilities had to be imposed and old entitlements shifted.

VI. CHILD ABUSE

Although I cannot properly address the issue of child abuse in this chapter, I do want to note the connections between that issue and the violence against women that I have been discussing. The connections highlight shared problems and the advantages of the relational approach in resolving them. These advantages, in turn, will lead us back to Shklar's concern with the scope of the state and my earlier claim that transforming the relations between men and women must be a legitimate objective because it is necessary to prevent violence against women.

The North American public has only recently come to recognize the prevalence and long-term consequences of child abuse (though the history of our not knowing is itself fascinating).[114] I see it (as does Judith Herman) as related to the overall pattern of sexual domination and the eroticization of dominance that MacKinnon describes.[115] If this is so, then preventing child abuse involves the same sort of scope of change. I think the issue of the protection of children also makes clear the problematic nature of relying on traditional conceptions of rights. Some have argued that what we need is more rights for children and better enforcement of those they already have. But I think that the conventional nature of rights as boundaries cannot (at least in many cases) be the best path for transforming the relations that bring about and result from child abuse.

As with rape of adult women, without changing the structure of relations that systematically produces the behavior, simply trying to enforce prohibitions (trying to police the boundaries of rights) will not work. In the case of rape, some serious effort at enforcement (or as serious as the culture is capable of) has been under way for at least thirty years.[116] But overall there has been little change in the incidence of rape in North America.[117] Of course, in the case of child abuse, as in the case of rape and wife assault, I am all for interim efforts at prevention in the sense of educating people about their rights and trying to enforce those rights. My point is that rights will work to protect only when they also serve to restructure relations. I do not think the violence can be stopped by treating rights as a barrier for protection, as a tool for policing the boundaries of the vulnerable without changing their vulnerability.

I should also note that a relational approach would not exclusively focus on the difficult problem of what motivates individuals to commit sexual, emotional, and physical abuse of children. It would also try to identify the kinds of practices that facilitate and hide child abuse and the kinds of laws that support those practices.[118]

Again, my point is that we cannot say that transforming the relations that foster and hide child abuse is beyond the scope of the law, if it is necessary for the basic security promised by the liberal state.

Finally, the issue of child abuse points to our society's astonishing indifference to the well-being of children. When we add the pain of poverty[119] to the shocking incidence of child abuse, we have to recognize that we permit fear, cruelty, and violence to dominate the lives of a huge percentage of our children. This toleration of evil is a puzzle to me, for children are hardly "others" in conventional ways. I think the inexplicable turns out to be accounted for, at least in part, by the unimaginable. It is inexplicable how we (here meaning those with relative power and privilege) can fail to act, to find ways of mitigating the pain, poverty, and abuse of children. Yet to face it, to let in the full scope of the horror, threatens to take over our lives. The degree of change entailed to ensure high-quality care for all children and to radically reduce child poverty, neglect, and abuse[120] seems overwhelming and, thus, unimaginable. So we manage not to see the pain even though we know it's there. How could we continue as we do if we did not protect ourselves by willful blindness, by a kind of radical dissociation from the pain around us?

VII. LAW AND THE SCOPE OF THE STATE

This brings me back to a question I raised at the outset. If our notion of rights as boundaries helps provide this blindness and dissociation, will not abandoning this metaphor and embracing a conception of rights as relationship overwhelm us with responsibility? As I noted in chapter 2, it *will* increase our responsibility, but it need not be as overwhelming as it appears. I think part of the problem is that in our attachment to the apparently secure limits of rights, including the security of limited responsibility, we have had little training in compassion. We know little about how to face the reality of suffering, how to hold it in our minds and not turn away from it, without having it overwhelm us[121] and how to make reasonable decisions about our responsibility in light of this knowledge.

I think habits of relational thinking, in the realm of rights as in others, would foster both compassion and intelligent responsibility. Seeing ourselves in relation to others would not generate inflated and overwhelming ideas about the scope of our responsibility to cure all evils. It could be the basis for a more reasonable judgment about the limits of our power as individuals as well as the desirable forms of power we exercise collectively.

Perhaps the most important point, however, is that the fear that relational responsibility will lead to the unconstrained power of the state rests on a misunderstanding about the role of law. In many, perhaps most, cases, the relational approach leads *not* to an expansion of the scope of the state, but simply to a change in the way *existing* state power is exercised. In the case of the change to the Canadian law of sexual assault, the old law shaped relations of power and responsibility between men and women by insulating men from legal accountability for violence. The new law created legal responsibility to ascertain consent. The scope or ambit of the law in terms of the kinds of actions it governed, the kinds of relationships it shaped, did not change. But its effect did.

When the law (together with social norms) has long provided impunity for harms done by members of one group to another, and then changes in the law remove that impunity, it often *seems* as though the scope of the state has increased. This is especially so when the social norms that backed the impunity have not fully changed. In the case of the sexual assault law, irresponsible behavior that caused violent and traumatic harm had been legally excused: if a man got so drunk that he couldn't tell whether a woman consented, he also couldn't form the intention to rape that was a necessary component of the crime. It became the woman's responsibility to stay out of harm's way, even if (especially if) the drinking took place in her own home. As I noted earlier, if a woman consensually engaged in sexual activity and then did not want to have intercourse, a man could take her "no" for a "yes" and argue that "she must have wanted it" if she had agreed to the initial sexual activity. In this latter case, especially, I think there is no clear consensus on social norms that "no means no" and that a woman's consent to some sexual activity is not an open-ended invitation to whatever the man wants.[122]

One could see the disjuncture with social norms particularly clearly in the outrage expressed over the provisions with respect to drunkenness. Critics pointed to the alleged inconsistency between holding a man responsible for sexual assault despite being too drunk to form the traditional "intent" and the new law's provision that having intercourse with a woman too drunk to consent cannot be considered consensual. (Again, this is a claim of a failure of neutrality.) Similarly, I think there is no clear social consensus on the imposition of responsibility for men to take "reasonable steps" to ascertain consent. One can get a sense of social attitudes toward such responsibility in the context of university codes of conduct and residence training about sexual responsibility. For example, in the early 1990s, Antioch College imposed a code of conduct that tried to capture the idea that a woman can withdraw her consent at any time during sexual activity.[123] It was met with a series of lampoons across the country, suggesting, for example, that men needed written consent for the next kiss, the next touch.[124]

The emphasis in the objections both to the changes to the law and the code of conduct was on the unreasonable demands made on men (by the state or the university).[125] But, in fact, these changes require new forms of responsibility for both men and women. Men have the obvious responsibility of ascertaining consent. (Obvious, that is, in the law or rules. My point, of course, is that prior to these legal and institutional interventions, what should have been obvious was not.) But women also now bear the responsibility for acknowledging and communicating their sexual desires; if no means no, then women will have to say yes, and perhaps even articulate what they want. The deep social myth that sex is something that men want and women provide is (partially) challenged under these rules. Both men and women have to take up new responsibilities as they learn to relate to each other with the kind of mutual respect befitting equals.

The new rules require a new way of understanding what it means to be a man or a woman in relation to sexuality. Transformation of gender roles is a deep kind of transformation that is almost certain to be difficult, complex, and probably slower than equality advocates would wish. In the 1990s, a law student who ran orientation sessions for first-year dorm residents at the University of Toronto reported that during sessions on sexual harassment and consensual sex the male students expressed anxiety about how they could tell what was permissible, a sense that the ground rules were shifting beneath them. The women seemed less conscious of, or less vocal about, the new responsibilities they were facing as part of their greater security and equality.

It is not surprising that in the face of shifting roles and responsibilities in something as emotionally loaded as sex, men feel resentment toward an unwanted intrusion into a private domain. This sense of intrusion can then take the form of complaints about the university or the state as "Big Brother" or the more formal objection to the increased role of the state. But my point here is that the amendments to the *Canadian Criminal Code* do not involve the state stepping in where it was previously absent. The law participated in constructing the responsibilities and expectations of men and women with respect to their sexual relations. To repeat, it did so in ways that provided men with impunity for sexual assault—and when long-standing impunity is removed, it looks like the state is stepping in. But it was the law that gave force to that impunity. (Of course, the impunity is itself a nonneutral exception to the legal and social norms against assault.) And when it (finally) becomes clear that the impunity is inconsistent with equality, the law must change to impose the kind of mutual responsibility consistent with "equal concern and respect," to quote a leading liberal theorist.[126] There is not more law, there is different law.

When, however, the law faces resistance rather than reinforcement from social norms, its presence may be more obvious, more keenly felt. It is also true that the enforcement of the old social norms of sexuality was done more by private violence (for which there was legal impunity from the state) while the newer, not fully accepted, norms are enforced more directly by the state. We can see, then, how the false belief might arise that the scope of the state has increased.

The comparison with Robert Cover's argument is again interesting. In the American south, the private violence that sustained apartheid was left uncontrolled by the state but it was not officially sanctioned by the law. Lynching was never legal, even though segregation was. But neither was lynching ordinarily prosecuted. In the case of violence against women, the impunity for irresponsible violence (whether through drunkenness or failure to ascertain consent) came directly from the law. What would now constitute rape—and would have been experienced by the woman as rape—was legally sanctioned behavior.

In the United States, the judicial enforcement of racial equality ultimately challenged the "private" discrimination and private violence. (The challenge to private violence continues to this day, as prosecutions for decades-old racially motivated crimes continue to go forward.[127]) Similarly, in the case of sexual assault, the change in the law reverses the impunity and authorizes the state to protect women from "private" violence.[128] In both cases, when the state's collusion with private violence is removed (or at least shifted), there is a shift in power between the relevant groups that moves toward equality. The change in the law allows blacks in the American south and women in Canada not to make it their primary responsibility to stay out of harm's way by controlling their own behavior—whether by stepping aside when white people walk down the street or trying to be on guard against the predatory behavior of men they socialize with.

The ongoing incursions on women's freedom and equality—their need to stay indoors or be accompanied after dark—is not affected by the change in the law since those protective behaviors are designed to avoid stranger rape, not the acquaintance rape targeted in the amendments to the *Criminal Code*. Ironically, as I have noted, it is the men providing the needed accompaniment who are actually most likely to be the threat.

Of course, the change in the law cannot single-handedly change deeply entrenched social relations. New forms of predation—like spiking women's drinks with knock out drugs—continue to generate advice to women about how to be on guard. But at least there is no ambiguity about the legality of this behavior or of the nonconsensual[129] sex following it.

In sum then, the change in the law has the potential to change important dimensions of the relations between men and women—even if it cannot wipe out all fears and threats of violence. It creates new relations of responsibility between men and women. It commands that men offer women a respectful attention to their wishes about sexual contact, and it requires women to be more forthright about their sexual desires. It is no longer women's primary responsibility to stay out of harm's way—by constraining her dress or her ability to invite a man to her home or avoiding sexual activity out of fear it will be interpreted as a blank check for men's desires. Women can enjoy a greater freedom to act (closer to men's scope of freedom) and can command greater respect for the autonomy of their choices. The change in the law moved the relation between men and women closer to mutually respectful equality. This transformation takes place not by expanding the scope of the state, but by changing the way the previous law of sexual assault had worked against the equal protection of women. (These changes in legal responsibility do not seem to change the cultural norm that women should modify their behavior in order to avoid illegal assault. The prevalence of guides on how to guard one's drink against knockout drugs is an ongoing example.[130])

Finally, I should note that the relation between law and social change is, of course, not unidirectional. I have been focusing on the potential for the change in law to change the way law structures social relations. But this change in the law itself came about because of changes in women's effective political power combined with the growing acceptance of feminist arguments about violence against women. It was initiated by the legislature in response to a judicial decision that had provoked widespread outrage.[131] Kim Campbell, then minister of justice, set up a nationwide series of consultations with women's groups involved in issues of violence to provide guidance for legislative change.[132] This law could not have come into being had there not already been significant changes in beliefs and norms about gender and violence. But the new law can, in turn, foster and reinforce change—and it can face resistance because the relevant norms and beliefs are in flux and still vary greatly across the population.

VIII. LIMITS AND POTENTIAL OF RELATIONAL TRANSFORMATION THROUGH LAW: FURTHER REFLECTIONS ON THE CANADIAN LAW OF SEXUAL ASSAULT

As I said at the outset, neither changing the law nor adopting a relational approach to rights can, by themselves, stop violence against women. The change in Canadian law will not stop men's anger at women; it will not stop a widespread cultural propensity to make women the target of rage and frustration (generated, for example, by workplace humiliations or the inability to find work[133]); it will not stop the projection of evil onto women and their sexuality or the sense that violence is justified as a means of controlling their dangerous sexuality. I believe all these patterns must change in order to end systemic violence against women, whether sexual assault by a stranger or an acquaintance or the alarmingly common practice of men beating their intimate partners.

Nevertheless, the Canadian law of sexual assault does challenge a set of beliefs that are part of these deep patterns. The idea that women welcome a show of force in sex—that not just power, but coercion, is a turn-on—can no longer be safely presumed (a reasonable effort to ascertain consent is necessary). Similarly, it is no longer safe for men to act on the idea that women are temptresses who cannot expect men to control themselves if they have been "led on." Women who dress "provocatively" and do not stay out of harms way are no longer fair game for assault.[134] Men must thus relate to women differently in a variety of ways. Powerful images of the nature of sexuality and men's and women's roles with respect to sex are challenged, and men who ignore that challenge risk being held accountable for violence they used to get away with. Modifying their behavior may cause stress and resentment, but is also likely, gradually, to yield a change in everyone's understanding of men, women, and sexuality.

A relational approach also helps us see why the change in the Canadian law of sexual assault was justified despite the incursion on long-standing rights of the accused not to be convicted unless subjective intent to commit the crime was proven. This matters a great deal because of the point I noted above: in the case of sexual assault, as in so many areas, it did not turn out to be possible to promote equality without changing the existing rights of the dominant group (since virtually all of the accused in sexual assault cases are men).[135] The conventional liberal aspiration to achieve equality by taking existing rights and finally applying them equally to all is only possible if "rights" are understood in the most general terms of big, abstract rights, such as freedom, equality, or security. These broad rights can and should be made to apply equally to all. But to do so will very often involve removing particular existing legal rights and immunities, imposing new obligations, and creating new legal entitlements for those who have been disentitled. Existing rights and immunities too often have systemic advantage and disadvantage built into them.

The Canadian law of sexual assault gives us a good example of why simply extending existing legal rights will not be sufficient to achieve equality. To dismantle law's role in sustaining men's power and advantage over women, some of men's traditional rights and immunities had to be taken away. This does not mean that the law is being used to harm or disadvantage individual men accused of sexual assault in order to redress the historic disadvantage of women. It means that those traditional rights and immunities are now understood to be inconsistent with basic liberal commitments to the equal protection of the law.

It is important to emphasize here that while particular legal rights and immunities may need to be changed in order to advance equality (or security of the person, or free speech, etc.), there is no reason to believe that a relational approach would cast doubt upon the value of any of basic rights outlined in the *Charter* or most other Western constitutions. As we will see in more detail in the next chapter, all constitutional rights (indeed all rights) require interpretation, and a relational approach will support some interpretations over others. For example, interpretations of equality provisions that recognize and attempt to redress systemic disadvantage lend themselves to, and will be supported by, relational analysis. Interpretations that focus on intent to discriminate will receive less favorable analysis from a relational approach. Again, as we will see shortly, a relational approach offers reasons for not treating property as a constitutional right (as the *Charter* does not, but most other constitutions do).

It is hard to imagine, however, that the big broad rights, such as freedom of speech, press, and conscience, freedom of assembly and movement, due process or fundamental justice, liberty or security of the person, could be shown in principle to foster relationships that undermine the core values of society. Particular interpretations will, of course, be contested, and particular notions of rights—such as the right of an accused never to be convicted without proof of subjective intent—will change. In the inevitable cases where rights conflict, a relational analysis can be expected to yield outcomes different from an individualistic, boundary-focused approach. Each side may think that the other's interpretation undermines a core right—as happens in a wide variety of conflicting interpretations. Nevertheless, there is nothing in the relational approach that threatens basic rights. My claim is that the inevitable challenges of definition, interpretation, and debate about the meaning of those rights will be best facilitated by relational analysis.

IX. CONCLUSION

Judith Shklar's liberalism of fear provides a powerful indictment of the liberal state she seeks to defend. She offers some of the most effective language I have seen to describe the horror of the failure to protect women and children from pervasive fear. One of Shklar's central purposes was to limit the power of the state because the state is the most dreaded source of fear and cruelty: "systematic fear is the condition that makes freedom impossible, and it is aroused by the expectation of institutionalized cruelty as by nothing else."[136] My approach to systemic fear appears to cut against this purpose in the sense that it asks us to expand our conception of the appropriate tasks of the liberal state to include the transformation of the relation between men and women. But, in fact, the relational approach reveals that the issue is not the expansion of the scope of the state, but the expansion of our understanding of what that scope *is*.

My relational analysis reveals law's complicity in subjecting women to "systematic fear," the condition that Shklar rightly says is incompatible with freedom. The cruelty of private sexual violence is not institutionalized, but a great deal of male impunity for that violence is. The change to the Canadian law of sexual assault shows how law structures—and can restructure—patterns of relationship that are inconsistent with the basic liberal values of equality and security from fear.

The relational approach does require a rethinking of the categories of public and private; it does acknowledge that existing rights and impunities needed to be withdrawn; it does raise the wider challenge of how to articulate the legitimate scope of the state if the categories of public and private cannot be used in traditional ways to demarcate that boundary. But the amendments to the law did not expand the scope of the state, and neither will many demands to change the way existing law structures relations of inequality or insecurity. In some instances, a relational analysis of the many dimensions of society that foster such inequality and insecurity might lead not only to a greater awareness of law's complicity but also to the inclination to actually expand the reach of the law. (Some of the laws and regulations regarding sexual harassment might count as such expansion. Although, again, much of sexual harassment is a matter of impunity for already regulated actions, such as assault [nonconsensual touching] and abuse of authority.) But the case of Canada's sexual assault amendments offers a concrete example of Shklar's insights into the centrality of fear, which reveals the limitations of the traditional liberal approach and the advantages of a relational one.

The liberal state has systematically failed to provide its most basic protection to women and children, and the nature and harm of that failure is best captured in relational rather than boundary terms. Men routinely do violence to women and children in part because the law and social norms have permitted them to do so with impunity. In addition, men do violence to women because the construction of gender has built into it a superiority and dominance of men over women as well as a picture of sexuality that entails a deep asymmetry between men and women. One might even say that the very construction of sex as something men want/need and women can withhold or provide supports the relation of domination: men must have the power to extract the sex they want—or they risk becoming subordinate supplicants. The law has helped sustain this ugly, dangerous, and inherently unequal pattern of relationships. Changes in the law are generated by changes in social norms and are, in turn, able to advance these changes in the direction of law's core value of equality.

In reflecting on the unease that might be generated by my relational project of transformation, it is important to remember that I began my argument not with contested claims about equality and dignity, but with the uncontested, minimal objective of the liberal state to protect its members from violence. If I have persuaded you of the liberal state's failure on *these* terms, and the need to go beyond an approach of trying to "stop men" from committing violence, then I hope the relational approach emerges as plausible. It does not follow that the state would wield more power, control more dimensions of people's lives, if we were to focus our attention on the way the law and the state's delegated power (economic as well as familial) *currently* structures relationships, not only to the detriment of women but also in ways inconsistent with liberalism's basic goals.

A relational approach will help guide an inquiry into how inequalities and failures to protect basic rights should be redressed. To use Shklar's concepts, it will help us figure out how to reduce systemic cruelty. Because of Shklar's concerns (which I take to be widely shared), I have focused on assuring readers that a relational approach does not necessarily increase the scope of state power. But a better formulation is, as I said in chapter 1, that its use will not predetermine an increase, a decrease, or a redirection of state power. I believe it matters that the relational approach does not necessarily entail an expansion of state power. But there is also no reason to believe that whatever the status quo of state power is, it is optimal from a relational perspective. This will surely vary among jurisdictions and among spheres of human activity. Understanding how state power does structure relations is an excellent starting point for a judgment about how it should do so—whether by stepping in, stepping aside, or using existing power in new ways.

In rethinking the tasks of the state from a relational perspective, it is clear that we need to think in new and challenging ways—but these challenges are what we need to take on the violence that is so deeply rooted in society. The disturbing dimensions to the relational approach—such as the unnerving scope of the task and of collective responsibility and the renegotiation of public/private relations—are what makes it suitable for addressing the dramatic failure of the liberal state to protect well over 50 percent of its members from systematic fear. The relational approach does not offer pat answers, but a framework to analyze the problem in ways that can facilitate the necessary change so urgently required.

6

Reconceiving Rights and Constitutionalism

I. INTRODUCTION
A. Context and Objectives

"Rights" are a powerful rhetorical tool in struggles for justice all around the world. And systems of constitutional rights as limits to the legitimate power of governments have been important institutional means for articulating a society's core values and for holding governments accountable to those values. This has been especially true in liberal democracies, despite the puzzle of why democratically elected legislatures should be limited by rights set out in a constitution the democratic origins of which are often problematic or at least far less clear than the democratic legitimacy of the current legislatures.[1]

At the same time, rights and the entire discourse of rights have been the subject of a variety of compelling critiques. Part of the critique is focused on the fact that in Western democracies courts have long been the institutions that define and enforce rights. Courts are, of course, among the least democratically accountable institutions of government. And the legal language of debate over the meaning of rights is among the least popularly accessible forms of public deliberation. This feature of rights is even more prominent (though not perhaps more important) in the context of constitutional rights. The primary institutional mechanism for enforcing constitutional rights as limits has been judicial review, where courts are authorized to determine whether governmental action (legislation, regulation, or executive action) violates a constitutional right. If so, the courts can declare the action invalid. This use of courts to strike down legislation they find to be inconsistent with constitutional rights has been widely criticized as being undemocratic.[2]

In this chapter I argue that a relational approach to rights meets many of the objections to rights discourse. I also make a separate, but related, argument for an understanding of constitutional rights not as "trumps" (as they are famously described in the American model of constitutionalism[3]), but as triggers for a dialogue of democratic accountability. This shift in understanding of constitutionalism allows governments to be held accountable to rights in a democratically defensible way. The approaches I propose make it possible to draw on the many advantages of rights while avoiding some of their greatest limitations. Similarly, in the accountability approach, the useful tension between rights and democracy that is at the heart of constitutionalism can be sustained in a way more in keeping with the best understanding of both.

For most of the twentieth century, the American model of judicial review and a corresponding notion of rights as trumps was the dominant model of constitutional protection of rights. This dominance has now significantly eroded. Canada and South Africa, for example, have constitutions that explicitly invite courts to consider when limitations on rights might be justified—and thus deny their trump-like status.[4] The proportionality approach in many European contexts also makes a balancing of competing values integral to the interpretation of rights.[5] Nevertheless, the rhetorical use of rights still very often carries with it the idea that to invoke a rights violation is to proclaim unequivocally the illegitimacy of what a government has done. And there has been a striking failure of institutional imagination with respect to the kinds of structures that could foster democratic dialogue about the meaning of rights as well as effective protection of rights. In liberal democracies, judicial review remains an almost universal mechanism.[6]

I have, therefore, a range of objectives for this chapter. I think that my arguments for a relational approach to rights can and should be used in all contexts where rights are invoked, defined, debated, or defended. While a relational approach may ultimately suggest institutional changes, the approach can be used right now in every existing legal system. I recommend it to judges, to lawyers, and to activists who use rights language. The understanding of constitutional rights protection in terms of a dialogue of democratic accountability will, on the other hand, fit more readily within some existing structures than others. While in the United States there can be modes of writing judicial opinions that invite more or less openness to public deliberation and institutional dialogue,[7] some version of the idea of rights as trumps is deeply ingrained.[8] And there is virtually no chance of experimentation with alternative institutional forms. Canada's *Charter of Rights and Freedoms* is, by contrast, well suited to both a relational approach to rights and a dialogical understanding of constitutionalism. But even in Canada, no institutional changes are likely in the short term. The alternative I discuss at the end of the chapter was proposed in Canada as a means of giving effect to social and economic rights, but it was to serve as a supplement to the existing structure of judicial review. While I neither envision nor advocate immediate institutional change, I hope that people everywhere will begin to think more creatively about how to protect rights in ways that acknowledge their constructed and contested character. And, to circle back,

I advocate thinking through the many puzzles of rights in terms of the way rights structure relationships.

B. Outline: The Problem and the Proposed Solution

Human rights invoked in the international context are often treated as having self-evident content. The focus is on implementation and enforcement. The urge to enforcement is especially strong when people are suffering violence: the language of rights is invoked to inspire moral outrage and the will to intervene, to create a bulwark against government tyranny, or ethnic cleansing, or deeply embedded practices, such as wife assault.

This focus buries the highly contested nature of the meaning of the rights themselves. Rights must be defined before they can be protected.[9] In this chapter, I highlight the problem of how decisions about definitions are made. I argue that rights are collective decisions about the implementation of core values. Constitutional rights, in particular, are means of holding governments accountable to core values. I argue that a relational approach to rights provides a useful framework for understanding and evaluating the collective choices entailed both in constitutional rights and in the laws challenged as violating them.

This chapter thus takes up a core problem of constitutional rights: how they can simultaneously function as a bulwark against illegitimate force *and* be understood as the products of collective choice. This same problem arises (though in different institutional form) in the context of international human rights. Another way of posing the puzzle is this: if rights are recognized as collective choices, then why should they have the (moral or legal) authority to set limits to democratic outcomes (or to the scope of national sovereignty, in the case of international human rights)? I think that people imagine that rights could only have the authority to limit democracy or sovereignty if they somehow have a transcendent meaning that is above and beyond politics.[10] It seems, then, that if one brings attention to the fact that rights are (evolving) commitments that societies make to their core values, rights will (rightly) be seen as human choices, which then (wrongly) will be seen as having insufficient weight to stand up against democratic outcomes.

Thus my project might be seen as an unworkable paradox: how can an optimal means (both institutional and rhetorical) of protecting rights also be asked to highlight the contingent and contested quality of their meaning? The core of the answer that I elaborate here is that this is only a variation of the fundamental paradox of constitutionalism: how can a government democratically bind itself against future democratic decisions, and how is this binding to be implemented in a democratically defensible way? I think the approaches I outline in this chapter offer a better answer than the traditional (American-influenced) models of rights and constitutionalism.

As I noted above, in taking up this puzzle I make two related points. The first is that all the inevitable decisions about rights are best analyzed in terms of the way rights structure relationships—of power, trust, responsibility, and so on. The second is that the constitutional protection of rights is best understood as a dialogue of democratic accountability. These points are separable, but they reinforce one another: a relational approach to rights highlights the contested decision making involved in rights, which then makes an accountability approach preferable to rights as trumps; and my proposed dialogue of democratic accountability works best with a relational approach because it is an optimal way to describe conflicting interpretations of rights.

I should note at the outset that when I refer to constitutionalism my focus will be on constitutionalism as a means of protecting rights from violation by democratic decision making—usually through judicial review.[11] Although judicial review is only one part of the institutional structure by which governmental decision making is shaped—and indeed is only one part of what makes rights secure—it has become an important part of international rights discourse and a key project for countries trying to develop democratic institutions consistent with a respect for rights. Thus it is constitutionalism as rights protection that I want to reconceptualize rather than its fuller meaning as the structuring of governmental institutions (although, as we will see, the reconceptualization invites new institutional structures of rights protection).

I begin in section II with a brief canvas of the different contexts in which rights are invoked and introduce my relational approach to rights. In section III, I take up the core of my argument: rights are collective choices, and constitutionalism must be reformulated accordingly. In section IV, I take up and respond to critiques of constitutional rights and, more broadly, rights talk, arguing that a relational approach meets or mitigates these concerns. In section V, I provide examples of how a relational approach can help analyze debates over which rights should be constitutionalized and guide interpretation of existing constitutional rights. I also offer my conception of the purpose of constitutional rights as structuring relations of equality not only between citizen and state, but also among citizens. Finally, section VI presents a concrete proposal for a model of protecting social and economic rights that is consistent with my picture of constitutionalism as a dialogue of democratic accountability. This model encourages a relational approach and highlights the limits of the dominant court-centered understanding of rights and constitutionalism.

II. THE LANGUAGE OF RIGHTS AND A MOVE
TO A RELATIONAL APPROACH
A. The Ubiquity of Rights

In the United States, the language of rights has long dominated both political debate and casual conversation. Today, people throughout the world formulate their claims, concerns, and protests in the language of rights. Institutions such as international criminal courts operate on the basis of claims about universal human rights.[12] Tragedies, such as the massacres in Rwanda, are discussed in the language of rights, as are the debates over when international intervention is appropriate. Virtually every state that has made a transition to democracy has created a constitution that outlines protected rights. In Europe, the *European Convention on Human Rights*[13] recognizes rights, the *Treaty on European Union*[14] makes membership conditional on their protection, and the European Human Rights Tribunal adjudicates claims of state violation. Most Latin American countries have rights listed in their constitutions, and legislation is subject to judicial review for compliance with those rights.[15] In addition, most Latin American countries are part of a regional human rights system integrated by the Inter-American Commission on Human Rights and the Inter-American Court of Human Rights.[16] And there is the *African Charter on Human and Peoples' Rights,* which established both the African Commission on Human and Peoples' Rights and the African Court of Human and Peoples' Rights.[17]

In short, the prevailing language of justice and entitlement is overwhelmingly that of *rights.* Thus in my view, the debate over the desirability of rights (as concept and legal institution) has, in practical terms, been decisively won by those who advocate the language of rights. Despite the merits of the (ongoing) scholarly objections,[18] the practical issue is not *whether* but *how* the language of rights will be used. The best hope for meeting the concerns of its opponents is to shift the understanding of rights—both what the term means and how rights are best defined and protected by state institutions. That is my project here.

Rights are claimed in many contexts. Casually, such claims usually assert abstract entitlements rather than actual legal claims, as in "I have a right to my privacy" or "I have a right to my opinion." In international human rights debates, rights claimants often refer to rights outlined in international documents, such as the United Nation's *Universal Declaration of Human Rights.*[19] There are also claims that there are rights that *should* be enshrined in such documents, as in the twenty-five-year struggle to get the UN to adopt the *Declaration on the Rights of Indigenous Peoples* (in September 2007).[20] Sometimes these arguments invoke claims that certain legal rights should follow from a universal *moral* right, such as dignity or equality.

When I use the term "rights," I will be talking about legal rights. Some legal rights, such as spousal rights to support or to a share of the matrimonial home, are created by legislative enactment. Others, such as property and contractual rights, take form in common law[21] countries through court rulings as well as legislation. In this chapter I focus primarily on constitutional rights. These are invoked either to make broad claims of values or entitlement ("There is freedom of speech in this country") or to make legal claims to a right that the government cannot (ordinarily) violate, such as a right to privacy against government wiretapping.

In all these contexts, there are debates over rights. My claim is that they are best analyzed in terms of the ways rights structure relationships.

B. A Relational Approach to Rights

The relational approach I propose[22] has four steps. The first is to examine the rights dispute to determine what is structuring the relations that have generated the problem. (Rights debates, even highly abstract ones, like which rights belong in a constitution, do not arise in a vacuum.) Specifically, in a legal case, how is law structuring the relevant relations, and how is that structuring related to the conflict? Having established this context, the next question is what are the values at stake. The third is to ask what kinds of relationships would foster those values. The fourth is to determine how competing versions of a right would structure relations differently.

The basic premise of this approach is that what rights do and have always done is construct relationships—such as those of power, responsibility, trust, and obligation. The decisions about how the law *should* construct relations are best made on the basis of inquiry into the questions listed above.

In some cases, both the role of the law in generating the problem and the value at stake will be obvious. For example, in the debate over same-sex marriage, it is clear that the problem is the legal exclusion of same-sex couples, and it is clear that the values of equality and dignity are at stake for those arguing in its favor. The values at stake for the opponents are somewhat less clear and take various forms: the stability of society; the stability of an institution (marriage) that long predates our particular legal and political arrangements and that is said to be essential for the well-being of society and its members; the collective norms of sexual morality and the importance of having the state reflect and support them.

Attending to this last issue may help people understand the inevitable loss some will feel when state support is withdrawn from the norms they had seen as simply natural. It becomes clearer that the law has the coercive power to change the meaning of one's social world (even if no one is coerced to participate in a same-sex marriage). Articulating the value of having the law mirror one's understanding of social reality (in this context the "normalness" of heterosexual marriage) highlights the fact that many of the most important social contests are over the form this sort of inevitable coercion should take. (I return to this example in section V.B.)

Sometimes in technical legal debates over, say, the scope of copyright protection or fiduciary obligations of corporate CEOs, it is an important contribution to the debate to make clearer what the competing values at stake are. For example, the rules of copyright may have nonobvious implications for access to intellectual resources in developing countries. The obligation of CEOs to maximize profit may interfere with (or be so interpreted as to interfere with) their capacity to take issues of social and environmental responsibility into account in their decision making.[23]

Once the relevant values are clear, it will be easier to move to the stage of deciding on what form of the legal rights (and obligations) in question will actually foster the values at stake. This question, in turn, will be clarified by asking what kinds of relationships the competing forms of the right will structure and whether those relationships will foster the values at stake.

For example, will the very fact of exclusion from marriage, a central legal institution, construct relations of inequality? Is it a badge of inferiority that *must* generate relations of inequality? Or is it possible that access to civil partnership (as in England) will ultimately generate relations of equality and respect just as effectively as access to marriage? In which case the claim that *only* access to marriage can meet the requirement of equality and dignity might be wrong. As this brief example suggests, there is an inevitable element of uncertainty, even speculation, in the claims that a given form of law would promote a certain structure of relations. In the case of same-sex marriage there is a sufficient variety of legal solutions in different countries that it may be possible later to make some empirical claims about which forms of legal rights best shaped relations of equality and respect. Similarly, a decade from now, the dire predictions about the consequences of a legal change in the meaning of marriage can be examined for their accuracy.[24]

This relational approach to rights works as well for the law of property and contract as for areas like family law in which the law obviously structures relationships. (In the example from family law above, of course, the relationships in question were not just those within families, but the wider structures of social relations that would be affected by legal change.) For example, as lawyers know, property rights are not primarily about things, but about people's relation to each other as they affect and are affected by things.[25] The rights that the law enforces stipulate limits on what we can do with things depending on how our action affects others (for example, nuisance law), when we can withhold access to things from others, and how we can use that power to withhold to get them to do what we want (we are now into the realm of contract and how it is backed by property), and what responsibilities we have with respect to others' well-being. For example, tort law invokes the explicitly relational question "who is my neighbor" to determine to whom people owe an obligation to take reasonable care (such as shoveling one's sidewalk or preventing contaminants, such as decomposing snails, in the soft drinks one manufactures).[26] The common law also defines fiduciary relationships: it defines particular relationships of trust and responsibility, such as those between doctor and patient. In the realm of contract, the law takes account of relationships of unequal bargaining power, and it defines certain parameters of employment and of landlord–tenant relationships. In deciding on the importance to give instances of reliance, judges must make choices about the patterns of responsibility and trust the law will foster in commercial relationships.[27]

I run through this list to make it easier to think about my claim that in defining and enforcing rights the law routinely structures and sometimes self-consciously takes account of relationship.[28] What I propose is that this reality of rights structuring relationships become the central focus of the concept itself and, thus, of all discussion of what should be treated as a right, how rights should be enforced, and how they should be interpreted. It is really a matter of bringing to the foreground of our attention what has always been the background reality. My claim is that people will do a better job of making all the difficult decisions involving rights if they focus on the kinds of relationships they actually want to foster, what the values at stake in that fostering are, and how different concepts and institutions will best contribute to that fostering.

Finally, it is important to see that the relational approach is not some sort of collective *alternative* to protecting and enforcing individual rights. It is, rather, a means of doing so. When I say that a right structures relationships, that also means that those relationships make possible the enjoyment of the right. To enjoy one's property rights, for example, requires that most people will defer to one's power to exclude (even if they are cold and homeless). This hierarchy of power relations also structures employment relations: people agree (via contract) to perform labor in order to have property (payment in wages otherwise withheld) transferred to them. In a factory, everyone understands the relations of ownership: the people who build the computers do not own them; their employers do. And they understand that the power to hire and fire is part of the hierarchy of power relations that flows from the relations of ownership.

One could also tell a story of the relations of freedom made possible by property and contract law. Indeed, there is a long history of competing narratives about the values fostered by relations structured by property and contract law. (There are particularly clear examples of this in the debates in the early twentieth century over U.S. and Canadian minimum wage and maximum hours laws.)[29]

Thus to engage in debates about what the relations of property should be—how property law should structure relations (the relations that largely *constitute* the right of property)—is to deliberate about what the rights of property should mean by attending to the concrete manifestation of that meaning. To attend to the relationships that constitute property rights and that are constructed by property law is to deliberate about rights, not some other collective value.

III. JUSTIFYING CONSTITUTIONAL RIGHTS
A. Constitutional Rights as Collective Choices

I begin with the still powerful American conception of constitutional rights in order to highlight the need for an alternative paradigm. The notion that there are certain basic rights that no government, no matter how democratic, should be able to violate is a central idea behind the U.S. Constitution and its institution of judicial review.[30] On this view, basic rights should be enshrined in the constitution, and democratically enacted legislation that violates those rights should be struck down by the courts. But the simple, compelling clarity of this idea is difficult to sustain in modern times. The Framers of the U.S. Constitution did not worry much about whether there were such basic rights and what they were.[31] Their confidence was the foundation for their vision of constitutionalism. Today, however, we have a two-hundred-year history of the vicissitudes of rights jurisprudence in the United States. For example, neither property nor equality look today like they did in 1787. Even core values seem not to take a constant form. There are disputes about rights at every level: What should be called a basic right? Is there a right to food? To health care? Are natural rights the source of legal rights? Which rights should be constitutional? What is their practical scope? Debates over the meaning and implementation of rights are inherent in rights themselves.

If rights are to serve as constraints on democratic outcomes, they must do so in a way that is true to their essentially contested and shifting meaning. It is, therefore, important to acknowledge the depth of the changes over time in both popular and legal understandings of rights. Consider, for example, equality. Until recently, in all Western countries significant restrictions on the legal rights and actual opportunities for women were widely (though not unanimously) believed to be consistent with a basic commitment to equality.[32] Most of these restrictions are now unacceptable as a matter of both law and public opinion. Consider also the changes in common law conceptions of contract since the mid-nineteenth century. People have come to expect constraints on individual contracts, such as minimum wage legislation, and courts continue to work out concepts of fairness in contract—such as unjustifiable enrichment and unconscionability—in ways that would have been hard to imagine in the middle of the nineteenth century.[33] These shifts are ongoing, and a workable conception of rights needs to take account of the depth of the continuing disagreement in democratic societies about rights. For example, what does equality mean, and how does it fit with our contemporary—and contested—understanding of the market economy and its legal foundations, property and contract? How much economic inequality is the normal or necessary consequence of the efficiencies of a free market, and how much is inconsistent with equal citizenship?

Once we acknowledge the changing and contested quality of basic rights, the problem of protecting them from democratic abuse is transformed. We do not have to abandon the basic insight that democratic majorities can threaten individual rights (such as the internment of Japanese–Canadian and American citizens). But we must see that the problem of defending individual rights is inseparable from the problem of defining them. Even if deep immutable truths underlie rights, the terms that capture those truths shift; the ongoing problem of defining rights remains.

We can then see that the neat characterization of constitutionalism as balancing a tension between democracy and individual rights is not adequate for the actual problem. In a society that gives voice and effect to its collective choices and values through government institutions, *both* the courts and the legislatures[34] must be seen as expressing those choices and values. Courts have traditionally expressed those shifting collective choices in terms of rights, but we must recognize rights to be just that: terms for capturing and giving effect to what judges perceive to be the values and choices that "society" has embedded in the "law." (I am being deliberately vague as to how values come to be seen to be basic to the legal system and which components of "society" end up influencing the choice of values.)

The judicial implementation of societal values (and the choices and conflicts they entail) is present at every level of legal rights from the common law of property to the most obviously contested constitutional cases involving a woman's right to terminate her pregnancy or the question of whether anti-hate speech laws violate free speech. Consider, for example, the competing values of the right to use one's property as one wishes and the right to the "quiet enjoyment" of one's property. In the nineteenth century, judges had to find ways to accommodate the noises and smells of early industrialization that would have clearly violated the right to quiet enjoyment of traditional nuisance law.[35] Today nuisance law continues to mediate conflicts over what constitutes legitimate land use, such as complaints by neighbors of huge hog farms,[36] and property law adjudicates the reasonableness of the restrictions condominiums place on the use of units.[37]

Judges, in effect, make and enforce evolving collective choices about the practical meaning of legal rights, such as property and equality. Where judges are, inevitably, forced to make difficult interpretive decisions, they generally justify their decisions on the basis of some form of collective choice, though that language is not used. Such choices may include the original collective choice of the Framers (or ratifiers) of the Constitution, the tacit choices (of custom or judges) accumulated in the common law, or society's commitment to basic values reflected in the language of the Constitution—these are all forms of collective choice as the basis for the interpretation of rights.

Even if one believes that that there is a form of natural law or a philosophical foundation for the nature of rights, one must also believe that society has somehow made a collective choice to embrace those principles and to *authorize judges* to enforce them (by interpreting rights according to those principles).

My first point, then, in seeing the hidden complexity of "rights versus democracy" is that judicially defined rights are as much collective choices as laws passed by the legislature. And if rights no longer look so distinct from democratic outcomes, democracy also blurs into rights. Democracy is, of course, not merely a matter of collective choice; it is also the expression of "rights" to a voice in the determination of those collective choices.

The problem of constitutionalism thus can no longer simply be protecting rights from democracy. The more complex problem can be posed in various ways, with either rights or collective choice on both sides of the balance. In one formulation, using the language of rights, the problem is why some rights (constitutional rights) should limit others, namely, the rights to democratically make collective choices. For example, why should freedom of speech constrain the right of the people to legislatively restrict violent pornography or hate speech? In another formulation, using the language of collective choice, the problem is why some collective choices, that is, those we constitutionalize as rights, should limit other collective choices, that is, the outcomes of ordinary democratic processes.[38] For example, why should the collective choice to treat equality as a constitutional right limit the collective choice to democratically define marriage as between a man and a woman? Since the idea of a limit is itself problematic, I think a more helpful way to put it is this: we need a better way of thinking about how and why we measure democratic outcomes against core values.

B. *Rights and Values*

Here it is important to clarify the way I am using the term "right" in relation to the term "value."[39] By value I mean any of the big abstractions used to articulate what a given society sees as essential to humanity or to the good life for its members. That could include such core values as equality, dignity, security, harmony, peace, bodily integrity, autonomy, liberty, freedom of conscience, freedom of expression, adequate material resources, individual and/or collective spiritual expression, respect and care for the earth and the rest of creation, scope for individual and/or collective artistic expression. These values can, of course, be understood differently by different people and societies, and they can conflict with one another in practical implementation. And different societies (and individuals) will place higher priority on some than others. By "rights" I mean a particular institutional and rhetorical means of expressing, contesting, and implementing such values. Although some people use "right" and "value" interchangeably, or claim that there is a basic (usually moral rather than legal) right to whatever is a core value, I prefer to distinguish the terms.

The distinction between rights and values is, of course, necessary for my relational approach to rights. The distinction allows for the multistage inquiry into rights debates I outlined above: What are the values at stake? What kinds of relations will foster the values in question? What kinds of relationships will a contested version of the right structure? But I think it is also justified for a variety of other reasons.

One virtue of this distinction is that it makes it easier to discuss whether all societies share certain core values, such as human dignity or liberty, and whether they express and implement them in terms of rights or not. This makes comparison across both time and culture more useful, since it is clear at least that the Anglo-American institutions of rights are not universal. And not all societies conceptualize their core values in ways that are like the Anglo-American liberal understanding of rights as individual entitlements. The distinction then allows one to say that there are instances of shared core values but different rhetorical and institutional ways of expressing and implementing them. For example, both equality and dignity might be expressed through norms of showing mutual respect, without those norms being cast in the language or institutions of legal rights. A value such as liberty can be understood as something that comes into existence through mutual obligation and modes of life made possible by shared commitment and a thriving collective life. Liberty can then be understood as important to every person without conceptualizing it as an individual entitlement. For these reasons I find the language of inherent individual rights to be far too particular to use for empirical claims about universally shared values.

Similarly, I find values to be a more capacious term for articulating what matters most to people—whether understood in terms of their well-being or their ability to develop or express their nature (as, say, rational beings or affective, embodied, and relational beings or as spiritual beings). Thus if the project is to express the foundational normative commitments that should guide a legal system, it is not at all clear to me that the best way to capture a value such as liberty is in terms of an individual entitlement to a right to liberty. As I noted in chapter 1 (and return to in "Closing Reflections"), I have a lot of sympathy for Linda Zerilli's Arendtian view[40] that freedom exists only as relations of freedom. If this is so, the language of individual entitlement is arguably not the best way to think about how to make this value real in human lives.

This conceptual limitation of rights language is even clearer with respect to such evolving values as environmental sustainability. Of course, there are efforts to express this value in rights language.[41] There is always a political advantage to get a value recognized as a right. But I doubt that what is really at stake in developing a collective commitment to an environmentally respectful and sustainable mode of life is essentially about individual entitlement.

The example of the environment points to a practical advantage of maintaining the distinction between rights and values and to treating values as guiding principles for the meaning and implementation of rights. There are values that are widely recognized as such but have not achieved the status of rights. Whether such status is ultimately optimal or not, using values as a guide in reflecting on the legitimacy of governmental action allows for a fuller engagement with what is really at stake. The importance of the parent–child relationship is an example of a value (not recognized as a right) that is at stake in governmental policies of extradition and incarceration.[42] The value of cultural and linguistic integrity is at stake in claims about the harms done by the residential schools aboriginal children were forced to attend.[43]

In arguing for the usefulness of the distinct language of values, I do not try to specify the ultimate source of what I call the core values of society. It is enough for my purposes that all societies have values they see as fundamental—to individual well-being or to the nature of individuals as rational agents or to the nature of their collective life or to living in accordance with the laws of nature or with the values of a Creator. And I do not suggest that, unlike rights, core values are immutable or uncontested.

To refer to the core values of a society suggests that there is some level of consensus— or at least that it is relatively clear which views about values are dominant. Equally important, however, is the idea that the understanding of these values—especially the beliefs about what actions or institutions are most consistent with them—will be contested by some and will shift over time. Equality, for example, has long been a core value in the United States. Consider the ringing language of the American Declaration of Independence: "We hold these truths to be self-evident, that all men are created equal, that they are endowed by their Creator with certain unalienable Rights, that among these are Life, Liberty and the pursuit of Happiness." Yet those famous words were, infamously, written by a slaveholder for a society large parts of which depended on slave labor. And, for more than a century after these words were written, women could not vote and African Americans and Native Americans were effectively disenfranchised for even longer.[44] Rather than simply accuse the authors of hypocrisy (although I think some of that is justified), I would say that equality is and long has been a core value of American society and that the meaning of that value has always been deeply contested. It is not just that long ago what was seen as somehow consistent with equality now seems obviously a violation of equality. Today there are profound differences in people's views about important issues of equality, such as the levels of poverty and child welfare in the United States and Canada. And yet it is also true that one can engage in argument about whether such levels are consistent with a commitment to equality without having to make an argument either about inherent human equality or the right to equality before the law. I think it is equally important in understanding core values that there will be no agreement about what this means in practice, that ideas about practical meaning will change over time, and that there is widespread commitment to the abstract principle of equality.

In my understanding, then, not only does the meaning of rights change over time, but so does the understanding of core values. As noted above, one might say that respecting and protecting the environment is gradually becoming a core value in a way that it simply was not for mainstream North American society for the past two hundred years. (This value may or may not ultimately take the form of a right.) It will also frequently be the case that both the core values of one's own society and those of others will be contested as inadequate or inappropriate. It is often the project of reformers to persuade others (internal and external to one's society) that they should change their understanding of core values.[45]

There is always a question in imperfectly democratic societies (which include all large-scale societies) of whether what are widely taken to be the core values of the society—and what those values should mean in practice—are disproportionately articulated and enforced by some powerful subset of the members of the society. Within both Canada and the United States, for example, there are aboriginal groups for whom the language of rights, and perhaps particularly private property rights, does not adequately express their understanding of core values. This means that the relational approach has to include attention to ways of equalizing access to public deliberation and decision making about what society's core values should be. It also means that tacit claims of consensus about core values must always be read in light of the inevitability of contestation and the possibility of transformation.

Despite all these complications about what the core values of a society are, I think that they are useful in sorting through the questions of how rights ought to be defined and implemented. Societies that choose to use the language and institutions of rights to implement their core values often name many of those values as rights. But it is common that they do not do so with respect to all values, even those relevant to the legal and political realm. For example, the values of the rule of law and dignity are not listed as rights in either the U.S. Constitution or the Canadian *Charter*.[46] But both concepts are used as part of an interpretive framework. In Canada, questions about the impact of governmental action on dignity or whether such action would undermine the rule of law have been basic parts of the jurisprudence. The use of values not enshrined as rights to guide the inquiry is similar to the role values play in my approach (though the steps of analysis are not the same).

Finally, I would note that I do not see the relationship I propose between rights and values as entailing a *denigration* of rights. It is true that I deliberately distinguish the two so that we can see legal rights as a particular institutional and rhetorical way of implementing values. But some such distinction is common in many theories of rights. Sometimes legal rights are seen as means of implementing moral rights. Another example is Martha Nussbaum's treatment of rights as a crucial way of enabling and protecting human capabilities. In all such theories, legal rights are instrumental, but they are not thereby denigrated. They *are* subject to inquiry about the circumstances in which they may not be the best means of advancing values.

I return now to the question of justifying constitutional rights and, in particular, to objections to constitutional rights as violations of democratic principles. Here we begin to see the links between a relational approach to rights and an alternative conception of constitutionalism.

C. Beyond the "Pure Democracy" Critique

The pure democracy critique is primarily aimed at rights as judicially enforced limits on democratic outcomes (rather than rights talk more generally, which might include common law rights or statutory rights). The argument comes in two forms. One rejects any judicial oversight of democratic bodies. The underlying claim can be that, in principle, there are no rights claims that can legitimately stand against democratic outcomes or that there is no justifiable way of *enforcing* such claims or that, in practice, the best way of ensuring rights in the long run is through democratic procedures, not through efforts to circumvent them. The more common form of the argument acknowledges that even if democracy is accepted as the sole or supreme value of a political system there may be times when the courts can play a useful role in making sure the procedural conditions of democracy are met. John Hart Ely in the United States and to some extent Patrick Monahan in Canada defend judicial review in these terms, and each has claimed that the Constitution in his country[47] authorizes judicial review primarily or exclusively for democracy-enhancing purposes.[48]

My view is that democracy has never been the sole or even primary value of the political system in either the United States or Canada and that it could never be the *sole* basis for a good society. There have been and always will be other values that are not derived from democracy. Autonomy is one; although it is necessary for democracy, democratic participation does not exhaust the value of autonomy. The development of people's spiritual nature is another, captured by notions of freedom of conscience and religion.[49] And, of course, these values can be threatened by democratic majorities wielding the power of the state. If one accepts that there are values we cherish for reasons other than their relevance to the functioning of democracy, and that these values may need protection from democratic outcomes, then neither form of the pure democracy critique of rights is persuasive.[50] Even an optimal democracy could threaten core values. Despite the importance of this potential threat, I think that the conventional formulations of rights as limits to democracy are not adequate.

Fortunately, I think it is possible to do a better job of capturing the multiple values that people care about and that may need protection against state power.

For example, autonomy is best understood in terms of relationship, and once we see that, we can begin to rethink what it means conceptually and institutionally for autonomy to serve as a standard for democratic outcomes. As I have argued in previous chapters, the relational approach shifts the focus from protection against others to structuring relationships so that they foster autonomy. Interdependence becomes the central fact of political life, not an issue to be shunted to the periphery in the basic question of how to ensure individual autonomy in the inevitable face of collective power. The human interactions to be governed are not seen primarily in terms of the clashing of rights and interests, but in terms of the way patterns of relationship can develop and sustain both an enriching collective life and the scope for genuine individual autonomy. The whole conception of the relation between the individual and the collective shifts: we recognize that the collective is a source of autonomy as well as a threat to it.

The constitutional protection of autonomy is then no longer an effort to carve out a sphere into which the collective cannot intrude, but a means of structuring the relations between individuals and the sources of collective power so that autonomy is fostered rather than undermined.[51] In this approach, the relation between autonomy and democracy is not simply one of threat and tension—just as the relation between the individual and the collective is not simply a matter of threat.

With this relationship-focused starting point, how do we move beyond "rights as limits to democratic outcomes?" We shift our focus from limits, barriers, and boundaries to a dialogue of democratic accountability—which does not make the mistake of treating democracy as the sole value. We require two things for this dialogue. We need (1) an institutionalized process of articulating basic values that is itself consistent with democracy and (2) ways of continually asking whether our institutions of democratic decision making are generating outcomes consistent with those values. For example, if autonomy is the value at stake, the question would be whether the contested outcome (e.g., legislation) so seriously undermines the structures of social relations that make the development of autonomy possible that it should be found to be a violation of a constitutional right (such as liberty). This mechanism for holding governments accountable to basic values should take the form of institutional dialogue that reflects and respects the collective as the source of the shifting form of those values. Of course, judicial review has for a long time in the United States and recently in Canada and many other countries been the primary vehicle for the articulation of values against which democratic outcomes can be measured.

Judicial review also serves the second purpose: it provides a mechanism for publicly asking whether the outcomes of democratic decision making—primarily legislation— are consistent with the core values articulated in the constitution. But judicial review as practiced in the United States, or even Canada, does not do an optimal job of either objective: leaving these determinations in the hands of judges is questionably consistent with democracy, and the process is equally questionable in its ability to reflect and respect the collective source of the form values take. The issue is not just that judges are unelected and thus not democratically accountable. There is a question of whether judicial opinions encourage reflection on the sources of the rights they interpret and on the way such interpretations have changed over time. And there is a broader question of whether judicial review, like any judge-made decision, fosters informed public deliberation on the issues.

Of course, sometimes controversial constitutional issues, like same-sex marriage, attract a lot of public attention. But part of the issue is whether judges are, or should be seen to be, uniquely qualified to resolve constitutional disputes. To the extent that they are held out to be so, or that formal legal expertise is required to understand the issues, the public capacity for democratic deliberation on core values is undermined. At the end of the chapter, I will outline a proposal for a mechanism of democratic accountability that is significantly different from judicial review and that holds out the promise of upholding core values while also promoting constructive public deliberation about their practical meaning.

The example of relational autonomy together with the idea of democratic account-ability help solve one of the puzzles of justifying rights as limits: how to justify their supremacy over democracy when constitutional rights themselves have shifting content. First, we no longer have, and thus need no longer justify, simple supremacy, but a more complex structure of democratic accountability to basic values—as we will see more clearly in the example at the end. Second, the shifting quality of the rights to which democracy is held accountable makes more sense when our focus is on the structure of relations that fosters the underlying values. It is not at all surprising that what it takes to foster autonomy, or what is likely to undermine it, in an industrialized corporate economy with an active regulatory-welfare state, is quite different from the relationships that would have had those effects in mid-nineteenth-century Canada. These may be different still in twenty-first century Eastern Europe or South Africa. A focus on relationship auto-matically turns one's attention to context and makes sense of the commonly held belief that there are some basic human values *and* that how we articulate and foster those values varies significantly over time and place.

In this vision, rights do not trump democratic outcomes, and so they and the institu-tions that protect them do not have to bear a weight of justification that is impossible to muster. Rather, when we begin with a focus on the relationships that constitute and make possible the basic values—which we use rights language to capture—then we have a better understanding not only of rights but also of how they relate to another set of values, for which we use the shorthand "democracy." The mechanisms for institutionalizing both sets of values must aim at maintaining an ongoing dialogue that recognizes the ways in which democracy and autonomy are both linked together as values requiring each other *and* potentially in conflict with one another.

It will probably have already become apparent to readers familiar with the Canadian *Charter of Rights and Freedoms*[52] that it is much better suited to implementing such a dialogue than is the American system of judicial review, for which, at least formally, rights as trumps is an accurate metaphor. The *Charter's* "override" provision in Section 33 may be seen as an effort to create a dialogue about the meaning of rights that would take place in public debate, the legislature, and the courts.[53] Section 1 invites a dialogue internal to the courts, or to any body considering the constitutionality of a law, by opening the *Charter* with an assertion that rights are not to be seen as absolute: Section 1 reads: "The *Canadian Charter of Rights and Freedoms* guarantees the rights and freedoms set out in it subject only to such reasonable limits prescribed by law as can be demonstrably justified in a free and democratic society."[54] Those reasonable limits cannot be specified in advance; they are, implicitly, open-ended and shifting, requiring judgment and debate.[55]

Perhaps some readers have had occasion to try to explain Section 1 and Section 33 to incredulous Americans—who often conclude that Canadians simply still do not *really* have constitutional rights. The American vision of rights as trump-like limits is so central to the mainstream understanding of constitutionalism that they have a hard time imagining that "rights" could mean anything else. This it true despite the fact that the increasingly obvious problems with this notion drive American scholars to produce thousands of pages each year in efforts to explain and defend it. "Rights as trumps" is a catchy phrase and an apparently graspable, even appealing, concept, but it cannot capture the complex relations between the multiple values societies actually care about.[56] I think *dialogue of democratic accountability*, though not quite as pithy, is truer both to the best aspirations of constitutionalism and to the structure of the Canadian *Charter.*

IV. CRITIQUES OF "RIGHTS TALK"

Let me turn now from the issues of justifying constitutional rights to some of the critiques of rights talk in general: (1) rights are undesirably individualistic, (2) rights obfuscate the real political issues, and (3) rights serve to alienate and distance people from one another. I will not be trying to present these critiques in detail but merely to sketch them to show how a focus on relationship helps construct a response.

Although I will turn to the critiques of rights shortly, I want to begin with the basic question of whether to use the term "rights" at all. Over about the past twenty years there have been two somewhat contradictory phenomena respecting rights. The first is a wide-ranging academic debate about the meaning and usefulness of the term "rights." Some critics, particularly those associated with the critical legal studies movement, have suggested that the term "rights" should be abandoned. They argue, as we will see later, that the purposes intended to be served by "rights" would be better served by avoiding the term altogether.[57] Others suggest that what contemporary legal and political issues need is attention to individual and collective responsibility rather than an ongoing pre-occupation with rights.[58] I have sympathy for both arguments. But the other phenomenon is the global expansion of rights language.

As I noted at the outset of this chapter, I think this global phenomenon is decisive. Since rights *are* being used, the real question is whether there are ways of overcoming the important critiques leveled against them. My argument here is that a relational approach can make a significant difference.

I will begin with the claim that rights talk is excessively individualistic, noting the core of the critique that I find persuasive (and have participated in myself). Implicit in the critique is usually a suggestion that rights are either inherently individualistic or that their historical association with liberal individualism so taints them that they are undesirable tools for political transformation. My argument is that rights are not inherently individ-ualistic because rights are, in fact, inherently relational in nature. I then hold out the hope that if this relational nature is recognized and becomes a regular tool of analysis in rights debates, the historical taint of individualism can be overcome.

A. Individualism

Critics of the individualism of rights point to both practice and theory.[59] In practice, for example, the failure of American constitutional jurisprudence to adequately recognize systemic disadvantage can be attributed to the excessive focus on intent to discriminate and individual harm. Similarly, the American rejection of hate speech legislation as con-stitutionally impermissible can be seen as a failure to understand the collective harm and collective silencing (thus interference with free speech) of hate speech. While Canadian jurisprudence takes a less individualistic stance on these issues, critics also see *Charter* rights as shaped by the heritage of liberal individualism. For example, the charge that *Charter* rights express individualistic values is offered as an argument about why they should not apply to the collective decisions of First Nations.[60]

There are good reasons to believe that all contemporary systems of constitutional rights draw on a powerful legacy of liberal political thought in which rights are associated with a highly individualistic conception of humanity.[61] Indeed, the rights-bearing individual may be said to be the basic subject of liberal political thought. What is wrong with this individualism is that it fails to account for the ways in which our essential humanity is neither possible nor comprehensible without the network of relationships of which it is a part. Most conventional liberal rights theories do not make relationship central to their understanding of the human subject.[62] Mediating conflict is the focus, not mutual self-creation and sustenance. The selves to be protected by rights are seen as essentially separate and not creatures whose interests, needs, and capacities are mutually constitutive. Thus, for example, one of the reasons women have always fit so poorly into the framework of liberal theory is that it becomes obviously awkward to think of women's relation to their children as *essentially* one of competing interests to be mediated by rights.[63]

I share the critics' concerns about how the limitations of history and theory may affect the way rights are actually implemented. Nevertheless, I think that rights can be rescued from their long association with individualistic theory and practice. The best understandings of the nature of the human self and the way rights function are on the side of a realignment of the liberal tradition. Human beings are *both* uniquely individual and essentially social creatures. The liberal tradition has been not so much wrong as seriously and dangerously one-sided in its emphasis.

The relational approach redresses this historical imbalance by making clear, as I said above, that what rights in fact do and have always done is construct relationships. Legal rights *can* protect individuals and the values that matter to them, but they do so by structuring the relations that foster those values. Thus all rights, and the very concept of rights, are best understood in terms of relationship.

My point here is that once rights are conceptualized in terms of the relationships they structure the problem of individualism is at least radically transformed. At the most basic level, the focus of analysis will shift from an abstraction of individual entitlement to an inquiry into the ways the right will shape relations and those relations, in turn, will promote (or undermine) the values at stake. Sometimes a relational analysis will cut through individualistic logic that denies the relevance of context. Sometimes a relational analysis will reveal deep disagreements about underlying values. There will almost certainly still be people who *want* the kind of relationships of unequal power and limited responsibility that the individualistic liberal rights tradition promotes and justifies. But at least the debate will take place in terms of why people think some patterns of human relationships are better than others (for promoting liberty values, for example) and what sort of legal rights will foster those relationships.

For example, there will surely be those who believe that my conception of autonomy involves relationships of individual and collective responsibility that will ultimately undermine autonomy itself. But it will be more helpful to have a debate in those terms than to assert, say, that the rights to private property preclude the taxation necessary for a guaranteed annual income.[64] This is not to say that the debate must proceed on high levels of abstractions about the nature of human autonomy. On the contrary, conflicts over the individualistic views of rights and self can take place at the concrete level of why one thinks that a particular property regime (with high levels of inequality) will better promote true autonomy than a guaranteed annual income supported by progressive taxation. An analysis of the relations of power, of dependence and independence that the different systems would promote, of the kinds of relations that foster initiative, individual responsibility, and mutual respect and how they would fare under the different rights regimes will yield a more fruitful ground of deliberation than will claims about inherent individual rights. The nature of the commitment to individualism can be transformed from a tacit assumption to a position that requires justification in particular cases.

In short, an understanding of rights as constructing relationships will dispel or rebut many of the individualistic assumptions built into the liberal tradition of rights. And those beliefs that lie at the heart of the deepest disagreements will be revealed in a way that fosters understanding of the nature of the disagreement.

B. Obfuscation

Next, let me offer some brief suggestions about how this approach can meet the diverse body of criticism (often associated with critical legal studies) that I have lumped into my second category of objection to rights talk as obfuscation. One of the most important parts of this set of critiques is the objection that when rights are central to political debate, they misdirect political energies because they obscure rather than clarify what is at issue, what people are really after. As with the objection of individualism, this critique points to serious problems. But as I have just argued, those problems are transformed when we understand rights as structuring relationships. A relational analysis will clarify rather than obscure what is really at stake.

If we approach property rights as one of the most important vehicles for structuring relations of power in our society and as a means of expressing the relations of responsibility we want to encourage, we will start off the debate in a useful way. For example, if we ask whether ownership of a factory should entail some responsibility to those it employs and how to balance that responsibility with the freedom to use one's property as one wishes (a balance analogous to that in traditional nuisance law), then we can intelligently pursue the inevitable process of defining and redefining property. We can ask what relationships of power, responsibility, trust, and commitment we want the terms of ownership of productive property to foster, and we can also ask whether those relationships will foster the autonomy, creativity, or initiative we value.[65] By contrast, to say that owners can shut down a plant whenever and however they want because it is their property is to assert either tautology (property *means* the owner has this power) or a historical claim (property has in the past had this meaning). The historical claim does, of course, have special relevance in law, but it can only be the beginning, not the end, of the inquiry into what property should mean. The focus on relationship will help to give proper weight and context to the historical claims and to expose the tautological ones.

One common form of the allegation of obfuscation is the objection that rights are "reified." They appear as fixed entities with meanings that are simply taken as a given. This thing-like quality of rights prevents the recognition of the ways in which *the form rights take* are collective choices that require evaluation. (This precise formulation captures my argument above that the underlying values are not simply collective choices, but that rights can take different forms and that there can be forms other than rights to express and effect those values. But since it is too awkward to keep repeating that more precise formulation, I will use the shorthand "rights are collective choices.") Descriptively, I think reification is a valid concern about the dominant traditions of rights. But, as is no doubt already clear, I do not think it is inevitable. I think that if we always remember that what rights do is structure relationships, and that we interpret rights in that light and make decisions about what ought to be called rights in that light, then not only will the existing reification loosen up, but our new conceptions of rights as relationship will not be as likely to once again harden into reified images that dispel rather than invite inquiry.

There is another form of the critique of obfuscation that a relational approach to rights cannot meet as fully. That is the concern that a focus on rights leads to the misdirection of political energies to courts rather than legislatures, the use of lawyer-run litigation strategies instead of grassroots political organizing for democratic transformation.[66] This remains a problem, even with a reconceptualization of rights, as long as courts (as the Anglo-American system has understood them) remain the primary locus for the interpretation, defense, and implementation of rights. I think, however, that it is reasonable to hope that widespread habits of relational analysis will lead to a recognition that courts are not the only bodies suited to, or responsible for, the (re)structuring of relations necessary for core values to flourish for all.[67] The proposal at the end of this chapter for an alternative mechanism for democratic accountability also shifts the institutional locus of responsibility for rights.

C. Alienation and Distance

Finally, there is the important critique that rights are alienating and distancing, that they express and create barriers between people.[68] Rights have this distancing effect in part because, as they function in our current discourse, they help us avoid seeing some of the relationships of which we are in fact a part. For example (as I noted in chapter 2), when we see homeless people on the street we do not think about the fact that it is in part our regime of property rights that renders them homeless.[69] The dominant conception of rights helps us to feel that we are not only not responsible but are not in any way connected to these "others." If, however, we come to focus on the relationships that our rights structure, we will see the connection between our power to exclude and the homeless persons' plight.[70]

Thus my response to the critique of distancing is that rights conceived as relationship will not foster the same distancing that our current conception does.

Relational rights *could*, however, still serve the protective function that thoughtful advocates of rights-based distancing, like Patricia Williams, are concerned about.[71] Williams points to contractual transactions as instances of relationships in which the parties stand in a highly formalized, abstract relationship to one another. The right of access to these relationships guarantees that inappropriate considerations, such as one's gender, one's sexual preferences, or whether one is seen as a racialized person, do not exclude one from participating in market transactions. This is essential when these transactions are largely responsible for the allocation and distribution of material resources. Her point is that to those historically excluded, what is important for equality, dignity, and security is access to the impersonal transactions, not their replacement with highly personalized relationships. (I don't take Williams's argument to make claims about which transactions would, in an ideal world, be characterized by impersonal rather than more personalized relationships.)

My vision of rights as relationship can respond to this concern. Not only does it have equal respect at its core, but its optimal structures of human relations will always provide both choice about entering relationships and space to withdraw from them.[72] It seems likely that people would choose to have a legal system that allows for the kind of "arms-length," impersonal transactions that Williams sees as functioning as markers of equal respect in a market economy.

Williams's concern points to the question of how one determines when formal relations based on highly abstracted conceptions of the agent construct the kinds of relations one wants—say of equality, mutual respect, and privacy. And when, on the other hand, details of context and even individual identity are essential for rights to foster the values at stake, for example, the use of affirmative action programs to foster equality. My point here is that distance and impersonality are forms of relationship. Sometimes they foster desired values. As such, they are no more ill-suited to a relational conception of rights than, say, more obviously "relational" claims that relations of support, trust, and responsibility foster the autonomy of children.

In sum, then, a relational approach to rights avoids or mitigates the core problems that have given rise to the critiques of rights as individualistic, obfuscating, and alienating. There is also an additional advantage that is central to this approach: it is both an important transformation *and* practical within existing legal systems. No radical restructuring of existing law and courts would be necessary; a move toward habits of relational analysis could begin immediately. Of course, an understanding of the relational nature of rights may encourage changes in legal institutions. My point here is that the use of relational analysis need not wait for such changes. This is because the core of my argument is *not* that rights should begin to structure relationship while previously they have not. My argument is that rights have always structured relationships. Recognizing rights as relational brings to consciousness, and thus open to considered reflection and debate, what already exists. My claim is that this recognition and reflection is capable of transforming the legacy of individualism, obfuscation, and alienation in the tradition of liberal rights.

V. APPLYING "RIGHTS AS RELATIONSHIP" TO CONSTITUTIONALISM
A. Constitutionalizing Rights: Property

I turn now to my sketches of how a relational approach to constitutional rights helps with some specific problems. I begin with an example of the question of which rights should be constitutionalized: should property be among the rights specifically protected in the Canadian *Charter*? This question was debated during the writing of the *Charter*, and property was not included.[73] In the early years after the adoption of the *Charter* there were a few efforts to reopen the question of the inclusion of property. None of these efforts got very far.[74] Nevertheless, I think the example of property remains important because virtually every other Western constitution includes it among the rights that are constitutionally protected. There was a particularly interesting debate on this question during the writing of the postapartheid South African constitution.[75] I pose the question in terms of the Canadian *Charter* rather than as an open-ended one about constitutionalizing property because I think the answer must always be context-specific. Although my argument below is quite general, it relies on my understanding of the core values of the *Charter*.

I use the question of property to make more concrete the abstract question I began the chapter with, how we are to understand the idea of constitutionalizing rights. Once we acknowledge that constitutional rights are collective choices, we not only make the simple "democracy versus rights" formulation untenable; we also make it a great deal more difficult (or we make it more obvious why it is difficult) to explain why some things we call rights (like freedom of speech or conscience) should be constitutionalized in my dialogue of democratic accountability and why others, like property, should not.

My idea of constitutionalism is to make democracy accountable to basic values, to have mechanisms of ongoing dialogue about whether the collective choices people make through their democratic assemblies are consistent with their deepest values. There is a certain irony to this idea of "deepest values" as what constitutionalism protects. When a society chooses to constitutionalize a value, to treat it as a constitutional right, they are in effect saying *both* that there is a deeply shared consensus about the importance of that value *and* that they think that value is at risk. The same people (collectively) who value it are likely to violate it through their ordinary political processes. Although an apparent paradox, this duality makes sense. There are lots of values like that. It may be that the fear is that different majorities at different times will be willing to violate rights they care about if the violation primarily affects a minority to which they do not belong. Many of those who supported the segregation of the American south did not oppose equality in principle. Presumably, they wanted the equal protection of the law for their own class of people. The abrogation of civil liberties in the name of a "war on terror" is another example. It is not that those who support such violations do not value liberty or security for themselves, but that they are (presumably) confident that they (and their friends and family) are not the sort of people whose basic rights will be affected. (They may say that they are willing to bear the costs of inconvenience, like long lines in airports, but they do not expect to be apprehended in airports and whisked off to detention and torture in foreign countries.) This sort of differential commitment to core values can even affect majorities. The exclusion of women from the vote or the professions is an example. The current failure of most states to provide women with the basic security of bodily integrity is another. The incidence of violence against women is not indicative of a general indifference to dignity, security, or bodily integrity (though it may be part of a more generalized glorification of violence, with unrecognized implications for the security of all).

Constitutional rights may also protect against a nonmajoritarian threat by those in power. Tyrannical governments may abuse their power in ways that put most citizens at risk and that violate rights to which the society in general is committed. But this danger does not as clearly capture the puzzle of simultaneous commitment to and propensity to violate core rights in democratic systems.

Once we recognize the duality, we know that it is not a sufficient argument *against* constitutionalizing a right to say either that it is contested and so does not belong in the *Charter of Rights and Freedoms* or that it is so well accepted that it does not need to be in the *Charter.* Of course, those are both arguments one might make about property.

In Canada, and probably more generally in contemporary constitutional democracies, the fundamental premise of constitutional rights is equality.[76] Basic constitutional rights define the entitlements that *all* members of society must have, the basic shared norms that will make it possible not just to flourish as individuals, but to relate to each other as equal members of society.[77] (This is not to say that constitutionally protected values— autonomy, privacy, liberty, security—are themselves identical to or derivative from equality.) This might sound at first perilously close to the basic notion of liberal theory: people are to be conceived of as rights-bearing individuals who are equal precisely in their role as rights bearers abstracted from any of the concrete particulars, such as gender, age, class, abilities, which render them unequal. This conception has been devastatingly criticized by feminist scholars such as Iris Young.[78] My notion is subtly, but I think crucially, different.

The challenge is to capture in constitutional rights the meaning of equal moral worth *given* the reality that in almost every conceivable concrete way we are not equal, but vastly different, and vastly unequal in our needs and abilities. The object is not to make these differences disappear when we talk about equal rights, but to ask how we can structure relations of equality among people with many different concrete inequalities.

The law will in large part determine (or give effect to choices about) which differences matter and in what ways: which will be the source of advantage, power, privilege and which will be the source of disadvantage, powerlessness, and subordination. One might say that whatever the patterns of privilege and disadvantage that the ordinary political and legal processes may generate (such as economic inequality), equal constitutional rights are supposed to ensure that these patterns are consistent with basic equality. Of course, as I noted earlier, there will always be disagreement about which forms of power and advantage are consistent with the basic constitutional commitment to equality. Nevertheless, constitutional rights (in my terms) are a standard, a framework by which to assess the acceptability of these patterns of privilege. Constitutional rights hold ordinary laws to account: the relations they structure must be consistent with basic mutual respect and dignity. Constitutional rights thus define indicia of respect and requirements for dignity—including rights of participation. They define basic ways people must treat each other as equals as they make their collective choices.

Property fits very awkwardly here. It is, at least in the sorts of market economies we are familiar with, the primary source of *inequality*—of power, privilege, and access to goods, including education and health care, as well as material resources.[79] Of course, formally, everyone who *has* property has the same rights with respect to it. Nevertheless, property is a primary vehicle for the allocation of power from state to citizen, and in market economies the presumption has been that that power must and should be distributed unequally—for purposes of efficiency and prosperity and, on some arguments, merit. The unequal distribution of property yields, in market economies, social and political as well as economic inequality. The result, of course, is an ongoing tension between the inequality of power generated by property through the market and the claims of equal rights. We see this, for example, in debates over free speech and access to the media, in campaign spending debates, and as I will note shortly, in arguments for a charter of social and economic rights.

All of this suggests to me that debates over the meaning of property, of the kinds of power that should be allocated to individuals and the limits on that power (as in my earlier examples of landlord–tenant law, environmental regulation, and plant closing legislation), should be part of the ongoing vigorous debate of the most popularly accessible bodies, the legislative assemblies.

There is another, more straightforward, argument against constitutionalizing property: property is really a second-order value; it is a *means* to the higher values the *Charter* treats as constitutional rights—such as equality, life, liberty, or security of the person. It does not really belong with that list, treated as a comparable value. Property, on this account, should be treated as instrumental to both rights and values, not as a primary value or a fundamental right. Remember that in creating a constitutional right the question is whether the value in question is the sort of value to which all governmental decisions should be held accountable. So, in the case of property, if property rights are *not* constitutionalized, it will be easier to challenge a law of property as inconsistent with equality (say, for example, rules of property that permit unilateral plant closings or an interpretation of patent law that allows the monopolistic patenting of life-forms, such as genetically modified white mice). But if property rights *are* constitutionalized, then laws aimed at promoting equality can be challenged as violating property rights (laws giving employees a say in plant closings, laws providing public access to beaches).

Thus one might say that the question is whether one wants property to be held accountable to equality or equality to be held accountable to property. Of course, equality is not the only constitutional value that can conflict with property rights, but this summary question remains apt because property is, as I said, a basic source of inequality. And a choice between these forms of accountability is not literally necessary; constitutional rights can conflict, so there could be both kinds of accountability. But if property is an instrumental, second-order value, it does not make sense for first-order values such as equality to be held accountable to it.

Property is really a proxy for other values—such as liberty, autonomy, security, privacy—that are already protected by the *Charter*. So much of ordinary governmental decision making has an impact on property that it becomes extremely awkward and artificial to determine which of these impacts ought to be described as a violation of property rights. What is actually important is determining when the impact amounts to an infringement of one of the basic values that is in the *Charter*—most likely liberty or security.[80] For example, arbitrary or punitive confiscations, or confiscations without compensation, could surely be deemed to be an infringement on security of the person not in accordance with fundamental justice. People cannot feel secure or free among their fellow citizens, or count on being treated as an equal worthy of respect, if they feel that at any time they could be capriciously deprived of their material possessions. That kind of insecurity would destroy relations of trust, confidence, and equality necessary for a free and democratic society.

In short, the values at stake, such as security, dignity, and equality, do not need a constitutional property right to protect them; they can be better protected by a direct inquiry into the relations that foster those values, including relations with respect to material possessions. I should add that in a different historical context a concept of property as a basic right might serve to guide such an inquiry. But the prevailing conception of property is so infused with inequality (and with presuppositions about the market) that it is not well suited to serve as a constitutional right against which to measure democratic outcomes.

B. The Purpose of Constitutional Rights

There is a possible objection to the argument above, which is important because it goes to the meaning of relational rights in the constitutional context. The focus of the objection would be my claim that "constitutional rights hold ordinary laws to account: the relations they structure must be consistent with basic mutual respect and dignity." My argument is that because all laws structure relations among citizens, part of holding laws accountable to constitutional values is assessing whether those relations—for example, of hierarchy, exclusion, or advantage—are consistent with core constitutional values. Similarly, a relational approach highlights the fact that constitutional rights, too, will structure relations among citizens. Those relations then must be assessed in evaluating competing interpretations of constitutional rights.

The opposing view would be that the purpose of constitutional rights is to limit the scope of government in order to prevent the use of governmental power to violate rights, not to structure relations among citizens. On this view, constitutional governments must treat citizens equally, and thus one might say constitutional rights structure relations of equality between *citizen and state*. But relations *among* members of society are not the object of constitutional law; they are a matter of private choice facilitated by private law. A libertarian might elaborate that these freely chosen relations will in fact be characterized by inequality, social as well as economic. It is only qua citizens that people are equal, thus only in relation to government. Indeed, he might add that this is the only kind of equality that is either possible or a legitimate aspiration. It isn't just that efforts to create social and economic equality are doomed to failure; it is also that their inevitable expansiveness will lead to a totalitarian state.

The issue before us, then, is whether the purpose of constitutional rights is only to structure relations of equality between citizen and state or whether the purpose of constitutional rights must extend to structuring relations among citizens. The first and most familiar form of response involves a limited relational analysis. It is the egalitarian liberal position that because liberal democracies require political equality some degree of economic and perhaps social equality is necessary to make equal participation possible. There are, of course, debates over the kind of equal access to participation required. Those who focus on minimum requirements as opposed to comparative inequality of access offer the least relational analysis. All versions of this approach recognize that the structuring of relations of economic and social equality cannot be left to the rules of property and contract alone (at least as they are currently constructed). While ordinarily the role of "private law" in this structuring is not analyzed as such, these approaches argue that the unequal distribution generated by these rules—that is, by the market—needs to be redistributed or mitigated by welfare, tax systems, subsidized day care, and so on. Here the position is that government must concern itself with relations of social and economic equality (to contested degrees) in order to achieve the political equality necessary for democracy and thus for citizens to, in fact, be equal qua citizens.[81]

The next, more fully relational, approach is to ask (at least tacitly) what kinds of social, economic and political relations are necessary for the core constitutional values, such as equality, dignity, liberty, security of the person to be available to every member of society. One could say that this approach was used in ending legal segregation in the American south. The U.S. Supreme Court ultimately determined that certain kinds of "private" relations of hierarchy and exclusion via the existing legal regime of private property were incompatible with the meaning of equal protection of the law. Privately owned restaurants could no longer be for whites only. It was only after these legally backed relations were held accountable to constitutional norms of equality that significant headway was made in the slow transformation toward equal access to constitutional rights for black Americans.[82] (In the north, it turned out to be much harder to challenge the "private" exclusions of real estate practices that still shape the black ghettos of cities like Chicago.)

It is now largely uncontested that there are legal requirements of equal access to public accommodation whether privately or publicly owned (actually a very old common law principle).[83] Restrictions on the power of employers to hire or fire on the basis of prohibited categories, such as race, gender and religion, are routine—though in some jurisdictions it remains unsettled whether homosexuals are entitled to such social and economic relations of equality. Canadian courts have concluded that the social and legal institution of marriage has such far-reaching implications for relations of equality that the constitutional rights of equality and dignity are only possible if the legal institution of marriage includes same-sex couples.[84] Opponents argue that this inclusion will have such a profound effect on social relations as to destabilize the family and to promote the marginalization of those whose religious beliefs oppose same-sex marriage. The same-sex marriage debate is one of the clearest examples of the significance of structures of relations for core constitutional values.

The links between marriage as a legal, social, and religious institution are particularly complex. But the point the issue reveals is a general one: laws inevitably shape social relations, and the way they do so may conflict with core constitutional values. When that is the case, it makes no sense to say that the relations among citizens are not the concern of constitutional rights.

This brings us then to the fully relational position on the nature of constitutional rights. We have already seen that certain structures of relations are necessary for effective constitutional rights and that law structuring those relations must be held accountable to constitutional norms. Now we can also see that the definition and implementation of constitutional rights will, like all legal rights, inevitably structure the relations between citizens. Whether or not a constitution is held to require same-sex marriage, either interpretation will shape relations among citizens. Since all law shapes social relations, those relations must be part of the responsibility of legislatures and courts seeking to implement, interpret, and protect constitutional rights. Thus a constitutional guarantee of equality—and the equal entitlement to all constitutional rights—*must* engage the question of relations of equality among the members of a polity, not simply between citizen and state.

Indeed one might say that the crucial issue of systemic inequality (which Canadian jurisprudence formally recognizes[85] in ways American jurisprudence does not) can best be understood through the kind of relational analysis I outlined above. The issue at stake is the way law structures relations of hierarchy and exclusion that cannot be understood or transformed in terms of individual intent.[86]

The most straightforward form of this engagement is attention to relations of equality among citizens when considering competing interpretations of constitutional rights. This is what I have been referring to above and will give brief examples of below. But I should note that there is another, much more contested, form it can take: the direct application of constitutional values like equality to "private law" in cases that do not involve state actors. This is sometimes called horizontality.[87] This seems to me also supported by a relational approach. However, it does not follow that existing institutions of judicial review are the best way to implement it.

C. Examples of Relational Interpretation

I begin with a relational comparison between Canadian and American equality jurisprudence. Then I return to the question of property with a brief discussion of how a relational approach would assess when an interference with economic liberty violates the *Charter*, given that property is not listed as a constitutionally protected right.

The contrast between the equality jurisprudence of the American and Canadian Supreme Courts offers an example of the advantages of a relational approach. Of course, equality jurisprudence is an extremely complicated area of law, and a thorough comparison in these terms would require at least a chapter. Nevertheless, I think a brief comparison can give a sense of what a relational approach can offer.

Section 15 of the Canadian Charter of Rights and Freedoms provides that:

(1) Every individual is equal before and under the law and has the right to the equal protection and equal benefit of the law without discrimination and, in particular, without discrimination based on race, national or ethnic origin, colour, religion, sex, age or mental or physical disability.

(2) Subsection (1) does not preclude any law, program or activity that has as its object the amelioration of conditions of disadvantaged individuals or groups including those that are disadvantaged because of race, national or ethnic origin, colour, religion, sex, age or mental or physical disability.[88]

Charter jurisprudence has read the language of "in particular" and "including" to mean that the list of grounds in these sections is not exhaustive and has developed the concept of "analogous grounds." This allows the court to inquire into whether other groups (for example, noncitizens and homosexuals) stand in relations of inequality that have systematically disadvantaged them. In virtually all Canadian equality jurisprudence, the courts look to how a group has been disadvantaged in the past and how the challenged law or practice may exacerbate (or alleviate) that disadvantage. So, for example, in 1989 the Supreme Court of Canada affirmed the template in *Andrews v. Law Society of British Columbia*[89] as "a two-part test for showing discrimination under s. 15(1): (1) Does the law create a distinction based on an enumerated or analogous ground? (2) Does the distinction create a disadvantage by perpetuating prejudice or stereotyping?"[90]

The idea of the perpetuation of prejudice or stereotyping has developed in the context of an understanding of systemic inequality. It is the effect of a law or practice in the context of a history of disadvantage that matters. "Intent" to discriminate is not the issue.

The analysis is framed in terms of an understanding of equality that is essentially relational. One of the first questions a court should ask of a law that is being challenged is whether it fails "to take into account the claimant's already disadvantaged position within Canadian society resulting in substantively differential treatment between the claimant and others on the basis of one or more personal characteristics." The court should always undertake their analysis in light of the purpose of Section 15(1) of the *Charter*, which is to *remedy* inequality. So the question is, then, does the "differential treatment discriminate in a substantive sense, bringing into play the *purpose*...in remedying such ills as prejudice, stereotyping, and historical disadvantage"?[91]

Thus the purpose of Section 15(1), not just of Section 15(2), is to transform existing structures of inequality. Claims under Section 15(1) must always be assessed in terms of the broad context of whether the claimant already stands in relations of inequality, which the challenged law is worsening. I think this question would dispose of a number of challenges to affirmative action in the United States.[92]

An example of this relational jurisprudence is the gradual expansion of the judicial recognition of sexual orientation as an analogous ground of discrimination, finally supporting same-sex marriage. In the case that led to the Supreme Court of Canada's 1999 ruling on same-sex marriage, *M v. H*,[93] we can further see the relational nature of their analogous ground reasoning. (This case raised the question of whether a woman who had been part of a long-term lesbian relationship could seek support under the Family Law Act, which covered unmarried heterosexual couples in a "conjugal" relationship.) Justice Cory framed the issue in terms of earlier analogous ground jurisprudence:

> In *Egan*, this Court unanimously affirmed that sexual orientation is an analogous ground to those enumerated in s. 15(1). Sexual orientation is "a deeply personal characteristic that is either unchangeable or changeable only at unacceptable personal costs" In addition, a majority of this Court explicitly recognized that gays, lesbians and bisexuals, "whether as individuals or couples, form an identifiable minority who have suffered and continue to suffer serious social, political and economic disadvantage."[94]

He further elaborated (drawing on Justice Iacobucci in *Law v. Canada*):

> [T]he discriminatory calibre of differential treatment cannot be fully appreciated without considering whether the distinction in question restricts access to a fundamental social institution, or affects a basic aspect of full membership in Canadian society, or constitutes a complete non-recognition of a particular group. In the present case, the interest protected by s. 29 of the *FLA* [Family Law Act] is fundamental, namely the ability to meet basic financial needs following the breakdown of a relationship characterized by intimacy and economic dependence. Members of same-sex couples are entirely ignored by the statute, notwithstanding the undeniable importance to them of the benefits accorded by the statute.[95]

He concludes this part of the analysis with another explicitly relational framing of the issue:

> The societal significance of the benefit conferred by the statute cannot be overemphasized. The exclusion of same-sex partners from the benefits of s. 29 of the *FLA* promotes the view that M., and individuals in same-sex relationships generally, are less worthy of recognition and protection. It implies that they are judged to be inca-

pable of forming intimate relationships of economic interdependence as compared to opposite-sex couples, without regard to their actual circumstances. As the intervener EGALE submitted, such exclusion perpetuates the disadvantages suffered by individuals in same-sex relationships and contributes to the erasure of their existence.[96]

Finally, I want to offer an example of the Supreme Court of Canada's engagement with the issue of systemic racism. The quote below comes from *R. v. S (R.D.)*, a case raising the issue of whether a (black, female) judge's conduct (in remarking on racism among Halifax police) gave rise to "reasonable apprehension of bias."[97] Part of the issue was what a reasonable person would think upon hearing the judge. I quote at length the joint reasons of Justices L'Heureux-Dubé and McLachlin:

> The reasonable person must be taken to be aware of the history of discrimination faced by disadvantaged groups in Canadian society protected by the *Charter*'s equality provisions. These are matters of which judicial notice may be taken. In *Parks, supra*, at p. 342, Doherty J.A., did just this, stating:
>
> "Racism, and in particular anti-black racism, is a part of our community's psyche. A significant segment of our community holds overtly racist views. A much larger segment subconsciously operates on the basis of negative racial stereotypes. Furthermore, our institutions, including the criminal justice system, reflect and perpetuate those negative stereotypes."
>
> The reasonable person is not only a member of the Canadian community, but also, more specifically, is a member of the local communities in which the case at issue arose (in this case, the Nova Scotian and Halifax communities). Such a person must be taken to possess knowledge of the local population and its racial dynamics, including the existence in the community of a history of widespread and systemic discrimination against black and aboriginal people, and high profile clashes between the police and the visible minority population over policing issues. The reasonable person must thus be deemed to be cognizant of the existence of racism in Halifax, Nova Scotia. It follows that judges may take notice of actual racism known to exist in a particular society. Judges have done so with respect to racism in Nova Scotia. In *Nova Scotia (Minister of Community Services) v. S.M.S.,* it was stated at p. 108:
>
> Racism "is a pernicious reality. The issue of racism existing in Nova Scotia has been well documented in the Marshall Inquiry Report. A person would have to be stupid, complacent or ignorant not to acknowledge its presence, not only individually, but also systemically and institutionally."[98]

Racism, from a relational perspective, is a deeply embedded structure of relations sustained by beliefs, practices, and institutions. Law participates at all of these levels. It has been complicit in shaping racism and must take an active role in restructuring relations toward equality. Neither individual nor institutional intent is at the heart of systemic racism. The Canadian recognition of the concept of systemic racism as the necessary context for equality analysis stands in sharp contrast to American jurisprudence, as we will see shortly.[99]

Canadian courts do not always use the textual and jurisprudential openness to a relational approach to full effect.[100] Nevertheless, the core recognition of systemic inequality and governmental responsibility to redress it provide grounds for relational analysis. It is a key part of what distinguishes Canadian equality jurisprudence from American.

The United States, of course, has a different constitutional text to work with. But while the Canadian *Charter* facilitates a relational approach, the American constitution does not preclude it. Nevertheless, the current American equality jurisprudence consistently rejects it. Equality jurisprudence under the Fourteenth Amendment requires a showing of intent to discriminate.[101] The inquiry is thus not fundamentally about whether the challenged law or practice contributes to disadvantage. Civil Rights legislation is broader: "Title VII of the Civil Rights Act of 1964, 42 U. S. C. §2000e *et seq.*, as amended, prohibits employment discrimination on the basis of race, color, religion, sex, or national origin. Title VII prohibits both intentional discrimination (known as "disparate treatment") as well as, in some cases, practices that are not intended to discriminate but in fact have a disproportionately adverse effect on minorities (known as "disparate impact")."[102] But there are currently stringent restrictions on what a government can do to try to avoid disparate impact, and indeed on what counts as disparate impact. As is clear in *Ricci v. DeStafano*, the focus of the jurisprudence is on the use of categories, such as race, and whether those categories discriminate against the group bringing the complaint (white and Hispanic firefighters in *Ricci*).[103]

The jurisprudence does not begin with a question of whether the complainants are members of a disadvantaged group,[104] and it does not focus on the ameliorative or harmful effects of the categories. It does not, therefore, ask the key relational question of whether the challenged practice creates a disadvantage through the perpetuation of prejudice or stereotyping. In *Ricci,* for the majority, the focus is on the right of an individual (whether part of a disadvantaged group or not) not to be subjected to treatment based on race. The practical meaning of this right is not to be examined in the context of whether the purpose of Title VII is to restructure relations of systemic disadvantage. On the contrary, the individual right is understood as setting limits to efforts to restructure historical (even recent historical) disadvantage.

Of course, as I said above, a more relational approach is possible for American jurisprudence. Working within precedent prior to *Ricci*, Justice Ginsberg, in dissent, read both the facts and the law in a very different way from Justice Kennedy. One of the particularly striking parts of her opinion, for my purposes here, is her use of context. She begins with a historical account of racial discrimination in hiring and promoting firefighters;[105] she then looks at the recent history in New Haven and returns repeatedly to the historical context of the Civil Rights Act, Title VII. It is, in part, an argument that without attention to disparate impact (the actual effects of a practice), the United States had proved unable to end racially discriminatory practices. In other words, she attends to the past and present structures of inequality and to the history of efforts to shift that deeply embedded structure of relations. This relational context of past discrimination and the inability to end it without attending to context and effect are an important part of her different interpretation of both law and fact.

Indeed, one of the striking things about comparing Kennedy's and Ginsberg's opinions is the way in which their different frameworks lead them to see the facts so differently. For example, Ginsberg challenged the characterization of refusing to use test results with a clear disparate impact as subjecting anyone to race-based treatment.[106] The results for all candidates were discarded. By contrast, she sees race as playing a role in the relational context of how the candidates were able to prepare for the exam:

At least two candidates opposed to certification noted unequal access to study materials. Some individuals, they asserted, had the necessary books even before the syllabus was issued. Others had to invest substantial sums to purchase the materials and "wait a month and a half for some of the books because they were on back-order." These disparities, it was suggested, fell at least in part along racial lines. *While many Caucasian applicants could obtain materials and assistance from relatives in the fire service, the overwhelming majority of minority applicants were "first generation firefighters" without such support networks.*[107]

A relational approach directs inquiry into how law enhances or impedes relations of equality. It can highlight relevant facts that permit one to see the ways relations of inequality work. There will always be disagreements about the kind of equality to which law should aspire and the practices that best promote optimal relations of equality. But without an attention to the way a contested law or practice actually shapes relations (and has done so in the past), a focus on the presence or absence of such categories as race in a given practice, or on "intention," cannot get at either the ways law remains complicit in reinforcing systemic disadvantage or the ways it can best work to overcome that disadvantage.[108]

I return now to the example of property. Since property is not in the *Charter,* how should Canadians determine when impacts on property or economic interests amount to violations of liberty or security of the person?[109] Here I will just outline the kinds of questions a relational approach would address to a case of economic liberty. I use the British Columbia "doctors' case," *Wilson v. Medical Services Commission.*[110]

In an attempt to make sure that all areas of British Columbia were adequately provided with medical care, the provincial government decided to restrict the number of doctors to whom it would provide billing numbers in popular areas like Vancouver. In effect, doctors could not practice wherever they wished if they wanted their services paid for by the government. Does this amount to an infringement of liberty?[111] Suppose we begin by looking at the network of relationships in which these doctors are embedded—public funding for medical school, for hospitals, for their salaries (hence the problem in the first place). We should then consider more broadly the interdependencies we already formally recognize in a wide variety of schemes that limit access to jobs ranging from chicken farming to taxi driving. Of course, constraints on one's livelihood are serious constraints and come close to our understanding of liberty. But we cannot view any case, like *Wilson*, in isolation. The relationships in society will be different depending on how much scope for individual choice we allow and how much we constrain that choice by notions of mutual responsibility.

In any given case we have to ask whether the alleged infringement is designed to foster or enforce social responsibility in ways consistent with other forms of social responsibility in Canada. Or is the infringement arbitrary, gratuitous, or disproportionate to its purpose? Of course, consistency with other policies might not itself be sufficient. We could ask if the network of mutual responsibility seems to be drawing such a tight net that we cannot imagine those relationships being conducive to individual autonomy—having recognized, of course, that autonomy is not a matter of *independence*, but of interdependent relationships that foster it. I will not go into any more detail here, beyond saying that I think in this example, as in others, the difference a focus on relationship makes is not stark, but subtle. Many of the questions sound familiar and can be generated by other frameworks, but I think the emphasis will be different. Our attention will be drawn to different matters, and the overall result will be better.

D. What I Do Not Mean

Finally, a note about what the relational/dialogical approach does not mean. Conceptualizing rights as institutional methods of protecting values does not mean that judges can simply disregard entrenched rights in the name of an underlying value. The choice of the institution of judicially enforced rights brings with it institutional constraints on judges. For example, even if an American judge were to be persuaded that property was not the kind of right that should be constitutionalized, she could not simply discard it in the name of the values (like liberty) that property is supposed to promote. Until the Constitution is amended, judges have to (as they always have) weigh competing values within the constraints of entrenched rights.

I argue that judges should ask whether a given interpretation of a right will structure relations in a way that will foster or undermine the value at stake. This could mean, for example, that judges would interpret the property rights of those who own shopping malls to be limited by the freedom of speech of protestors or pamphleteers. The value here would be the democratic importance of (privately owned) "public" spaces in which people can exchange ideas. The ordinary right to exclude—say, those whose presence interferes with the ambience conducive to consumption—fosters some values (the freedom to decide for oneself the use of ones' property, commercial success) at the expense of others (freedom of expression and the availability of public spaces for the free exchange of ideas).[112] In invoking the value of democratic exchange as a guide to interpreting contemporary property rights, one could argue that the traditional hierarchical power to exclude is inconsistent with the relations of equality and freedom necessary for the free speech of democracy to thrive. The supreme courts of neither the United States nor Canada have accepted this argument, though there are dissents from both countries that do.[113] In no case would a judge simply replace the analysis of rights with an argument for a value. The value would be a guide to interpretation of competing rights.

A similar argument would hold with respect to rights and responsibilities. If a judge were to decide that responsibility is actually a better framework than rights for articulating the requirements of protecting the environment, it would not be open to her simply to abandon rights analysis because she thought the underlying values (say in disputes about environmental regulation) were better promoted by responsibility. She would have to analyze cases in terms of the way competing interpretations of rights structure relations of responsibility necessary for the protection of the environment. To repeat, then, the idea that rights are means for implementing values does not free judges from the constraints that come with the institutional choice of judicially enforced rights.

The second point is that the relational/dialogic approach does not mean that there will simply be more—or less—protection for individual rights as they are currently understood in, say, Canada or the United States. As I have already suggested, I think equality rights are better protected by a relational analysis that can encompass the idea of systemic inequality. But, I think a relational analysis is often likely to give precedence to environmental protection or public deliberation over traditional property rights. If rights to give and receive care were to come to be recognized (probably through legislation, such as family leave policies), the prerogatives of employers would be limited (as they have been in most Western countries through mandatory pregnancy leave). Freedom of contract would then be limited in yet another way (in addition to maximum hours, minimum wage, social security/insurance contributions). Some rights would get more protection than currently, some less. The question of whether a core value such as liberty would be increased or decreased—for all—would be a complicated and inevitably contested question.

VI. INSTITUTIONALIZING A DIALOGUE OF DEMOCRATIC ACCOUNTABILITY AND RELATIONAL RIGHTS: A PROPOSAL

Finally, I offer a concrete proposal for implementing a dialogue of democratic accountability: the Alternative Social Charter that was proposed in Canada in the early 1990s. I offer a fair bit of detail so that readers can see how a system not centered around the courts can both protect rights and foster democratic deliberation about their meaning.[114]

In the early 1990s, Canada went through one of its periodic rounds of constitutional negotiation. The Charlottetown Accord, a set of proposals for constitutional amendment, was rejected in a national referendum. But such periods of debate (whatever their other disadvantages of time, money, and energy) open up people's imagination to new constitutional possibilities. The Charlottetown Accord had included a (rather vague) social union provision modeled on a proposal for an entrenched charter of social rights put forward by the New Democratic government of Ontario. There was widespread interest in this possibility among equality-seeking nongovernmental agencies or NGOs. The Alternative Social Charter (ASC) was put forward by a coalition of antipoverty groups.[115]

At the time, I found the ASC exciting not because I believed it could single-handedly transform the deep structures of inequality in Canada, but because I thought it offered the hope, not only of ameliorating the conditions of the disadvantaged but also of transforming the meaning of rights and of constitutionalism. In 2010, Canada is no longer in a political moment where "the idea of a constitutional charter of social rights ha[s] some prospect of becoming a reality."[116] But the ASC continues to provide an interesting model for institutionalizing a "dialogue of democratic accountability" and a structure that invites a relational analysis of rights.

The ASC was an effort to carry through a vision of what it would take for all members of Canadian society to be full, equal participants; to be truly treated with equal respect and dignity. I think the ASC grew out of an awareness of the ways the relations of disadvantage in Canada preclude that equal membership.[117] Thus while the ASC uses the language of rights, I see it as tacitly recognizing that traditional, individualistic rights can obscure the impact of disadvantage. The language of the ASC makes disadvantage (an inherently relative and thus relational category) central and thus invites a relational approach to rights—which can sustain, rather than deflect, the focus on vulnerability and disadvantage.

Perhaps most importantly, the structure of the ASC avoids treating courts as central means for institutionalizing rights. The initial debates around a social charter hit an impasse. Among those advocating for a social charter there was no consensus about the appropriate role for the courts in its enforcement. Once a social charter was proposed, there was immediate resistance to the idea that courts should adjudicate constitutional issues for which public spending was central. For many, the conclusion then seemed to follow that a social charter could not be enforceable; it would have to be merely a statement of principle. The ASC breaks through this impasse with an enforcement mechanism that is a viable, indeed preferable, alternative to a court-based system of rights.

The ASC opens with a statement of "Social and Economic Rights":

1. In light of Canada's international and domestic commitment to respect, protect and promote the human rights of all members of Canadian Society, and, in particular, members of its most vulnerable and disadvantaged groups, everyone has an equal right to well-being, including a right to:

(a) a standard of living that ensures adequate food, clothing, housing, child care support services and other requirements for security and dignity of the person and for full social and economic participation in their communities and in Canadian society;

(b) health care that is comprehensive, universal, portable, accessible, and publicly administered, including community-based non-profit delivery of services

(c) public primary and secondary education, accessible post-secondary and vocational education, and publicly-funded education for those with special needs arising from disabilities;

(d) access to employment opportunities; and

(e) just and favourable conditions of work, including the right of workers to organize and bargain collectively.

Among other stipulations, the ASC asserts that the *Charter*, as well as statutes, regulations, policy, practice, and the common law, shall be interpreted and applied "in a manner consistent with the rights in s. 1 and the fundamental value of alleviating and eliminating social and economic disadvantage."[118] And in case there was any doubt that the document was intended to create positive obligations, "governments have obligations to improve the conditions of life of children and youth and to take positive measures to ameliorate the historical and social disadvantage of groups facing discrimination."

The ASC created two nonjudicial institutions for implementing these rights. The Social Rights Council and the Social Rights Tribunal were both designed to enhance public and governmental debate about these rights. For both, rights are not just claims against a government, but an occasion of ongoing dialogue about the meaning and implementation of these rights. And both institutions were designed to ensure that the experience of those to whom these rights mattered the most was part of the deliberations. Both bodies were to be appointed by the (reformed) Senate, with one-third of the nominations from the federal government, one-third from provincial and territorial governments, and one-third from nongovernmental organizations representing vulnerable and disadvantaged groups.

The council's primary job was to evaluate federal and provincial compliance with these rights. In doing so, they were charged to

(a) establish and revise standards according to which compliance with the rights in s.1 can be evaluated;

(b) compile information and statistics on the social and economic circumstances of individuals with respect to the rights in s.1, especially those who are members of vulnerable and disadvantaged groups;

(c) assess the level of compliance of federal and provincial law and practice with respect to the rights in s.1;

(d) educate the public and appropriate government officials;

(e) submit recommendations to appropriate governments and legislative bodies;

(f) encourage governments to engage in active and meaningful consultations with non-governmental organizations which are representative of vulnerable and disadvantaged members of society; and

(g) carry out any other task that is necessary or appropriate for the purpose.

They were also authorized to hold inquiries, compel governments to provide documents, and report on relevant matters. When the council did submit recommendations, the body to which they were submitted was required to reply in writing within three months.[119]

A particularly interesting part of their mandate was to participate in the preparation of reports to international bodies, such as the United Nations Committee that oversees the implementation of the International Covenant on Economic, Social, and Cultural Rights. The council was to assist in the preparation of reports, append separate opinions if they saw fit, and "actively consult with non-governmental organizations representative of vulnerable and disadvantaged groups, and encourage governments to engage in similar consultations."[120]

A reporting process that ordinarily receives very little public attention could thus become a focus of public conversation about the extent of Canada's compliance with its international commitments. This offered the interesting prospect of making international human rights an active part of domestic Canadian political debate. Canada sees itself as a leader in protecting human rights around the world. An institution like the Social Rights Council could use this self image as a lever to generate serious debate about Canada's domestic human rights record on such issues as child poverty, homelessness, violence against women, and aboriginal rights.

Perhaps most important, for my purposes, is the second institution, the Social Rights Tribunal. It offered an alternative to the courts as a mechanism for hearing specific rights claims from individuals and groups. The tribunal would hear selected complaints alleging infringements "that are systemic or that have systemic impact on vulnerable or disadvantaged groups and their members."[121] Thus this form of rights adjudication was aimed at a structural analysis that would not just provide redress in particular cases but also examine the underlying sources of the rights deprivation.

Taken together with the language of the Section 1 rights, the ASC invites a relational analysis. Section 1(a) refers to the "requirements for security and dignity of the person and for full social and economic participation in their communities and in Canadian society." Thus to determine what the rights in Section 1(a) are (and what would constitute violations of them), one would have to ask what will make security, dignity, and full participation possible. The consistent focus on disadvantage suggests that until the relations of inequality are changed, security, dignity, and full participation will not be possible for everyone.

For example, if the system of social entitlements did not enable single mothers to get the kind of training and education that would allow them to break free of their roles as dependent, marginalized citizens, or did not enable a parent to stay home with a young child at a level of support sufficient for full social and political participation, then we would judge that system to fail the standards of the ASC. Where the choice has been made to provide benefits related to goods like food or shelter (whether in terms of in-kind provision of or financial entitlement sufficient to secure these goods in the marketplace), the quantity of the benefits alone could not tell us whether the standard has been met. The recognition that rights structure relations of equality and respect (or their opposites) would focus adjudicators' attention on the network of relations established or maintained by the system of benefits—and on whether that network was one within which people could be full participants in society.

The overall framework of an equal right to well-being in the context of responsibility for the most vulnerable and disadvantaged invites a structural, relational analysis that would take us beyond the social services or welfare model that has been criticized from both the left and the right. If the basic rights are to well-being and full, equal membership in the community, then the provision of social services is only one possible means to be measured against the broader ends. The ASC invites a more open-ended, creative inquiry into the kinds of legal structures that will actually promote equal citizenship.

Even the adjudicative tribunal is designed to promote ongoing dialogue about the rights in question. First, the tribunal holds hearings to determine if there has been a violation of the Section 1 rights that is systemic or has significant impact on vulnerable or disadvantaged groups. Then there is a second-stage hearing on the appropriate remedy, in which the tribunal hears the views of both governments and petitioners as to "measures . . . required" and "time . . . required."[122] The tribunal can then "order that measures be taken . . . within a specified period of time"[123] with this order then making its way into the policy making and legislative process.[124] But the tribunal can also let the government take the initiative and order the appropriate government to report back on the measures that the government has taken or proposes to take.[125] The tribunal can then endorse that proposal, send it back for further consideration, or decide at that stage to issue its own order. The conversation can go back and forth as long as the tribunal thinks it appropriate. Once it issues an order, the relevant legislature has a chance to consider it. The order "shall not come into effect until the House of Commons or the relevant legislature has sat for at least five weeks, during which time the decision may be overridden by a simple majority vote of that legislature or Parliament."[126]

Thus the tribunal is set up to maximize democratic deliberation. It has the authority to command the attention of the legislature by issuing its own order for a remedy—which would normally involve some kind of legislative or regulatory change, since its focus is systemic rights violations. The default rule (which, of course, is sometimes important on politically contentious issues) is that the order comes into effect if the legislature does not act. The legislative body has the final word in its power to override, but the presumption is that this would be politically costly.[127] The back and forth structure of order and response allows for ongoing public debate about the tribunal's determination that existing policy constitutes a rights violation.

Finally, the democratic nature of this public deliberation on the meaning of rights is sustained by closely circumscribing the role of the courts in overseeing the tribunal: only the Supreme Court of Canada is capable of reviewing decisions and orders of the tribunal and only on the grounds of a "*manifest* excess of jurisdiction."[128]

In sum, the ASC provides an institutional structure that recognizes rights as entailing an ongoing process of definition. It creates a democratic mechanism for that process without simply giving democracy priority over rights. At the same time, it provides a means of ensuring that democratic decisions are accountable to basic values without treating rights as trumps. The ASC thus provides us with an outline of a workable model of constitutionalism as a dialogue of democratic accountability.

Of course, it is an outline only. It never reached the stage of being incorporated into the proposal for constitutional change and thus having its details receive further rounds of debate and refinement. I think the question of exactly how appointments would work is one of the areas where further detail would be needed. While the role of NGOs in providing for one-third of the nominations is important, it is not sufficient to ensure the democratic nature of the council and tribunal. Were such bodies to be created, there would difficult challenges of ensuring their independence (which is stipulated), their democratic nature, and their capacity for impartiality. In other words, the challenge to be optimal adjudicators as well as policy makers (common to many tribunals) would be especially demanding in this context.

Because the ASC was conceived as an addition to the existing structure of *Charter* adjudication, the authors did not have to work through the questions of whether or how a similar system could *replace* judicial review by courts. I think it is important to imagine and experiment with alternatives to judicial review, and it seems likely to me that experiments might take the partial form of the ASC. While there are still unresolved questions, I think it provides an important model of rights adjudication where public deliberation about the content of rights is an integral part of the process. In the ASC the rights to be protected derive from a many-layered inquiry into what it would take to create the relationships necessary for a free and democratic society.

VII. CONCLUSION

When we understand the constitutionalization of rights as a means of setting up a dialogue of democratic accountability, we redefine the kinds of justification necessary for constitutional constraints on democratic decision making. Perhaps even more importantly for the world outside of academia, we provide a conceptual framework that will help us to design and assess workable mechanisms for constitutionalizing rights in modern democracies. This conception of constitutionalism fosters an alternative understanding of rights—rights as structuring relationships. This approach to rights, in turn, helps to overcome the most serious problems with the dominant conceptions of our liberal tradition. When we understand rights as relationships and constitutionalism as a dialogue of democratic accountability, we can not only move beyond long-standing problems; we can also create a conceptual and institutional structure that will facilitate inquiry into the new problems that inevitably will emerge.

In the context of international human rights, this approach suggests that the focus cannot be on implementation alone. Equal attention must be given to the question of who has defined the rights in question. What processes are in place to facilitate (at least periodic) deliberation about the practical meaning of rights? Who has actual access to these processes? Some might say that inviting attention to who gets to define rights will undermine their rhetorical efficacy, their power to command attention and insist upon response. On this view, it is only when rights are seen to stand above the fray of politics that they can have the authority necessary to resist illegitimate force or deeply ingrained harmful practices or inequalities. But as virtually everyone who works on human rights knows, the question of definition is already on the table. Its most common form is the allegation that universal human rights are really just the creation of Western/Northern Hemisphere countries and a tool for the imposition of their power.[129]

One need not reject the possibility of universal human values to recognize the real problem of who participates in the definition of the rights that are supposed to set limits to legitimate sovereign power. If human rights really are to attain universal legitimacy, then the processes by which they are defined must themselves be universally recognized as legitimate. Giving up the allure of rights as trumps that can decisively shut down counterclaims of culture, religion, or democracy is not to give up the hope of workable international processes for holding all nations accountable for rights violations. In the end, only rights that have the legitimacy of a democratically justifiable process behind them will be able to serve that purpose.

VIII. APPENDIX I: DRAFT ALTERNATIVE SOCIAL CHARTER (ASC)

PART I
i. Social and Economic Rights

1. In light of Canada's international and domestic commitment to respect, protect and promote the human rights of all members of Canadian Society, and, in particular, members of its most vulnerable and disadvantaged groups, everyone has an equal right to well-being, including a right to:

(a) a standard of living that ensures adequate food, clothing, housing, child care support services and other requirements for security and dignity of the person and for full social and economic participation in their communities and in Canadian society;

(b) health care that is comprehensive, universal, portable, accessible, and publicly administered, including community-based non-profit delivery of services;

(c) public primary and secondary education, accessible post-secondary and vocational education, and publicly-funded education for those with special needs arising from disabilities;

(d) access to employment opportunities; and

(e) just and favourable conditions of work, including the right of workers to organize and and bargain collectively.

2. The *Canadian Charter of Rights and Freedoms* shall be interpreted in a manner consistent with the rights in s.1 and the fundamental value of alleviating and eliminating social and economic disadvantage.

3. Nothing contained in s.1 diminishes or limits the rights contained in the *Canadian Charter of Rights and Freedoms*.

4. Governments have obligations to improve the conditions of life of children and youth and to take positive measures to ameliorate the historical and social disadvantage of groups facing discrimination.

5. Statutes, regulations, policy, practice and the common law shall be interpreted and applied in a manner consistent with the rights in s.1 and the fundamental value of alleviating and eliminating social and economic disadvantage.

6. Any legislation and federal–provincial agreements related to fulfilment of the rights in Section 1 through national shared cost programs shall have the force of law, shall not be altered except in accordance with their terms and shall be enforceable at the instance of any party or of any person adversely affected upon application to a court of competent jurisdiction.

7. (1) The federal government has a special role and responsibility to fund federal-provincial shared cost programs with a view to the achievement of a comparable level and quality of services throughout the federation, in accordance with s.36.

   (2) Accordingly, federal funding shall reflect the relative cost and capacity of delivering such programs in the various provinces, with equalization payments where required to address serious disparities in relative cost and capacity.

   (3) The federal government and provincial government shall conduct taxation and other fiscal policies in a manner consistent with these responsibilities and with their obligations under shared cost programs.

8. The provisions of sections 1 to 7 shall apply to territorial governments where appropriate.

PART II

ii. Social Rights Council

9. (1) By [a specific date], there shall be established by the [REFORMED] Senate
   of Canada the Social Rights Council (the Council) to evaluate the extent to
   which federal and provincial law and practice is in compliance with the rights
   contained in s.1.

   (2) In evaluating compliance the Council shall:
       (a) establish and revise standards according to which compliance with the
            rights in s.1 can be evaluated;
       (b) compile information and statistics on the social and economic circum-
            stances of individuals with respect to the rights in s.1, especially those
            who are members of vulnerable and disadvantaged groups;
       (c) assess the level of compliance of federal and provincial law and practice
            with respect to the rights in s.1;
       (d) educate the public and appropriate government officials;
       (e) submit recommendations to appropriate governments and legislative
            bodies;
       (f) encourage governments to engage in active and meaningful consulta-
            tions with non-governmental organizations which are representative of
            vulnerable and disadvantaged members of society; and
       (g) carry out any other task that is necessary or appropriate for the
            purpose.

   (3) In evaluating compliance with Part 1 the Council shall have the power to:
       (a) hold inquiries and require attendance by individuals, groups or appro-
            priate government officials;
       (b) require that necessary and relevant information, including documents,
            reports and other materials, be provided by governments; and
       (c) require any government to report on matters relevant to compliance.

   (4) The government or legislative body to which recommendations in s.9(2)(e)
        are addressed has an obligation to respond in writing to the Council within
        three months.

   (5) With respect to Canada's obligations under international reporting proce-
        dures that relate to the rights in s.1, the Council shall:
       (a) assist in the preparation of Canada's reports under such procedures;

(b) actively consult with non-governmental organizations representative of vulnerable and disadvantaged groups, and encourage governments to engage in similar consultations;

(c) have the right to append separate opinions to the final versions of such reports before or after they are submitted to the appropriate international body; and

(d) make available a representative of the Council to provide any information requested by the appropriate international body.

(6) The Council shall respond to any request for information or invitation to intervene from the Tribunal established under s.10 and the Council shall have the right to intervene in any proceedings before the Tribunal.

(7) The Council shall be independent and shall be guaranteed public funding through Parliament sufficient for it to carry out its actions.

(8) Persons appointed to the Council shall have demonstrated experience in the area of social and economic rights and a commitment to the objectives of the social Charter.

(9) (a) All appointments to the Council shall be made by the [REFORMED] Senate of Canada.

(b) One-third of the appointments shall be from nominations from each of the following sectors

(i) the federal government;

(ii) provincial and territorial governments; and

(iii) non-governmental organizations representing vulnerable and disadvantaged groups.

(10) [self-governing aboriginal communities]

PART III
iii. Social Rights Tribunal

10. (1) By [a specified date], there shall be established by the [REFORMED] Senate of Canada the Social Rights Tribunal of the Federation (the Tribunal) which shall receive and consider petitions from individuals and groups alleging infringements of rights under s.1.

(2) The Tribunal shall have as its main purpose the consideration of selected petitions alleging infringement that are systemic or that have significant impact on vulnerable or disadvantaged groups and their members.

(3) The Tribunal shall have the power to consider and review federal and provincial legislation, regulations, programs, policies or practices, including obligations under federal-provincial agreements.

(4) Where warranted by the purpose set out in s.10(2), the Tribunal shall

(a) hold hearings into allegations of infringement of any right under s.l; and

(b) issue decisions as to whether a right has been infringed.

(5) Where the Tribunal decides that a right has been infringed it shall

    (a) hear submission from petitioners and governments as to measures that are required to achieve compliance with the rights in s.l and as to time required to carry out such measures; and

    (b) order that measures be taken by the appropriate government within a specified period of time.

(6) (a) In lieu of issuing an order under s.lo(5)(b), the Tribunal shall, where appropriate, order that the appropriate government report back by a specified date on measures taken or proposed to be taken which will achieve compliance with the rights in s.l.

    (b) Upon receiving a report under s.lo(6)(a), the Tribunal may issue another order under s.lo(6)(a) or issue an order under s.19(5)(b).

(7) (a) An order of the Tribunal for measures under s.10(5)(b) shall not come into effect until the House of Commons or the relevant legislature has sat for at least five weeks, during which time the decision may be overridden by a simple majority vote of that legislature or Parliament.

    (b) The relevant government may indicate its acceptance of the terms of an order of the Tribunal under s.lo(5)(b) prior to the expiry of the period specified in s.lo(6)(a).

(8) Tribunal decisions and orders shall be subject to judicial review only by the Supreme Court of Canada and only for manifest error of jurisdiction.

(9) The Tribunal may, at any stage, request information from, request investigation by, or invite the intervention of the Social Rights Council.

(10) The Tribunal shall be made accessible to members of disadvantaged groups and their representative organizations by all reasonable means, including the provision of necessary funding by appropriate governments.

(11) The Tribunal shall be independent and shall be guaranteed public funding through Parliament sufficient for it to carry out its functions.

(12) (a) All appointments to the Tribunal shall be made by the [REFORMED] Senate of Canada.

    (b) One-third of the appointments shall be from each of the following sectors:

        (i) the federal government;

        (ii) provincial and territorial governments; and

        (iii) non-governmental organizations representing vulnerable and disadvantaged groups.

(13) [The Province of Quebec] [Any province] may exclude the competence of the Tribunal with respect to matters within its jurisdiction by establishing a comparable tribunal or conferring competence on an existing tribunal.

(14) [self-governing aboriginal communities]

PART IV

iv. Environmental Rights

11. In view of the fundamental importance of the natural environment and the necessity for ecological integrity,

  (a) everyone has a right:

    (i) to a healthful environment;

    (ii) to redress and remedy for those who have suffered or will suffer environmental harm; and

    (iii) to participate in decision making with respect to activities likely to have a significant effect on the environment;

  (b) all governments are trustees of public lands, waters and resources for present and future generations.

A Note on Enforcement of Environmental Rights: The Canadian Environmental Law Association, Pollution Probe, and the Constitutional Caucus of the Canadian Environmental Network endorse an amendment to the *Canadian Charter of Rights and Freedoms* protecting the right to a healthy environment

This is not to say that the mechanism for enforcement of environmental rights must rely solely on the courts. The proposed Environmental Bill of Rights for Ontario provides an example of an enforcement mechanism by a specialized tribunal.

7

Relinquishing Control

AUTONOMY, THE BODYMIND, AND THE PSYCHE

I return here to reflections on the nature of autonomy. In chapter 3 I argued that we should reject the common identification of autonomy with independence. Here I make a similar argument about autonomy and control. While control may not figure as prominently in the list of philosophical characterizations of autonomy, I think it is widely associated with autonomy in the popular imagination. In North America there are offers everywhere to learn to take control of one's life and corresponding expressions of dismay at one's life being "out of control." I think the suggestion that autonomy is about being in control is as dangerously misleading as the idea that independence is a good synonym for autonomy.

People can best exercise their autonomous capacities for creative interaction when they relinquish control as a goal.[1] Seeking control is not a path to autonomy, and control is not a component of autonomy, even though experiencing one's life as "out of control" is a sign that one's autonomy is not thriving, and having others control one's life is inconsistent with autonomy. Control is not a respectful stance toward others with a capacity for autonomy. Indeed, the link between autonomy and control (and independence) is also a link to domination: the illusion of control and independence can only be sustained through domination.

In section II, I use the fact of our embodied nature and the puzzles of the mind–body relationship to examine the puzzles of a capacity for autonomy whose actuality depends on relationships beyond one's control. In particular, I look at the question of the responsibility for one's health as a way of disentangling the conventional links between autonomy, control, and responsibility. In this discussion I use the conventional dichotomized terms "mind" and "body" for the purpose of challenging the dichotomy. Occasionally I use what I think of as the better term, "bodymind,"[2] which can encompass the ongoing flow of information and energy that characterize the whole—that we dissect into body and mind.

I open my discussion of embodied autonomy with a quote from Hannah Arendt about the separation of the body and the soul. I return to this language of the soul at several points. I note the ways in which the puzzles of autonomy are reflected in theological language and debates. Since not everyone is sympathetic to invocations of the spiritual, I take the use of this language to require some explanation: it seems useful to me to note some of the many, and ancient, forms these puzzles of autonomy and creativity have taken; I also find that the theological metaphor of our creative capacity as the "spark of the divine" is a helpful way of capturing the mysterious dimension of the human capacity for autonomy.

The autonomy-control-responsibility connection is also central to law. Law is in the business of holding people accountable for their actions. To do so, it often assumes autonomy (as we saw in chapter 4). But a relational approach cannot presume autonomy. This chapter anticipates the discussion in chapter 8, "Restructuring Relations," raising the question of whether law can deal with the nuance and contingency of a relational approach to autonomy and its implications for a similarly contingent approach to responsibility.

I see control as central to the conventional link between autonomy and responsibility: when we are acting autonomously, our actions are thought to be under our control and we can be held responsible for those actions. But I want to disrupt the autonomy-control-responsibility nexus. To better understand both why it is important to disentangle autonomy from control and why it will be difficult to do so, I turn in section III to a psychoanalytic account of the role of control and domination in the prevailing conception of autonomy. Here we also encounter the link between an optimal conception of autonomy and the capacity to engage with difference in a way that advances equality. It is in this section that I address the understandings of the psyche (in the chapter title) as an important part of what keeps dominant understandings of autonomy and the self in place.

At the end, in section V, I return to our embodied nature to offer some clarification of my rejection of both independence and control as components of autonomy. I also suggest that a focus on the body offers paths out of the difficulties of conventional understandings and practices. In this final section, I return to the language of soul with which I begin the next section.

II. MEDITATIONS ON EMBODIED AUTONOMY

In describing Greek philosophy, Hannah Arendt says, "death, being the separation of body and soul, is welcome to [the philosopher]; he is somehow in love with death, because the body, with all its demands, constantly interrupts the soul's pursuits. In other words, the true philosopher does not accept the conditions under which life has been given to man."[3] My purpose here is to explore how accepting those conditions, accepting our embodied nature, invites us to rethink core values such as autonomy. And I want to ensure that the acceptance is deep and realistic.

Susan Wendell reminds us that the feminist embrace of the body, the rejection of the mind–body split with its denigration of the female as body, has served an important function; but it has glorified the body as a site of pleasure and connection without taking seriously the ways in which the body is a source of pain and incapacity.[4] When we see the body in all its dimensions—as a source of joy and of intimacy, as a part of the interdependency of all living beings, as that which links us to the cycles of death and decay and rebirth, as a source of suffering and limitation—the body offers an ideal focus for exploring the puzzle of autonomy. In particular, the complexity, paradoxes, and tensions of the mind–body relationship reveal and illuminate analogous difficulties in conceptualizing human autonomy. Finally, the language of the soul that Arendt invokes offers another metaphor for the relation between parts of a whole: when we see the body as ensouled, as well as the soul embodied, we can honor the body—and the material world—in a new way as we focus on the limitations that inhere in it.

As we have seen in previous chapters, I object to political and legal theories that simply presuppose human autonomy. I have argued that the proper subject of inquiry is *how* autonomy is fostered, what relationships are required for it to thrive and what institutions and laws will foster those relationships. We have also seen why law seems to need this presumption: we cannot hold people responsible for an action unless we believe the action was genuinely "theirs," unless it was the result of their autonomous agency.[5] In a relational approach, where the starting point is interdependence and interconnection, we can see the question of the autonomy–responsibility nexus as follows: in what sense or under what conditions do we think a person's actions are "hers"? Given the complex network of interaction that led up to the moment of action, *when* or *why* would we attribute such "ownership" or authorship of action so that we could then attribute responsibility?

I think the core of the answer to *why* is a belief in the genuinely creative capacity in human beings to bring forth something new, something not determined by all that went before. We live in a web of relationships that shape us, that are necessary for our very capacity for autonomy; the web interacts with and enables an irreducible capacity to initiate, to be ourselves a shaping force, to interact in ways that create. Our conception of autonomy must, then, capture this capacity for creation at the same time that it is built upon the interdependence that makes autonomy possible. The autonomy that is linked to this capacity for creation is not to be confused with control, just as it must not be seen to have independence as its essence.

The body provides an ideal focus for working through such a conception of autonomy. We did not create and cannot ultimately control our bodies, just as we did not create and cannot control the world we live in. But we are responsible for our bodies (and our world), and the complex nature of that responsibility can help us think through the more general problem of reconceptualizing autonomy and responsibility—and thus of *when* to hold someone responsible.

Let us begin with the problem of what it means to think of ourselves as autonomous within our bodies. In law we have an example of the opposite of the autonomy we require for responsibility: the automaton, who, sleepwalking or drugged, is seen not to control the actions of his body. The implicit contrast suggests that under normal circumstances we can assume that the actions of our body are under our control and thus are "ours." One might think that for the purposes of pulling the trigger of a gun that is surely true. But to explore the complexities of embodied autonomy, it is helpful to look at the full nuance and ambiguity of "voluntary" action. In *Job's Body* (1987), Deane Juhan explains that in picking a flower,

> I am certainly not...aware of each of the millions of individual muscle cells whose contractions are coordinated to make the necessary movements of my limbs and torso. I am aware that I want the flower, that I stoop, and that my hand reaches out, stops at the correct place, grasps and plucks the flower, and then raises it to my nose. But can I then say that I have "consciously directed" the countless internuncial circuits in my spinal cord, the constant refinement of my movements by my cerebellum, and the complex participation of my gamma motor system, all of which are necessary to make this simple voluntary gesture possible?[6]

He concludes that "a large part of every voluntary movement is both involuntary and outside consciousness."[7] And to further complicate the dimension of consciousness that is a crucial link in our tacit chain of autonomy-control-responsibility, Juhan notes, "I know with complete certainty when I am doing something that I want to do, but I have no precise idea how it is that I came to want to do it."[8]

The example above might be seen as revealing uncertainties about how the mind controls the body. There are, of course, also many instances where the body appears to control the mind—in ways that are perhaps even more disruptive of conventional notions of autonomy. There are the dramatic cases where severe depression seems to be caused by a chemical imbalance in the brain or by a disease that affects the brain. And there are the more mundane, but still compelling, examples of bodily cycles affecting mood. I was in my midtwenties before I finally realized that I had predictable mood swings associated with my menstrual cycle. I was both amazed that I had been so cut off from my bodily rhythms as not to notice this and relieved that I had an account for the extreme reaction to a disappointment that finally precipitated the insight.[9]

I think my early resistance to recognizing these effects stemmed from a distress at the idea that something as integral to "me" as my mood, my modes of reaction, my feelings about those around me could be "dictated" by hormonal changes which seemed like alien forces beyond my control. And perhaps it was that affect (widely shared in the culture) that impeded my learning about ways of responding to the natural shifts in my body. It is as though once I recognized the bodily source of my feelings I abandoned any further effort at reflection, inquiry, interaction. My body had become an external object that regrettably—even outrageously—had the capacity to control my feelings, and there was therefore nothing to do but accept it with as much grace as possible.

While women (in Western culture) are particularly compelled to acknowledge the effects of body on mind, the phenomenon is, of course, much more general. One often hears of toxins in the environment causing irritability and poor concentration. And perhaps the most common example is the way the body's reaction to stress affects a wide range of complex phenomena ranging from fatigue, to experience of pain, to susceptibility to disease. And here, of course, we come to the real crux of the issue: the interaction of the mind and the body is exactly that, an ongoing interaction which is not simply about the mind's (limited) capacity to control the body or the body's ability to influence the mind.[10] The body reacts to emotional stress in ways that affect so many dimensions of bodily function that it manifests in ways that we think of as "physical" as well as ways that we think of as "mental." And we know that we can learn to change how our bodies react to stress, which we might characterize as the mind controlling the body. But, in fact, as most people already know (in the sense that they have heard it) the ways of changing reactions to stress include both physical exercise and mental exercise, such as meditation. And if the trigger of the whole process is emotional stress, do we properly describe this as an instance of the mind controlling the body or the body controlling the mind, because of the bodily response that in turn affects our thinking and our feeling? As Juhan notes, "over and over ... we find ... that the strict separation of what is 'in the head' from what is 'in the tissues' is not an accurate representation of reality."[11]

In what sense then are "normal" actions autonomous actions? What is it, actually, that we mean by such a question? The question can be rephrased as, "when are the actions of the body the result of our autonomous choices?" I think the ordinary, implicit meaning is "when are the actions of our body governed by the autonomous choices of our mind?" But that, of course, is to reinscribe the mind–body split that the above discussion was intended to cast doubt upon. It is not that the last phrased question has no meaning but, rather, that our inquiry into autonomy should be informed by the complex interactions of mind and body.

Our preferences, our judgments, our feelings, and thus our choices may be shaped by dimensions of ourselves that we would ordinarily describe as physical, bodily. And the choices that we think of directing our bodies to carry out are not in any simple sense under our conscious control. Moreover, the bodymind implications of those choices are often so little understood that they scarcely merit being called conscious choices. For example, we may react to stress by "choosing" to smoke, to overeat, to hold our body in rigid and painful ways. At some level (as I will return to shortly) these are indeed choices, which can be replaced with other choices, such as focused breathing, going for a run or a massage. But the ways in which the habitual actions flow from complex pathways of response in our bodies make the simple language of choice inadequate.

Of course, choice implicates responsibility, and thus the inadequacy of a simple language of choice raises problems for responsibility. Here we can see some of the ways the conception of embodied autonomy provides a helpful analogue for other debates. Consider for example, the familiar question of whether it is appropriate to say that a child from an impoverished neighborhood *chooses* to steal. We may talk about role models, about poverty, about a failure of the environment to provide a sense of options. And we may believe that his choice to steal is in some ways less autonomous than that of the bored, disaffected, wealthy kid from the suburbs. But we also know that there are kids from poor neighborhoods who do not steal. Maybe we can identify differences in families, but there are also cases where one sibling seems to be able to surmount adversity in ways the others are not. There seems to be something wrong with a language for describing these situations that has no place for choice, that tacitly denies autonomy to those in terribly difficult circumstances, just as simplistic assertions that they *chose* a life of crime seem callous and smug.[12]

A relational approach to autonomy adds an additional twist of complexity: autonomy is not generated autonomously (in conventional terms of independence or control). When we focus on the relationships that make autonomy possible, we must recognize that we do not choose many of the relationships most central in developing our capacity for autonomy: parents, teachers, the structures of state assistance. In a relational approach, where autonomy is not simply posited as an attribute of humanness, we are forced to recognize both the interdependence that makes autonomy possible and our lack of control over it.

The puzzle of whether autonomous choice (and thus responsibility) really exists is an old one. We see it in the theological debates about how we are to understand free will and human responsibility for sin, if God is all powerful. The theological version, like all constructions of the puzzle, gives rise to the temptation to determinism: God really does determine all of our actions. In the social science version, if we really could identify and understand all the variables, we could predict and know why one kid becomes a drug dealer (without a license) and the other a physician (with a license). The physical science approach holds out the promise that if we ever really understand the chemistry and biology of the brain, we could understand and control our actions and reactions. In its various forms, the debate over determinism has gone on for centuries. For our purposes here, it is enough to say that determinism denies our creative power. If we are to take autonomy seriously, we cannot succumb to the temptation of determinism when we turn our attention to interdependence and interaction.

The challenge of embodied autonomy shows that we need an approach that focuses on the ongoing and inevitable interaction of what we call body and mind. In the domain of sociology or environmental factors we can make the mistake of thinking that we must choose between choice and autonomy, on the one hand, and environment and determinism, on the other hand. But, in fact, each of us is constantly acting on, and thus changing, our environment, just as it is acting on and changing us. Our capacity for autonomy itself will develop in such a dynamic interchange. And so our concept of autonomy must have dynamic interaction as an essential component.

I will return now to the question of responsibility as a way of coming closer to understanding what autonomy is, if it is not control and independence. Again, the body provides a helpful focus: what is the nature of our responsibility for our health? A closely related question is what is an optimal relation to our sick or disabled body? I use *Job's Body* to explore these questions because Juhan's primary purpose is to persuade his readers that they are responsible for their health and that they can only exercise that responsibility by maintaining a certain kind of relationship with their body. To begin to capture that relationship, he introduces the biblical parable of Job.[13] In Juhan's interpretation, Job found that neither his former beliefs and practices nor the advice of others could help him.

> Left with nothing but his own resources, Job discovered that those resources had an authority of their own, and they spoke to him of a very different God than the old law-maker to whom he had been supplicating. "Who hath put wisdom in the inward parts? or who hath given understanding to the heart?" he asked as he looked inside himself. He found within his own substance and his own sensibilities a relationship with the powers which was more direct, more intimate, and more complete than anything he had known before: "Deep in my skin it is marked, and in my very flesh do I see God."[14]

For Juhan, to thrive (as well as to know God) we must engage in an active, ongoing, attentive relationship with the creative forces that manifest in the world around us and in our bodies. We both participate in these forces and are subject to them. *How* we are subject to them will depend on how we use our own conscious creative capacities to engage with them: "the conscious exercise of our own perceptions and our own will is a decisive factor in our relationship with the laws of nature."[15] The engagement that is required must be conscious, continuous, and ever responsive to change.

> Any conception that is not constantly rediscovered or reconfirmed by the efforts of our own participation and scrutiny cannot continue to be actively true for us, cannot continue to be the basis for right actions and just rewards.... The forces that mold us cannot be good or just to an individual who is unwilling to struggle toward a first-hand understanding of his relationship to them, who is not actively engaged with expanding his capacities, who is not himself taking a conscious part in the creation of his own circumstances.[16]

The role of the body here is complex and subtle. At the most obvious level, the health of our bodies requires this engagement. If we want healthy bodies, we must exercise this responsibility. Put somewhat differently, it is because we are embodied beings that our engagement with the creative forces must take this form. We are part of an ongoing process of creation and transformation with which we can choose *how* to interact but with which we cannot choose *not* to interact:

> This incessant formation we cannot stop. We can only make the choice to let it go its own way—directed by genetics, gravity, appetites, habits, the accidentals of our surroundings, and so on—or the choice to let our *sensory awareness* penetrate its processes, to be personally present in the midst of those processes with the full measure of our subjective, internal observations and responses, and to some degree direct the course of that formation. We do not have the option of remaining passively unchanged.... Like putty, we are either shaping ourselves or we are drooping; like clay, we either keep ourselves moist and malleable or we are drying and hardening.[17]

I added the emphasis to "sensory awareness" because it relates to another way of seeing the role of the body here. The body is a crucial source of knowledge. We must learn to tune in to it. It is a source of knowledge of ourselves and of how we are to engage in the ongoing act of self-creation (something far beyond keeping our bodies free of pain or disease). For Juhan, the body is even more: it is our path into the forces of creation themselves. That is why he begins with Job, who learns to find God within his own body. Indeed, Juhan ends his chapter on Job with a still broader claim from Rainer Maria Rilke (in Robert Bly's translation):

> Take your well-disciplined strengths
> And stretch them between two
> opposing poles. Because inside human beings
> is where God learns.[18]

Juhan makes a compelling case for responsibility for our own health without claiming that we can become master of all the physical forces that affect us. But he does repeatedly use the word "control," sometimes with qualifications, sometimes not. And "will power" recurs a lot. I find Juhan's model of what I call the interaction of creative forces interesting, even promising. But in his urge to impress upon his readers that they have choices to make and a responsibility to assume, he has little space for some of the fears and anxieties that such an approach can generate. Attention to these anxieties will add a useful element to the problem of autonomy and responsibility.

I first became conscious of these anxieties years ago when I had a friend who suffered from a chronic health problem. I suggested, several times, something I thought might help and was always met with resistance. Finally, I understood her to say that if she accepted my suggestion, it would mean that she could and should have done something all along to alleviate or prevent the problem, and that would mean that the years of suffering would have been *her fault*. That thought was too much to bear. It had been very important to her (like most people) to present her physical problems as something beyond her control, which in turn accounted for why she had been unable to do certain things. If this whole story had to be revised, the sense of responsibility and failure would be overwhelming. It was not worth finding out whether my suggestion could make a difference; the cost was too high. It was better to put up with the suffering in a framework she could live with.

I think this story captures an important element of the problem with the responsibility–control approach. In our culture, responsibility is so closely associated with accountability, with fault, that an emphasis on responsibility for our health can easily get translated into fault for ill-health. This is the dark side to many forms of popular inducement to take up physical and mental practices to ensure good health. There is an implicit message that if we get sick it is because we have done something wrong. And this taps into a preexisting tendency to feel that if we get sick, it is our fault. (Perhaps this is a residue of the very old notion of sickness as sin.[19])

Susan Wendell points out an interesting parallel to this problem in feminist writings: "Feminism's continuing efforts to increase women's control of our bodies and prevent unnecessary suffering tend to make us think of bodily suffering as a socially curable phenomenon."[20] This collective approach does not induce individual guilt—indeed it is often intended to provide an alternative to such guilt—but it still treats bodily suffering as something that can be prevented if we do things right. Wendell wants feminists to not only face the inevitability of sickness and pain but also to think differently about the kind of control we can exercise over these phenomena. We need to attend to the ways in which even positive approaches to responsibility for our health can lead to an oversimplified picture which has control at its center—with disturbing overtones of both infinite optimism and fault and failure.

Trying to figure out the optimal way of conceptualizing responsibility for our health is a way of exploring the seeming paradoxes of our autonomy as embodied beings who participate in creating ourselves and our world but control neither. Wendell's work provides a subtle counterpoint to Juhan's emphasis on responsibility and control. She does so in part by objecting to approaches that "give the body too little importance as a *cause* in psychological and spiritual life."[21] She knows there are those who "insist that the sufferings of the body have psychological and/or spiritual meanings, and that I should be searching for them in order to heal myself."[22] In her view though, this "reduces the body to a mere reflector of other processes, and implicitly rejects the idea that the body may have a complex life of its own, much of which we cannot interpret."[23] In coping with her own debilitating disease with its chronic pain she found that, "I must remind myself over and over again that the pain is meaningless, that there is nothing to fear or resist, that resistance only creates tension, which makes it worse."[24]

This stance toward the body challenges not only the implicit optimism of approaches like Juhan's but also the "social" optimism of the feminists:

> On the one hand, there is the implicit belief that, if we can only create social justice and overcome our cultural alienation from the body, our experience of it will be mostly pleasant and rewarding. On the other hand, there is a concept of the body which is limited only by the imagination and ignores bodily experience altogether. In neither case does feminist thought confront the experience of bodily suffering....Unless we do...I suspect that we may not only underestimate the subjective appeal of mind-body dualism, but also fail to offer an adequate alternative conception of the relationship of consciousness to body.[25]

Wendell does not exactly advocate mind–body dualism, but the sort of alternative she wants to develop has quite a different feel to it than that of either Juhan or the feminists who celebrate our embodiment. Wendell offers striking and thoughtful descriptions of "strategies of disembodiment."[26] In her own case,

> being able to say..."My body is painful...but I am happy," can be very encouraging and lift my spirits, because it asserts that the way my body feels is not the totality of my experience, that my mind and feelings can wander beyond the painful messages of my body, and that my state of mind is not completely dependent on the state of my body....In short, I am learning not to identify myself with my body, and this helps me to live a good life with a debilitating chronic illness.[27]

I do not think Wendell and Juhan are really so far apart, but the differences in their emphases are instructive. Wendell reminds us that in rejecting traditional mind–body dualisms we must be careful not to tacitly assume that the mind can control the body or even that the body is *merely* a reflection of processes going on in some higher plane of meaning. While she seeks transcendence of the body, it is a transcendence based in a kind of respect for the body as such. I think the concept of control is key to their differences and what they can teach us. In my view, Juhan offers too little sympathetic understanding for the forces that may impede our ability to take up the responsibility he so persuasively advocates.

There may be many reasons why we are unable to interpret our bodies in ways which allow us to constructively engage with them.[28] Some people have never had access to books such as Juhan's or to practitioners who could teach them a form of interaction that did not simply induce helplessness, guilt, or panic. Some who suffer may be so beset with worries about money and care for their children that they can never find the moments of stillness to tune into their bodies, to develop the attentiveness without resistance that Wendell describes. This approach requires not only concentration but also a willingness to let go, to not to try to control. I can easily imagine situations in which a woman cannot see how she can responsibly relinquish efforts at control—given, for example, her responsibility for her children. Some may have had their self-esteem and their capacity for autonomy so eroded that they do not believe they are entitled to find doctors and therapists who treat them with respect, who enable them to participate in constructive care of their bodies. The capacities required to be able to take on Juhan's kind of responsibility are themselves developed by a myriad of factors that are beyond an individual's control.

I understand that there is a danger in my argument: a kind of passivity before the forces of fate. But that, of course, is a kind of restatement of the puzzle of autonomy itself. We should neither believe that we have no creative powers, no ability to shape and transform ourselves and our environment, nor imagine that that ability is unlimited or constant across the course of our lives or across the population at large. The autonomy required for responsibility for one's health (as for other things) is not simply present or absent as a static characteristic. It is itself a matter of ongoing relationship and interaction.

I think one of the things that fosters autonomy is a sympathetic response to its limitations at any given point. If an exhortation to responsibility makes someone feel inadequate, if a description of the benefits of meditation, exercise, or a healthy diet make a sufferer feel that the suffering is her fault, then her autonomy, her capacity to engage positively with her body, will be undermined. (Of course sometimes the problem will lie primarily in the nature of the exhortation or description, sometimes in the predisposition of the sufferer, and sometimes in the chemistry of the interaction.) In short, our understanding of responsibility must be tempered by a compassionate understanding both of the ways in which our autonomy, our capacity for responsibility, is not itself entirely under our control and of the ways in which compassion fosters autonomy.

Before pursuing the general relation between control and autonomy further, I want to note the way in which I think the issue of control may affect Wendell's approach. Remember that Wendell advocates what might be described as a kind of humility about our capacities to understand and interpret the body. The body may have a kind of autonomy of its own, rhythms and patterns that come from its own dynamic, that we cannot fully understand and ought not try to assimilate to the "meanings" of psyche or spirit. I think that even if there *is* always some such a meaning, because of the body's ongoing interaction with psyche and spirit, we should not imagine that we can always understand it. But Wendell herself is less equivocal: "If I had insisted on seeing [my body] as reflecting psychological or spiritual problems, and devoted my energy to uncovering the 'meanings' of my symptoms, I would still be completely absorbed in being ill."[29] I think that part of why it seemed important to Wendell to stop trying to find meaning in her symptoms had to do with a sense that to find meaning entailed *doing something* about the symptoms. Finding meaning was tinged with an implicit picture of responsibility that was about taking control of her body (and perhaps also about fault). In the same paragraph as the quote above, she says that "when I began to accept and give in to my symptoms, when I stopped searching for medical, psychological or spiritual *cures*, when I began to develop the ability to observe my symptoms and reduced my identification with the transient miseries of my body, I was able to reconstruct my life."[30] In other words, when she stopped trying to do something about her symptoms, to control them, and could observe and accept them, she was able to have very much the kind of creative engagement Juhan advocates. For her, treating her body as a kind of independent cause freed her to let go of efforts at control.

I think the lesson here is, again, that when we talk about responsibility it must be distinguished from control. If people think that to learn from their symptoms is to find ways of controlling their body, their capacity for learning may be inhibited. It may even be that Wendell chose the wording she did because even trying to understand a message or meaning from symptoms has too much of a control dimension.

What we need instead is a stance of receptivity, acceptance, attentiveness, and creative responsiveness. With such a stance and the release of control, we may paradoxically find that our lives are no longer governed by things beyond our control—with the result that our lives feel more under our control. Consider, for example, Jon Kabat-Zinn's approach, which both clearly rejects control as a model and offers relief from the pain and fear that can control one's life. He says,

> Being the scientist of your own mind/body connection doesn't mean you have to control it.... It's not as if we're trying to get hold of our superphysiological control knobs and then tune up our immune system, and tune down something else.... What we're learning is a new kind of science. It's an inner science that marries the subjective and the objective, in which you become more familiar with the workings of your own body.... You'll make decisions that are more apt to bring you in touch with the way things work for you in the world.[31]

Then when describing the benefits of his "mindfulness" approach to meditation he says that "you can live your life with a greater sense of control, especially in relation to situations that previously might have sent you spinning out of control."[32]

The examples Kabat-Zinn was discussing in the context of gaining control were phobias and panic. These problems of the "mind" add an important dimension to Wendell's discussion of "strategies of disembodiment." Heather McKee, the student who introduced me to Wendell's work, raised the problem of disabilities that are mental. How would Wendell's approach help there?[33] What Kabat-Zinn makes clear is that the strategies can actually be the same. Using the example of panic, he says, "You realize, 'Well, those are thoughts, too.' and you come back to your belly and back to your breathing. In that way, you begin to experience what I mean when I say 'your wholeness.' You realize that you are more than a body. You are more than the thoughts that go through your mind."[34] There is thus a way in which "you" can gain some distance from both your body and your mind. This notion of distance does not presuppose the "higher" mind controlling the body or a mind/body split.

This broader context shows more clearly the paradox of control: optimal forms of conscious creation of our lives are best fostered when we relinquish control as a goal. As I noted at the outset of this chapter, seeking control is neither a path to nor an element of autonomy, even though having a sense of one's life as out of control or controlled by external forces is surely antithetical to autonomy. And recognizing that such forces can include thoughts and feelings helps overcome the unease that feminists may feel at Wendell's language of "strategies of disembodiment." What we need is some broader term that, in encompassing the mind as well as the body, avoids connotations of hostility to the body or superiority of the mind. (It is after all attention to the breath in the belly that is the focus for the centering Kabat-Zinn describes.) Kabat-Zinn's term "wholeness" seems aimed at capturing a capacity for transcendence that does not imply rejection or superiority of one dimension of us.

When I initially read Wendell, I thought she was unnecessarily rejecting the quest for meaning in symptoms. But I find that as I think back about my own engagement with chronic fatigue syndrome, I am in closer agreement than I had thought. In the beginning I devoted a lot of energy to trying to find psychological causes for the fatigue. And I think I did actually gain some important insight into the state of my psyche. But I'm not sure that psychological causes really had anything to do with the fatigue. And as long as my approach was to find a psychological cause, I did think of it as somehow my fault. Although the disease was seriously constraining what I could do, I told almost no one about it. It was not until I finally saw my family doctor—a very sympathetic doctor who had suffered from what he called postviral fatigue syndrome himself—that I began to be cautiously willing to go public with the problem. Once I had a medical name, and thus a sense that there was some bodily cause (just as Wendell said), I was also able to be more responsive to the needs of my body. Partly it was that my doctor told me to rest as much as I needed to and thus authorized me to do so. (People I talked to who had the disease all said that they had made it much worse by trying to ignore it in the beginning.) But I think also that I shifted my energies from trying to find out *why* I was feeling this way to figuring out what I needed to do to feel all right. I wasn't trying to change my symptoms; I was trying to give my body what it needed, given my symptoms. The paradoxical virtues of this approach are particularly obvious in the case of fatigue: the response the symptoms required was rest, which then made the symptom go away—although not, of course, the underlying need for a huge amount of rest.

In a way consistent with Wendell's approach, I think I was initially aided in my response by a kind of abandoning of responsibility for the fatigue. My body was sick. It wasn't my fault. All I needed to "do" (and all I could do) was try to give my body the rest it needed and find a practitioner, a naturopath, who could do something about the disease. In a way that still rather surprises me, I initially wanted to turn responsibility for "curing" the disease over to someone else. As the months went on, I felt helpless and very scared that I would never be all right again. I wanted to hand the disease over to someone who could do something about it.[35] Once I started to feel better, I was able to take more active steps, such as changing my diet.[36]

Even in the beginning, however, I was not simply being passive. I used the enforced rest to pay attention to my dreams, turn inward, and be contemplative. I learned a lot from this period, and I think I was able to benefit from the rest and contemplation in part because I was not constantly trying to understand my symptoms or cure them. I was in an ongoing state of reflection, not (generally) an attempt at control.

I was conscious throughout that I was able to engage constructively in part for external reasons. I cancelled all travel and conference participation and postponed all writing until after classes were over. This was possible for me to do without high anxiety for a variety of reasons, which reflect the complex range of factors affecting one's capacity for conscious, creative, engagement. I had tenure. I did not have to be frantic about the implications of a year without research and writing. I was able to be clear and confident about my judgment that I could fulfill my teaching responsibilities if (and only if) I stopped trying to do anything else. I felt very satisfied with my ability to successfully make that accommodation[37] (though the better I felt, the more the anxiety about productivity returned). I also had the vast flexibility of an academic job, where I could nap regularly. And I had a sympathetic husband whose own academic job made it possible for him to take on additional household responsibilities—beyond the 50 percent he was already assuming. And I had an excellent, responsible, full-time nanny. I missed playing with my five-year-old at lunchtime, which became naptime, but I knew he was happy and well cared for. All of these factors were crucial to my ability (much of the time) to relax into the situation.

I believe I should take credit for finding a variety of excellent body/psyche/soul workers who helped me enormously in learning from the experience. And I can claim responsibility for the ways in which what I did took a kind of hard work, courage, and perseverance. But it does not detract from that to know that I could not have done this work alone, and that it would have been vastly harder, if not impossible, without the external supports (including an insurance plan that covered all the expenses except the naturopath).

We can now circle back to the beginning: the body as a path into the puzzle of autonomy in connection. In what ways are we autonomous, and in what ways subject to forces beyond our control, which at some point we would say negate our autonomy? The images of "embodied spirit" and "ensouled body" are statements of that problem, of the tensions inherent in the notion of autonomy for embodied human beings who live together in the material world. The solution lies in a restatement of the question about autonomy and forces beyond our control.

We are not simply *subject* to these forces; we are also part of an interplay with them in which we have a genuine, autonomous capacity to shape and create—a capacity that should not be mistaken for control. This holds true whether we experience the forces in question as lying in our body, in the body politic, in the earth, or in the universe. If we do not pay attention to this core interactive element, we can make a series of common mistakes: we can say that if we do not have control over something, we surely cannot be responsible for it. But that is true neither for our bodies nor our children. If we mistake our task as control in either case, we can do terrible damage—just as we can if we abdicate responsibility (perhaps because we despair of control). Similarly, if we deduce the need to control from a sense of responsibility, we will do damage.

If we start from the notion that we must be able to hold people responsible for their actions, and must therefore posit autonomy, we will turn our attention away from where it belongs: an inquiry into the forms of interaction that foster autonomy and the kinds of interactions that are responsible. In fact, we can be responsible and creative even when we have very little control. But in many instances, we cannot know in advance the scope or form of our creative powers or those of others. We cannot simply assign the responsibility someone has for, say, their health because of some presupposition about their autonomy. There are too many varied and contingent factors.

Our actual capacity for autonomy shifts; it flourishes or declines depending on circumstances—some of which might be said to be under our control and others not. We cannot assume a simple nexus between autonomy, responsibility, and control—and it is control that is the core of the problem. There is almost nothing that we completely control. (Perhaps there *is* nothing, but I leave the "almost" in to avoid sweeping claims.) What we have is a creative capacity to interact. We do not know the scope of the power potential in that capacity. We do not know the limits of our powers to shape and create as we interact—whether that is mind to body, body to mind, mind to mind, body to body, or mind to other bodies. But we must conceptualize that creative power—of which our autonomy is a part—as itself an ongoing subject of interaction that we can shape but not control.

This interactive picture of autonomy seems well suited to any project of governing the interactions among people. (I will come back to the particular problems it poses for law.) If we imagined that autonomy and its attendant responsibility corresponded to situations where we were in control, we would either have to imagine a situation of isolation or deny, denigrate, or undermine the autonomy of others. In interactions with others we are never in control and should not seek to be so, for, as I said in the beginning, control is not a respectful stance toward the autonomy of others—including children.

The alternative I proposed to the effort to control the body seems as appropriate, and perhaps even more important, in this broader context of human interaction: what we need, as I said earlier, is a stance of receptivity, acceptance, attentiveness, and creative responsiveness. Just as our consciousness engages in a complex shifting interaction with our body, in our interactions in the world we are constantly affecting and being affected by other autonomous beings. At some level, we must acknowledge our inability to conceptualize the infinity of interactions among animate and inanimate objects that we affect and are affected by. And the ideal conceptualization would not be one of perfectly comprehended determinism, but of infinitely malleable and shifting interactive creative powers. The power to control is illusory; the power to create is real.

Is there then nothing valuable in the many forms of the admonition to "take control of your life"? And is it simply a mistake to see such admonitions as invocations of autonomy? As is the case with seeing autonomy as independence, there is a grain of truth in the autonomy–control connection. (I will return to independence at the end of this chapter.) If taking control is understood to mean not being passive or merely reactive in the face of the events and interactions of one's life, then it can be valuable. It is only by consciously formulating intentions and hopes and trying to shape one's life accordingly that people can be autonomous.[38] Their capacity for creation becomes manifest in the world when people consciously shape their interactions with it. But "control" (which is also not the same as discipline) is not optimal language for understanding or fostering that capacity.

I think there is some irreducible element of mystery in our power to create, to autonomously interact, in ways that create new, previously undetermined, unimagined interactions. Reflecting on the puzzles of consciousness and the body, on the meaning of responsibility for our health, does not eliminate the mystery. It provides a concrete focus for thinking about autonomy in interactive terms that reject control as well as independence as core elements of human autonomy. The puzzles of consciousness and the body provide a focus for meditating on the inherent mystery of autonomy that can move us forward in our efforts to conceptualize autonomy without trying to eliminate its illusive dimensions.

Religious metaphors also try to capture this capacity. One that makes sense to me is that the capacity for undetermined creation is the spark of the divine within us—and within all life.[39] In the language of the Judeo-Christian tradition, it is as creators that we are created "in the image of God." To create is to take what previously existed before and by a conscious action to make something new, something that not only did not exist before but that would not have come into being (in this precise form) without the act of creation. It could not be predetermined, for the spark of creation was necessary and could not itself be predetermined.

I think this spark is innate and can never be completely extinguished—and thus the philosophers who posit autonomy as a given of human nature are, in a way, correct. But the ability of the spark to ignite in creative interaction is not simply a given, and it is not static; it is dependent on the interactions I have tried to indicate above. Thus while one might say there is always hope, and even some kind of moral responsibility to nurture that spark and use it constructively, I think one must be very wary about assigning blame.[40] If we want to assess responsibility, we cannot simply posit autonomy; we will have to inquire into the nature of its flourishing.

In my reflections above, I have made several, sometimes oblique, connections between consciousness and autonomy. Trying to work through just what those connections are returns us to the issue of law. In the automaton example I used at the beginning, it is the absence of conscious control that is at stake. In the discussions of Juhan and Kabat-Zinn, it is bringing consciousness to the processes of one's bodymind that is crucial. I think it is fair to say that the higher the degree of consciousness, the greater the autonomy. The problem is not only that there are different degrees of consciousness but also that the norm in North America is a fairly low level of consciousness about the inner workings of our bodies and minds and their interconnection. This compounds the challenge for law to construct an approach to legal responsibility that is consistent with the shifting and contingent relational and embodied conception of autonomy.

Reflecting on embodied autonomy helps us see that the link between autonomy and responsibility is complex and cannot simply be mediated by control. Despite its seemingly commonsense links to both autonomy and responsibility, control is not an optimal concept for understanding either. Control is not a relationship consistent with equal respect. Thus the conventional autonomy-control-responsibility nexus is disrupted: control is not a component of autonomy; the existence of responsibility (say for children) can neither dictate nor presuppose control. The connection between autonomy and responsibility must be understood in the context of the relationally contingent nature of both.

The question remains whether these nuanced complexities can be translated into the task of assigning legal responsibility.

III. PSYCHOANALYTIC REFLECTIONS ON CONTROL

Having identified this challenge, I will postpone my response.[41] First, I want to switch gears somewhat and locate the issue of autonomy as control in still another context: psychoanalytic conceptions of the self as presented in the work of Jessica Benjamin.[42] Her work offers another way of seeing how powerful the connection between autonomy and control is in the culture, why it so important to break that connection, and why there is likely to be fierce resistance to such an attempt. This feminist psychoanalytic context will help me draw links between the fearful relation to the body and the fearful relation to others (noted in chapter 2)—and how each is linked to control. It will also link us back to the broader transformations necessary to end violence against women that I noted in chapter 5.

Benjamin is interested in the psychodynamics of child development and in psychoanalytic theory. She is interested in these in part for purposes very close to mine here: she wants to show the destructive consequences of existing practices and theory and to show that there is a psychologically viable alternative consistent with the equality and mutual respect necessary to end deeply engrained patterns of domination. These patterns characterize relations between all people, not just between men and women. But since they arise in the context of gendered theories and practices of child development, yielding gendered conceptions of adult autonomy (and domination), the larger patterns of domination will not change until the underlying gendered conception and enactment of individuation changes.[43]

Benjamin also explicitly makes links to another political aspiration she shares with my project: equality in which difference is not peripheral.[44] She offers a psychological perspective on how to recognize both difference and universal equality: when the mature self sees the other, she can recognize her in the particularity of her difference (and potential opposition) *and* recognize her as another self, a possessor of subjectivity just like herself. She can recognize others' equal entitlement to this recognition and their mutual need for this equal recognition. This is the alternative, a psychologically possible alternative, to autonomy as control and independence, with its inevitable link to domination and, ultimately, violence.

Benjamin is a relational psychoanalyst who shows how the traditional Freudian conception of the self entails a conception of (male) autonomy as independence, control, and domination. Her analysis shows how breaking the links to control and independence is essential to breaking the link to domination.

Before turning in detail to Benjamin, I want to note three things about the argument here. First, psychoanalytic theory is, of course, concerned fundamentally with the unconscious. As Jane Flax reminded me, the concept of the unconscious is itself one of the greatest challenges to a control-based discourse of autonomy: "Freud thought this was the third blow to human pride of Enlightenment. (Copernicus's sun centered universe and Darwin's [theory of] evolution connecting us to the primates were the other two.) If much of our subjectivity is not accessible to or controllable by reason, what happens to autonomy? It has to be shifted to practices of constant subjective interrogation and suspicion."[45] Despite the centrality of the unconscious to psychoanalytic theory, I will not be focusing directly on that concept here.

The second note is that all theories of infant experience have an inherent degree of speculation. But Benjamin relies heavily on Daniel Stern's highly regarded empirical observations of infant behavior.[46] She does not just deduce her claims from her theory.

Third, Benjamin is very conscious of the particular cultural context that spawned and sustains the Freudian concepts she challenges. And what makes her work so helpful here is the confluence between her understanding of the need for an alternative to the Freudian conception of the self and my own efforts to provide an alternative to the dominant understandings of self and autonomy in legal and political thought. While both of us self-consciously situate our critique in a historical–cultural context, our claims for the desirability of the alternatives we propose may veer toward universal language. I think the best reading of both her argument and mine is that in the context of the (still) dominant framework, our alternatives are an improvement.

According to Benjamin, psychoanalytic theory has for a long time sustained the links between control, independence, and domination. Traditional Freudian theory had different stories about how little boys and girls deal with the recognition of their differences from their mothers and fathers. It involved a repudiation of the boy's early identification with his mother but also a fearful and idealized relation to the father. Nevertheless, according to the theory, if he properly internalizes the father's rules and attributes, he can hope to grow up to be like him, to have his power and capacity for action in the world. The little girl must accept that she can never be like the father whose power in the world (and the household) she admires. And, of course, she cannot actually have him. She must accept the comparatively passive position of the female in the hope of attracting a man who has the power and capacity for action she admires and longs for. Neither boys nor girls in this model learn to truly recognize the different other as an equal.

Benjamin argues that there is an alternative theory, and practice, of individuation in which both little boys and girls come to recognize other people—in their different particularities—as having the same capacity for subjectivity as themselves. Indeed, it is only by recognizing others as such that young children (and ultimately adults) can receive the recognition they require for the development of their own subjectivity. She uses Hegel's analysis of the master–slave relationship as an analogue, but as with her critique of Freud, she rejects the impasse of domination.[47] By focusing on the intersubjective play between mother and infant, the story of individuation comes to include this key element of learning the possibility of true mutual recognition—which is the only outcome that does not entail domination and subordination.

The issue of control is central here. It is the infant's encounter with the fact that he cannot control his mother and thus whether his needs are met that sets the stage both for the Freudian account (in which the Oedipal conflict then becomes predominant) and for Benjamin's alternative. The Freudian account rests on the idea that sensing the external reality of others involves recognition that one cannot control them and, for the infant, the doubly terrifying reality that one is dependent upon what one cannot control. The Freudian story may be read as a way (for the male) to transform this terrible reality in ways that deny dependency and create a picture of individual autonomy very close to the one I have critiqued in political and legal theory. But this story requires women not to try to appropriate the same form of autonomy. They have to get it vicariously through a man to whom they are attached. In Benjamin's alternative there is the possibility for both boys and girls to identify with (and differentiate from) both their mothers and fathers and to learn a capacity for mutual and equal intersubjectivity.

In order to enable the development of the child's capacity for mutual recognition, the mothering parent[48] must be able to show the young child that she will neither abandon him with withdrawal nor try to annihilate him with punishment (nor fall apart) when the child thwarts or challenges the parent. The child must be able to run up against this genuine other in conflict and find her (and her love) intact. The child learns to give up the fantasy of control and the quest for domination in favor of the pleasure of mutual intersubjectivity and the exciting possibilities of new development it provides. The child comes to recognize equal others and their potential for harm and conflict; simultaneously, she learns to embrace the pleasure of mutual recognition and its necessity for her to thrive.

The potential for the other to hurt, disappoint, thwart, and challenge is always there in Benjamin's alternative. It is not denied in a picture of blissful merging or idealized relations. The self becomes differentiated from the other, and in so doing opens itself to both threat and joy and, thus, to the possibility of the mutual recognition. This mutual recognition, together with acknowledgment of the need for this mutuality, are what constitute the mature self—not the separateness that denies dependence and seeks control through domination. To meet the other with openness to intersubjective exchange entails risk—of misunderstanding, hurt, rejection, betrayal. One can never be certain that the other's defensive urge for domination and control will not take over. It is just as important to acknowledge the risks as to recognize that to be open to mutual engagement is not to slide into the dependency of infancy, with either its helplessness or its unconscious bliss.

Benjamin thus holds out an alternative picture of the process of individuation that still respects and uses many of the concepts of psychoanalysis. She transforms the basic story of individuation to one of mutual, equal intersubjectivity rather than the gendered story of separation, mastery, and dominance as the attributes of the autonomous male accompanied by the lack, loss, and objectification of the necessarily subordinate female. This matters so much not just because of the influence of psychoanalysis as theory and therapeutic practice but also because the gendered story of autonomous independence and constrained, subordinate dependence is actually enacted in children's development.

Benjamin is a bit vague on the relation between the theory and the actual dynamics of child development. She does not try to spell out the ways in which the power of the psychoanalytic framework itself actually shapes people's behaviors. Nevertheless, I think she is right that unless there is a compelling alternative articulation of mature individuation, the many diffuse ways in which the Freudian picture infuses the culture will go unchallenged and unchanged.[49] And it *is* clear that Benjamin thinks that social practices, not just gendered parenting but also the roles men and women play in society, interact with collective norms, values, and conceptions—such as autonomy, power, and masculinity—to reproduce these patterns of child development.

Her argument helps us see that there is a mutual reinforcement between the political and legal conceptions of autonomy that I have been critiquing and the conception of autonomy built into the traditional psychoanalytic framework.

I think it is worth noting that in her presentation of the traditional psychoanalytic picture of autonomy, she does not try to address the question of how it managed to sustain itself in the face of its manifest unavailability to millions of men whose work lives deny them control or meaningful autonomy and whose subordinate positions in society severely constrain their ability to enact the role of the independent autonomous individual in control of his life. Similarly, Benjamin does not try to take up Elizabeth Spelman's compelling critique[50] of Nancy Chodorow's related analysis of the relation between gender and domination.[51] (Spelman shows in effective detail that child rearing cannot be characterized by a simple connection between maleness and superior power and domination. For example, for most of the twentieth century in the racist society of the United States it would have been dangerous for black mothers to raise their sons to believe that all [including black] men should behave as though they were superior to all [including white] women.[52]) Benjamin's language sometimes expresses an overgenerality similar to

Chodorow's. But this limitation shows how the psychoanalytic picture of the autonomous man, like that of the autonomous man in political and legal theory, are pictures from the view of the privileged.

Indirectly, Benjamin's picture helps us see how the impossibility of living up to the cultural ideal of the autonomous man can lead to dangerous rage and frustration. For example, we see in analyses of wife battering the role of rage at humiliation in the work world (whether through unemployment or demeaning employment). It is also common to find descriptions of the battering partner exerting control over every aspect of the woman's life. One might see wife assault as a desperate attempt by the batterer to claim the indicia of autonomy—independence and control—by reducing his female partner to an extreme of dependency and helplessness.[53] How many other forms of male violence are expressions of the necessary failure of even the illusion of autonomy for the millions of men who work in environments of assembly line production or managerial control that are inimical to both real autonomy and the image of autonomy as independence and control?[54]

In the earlier chapter on "Violence against Women" (chapter 5), I noted the range of deep cultural and psychological transformations necessary to end this violence. Benjamin helps us see that the transformation of the understanding of autonomy is itself part of this transformation: the dominant conception of autonomy is itself inseparable from domination because the illusion of control and independence can only be sustained through domination. She also helps us see that the relation of domination between men and women is part of a broader structure of relations of domination. The one cannot be transformed without the other.[55]

It is explicitly part of Benjamin's project to show that a society characterized by equality and respect for difference requires a model of mature autonomy that is based on mutual recognition. The mature self recognizes others as autonomous, interconnected selves with minds and spirits (and, in intimate relations, bodies) that—because of their inherent equality—can be shared. It is the mix of difference and equality that makes the true intersubjective exchange exciting. In such exchange, women know themselves as desiring subjects, not merely the objects of desire. (We saw the importance of this in chapter 5.)

Here we can connect the discussion of Benjamin back to the fear of others I discussed in chapter 2 and to the fear of the body. Both are part of the striving for (impossible, illusory) control that is part of the dominant picture of autonomy. Other people—whether constructed as particularly different and dangerous "Others" or not—are always potential threats. They inevitably remind us of our dependency and of the fact that our will is not all powerful, that it can only be made manifest with the (sometimes coerced) cooperation of others. Standard means of coping with the fears others arouse are incompatible with equality. For example (as I noted earlier in chapter 3, "Reconceiving Autonomy"), people try to sustain a sense of autonomous independence by using power hierarchies to control others and to meet their needs without having to recognize that their "independence" depends on help from others. Of course, such people are not treating their helping others with the respect due to autonomous beings.

The problem is that the autonomy of others is incompatible with control. All autonomous others are threats to the desire for control, a reminder that being in control in a world of others is impossible.

Autonomy as control is an illusion, but the danger it poses is real. Real efforts to control do real harm, and those harmed *are* likely to be threats. The control will never be complete, and the others will always resist in some ways.[56] Resistance to domination and control is reasonable and probable. In sum, the quest for control will always fail—and others will always remind us of that.

Distance sometimes seems to provide safety from the threatening others. For those in power, others can be kept at bay by a variety of rights—in particular, property and the power it provides. Similarly, techniques of emotional distance can deny the basic recognition of intersubjective exchange, of course, denying the vital benefits of such exchange to the denier as well as to the one she refuses to recognize. Remember my comment in chapter 2 that the property metaphors suggest that the most autonomous person is the most perfectly isolated. Benjamin helps us see that such isolation is not just metaphoric. It becomes an emotional reality for those who seek the autonomy of control and independence.

I think the common relation people in North America have to their bodies reflects and reveals a similar destructive role of control. It is in part our embodiment that makes us inevitably dependent on others. As I said in chapter 4, in sickness and death we are forced to recognize both our need for others and our ultimate lack of control. And it is this dependency and inherent lack of control that, in our culture, breeds fear, distaste, and hostility toward all things bodily. The visions of freedom from necessity falter in the face of the sick or dying body. The image of autonomy becomes muddied.

In transforming the conception of autonomy as I suggest, we must also recognize and transform the fears that are embedded in traditional conceptions. It is exactly the elements I want to change—control and independence—that are tenaciously held in place by fear.[57] Benjamin offers a psychoanalytic account of the source of that fear: the primal experience of the infant's helplessness. This account also tacitly warns that those same primal fears may be stirred up by efforts to loosen the grip of control in dominant understandings of autonomy.

The focus on control reveals another link: just as the model of autonomy as control precludes true intersubjective exchange with other people, it precludes an openness to communication with our bodies. When the other is a threat or an object to be possessed, controlled, or vanquished, real intersubjectivity is impossible. Similarly, the attention most North Americans do give to our bodies—to whip them into shape, to achieve peak performance and ideal appearance—is a form of control. It is almost the opposite of open communication with our bodies in which our conscious mind becomes a self-conscious participant in the ongoing flow of information that constitutes our bodymind. In such communication we recognize our bodies as sources of the knowledge we need for optimal consciousness.[58]

We can also see an interesting parallel with the fear of "Others," who are often constructed as mere bodies. (We can see this with women and many people of color. Their construction as mere bodies usually goes together with a denigration or denial of their capacity for reason.[59]) Thus just as we treat Others as bodies, we treat our bodies as Others—to be disciplined and controlled but not listened to and respected.[60] When autonomy is understood as control, we dominate not only others but also ourselves.

IV. LAW, RESPONSIBILITY, AND THE CHALLENGES OF RELATIONAL AUTONOMY

Benjamin helps us see both the urgency and the psychic possibility of a transformation of our collective understanding of autonomy, releasing it from its destructive connection to control and independence. And it is easy to see that for the deep cultural transformation she is talking about to take place, law must be a part of it. In North America, law infuses culture (and vice versa, of course), and law structures relations from the most intimate to corporate to international and environmental. The law cannot, of course, teach people the openness to intersubjective engagement that allows the self to develop and thrive in equal mutuality. But it can stop reinforcing a picture of autonomy that has control and independence—and thus domination—built into it.

Let me sketch some of the forms this transformation can take. The first is that which is already familiar from preceding chapters. The constructive relationships that autonomy requires to flourish are not simply those of parent and child; they are also the relationships law shapes as it defines responsibility for male violence, as it shapes clients' interactions with government bureaucracies, as it defines contractual obligation and the responsibility for reasonable care we owe to our neighbors.[61]

From this perspective there are two ways the law can contribute to the cultural reconstruction of autonomy. First, legislators and judges can actually promote relational autonomy by implementing law in ways that shape the kinds of relations that foster autonomy. Second, by paying overt attention (in debates and opinions) to this issue, they can foster a wider understanding of autonomy as relational. When judges and legislators talk about how different forms of the law can affect structures of relationship, and how these can undermine or enhance autonomy, autonomy can come to be collectively understood as requiring constructive relationship. An understanding of autonomy as dependent on constructive relationship will erode a conception of autonomy as independence. When autonomy is seen as shaped by both large- and small-scale relationship, its identification with control will be undermined.

Of course, one could still have the idea that, *once achieved,* autonomy is a matter of independence and control—however much that achievement is dependent on forces beyond one's control. This is part of why it is important to see that autonomy is never simply achieved; for the capacity for autonomy to thrive it is continually dependent on constructive relationship. For example, however much optimal parenting provides groundwork, autonomy can always be eroded by oppressive governments or work environments. Here it is important to remember that the picture of autonomy as independence and control is a picture from the top of a hierarchy. And attachment to this picture might yield a determination to stay on top; domination and control of others is necessary to make sure that the "autonomous one" gets to keep his autonomy.[62] What is the law to do about this?

In a society committed to equality, judges and legislatures can try to see where the law is implicated in structures of inequality, domination, and the kind of control inimical to autonomy—so that the core value of autonomy is available to all, not only those on top.[63]

Again, when judges and legislators articulate their concern in these (or similar) terms, they convey a sense that *equal* autonomy cannot be the autonomy of control. Autonomous equals do not want to be controlled. One can see privacy rights of renters and antidiscrimination limits on employers' ability to hire and fire at will as examples of constraining the control of those in power in ways that foster equal autonomy. Freedom of information laws also might be an example. Contested areas where one might advocate constraints on employers' powers of control would be additional limits on their power to fire at will and to structure workplace environments such that employees have little say about the conditions, pace, or nature of their work.[64]

In sum, if judges and legislators take a relational approach to autonomy they can both actually promote it and can contribute to a shift in the collective understanding of it.

Here the question may arise whether it is possible for lawmakers and judges, in particular, to build decision making around such a highly contingent conception of autonomy. I want to note two, contradictory, answers. The first is that throughout the twentieth century law did just that, recognize that social context, power relations in particular, constrain autonomy and that the law must take account of this. Minimum wage and maximum hours legislation is the clearest example: it is not reasonable to assume that workers can simply bargain with their employers around these issues because of power disparities. Fostering workers' real autonomy requires collective constraint on the terms of work. Of course, notoriously, American judges in the early twentieth century argued that such laws denied the liberty of workers who, as autonomous agents, should be respected as competent to set their own terms in private contract.[65] And while that particular argument might be (virtually) settled, the wider debate continues over what should be left to the "autonomous choice" and bargaining power of employees and what should be regulated for their health, safety, equality, or dignity. Accommodation for disability, regulations regarding hazardous working conditions and the nature of employees' control over the use of their pension funds are all examples of contestations over the nature and reasonable scope of individual choice and autonomy. One might also say that in modern contract law judges have recognized the ways in which power relations between consumers and producers have to be taken into account when judging the enforceability of standard form contracts and liability waivers in particular.[66] Family court judges, as well as legislators, often recognize that the concept of choice is not adequate to capture why women stay home with their children and thus the kind of compensation or support they should be entitled to when marriages end.[67] Judges have recognized that courts should not simply assume that a wife's signature on a loan against the family home constitutes autonomous consent.[68] All of these involve a relational approach to autonomy.

The contrasting claim is that law cannot accommodate the contingency of a relational conception of autonomy. This brings us back to the beginning of this chapter and the claim that law must assume autonomy in order to assign responsibility and legal liability. One might say that to presume autonomy is not to presume any particular conception of it. But the presumption itself reflects a picture of autonomy as a given (barring exceptional circumstances), not something that is necessarily shifting and contingent, as a relational conception must be. Here the argument would be that judges cannot spend their time trying to unravel the situational intricacies that might reveal the exact level of autonomy that any given litigant or defendant might have—and then try to assign responsibility accordingly. This is beyond the scope of what judges can reasonably be expected to do.

This argument engages us in the fascinating complexity of law, the common law in particular. Law inevitably involves abstraction and categories that cannot capture the particularities of every human interaction.[69] But the common law is case-based. Its rules, for the most part, are just generally accepted distillations of holdings in previous cases.[70] The actual binding precedent is the entire case, with all its particularity. And each new case is to be heard in all its particularity. Similar previous cases can always be "distinguished" on the facts. The common law system is characterized by a combination of general principles articulated over the course of many cases, and attention to the particularity of each new case. Can that particularity include an attention to the particulars of an individual's autonomy—beyond the grossest conditions of a gun to the head, insanity, or drug-induced incapacity? Can there be a corresponding form of legal responsibility that matches the subtleties of the responsibility for one's body that I discussed earlier?

My answer is a qualified yes. To ask judges to attend to some of the particularities of the continuum along which people experience autonomy, and the conditions that affect it, is not to ask them to dispense with precedent and the sorts of generalization, rules, and guidelines it provides. Cases would come to stand in as shorthand for common forms and degrees of autonomy, as with all other complex legal concepts. Judges would not have to approach each case from scratch. They would, as always, need to attend to the particulars before them in light of their understanding of the general principles (including the value of autonomy and its relational nature).

Let us look briefly at some of the examples we already have of judges' attempts to assign responsibility in ways that reflect an awareness of the contingent, relational nature of autonomy. First is the example we already saw of the responsibility of women who kill their battering partners (chapter 4). While I argued that the real issue there was the failure of the state to provide such women with protection, I noted the question of women's responsibility for protecting their children from abuse. This issue arises particularly in the context of sexual abuse. Here we might see not only a question of diminished autonomy arising out of the battering relationship and the state's failure to protect the woman but also a parallel failure of the state to intervene to protect the child. Thus we might say that the woman's responsibility should be judged in the context of the consequences of both her personal relationship and how that relationship is situated in the wider structure of social and governmental relationships that effectively tolerate the abuse of children as well as women.

In the very different context of administrative law, we saw judges assign bureaucratic decision makers the responsibility to provide reasons for their decisions and to conduct their investigations in ways that promote rather than undermine clients' autonomy.

Another form of legal response to these issues is the split that takes place within criminal law between assigning liability for the crime and considering the appropriate sentence. The assignment of liability usually takes place with the presumption of autonomy (barring exceptional circumstances) that I have characterized as the dominant conception. But then at the time of sentencing, a wide range of factors—both mitigating and aggravating circumstances, including harm to the victim and its impact on family and even community—can be taken into account.

One might say that responsibility in the sense of the penalty that should be imposed is assigned in a relational context, with the ability to consider the relational dimensions of autonomy. The more basic question of guilt or innocence, of whether the state gets to impose a sentence at all, is handled without trying to assess the full complexity of individual autonomy. (One might note here that criminal law is a context in which, in order to ascertain intent, judges do take upon themselves the responsibility to evaluate evidence of the internal working of the mind of the accused. So we should not underestimate the kind of complexity judges are used to working with.)

There is a norm in the criminal law that there should be stringent protections of the rights of the accused—given that the accused confronts the power of the state. But as we have seen in the case of women accused of killing their battering partners, using a relational approach to autonomy does not necessarily put the accused at greater risk. Or to put it the other way around, a less contingent approach to autonomy does not simply yield greater protection for the accused. Using a relational approach to autonomy to determine criminal liability may give judges a greater scope of discretion, but since the existing norm is a presumption of autonomy, turning to a more contingent conception should enhance rather than undermine the protection available to the accused.

In the sketch of issues above, I have not tried to show in detail how a relational conception of autonomy would be used in deliberations assigning liability or interpreting the law or in judgments about the kind of law legislators should impose. The common law is a rich and diverse system, not a uniform, seamless whole. It is to be expected that the approaches to autonomy will be more relational in some areas of law than others and that the forms of relationality will vary. The claim that matters here is that using such a conception is well within the range of legal possibility.

In making this claim, I also want to insist that a relational conception of autonomy is not one based on utopian visions about human relations. In the general absence of equal relations, law must be able to deal with people's fears, both those that are inevitable and those that are generated in part by hierarchy and our existing constructions of autonomy as control and thus domination. When people feel threatened, humiliated, and unjustly deprived, they may attack both persons and property. And people can reasonably hope that the state will use the law to protect them from such attacks. (This means, of course, that the law will often protect unjust privilege.) Even with much greater equality, dangers will not simply disappear. As we have seen in looking at Benjamin's work, to meet the other on equal terms is always a risk, and it is part these risks that law must mediate.

In a relational approach, it is not just the law's job to construct relations that foster autonomy. It remains law's job to try to provide security—another basic value. And to do so will require attending to people's fears and their capacity to do harm. Human relations generate violence, threat, anxiety, rejection, and betrayal as well as the best of intersubjective mutuality. Law will always have to consider all of these.

In a final word here on the viability of the relational approach, it is worth remembering that, for Benjamin, the origins of the intersubjective capacity is the mother–infant relationship. This is a relationship characterized at its best by intersubjective mutuality but also, inevitably, by dependency and huge power disparity. We thus see that true mutuality can be consistent with the inevitability of power disparity. The relational approach does not require a utopia of (impossible) relations of perfect equality. It can address the dangers of our existing arrangements, guide their transformation, and give us a picture of optimal relations of equal mutuality—which will always have some forms of power hierarchy.

In sum, Benjamin helps us see the urgency, possibility, and difficulty of conceptualizing—and developing—autonomy without control. To genuinely meet others as equals is a risk. To abandon the illusion of control and independence will feel like a risk. But the dangers of domination are certain.

V. CONCLUSION: OUR EMBODIED SELVES

Before closing this chapter, I want to offer a clarification of my rejection of control and independence as core components of autonomy. In keeping with my opening invocation of Susan Wendell's critique, I want to ensure that my reflections on the body capture both its joys and its limitations. Thus I begin this clarification with two images: the joy of bodily independence that a toddler feels and the sadness about loss of independence and control that many feel with the debilities of age or illness.

The body invites us to see both sides. We are never really independent or in control of our lives. But there are degrees of independence and degrees to which we find ourselves under the control of others. Bodily infirmity may mean that others are "in control" of things like when or what one eats, when one can get out of bed, go outside, listen to music, or read a book. I think that the anguish many feel at the loss of physical independence is compounded by the false sense of autonomy perpetuated in the culture: when people know that they are dependent on others they feel they have lost not just mobility but also one of the highest values of the culture, autonomy. Thus they no longer have the indicia of successful adulthood, the basis and measure of respect, and so they feel diminished.

I think an acceptance of a relational conception of autonomy with neither control nor independence at its center could mitigate that sense of loss. But I do not imagine that even the fullest sense of the inevitability of dependence and its consistency with autonomy would eliminate grief over the loss of the ability to move when and where one wants to, to get what one needs for oneself without having to trouble others or be subject to their moods or busyness.

The joy toddlers display in increasing control over their bodies, of being able to walk by themselves, to climb, to grab things, and open cupboard doors at will is itself a joy to behold (as well as a threat to peace, order, and security). Their pleasure in physical competence and the independence it brings—as they can feed themselves, dress themselves, build their own block towers—is obviously not the result of some misconception about autonomy. Indeed, these same stages are linked to increasing capacity for autonomy. To say that we should not mistake the essence of autonomy for either independence or control is not to say that there is no value to relative independence or freedom from the power of others (which may or may not be exercised in disrespectfully controlling ways).

Our bodies invite us to relish the joys of physical strength and competence (whether playing the cello, dancing, or walking), and the decline of that competence is a genuine loss. Big declines can make us more, and more obviously, dependent on others. That dependency can generate both unnecessary, disrespectful control and the inevitable sense of not being able to control certain dimensions of one's life. In the echo of infant helplessness and the seeming reversal of the child's joint development of autonomy and physical competence, there may be a primal sense of threat to autonomy—that is, again, not about cultural misconceptions.

Nevertheless, these real losses need not be a threat to autonomy itself. One can recognize that it is harder to sustain a sense of, say, the autonomy of consciousness when one is physically dependent (and one's mental capacities are shifting as well). One can acknowledge the experiential links between physical competency and autonomy. Full recognition of these links, of the pleasures of physical competence and independence (with their links to control) and the pain of grief over their loss, is consistent with my insistence that autonomy should not be misconstrued as independence or control. To treat autonomy as independence or control is to deny its inherently relational nature and thus to foster illusions of independence and control that can be sustained only through domination. Accepting the many forms of our dependence (including dependence on autonomy-fostering relations) and the inherent disrespect of relations of control does not require denying the joys or losses of physical competence and the forms of independence and material control it can bring.

Finally, a note to suggest that while law can play a partial but important role in the reconception of our autonomous selves that I advocate, the body (and its metaphors) can provide a path to transformation for anyone engaged in the project of reimaging autonomy. Paying attention to our embodiment can allow us to see that the very forms of physical dependency that seem such a threat to autonomy are themselves forms of connection through which intersubjective mutuality develops and thrives. This begins, of course, with the physical care of infants. The general denigration of physical caretaking in the culture—itself related to the denigration of the body with which I began this chapter—has meant that forms of care, such as changing diapers, are constructed as distasteful chores. Even feminists have surprisingly little to say about the irreplaceable connection created by physical caretaking. Changing diapers and feeding an infant (by bottle as well as breast) creates intimacy, builds a relationship that just playing with him cannot. (I discovered this during a period of intense work when my husband took over many of the "chores" in caring for our first baby. I came to feel something missing in my bond, despite many hours of other kinds of interaction with him.) People who have cared for their dying parents report similar bonds arising from the interaction of physical care. True mutuality can be enacted and created in the context of extreme dependency.

Many feminists have noted the links between the denigration of the body and the despoiling of the earth.[71] I think a respectful relation of mutuality with our bodies is likely to generate a more respectful relation to the earth and to all the forms of physical caretaking such a relation might entail. A respectful relation to all forms of physical caretaking would transform the hierarchy of the value accorded to work. A stance of respectful care toward the material world could replace the stance of control, which is as destructive in relation to the earth as it is to ourselves and autonomous others.[72]

There is a metaphoric alternative to the separation between body and soul that Arendt ascribed to Greek philosophy, with which I began this chapter: the ensouled body. In this image, our soul resides not in our head (or even our heart), but in every cell of our body. Thus spiritual uplift can rejuvenate the body, and the body can be a path to spiritual renewal. Almost every tradition recognizes some form of this path, whether chanting, singing, dancing, or fasting.

The body is then not simply an imperfect, interfering and gradually deteriorating container for what is truly valuable (for some that would be mind rather than soul). It is not merely the mechanism by which this higher part makes itself manifest. In this alternative image, every cell of our body is part of what we think of as the soul. (The image works for the mind as well in the sense that what we think of as mind involves a constant chemical and electrical exchange of information throughout the body.) There is no cell that is not itself ensouled; every part of our body carries the divine creativity within it. Our selves are not just embodied in the sense of being encased in our bodies. Our selves are fully embodied, in the sense that our bodies are constitutive, interactive dimensions of a whole.

With such an image, it should be easier to treat bodies—our own and those of others—with care and respect. It might then also be easier to recognize the joy and beauty of our physical interdependence instead of construing it primarily as a threat or impediment. Such an image can be an additional aid to focusing on the special forms of interaction made possible by bodily connection, whether pregnancy, lovemaking, or feeding a child or a sick loved one.

Whatever the path, what ultimately matters is that people learn to see our inherent lack of control as the necessary corollary of our embodied nature and our interaction with other embodied beings and the world we share. This interaction takes a particular form in the company of other free beings who mirror our creating selves back to us and co-create with us. Those on the top of hierarchies might be able to meet some of their bodily needs by controlling and dominating others. But everyone needs autonomous others to exercise their creative human potential. The autonomy of all cannot be an autonomy of independence and control.

8

Restructuring Relations

THE HEART OF my argument has been that values like equality or autonomy are made possible by structures of relationship. Thus transformative projects, such as feminism, involve restructuring relations. (This is equally true of attempts to end racism or discrimination against gays. Trying to achieve greater economic equality would, of course, also involve restructuring relations.) This chapter turns to a variety of scholars, each of whom provides an example of what it means to bring a relational analysis to bear on the problem of violence against women. It also takes up some of the most important challenges to projects of restructuring relations though law.

I. INTIMATE PARTNER VIOLENCE: THE NATURE OF RELATIONAL ANALYSIS

I begin with a discussion of intimate partner violence as an example of a problem that cannot be solved without a restructuring of relations. This problem is particularly challenging because it involves so many state and nonstate relations; because those relations in turn are shaped by deeply held, sometimes unconscious beliefs, needs, and desires; and because this problem brings home especially acutely the recognition that restructuring gender relations involves the inherently "tricky, risky"[1] and fiercely contested problem of transforming sexuality.

These issues help us see the complex interplay among ideas, state and nonstate practices, and the structures of relations that enable or undermine such core values as bodily security. The invocation of legal rights works at all these levels: when rights are claimed, people's beliefs about who is entitled to what can shift; the way rights are implemented institutionally shapes both people's relation with the state and their relations (of, say, power and trust) with each other. I intend the discussion below to offer further evidence that judgments about invoking and implementing rights are best made through a relational analysis—even when that analysis highlights the conflicts and uncertainties inherent in the judgments.

I begin this section with my own affective response to reading about women who are routinely assaulted by the men with whom they are in intimate relations. I then turn to Ann Jones's *Next Time, She'll Be Dead*,[2] which offers a combination of what I see as a compelling example of a relational analysis of the causes and cures for battering together with a repeated invocation of women's absolute right to bodily security as the key to the necessary transformation. I use this absolute language to ask whether it is a tacit challenge to my relational approach to rights—allowing me to take up the question of whether a relational approach to rights makes rights more contingent and less effective rhetorically.

Next I turn to Sally Merry's 2003 article "Rights Talk and the Experience of Law," which offers an analysis of rights consciousness as a choice of subjectivities.[3] In her take on the role of rights in ending battering, she provides another set of examples of how rights structure relationships and the contestations and losses involved in the restructuring. This discussion also allows me to make clear that I do not see rights as always the best vehicle for restructuring relations. I conclude this section with "The Question of Men," in which I argue for the need for a symmetrically deep relational analysis of men's role in intimate partner violence against women.

A. The Problem: The Pervasiveness of Relations of Violence

Violence against women by their intimate partners should be shocking. People should be shocked by its prevalence, the severity of the violence, the scope of the harm, and the fact that it continues more or less unabated decades after it has been recognized and widely proclaimed to be unacceptable.[4] But it is one of those things that most people know and yet don't know. So they are only occasionally shocked by a graphic story. One cannot, after all, sustain shock, and it is hard even to sustain awareness of brutality. And it is hard to sustain awareness of collective indifference when most people are complicit in it.

My problem is how to temporarily bring home to my readers what they already "know" so that a sense of the shocking nature of the problem is the context for arguments about the need to restructure relations. I cannot know or control how my readers will respond to information I find shocking. In the end, I have opted to put much of the detail in extended notes so that those who want to can see if this information shifts the way they know about this violence. But I begin with a paragraph about my own experience of temporarily experiencing the shock.

I find that I am always shocked anew by detailed information about the prevalence and seriousness of the violence, its relation to control, what it does to women and children, and what it costs all of us. When I read the stories[5] of women who have been terribly injured in body and soul, who have had their hearts broken as well as their teeth and their jaws, I feel a terrible sadness. I hear the urgency with which scholars, activists, and front-line workers try to communicate how horrible the situation is, how common it is, and how often injured women cannot find the help and protection they need to keep them-selves and their children safe. I can feel the pain of a woman having to give up her kids ("into care") because, having left a dangerously violent partner, she does not have the money to feed them. And I also feel—or imagine—the safe remove of my life from theirs. I can choose not to read another book or article about women who suffer this violence, and then, after a while, when the disturbing memories and thoughts fade, I won't have to think about it. For me, the problem can go away. But the message of almost all the stories is that that is an illusion.

The problem is so pervasive that it casts a net of relationships that encompass us all. Women in desperate situations commit crimes (generally nonviolent) and end up in prison at vast cost to society[6] (as well as to themselves, suffering not only the deprivations and indignities of prison but also separation from their children). Children who witness violence against their mothers are at high risk of being violent in their adult relationships. Children living with violence, or escaping violence into poverty, have their ability to suc-ceed in school compromised. And the incidence of violence in intimate relations is so high (though the numbers are contested) that most people will have some connection to women and children whose lives are shaped by this violence. In a society such as Canada's, where the collective responsibility for health care is assumed, everyone shares directly in the costs of the physical (and sometimes the emotional) injuries. Even in the United States, society bears the cost of emergency room treatment as well as the indirect costs of impaired workers, parents, and neighbors.

And then there are the subtler forms of the costs to women (and men) of the knowledge that violence against women is endemic—whether sexual assault by strangers or "dates" or the violence within battering relationships. Frontline workers bear the cost of directly confronting the harm of that violence: As one worker put it, "Vicarious traumatization is a lie. The label pathologizes compassion and political struggle. It divides us from one another. There is nothing vicarious about the traumatization of hearing another woman tell the truth about her life."[7] Those who work in this area in other ways also bear the cost of the daily pain of thinking about the harm, the scope, and seeming intractability of the problem as well as of the apparent indifference of most of society.[8] The rest of us who do not work on this issue bear the knowledge that we collectively tolerate a society with sick and dangerous patterns of relationship between men and women. That is a cost to everyone whether the knowledge is repressed or not.

Finally, the violence of men against women cannot be understood just as a matter of gender relations or sexuality—though the construction of both gender and sex plays a part. Male violence against their intimate partners is shaped by the wider patterns of violent inequality—whether the physical forms of police brutality or their failure to protect[9] or the routinely tolerated violence toward children or the humiliations of poverty and the indignities suffered by welfare recipients or the insult and deprivation caused by prejudice and discrimination.[10] These are all harms that can be experienced as violent and can give rise to violent rage.

Our collective participation in all these forms of violent relations is part of a deeply embedded norm not just of hierarchy but also of violence: violence in North American culture is seen as normal, reasonable, and appropriately used in service of our highest values. Our children (especially boys) are given games and fed stories in which violence is the path to heroism, fame, excitement, adventure, maturity (becoming a man), courage, fraternal bonding, exhilarating strategy, and glorious rescue of those in need. In the so-called real world, wars are fought to spread democracy, to advance civilization, to defend civilization as well as home and hearth, and to protect human rights.

In this context, it is worth noting that violence is organized around gender in many ways, not to the disadvantage of women only. It is overwhelmingly men who are sent into combat and boys who are recruited to be child soldiers. Far more boys than girls are expected to cope with routine physical violence in school yards. When we are surrounded by relations of violence and hierarchy—from the most intimate to international—it shapes and damages us all. A relational approach invites the project of identifying, analyzing, and articulating the nature of that damage.

How then do we best understand and transform the deeply embedded patterns of violence between men and women? The violence I want to focus on in this section is the violence of men against their intimate female partners. This is sometimes called "domestic violence," a term that threatens to domesticate, privatize, and trivialize frightening and horrific male behavior to which millions of women around the world are commonly subjected. The term recommended by the Atlanta-based Centers for Disease Control and Prevention is intimate partner violence (IPV).[11] This term seems useful to me because it remains open to inquiries into female against male violence and into the extent to which the well-known patterns of male violence against female intimate partners may be found also in same-sex couples. Nevertheless, my focus here is on the well-documented, widespread violence that men inflict on women. And I will try to avoid forms of language that hide this brutal reality, thus heeding Ann Jones's warning.

> We are likely to be betrayed by syntax as well, ambushed all at once by the passive voice, just as women *are beaten*, wives *are abused*, children *are abandoned*. By whom?…Women are victimized by *abuse*, they are threatened by *aggressive behavior*, they are battered by *the relationship*,…and murdered by *domestic incidents*.…Rarely in the authoritative literature does a man hit a woman: in the gut, for instance, or the face, with his fist, hard—hard enough to split her lip, loosen her

teeth, break her nose, lace her eyeball with the red web of ruptured veins—hard enough to make the blood run down the page. In real life it happens all the time.[12]

Later I will talk about the ways men also seem to disappear in feminist analyses of this violence, that is, men as individuals embedded in relationships as opposed to instances of a violent class.

B. The Nested Relations That Sustain Violence

The law has a long standing role in providing men with impunity for the violence they inflict on their intimate female partners. In the name of privacy judges (and other agents of the state) have long resisted "interfering in the home."[13] (Although I will not be discussing privacy as one of the competing values at stake, it remains a powerful force in the debate, together with the related idea that "domestic relations," including violence, are a private domain that must be handled differently from matters of public concern.[14]) Despite this long-standing complicity—and because of it—a great deal of feminist scholarship and activism is aimed at trying to enlist the help of the legal system. The projects take the form of passing new laws (for example, the 1994 American Violence against Women Act), educating police, prosecutors, and judges and perhaps most importantly, trying to develop systems of coordination between the many branches of the state that interact with women who have been assaulted by their partners and are at risk of further violence.

A great deal of this advocacy and analysis is relational. It insists that women in battering relationships cannot be adequately protected and assisted unless the nature of that relationship is understood. And understanding a battering relationship involves seeing how it is embedded in other relationships—from familial to local community to economic structures to citizenship and hierarchies of racialization. Indeed I would say that the need for a relational analysis of IPV is now widely assumed among both scholars and activists, even if not named in these terms. But state authorities continue to try to account for IPV in terms of individual psychological problems—whether the woman's failure to leave or the man's problem with anger management.[15]

For courts, as well as popular conceptions of IPV, the recurring question has been, "If it was that bad, why didn't she leave?" For courts, the individual psychology of battering relationships has been crucial to overcoming the hurdle of that question. In the absence of an answer, the abuse itself seemed implausible. As we saw earlier in chapter 4, battered women's syndrome seemed to provide an answer courts could use via expert testimony. But as we have already seen, this story of autonomy-impairing personal relationship is not adequate to understanding the problem. In chapter 4, I focused on understanding the rationality of women's killing in self-defense in terms of the state's failure to protect women from their homicidal partners. Here we look at a wider relational account of the violence.

There are dozens of books and articles that dissect the nature of the state's failure to protect. Research shows that when state actors focus on women's personal relationships of violence they may deny women the protection they need—and thus participate in the societal structuring of relations that perpetuate violence.[16]

It should not be surprising that the move to see women in terms of their intimate relationships impedes both protection and structural analysis. Intimate relations have traditionally fallen into the private domain, and even when a "syndrome" is recognized it invites individual psychological analysis—rather than systemic relational analysis.[17] Poverty, lack of shelters, restrictive welfare regimes, and cultural tolerance of violence are all issues relevant to the common question "why doesn't she just leave?" [18] An enormous amount of scholarship and advocacy show that women who are abused find themselves without the social structures that would make it less than a desperate struggle to survive once they leave the men who were abusing them.

In some ways making it possible for women to leave is a kind of solution—even though it doesn't necessarily change the behavior of violent men. Ann Jones argues that most women in abusive relationships want to leave and that if adequate resources are available to them they will leave.[19] That is, the prevalence of abusive relationships is in part caused by the many layers of difficulty of getting out of them: the autonomy-impairing fear and dependency created by the relationship itself; the difficulty of supporting one's kids once one has left; and the increased danger of getting killed, a danger the police are not good at preventing.

Almost all of this analysis and advocacy is aimed at improving the situation of women who are already in violent relationships. It does not address the question of why so many men are violent and abusive to their intimate partners, women they often claim to love. Consider, for example, this description of one of the "success stories" of institutional intervention:

> In almost twenty years of the Domestic Abuse Intervention Project, approximately one in twenty men living in the Duluth area (population 150,000) has been ordered by civil or criminal court to attend the twenty-six week non-violence programs designed and conducted by profeminist women and men. The program has provided safety for thousands of women and children, *although the number of men using violence has not decreased.* Men who batter often turn on the charm to snare another victim and are arrested again and again for assaulting a succession of women; yet 80% of women who have used DAIP report five years later that they are living free of violence, most no longer living with the man who assaulted them. Duluth also maintains, year after year, a low rate of domestic homicide. The Duluth coordinated community response has become a model for other communities.[20]

Jones also argues that the availability of shelters decreases the number of women who end up killing their violent partners,[21] from which she concludes that women want to escape, not kill.

Of course, as we will see more fully, the widespread male violence against intimate female partners is sustained not just by women's relationships with the state—law enforcement officers, the courts, welfare agencies. Women are often embedded in relationships with family and community who encourage them to tolerate, forgive, or change their behavior in order to prevent the violence.[22] Family and community may not see the violence as a serious problem, or they may think it is a private problem to be solved by the couple—or the woman. Thus a woman's personal relations as well as relations with the state may be shaped by understandings of this violence as legitimate, exaggerated, or her fault.

Even if family and community take the violence seriously, they may think that it is not worth the risk of calling in the state. There may be good reasons for such fear and distrust of state authority, but it may also lead family and community members to see a woman's call for police help as a betrayal.[23]

These particular problems of women living in subcommunities with distrust of the state and/or high tolerance of male violence toward their female partners are real and call for particular kinds of responses to protect those women. But acknowledging this should not obscure the wider issue that violence against women is tolerated throughout North American society. Otherwise it could not continue at its current (and long-standing) rates. As Jones says, the common question is "why doesn't she just leave?"[24] In her view, the appropriate question is "what can we do to stop the violence?"

C. Restructuring Relations through Rights and Why Relational Rights Can "Work"

Jones has an entire chapter of detailed ideas about what could be done. I will return at the end of this section to an analysis of her list. But here I want to focus on her repeated claim that the heart of the problem—and the solution—is a matter of rights:

> The battered women's movement arose among women from immediate need, not abstract theory.... So we have a situation in which social action *precedes* the premise from which it should follow: namely, that all women have an absolute right to be free from bodily harm.... Grant the principle and all the rest falls into place. For women in the United States, that principle has not yet been recognized.[25]

One of reasons I want to focus on this central theme in her book is that her use of rights language helps me to clarify what I do and do not mean by a relational approach to rights. It also indirectly raises the question of the usefulness of rights as a central strategy for change.

The following lengthy quote captures Jones's use of rights:

> It is now long past time to admit that the right to be free from bodily harm, the right that belongs to all men under the [American] Constitution belongs to *all*

women as well. A fundamental *human* right. Not contingent upon the status, character, or behaviour of the individual. That means that *no* woman anywhere should be subjected to bodily harm at any time for any reason. Today, given our immense burden of sexism and racism and class bias, our tendency to blame victims and to whitewash violence in the language of love, the *only* way to combat violence against women is to acknowledge this fundamental right of every woman—every "masochist," every "narcissist," every neglected and abusive and "unfit" mother, every prostitute and junkie and drunk, every mother of an "illegitimate" child, every "bimbo," every "slut," every "bitch" and "fox" and "whore" and "cunt" and "piece of trash." Women are just women, after all: no better than we should be, and often a good deal worse. But rights do not have to be earned. Human rights, by definition, are ours by virtue of our humanity.[26]

Jones is not a lawyer or an academic, and there is something almost touchingly naive about her faith in rights. But there is nothing naive about her depiction of violence against women or her intention in invoking rights.

The first point to notice, for my purposes, is that one might (at first glance) read the lengthy quote above as an explicit rejection of a relational approach to rights. Her point is that a woman's right to be free from bodily harm must not in any way be contingent on her relationships, on where she is situated in relation to others and their prejudices and preconceptions. The point of rights language for Jones is that a right is simply and absolutely a right. If women really had rights—if these rights were recognized—it wouldn't matter if her violent spouse said he loved her or if the local cop knew him or if she was a prostitute or an aboriginal woman or a welfare mother. No one would tolerate her partner beating her—not her friends, family, neighbors, police, prosecutors, judges, welfare workers.

What Jones has in mind when she invokes rights is a transformation of consciousness as well as institutional practices. She sees rights as central because she thinks that the absence of women's rights—which includes their recognition—is a way of characterizing the tolerance, indifference, blindness, woman blaming, and excuses for men that are currently the common responses to women being assaulted by their male partners. If women's rights were really recognized, these responses would, by definition, go away. They are incompatible with real, absolute rights for all women regardless of their situation or relational context. Rights for *some* women are not really rights in Jones's terms. Amelioration of harm is not recognition of rights. "It is no longer enough to offer some victimized women safety and sympathy, any more than it would have been enough to offer Rosa Parks that seat at the front of the bus without granting the principle of equality behind it."[27]

Of course, one might think that calling up the image of Rosa Parks starting the civil rights movement would be a reminder of the complexity and imperfection of rights. There are few people in North America today who would deny that "blacks" and "whites" should be entitled to equal rights. That recognition is a tremendously important transformation in both consciousness and institutional practice. But it is a far cry from equality. Both prejudice (consciousness) and discrimination (systemic practice) continue to coexist with widespread acceptance of "rights." (Indeed the legal recognition of rights is sometimes seen as proof that continued disadvantage must be the fault of those who continue to suffer disadvantage.)

One might say that the advocacy on behalf of "battered women" has shifted popular understandings in the direction Jones has in mind. Far fewer people would simply assert that men have a "right" to beat their female partners.[28] But the shift is far from complete. The literature is replete with examples of men—not only batterers but also police and state officials—who continue to trivialize such violence and treat it as properly a "private matter." I think it is fair to say in 2010, as Jones did in 2000, that a clear and universal right for women to be protected from bodily harm has not yet taken hold in either popular consciousness or institutional practice.[29]

Is Jones's insistence on the noncontingency of the right a tacit challenge to my relational approach? Or, put differently, does my insistence on a relational approach undermine her project of universal, unqualified recognition? In answering these questions it is important to note that Jones (rightly) sees no conflict between her invocation of individual rights and (what I see as) her thoroughly relational analysis of cause and potential solution.

The first answer is that a relational approach to rights means that people should see rights as structuring relations—not that the rights one has are contingent on one's relationships. This is crucial not just for the particular problems of women whose partners assault them but also more generally to combating the continuing ways in which (all over the world) women's relational status—as wives, mothers, welfare recipients—define and limit the rights they can enjoy and the resources they can access.

At this first level, the answer is simple. The relational project is to ask how defining (and protecting) rights in one way rather than another will structure relationships and how those relationships will, in turn, promote or undermine the value at stake. So, for example, if a woman's right to be free from bodily harm is contingent—in practice—on her not being a prostitute, then she is in a relation of vulnerability and relative powerlessness with respect to the men who hire her and to her pimp and, indeed, to strangers and serial killers. Those relations would be shifted if everyone involved knew that the police would respond promptly to a prostitute's call for help and arrest the man who had injured her and that prosecutors would follow through with charges. The relations of vulnerability would shift similarly if everyone knew that a report of a missing prostitute would generate the same prompt response as a missing lawyer.

In this context, the formal rights do not need to change—the laws against assault would be adequate if enforced in ways that protected and empowered sex trade workers. The problem does not lie with rights definitions, but with the way enforcement is practiced. Jones's point in invoking rights is to capture the sense that if everyone—neighbors, police, prosecutors, judges, johns, and pimps—recognized the right of *all* women to be free of bodily injury, people would behave differently. The practices of enforcement would shift, as would the sense that some women can be harmed with impunity.

My approach would ask whether there is a problem with the definition or interpretation of the law that is generating a failure to protect these women. In Canada, where prostitution is not illegal, the question would be whether the criminalization of soliciting, living off the avails, and brothels contributes to the vulnerability of sex trade workers. If there is no legal right to work as a prostitute, the criminalization of the sex trade is itself likely to increase a prostitute's vulnerability to violence. In that case, the criminal law (and its enforcement, for example, whether prostitutes or their clients are to be the primary target[30]) structures power between prostitutes, pimps, and johns. These power relations in turn shape prostitutes' vulnerability to violence and their ability to seek redress for the violation of their formal rights to bodily security (as found in laws against assault). Thus a relational analysis would probably generate an argument in favor of decriminalization of prostitution and perhaps of related activities, such as solicitation, that also are prohibited in the *Canadian Criminal Code*. (A full relational analysis would require a broader scope than this sketch of an example.)

Of course, it is not just the legal system that gives effect to rights. As already noted, shelters and adequate welfare support are needed to shift relations of power between men and women so that a woman has a (relatively) easy exit if her partner is violent. His success in trapping her in the battered women's syndrome requires a whole set of external relations, some of which can be shifted by state policy (see chapter 4). These policies, in turn, can be guided in the first instance by what is necessary to make real her right to be free from bodily harm. Here we confront a wider problem of the extent of society's collective willingness to make it possible for everyone to actually enjoy *any* rights. The right to be free from violence might seem like a negative right,[31] but it takes a lot of restructuring of relations to make it real for many women.

Jones's own invocation of absolute rights is intended to restructure relationships. She thinks that if people believe women have these rights that relations of indifference or contempt will be replaced by relations of respect and active protection; relations of dependence and powerlessness, by mutuality and equality. When faced with repeated violence, women will end the relationship—for they will have the power and resources to leave. But this picture of what a commitment to rights entails assumes that the commitment carries with it a willingness to do the restructuring, provide the services, mobilize the resources to make the right a reality for everyone. That form of commitment is generally lacking. And as U.S. history has amply shown, the rhetoric of absolute rights does not supply that commitment.[32]

Of course, a relational approach alone will not provide it either. But I think people are more likely to recognize the need for that commitment with a focus on how rights structure relationships and the recognition that it is the actual form and practice of those relationships that either ensure security or render it tenuous or unevenly distributed.

When looking at Jones's claim that women should finally have the absolute right to bodily security that men have, it is important to remember that in North America it is not the case that men actually have an absolute right to be free from bodily harm. *Some* men can effectively claim such a right. Very often gay men cannot. Young black men in American cities cannot. Male children often cannot. Men who are homeless or in prison or addicted to drugs or alcohol often cannot. Men in mental institutions and nursing homes often cannot. Under our current arrangements the right to be free from bodily harm is very unevenly distributed. Gender is a powerful factor in that uneven distribution, but it is not the only one. White, middle-class, professional women in Toronto are almost certainly at less risk of bodily harm than are black sixteen-year-old males in parts of Harlem.[33]

In North America we are now past the point of the law formally legitimating such unequal distribution of security. Laws do not (any longer) define the crime of assault differently if the victim is a woman, a wife, a young black man, an aboriginal woman. (Assault of children *is* an exception to the criminal law in both Canada and the United States, through provisions that allow for corporal punishment.) The *legal rights* to women's bodily security are largely in place. What is not in place is either the moral or institutional commitment that Jones means when she declares that women have an absolute right to be free from bodily harm. Other advocates who invoke rights language on behalf of subordinated, disadvantaged, and injured groups often mean something similar.

So I return again to a slightly different version of the question whether a relational approach to rights will undermine or advance the achievement of this deeper and more practical commitment to rights. This, in turn, is a version of the question "can a relational approach to rights work?" In this context, that means *will the rhetorical efficacy of rights language be undermined*? If the rhetorical power of rights lies in part in its language of absolutes, will the insistence on thinking about rights structuring relations dilute the effect of the simpler, uncomplicated claim of absoluteness? I don't think so. Or it won't any more than it should.

There are two parts to my response. First, a consciousness of the complexity, inevitable tensions, and implications both for resources and for other rights, values, and interests is a good thing when one goes about proclaiming and trying to enforce rights. We will see more about such costs and complexity when I turn to Merry, Kennedy, and Halley.

Second, in slight tension with the first, I see no reason why shorthand forms of rights claims—with their emphasis on universality and absoluteness—cannot coexist with an underlying relational analysis. Most theories of rights and understandings of the practical meaning of rights implementation by practitioners and advocates coexist with shorthand forms. Lawyers who spend their time working through the nuances and compromises of legal defenses can still say with conviction, "My client's rights have been vindicated (or violated)" by a particular judicial outcome. Activists who spend time assessing competing policies for promoting values, such as security, privacy, or autonomy, and formulating different strategies for getting a chosen policy implemented can (and do) still say things like "the right of privacy is inconsistent" with a given welfare regulation or that "women's right to bodily integrity requires mandatory arrest of male partners who assault them."

Rights language has always had this two-sided quality. Those who work closely with issues of rights, whether as theorists, members of the legal profession, or activists, know that there are many layers of complexity to the meaning and implementation of rights. Yet they all use shorthand claims that have an absolute quality that belies their own deeper understanding. Indeed this is true of Jones herself. Her repeated invocation of absolute rights exists side by side with a detailed (relational) analysis of the many levels of transformation that will have to be accomplished before those rights could become a reality. I take it that, in her case, coexistence is intended to harness the rhetorical power of rights to accomplish difficult changes to deeply embedded practices and beliefs. Such use of rights language seems reasonable to me.

There can, however, be a danger of coming to believe in the simplicity of the absoluteness, when a stark denial of rights is uppermost in the minds of advocates. I think this danger is sometimes to be seen in Jones's apparent lack of interest in what the costs might be of her approach. Indeed, sometimes that is the point of invoking rights: to make mentioning costs—including competing values—seem outrageous and inhumane. I think sometimes the simplicity and absoluteness of rights claims is a calculated (and not unreasonable) strategy to mobilize support to redress violence and atrocity. Sometimes the consciousness of the complexities recedes in the press to accomplish change. To the extent that a relational approach exerts a pull in the direction of recognizing complexity, I think this is a good thing. I do not think it need undermine the appropriate availability of a shorthand language of rights that does not attempt to capture the inevitable complexity.

In sum, then, I do not think that the focus on how rights structure relationships gives rights a more contingent or conditional meaning than do conventional liberal understandings.[34] I do think that a relational approach highlights rather than obscures the contested nature of underlying values as well as conflicts over which relations and what forms of rights will best foster them. (We will return to these contestations later.) The question is really one of emphasis and overtness. All sophisticated versions of rights—and all actual practices of implementing them—involve assessment of competing values and conflicting judgments. To the extent that a relational analysis draws attention to this contestation and complexity, it may shift the kind of rhetorical use that can be made of rights claims. But that shift is likely to be subtle, and I do not see it as a serious threat to the rhetorical efficacy of shorthand invocations of rights.

D. Merry: Rights, the (Painful) Choice of Subjectivity, and the (Contested and Nested) Structures of Gender Identity

I turn now to Sally Merry's "Rights Talk and the Experience of Law" (2003), a study of the role of rights in changing the patterns of men's violence against women who are their intimate partners.[35] Once again, this study shows how law and rights can and do restructure relations. Merry helps us see the subtle and deep forms of transformation that can be involved in invoking legal rights to protect women from violence. She not only provides an example how women's use of law can reconstruct gender relations she also shows how this reconstruction entails a shift in identity, a choice of "subjectivities." Thus we see the complex interplay between rights, gender relations, and identity. Merry also highlights the way intimate partner violence is embedded in a wide set of relationships.

As Merry sees it, the rights consciousness that Jones presents as the key to transformation should be understood as a choice, often a difficult one, for women facing violence from their partners. In Merry's study of Hilo, a community in Hawaii, she provides examples of how law participates in constructing the relationships of gender and how the encounter with "law" involves multiple relationships—with police, judges, shelter workers, and staff of Alternatives to Violence programs (required for offenders).

She also shows how women's experience of law and rights is framed by their other relationships—with family, community, and religious institutions. As Merry sees it, each of these sets of relationships and experiences constitutes a different subjectivity, and the two are in tension with one another. Women in violent relationships who call upon the law are thus faced with a "choice of subjectivities." Women can choose to embrace a sense of themselves as rights holders. To do so offers (sometimes precarious) protection, but it also often involves a transformation of their self-understanding and ruptures other important relationships. The following quote gives a sense of the framework of her argument:

> The law has constituted women as legal subjects no longer mediated by their embeddedness in family relationships, but now standing alone in relation to the state. At the same time, it has reduced the patriarchal privileges of males within the domain of the family. [The family becomes open to state surveillance.]
>
> Thus the new terrain is ambiguous, both offering a new legal self protected from violence by men, but providing in practice a far more limited and nuanced legal self whose protection is never fully guaranteed nor experienced. It is through experience, through encounters with the multiple responses of the police, prosecutors, courts, and probation officers, that a new legal subjectivity about gender violence is made, along with a new sense of marriage, family, and community, and the place of law. The law claims for itself the definition of gendered relationships within the family as well as outside the family, but ambivalently and uncertainly, creating areas of leniency and inaction that characterize this sphere of the law.[36]

Merry takes as her project figuring out what brings women to see themselves as the subjects of rights, to adopt this new subjectivity. Merry's tacit, and sometimes explicit, standpoint is that in adopting the subjectivity of rights bearer, women enhance their power, their autonomy, and their safety. She shows how important it is that women have positive experiences with the legal system if they are to adopt this new subjectivity. In practice they often have mixed experiences (often more negative with police, more positive with judges and shelter staff). Merry wants her readers to see that there can be high costs as well as benefits to this new sense of self, costs that make sense of women's ambivalence and vacillation in behavior:

> Taking on a rights-defined self in relation to a partner requires a substantial change both for the woman and the man she is accusing. Instead of seeing herself as defined by family, kin, and work relationships, she takes on a more autonomous self protected by the state. At the same time, her actions allow the law to define her husband/partner as a criminal under the surveillance and control of the state. A battered woman may be pressured by kin to feel she is a bad wife, while her partner may claim she is taking away his masculinity. The only way she can rescue him from this loss is to deflect the very legal sanctions she has called down upon him. It is hardly surprising that abused women will ask for help from the law, back away, and then ask again.... These women are tracking back and forth across a significant line of identity transformation.[37]

Like Jones, though somewhat less directly, in this article Merry presents the choice of rights subjectivity as the right choice. It is the choice that will enhance a woman's autonomy, power, and security. Merry is sympathetic to the difficulty of the choice. But her project is to understand how to facilitate the choice for rights. And the answer is to increase women's positive experience with the state.

Merry offers a rich and nuanced analysis of the way rights structure relationships, but I think the language in the quotes above requires some qualification, rather, clarification of how I would see the issue. Merry may aptly capture the experience of women who call on the law as now "standing alone in relation to the state."[38] This phrase may also capture the understanding of legal actors (and advocates) about how legal rights can free women from confining relationships. But the idea of standing alone in relation to the state is an illusion. As Merry clearly sees, the act of claiming rights reconstructs the relation between men and women; it does not remove women from their relationships.

Indeed, Merry does an excellent job of showing how gender mediates people's experience with the law and how the encounters with the law can constitute changes in the meaning of gender. For example,

> Gendered subjectivity is redefined by doing legal activities: through acting as a legally entitled subject in the context of these injuries. As women victimized by violence call the police, walk into courtrooms, fill out forms requesting restraining orders, tell their stories of violence and victimization in forms and responses to official inquiries, they enact a different self. Such performances reshape the way these women think about themselves and the relationship between their intimate social world and the law. Turning to the courts for help in incidents of violence by part-

ners represents a disembedding of the individual in the structure of kin, neighbors, friends, and churches in favor of a new relationship with the state.[39]

[...]

Because gender is produced by such performances, the way that women and men chart courses through the tensions of violence and its legal regulation shapes their gendered selves. As they do law, they also do gender.[40]

What Merry seems to attend to less is that calling on the law will often not simply "dis-embed" women from their wider relations but also restructure those relations. In the tacking back and forth that Merry discusses, women will not just be vacillating between alternative subjectivities but also shifting the relations in which they are embedded.[41]

Looking at the wider relations of kin and communities helps us see not only the reach of the law in structuring relations but also the ways in which nonstate relations are crucial to the experience of and accessibility of rights. These nonstate relations are not simply in opposition to (the image of) the autonomy of legal rights. In addition to being shaped by the use of those rights, these relations also shape the lived experience of those rights.

Relations outside the state can be shifted by legal rights, but rights are not the only—or best—way of doing so. Because Merry's focus here is on rights, she doesn't try to address the possibilities of changing the norms in these other networks of relationship without the use of rights language. Rights have an oppositional quality to them. The very rhetorical efficacy I discussed above lies in the language of absolutes that is intended to brook no opposition, reject compromise, and that can easily dismiss nuance and complexity. (A relational approach will shift this but not dispel it entirely.) Perhaps the sense of the zero-sum game of gender relations—women gain power, men lose it, and in the process both increase their (often costly) engagement with the state (whether as rights claimant or accused criminal)—would be less in another framework for transforming gender relations.

The acceptability of male violence in intimate relations could, instead, be shifted around shared community values of health, mutual care, and responsibility; the development of norms of mutual respect that are not always embedded in—and thus in tension with—hierarchy. Such projects of transformation would not pose the stark choice between bonds with community and entitlement to safety. I am not, of course, suggesting that such a shift would be easy or the strategies obvious. My point is that to recognize the role of rights in structuring relations—both with and outside the state—is not to insist that rights are always the best way of doing so.

Merry herself notes that even as women take legal steps to protect themselves and to come to see themselves as "entitled" to safety and security (thus shifting their subjectivities), they do not necessarily embrace the language of rights: "The [Alternatives to Violence] program talks about rights, but the women talk about finding themselves, about following their intuition, about having courage, and about surviving."[42]

E. The Question of Men

Merry's study also includes the results of interviews with men about their experience of this doing of law and gender through the Alternatives to Violence (ATV) program. They talk about a sense of betrayal when their partners call the police, about not being listened to by judges, about being treated unfairly. Some talk about improvement in their relationships and communication with their partners as a result of participation in the mandatory eight-month program. Merry interprets women taking on the rights subjectivities as an attack on the men's masculinity as they had understood it. When a woman takes on this subjectivity, she "inevitably excludes him from her life unless he is willing to adopt the new identity the law offers him."[43] Merry is particularly insightful about the way in which these shifting gender identities intersect with relations of class:

> This new subjectivity represents the masculinity of a different social class, one to which few of these men [assigned to the ATV programs] have the education, income, or job skills to aspire. In effect, through the ATV program, the men are offered a masculinity developed by men of wealth and education in which authority over women depends on resources and allows some negotiation of power, an authority constructed by dominant whites, in place of that grounded in strength, physical competence, sexual prowess, and control over women favored by the working class men in Hilo [the town in Hawaii].[44]

She concludes that "authority is displaced from control over women to control over property. It is not surprising that poor men often reject this identity, as the resistant conversation in the treatment groups reveal."[45]

While Merry thus shows some sympathy for the resistance of the men in her study, she shows little ambivalence about the desirability of the rights-based subjectivities for women and the corresponding changes in the meaning of gender—which, of course, involve both men and women.

All the feminist scholars who work in this area see gender in these relational terms, and virtually all of them want to invoke the power of the law to change those relations. They recognize the way the law has worked to construct those relations in the past in ways that have harmed women—including putting them at risk of bodily injury—and now they want to change the law and its practices to transform those relations. As is no doubt clear by now, I am generally sympathetic to this project.

I see this sort of engagement with the state as largely unavoidable if equality, autonomy, security, and other core values are finally to be made available to all. In ways I have discussed earlier, the law and the state are so entangled in existing relations of inequality, in the unequal distribution of access to core values such as security, that deep transformation will have to exceed, but cannot bypass, the state. Nevertheless, I want to turn now to set of issues around where men fit in the feminist project of ending intimate partner violence and the way that question points to wider concerns about the deliberate mobilization of the state to reconstruct gender relations. This reconstruction involves the meaning not only of masculinity but also of sexuality.

First, I want to note a common contrast between the treatment of men and women in much of the feminist scholarship I (otherwise) admire: it offers a sophisticated relational analysis of the factors affecting women's vulnerability to violence; men, by contrast, appear as a largely undifferentiated class of perpetrators or as those in power in the legal system who deny women the protection to which they are entitled. (Merry is an exception here.) Their motivations—other than to maintain power and control—or the sources of those motivations are not the subject of much inquiry.

One reason for this is a deliberate decentering of men. The traditional responses to violence against women are often said to be characterized by excuses for men and a willingness to put their interests first. Feminists are often determined to shift the attention to the horrible realities of battered women and to figure out what can be done to protect them. In this approach, men—as batterers or agents of the state—are the problem to be solved. The stance seems to be: "it's" time to pay attention to women for a change.

In my view, the anxiety about keeping women at the center of concern, about avoiding the constant pull in the direction of a focus on men and distortions in their favor, is appropriate. Failing to engage in a full relational analysis of men's role in the violence is not. A relational understanding of gender needs to take seriously actual relationships *between* men and women in which men are as much embedded in networks of relationship as women.[46] The absence of a consistently relational stance toward men's roles can lead to an oddly individualistic account of male behavior, embedded in a detailed and comprehensive analysis of all the relational contexts that shape women's experience of battering and the difficulty of escaping it. This often takes the form of focusing on individual men's *choice* to engage in violence.

The mix of relational analysis and invocation of male, individual choice is clear in Jones. Her point, like that of other feminist writers, is that the targeting of intimate partners is structured by relations of inequality, by patriarchal conceptions of masculinity.[47] These personal relations of male violence are comprehensible only when looked at in light of the broader picture of gender relations (sometimes combined with other like hierarchical relations, such as race and class). Jones's book includes an interesting and disturbing chapter about contemporary cultural validation of anger and aggression and the presentation of sex and violence as a natural mix. As she presents it, this cultural context helps explain male violence. But in the end (literally the last pages of her book), it is men's *choice* to engage in the violence: "men *choose* to use violence to get their way. They can just as well *choose* not to, as many men do who take a stand with women against violence and emotional abuse."[48]

Is this plausible as an adequate account of why some men batter their partners? Part of the volitional story is often that batterers seek total control over "their women." They use violence strategically to get it. But what makes them want total control? What makes them seem desperate to have it? Should we just dismiss the "language of love," the cries of "I can't live without you," as mere strategic posturing?[49]

Joseph A. Kuypers offers an interesting example of an effort at what I would call a relational analysis of male violence in *Man's Will to Hurt* (1992).[50] He situates men's violence against their intimate partners as part of a much wider pattern of male violence, which includes the violence of many sports, hunting for fun, entertainment that glorifies male violence, the violence of ruthless profit seeking, and violent crime (noting that females are one-tenth as likely as men to commit violent crimes[51]). He talks about how boys are socialized into both inflicting pain and taking it stoically and about the physical danger as well as social ostracism involved in refusing to comply with dominant norms of masculinity. This danger is just one of the ways male violence structures relations among men as well as between men and women. He sees male violence as the lynchpin of patriarchy:

> To end male violence is to seriously rearrange the power relations between men and women. If the male is given or claims a position of superiority, then he will use whatever means available to him to keep his position. Since no other unique means are left to him except his greater ability to control with force, this is what he uses. And he justified his acts as being in the service of a "natural order"—his position of power, authority, duty and domination. This view is simple: a man's ability to control other people and keep them in subservient positions is sufficient to explain violence. Violence serves his ends and keeps the patriarchal order in place. But this view is also profound, because it goes to the heart of relations between the sexes and focuses thoughts of change on fundamental structures of society.[52]

For Kuypers, this wider context is part of an inquiry into the benefits of compliance with violent masculinity, the pressures to comply, and the many forms of instruction into and enactment of violence. This wider context offers the best justification I have seen for not focusing on the *personal relational* dynamics of battering relationships. He notes that many such accounts end up being stories of "wifely complicity" (including such contradictory theories as "women provoke men's violence because they act helpless" and "strong, successful women provoke men's violence by 'showing them up'").[53]

More importantly, blaming the victim in IPV is part of a wider scenario in which violence is presented as a necessary move to rectify a wrong. "Construct your evil in a way the public will support...and you will be given free reign and public support to use pain, to send a message, to right a wrong, to even a score, to teach a lesson. The benefits are obvious and your violence is obviously necessary."[54] He links the story of provocation in IPV with one of the key elements of the male code of violence: someone else has to start it. This code is applied in international relations as well as violence against women and children.

Even Kuypers, whose interest is in the collective practices that generate and sustain male violence, uses the language of choice. He wants to emphasize (as Jones does) that men get something out of their violence and that they do so in large part because they generally get away with it. He not only wants to emphasize men's choice to threaten and use violence but also to challenge the routine violence they observe. "Men who plan war games, who hunt for fun or enact killing and call it entertainment are not confronted by less violent men. They go their way assured of general male approval."[55] If transformation is possible, there has to be choice—and responsibility for choices made. But I find his language of choice less troubling than Jones's because it is situated in an analysis of all the factors that drive the choice for violence. It is an insistence on individual responsibility even in the face of structures of relations that demand violence or complicity in it.

Of course, this is another example of the complexities of relational autonomy. Kuyper's analysis might be seen as revealing a way in which men's real autonomy also is undermined by the existing structures of gender relations.

Men's experience of what are viable choices, as well as the grounds for making them, are shaped by the structure of relations of which they are a part. But, of course, choices that are shaped by convention, advantage, and even threat are, nonetheless, choices. The question of the moral (as opposed to legal) responsibility that ought to be assigned to men who are complicit in the norms of violence is a complicated one.

Kuyper's project, like those of others trying to understand contemporary masculinity and the structures that generate it, is a necessary part of a relational analysis of violence against women. One might say that it is a reasonable division of labor for female feminists to focus on women and leave analyzing the impact on men to male scholars and activists. This is so as long as there is some self-consciousness about the asymmetries in relational analysis that sometimes characterizes female feminist scholarship. Whether through a division of labor or a more thorough relational analysis of men by female feminists, it is important to understand how gender intersects with other hierarchies and state structures for both men and women. It is this symmetry that can best promote the restructuring of relations between men and women and the reconstruction of the meaning of gender.

II. RESTRUCTURING SEXUALITY: CONFRONTING UNEASE ABOUT A RELATIONAL APPROACH

A. Kennedy: The "Tolerated Residuum," Contested Values, Inherent Uncertainties

Duncan Kennedy offers an extremely interesting step in that direction: an intriguing account of the costs and benefits for men and women of what he calls the "tolerated residuum" of sexual abuse of women by men.[56] In North America, despite laws against rape, intimate partner violence, and sexual harassment, society collectively tolerates a startlingly high level of ongoing abuse. This is the "tolerated residuum." Kennedy asks what men who do not engage in violence get out of it, what it might cost them to reduce that "acceptable residuum," and what they might get out of such a reduction. His version of cost-benefit analysis involves what I would call a relational analysis of consequences of a shift in state (and other) practices to reduce the level of abuse.

Kennedy's analysis also points to two important challenges to the relational approach: (1) the deep contestation over the values that relations are to foster and (2) the inevitable uncertainties about how law will affect relations.

It is important to be clear that the "tolerated residuum" is not a version of what society acknowledges as acceptable. Part of how abuse (and, I would say, violence) against women currently functions is as an ongoing disjuncture between formal law and practice: the legal system is set up "to condemn sexual abuse of women by men in the abstract, but at the same time operating the system so that many, many instances of clearly wrongful abuse are tolerated."[57] Indeed, this disjuncture operates not just within the legal system but also more broadly to constitute a kind of "cultural crisis":

> It seems to me that women would benefit enormously if they were free of the actual abuse, free to do the things they now can't risk doing, and free of the generalized fear that is a rational response to the pervasiveness of male violence. But the conventional view denies or ignores this whole range of costs. The various activist movements against battery, child abuse, rape, and sexual harassment, with their allies in social work, psychotherapy and the liberal media, have gradually forced them into public awareness, without managing to have a major impact on them in practice. The result is a situation of disequilibrium, a kind of cultural crises for the conventional view.
>
> The crisis arises because acknowledging the actual prevalence of abuse threatens to undermine the other elements of the gestalt: that abuse is a matter between a small class of abnormal perpetrators and a small class of victims; that apparent instances are often explained by the woman's behavior; and that the whole practice is of only marginal importance to the patterns of social life.[58]

To understand this cultural crisis, and the possibility of shifting it toward transformation, Kennedy argues that we need to understand that there are powerful conflicts of interest between men and women over how it should be resolved. We also need to see the many and varied ways in which the ongoing tolerance affects men and women and to envision the possible consequences of different forms of transformation. In making this argument, Kennedy offers insights into social relations and how they are shaped by the "tolerated residuum," which is itself constituted in part by law.

He thus offers us a good example of how law (interacting with other practices and beliefs) structures social relations. It is a particularly good example because he is always alert to the complexities involved. A given law, practice, or norm never simply determines conduct. There is always variance and contestation. Although it is important to see that, broadly speaking, men may enjoy benefits or bear costs from legal practice, there is not one homogenous group of men who will have the same experience.

Kennedy's analysis is also candidly speculative. In this way he reveals one of the inherent difficulties and limitations of a relational approach. It is possible to gather evidence about how, say, women constrain their behavior because of fear of violence or sexual abuse, but that behavior will almost always be "over-determined."[59] There will be so many different factors affecting it (even if one can tell a plausible story about how many of these factors are related to male power), that it will be extremely difficult to show that the constraints are caused by a given practice, such as the ratio of reported rapes to prosecutions. Kennedy is always conscious of these difficulties, which are then heightened when the objective is to project *future* changes in behavior, affect, or identity as a result of changes in policy and practices.

My version of relational analysis requires both forms of inherently difficult claims: (1) about how existing legal practices shape relations and (2) why we have reason to believe that certain kinds of changes will yield different relations, which in turn will better foster the core values at stake.

I have turned to Kennedy here in order to confront these difficulties as well as the depth of disagreement there is likely to be about the core values at issue. Of course, the degree of difficulty will vary. For example, there are some practices of welfare systems that seem obviously to put women at risk of further violence, such as the requirement of naming the father of dependent children and the failure to inform women who have been battered that they may be eligible for an exemption from this requirement.[60] There are strongly contested policies, such as mandatory arrest in the case of intimate partner violence, that some claim will restructure relations between men and women in ways that increase women's autonomy (of course, others claim it would decrease women's autonomy because it removes them from the decision-making process regarding arrest and the filing of charges).[61] And then there are crucial, but intrinsically contested, aspirations to "undo" certain constructions of gender, for example, to transform the complex relation between masculinity, dominance, and violence. Even the most straightforward arguments about the connections between a policy and women's vulnerability to violence involve uncertainty. And the most complex involve a disturbing level of speculation. Later I will consider whether other approaches are actually more certain or offer a path to transformation (or rights protection) that is less demanding.

Kennedy actually offers almost no concrete details about the sort of changes in laws, practices, or policies he thinks would shift the "tolerated residuum." His focus is on trying to figure out what the resistance to such changes would be and the kinds of effects such a change might have. He argues that this exercise in analysis, imagination, and speculation might help men see that while there would be costs, there also could be important benefits. And he acknowledges that even his picture of optimal benefits is contested. This is an important piece in the kind of analysis a relational approach requires.

I want to give a brief indication of how he tries to show that the ongoing tolerated violence and abuse is, in fact, central rather than marginal to "the patterns of social life."[62]
More specifically, and instrumentally, he argues,

> If men and women benefit in various describable ways from abuse, it is important
> to say so, because the vulgar male *interest* in abuse is likely to get translated into
> action through male control of the legislative, judicial, and administrative processes.
> If men have other, often unrecognized, non-moral, material, erotic or aesthetic
> interests in reducing or ending abuse, then it is important to say so. These interests,
> more fully recognized, might influence this same ruling male class.[63]

In order to understand what those interests might be, he proposes a cost-benefit analysis,
that starts from the claim that "men's and women's reactions to the particular line we've
chosen to draw between sanction and tolerance have extensive 'indirect' consequences
for everything from the details of day to day behaviour to the formation of male and
female identities."[64] In charting those consequences, he intends to challenge the conventional view of abuse and the way it interferes with an honest assessment of both the
advantages and difficulties of change:

> To my mind, the main problems with the conventional view are (a) that abuse is far
> too widespread to be understood through the categories of abnormality or
> pathology, (b) that the manoeuvre of blaming the victim allows both men and
> women to deny its reality, (c) that this denial keeps men and women *in situations*
> *that seem not to involve it at all*, and (d) that the result is blindness to the real conflict
> of interests between men and women in this area...the conventional view greatly
> understates both the costs to women of present practice and the potential costs to
> men of changing it. The conventional view is apologetic: it views the status quo
> through rose-colored glasses, and at the same time underplays the structural factors,
> and particularly male interests, that support it.[65]

The costs to women include the familiar feminist arguments about the constraints in
behavior driven by pervasive fear of violence and efforts to avoid assault and insult. The
costs to men of trying to *reduce* the residuum include both actual and anticipated
increase in surveillance and constraint, collectively having to deal with an increased
number of complaints, and a cruder definition of abuse to make it more "workable."[66]
The current arrangement "spares both abusive and non-abusive men the burden of
excess or inaccurate enforcement that any significant increase in social control would
almost certainly generate. And it spares them the burden of precautions against the
risk of excess enforcement."[67] A shift in who bears the burden would shift social
relations: "The argument that increased enforcement would make men hesitate to
take altogether innocent initiatives toward women is usually put forward without

considering that the tolerated residuum makes women hesitate to take altogether innocent initiatives toward men."[68]

The bottom line here is that there is a conflict of interest between men and women. This basic conflict is compounded by a belief that men and women see the issues of abuse differently. This means that for women to get a greater share of the power to interpret and enforce the law is likely to make men very nervous. Kennedy notes another interesting cost to trying to give women more protection: "Such an effort would force us men into conflict with one another. It would force us to define our positions and use our resources and energy in fights about definition and enforcement. We men can avoid these fights so long as the whole level of enforcement is low enough so that most of the time women know from the beginning that they have no effective recourse."[69]

Under the heading "Bargaining in the Shadow of Sexual Abuse Law," Kennedy makes a variety of arguments about how men's overall bargaining power in relation to women is increased by the background residuum.[70] Women's knowledge that their existing situation (whether in an intimate relationship or in the workplace) could be a lot worse, that is, that they could end up with a batterer or at a workplace pervaded by sexual harassment, makes them less willing to leave and more willing to put up with disadvantages of various kinds, making the threat to leave less credible. These are ways the background residuum works to enhance the power of nonabusive men.

What most engages Kennedy's interest and insight are subtler costs and benefits of the role of the residuum in the construction of gender and desire:

[T]he reality of male abuse of women burdens or discourages the activities of fantasy, play, invention and experiment through which we have whatever hope we may have of evolving or transcending our current modes of male and female sexuality. For this reason, I argue that men have at least a potential erotic interest in fighting against it.[71]

Thus while Kennedy want us to recognize the ways nonabusive men get something out of the ongoing violence, he also wants us to see the costs of that violence and the potential benefits of change to those same men. The background threat of violence operates in a kind of repressive way that undermines the sort of possibilities he is interested in and thinks many men might be interested in—if they turned their minds to it. For example, "I value the occasions when women surprise, disconcert and sometimes terrify men by suggesting possibilities of identity that have nothing to do with what men think women 'ought to' be like, but come at us (men) out of their irreducible differences. The system of abuse makes these occasions less likely than they might be in its absence, and indeed seems targeted to prevent them from happening at all."[72] Keeping women in their place, sustaining a whole regime of liberal patriarchy,[73] enforces men's superior power but at the cost of a kind of rigidity of roles and repression of women's active, playful, and imaginative sexuality. Kennedy wants men to think about whether that isn't a very high cost.

Kennedy addresses this question through a long, interesting discussion of "sexy dressing," its relation to abuse and its role in the construction of male and female sexuality. Thus he draws a picture of connections between a legal (and social) regime through a large "tolerated residuum"[74] of violence, everyday practices like dress codes (and the flaunting of them in sexy dressing), and people's experience of their sexual identity and desire. This ultimately brings him to the thorny issue of the eroticization of power. Here we confront a potential clash in objectives. His readers can agree with his imaginative analysis about the links between law, violence, and the construction of sexuality. To use my language, we can see how his analysis is helpful in revealing the complex ways the most subtle (as well as the crudest) relations between men and women are structured by practices that *could* be changed if there were a collective commitment to reduce the residuum of violence.

But what sorts of relations should a new regime try to structure? It is relatively easy to say that the value to be promoted is increased physical security for women. But having shown that the existing residuum is doing a lot more than failing to provide protection, the question inevitably arises about what sorts of gender identity and desire would characterize an optimal structure of relations. While Kennedy, as I noted above, does not try to spell out exactly what concrete changes in legal practices are likely to lead to the sorts of changes he has in mind, he does directly confront his readers with the reality that they are likely to disagree with one another (and him) about these subtler dimensions of relations between men and women.

To use a relational analysis for purposes of social transformation—which reducing violence against women would constitute—one needs to think not only about the connections between given practices (of say law enforcement) and relations (say of power and autonomy) between men and women but also about the kinds of changes one wants. If we acknowledge that the existing regime of gender identity and desire is shaped by the way the current residuum operates, then it is a bit disingenuous to suggest that the objective of change is simply an unproblematic commitment to safety and security.

So, for example, Kennedy looks at different ways of responding to the current structures, including the eroticization of dominance. He concludes his discussion of norms and practices of "sexy dressing" by saying that what is wrong with them politically is that these norms disempower women within the "male sphere" and that what is wrong with them erotically (from the perspective of a straight, white, middle-class man) is that they require "each party to give up a possible pleasure—that which might be found in the activity the regime allocates to the opposite sex. To say this is to make a choice between two plausible routes beyond asymmetry."[75]

One of these routes is to "try to get rid of sexual objectification and to de-eroticize power in sex."[76] I want to focus on the de-eroticization of power, both because it is important to so many feminist arguments and because it is a compelling instance of competing values. As Kennedy sees it, de-eroticizing power in sex means looking for the sexual charge, the excitement, that is sometimes present when the other is "just the same" while at the same time "different," without implying hierarchy. [Note the echo here of Benjamin.[77]] It also means trying to "deprogram" one's own excitement at images of domination and submission. Though this is unmistakably the liberal humanist sexual program, it seems to me what is often behind cultural and socialist feminist theorizing about sex as well.[78]

But this is not Kennedy's choice. First, he quotes Judith Butler to suggest that it is impossible: "sexuality is always constructed within the terms of discourse and power." Therefore, "the postulation of a normative sexuality that is 'before,' 'outside,' or 'beyond' power is a cultural impossibility and a politically impracticable dream, one that post-pones the concrete and contemporary task of rethinking the subversive possibilities for sexuality and identity within the terms of power itself."[79] He then endorses Robin Morgan's picture of taking turns with power positions in sex rather than trying to de-eroticize power: "a joyous competition which must include an assumption of defeat as (1) temporary and (2) utterly lacking in humiliation; of any triumph as, obversely, impermanent and meaningless. *The taking and giving of turns.*"[80]

There will be strongly felt disagreement—not just among feminists—about the project of de-eroticizing power or embracing it in a form of sexual turn taking. And while in this context Morgan's picture is presented as the more expansive, less disciplinary project, there are those who would contest her rejection of humiliation as having any legitimate place in sexual play. There is no uncontested picture of the sort of sexual freedom, empow-erment, or autonomy that should follow from the elimination of the forms of sexuality held in place by violence. And Kennedy reminds us at the end that the contestation can go deeper than that: "Both the idea of reducing the violence so we can get on with playing within while evolving the repertoire, and the idea of overthrowing the repertoire alto-gether, are open to the critique that people would end up worse off in fact with more freedom and less repression."[81]

What I find important here is both the confrontation with contested choices and the view that these choices matter because it *is* possible to reconstruct eroticism (even if he suggests that trying to de-eroticize power is impossible or perhaps undesirable because of the depth and scope of disciplinary work involved in collective "deprogramming"[82]). Erotic charges are, like everything else, open to interpretation and transformation. "We learn them, and unlearn them. Abuse, tangled into the cultural images through which we produce and interpret our own and other people's sexuality, seems to me to weigh heavily on this tricky, risky enterprise. I think men and women might fantasize, play, experiment, and innovate more, and *perhaps* more happily, if there was less of this danger."[83] Most attractively (to me), Kennedy holds out the prospect of eroticizing women's sexual autonomy.

One might say that for the purposes of his article and of this chapter, what matters is that the reduction of violence is a prerequisite for any of the desirable, contested reconstructions. But the depth of the conflict over competing pictures of optimal reconstruction also matters. Kennedy gives no real hint as to which policies, which paths, to the reduction of the residuum would move the transformation of the erotic charge in one direction or another. Even if the reduction is a prerequisite, the form it takes can matter. As we will see shortly with Halley, there are some legal forms that she thinks are dangerous. And her judgment is shaped by the sort of vision of sexual freedom she has.

As we have seen, my version of the relational approach requires attention to each step: (after seeing how the problem is shaped by current relational structures) what are the values at stake; what (new) structures of relations will foster those values; how will different forms of legal rights or policies foster those relations? The definition of values is inevitably contested, and the predictions about relations fostering values and law structuring relations are inevitably tentative or speculative. But these limitations are, I think, inherent in any project of social transformation. And given the existing failure to provide women with such *uncontested* values as physical safety and bodily integrity, the need for transformation should not be contested. Neither should its difficulties be obscured.

Finally, though I think Kennedy would find my position too close to the de-eroticization of dominance he rejects, his argument parallels mine in chapter 5, "Violence against Women." Violence is too deeply intertwined with existing constructions of gender and sexuality to imagine that something like more effective policing can simply stop the violence. (Better policing could, however, be part of a process of change.) Deeper changes in the relations between men and women are necessary because the violence sustains and is sustained by the existing structure of relations. There is a necessarily circular, or spiraling, structure to the change. If the residuum of violence is reduced, women will have more freedom and power in relation to men. If men are to accept this reduction and the changes that flow from it, their own sense of their gender and sexuality will shift—and not just for men who acted out a sense of entitlement to violence and now have to refrain from it. The new versions of sexuality that start to emerge may still eroticize dominance, but they will not entail a large residuum of violence and abuse.

The law involved in reducing the residuum is thus inevitably involved in the tricky, risky project of transforming gender relations and sexuality. Some versions of the language of rights, demanding simply that women have the same rights to safety and bodily integrity as men, can hide this larger, unnerving dimension of the project. But a relational approach will not. Kennedy's central point is to persuade men that, having faced these wider, contested, and unpredictable implications, they can see not just the real costs but also the less obvious potential benefits to the new eroticism that will emerge.

Abuse screws women up sexually, and that's bad for men. It discourages women from risking, disciplines them not to risk the forms of pleasure/resistance through which we might eroticize autonomy and soften the contrast between the straight white middle class cultural center and the imagery of exciting but dangerous margins that are often real-life sites of oppression. And it burdens both men's and women's fantasy, play, experiment and innovation with questions, risks, fears, and guilt that trap us in the reproduction of patriarchal sex. Being against abuse is not, for men, just a matter of human rights, empathy, protecting "our" women, romantic paternalism or political correctness, however valid and important each of those may be.[84]

In closing, I want to note a colleague's skepticism that men would ever be willing to give up power for more "play."[85] This goes to the issue of the extent to which the many forms of men's superior power and advantage are sustained by violence. The greater one believes that link to be, the less plausible Kennedy's argument. While he structures his argument as a cost-benefit analysis, one would have to weigh the advantages of "fantasy, play, experiment and innovation" very highly to give up such advantages as the effective control of corporations, the ongoing wage gap, and the structure of what Eva Kittay calls "dependency work"—through which men can count on women doing a huge proportion of the caregiving necessary for those inevitably dependent upon it, with little or no remuneration.[86]

Of course, men do not have to be conscious of the relation between their advantages and their tacit tolerance of the residuum of violence. Most probably are not. But Kennedy's argument does not try to assess what the whole picture of costs to men would be if women were really equal competitors for all men's advantages and if the distribution of care work were no longer organized around gender. Kennedy does not discuss care work as a crucial dimension of the gender roles that are sustained in part by the ongoing threat of violence. Despite his arguments about how the residuum backs up superior negotiating positions of various kinds, what he details is the way men might be subjected to greater constraint and surveillance if there were a serious effort to reduce the residuum. But the tacit picture is that men would continue more or less in their current positions while suffering this constraint. Those who believe (as he suggests he does) that the whole structure of male privilege is sustained by women's pervasive fear of violence, should anticipate a much deeper disruption of the power structure if the violence were to be significantly reduced. It is the willingness to trade off this deep disruption for the pleasures of freer play in sex and gender roles that seems unlikely.

If we are to be really candid about the values at stake, a greater acknowledgment of the potential disruption seems called for. I think it is helpful to bring to light the costs to "play"–which I think is an important and too often ignored human value. But as my colleague Pamela Shime also points out, through prostitution our culture makes available to men forms of play that are outside the normal bounds of their marriages and public performances.[87]

And, as we saw earlier, Joseph Kuypers[88] argues that a vast structure of social practices— from war to entertainment—is built around male violence. Violence against women is one piece of this. To give up the structures of hierarchy and privilege built on male violence would require a huge transformation. The benefits of sexual playfulness and openness to experimentation will surely not be sufficient incentive. And it seems unlikely that violence against women can be disentangled from other ways in which male violence is embedded in the meaning of masculinity and the many structures that enact and enforce that meaning. Kuypers tries to offer as motivation a catalogue of the harms the culture of male violence generates.[89] I think that, in the end, some combination of a justice argument and a deeper analysis of the collective and individual costs of patriarchy will be necessary to persuade men to make the changes necessary to end the violence that sustains it.[90]

B. Butler and Halley: Norms, Normalizing, and Deep Sexual Diversity—And the Problem of Transformation through the State

I turn now to Judith Butler and Janet Halley to look more deeply into the troubling dimensions of the social transformation part of the relational approach. While my point in chapter 5 "Violence against Women" was (as I just noted) that ending violence against women meant restructuring relations between men and women, I was focused there on showing that the engagement with the meaning of gender was inevitable if the violence was to be stopped. I was trying to confront the argument that such issues must be beyond the reach of the liberal state. But I was not trying to confront the extent to which such a project is tricky and risky. The reconstruction of gender I discussed had primarily to do with the role violence plays in masculinity and the role of dominance for both male and female constructions of gender. My argument there, like that of most feminists, treats violence as simply and unequivocally bad. Halley challenges us to ask, what is violence and is it always bad?

Both Butler and Halley warn that feminist projects of protecting women from men, and of trying to shift the dominant construction of masculinity to one that is less dangerous to women, may affect the wider meaning of gender—and the wider universe of diversely gendered persons—in ways feminists had not thought about. And when the law and the state are harnessed to these projects, they can pose real dangers.

While it might be self-evident that gender involves sexuality and, thus, that transformations of gender will involve sexuality, Halley reminds us that the full dimensions of human sexuality remain uncharted. She brings home to us that to take on a project that seems uncontested in the feminist world—reducing the residuum of violence—is to step into highly contested and unknown terrain. Halley reminds us starkly of the murkiness of sex: "I think most of us experience sex (when its not routinized) as an alarming mix of desire and fear, delight and disgust, power and surrender, surrender and power, attachment and alienation, ecstasy in the root sense of the word and enmired embodiedness."[91] She confronts us with how little we really know about sex and what would constitute optimum forms of sexual relations—in the workplace, in the "privacy" of the home, the value of privacy for sex, the role of public displays of sex. She reminds us that there are deep and contested judgments about the nature of sexuality, as well as about ideal forms of gender relations, that shape arguments and policies for reducing violence against women.

Before offering a sample of what Halley has to offer, I want to turn to Butler's useful discussion of "norms." This will provide a helpful framework for the question that hovers over all of this discussion: to what extent is it actually possible or desirable to adopt a hands-off, or at least a state-off, approach once we recognize the unknown and contested nature of sexuality.

Butler points out that the term "norm" can be used in two different ways. "On the one hand, norms seem to signal the regulatory or normalizing function of power."[92] Norms in this sense define the normal, the acceptable, and thus inevitably exclude those who deviate from the norm. Theorists who use the term "normalizing" tend to use it with a derogatory connotation, emphasizing the exclusion, the "disciplining" used to enforce conformity with the norm. "But from another perspective, norms are precisely what binds individuals together, forming the basis for their ethical and political claims. When... I oppose violence done by restrictive norms, I appear to appeal to a norm of non-violence. It would seem to follow that norms can operate both as unacceptable restrictions and as part of any critical analysis that seeks to show what is unacceptable in that restrictive operation."[93]

I find this neat juxtaposition of the two usages very helpful. She associates the two with different kinds of theory. They also track academic disciplinary boundaries. I was once at a conference of mostly legal academics who for an hour had been talking in highly affirmative terms about norms. Finally someone from sociology noted that he found the conversation odd, since, in the academic world he inhabited, "norms" connoted "normalizing" in the derogatory sense.

What I find useful is the reminder that the two forms are not, in practice, separable. When one talks about shaping norms in an affirmative sense—like norms of nonviolence—one must remember that those norms will inevitably also be normalizing and thus exclusionary.[94] As we will see, Halley points to the exclusion even in the seemingly uncontested norm of reducing violence.

As I read her, Butler tries to expand the space within the second usage to minimize the exclusionary. She associates the second usage with Habermas, who "relies on norms to supply a common understanding for social actors and speakers."[95] And she tries to disrupt his assumptions about what is common.

> Do we need to know that, despite our differences, we are all oriented toward the same conception of rational deliberation and justification? Or do we need precisely to know that the "common" is no longer there for us, if it ever was, and that the capacious and self-limiting approach to difference is not only the task of cultural translation in this day of multiculturalism but the most important way to non-violence.[96]

I think Butler rightly keeps pushing for ways to sustain openness, for example, "the necessity of keeping our notion of the 'human' open to future articulation."[97] At the same time, she acknowledges the inevitability of constraint: "Through recourse to norms, the sphere of the humanly intelligible is circumscribed, and this circumscription is consequential for any ethics and any conception of social transformation."[98]

One might even say that openness itself is a key norm for Butler. Here we can return to the issue of gender norms, for it is in part open-ended gender norms that Butler is after. Butler offers up as a hope, perhaps even a goal, a freeing up of gender constraints: so that more—the maximum number?—of people can perform gender in a way suits them, so that the possibilities of ways of performing gender is expanded, so that fewer people will find that their desires put them at risk—of violence or of being seen as sick or making some kind of fundamental mistake about what it means to be human. And she offers lessening violence as a normative standard for choosing among the kinds of orders a society might choose (and impose).[99]

But here there is a strikingly different resonance to the different contexts in which she is thinking about gender and violence (threats to all forms of the nonnormative) and those in which I am thinking about gender and violence (male violence against female partners). She wants to maximize the range, the scope for different ways of performing gender, and to minimize the "punishment" (not necessarily state inflicted) of those who do not conform to the (inevitable) norms. In particular, she wants to minimize the use of violence to enforce those norms—especially given their inevitably exclusionary character.

I, on the other hand—to be deliberately crude—want to eliminate a form of gender. I want to undo a particular form of gender—the intertwining of masculinity and violence. For example, I want to figure out how the state is supporting the particular (one might say pathological) version of this intertwining in male battering—through police behavior that amounts to failure to protect, to prosecutorial decisions, to the absence of public funding for shelters, to welfare policies that drive women back into battering relationships, and so on. And I want the state to stop supporting that form of doing gender and sometimes to directly intervene to stop particular moments of those performances.

I assume that Butler would agree that at some level the difference in our projects is not as stark as I have just presented it. The kind of violence she wants to get rid of (I think that is a fair statement) is itself a form of performing gender, too. People who use violence to enforce gender norms (say by beating up gays) are participating in the performance of gender. (Indeed, I think it is interesting that many of the reasons batterers give for their violence imply a kind of gender norm enforcement: the house is messy, she is fooling around with other men, she didn't do what I told her to.) So there are certain kinds of violent performances of gender that she—like I—would like to see stopped. And in at least some instances, we would both endorse the use of state power (like the criminal law) to stop them.

But now when we turn to Halley, we see how complicated both projects may be—because Halley wants to complicate what she sees as the standard feminist rejection of mixing sex and violence. In a way true to Butler's invitation to always see norms as fluid and contested, Halley wants us to see that trying to end the mix of sex and violence is likely to be just the sort of exclusionary, constricting, and dangerous norm that Butler is worried about. It is particularly dangerous because the state is likely to be drawn in.

Halley thus offers a troubling (because compelling) version of the concern that my relational project, like feminism generally, is far too likely to call in the state to participate in normalizing (in the bad sense) projects. Her argument might even suggest that my form of relational feminism is particularly dangerous because it so explicitly takes on the project of transforming relations, including intimate gender relations—and thus will almost certainly be intrusive and destructively normalizing.

The first question for me is whether I can make the same sort of answer to her that I made in chapter 5: in most cases, the state is already present. My project doesn't necessarily call for greater state involvement, though it will often call for different state involvement. The state helps construct relations in ways I think are bad (promote violence against women), and I want it to structure relations that will reduce violence against women.

Beyond the issue of the role of the state, the broader question would be: is the relational, transformational project intrinsically, or likely to be, more dangerously intrusive, more normative in the bad sense, than is optimal? As we have seen, the reduction of the residuum (including IPV) necessarily involves a reconstruction of masculinity. Kennedy is optimistic about new versions of gender that would create more room for playing sexual power games that evoke fantasies of sex and violence without actually doing violence. But while he may hope for a greater scope of freedom, his project still entails deep and contested transformation. Halley raises doubts about whether projects of reducing the residuum will actually leave the kind of scope for diverse sexualities she thinks there should be. She fears the inevitable normalizing function even of reducing the residuum (or at least of the forms it is likely to take). But she has her own contested project to transform norms (and their legal enforcement) in order to increase scope for diverse sexualities. And my transformative project would not be wholly in sync with either Halley's or Kennedy's. Kennedy is too optimistic about men's willingness to give up power and too little interested in de-eroticizing dominance. As we will see, from my perspective, Halley is (among other things) too sanguine about protecting desires for "unwantedness" in sex.

The second issue then, as I have already indicated, is the inevitability of deeply contested normative judgment in decisions about social transformation, including every protest or policy advocacy or claim about core values. The (implicit) question for me is whether my version of the relational approach makes adequate space for the contested nature of the values that I say law is supposed to advance as it (inevitably) structures relations. As I said, Butler, somewhat tentatively, suggests that lessening violence might work as a normative standard she is willing to sign on to. And both feminists and others often hold out ending or reducing violence as an uncontested norm. But Halley wants us to think twice about that—and even about whether "consent" is going to get us very far in resolving the difficulties.[100] Thus she brings home very clearly the depth of disagreement that may be revealed when doing the work of relational analysis.

Like Kennedy, Halley employs the language of costs and benefits. She wants us to see that they always entail one another and that hidden costs and benefits are everywhere. For example,

> I am assuming that we live in a world where gains for transsexuality might come at the expense of feminism. This can happen at the level of material distributions: safety and home for transsexuals might require the reaffirmation of precisely the social forms that have been deployed to make heterosexuality compulsory. And it can happen at the level of theory: thought practices that make transsexuality articulate might make intersexuality less intelligible, might render gender trouble less powerful an idea. Real social goods, real social costs are being allocated here.[101]

And the hidden costs are especially worrisome when they are embedded in legal decisions. At the end of *Split Decisions* (2006), Halley takes up two cases that she thinks have very serious costs. The first is *Oncale v. Sundowner Offshore Services, Inc.*,[102] in which a man working on an all-male oil rig alleged that he was repeatedly "menaced and harassed by his supervisor and two co-workers. They threatened to rape him; twice they held him down while placing their penises up against his body; once they grabbed him in the shower and did something (one cannot be sure quite what) with a piece of soap. His complaints were ignored and he quit under protest. Oncale complained in federal court that he had suffered the form of employment discrimination under Title VII that we call 'sexual harassment.'"[103] The U.S. Supreme Court held that he could sue under Title VII and laid out the terms for finding same-sex sexual harassment.

Although Halley describes the alleged facts as "disturbing,"[104] she argues that the Court's reading of these facts as "sexual harassment" may vindicate "antigay" or "antisex" rulings in future cases.[105] In order to illustrate these troublesome implications of the *Oncale* verdict, she posits alternate readings of the facts that "put [Oncale's] allegation of unwantedness aside, as a mere allegation."[106] In doing so, Halley seeks to show that a single fact scenario may yield a multiplicity of readings when we "Tak[e] a Break from Feminism (and any other single theory)."[107]

First, Halley suggests that the facts in that case might support a reading that the plaintiff "willingly engaged in erotic conduct ... and then was struck with a profound desire to refuse the homosexual potential those experiences revealed in him."[108] On this reading, Halley interprets *Oncale* as a "homosexual panic case," casting "Oncale as the aggressor, the other men on the oil rig as the victims, and the lawsuit (not any sexual encounter on the oil rig) as the wrong."[109]

Second, Halley challenges the reader to adopt "a more thoroughgoing queer approach" based on Eve Sedgwick's call to "detach male bodies from masculinity and superordination and female bodies from femininity and subordination…and generally 'get beyond,' discrete homo- and heterosexual identities" and on Bersani and Kennedy's view that "sexual super- *and* subordination can *both* be complex objects of desire."[110] Halley posits four "possibilities" for describing the gender and power relationships at play and urges the reader to "Mix, match and omit as you will."[111] On these readings, "uncertainty intensifies" and "we move from the homosexual panic hypothesis to the problematicness panic hypothesis."[112]

> On [the problematicness panic rereading] it was precisely the loss of certainty about wantedness [of sex] that the players were seeking. That *was* their desire. It's a risky desire: acting on it places one in the way of having some unwanted sex. Things can go wrong; we need to keep one eye on the cause of action for assault. But more profoundly, if things go right, the wantedness of the sex that happens will be unknowable. The queer theoretic reading of the case reminds us that we will always do violence when we decide.[113]

Halley's concern here is that the "mix-and-match volatilities of gender and sexual orientation work to make the question of who is submitting to whom extremely difficult to answer.…To the extent that the decision in *Oncale* allows one participant in scenes like these to have a panic about it afterward and sue, it sets courts and juries administering Title VII a deeply problematic function."[114]

In embracing the ambiguity of the "wantedness" of sex, Halley is, in effect, challenging one of the most sacred of contemporary feminist commitments: no means no. That mantra (which I think has done tremendous good) effectively claims that unwanted sex *is* what the law should protect us from. (Of course the slogan is used in the context of men forcing women, but I think the wider issue of unwantedness is [almost] the same.) Giving legal force to "no means no" thus denies that there are *desires* for ambiguity about wantedness, desires that should be respected and protected. And it allows people who get panicked about their own desires for ambiguities around wantedness to bring down the force of the law on others as a way of asserting their normalcy. And that, in turn, will enforce norms and relations among people in ways that discourage rather than promote experimentation with unwantedness in sex.

> Of course throughout we are concerned about sexual predators who make the workplace impossible for their victims. But we might also worry that Oncales who inhabit my fourth rereading[115] contradict their own past decisions when they claim access now to a less problematic set of norms about wantedness. We might want to estop them from claiming now that then they didn't want to put wantedness *en abime*, not only because we find this dishonesty repulsive, but also because the

social forces they will gather and sharpen, if they win, bid to make Title VII a vanilla-sex regime. It might turn the normative screw in the direction of less problematic sex, making problematic sex more unwanted by more people, and increasingly more actionable.... There are lots of people out there—card-on-the-table moment: I am one of them—who think the problematic of wantedness isn't just tolerable; we think it's beautiful; its brave; its complicated and fleeting and elaborate and human. Workplace discrimination rights to bring problematicness panic suits against it insulate a big part of the world from our political reach.[116]

I think that statement is very brave, complicated, human, and very problematic. It's as tricky and risky as the desire for ambiguously (un)wanted sex. But I am persuaded of what I see as Halley's main point: an open engagement with the ambiguities and unknowable dimensions of sexuality reveal costs to what look like unambiguous benefits of a legal regime of protection against sexual abuse and violence. As she says,

[There] are some pretty striking downsides to the *Oncale* decision. They might not be worth it. Protecting feminine gay men is a good thing to do; same-sex wrongdoing should not be exempted from regulation; people should be made to worry about how their sexual desires affect other people; everybody has to work and should be able to do so without running irrelevant and acute dangers; and so on. But we don't get those social gains without the social costs. The benefits have costs. And the costs have benefits: as long as erotic masochism is a powerful position, we face the problem of infinitely unknowable preferences.[117]

Halley has an equally disturbing (and compelling) rereading of the facts of *Twyman v. Twyman*,[118] a 1993 Texas case in which a woman successfully claimed damages for intentional infliction of emotional distress on the basis of her husband's imposition of "deviate sexual acts,"[119] which Halley describes as "mild sadomasochistic sex."[120] (Especially disturbing is her parenthetical dismissal of ongoing reactions to past trauma and/or the possibility that rape might be experienced as trauma.[121]) Earlier in the Twymans' relationship, Mrs. Twyman had participated in sadomasochistic sex. But then she was raped and said that after that she found that form of sex intolerable. She found out that her husband was having an affair with a woman who engaged in such sex, and he told Mrs. Twyman that he thought the marriage had no future if she would not participate in sadomasochistic sex. This is what Halley suggests the judges treat as "the divorce threat."[122] Halley paints a picture in which we can see the possibility that the husband was trying to tell her that he couldn't see staying in the marriage if his sexual needs were not met—rather than his using the threat of divorce to coerce sadomasochistic sex. I can imagine that the wife felt frightened, intimidated, humiliated, and sexually inadequate for being unable to meet her husband's sexual needs—which his lover was meeting. (There is the barest hint that Halley thinks the wife—on this reading of the facts—is sexually inadequate; she should have gotten over the rape and gotten back into the sex they had previously engaged in.[123]) The wife then uses the law to punish him for her pain. As Halley reads it, Sheila Twyman's project was to seek a public finding that his conduct is "outrageous, beyond all possible bounds of decency, atrocious, and utterly intolerable in civilized society."[124] And she won because that is, roughly speaking, how the judges see sadomasochistic sex.

Even without Halley's expansive understanding of sexuality, I can see this as a role I don't want the law to play. Halley suggests that it would restructure relations between men and women, giving women more power—in particular power to insist on their own sexual preferences.[125] But here I would agree with Halley: the cost of such benefits are too high. This is a form of tacit policing of "normal sex," of what reasonable men can ask of women, that is unnecessarily intrusive.

Part of what we see in Halley is that the law continues to be engaged in (indirectly) defining "normal" sex in ways I thought had gone the way of criminal sanctions against sodomy. For example, Ummni Khan's work analyzes several judicial decisions from the United Kingdom, Canada, and the United States in which consensual sadomasochistic practices and pornographic depictions of sadomasochism have been characterized as deviant and harmful to the "public interest" of the communities in question.[126] She has particularly compelling discussions of the court's unwillingness to disrupt "normal" gender roles in which the male partner is "naturally" dominant and the female, submissive.[127]

Paying attention to the vast range of sexual preferences that people have, the extreme difficulty of adjudicating among them to determine which are really harmful or dangerous (sex with children would be a candidate, but who counts as a child is not always obvious), leads me to agree with Halley that we must always be alert to the hidden costs when we look to the law. This may be especially true when sex is involved. The scope of the unknowability is daunting, making one want to tread lightly. But what would it mean to tread lightly? Sex is always involved if gender is involved, and that covers most projects aimed at women's equality, safety, and well-being.[128] Moreover, the unknowability around sex may be just more evident or more extreme than the inherent unknowability in other domains.[129]

As I read Halley, she doesn't think that the libertarian hands-off/state-off solution is a real one.

Once we really do admit masochism into our vocabulary of sexual pleasure, we make it hard to know that any particular social outcome involving sexuality broadly conceived is a cost or a benefit, a good or a bad. Even there, we must—constantly, existentially, pragmatically, and in uncertainty decide.[130]

One of the reasons we must decide is that the law is already actively constructing sexuality. There are a few instances in which one can actually say that the law should just stop doing what it is doing (as opposed to doing it differently). Sometimes getting the state out will advance the sort of reconstruction one hopes for. Some people argue for getting the state out of marriage. Decriminalizing homosexual activity is another example. But as the conservative voices make clear, that is not doing nothing. And most advocates of gay rights would see this as only a first, though vitally necessary, step. The state must also protect against discrimination. In most cases the choice is between forms of law, of enforcement, of policy, not between law and no law.

Thus, in the end, I *can* offer Halley the same answer I put forward in chapter 5. In most cases, my project does not call for greater state involvement; it calls for different state involvement. But the values that guide that involvement remain (inevitably) contested.

III. RELATIONAL TRANSFORMATION
A. Openness, Intrusion, and Self-Consciousness

Feminism created a new normativity. It offered a language of justice and entitlement to challenge long-standing social and legal practices.[131] It is the self-conscious project of many feminists to get the state to support that normativity instead of an older one that authorizes and protects male power and provides an impunity to men for harms to women that are (or should be) formally legal wrongs. As we will see shortly, when I turn to Ann Jones's "to do" list, in case after case an existing state practice is identified and its modification called for. What then should feminists do about Halley's arguments about the costs, and potential costs, of such projects? While Halley's target is feminism, for my purposes her argument raises broader problems.

The feminist project of social transformation is not structurally very different from most projects of egalitarian transformation. They virtually all call for a recognition of the way the existing law is complicit in sustaining inequality and for changes in the law to advance equality. Other egalitarian projects may not engage sexuality in such a central way. (Although in North America sexuality is a big part of how racialization and class identity work.) But I have turned to Halley (and Butler and Kennedy) to see how they trouble my relational approach to transformation generally. Most transformational projects that I would want to encourage to use my approach have a transformational normativity (e.g., ending racism, poverty) that they want to use to guide changes in the law. And this normativity will have its normalizing dimension. All projects of greater inclusion may have a hidden dark side of exclusion. (Remember, for example, Halley's comments about transgender.) And all aspirations to transformation have to deal with inherent uncertainty.

I want to begin my reflections on these problems by starting with Butler's call for openness. Halley warns us that feminists (and I would say most reformers guided by strong normative commitments) run the risk of being blinded by their particular construction of the core of injustice. So, for example, by focusing relentlessly on the categories of male and female and the oppression of women by men, they fail to see the other dimensions of the problems before them. And they are likely to fail to see the costs of the benefits they propose. So what would foster a kind of ongoing commitment to open-end-edness, to open-mindedness, in a way that could work together with a passion for justice (which will always have a particular construction that highlights some things and hides others)? I think my version of the relational approach has something to offer here. And what it has to offer is the flip side of one of its potential weaknesses, so it is helpful to see its contribution in this context.

A relational approach to rights calls for a constant inquiry into the values that are at stake in any given problem (e.g., of interpreting, implementing, recognizing new rights). It then requires an engagement with the inevitably difficult, sometimes even speculative, process of figuring out what kinds of relations would foster those values and then, again, what kind of interpretation, policy of enforcement, or legal recognition would structure relations one way rather than another. I think this process itself requires a high level of ongoing self-consciousness about the difficulties and ambiguities of each of the steps. As I noted earlier, this approach to rights resists simple reification. Workable shorthands for past decisions can emerge so that every new problem does not have to be resolved from scratch. Nevertheless, it is harder to slip into a language of absolute rights or claims that only one policy or interpretation can protect the values at stake. When one starts to think about the problems of how social relations foster or undermine a particular value, there should be a tendency to see how one set of relations intersects with another. This can make a problem seem unmanageable in scope; it can also encourage an attention to relations that were not originally on one's horizon.

I have to acknowledge, however, that a relational analysis does not guarantee the sort of openness I have in mind. I think there are many feminists who are quite sophisticated in thinking through forms of relations and the legal structures that shape them *in terms of the relations of power between men and women*. But they can remain blind to other structuring of relations. So, for example, Halley says of *Twyman*:

Twyman as background family-law rule that husbands with enduring ineradicable desires for sex that their wives find humiliating must either stay married to those wives or, if they seek a divorce (which they might well want to do simply to remarry and have non-adulterous sex with women who do not find their desires humiliating), pay a heavy tax in shame, blame, and cash. *Can feminism acknowledge that women emerge from the court's decision with new bargaining power in marriage and a new role as enforcers of marital propriety? And can feminism see how costly this bargaining endowment might be to women, who can tap into it only if they find the sex in question painful and humiliating? Can feminism read the case as male subordination and female domination—and still as bad for women?*[132]

Even feminists using a relational approach will need the reminders, the insights, that thinkers like Halley, Butler, and Kennedy offer. But I want to claim that although reminders will often be necessary (as they were for me), once alerted to them, relational thinkers should be especially receptive to those insights. They direct our attention to impacts on relations that we might have missed. And those relations are likely to be relevant to the core values of equality, dignity, safety, and so on. A relational approach should stand ready to receive them, even if they are disruptive of initial judgments about desirable structures, about what law, which relations, will actually foster the values feminists (or other social transformers) care about. And relational reformers should engage with such insights even if, as I will come to shortly, they disrupt the initial construction of what those values are.

The downside, or limitation, of the relational approach that I noted above is exactly its fluidity. The resistance (not imperviousness) to reification and simplified absolutism or certainty comes at the cost of the uncertainty inherent in ongoing, open-ended inquiry. The project of relational rights interpretation (or implementation) requires self-consciousness about the difficulties of the judgments involved, the unavoidable uncertainty not only of imperfect information but also of the predictions involved in the claims of links between law, relations, and values. It asks judges and others invoking rights and projects of transformation to be self-conscious about the contested quality of the values and the uncertainties about what will advance them. But all these limitations seem to me to encourage the illusive openness Butler advocates—in a way still consistent with the functioning of a legal system committed to rights and the rule of law.

Indeed, I think perhaps the only hope for the openness Butler calls for is self-consciousness. We will all, inevitably, get caught in our preconceptions, our commitments, our predilections in ways that blind us to the full scope of the issues we actually care about—or would wish to care about if we could see them. Only an ongoing self-consciousness of the inevitability of this blindness will welcome disruptive insight that literally allows us to see things differently.

I think my version of a relational approach requires and promotes just such self-consciousness. That is what makes it so demanding—so demanding that some may see it as unworkable in practice. This is the heart of my answer to the danger of the intrusion inherent in the project of restructuring relations: the "intrusion" is already there. The law and state policy (among other forces) *do* structure intimate relations. They can't just not do it. For example, the state *could* get out of the business of defining and authorizing marriage. (I think that might be a good idea.) Legislators could then engage in self-conscious reflection about what sorts of intimate relations the state should support— long-term friends living together, stable but shifting communal living arrangements, siblings living together, long-term or short-term sexual partnerships—and what policies would best provide that support. Legislators could decide in which contexts the state should supervise the dissolution of intimate financial entanglements in an effort to protect vulnerable parties. Or legislators could decide that none of those things are the state's business: there should be no special deals mandated for division of assets or pensions or health care or participation in medical decisions on the basis of intimate relations. Such arrangements should be left to private or collective contract. Or the state could decide that such arrangements are more like promises to go to a dinner party and are not enforceable at law. Legislators might also decide that more *direct* state involvement would better serve the purposes now served by state support of marriage. Maybe generous state funding for a range of child care options would serve the interests of children better than tax benefits for married couples with children. Maybe a guaranteed annual income and state-supported health care would better protect everyone's well-being—and equality—than a system of tying pensions and private health care benefits to intimate partners and their children.

There is a huge range of ways the state and the legal system could engage with intimate relations. All of them would structure those relations—make it easier or harder to dissolve the relations, provide incentives for forming legally recognized relations, making partners more or less dependant on one another, giving the partner who controls access to shared benefits greater bargaining power, fostering equality or dependency within relationships. As I hope is obvious in these examples, withdrawing current forms of state engagement would not stop structuring relations; it would structure them differently. Differently in each of the forms of withdrawal I listed.

What a relational approach offers is self-consciousness about this inevitability of structuring—as well as a way of thinking about the implications of different forms of structuring. It is the overtness of the relational approach that sustains the self-consciousness about what is involved, including its tricky, risky encounters with sexuality.

So for example, one might try to imagine the project of fostering an openness, a fluidity in the meanings, practices, experiences of gender. One might want to make all forms of sexual or familial partnering equally accessible to benefits traditionally associated with marriage. One might want to say the state shouldn't try to support or subsidize long-term relationships in preference to multiple, short-term shifting relationships. Here one might hope for a debate over the benefits of supporting long-term relationships (requiring a clear articulation of what those benefits are and who exactly should enjoy them) versus the exclusionary "normalizing" effects of preference for long-term relationships. One might see calls for more serious state protection against violence directed, say, at gays or transsexuals based on arguments quite similar to those about violence against women. These would all be ways of making life more livable for a wider range of performances of gender, of reducing the costs of acting on desires that are not (currently) those of the majority.

For people who see themselves as equality advocates, the above list of possible legal and policy moves might generate disagreement (say about long-term relationships), but I think the disagreements are likely to be of moderate intensity. There would be some widely shared set of values and disagreements about their priority and the best means of achieving them. I think the situation is different if people were to try to figure out what it would mean in practical terms to embrace, reject, or be relatively neutral toward Halley's invocation of the erotic charge of "unwantedness." As I noted above, it is a direct challenge to many parts of the feminist agenda of transformation of norms, belief, policy, and law.

Halley's project, as I see it, would be to figure out how to make space for those who like
to play with unwantedness to do so with relative safety (which would have to include
protections against one partner changing her mind and deciding to invoke the law to
reassert her "normalcy") without radically shifting the norm that ordinarily the law
should protect against unwanted sex. Part of the problem is that the law is still a long way
from actually providing that protection. If it were fairly secure, one could imagine a
warmer reception (or at least not fierce resistance) from feminists whose projects are to
provide better protection for women. I think I can see a possible path forward that
accommodates both standpoints.

It begins with the recognition of what Khan successfully shows: judges have quite fixed
and unexamined views about what normal sexuality is.[133] These views are so fixed that
they are prepared to tacitly deny that "real" women could want sex that involved, say,
"power plays" of humiliation and masochism. If judges were to become more self-
conscious about their views on sexuality, and open themselves to education about the
scope of adult sexual desire (as they have, for example, about patterns of relations where
women are battered), then they might be able to carve out reasonable ways of trying to
ascertain consensual engagement. This broader scope of recognition would, for example,
shift judges' readiness to see Mr. Twyman's desires as intrinsically unacceptable and, thus,
their capacity to contemplate the possibility that what was happening was not intentional infliction of emotional distress, but the pain of sexual incompatibility. It would
provide some protection against changes of mind.

B. (Fiercely) Contested Values

I can imagine versions of such shifts in legal practice and norms that I would see as bringing more benefits than costs. But I can also imagine that there would be feminists, and
women who have been victims of sexual violence who would not identify as feminists,
who would reject any legal or normative accommodation for playing with "unwantedness." They would see it as too dangerous, given the risks women are already subject to.
I can imagine them saying that those who want to play with unwantedness must do so at
their peril (the peril Halley acknowledges of unwanted sex and the peril she would like to
reduce of paying a heavy legal penalty if someone changes their mind about the game.)
Better their peril than increasing the already considerable risk of unwanted sex all
women face.

Now we are in the realm of deeply contested understandings of the values at stake.
Again, I can imagine feminists who are not the least interested in making any space for
playing with unwantedness. They might want to work toward reconstituting gender so
that unwantedness disappears as a form of desire. From that perspective, people who have
it should get over it—kind of like Halley seems to think women who have been raped
should get over it.[134] Maybe it comes from childhood sexual abuse, and one should have
some sympathy. But, from this perspective, that just means they should get therapy or

whatever it takes to keep them from trying to enact their pathology in law, policy, or collective norms of sexuality.[135]

I don't think I can distance myself from such a stance quite as much as I might like to. Halley, Kennedy, and Butler have taught me to be wary of such a perspective. They have a persuasive story that eradicating forms of sexual desire is a dangerous legal project. But as I noted above, none of them can simply reject all such projects. To successfully reduce the residuum will involve shifting the connection between violence and masculinity. It will have to involve shifts in desire. Maybe the nuance matters. Maybe its one thing to focus on reducing the residuum knowing that the reconstruction of gender and desire will ultimately be involved. And it may be another thing to say straight-out, that the norm which law should enforce has no scope for unwantedness. To say this would not, of course, require criminalizing such sex play. But this position would reject any accommodation that threatens the project of protecting women and normalizing legitimate sex as that which is wanted. This position is incompatible with Halley's.[136]

So does the relational approach founder on such deep contestation over values? I have said one should start an analysis with the values at stake in a case (or policy) so that we can inquire into the relations that would foster them. But what if at step one we encounter irreconcilable difference? I have three answers.

First, this problem is in no way peculiar to my approach. Part of what Halley helps us see is that values over which there are deep differences are already present in existing cases. What the relational approach does, as I have already noted, is bring to consciousness what those values are. Where judges may now routinely make assumptions about the values at stake and that they are the shared values of society, a relational approach would encourage a more self-conscious articulation of the values and then a recognition of their contested nature. For example, if these relational formulations of the relevant questions became routine, lawyers would construct their arguments around the competing conceptions of values at stake. Judges are de facto making choices among competing values now. A relational approach would make those choices more apparent.

My first answer, then, is that the problem of irreconcilable differences over the values at stake is always there, just more obvious with the relational approach. My second answer is that the self-consciousness entailed in the relational approach is, again, the best solution to the problem. If we must entrust judges (and policy makers) with choices between values about which there is deep disagreement in society, it will not be possible to make informed, responsible, or accountable decisions unless there is a high degree of self-consciousness about the choices. The more judges and policy makers are articulate about the choices they face, the better the possibility that their decisions (and opinions or debates) will foster good democratic deliberation about those choices. And of course, democratic deliberation can and should take into account the importance of protecting minority rights and interests. So, for example, even if Halley's view about unwantedness might not prevail in the first cases in which it was articulated as a value, the recognition of the existence of the costs of denying it might well come to be seen by legislators as a cost to be taken into account. The mere fact of a form of public debate around it might challenge the norms around legitimate sex and make space for a more encompassing stance.

My third point follows from this. As I argued in chapter 6, "Reconceiving Rights and Constitutionalism," I see the relational approach as encouraging a form of constitutionalism that is structured to foster democratic debate over the form and content of rights. In this chapter we can see the need for such debate from another perspective: we see the deep disagreements about the most basic values even among those committed to women's equality. (I include Halley in this group. I see her resistance to a framework that takes women's subordination as its starting point to be about the forms of precommitment that generate blindness to other issues, not about a lack of concern with women's equality.) And we see that it is not just the structure of constitutionalism as such that needs the benefits of public deliberation about rights.

One of the important democratic weaknesses in Canada and the United States is the extent to which judge-made law—the common law of torts, property, and contract—is essentially removed from democratic debate.[137] Few who are not trained as lawyers know anything about it. But as Halley's discussion of *Twyman* shows, tort law (here the intentional infliction of emotional distress) plays a part in the legal enforcement of gender norms and the normalization of sexuality. So-called private law also defines rights that are crucial to the structure of power (property most obviously), and private law is equally guided by contested norms in its inevitable structuring of relations. This is so whether that guidance is self-conscious or not. Unarticulated norms lead judges to define rights in ways that structure relations—in ways that, in turn, are of great concern to Jones as well to Halley, Butler, and Kennedy. The same is true for judicial interpretation of criminal law, whether statutory or common law, and for statutory interpretation, such as the ability to sue under Title VII.[138]

A relational approach would increase the transparency of judicial decision making in all these areas. It would have a similar effect in structuring the debates around legislation and regulation so that identification of competing values was routinely called for.

C. Contested Strategies: State Power, "Governance Feminism," and the Relational Approach

In this section I use the contrast between Jones and Halley to turn again to concerns about a relational approach involving excessive state power and intrusion into people's lives. The two authors are starkly different in the way they talk about violence, and there is a kind of implicit mutual contempt for the other's approach. Of course, Halley does think women should be protected from assault. And there is not a direct contrast in their approaches to battering, since Halley doesn't talk about it much. The aspersions she casts in her asides about feminist advocacy have more to do with sexual harassment, though she comments briefly about other issues. For example, her discussion of "governance feminism" (which one might say is what Jones aspires to):

There are plenty of places where feminism, far from operating underground, is running things. Sex harassment, child sexual abuse, pornography, sexual violence, antiprostitution and anti-trafficking regimes, prosecutable marital rape, rape shield rules: these feminist justice projects have moved off the street and into the state.

[...]

It would be a mistake to think that governance issues only from that combination of courts, legislatures, and police which constitutes the everyday image of the "the state." Employers, schools, health care institutions, and a whole range of entities, often formally "private," govern too [this list closely maps Jones's list in "what we can do"]—and feminism has substantial parts of them under its control. Just think of the tremendous effort that U.S. employers and schools must devote to the regulation of sexual conduct at work, through sexual harassment policies that have produced a sexual harassment bureaucracy with its own cadres of professionals and its own legal character....[O]ne result of feminist rape activism is the elevation of child sexual abuse as a serious enforcement priority complete with "zero tolerance" enforcement attitudes; other kinds of child neglect and abuse, other kinds of adult/adult interpersonal violence, lack the charisma of the sexual offences. They fall into the background. And this is the effect of governance feminism.[139]

Halley offers no evidence for these claims, no evidence about increased success in identifying and prosecuting child sexual abuse (to the neglect of other forms of harm), no evidence of greater use of legal resources to constrain harassers than, say, to policing street level drug deals.

Jones, by contrast, suggests that

police departments, prosecutor's offices, courts, and probation/parole agencies can designate staff members with special expertise to handle domestic assault cases and ensure that these employees are well trained [thus generating the sort of feminist influenced bureaucracy Halley is worried about]. They can adopt a consistent policy of arresting primary offenders and handing out serious consequences. Given limited resources, police policy makers can reorder their arrest priorities, recognizing that domestic assault, the leading cause of injury to women, is far more serious, violent, dangerous, and costly to the victim and the public than the petty thefts, car thefts, burglaries, and minor drug use offenses that typically engage police attention.[140]

This seems to me both a sober acknowledgment that priorities will need to be shifted and a persuasive argument that they should be. Over and over again Jones argues (and marshals considerable supporting evidence) that the priorities of all of these forms of governance fail to take seriously the harm of domestic assault and what it would take to allow women to escape from it.

As we will see shortly, Jones also makes the sort of sweeping, absolute statements rejecting all forms of mixing sex and violence that fuels Halley's unease (fury?) about feminist justice projects.

D. Foundational Relations: Restructuring Root Causes versus Responding to Existing Problems

I initially chose to contrast Halley and Jones to see the ways their deep difference reflected basic difference in values and their priorities. Some of this difference does emerge. But upon rereading Jones, I was struck by how the foundation of her argument is one Halley is likely to endorse, or at least not resist. What Jones thinks is most important is a change in the "material conditions" that make women's equality possible, thus enabling them not to be dependent on men:

> If we are to make progress against battering and child abuse, we must understand that neither the problems nor the solutions lie in the individual psyche, and that the material conditions necessary for women to become free and equal and independent will not be found in our heads. Nor in the long run will they be found in our court-rooms and jails. When the material conditions of women's lives change—when women have access to affordable housing, child care, health care, adequate welfare benefits, job training, and jobs that pay a *living wage*—most women can free themselves and their children from violence. But for that to happen, sex discrimination must end.[141]

While Halley would resist a single-minded focus on sex discrimination, especially one that presupposed women's subordination by men as the core of the problem, there is no reason to suppose that she would reject the argument that redressing women's economic inequality would make a big difference for intimate partner violence as well as other feminist justice projects. Leaving aside for a moment the role of the state in accomplishing this redress, and the inevitable disagreements about what it would take to accomplish it, Jones points to a way of restructuring relations between men and women without engaging in the sort of direct regulation of intimate relations that makes Halley particularly nervous. Indeed, I think that when one compares what Jones thinks is most important with the long list of interventions she thinks are currently necessary, we see something significant about approaching social transformation in relational terms.

When systemic harms are embedded in deeply entrenched structures of social relations (and corresponding patterns of beliefs), trying to respond to those harms without transforming the underlying structures creates dilemmas, situations in which there are no solutions without high costs. So in the case of the battering of women, as long as the conditions for women's economic self-sufficiency are not in place, it will be difficult for many women to leave men who batter them. As Jones sees it, if these conditions were in place, most women would leave. The phenomenon of long-term battering relationships would be vastly reduced, if not eliminated.

Women would take care of the problem themselves if they could. It is when they can't that a vast apparatus of support, intervention, and coercion come into play. And it is here that Halley and Jones are at odds. The conflict and danger (which each implicitly sees in the others approach) arise because the root problem of inequality has not been addressed.

Halley and Jones could agree that women (and men) would be better off without all the state intervention (and other forms of governance) that a failure to solve the root problem gives rise to. Jones herself points to this indirectly:

In the United States, "domestic violence" is addressed in terms of the personal psychology of individual victims and (far less often) perpetrators. "Domestic violence" is a "social" problem only in the sense that if affects an aggregate of those supposedly aberrant individuals.... When problems long neglected threaten to overwhelm us, we send in the cops, as though imprisoning aberrant individuals in sufficient numbers will achieve social justice. The 1994 Violence Against Women Act is a case in point—necessary and long overdue, yet essentially a law enforcement fix for a social problem eradicable only by profound changes in the status of women's lives.... advocates always knew that shelters and criminal justice served only a small fraction of American battered women, and that criminal justice was more likely to harm than help them.[142]

The project of providing economic equality for women is by no means a simple one. In my judgment, history has conclusively shown that the problem will not be solved by the market driven by the supposedly obvious benefits of having the full range of talents of men and women available in all spheres of work and life. So various ways of redefining the legal rules that structure the market (such as equal pay and antidiscrimination legislation, paid maternity leave, family care leave) will be required—and resisted as "intervention" in the market. The project of economic equality between men and women (and one might add reducing and ameliorating poverty) is a project of restructuring relations. And the arguments for it are arguments about how transformed structures will better advance such values as dignity, autonomy, security for all. The debates over these issues can call forth deep divisions over the meaning and priority of say freedom, dignity, and equality. But I do not think that Halley and Jones would find themselves pitted against one another in a sharp split over values in this context.

The conflicts arise, as I said, when trying to respond to some of the intractable problems caused by the failure to secure women's equality and their consequent dependence on men.

E. Competing Visions of Sexuality and the Possibility of Policy Compromise

Briefly, then, what are those conflicts? Faced with centuries-old patterns of men's violence against their female partners, and the absence of the material conditions that would make it relatively easy for women to leave, Jones advocates sweeping prohibitions on violence in intimate relations. For example, she says,

> The point is that as long as "a certain amount" of sexual and physical "fighting" is thought natural, civilized, desirable, or necessary in marriage, violence will always be thought to occur with the woman's consent, the woman's provocation, the woman's solicitation, the woman's pleasure, just as rape was once thought to be provoked, solicited, consciously desired, and unconsciously needed by women victims of rape.
>
> [...]
>
> battering is *always* wrong no matter who the woman is or what she does, no matter what she provokes or solicits or submits to or consents to or consciously desires or subconsciously needs and no matter how much the assailant *loves her*.[143]

It might be that a full definition of battering, including, say, "a crime in which the perpetrator does not consult the woman's wishes and from which he does not let her escape,"[144] would be sufficient to distinguish battering from any of the forms of sex play or openness to multiple forms of gender that Halley and Butler advocate. But note that Jones includes "consent" in her list of what cannot justify battering. I think this might give Halley pause (although we have seen that Halley thinks that consent provides no simple solutions). But even if they disagree about the role of consent, it seems likely to me that the kind of relationships that feminists like Jones describe as characterized by battering actually look quite different from relationships in which there has been violent sex play or even play with the edginess of unwantedness. So even if the kind of person for whom Halley wants space and protection changes her mind and calls in the law, it seems to me to be a manageable project to have evidence requirements that are capable of distinguishing between the two relationships.[145] It is likely, however, that consent would play a role that Halley would not be entirely happy with. So consensual violence might be protected, but play with unwantedness probably would not be.[146]

Of course, as in all areas of law, there might be grey areas and mistakes.

In short, it matters that Jones and Halley might be able to agree on at least some dimensions of what the law should prohibit. It also matters that they have deep differences in their visions of optimal sexuality. Both play a role in the forms of relational restructuring they would support.

Jones spends pages raging against the dangers of popular psychology's advocacy of anger, aggression, and violence in sex. In the many books she quotes, aggression and violence is a normal and thus a legitimate, perhaps necessary, component of fulfilling sex.

She thinks this is dangerous because it is part of what sustains a way of talking about these issues that consistently trivializes or denies women's experience.

> Women report rape, battery, broken bones, miscarriages, knife and gun shot wounds. Men talk about "marital problems." Women walk around with bruises, brain damage, paralyzed limbs, shredded genitalia, bullets in their heads. Men mention domestic disputes.
>
> [...]
>
> In defining common experience, batterers are backed up by the best authorities.[147]

For example, she quotes (with contempt) Alex Comfort, in *The New Joy of Sex* (1991), "an updated version of the perennial bestseller":

> Our image of love is uptight about the very real elements of aggression in normal sexuality.... To need for some degree of violence in sex, rather than the glutinous unphysical kind of love which...tradition propagates, is statistically pretty normal. [She adds that he does not provide statistics.]...If you haven't learned that sexual violence can be tender and tenderness violent, you haven't begun to play as real lovers.[148]

This sounds like a position Halley would endorse.

Jones is intensely preoccupied with trying to secure for women some basic values: security, bodily integrity, and the equality necessary to give real effect to those values. Halley has a passion for promoting freedom in the basic human realm of sexuality. Halley is worried about the law (such as Title VII) being enlisted to promote a so-called vanilla sex regime (like the tradition Comfort denigrates) and being available to punish (not necessarily via criminal law) those who deviate from it.[149] Jones is worried that stories of the "thrilling intermingling of sex and violence"[150] will justify and trivialize what batterers do so that all the various mechanisms of governance Halley identifies will—far from being controlled by feminists—fail to provide women with the most basic entitlements to security.

They both have subtle inquiries into how relations between men and women are shaped by understandings of sexuality and the way law affects and is affected by those relations and understandings. They would see each other's approach as dangerous, even if they would both, in principle, sign onto security, bodily integrity, sexual freedom and autonomy, and equality as core values. We will see shortly how these deep differences play out around issues of education.

Here, the important point is that each approach highlights different consequences of the ways law can restructure intersecting relations of power and sexuality. Halley's and Jones's books should be read together so that the perspective of each informs the other.

I think Halley is right in her central point: feminists can be blinded to the consequences (costs) of their projects by their single-minded focus on the categories of men and women and the subordination of women by men. Laws that will restructure relations in ways that give women more power and control over intimate sexuality could limit everyone's freedom to play, experiment, and love sexually. But it seems equally clear to me that before heeding Halley's warnings in any given case (she is careful to keep her language to warning rather than prescription, though the difference gets pretty thin at times), Jones's warnings should be taken into account. A move to protect diverse sexual preferences might work to endanger women by legitimizing stories about sex and violence that sustain men's power to inflict violence with impunity—and to make women feel guilty and inadequate. Such legitimacy and inadequacy help provide the conditions for battering relationships.

Taking the two perspectives together, the objective would become for law to provide the protections that Jones thinks are crucial without endangering the relationships Halley cares about. Of course, this will work best if all actors in the legal, political, and social services systems have some familiarity with (and respect for) the concerns of both Jones and Halley. Without Jones's perspective, there is the danger of reinforcing old stereotypes and of continuing to provide impunity to men who batter their wives. Without Halley's perspective, there is the danger that the law will (in effect) enforce a notion of legitimate sexuality that is far narrower than is necessary to protect women from the violence feminists are concerned about.

I think it also worth remembering Kennedy's argument that by reducing the residuum of violence there will be *more* scope for the play, experiment, and openness that he, along with Halley and Butler, advocate. Thus to the extent that Jones is right in her analysis of what will reduce the violence, they may have an interest in supporting her project.

F. Jones's "To Do List": Dangerous State Expansion, Repressive "Governance Feminism," or (Inevitably Contested) Redirection of Existing State Power

Jones has an entire chapter detailing her recommendations for change in areas of state and society that affect women's vulnerability to violence. As I see it, it is her relational analysis of the problem that leads her to identify such a wide range of institutions and practices and to see how changes could improve women's chances of avoiding and escaping violence. I use portions of her exhaustive list as yet another way of showing how—despite appearances—a relational approach rarely requires an expansion of state power.

Overwhelmingly, the call is for existing state power to be redirected so that the relationships it is currently structuring can be restructured in ways that enhance rather than endanger women's security. And, again, I take up Halley's challenge to see if such redirections are dangerously intrusive or restrictive, even if they aren't an expansion of state power.

Jones opens her chapter "What Can We Do" with an interesting reflection on the kind of change that *has* occurred in popular norms about a woman's relation to her family. It also contains a summary of the institutional changes she thinks are necessary:

> In the nineteenth century and a good part of this one [the twentieth century], when a woman left her husband, the public asked: Why did she leave?…What kind of woman walks out on her husband and family, the sacred duty entrusted to her by God and Nature?
>
> [...]
>
> Today, family, friends, clergy, courts and counsellors still urge a woman's duty upon her, but when…some "real" trouble occurs—a homicide perhaps, or the battery of a child—the public wants to know: Why *didn't* she leave?
>
> [...]
>
> The danger is now that we overestimate society's changes. Implicit in the question, "Why didn't she leave?" is the assumption that social supports are already in place to help the woman who walks out: a shelter in every town, a cop on every beat eager to make that mandatory arrest, a judge in every courtroom passing out well enforced restraining orders and packing batterers off to jail and effective re-education programs, legal services, social services, health care, child care, child support, affordable housing, convenient public transportation, a decent job free of sexual harassment, a living wage. The abused woman, wanting to leave, encouraged to think she will find help, yet finding only obstacles at every turn, may grow disheartened and doubt herself.[151]

Jones's first category of things to do is "institutional change." She is self-conscious about the dilemma of the urgent need for remedial change and its ultimate inadequacy because (in my terms) most of it cannot change the underlying relationships of inequality and vulnerability:

> Keeping in mind that no institutional change can "save" women and children set up by economic dependence and poverty, real or threatened, to be easy marks for male violence, we must change the way our institutions operate.[152]

She quotes Susan Schechter's argument that existing institutions fail to carry out their responsibilities properly:

> In the last fifteen years of testimony before Congress and state legislatures, in newspaper accounts, in proposals to foundations and state agencies, the same problems have been identified again and again: judges fail to hold offenders accountable or take victims fears seriously, doctors patch wounds and send women back to their

assailants, clergy tell women to try harder, courts issue visitation orders requiring children to see fathers who sexually assault them.[153]

This is by and large *not* a call for new agencies or new laws. It is about existing institutions doing their job "right"—that is actually carrying out the task that legislatures have already assigned to them.[154] (As we shall see, the potential for conflict with Halley is clearest in the kind of education Jones sees as necessary for all these actors to start carrying out their jobs properly.) Few of Jones's many recommendations involve an expansion of existing state power. She calls for aggressive enforcement of existing laws: "Courts can make it easy and *safe* for battered women to get restraining orders, and police can enforce them by *seeking out* and arresting violators. They can and should confiscate the guns of all men subject to restraining orders or convicted of domestic assault."[155] (It is not clear whether this last point might sometimes require additional legislative authorization.)

Her discussion of child protection policies is about paying attention to the reality of domestic violence in decision making about placing children, especially taking them from their mothers when adequate protection against the batterer would protect both mother and child. Similarly, there are many discussions in the literature about the way welfare regulations put battered women at risk[156] and provide such inadequate support that women face terrible choices between feeding themselves, feeding their children, giving their children up to "state protection," or returning to the batterer. Some of the remedies suggested call for increased funding, but most are about shifting policies and regulations rather than expanding their scope.

The health care system is another target for change. As Jones says,

Most battered women never call the police or go to court or flee to a women's shelter, but battered women in great numbers visit doctors and hospitals—often repeatedly—for treatment of injuries and other stress-related illnesses, both their own and those of their children. Most doctors fail to recognize these women as victims of violence—a blindness that in itself is harmful to battered women.[157]

Here the primary target is education and protocols for recognizing IPV and providing appropriate guidance and assistance. In a system of health care that is primarily private, the state is not involved. (Although in commenting on doctors' practices she notes that they didn't report child abuse either until they were required to do so by law.) Even in a public health care system, the primary actors are likely to be doctors' and nurses' associations and the institutions that educate health care professionals. "Colleges and universities that offer degrees in medicine, nursing, social work, psychology, and pastoral care can require education about male violence, battering, sexual assault, and child abuse in their standard curricula."[158]

As Halley made clear, her concern with "governance feminism" is not with formal state power alone; it extends to exactly such proposals as this one, for required courses about male violence. Jones's repeated insistence about the need for education at every level is not just about providing missing information or statistics. The existing ignorance and misunderstanding are part of a "story" about "domestic violence" that trivializes it, blames the victim, provides excuses for the perpetrator, and, in effect, allows large scope for violence with impunity. Jones wants education that will counter that story with an alternative, the feminist analysis she presents, which is the result of decades of research and activism. Jones's own version (like that of many, but not all, feminists) would, as we have seen, also come with an unequivocal rejection of mixing sex and violence.

This desire to "impose" (to use Halley's framework) an alternative understanding of battering is not, in my view, a gratuitous imposition of the feminist agenda. Jones's call for education is, as I see it, part of a recognition that "battering" is not just a characteristic of particular intimate relationships but also part of a wider structure of relationships—and corresponding ideas—that sustain the practice. The practice of battering cannot be changed until the understanding of that practice changes, among health care professionals, criminal justice personnel, social workers, and the public at large. As long as they see battering in a certain way, men will have the power to practice it, women's dependence on men will make it difficult to leave, and the external supports (shelters, adequate welfare with reasonable regulations) to enable women to leave will not be there. The power relations between men and women, the patterns of women's dependence on men, are sustained not just by economic inequalities but also by ideas and beliefs. Thus Jones (and many others in the field) see education, what one might (tendentiously) call reeducation, as a central part of the task of ending battering.

I use the term "reeducation" (despite its totalitarian overtones) to emphasize that there is an existing story about battering that is told (both tacitly and directly) and supported by multiple institutions. The question is not should these institutions be promoting a contested story about the nature of battering, but should the story they are promoting be challenged and changed. As with withdrawing impunity, overt projects of changing the story look like imposition, they seem like expanding intrusive power (whether of the state or other institutions with power over people's lives). But it really is a matter of making overt what has been covert and then trying to mandate change. At this historical juncture, it is not possible for doctors, social workers, or criminal justice officials to simply be neutral about battering, to promote *no* story about battering.

The virtue of Jones's education project, which I think Halley, Kennedy, and Butler all ought to endorse, is that it makes the covert explicit. The contested nature of the "story" then becomes obvious. By seeing the links—battering cannot be stopped without restructuring relations, part of that restructuring involves changing the prevailing (but often unstated) ideas about battering—the contestation over ideas and values becomes an explicit part of the policy debates. (Of course, Jones wants her version of the story to be accepted, not just reveal the contested nature of competing stories.) Sometimes policy makers (of both Halley and Jones persuasions) might be able to compromise on a practical agreement. For example, one could imagine a compromise on an education project that acknowledged the phenomenon of consensual violence (which is not battering) while successfully resisting the stereotypes that had sustained battering. In other instances, policy makers would have to acknowledge and debate competing visions of sex, violence, privacy, and the role of the state in ensuring women's security.

Halley's perspective provides another caution about what doing the job "properly" entails. While it is important to resist the stereotypes and tacit blaming of the victim that are all too common, it cannot really be appropriate for health care, social work, or criminal justice workers to take on the assumption that the injured woman is always right or blameless (as some of the literature implies). The unquestioning, supportive stance appropriate to counselors or shelter workers cannot be adopted by all the other institutional agents called upon to make judgments in cases of violence between intimate partners. It is a common tendency to think that the huge job of transforming stereotypes or conventional thinking or hegemonic ideology is a justification for counter distortions, simplifications, or exaggerations.[159] But my version of a relational approach requires attentiveness to all the dimensions, even nuances of relational structures. A single-minded focus on the victim cannot provide that. (Although, as I just noted, there are times when it may be appropriate in the context of counseling.) Such a focus cannot, as I discussed ealier, help us understand why large numbers of men (though, of course, a minority) feel driven to the violent control and domination that is characteristic of battering relationships.

Jones's long list indicates the huge cost of *responding* to the problem of battery. How much does the response shift relations? Collectively the ameliorative projects can give women the means of leaving battering relationships. As such they shift power relations between men and women, rendering women less dependent on men who batter them. In that sense, the overall project is one of restructuring relations. But each particular component is usually aimed at meeting a particular need or problem, without trying to address large-scale relational issues. Again, this is part of the frustration one can see in Jones's analysis. The needs are urgent. They are being exacerbated by existing practices, which must therefore change. But vast resources—with their inevitable scope for mistake, intrusion, coercion—must be marshaled because the underlying structure of relations invites women's vulnerability to violence from intimate male partners.

IV. CONCLUSION

The many-layered problem of violence against women shows the importance of a relational approach—for both analyzing the problem and envisioning alternatives.

This problem also helps us engage with some of the difficulties built into the approach. Identifying the values at stake in an issue reveals the depth of disagreement over some of those values as well as how best to implement them. Relational analysis makes explicit the judgments about the effect of relational structures on values and the equally uncertain judgments about the effect of law on those structures. But a relational approach does not actually generate any more contestation over values or uncertainty about effects than does any other form of legal or policy analysis. It brings them to the surface and, in making them conscious, improves the chances of good judgment.

Finally, this discussion of a relational approach to violence against women helps us see the often hidden complexities of the issue of state power. Both Judith Shklar (whom I discussed in chapter 5) and Halley are concerned about the dangers of state power. Halley, as we have seen, is particularly concerned about using the law for feminist transformational projects. Both of them end up raising the concern of turning to the state for solutions and thus expanding the scope of state power.

My discussion above, however, shows that turning to the state for solutions does not necessarily expand the scope of state power. Indeed the question of increasing or decreasing the extent of state power is usually the wrong question. Wherever the law is, the state is. And the law is virtually everywhere.[160] The question is how it is structuring relations, and how it should be. This is the appropriate question whether the law in question is the common law[161] of property and contract, a legislative regime of family law, an administrative structure such as welfare, or the criminal law of assault. Whatever the source of the law, courts will end up interpreting it—and should do so using a relational approach.

I have engaged here and in chapter 5 with the preoccupation with the danger of expanding the scope of the state, showing that a relational approach does not necessarily lead to such an expansion. Indeed, bringing a relational approach to bear does not necessarily involve turning to the state for solutions.[162] But let us look now at the ways the discussion in this chapter reveals the limitations of this preoccupation.

First, one of the issues the problem of violence points to is when the *forms* of state involvement are intrusive and crude, in ways that undermine values such as privacy and autonomy. I have argued that if the legal and political system successfully provided for women's equality the need to intervene in acts of violence against women—say, police physically stopping an assault and prosecuting the assailant—would be dramatically reduced. With adequate opportunity and support, far fewer women would stay in relationships characterized by battering. Acting at the source of the problem would reduce ongoing, and inevitably crude, intervention.

It is hard to say (and probably not very useful to try to determine) whether less state action would be required to ensure women's economic equality[163] than to step in when battering has become a pattern in a relationship. But the criminal law is always a rather blunt instrument and its exercise almost always highly intrusive. In addition, most people would agree that ordinarily prevention of violence is preferable to punishing it. The choice between using state resources to advance equality or intervene in preventable violence seems an easy choice.

The point is that although I said earlier that the relational approach shows that solving the problem at the source would generate *less* state involvement, what it would really do is change the nature of the involvement from crude, intrusive, and highly contested[164] intervention (such as arrests) to the creation of opportunity by enforcing rules of equality (which, of course, would also be contested).

What matters here is that the important question is what *form* state engagement should take. A relational analysis should always look beyond the immediate choices— say, mandatory arrest or not—to the ways the whole structure of relations could be reshaped such that those choices are not necessary. The state, through law, will almost always be involved in that restructuring. But it could be in a far more constructive, less intrusive, and more deeply effective way than police reaction to violence. (I believe this is Jones's view as well.)

We see the same question of how intrusive or obvious the role of state is in the question of withdrawing impunity for violent action—but with a somewhat different conclusion, at least in the first instance. In responding to a framework of anxiety about the scope of the state (both here and in chapter 5), I made the point that when the state starts to take action against those who commit violence against women, it will appear to the perpetrators (and some male onlookers) as though the scope of state power has increased. And while it is true, as I pointed out, that this new exercise of power is really just enforcement of laws (against assault) that had long existed—and thus in this sense *not* an increase in state power—the reality for perpetrators is that they are now subject to an exercise of state power from which they had long been immune. One might say that something similar happened when law enforcement officials started interfering with and prosecuting lynching in the American south.

Interference with violence through the criminal law is often violent and always intrusive. But when the state has failed to enforce the law to protect all equally, and then begins to do so, few would say (in the abstract) that this is the kind of exercise of state power to be concerned with. On the contrary, in principle, this is one of the least contested exercises of state power. It matters both that the authorized scope of state power has not increased (the laws were already on the books) and that people's experience— both victims' and perpetrators'—is that new forms of state power are being exercised. From a normative perspective, it matters that this new exercise arises to remove an unjustifiable, often illegal, impunity. From a relational perspective, what matters is how that new exercise is shaping relations—whether it is enhancing or undermining such values as security or equality. If the choice is between using state power to protect against illegal violence or providing impunity for the perpetrators, protection will normally foster relations conducive to security and equality. But restructuring the relations that generate the violence will almost always be better still.

The question of whether there is more or less state power at work in the structuring or restructuring will, as I noted, often be hard to tell. In most instances the changes will be in forms of state engagement, since there are so few areas of life in modern societies that are not governed by some existing form of law. Halley is worried about the decision in *Twyman* becoming a rule of family law. But if it did, it would not be entering a vacuum.

It would be replacing another rule of family law. In the area of violence against women, responsibility might replace impunity. The law structures both.

I have argued over and over again that what is at stake is not more law, but different law. This does serve to respond to the concern that the relational approach would expand the scope of the state. But the version of that concern that I actually think matters is not some kind of measurement of an increase in the total level of state power but how the power is exercised. Is it crude and intrusive? Is it exercised in an accountable and democratic manner? Who has a say in what the rules are and how they are implemented? These questions matter, and the relational approach can help answer them.

When trying to figure out how to solve a problem, we need a clear picture of what the problem is. The relational approach leads to clarity about the ways existing uses of state power generate and exacerbate problems, such as violence against women. And it can help assess the advantages and disadvantages of different forms of law to restructure the relations that have given rise to the problem.

In sum, the relational approach I advocate offers clarity in the analysis of problems and in the inevitable debates over both core values and ways of achieving them. It brings to the fore the basic interconnection of human beings and, with it, an attentiveness to both the harms and the benefits of human relations. I advocate its use for the transformational aspirations of equality-seeking projects—the necessary restructuring of relations. But as we shall see shortly, in the conclusion, a relational approach encourages humility rather than hubris in facing the inevitably tricky, risky nature of trying to undo the harms that existing law has generated.

Closing Reflections

MY CLOSING REFLECTIONS focus mostly on the implications of the relational approach for law. In particular, I address what I see as remaining puzzles and challenges, both the issues that I have puzzled over and those that I think others might (still) be troubled by. But before turning to these, I want to reiterate my opening intention: to shift the everyday framework of thought to include a relational perspective. Law is only one of the domains of life in which I see this approach as valuable. The explorations of alternative conceptions of self and autonomy laid out in the preceding chapters are intended to enable everyone to give clearer voice to the ways that these conceptions make sense to them—and thus to contribute to their development and use.

I begin (section I) with the central claim that law should be understood as a combination of the conceptual and the institutional and thus as an important vehicle not only for giving norms institutional effect but also for deliberating about what those norms should be and how they can best be realized. I then turn in section II to the question of nonlegal norms. Here I take up the question of the increased responsibility implicit in the relational approach. The shifts the relational approach calls for normatively, conceptually, and institutionally are significant, and, of course, I argue for the deliberate attempt to use the law to restructure relations. This raises what I call the "Burkean problem"[1] of the hubris implicit in any effort to use the law for social (and intellectual) transformation. I address this in section III. I then return in section IV to the issue of contested values (addressed in chapter 8) to ask what the relational approach can contribute in the light of the inevitability of deep disagreement over the very values relational structures are to advance.

In section V I address the disruption of existing categories, which is both an intention and a consequence of the relational approach. First I look at the issue in the context of the question of whether the relational approach subordinates the individual to the collective (a question I began with in chapter 1). Then I note a wider range of categories the relational approach disrupts to reflect on how I can simultaneously claim that the relational approach is immediately usable in existing liberal democratic legal systems and claim that the relational approach entails a significant divergence from the individualist assumptions underpinning those systems. I conclude that the tension is a productive one and can foster new and better ways of thinking about such age-old problems as the optimal scope of the state. Thus, at the end, I return to the issue of state power I have noted throughout the book and argue, again, that the question of whether the relational approach would increase state power is rarely the right question. The disruption of categories of public and private and the attention to how all law shapes relationships provides a constructive way to think about the inevitable choices about how to use state power.

I. ENGAGING WITH THE LAW
A. *The Conceptual and the Institutional Intertwined*

I conclude where I began, with a description of the project of this book as "engaged in an institutional project of finding a new language and new concepts in which to express our subjectivities and through which to enact law."[2]

The preceding chapters have worked through both conceptual and practical puzzles of relational autonomy. We have seen how a conception of autonomy is interconnected with conceptions of rights and of the self. At the same time, I have offered examples of how all of these conceptions take form in and give shape to the law. Thus an optimal legal system needs optimal understandings of its core concepts and values. And if ideas of rights or autonomy are to matter in people's lives, they must take root in practices; they must become manifest institutionally. Law is thus one of "the social and cultural institutions within which ideas of selfhood [and I would add, autonomy and rights] are played out, and which are needed to stabilize and co-ordinate them and indeed to make them livable."[3]

Thus my approach to the puzzles of self and autonomy is simultaneously theoretical, legal, and political. To make important changes in the legal and political system, people require an adequate conceptual framework. As long as they are locked in a notion of autonomy as independence, for example, they will not be able to see clearly what is needed to protect autonomy in the modern administrative state. A relational conception of autonomy facilitates recognition of practices that undermine it and of the shifts in those practices (such as a different interpretation of a law) that could restructure relations in an autonomy-enhancing way. For example, chapter 3, "Reconceiving Autonomy," looked in detail at how this has worked in the sphere of administrative law and how law could continue to change to enhance autonomy further.

This approach to law is not without its risks. Whenever one uses law as a tool of transformation, one runs the risks associated with using "the master's tools"[4]—for law is almost by definition controlled by those with power. By turning to law, one risks having one's project shaped by the dominant frameworks, priorities, and preoccupations. But I have argued that this is a necessary risk: the law must be engaged because it shapes so many dimensions of people's lives. It is thus essential to try to shift the dominant conceptual framework and to use the law in ways that foster rather than undermine such values as equality. I have offered examples of both actual and potential progress toward a more egalitarian and more relational use of the law.

Of course law is always in interactive relation with other social and cultural institutions, other relational structures, as well as with other conceptual frameworks through which people interpret their worlds. I have presented ways of stepping into that complex interaction at the levels of both legal interpretation and conceptual formation. The issues of violence against women, for example, involve deep cultural norms about masculinity, class, and familial expectation as well as the capacity of the law to provide impunity for male violence or to create new norms of responsibility, as in the change in the Canadian law of sexual assault (chapter 5). An example I have only noted, the gendered division of household care-work, invites us to see that existing relational structures prevent full social, economic, or political equality for women. "Private relations" interfere with public rights. These relational structures are sustained by a complex mix of deeply internalized gender norms, expectations entrenched in families and workplaces, and legal structures that permit or encourage discrimination flowing from these household relations. Law alone cannot change these patterns, nor are they likely to change without support from law.

B. Democratizing Law/Participation in Norm Creation

One of the ways in which I have tried to mitigate the risks of what I see as a necessary engagement with law is to democratize law itself. Because law is a central means of giving effect to and enforcing values, it is crucial that law become more open to public deliberation about what those values should be and how they should be implemented. To use the language of a postcolonial critique, my approach to law is "as a site of discursive engagement, and not merely as capable of promoting [ostensibly uncontested] universal norms and values in which everyone will ultimately be included."[5] I have argued that one of the virtues of a relational approach to law is to help make law genuinely "a site of discursive engagement" by making it more widely accessible to public deliberation. A relational articulation of what is at stake in legal cases should make the law more broadly intelligible. In addition, the version of constitutionalism that I have laid out invites popular deliberation about the meaning of rights.

Among the central relational dynamics this book has engaged with are the relations of freedom and autonomy. An important component of those relations is the participation in norm creation. That is, the relations of freedom and autonomy (or their absence) shape who gets to have a say in the formation of the norms that govern people's lives. The relational approach focuses attention on this question and its significance for law as one important form of norm creation. From the advocacy of meaningful participation in bureaucratic decision making to the greater accessibility of debates about law, my arguments have been intended to make law a vehicle for, rather than a barrier to, democratic participation in norm creation.

Of course, law is not the only institution that requires and gives life to conceptual underpinnings. The explorations of alternative conceptions of self and autonomy laid out in the preceding chapters were intended to invite people to give effect to them in many spheres. Sometimes relations should be restructured in ways that need not directly involve the state, for example, enhancing autonomy in a workplace. Employers can be helped to see that hierarchical relations and nonparticipatory structures of decision making are inconsistent with core values and unlikely to promote optimally creative and satisfying productivity. The relational approach works in all contexts. When rights are understood as structuring relations, and relations are seen as essential for rights to be realized, the relational approach to implementing values extends far beyond the state. It helps to recognize that even when rights are at stake, the state is not the only relevant actor.

II. COLLECTIVE POWER AND RESPONSIBILITY: THE CHALLENGE OF CHANGING NORMS

The state (and law) are not the only means for imposing norms, even norms that are, in effect, highly coercive. Gender norms are an example. The law may participate, but it is hardly the only source of coercion. Here I turn to the implications of my argument for nonstate norms. But first I situate that issue in the context of what I have said about the implications for the use of state power.

I have argued (particularly in chapters 5 and 8) that the primary effect of the relational approach will be to clarify the ways the existing exercise of state power shapes relationships in ways destructive to values, such as autonomy, and to help envision different (rather than additional) exercises of state power. In addition, my approach would foster a clearer understanding of the relational source of problems like violence against women. Solutions to underlying problems (often through different uses of law) would then lead to far less direct—and often problematic—state intervention, such as that required once women have been subjected to violence. I have tried to meet concerns about the scope of state power by showing that the use of a relational approach for transformational projects like feminism need not involve an increase in the scope of the state. But I have also argued that measuring what would constitute an increase in state power is not at all straightforward (chapter 8, section IV). And in any case, there is no reason to presume that an existing level of state power is optimal. It might, as in the dramatic cases of failed states, be seriously deficient. In most cases what really matters is how, not whether, the state is structuring relations in ways that enhance or undermine such core values as autonomy or security.

As I said in the first chapter, I do not see a concern with how states exercise their power as exclusively a liberal preoccupation. People with many different ideological and scholarly orientations can agree that state imposition of someone else's idea of the good life (or even good sex) is a serious problem—even if they also agree that simple neutrality with respect to the values that shape societies' relations is not possible. One could say something similar about ideas about rights. Consider, for example the threats to constructive relations from the imposition of a libertarian conception of liberty or a particular conception of a free market.[6]

The seriousness of the threat state power can pose does not turn on whether the state's objective is cast in the language of rights or the public good or universal values. The relational approach can help assess whether state action couched in any of these terms is actually fostering or undermining core values, such as autonomy or security.

The question I now turn to is the effect of the relational approach on collective norms. Even if the relational approach helps foster optimal use of state power, might a relational habit of thought generate notions of responsibility that would curtail individual freedom?

I have said that I aspire to a change in people's framework of thinking. Were this to be successful, people's sense of their responsibilities would shift. As in the example I discussed in earlier chapters of seeing the homeless person on the street, a relational stance would not permit shielding oneself with a story about not having caused her situation or violated her rights. People's habits of thought would reveal the interconnection between their right to exclude and her immediate plight. Perceiving that interconnection would not tell them what to do or even what the right policies would be. But it would make willful blindness to the problem much harder. Figuring out what kind of personal compassion is called for and turning one's attention to the issues of poverty, the care of the mentally ill, and the availability of social housing would command more of people's time. As I also suggested earlier, I think new skills of judgment would be called for with relational habits of thought.

I do not think the state would make greater incursions on the scope of individual freedom, but I do think people's sense of what responsible freedom consists in would shift. I think people would not experience their current sense of "free choice" about whether to pay attention to the homeless, to the number of children in poverty, to violence in prisons, to the high rates of violence against women and abuse of children, to cruelty in the production of meat. Of course, part of the problem is that I could have made a much longer list of issues claiming attention, even without getting to the question of the international distribution of wealth. Learning to exercise individual and collective judgment about the moral responsibilities that flow from a full awareness of human interconnection will be a bigger challenge than learning to see those interconnections. And, of course, wanting to avoid that challenge might be a reason to reject a relational approach in the first place. But it would not be a responsible or well-justified reason.

The Western conception of freedom has always had some form of responsibility attached to it—obeying laws, respecting others rights. And there have always been important norms of responsibility outside the scope of law. But the individualism of traditional liberalism encompassed a wise recognition of the potential dangers of the coercive powers of public opinion (John Stuart Mill, in particular[7]). This recognition has engendered a tolerance for a wide diversity of norms of individual responsibility. I think a widespread adoption of the sort of relational perspective I advocate would shrink the scope of that tolerance. People who said, or just behaved as though, they were too busy to worry about global warming or the homeless on the streets would be seen (and treated) by others as morally deficient. While there would have to be some recognition that different people would focus their energies on solving different problems, certain kinds of disregard would trigger disapproval. Relational norms would have their own normalizing (and thus exclusionary) effect.

I think this kind of nonstate-enforced reduction of personal freedom of choice about how to spend one's time, energies, and resources would be a loss, especially to those in privileged positions. I think of an analogy with the differences between the anonymous autonomy of city dwellers and those who live in small communities where everyone knows (and has opinions about) what everyone else does. As one who enjoys some of that anonymity, I can see the downside of collective norms with higher demands of responsibility. Relational connection can have its costs. But I also think about the reaction of law students first exposed to the horrors of the residential schools which aboriginal children were forced to attend.[8] Their reactions included wonder at: how it was that they were first learning about this in law school (after twelve years of education); how it could have been allowed to go on for so long; how the churches who ran the schools and the governments that funded them could have permitted the abuses inherent in the schools (efforts at cultural extinction) as well as the widespread physical and sexual abuse. I asked the law students what they thought a future class might be studying in fifty years, what practices are normal now that will be seen as abhorrent then.[9]

The point of the example of the residential schools is not the specific lessons one might learn but the general point about the scope of the harm done by indifference, blindness, and even nonrespectful efforts to confer benefits.[10] This is the kind of harm that I think must be balanced against the loss of scope of personal freedom for irresponsibility that a relational framework would involve.

In addition to this sense of balance, one must consider norms that would increase individual responsibility in the context of the recognition that all social systems generate norms that shape and constrain behavior.[11] If one wants to ask whether this kind of increase in (normatively compulsory) responsibility amounts to a real decrease in freedom and autonomy, one needs to compare the norms fostered by a relational stance with those fostered by, say, contemporary liberal capitalism in North America. Consider, for example, consumption norms which also have a compulsory, or compulsive, quality to them: people feel they need to have certain clothes or cars for their self-respect or for others' recognition of their success or even adequacy.

It seems likely to me that the responsibility that would come with a relational framework would also come with a greater level of self-consciousness about the reasons for that norm. Norms, such as consumption, which are not attended by self-consciousness or training in good judgment, seem more likely to me to be real barriers to freedom and autonomy than normative responsibility. Indeed, the prevalent idea that consumption choices are a fundamental exercise of freedom and autonomy contributes to a distortion of the understanding of those values and thus the capacity to enjoy them.

Shifting norms of individual responsibility and a growing awareness of interconnection would also shape norms of collective responsibility (which, of course, currently vary significantly among liberal democratic states, ranging from the United States to the Nordic countries, with Canada somewhere in between). At some point the stronger norms of collective responsibility would have an impact on state policy. I think this is particularly true with respect to the organization of the care work that is essential for both individual and collective well-being. And, as I discussed in chapter 1, making human interdependence (including dependence on care) a central part of the relational self means that responsibility for care will take a priority not found in more individualistic accounts. But as I have argued, these new forms of responsibility need not always take the form of direct state regulation or provision of services. A relational framework of thought should foster more creativity about the different forms collective responsibility can take (chapter 1).

Global warming has already made people more accustomed to public policy arguments that are guided by attention to interconnection and interdependence (of both people and planet). And in some instances, the shifts in habits that will be required to contain global warming can be seen not just as a loss but also as part of a deep rethinking about, say, the role of food in our lives and the many kinds of values connected to it—values that the dominant North American habits of consumption and eating had rendered invisible.[12]

Similarly, the approach I advocate would bring a renewed attention to the centrality of relationship in the quality of people's lives, which is likely to have compensatory benefits for the loss of irresponsible (yet cherished) freedom. Relationship brings not just burdens of responsibility but also joy, meaning, and the actuality of the abstract values people care about. There is a danger in closing this book with discussions of the potential problems of my approach. It makes everything seem hard, when some things will be easier. It will be easier to see, for example, that relationships themselves are part of what we create with our creative capacity. It will be easier to see their value and thus, perhaps, to take time to enjoy them.

III. RESTRUCTURING RELATIONS AND THE BURKEAN CHALLENGE

Nevertheless, I turn to another problem, what I might call the Burkean[13] objection: shouldn't one be wary about enlisting state power to change deep, long-standing structures of relations? Even with much more democratic participation in the ways law structures relations, shouldn't one doubt the wisdom of ideas (even relational analysis) compared to the wisdom of long tradition? Even the ethic of care, as I noted in chapter 1, has its own version of this caution: one should be wary about coercive and sudden disruption of long-standing relations, even relations of domination.[14] I think this is a serious concern, particularly when combined with alertness to the inevitability of unintended consequences and the inherent unpredictability of the consequences of human action.[15] (Remember that for Arendt this unpredictability is an inevitable consequence of freedom.)

It is worth remembering in this context that no industrialized society has ever really tried full gender equality—in the workplace, in government, or in the allocation of caretaking tasks or household labor. We cannot know the full consequences of such an experiment. Indeed, all industrialized societies have been characterized by many forms of inequality, such as those organized around class and racialization. Aspiring to equality in the modern context is itself a huge social experiment. And because the law is always in interaction with other social norms and structures, in an unequal society the law always plays a part in sustaining that inequality. Once one is committed to shifting social relations in the direction of equality, law will have to be a part of it—especially since contemporary liberal notions of law have conceptions of equality built into the very meaning of the rule of law. Law's role in structuring unequal relations (as in violence against women) will need to be redirected toward shaping relations of equality. There really is no morally justifiable alternative even though the outcomes of any given attempt are unknowable in advance. (Of course, there is a huge range of different ways of promoting such change, including degrees of direct engagement with law.)

The relational approach I have presented here is a way of thinking through that project of redirection at many levels: legal interpretation, legislation, and bureaucratic policies as well as restructuring in the nonstate realm, such as employment practices and the allocation of caretaking labor in the home.

So if there is no real alternative to trying to transform law's complicity in inequality, what is that we can learn from reflecting on the Burkean challenge? First, in thinking about the admonition to be cautious, one can take comfort from the observation that social relations are never static. Change is part of the fabric of life. Trying to hold onto past practices as a security against the unpredictable consequences of deliberate change will only generate a rigidity with its own unpredictable consequences. Nevertheless, I have turned to this issue in the conclusion because I think it is wise to be humble and cautious about the capacity of people to (wisely) engineer broad social change. It is usually easier to identify—and to reach agreement about—what are wrongs (violence against women) than what are desirable solutions to those wrongs. My earlier argument about solutions to the core of the problem, rather then constant, intrusive interventions in its manifestation, does not help in this context. It is the core solution, say, real gender equality, including economic equality, that raises concern about deep transformation—particularly via the law.

Since there is no responsible alternative but to try, is there some guidance as to how to try? The first answer is the humility I just suggested. Another is awareness of unpredictability and thus attentiveness to unforeseen consequences. This might take the form of mechanisms for trying to track significant changes and openness to the need for further adjustments. It might also take the form of recognition of the experience of loss for those who have lost important privileges: for example, those who no longer see their understanding of marriage and family reflected back to them in Canadian law, whose sense of meaning has been significantly disrupted; or men whose sense of authority and entitlement (say to women doing the caretaking in the home) would be significantly disrupted by moves toward equality.[16] The loss of unjust privilege can be a real loss, and acknowledgment of that loss might make the transition easier.[17]

Perhaps the most important thing offered by the relational approach presented here is the contribution to public participation in legal decision making as well as policy deliberation more generally. One answer to the question of how the residential schools could have happened, how (some) well-meaning people could have taught in them and helped to set them up, is also the answer to the question "how could they have known how wrong this was in their historical context?"[18] They could have known if they had respectfully consulted the children or the parents whose children were put into the schools.

If bureaucratic decision making, as in social assistance offices, was designed to respectfully take account of the views of the recipients, some of the worst abuses would disappear. When not just lawyers, but large segments of the population have some sense of how the relations that matter to them are structured by the law, they are better able to participate in public deliberation about transformation. If part of the concern about the relational approach is its potential for social engineering by lawyers and policy experts, part of the answer is that the "relations of freedom and autonomy" I have advocated include a widespread ability to participate in such deliberation. Of course, more than a relational analysis of law would be necessary to achieve such a transformation in knowledge and forms of participation. But I see the relational approach I advocate as contributing to both. This relational approach requires attention to democratic process as well as to results consistent with core values, such as autonomy.

IV. CONTESTED VALUES

In chapter 8, I took up the point that there is nothing simple about core values. From a relational perspective, as from any other, there can be disagreements about the practical meaning of a core value like autonomy, about what to do when the implementation of

that value conflicts with another value, as well as disagreements about the kinds of relationships that would most effectively foster a value. Here I want to say a bit more about
how a relational approach can help resolve these conflicts. Looking back over the chapters, we can see what the approach can and cannot do.

First, my version of a relational approach does not rank order core values in the abstract.
I offer no relationally grounded hierarchy between, say, autonomy, security, dignity, or
equality—as abstract values. In this, my approach is no different from the constitutional
jurisprudence of Canada or the United States or—to expand the framework I have used
in the book—the United Nations Declaration of Human Rights. There is no hierarchy of
rights in the documents nor (formally) in the jurisprudence.[19]

In concrete contexts, however, rights and values can conflict, and judgments of courts
thus must often give one priority over another in that particular context. For this project,
the relational approach is helpful. For example, as we saw in the change to the Canadian
law of sexual assault (chapter 5), the requirement of the accused to show that he had taken
"reasonable steps" to ascertain consent placed an additional burden on the accused and
thus shifted his rights at trial. But the impact on relations of equality of the previously
existing law and its failure to adequately protect women's rights to bodily integrity and
security could be weighed against the way the imposition of this new responsibility
would not only better protect women's security but also shift relations between men and
women toward equality. This analysis is not based on a general ranking of rights of the
accused, security, and equality. It is based on an evaluation of the relational implications
of a particular change in law as it would affect the core values in question. The relational
claim is, in part, that the impact will go far beyond the outcomes of particular trials
without putting defendants significantly at risk—just as the previously existing law
affected not just particular trials but also women's willingness to report rape and prosecutors' willingness to bring cases to trial.

Next, as I said at the outset, the approach I have presented does not include prescriptions
for, or visions of, ideal relations. At the most abstract level, my approach, like liberalism, like
all versions of feminism, begins with a commitment to equality. In that sense, equality is an
ideal. And I have argued that looking at how particular interpretations of rights structure
relations can help us figure out how to move toward equality. But that is not the same thing
as a picture of what optimally equal relations would look like.[20] Many questions remain,
such as the level of economic inequality that can be consistent with political equality or
what kind of equality in education or health care is necessary for full political equality. The
relational approach I have presented offers a framework for analyzing these questions, but
it is not based on a starting point of an ideal picture of equal relations.

Even with autonomy, to which I have devoted a lot of attention here, I do not offer a
picture of the ideal "relations of autonomy." This is in part because the kinds of relations
that will optimally foster autonomy are context-specific. What could work in one bureaucratic context, for example, might not work in another. The relevant power relations
might be different. A relational norm of listening to those whom the decisions will affect

will always be useful, but its practical meaning for the regulators of big pharmaceutical companies will be different from that for caseworkers in social assistance agencies.

The core of my claim is that a relational analysis will consistently reveal what is really at stake in a problem (or case) and that it will add clarity and insight to the task of making judgments about an optimal solution. For example, we have seen that the basic problem in the defense of women who kill their battering partners is that society systematically fails to protect them. And then we can better understand the rationality of their decision to kill in self-defense. But I do not claim that relational analysis yields determinative answers. (No complex system of analysis does.) For example, serious relational feminists might disagree on difficult autonomy problems, such as prostitution and mandatory arrest for people who assault their intimate partners. And there is room for disagreement about the argument I made above about Canadian sexual assault law. A feminist defense lawyer might engage in a relational analysis and argue that those accused of sexual assault would be exposed to a kind of vulnerability (say, to false accusations) that is too high a cost. She might argue that this change would exacerbate the huge power disparity that already exists between the state and persons accused of a crime. As I argued in chapter 1, I think those who differ about the results of a relational analysis will have a more fruitful conversation about the nature of their differences than if they had not used a relational approach; but it doesn't mean they will agree.

Even the kind of nonlegal norms a relational approach should generate is likely to be disputed. For example, as I have already suggested, a relational framework offers a way of tracing the interconnections between household inequalities and economic and political inequalities. But it cannot itself resolve a dispute between those who oppose the (non-legal) constraints of norms about gender equality in intimate relations on grounds of freedom or autonomy and those who advocate it on equal freedom and autonomy grounds. However distorted some of the traditional liberty versus equality disputes have been, I think some forms of them are likely to persist. A relational analysis should always be illuminating, but it cannot be dispositive.

The unavoidability of disagreement does not, of course, prevent me from making relational arguments for the importance of developing norms, such as those of mutual desire and pleasure in sexual relations. It does not prevent me from reflecting on the ways changes in the law (such as the change in the Canadian law of sexual assault) can support shifts in norms (and vice versa). I think the relational arguments are compelling. I do not think they can "prove" that I am right, even to those sympathetic to a relational approach. But, of course, these limitations are not distinctive to the relational approach—as the routine disagreements of judges and scholars demonstrate daily.

Finally, I would note that the contested and competing values I have focused on in this book have largely been "rights-like." Virtually all of them are recognized within Anglo-American law as constitutional values and most as constitutional rights (remember autonomy is not listed as right). One exception is that I have briefly mentioned harmony as a value that some societies might treat as a core value[21] and that might be important to the capacity for creative interaction. Harmony is not a value recognized in Western constitutions, and it cannot easily be cast in terms of an individual right. Unlike freedom of speech, which can fairly easily be understood as both an individual right and a public good, harmony is more obviously a characteristic of social relations.

The relational approach is receptive to such values, which do not have a traditional rights-like structure in the sense that they are obviously something no individual can just "have" and which it therefore sounds a bit odd to describe as an individual entitlement. I think this receptivity is a valuable feature of the approach. Proposals for recognizing a right to a clean environment are becoming more common. One might easily envision environmental sustainability becoming a core value (whether articulated in a constitution or not). The use of rights language with respect to the environment disrupts (as does the relational approach) the distinction between individual rights, on the one hand, and collective goods or welfare concerns, on the other hand. From a relational perspective one might say that it is just more obvious (than, say, with freedom of speech) that individuals can enjoy environmental sustainability only if it is respected and enacted as a public good, that is, if societal relations are structured in such a way as to promote sustainability. As the urgency of environmental concerns becomes increasingly obvious, the relational approach will be a welcoming framework for integrating those concerns into a language of rights that no longer draws sharp distinctions to the collective good.

V. DISRUPTION OF CATEGORIES
A. Rights and Respect for the Relational Individual

I have argued that a relational approach can make existing liberal democratic legal systems work better to protect and implement core values, such as autonomy. This is the "working with the master's tools," dimension, and it is important to me.[22] But, as I just noted, my approach also disrupts some important conventions of Anglo-American legal systems and traditions of legal and political thought. I argue that rights are not best thought of as trumps. The idea of rights as means of structuring relations to promote core values may seem dangerously instrumental from some liberal perspectives. The idea that rights can only have meaning when there are the relational structures that give effect to them disrupts category distinctions, such as rights versus the public good. As we have seen, from my perspective, most rights can only exist for individuals if they exist as structures of relations among people and, thus, also as public goods.

So in conclusion, I return to one of the issues I addressed in chapter 1: these disruptions can give rise to a concern that the individual is no longer properly valued, that the attention to relational structures has a collective quality to it that means that the individual will be subordinated to the collective. If individual rights cannot trump collective projects, what is to protect individuals? (It is useful to remember, as noted in chapter 6, that the American focus on rights as trumps is no longer the model followed by many other constitutional democracies.)

If what is really at stake in these concerns is that each individual is respected in some fundamental way, then that is consistent with my approach. My version of a relational approach is very attentive to and concerned with the particular individual. Indeed, I would say that have I insisted on such attention. Much of the relational approach is a call to attend to the individual in her particularity, which must include her particular context.

The particularity of the individual is well captured by her unique place in the nested webs of relationships she inhabits. The examples in the book help show that no one can know what will serve to recognize and protect a person's dignity, her security, or her equality unless we know where she sits in the structure of relations with which she interacts. Legal and political institutions cannot adequately express respect for her as an individual without attending to this relational context. And they cannot make those values real for her except by shaping the relations that give effect to them.

The examples throughout this book were intended to show that the call to attend to relationship is not a call to subsume individuals in some kind of concern for the collective. It is a call to recognize the structures of relations that give a pattern to the collective, that shape the way collective power is exercised, and to recognize how individuals are differently shaped by these patterns and powers. And since these structures of relations are shaped by collective (as well as individual) decisions, those decisions must be a central focus of the project of giving effect to core values—whether that decision making takes place at what is normally called the political level of legislation or regulation or through the processes of legal interpretation.

Rights have been central to how liberalism expresses and institutionalizes respect for individuals. In this book, I have taken this use of rights and proposed a reorientation. Rights are still to serve this purpose but through an attention to how rights themselves structure the relations that express or deny respect, that foster or undermine autonomy, security, or dignity. Making real the possibility of every individual, in all her embodied uniqueness, enjoying respect, equality, dignity, autonomy, or security is a central concern of my project as it is of liberalism (at least in its egalitarian forms). The difference—of orientation—is that I don't think this can be achieved without a central focus on the structures of relationships in which individuals develop their capacities.

As I noted above, this approach to rights disrupts the sharp distinction between what is an individual value and what is a collective value. Nevertheless (as we saw in chapter 6), institutionally, constitutionalism understood as a dialogue of democratic accountability still treats the traditional individual values—liberty, equality, dignity—as standards against which collective decision making must be held accountable. In this way, it protects individuals (as well as minority groups) against the abuse of power. I have argued that this is both a truer description of how constitutionalism does work and a better way of capturing the aspirations of optimal forms of constitutionalism. In particular, it is better because it fosters democratic deliberation about the meaning of the values that are to function as standards.

The relational approach I have presented does pose a kind of tension between different modes of language used to capture the core values that matter both to individuals and societies. The traditional liberal language speaks of rights as the inherent properties of individuals. My argument does not imply that this is always objectionable; it is a way of expressing the intrinsic, immeasurable worth of each individual. But there are always practical puzzles about how to effectively express and protect this worth. Each of the chapters has provided a different lens through which to see my claim that the best way of understanding how to treat each person with "equal concern and respect"[23] is to understand how the relationships of which they are a part enable the core values that matter to them.

It is, therefore, often more helpful to say that for people to enjoy values such as freedom, they need to be in relations of freedom with each other rather than to assert that each individual has an entitlement to it. Sometimes the entitlement language will sound appropriate (and therefore helpful), such as when making claims against a state on behalf of an individual (who, say, has been imprisoned for political speech). But the problem with entitlement language is that it suggests that freedom is something a person can simply "have" as an individual.

Freedom—or autonomy or dignity or equality or security—is not something an individual can just possess. It is a quality of human relationships that is precious to individuals, without which they cannot fully thrive. And people cannot treat each other in ways that respect values such as freedom, dignity, or equality except in so far as they shape relationships that express these values.

Thus, while people are familiar with language of individual entitlement, it is in part, misleading. It directs our attention to the individual who makes the claim rather than to the relationships that can enable the values claimed. I think the virtue of the language of individual entitlement is that it is good for expressing the idea that people have rights that are unrealized. This language sounds appropriate exactly where the necessary relations do not exist. Thus the "right" is a moral right that exists only as a claim. And it may then seem appropriate to locate that claim within an individual. The problem remains that only a change in relations can make good on that claim, and thus it can never actually be realized only by an individual.[24]

This book has presented critiques and alternatives aimed at answering the question: why go to the trouble of disrupting powerful conventions of thought and language, which have served useful purposes in articulating claims of wrongdoing by states; in trying to figure out what justice entails; in thinking about how to organize state power? The preceding chapters have offered examples of the kinds of problems that arise when relationships are not seen as central, but merely background context, or an object of individual choice, or a byproduct of proximity to others and thus as a reason protection is needed. Put differently, we have seen a variety of problems arise when people's interconnection with and dependence on one another is not seen as an essential human characteristic and thus as not central to legal and political analysis.

We have seen that a failure to attend to interconnection can mean that the fact of dependence on the state (welfare recipients) can be treated as inconsistent with autonomy and, thus, no serious effort made to structure these relations of dependency so as to enhance rather than undermine autonomy (chapter 3). A failure to attend to the ways in which multiple relations in society enable intimate partner violence and make women's escape from it so difficult may lead to confusions about the rationality of women's acts of self-defense (chapter 4). The way in which law shapes relations between men and women is not now a primary subject of legal and political analysis. Efforts to change the way the law shapes those relations can, then, be misunderstood as an expansion of the law and the scope of the state (chapters 5 and 9). The requirement of "taking reasonable steps" to ascertain a person's consent to sexual contact may be misunderstood as a violation of defendants' rights if people are unable to see it as an important means of securing women's bodily integrity—enabled in part through the law's restructuring of relations between men and women. The genuine equality of this requirement may be misconstrued as an inequality if the change in the *mens rea* requirement is not understood in relational context (chapter 5). Another important example, which I have mentioned but not elaborated, is the legal recognition of systemic inequality (chapter 6). This recognition is greatly facilitated by a relational approach.

In sum, these are all examples of why it is worth the disruption and disorientation to shift the focus of rights to the relations they structure—so that they can better do their job giving effect to the values that enhance human life.

B. Implications of Desired Disruptions

The individual versus the collective and the rights versus welfare distinctions are not the only categories disrupted by the relational approach. Indeed, one of its benefits, as well as one of the difficulties it raises, is that it challenges categories and frameworks that have been heavily relied upon in Anglo-American law. Of course, as we saw in chapter 2, it challenges the boundary metaphor that has been so important to the approach to rights. And the conventional public–private distinction is difficult to sustain in light of a full consciousness of how rights shape relationships and relationships are essential to giving effect to rights.[25] (I discuss this in chapter 5.) To say that is not to deny that privacy is a value in a relational approach (see chapter 6). It means rather that matters often thought of as belonging to the private domain (like the distribution of caretaking work) are inextricably linked to public concerns like equality, including equal access to employment and political participation. It also means, conversely, that public practices, like the enforcement of assault law in the context of intimate partner violence, shape "private" relationships, enabling the phenomenon of the battered woman—which, in turn, affects her capacity for public participation.

For related reasons, my version of a relational approach unsettles the conceptions of law and the state and their relations to core values, such as equality. These conceptions, in turn, underlie concepts such as "state action" (or governmental action in the Canadian context) that are still used to determine the question of which practices are subject to judicial review to assess whether they violate the *Charter* or the Constitution.[26] Thus the relational approach offers another challenge to these concepts as providing an inadequate framework for this determination. For example, the question of whether "private law" is considered an act of government or the state for these purposes is complex and convoluted in the dominant jurisprudence. But from a relational perspective, when "private law" (such as property, contract, and tort) shapes relations that are central to the ways people stand in relations of hierarchy or equality to one another, it is not obvious why they should not be held accountable to the core value of equality.[27] Of course, following my argument in chapter 6, it is also not obvious that judicial review is the best form of that accountability. The point is that the categories that have been used for thinking through the appropriate scope of judicial review are disrupted by a relational approach.

I have not tried to offer new ways of articulating what should be understood as private, beyond a gesture in chapter 6 at the ways access to information is part of the nature of a relationship. Similarly, I do not elaborate the implications for judicial review (though I touch on it in chapter 6) or provide an alternative framework for defining the appropriate scope for review. Here I just point to these implications of the book's arguments. By contrast, I do offer alternatives to "rights as trumps" and boundary images for reflecting on the scope of state power. The dialogue of democratic accountability offers a picture of constitutionalism that can check abuse of state power by holding democratic decision making accountable to core values—without treating rights as trumps.

Of course, it is in part my purpose to disrupt the conventions of thought. The point of my argument has been to reveal the kind of shift in perspective that is involved in a relational approach and to see its advantages for basic concepts, such as self, autonomy, and rights. But I have also argued that these advantages extend to the daily practices of law. I have claimed that the relational approach can be used immediately in legal interpretation and policy assessment because law and politics always do structure relations in ways that either foster or undermine core values. Pointing to the disruption of categories highlights the fact that this immediate usefulness coexists with a pressure against the remaining individualism of the dominant legal framework.

Focusing on the relationships that will be shifted by a legal ruling often reveals the limitations of individualistic assumptions that may be embedded in the categories a judge is using (as we saw in the questions of autonomy and responsibility of women accused of murdering their battering partner). A relational approach may also facilitate connections between spheres of the law in which a tacit relational approach has been used and spheres where it is underdeveloped. For example, the recognition of unequal bargaining power in labor relations may be seen in the wider context of contracts routinely shaping and being shaped by power relations, including in the family. For example, this link might be fostered by a relational approach to the example in chapter 1 of a woman signing a form to allow the family home be used as collateral for a loan for her husband's business. The complex problem of consent in that context could be connected to the use of power in divorce negotiations (including the role lawyers play in using custody as a bargaining chip in negotiations over financial settlements). In all these cases, a relational approach would direct attention not just to the power dynamics between the individuals in the case but also to the wider structures of relations that shape those dynamics.

In short, judges can and should use relational analysis even though it will be in tension with some of the concepts and frameworks they use.[28] This tension can be productive, gradually revealing unpersuasive assumptions, questionable categories, and inadequate frameworks.

Judges, theorists, and everyday users of the relational approach can then all contribute to the articulation of alternative categories and frameworks for working through the problems that categories, such as the public versus private dichotomy, were once thought to illuminate. When people recognize the complex interpenetration of law, rights, and relations, they can take on the questions of how the law should be used and what kinds of things state power is well suited to organize (as well as what kinds of issues judicial review is well suited to). These are not small questions. But, of course, the relational approach does not itself create these puzzles. It points to the inadequacy of categories, such as public versus private, individual rights versus the public good, or state versus the market,[29] as tools for analyzing them.

The relational approach helps reveal the ways law has helped create the problems to be solved—and thus the many ways the state is already an actor in problems such as violence against women. The relational approach then helps us to see when the real question is whether law should structure relations differently than it currently does, and when the question is whether the state (via law) should enter a realm from which it has been absent or leave a sphere (such as marriage) it has long occupied.

As I discussed in chapter 8, the relational approach thus helps to clarify what is really at stake in the long vexed subject of state power. Those who are concerned about an expansion of state power often do not recognize the ways the state is already present. This is particularly true with respect to so-called private law, such as property and contract.[30] For example, people sometimes think of environmental regulation as a new intrusive form of state power controlling what they can do with their property. But it is really a question of existing law governing the rights associated with ownership being changed. It seems like a new entry of the state because the existing law was taken for granted as a given, as an appropriate and rights-based baseline from which the regulation is deviating. But, of course, the existing private law had been shaping relations all along.

I said above that sometimes the question is whether the state should enter a realm from which it has been absent. But, in fact, it is hard to think of an example in states like Canada or the United States. In most cases, there is preexisting law of some kind. It normally takes some kind of new phenomenon for there to be a true legal vacuum. For example, when radio broadcasting became widespread, this became a sphere of new state control via regulation. The Internet also may provide for new spheres of legal action—though here, too, the issue may be between the application of existing law (which may not fit well) or the creation of new forms of private law (such as property) or a regulatory structure or even criminal law, as in the case of child pornography.

Of course, from a relational perspective, as from most perspectives, it matters what form the law takes. Some forms, as I have noted earlier, are more intrusive, and some may be better subject to democratic control than others. There are a wide variety of questions about how different forms of law will structure relations. And as I noted in chapter 1, sometimes law can be used to reallocate power from one nonstate actor to another (as in the example of shifting control of pension funds) rather than to shift it from private to public control. Sometimes a change in law will withdraw monopoly power (as in the case of telephone companies) with the result that less public regulation is necessary. The law will then delegate power to private companies and the market. Sometimes, as in the dismantling of segregation in the American south, private property rights (to exclude blacks from restaurants) come under the control of constitutional norms of equality. These shifts should always be assessed in relational terms. But it is unlikely to be helpful to try to measure whether they add up to more or less law and, thus, more or less engagement with the state. A relational approach can help assess the advantages and disadvantages of relying on, say, power delegated to private companies rather than public regulation. But, again, it rarely will be useful to claim that one is a form of state power and that the other (structured by laws of property and contract) is not.

I have, as I noted earlier, tried to respond to the concern about the scope of state power. But, in the end, I think the relational approach is one more way of seeing that the real question is rarely whether the state is there or not. Traditionally, people have seen the state as the most important threat to liberty (or in Shklar's case, the most potent source of the threat of cruelty). And the puzzles of democratic control of state power are difficult ones (especially in the face of systemic inequality organized around wealth as well as such categories as gender and race). But it has long been recognized that the power allocated by the state to "private" entities, such as corporations, can create a form of concentrated power as dangerous to the relations of freedom and autonomy as the direct exercise of state power. Often it is the state's job to try to control that power to protect freedom and equality. The relational approach is, as I have said, one more way of reflecting thoughtfully about how state power should be exercised, how the law should structure relations.

Fears of state power can be corrosive and distort policy debates, as in the case of health care in the United States.[31] As always, a relational analysis would not dispel the depth of conflict around the issue. But one might hope for a more constructive debate based on an inquiry into the consequences of the different ways law has and could structure the relations affected by health care systems—rather than a misguided preoccupation with the presence or absence of the state.

In sum, having helped reveal the important questions and recurring puzzles of law in the modern state, a consistent focus on the relational dimension of human life can illuminate new and better ways of resolving them.

NOTES

INTRODUCTION

1. At the end of this introduction I comment on the use of the term "we." I preview it here with my first use of the term. In many places in the text I have avoided the use of the term "we," in order not make presumptions about what I and my diverse audiences share with one another. But in some contexts, I find the alternatives, such as "people," "they," or "one," rather distancing. These terms tacitly invite the reader to imagine that I am talking to and about *other* people. Thus sometimes when I particularly want the reader to imagine him- or herself as part of the proposal or claim I make, I use "we," despite the risk of presumption.

2. By liberalism I mean a tradition of political thought that, from a relational perspective, is too individualistic. I do not mean the distinction between "liberal" and "conservative" as these terms are used in the context of popular politics and political parties.

3. See note 3 in chapter 3.

4. O'Donovan, "With Sense, Consent, or Just a Con," 63.

5. Ibid.

6. Ibid.

7. See, for example, Brown and Halley, *Left Legalism, Left Critique.*

8. See note 14 below on egalitarian liberals.

9. Nussbaum, *Frontiers of Justice,* 91.

10. Ibid., 86.

11. See chapter 1, note 27 and accompanying text.

12. See, for example, the selection of quotes from *A Theory of Justice* in Michelman, "Rawls on Constitutionalism and Constitutional Law," 399. In chapter 4, section II.A, I discuss my own version of a formal dimension to equality.

13. Rawls, *Theory of Justice*. Rawls did not himself take up that invitation with respect to the role of "private law."

14. Among the best known egalitarian liberals who engage with these issues are Ronald Dworkin, Owen Fiss, Will Kymlicka, Frank Michelman, Joseph Raz, Cass Sunstein, and Jeremy Waldron. For some of them, one can see an increasing attention to relational concerns in their later work.

15. I was happy to read that the editors of the major anthology on relational autonomy found that, "As far as we know, Jennifer Nedelsky was the first to articulate a conception of relational autonomy from an explicitly feminist perspective" (see MacKenzie and Stoljar, *Relational Autonomy*, 26). But versions of a social self have been around for a long time. Colleagues have often pointed out the correspondence between my work and that of George Herbert Mead (1863–1931) and Georg Simmel (1858–1918).

16. Friedman, "Autonomy, Social Disruption, and Women," 40.

17. I see this as also part of Friedman's project.

18. In chapter 1, sections IV.A.i and iii, I take up the general question of the extent to which the relational approach is primarily methodological or whether it has substantive values built into it.

19. See Borrows, *Recovering Canada* and *Drawing Out Law*; Johnston, *Litigating Identity*; Napolean, "Aboriginal Self Determination," "Living Together," and "Looking beyond the Law"; Kennedy, "Reconciliation without Respect?" For scholarship that looks beyond the context of North America, see Kuokkanen, *Reshaping the University*.

20. See, for example, Wingo, "Akan Philosophy of the Person," on different interpretations of the conception of the person in the tradition of the Akan people of West Africa. My thanks to Jane Mansbridge for directing me to this article.

21. "After this concern for the integrity of the earth, the next concern is to see the human self as an integral member of the earth community, not some lordly being free to plunder the earth for human utility. The issue of interhuman tensions is secondary to earth-human tensions. If humans will not become functional members of the earth community, how can humans establish functional relationships among themselves?" Berry, *Dream of the Earth*, 219.

22. I use the term "affective" despite its relative unfamiliarity because the word "emotional" has strong connotations that mean something other than the capacity for emotion.

23. This is George Kateb's description of Shklar's argument in Kateb, "Judith Shklar (1928–1992)."

CHAPTER 1

1. See the introduction in Nussbaum, *Women and Human Development*.

2. Additional relevant questions are: Is there a dissonance between what she learns at school and what is modeled in the relations around her? If she comes from a low-income family, does she live in a place where postsecondary education is affordable? Where she can earn enough in a summer to pay tuition? What are the relations of social mobility she sees around her? If there is a serious economic downturn and her father loses his job, will she be expected to quit school and work to support her brothers? Children are shaped by teacher–student relations: are they authoritarian; is fear a much used incentive?

3. See the introduction in Ehrenreich and Hochschild, *Global Woman*.

4. McLeod, "A Feminist Relational Perspective on Conscience."

5. Mill, *On Liberty*, 12.

6. Statistics from the Canadian Centre for Justice Statistics (Statistics Canada) indicate that 37 percent of spousal assaults are witnessed by children; 70 percent of this violence was directed at mothers. Trainor and Mihorean, "Family Violence in Canada: A Statistical Profile 2001," 19. Furthermore, "In half of cases of spousal violence against women that were witnessed by children, the woman feared for her life." Johnson, *Measuring Violence against Women*, 13. The costs of witnessing violence as a child are profound: "The impacts on children living in a violent home can stay with them over the longer term and can result in a continuation of violence through generations" Ibid., 32. Moreover, the "costs to families and to society that result from children being exposed to violence against a parent can be severe and can include psychological, social, cognitive and behavioural maladjustment problems." Ibid., 33. See also footnote 13.

7. See chapter 5, note 63.

8. See Kuypers, *Man's Will to Hurt*.

9. For a compelling picture of sexual abuse of female children in rural America, see Jane Smiley's novel *A Thousand Acres* (1991).

10. Of course this is true for all the others in my position, which for these purposes includes those who rent apartments as well as those who literally own property.

11. Martin Niemöller, cited in Novick, *The Holocaust in American Life*, 221. Martin Niemöller was a German pastor and theologian; this quotation has been described as a "confession of his moral failure during the 1930s" (221).

12. Audre Lorde has a version of this saying: "I am not free while any woman is unfree, even when her shackles are very different from my own." Lorde, "The Uses of Anger," 132–133.

13. The negative effects of being exposed to violence in childhood are well documented. Psychological damage to children who directly witness violence manifests in the form of neuropsychiatric problems (i.e., attachment problems, eating disorders, depression, suicidal behavior) that may begin at childhood but persist into adulthood. Perry and Azad, "Posttraumatic Stress Disorders in Children and Adolescents," 312. Furthermore, children exposed to violence, whether at home, in the community, or through popular media, can experience a persisting fear or threat of violence that "alter[s] the development of the child's brain, resulting in changes in physical, emotional, behavioral, cognitive and social functioning." Perry, "Neurodevelopmental Adaptations to Violence," 2. Examples of this include a predisposition to violence and a persistent stress-response state; notably, there is a marked gender difference associated with this impact: males are more likely to display classic "fight or flight" responses while females are more likely to dissociate. Ibid., 4.

Negative effects of exposure to violence are not limited to childhood. Adults who experience or learn about a traumatic event face challenges to their sense of safety, leading to feelings of vulnerability and powerlessness, which can take the form of "horror, anger, sadness, humiliation, and guilt." Such exposure can also affect their coping resources, causing them to avoid thoughts and feelings associated with the traumatic event. Yehuda, "Post-Traumatic Stress Disorder." In the context of community violence, the limited research on adults exposed to violence suggests that age does not necessarily decrease the likelihood of developing PTSD in response to violence. Brown, Hill, and Lambert, "Traumatic Stress Symptoms in Women Exposed to Community and Partner Violence," 1481.

14. Of course, as I note throughout the book, exactly what equality means and how it should be implemented in law is widely and strongly contested.

15. Easton, "Survival of the Richest," 2.

16. Yeatman, "What Can Disability Tell Us about Participation?" 189.

17. See, for example, Nussbaum, *Frontiers of Justice*.

18. MacIntyre, *Dependent Rational Animals*. He particularly notes the important work of Eva Feder Kittay, *Love's Labor* (1999).

19. MacIntyre, *Dependent Rational Animals*, 1.

20. See Arendt and Beiner, *Lectures on Kant's Political Philosophy*.

21. In part two, Kittay elaborates the various dimensions of Rawls's theory that fail to ensure that those with dependency obligations include them in their justice reasoning as well as the disadvantage to those who do and thus are unable to consider only their own advantage as others do. Rawls says, for example, that the "assumption of mutually disinterested rationality, then, comes to this: the persons in the original position try to acknowledge principles which advance their system of ends as far as possible. They do this by attempting to win for themselves the highest index of primary social goods.... The parties do not seek to confer benefits...on one another; they are not moved by affection." Rawls, *Theory of Justice*, 144. Kittay also considers the problem of those cognitive impairments. (Nussbaum elaborates this latter problem in *Frontiers of Justice*.) One need not accept every step of Kittay's argument to see that Rawls's *Theory of Justice* does not adequately deal with the problem of dependency and dependency workers. Kittay, *Love's Labor*; Rawls, *Theory of Justice*.

22. Abrams, "Choice, Dependence, and the Reinvigoration of the Traditional Family," 533.

23. Thus societies should be moving toward a universal caregiver model rather than either a universal breadwinner model (which she sees prevailing in North America) or a caregiver parity model, which she sees as prevailing in Europe, and which one might see as the outcome of Kittay's proposals. Fraser, "After the Family Wage," quoted from *Justice Interruptus: Critical Reflections on the Postsocialist Condition* (New York: Routledge, 1997).

24. See Ruddick, *Maternal Thinking*, on the skills necessary for good mothering and what one learns (as well as teaches) from skillful mothering. See Tronto, *Moral Boundaries*, for what is still one of the most sophisticated engagements with care, including what good caring requires.

25. One of the sad failures of social relations in contemporary North America is the absence of norms of connection between overwhelmed parents and people who would like to have a close relationship with a child but do not have one of their own. Swedish Social Services runs an innovative program called Contact Person/Contact Family, which supplements traditional social work services by linking single parents with community members "offering support and relief to parents in need." Andersson, "Support and Relief," 61. Contact persons/families are provided a nominal stipend by the Swedish government and are not required to have professional qualifications as social workers in order to participate. Ibid., 55.

It is worth noting that despite the progressiveness of the program, the service seems to reinforce gender roles around caretaking: Andersson describes the program as being intended to relieve mothers, and most of those enrolled in the program as contact people are women. Ibid., 52.

26. For a brilliant exposition of the evolution of the Western conception of the separate self see Keller, *From a Broken Web*.

27. Nussbaum, *Women and Human Development*, 56–57. Nussbaum does say that the core idea "is that of the human being as a dignified free being who shapes his or her life in cooperation and reciprocity with others" (72). And in her later work, *Frontiers of Justice*, she takes up Kittay's work.

28. This is from the above quote. Nussbaum, *Women and Human Development*, 56–57.

29. Arendt, *The Human Condition*, 231–232.

30. Ibid., 233.

31. Ibid., 9, 11.

32. Winter, "Indeterminacy and Incommensurability in Constitutional Law," 1486.

33. I discuss care theory in section IV.D of this chapter.

34. The same is true for whatever differences may currently exist in how men and women take relationships into account in their thought processes or their values and preferences.

35. A classic invocation of this value and how it needs relations that support it is Virginia Woolf's essay *A Room of One's Own* (1929).

36. Free speech is an area in which there has been a lot of attention to the social dimension of the right. For example, Owen Fiss wrote that free speech "is predicated on a theory of the First Amendment and its guarantee of free speech that emphasizes social, rather than individualistic, values. The freedom the state may be called upon to foster is a public freedom. Although some view the First Amendment as a protection of the individual interest in self-expression, a far more plausible theory, first formulated by Alexander Meiklejohn and now embraced all along the political spectrum, from Robert Bork to William Brennan, views the First Amendment as a protection of popular sovereignty. The law's intention is to broaden the terms of public discussion as a way of enabling common citizens to become aware of the issues before them and of the arguments on all sides and thus to pursue their ends fully and freely." Fiss, *The Irony of Free Speech*, 2–3. For a discussion of the complexities of determining what are individualistic concerns and what are matters of enabling "social-structural conditions" (98), see Michelman, *Brennan and Democracy*, esp. 97–119. See also Raz, *Ethics in the Public Domain*, on free speech as a public good. I develop this argument later in this chapter in section III.C.

37. As she sees it, "relations of freedom" are only possible only within political community. Zerilli, *Feminism and the Abyss of Freedom*. For me, what matters is that freedom is understood as something individuals cannot "have" unless they stand in relations of freedom with others. While Zerilli is interested in political freedom, and the claim is clearest in that context, I think one could expand even a highly internal notion of freedom to examine the kind of relations that support its development. In any case, the point here has to do with the kinds of freedom to which people claim rights.

An example of a highly internal notion of freedom would be one associated with Buddhism. Jon Kabat-Zinn says the challenge is to "bring awareness to our moments as best we can, in even little and fleeting ways. [And] to sustain our awareness and come to know it better.... When we do, we see thoughts liberate themselves, even in the midst of sorrow, as when we reach out and touch a soap bubble. Puff. It is gone. We see sorrow liberate itself.... In this freedom, we can meet anything and everything with greater openness." But he also invokes what I would call relational support: "Yet to do so, practically speaking, over the course of a lifetime, usually requires some kind of overarching framework that gives us a place to begin, recipes to try out, maps to follow, wise reminders to give ourselves, all the benefits of other people's hard-won experience and knowledge." *Coming to Our Senses*, 92.

38. This is in opposition to Ronald Dworkin's famous conception of (individual) human rights as trumps over other justifications for political decisions within a community. Dworkin, *Taking Rights Seriously*.

39. I discuss this term further in chapter 7.

40. See the beginning of section I.C, above, and MacIntyre, *Dependent Rational Animals*.

41. Winter, "Indeterminacy and Incommensurability in Constitutional Law."

42. Lacey, *Women, Crime, and Character*, 49. Lacey also refers to the wider background of historical development of conceptions of the self traced by Charles Taylor, who "has shown how the key elements of modern individual self-hood—most notably for our purposes the idea of self-hood as involving a sense of 'inwardness' which generates the distinction between subject and object and the reflexivity of human being as self-interpreting creatures—were assembled, gradually and unevenly, over many centuries from Aristotle on" (25).

43. Ibid., 28. She is drawing the term "ancien regime" from Wahrman, *Making of the Modern Self*.

44. Lacey, *Women, Crime, and Character*, 26.

45. I thank Iffat Sujad for suggesting this language.

46. Government-run workability/employability programs, for example, are intended to provide welfare recipients with skills, knowledge, and other tools to secure and successfully maintain steady employment in order that recipients might support themselves and their families. However, Mosher et al. discovered that, for abused women, such workability programs presented multiple obstacles to autonomy, including "the ways that workfare discounts and devalues the work women do in caring for children, pays little attention to impediments (child care, health) to employment, while ignoring their strong commitment to employment, their specific aspirations, and the realities of the low-wage labour market. It is usually experienced as coercive and, very rarely, helpful." Mosher et al., "Walking on Eggshells," 21.

47. See ibid.

48. *Wyman v. James*, 400 U.S. 309 (1971), though not using the term autonomy. See next section for further discussion.

49. Of course, the protection is not perfect. During the McCarthy period in the United States, professors at some public universities were subjected to loyalty oath requirements passed by state legislatures. Some lost their jobs as a result of their principled refusal to take these oaths. See for example, Blauner, *Resisting McCarthyism*.

50. I return to this issue briefly in sections II.E and III.A of this chapter and in detail in chapter 3, section VI.

51. In Ontario, young children are tested to see if they can access programs for "gifted students," but failure to qualify does not cut them out of classes aimed at preparation for university.

52. Even within broad agreement about the kind of equal relations that are necessary, there will always be disagreement about exactly what is required and what constitutes a violation of equality rights.

53. Raz, *Ethics in the Public Domain*.

54. Perhaps this is why it is one of the concepts most fully elaborated in relational terms by feminist scholars. See MacKenzie and Stoljar, *Relational Autonomy*.

55. Nedelsky, "Judgment and Autonomy."

56. Walker, *Moral Contexts*, 194. She also notes, tellingly, the wide variety of philosophers whose views are shaped around a career self: "In John Rawls's theory of justice as fairness, a signal achievement of the century, Rawls conceives of a person as a human life lived according to a plan. He sees a person's good as determined by the most rational long-term plan of life for that person. Bernard William, a strong objector to Rawls's idea of the planned life, thinks of human lives in terms of 'constitutive projects,' important commitments and attachments that

carry us into the future with a reason for living. Alasdair MacIntyre, harshly critical of many facets of modern thought, describes a human self as the subject of a lifelong narrative that gets meaning from the climax toward which it moves. Charles Taylor, both critic and interpreter of the modern sensibility, endorses MacIntyre's idea of an individual life as a 'quest.' He judges those whose lives as a whole do not sustain a meaningful narrative severely: he says that have failed as persons.

"What is revealing in these otherwise ethically diverse views is the repetition of the idea of an individual's life as self-consciously controlled career. It binds a whole life or lifetime together in a unified way for which the individual is accountable. The individual's ability to account for this life—to bring forward its plan, project, or narrative plot—testifies to the individual's self-control. The imagery in each case recycles the cultural theme of autonomous agency, with its self-conscious individual enterprise." Ibid.

57. Ibid., 196
58. Ibid., 191.
59. Ibid., 192.
60. Ibid.
61. According to Sherry Sullivan,

In the last two decades, managers, older workers, and the more educated—those typically less affected by downsizing—have experienced the highest job loss rates from organizational restructuring. Many of these individuals are now underemployed or working one or two part-time jobs.... Those surviving these recent rounds of downsizing have also had to adjust; many individuals have increased job responsibilities and working hours, and reduced promotional opportunities [...]

The psychological employment contract between firms and workers has also altered. Under the old contract, workers exchanged loyalty for job security. Under the new contract, workers exchange performance for continuous learning and marketability. This change in the psychological contract has resulted in decreased job security, decreased employee loyalty, and increased worker cynicism.... Workers outside of the traditional career model, who have "boundaryless careers" [defined in the article as "a sequence of job opportunities that go beyond the boundaries of a single employment setting"] are becoming the norm rather than the exception.

Sullivan, "Changing Nature of Careers," 457–458.

62. Walker, *Moral Contexts*, 190. Sarah Hoagland offers a thoughtful critique of the term and offers an alternative: autokoenony. "I mean to invoke a self who is both separate and related, a self which is neither autonomous nor dissolved: a self in community who is one among many." Hoagland, *Lesbian Ethics*, 12.

63. See Radin, *Contested Commodities*, for a thoughtful discussion of these puzzles.

64. I explore these issues in "Judgment and Autonomy."

65. See, for example, Tamara Pierce's novels, the Alana series "The Song of the Lioness," in particular, about a girl who becomes a knight.

66. I have in mind the sort of stories one hears on the news and in magazines. For a deeply thoughtful example see Dorothy Allison's brilliant autobiographical essays "Context" and "A Question of Class" in *Skin*.

67. Of course, there are also disturbing male narratives of autonomy. Marilyn Friedman offers an excellent discussion of the heroic figure of the artist Gauguin abandoning his family to pursue his art. Friedman, "Autonomy, Social Disruption, and Women." Even when such abandonment is not valorized and romanticized, it is generally overlooked or forgiven for male artists (including authors). Jennifer Donnelly's coming-of-age novel *A Gathering Light* explores these tensions between autonomy and family commitment for women. The protagonist's dying mother extracts a promise from the young woman, and another character describes it this way: "She lost her life, and took yours." This novel also highlights the dangers of women challenging cultural expectations. The author succeeds in portraying the role of law in shaping the relations (such as the power of husbands) that constrain the protagonist. It would make a very interesting study to compare such novels across cultures and time to see the different roles and images of autonomy.

68. See also Friedman, "Autonomy, Social Disruption, and Women," 37.

69. In chapter 8 I discuss the question of whether autonomy is best understood as an individual characteristic, or as something that exists among people as "relations of autonomy." In that chapter I also introduce the idea of a field of autonomy.

70. Clement, *Care, Autonomy, and Justice*, 23.

71. Even the aspiration to control one's self does not reflect a loving, respectful stance toward oneself. It implies a battle and a victory in which one part of oneself successfully "masters" another. My thanks to Jess Eisen for this point.

72. See Kompridis, *Critique and Disclosure*, 199–209 for a discussion of the importance of receptivity.

73. I discuss later the implications of my belief that all life-forms possess this capacity in some degree. It is essential to life.

74. Arendt, *Human Condition*, 246. She continues, "Action is, in fact, the one miracle-working faculty of man, as Jesus of Nazareth, whose insights into this faculty can be compared in their originality and unprecedentedness with Socrates' insights into the possibilities of thought, must have known very well when he likened the power to forgive to the more general power of performing miracles, putting both on the same level and within the reach of man. The miracle that saves the world...is, in other words, the birth of new men and the new beginning, the action they are capable of by virtue of being born.... It is this faith in and hope for the world that found perhaps its most glorious and most succinct expression in the few words with which the Gospels announced their 'glad tidings': 'A child has been born unto us.'" (246–247). In the theology of my small faith community (Bathurst Street United Church, Toronto), the miracle of Jesus's birth is the miracle of every birth.

75. Winnicott quoted in Davis and Wallbridge, *Boundary and Space*, 65. I thank my friend Donna Freireich for first directing me to Winnicott.

76. Ibid., 64–65.

77. Ibid., 64.

78. Ibid., 63–65.

79. Ibid., 169.

80. Ibid., 167.

81. Keller, *A Feeling for the Organism*.

82. Jackson, *Regulating Reproduction*, 6.

83. I do, however, think that even thoughtful feminists sometimes make claims about defining one's own identity in ways that radically understate the relational nature of human beings. For

example, Beth Jamieson writes, "freedom depends on the argument that identity is best generated internally rather than imposed." Jamieson, *Real Choice*, 68. Drucilla Cornell, while clearly recognizing the inevitability of social construction, seems to make a similar argument in *At the Heart of Freedom*. While one can hardly endorse external imposition, the invocation of internal definition of identity needs, in my view, to be placed in relational context. As I say at the end of this section on Relational Autonomy, I think Judith Butler gets it right: "One can only determine 'one's own' sense of gender to the extent that social norms exist that support and enable that act of claiming gender for oneself. One is dependent on this 'outside' to lay claim to what is one's own. The self must, in this way, be dispossessed in sociality in order to take possession of itself." Butler, *Undoing Gender*, 7. The idea of "one's own" continues to make sense in my relational approach, but only if one is attentive to what makes claiming it possible.

84. See the Introduction in MacKenzie and Stoljar, *Relational Autonomy*, for an excellent overview of such debates.

85. I elaborate this rejection of property as the central metaphor in chapter 2. But I am intrigued by the obvious link between the term "one's own" and property. The same word is used to describe the relationship to material property, "ownership," and an autonomous relationship to a belief, choice, or value as "one's own. I understand that the same similarity exists in Spanish and French. It would be interesting to test this across a wider range of languages.

86. She made this point at a workshop on my manuscript in May 2008.

87. In addition to my own work, I have used, among others, essays by Marilyn Friedman ("Autonomy, Social Disruption, and Women") and Linda Barclay ("Autonomy and the Social Self") as well as Susan J. Brison ("Outliving Oneself: Trauma, Memory, and Personal Identity.")

88. *R. v. Lavallee*, [1990] 1 S.C.R. 852.

89. See Keller, *From a Broken Web*, on the link between conceptions of self and God.

90. See, for example, Kennedy, "Reconciliation without Respect?"; Borrows, *Drawing Out Law*; Simpson, "Looking after Gdoo-Naaganinaa"; Monture, *Journeying Forward*; and Johnson, *Two Families*.

91. See the essays in Downie and Llewellyn, *Being Relational*.

92. Brian Goodwin discusses the last example in the context of self-organization: "the capacity of…fields to generate patterns spontaneously [though predictably] without any specific instructions telling them what to do, as in a genetic program….What exists in the field is a set of relationships among the components of the system such that the dynamically stable state into which it goes naturally…has spatial and temporal patterns." Goodwin, *How the Leopard Changed Its Spots*, 51–52.

93. This paragraph is a very brief summary of a longer argument I make in "The Trap of Social Determinism: Insights for Contemporary Science and Theology," available from the author. In this essay I also use modern theologians as sources for a framework of relational conditions of creativity. They have tried to find language that captures the creative capacity of both Creator and humans in ways that do not invoke an unmoved (unconnected, unresponsive) mover.

94. Arendt, *Human Condition*, 246.

95. See Jane Bennett's discussion of "lively matter" in her *Vibrant Matter*.

96. See Beiner and Nedelsky, *Judgment, Imagination and Politics*.

97. See Nedelsky, "Judgment, Diversity, and Relational Autonomy" and "Communities of Judgment and Human Rights."

98. The reciprocal relation argument is drawn from Nedelsky, "Judgment and Autonomy."

99. For a discussion of these and other categories see the introduction to MacKenzie and Stoljar, *Relational Autonomy*.

100. Hirschmann, *Subject of Liberty*, 39.

101. Ibid., 236. I would add that this quote doesn't seem to engage directly with Hirschmann's own standards of internal freedom. I'm not sure how far apart her notion of internal freedom is from autonomy. At some point an absence of internal freedom will make her unwilling to accept just any answer as a free one.

102. She discusses the inherently disruptive nature of critical thinking in Arendt, "Thinking and Moral Considerations."

103. See Flathman, *Freedom and Its Conditions*, 163: "On the conception of freedom accepted and promoted here, that is, freedom of action and autonomy or a robust independence, forms of discipline—and the capacity for resistance that they create and help to sustain—that are in some meaningful sense adopted and maintained by the agent herself are more compatible with and contributive to her freedoms than those that are adopted and imposed on her by other agents and agencies."

104. Ibid., 169. William Connolly also uses the image of "self-artistry" in his relational account of the self: "The goal of self as modest artist of itself needs to be neither to discover a true self underneath those sedimented layers nor to create the self anew entirely by oneself." Connolly, *Why I Am Not a Secularist*, 150.

105. Sherwin, *Politics of Women's Health*, 33.

106. Butler, *Undoing Gender*, 7.

107. Mosher et al., "Walking on Eggshells."

108. Ibid.

109. *Falkiner v. Ontario* (Ministry of Community and Social Services), (2002), 212 D.L.R. (4th) 633.

110. See chart, ibid., at para. 77.

111. "Beyond purely financial concerns, more fundamental dignity interests of the respondents have been affected. Being reclassified as a spouse forces the respondents and other single mothers in similar circumstances to give up either their financial independence or their relationship. Many women, including three of the respondents in this appeal, have been victimized by alcoholic or abusive partners. Forcing them to become financially dependent on men with whom they have, at best, try on relationships strikes at the core of their human dignity." Ibid., at para. 101. He also noted that "the administration of the definition [of spouse] is highly intrusive of the privacy of single persons on social assistance. They are subject to heightened scrutiny of the personal relationships. They are required to complete a detailed questionnaire on their personal living arrangements." Ibid., at para. 104.

112. I discuss related cases *Goldberg v. Kelly*, 397 U.S. 254 (1970), and *Wyman v. James*, 400 U.S. 309 (1971), in chapter 3, section IV.

113. There is brief discussion of such differences in chapter 6, section I.A.

114. Christianity and Culture Program, St. Michael's College, University of Toronto. Discussion at the Faculty of Law Alumni Speakers series, University of Toronto, October, 2006.

115. The women in these situations are sometimes referred to as "surety wives"; see chapter 7 note 68.

116. *Royal Bank of Scotland v. Etridge*, [2001] UKHL 44 at para. 10.

117. Borrows, "Indian Agency," 16.

118. This issue is sometimes referred to as "the relative autonomy of the law." Yavar Hameed and Niiti Simmonds, for example, chastise the "appalling logic of our Courts in summarily and repeatedly rejecting the permeation of social and economic rights into the interpretation and application of the *Charter*" but observe that "in fairness to the Courts, however, they are loath to order ameliorative measures for social programs and to place positive obligations upon the State against the legislative backdrop of anti-vagrancy laws, trespass statutes and strong values of protection of private property and liberal notions of rights and freedoms." Hameed and Simmonds, "The *Charter*, Poverty Rights and the Space Between," 201. They point to the "political sphere" as providing a context for activism where "the question of dignity of the poor is not theoretical" (202).

119. See, for example, the introduction to Brown and Halley, *Left Legalism, Left Critique*.

120. See, for example, Eva Feder Kittay's *Love's Labor*, an excellent book on the responsibility for care, which calls for direct state action, and Nancy Fraser's invocation (not elaborated) of community-based responses to the need for child care in "After the Family Wage."

121. Davis, *Democratizing Pension Funds*. He opens his introduction with the following: "In 1976, Peter Drucker proclaimed that the United States had become the first truly socialist country because the ownership of the means of production by the workers had been achieved. He claimed that employees in the private sector owned at least 25 percent of American business' equity capital through their pension funds, while employees in public and non-profit institutions beneficially owned another 10 percent. Collectively, that was sufficient to provide them with control" (3).

122. The Supreme Court of Canada recently considered another exemption to the law of assault. In the so-called "spanking case" (*Canadian Foundation for Children, Youth and the Law v. Canada*, [2004] 1 S.C.R. 76), the Court upheld section 43 of *the Criminal Code*, which suspended the operation of the laws of assault in some cases where children were the victims: "Every schoolteacher, parent or person standing in the place of a parent is justified in using force by way of correction toward a pupil or child, as the case may be, who is under his care, if the force does not exceed what is reasonable under the circumstances." *Criminal Code*, R.S.C. 1985, chap. C-46, sec. 43. While the majority upheld the provision, Justices Binnie and Deschamps argued forcefully that the provision violated the dignity and equality of children and designated them as "second-class citizens" (at paras. 72, 109, 231). In Justice Binnie's view, "Few things are more demeaning and disrespectful of fundamental values than to withdraw the full protection of the *Criminal Code* against deliberate, forcible, unwanted violation of an individual's physical integrity" (at para. 106; Justice Binnie, however, found the violation ultimately justifiable). Justice Deschamps further posited that the provision "perpetuates the notion of children as property rather than human beings and sends the message that their bodily integrity and physical security are to be sacrificed to the will of their parents, however misguided" (at para. 231).

123. Siegel, "'The Rule of Love': Wife Beating as Prerogative and Privacy."

124. See chapter 5, section V.

125. Römkens, "Law as Trojan Horse," 285.

126. Stephen Waddams explains that the phrase "common law" has "a variety of meanings, according to the subject with which it is contrasted." Waddams, *Introduction to the Study of Law*, 75. In this case, I have contrasted common law with legislation. Waddams describes the meaning of 'common law' in this context as follows: "Common law is that area of law still largely dependent on judicial decisions, as opposed to areas of the law governed mostly by statute. Thus,

one can call contracts and torts common law subjects in a sense that income tax is not" (75). My point above is that this distinction is not important to my argument here. Nor is my argument specific to common law as it is defined by the other oppositions identified by Waddams: (1) common law as a legal tradition, as opposed to civil law (with common law as "a system of law based primarily on judicial decisions as contrasted with a system based on Roman law (usually, but not always codified))" (75); or (2) common law as opposed to the law of equity (two parallel sources of law within the common law legal tradition) (75, chapter 8). All of these oppositions fall within the broader realm of state-based law, which is what I mean when I refer to "law."

127. To say this is not to say that everyone uses the language of rights, even in the United States. John Gilliom conducted interviews with fifty welfare recipients in Appalachian Ohio. He found that, "for these women...the interplay of law, everyday life, and individual experience do not make a mix in which rights talk is a central theme as they struggle with welfare surveillance.... The law surrounds them as rules, as threats, and as commands; it is there as police officers, caseworkers, lawyers, and fraud control investigators; it is there in constructing their status as dependents of the state. The law is all over, but...rights are not all over. These emancipatory, empowering, entitling elements of our legal system evade the women studied here and rarely emerge in their ways of speaking or acting about their problems." Gilliom, *Overseers of the Poor*, 11, quoted in White and Tronto, "Political Practices of Care," 438.

128. "We should understand our entitlements as obligations we owe others with whom we are in relationship.... The shape and character we want those relationships to have...will determine the legitimacy of any property regime.... The scope of power we give owners gets its legitimacy for the relationships it enables and the forms of social life it creates. It gets its limits the same way. Owners have entitlements, but they also have obligations. The mix of entitlements and obligations we can legitimately claim depends on the kinds of human relationships we can defend, nothing more and nothing less" Singer, *Entitlement*, 216.

129. Williams, *Alchemy of Race and Rights*.

130. See Macaulay, "An Empirical View of Contract," and Macneil, "Relational Contract."

131. "Their importance to the common good, rather than their contribution to the well-being of the right holder, justifies the high regard in which such rights are held and the fact that their defense many involve a considerable cost to the welfare of many people. When people are called upon to make substantial sacrifices in the name of one of the fundamental civil and political rights of an individual, this is not because in some matters the interest of the individual or the respect due to the individual prevails over the interest of the collectivity or of the majority. It is because by protecting the right of that individual one protects the common good and is thus serving the interest of the majority." Raz, *Ethics in the Public Domain*, 52–53.

132. Ibid., 33. He goes on to say that this approach "derives directly from the conception of duties as fetters.... If duties are not essentially fetters detrimental to their subject, then rights need not be considered as essentially confrontational." Ibid., 33. Raz's language is that rights have "an interpersonal nature," which he says is a major barrier to regarding them "as foundational." The core of that interpersonal nature is that "rights are based on evaluating the interests not only of their beneficiaries, but also of others who many be affected by respect for them" (35).

133. Hohfeld, "Some Fundamental Legal Conceptions as Applied in Judicial Reasoning."

134. First Amendment to the U.S. Constitution.

135. *Canadian Charter of Rights and Freedoms*, Part I of the *Constitution Act, 1982*, being Schedule B to the *Canada Act 1982* (U.K.), 1982, chap. 11, sec. 7.

136. Of course, a relational analysis of any particular right, such as the right of an accused only to be convicted if subjective intent can be proven, might be varied to better serve rights of equality, security, and bodily integrity as well as the integrity of the criminal justice system. See chapter 5, section VIII.

137. Leckey, *Contextual Subjects*.

138. Ibid., 220.

139. See Nedelsky, "Property in Potential Life?" for similar arguments.

140. Leckey, *Contextual Subjects*, 20.

141. See chapter 4, section IV.B.

142. Leckey, *Contextual Subjects*, 18.

143. Nedelsky, "Property in Potential Life?" 364 and "Reconceiving Rights as Relationship," 10, cited in Leckey, *Contextual Subjects*, 18.

144. The relational approach I spell out here would also provide guidance for how to apply a contextual approach. For an excellent discussion of "contextualism" in the jurisprudence of the Supreme Court of Canada, see Sugunasiri, "Contextualism." Interestingly she notes that Justice Wilson—who she says first expressly propounded the contextual approach in *Edmonton Journal v. Alberta (Attorney General)*, [1989] 2 S.C.R. 1326, 64 D.L.R. (4th) 577 (cited to D.L.R.; ibid., 129–130)—says that in both the contextual approach and the conventional "abstract approach" "it is necessary to ascertain the underlying value which the right alleged to be violated was designed to protect" (at para. 581; cited in ibid., 132). Sugunasiri also quotes a majority of the Court in *R. v. Laba*, [1994] S.C.R. 965, 94 C.C.C. (3rd) 385, 411–412:

> It is now well established that the *Charter* is to be interpreted in light of the context in which it is being applied…[and that] the historical, social and economic context in which a Charter claim arises will often be relevant in determining the meaning which ought to be given to Charter rights and is critical in determining whether limitations on those rights can be justified under s. 1.

Sugunasiri, "Contextualism," 134.

145. Leckey, *Contextual Subjects*, 19.

146. See Koggel, *Perspectives on Equality*.

147. Joan Tronto provides one of the most systematic arguments in *Moral Boundaries*.

148. See Kittay, *Love's Labor*.

149. Shanley, "The Right to a Parent-Child Relationship."

150. Leckey, *Contextual Subjects*, 17.

151. "To be a feminism in the United States today, a position must posit some kind of subordination as between m and f, in which f is the disadvantaged or subordinated element." Halley, *Split Decisions*, 19. This is one of her three criteria (17–19). Of course, I do think there is some kind of subordination, but I also think that even some of the subordinated roles, such as "housewife," can be preferable to dominant male roles.

152. See Fraser, "After the Family Wage; Weir, "Global Caregiver"; and Nedelsky, "Feminist Constitutionalism."

153. See Williams, *Truth, Autonomy, and Speech*; Craig, "Reconstructing the Author-Self. For the application of a relational approach to health care, see Downie and Llewellyn, *Being Relational*.

154. This is a claim about the formal structure of liberal theory. There are, of course, complex and important questions about how liberalism developed in the context of colonialism, slavery, and the disenfranchisement and legal (as well as practical) inequality of women.

155. See Leckey's discussion in *Contextual Subjects*, 8–10.

156. In their generally excellent introduction, Catriona Mackenzie and Natalie Stoljar assert that "theorists influenced by the care perspective, such as Jennifer Nedelsky, argue for a reconceptualization of autonomy modeled on the mother-child relationship. Such reconceptualizations give normative primacy to relations of care and connection identified by Chodorow and Gilligan and articulate autonomy within the context of these relations." MacKenzie and Stoljar, *Relational Autonomy*, 9. While, as readers will see in chapter 2, I do refer to the helpfulness of the mother–child model, the major examples are drawn from administrative law. Thus it is odd to characterize my approach as focused on personal relationship.

157. "The ethic of justice prioritizes equality in some form, while the ethic of care prioritizes maintaining one's relationships to others and meeting the needs of those to whom one is related." Clement, *Care, Autonomy, and Justice*, 80.

158. "It is antithetical to care feminism to force the uprooting of existing attachments to people and values, even where those attachments might embody discrimination for or against a particular group, including women. The ethic of care is obliged to work through example and persuasion rather than through legislation or more direct coercion.... Care feminism does not push for the immediate overturning of existing social and political relations, it wants to work immanently and be sensitive to specificities of context." Hutchings, "Feminist Perspectives on a Planetary Ethic," 183.

159. Julie A. White and Joan C. Tronto provide a very precise articulation, which uses the language of entitlement rather than rights (but I think they function identically): "What is most important, then, is that there be democratic processes by which rights can be asserted for and by all.... There should be, in the end, a duty to care about public care, which requires a recognition of collective responsibility for all needs. The goal is to start from three presumptions: 1) everyone is entitled to receive adequate care throughout their lives; 2) everyone is entitled to participated in relationships of care that give meaning to their lives; 3) everyone is entitled to participate in the public process by which judgments about how society should ensure these first two premises are framed." White and Tronto, "Political Practices of Care," 449.

160. Hutchings, "Feminist Perspectives on a Planetary Ethic," 205.

CHAPTER 2

1. George Lakoff and Mark Johnson offered the important insight that "metaphor is pervasive in everyday life, not just in language but in thought and action. Our ordinary conceptual system, in terms of which we both think and act, is fundamentally metaphorical in nature. The concepts that govern our thought are not just matters of the intellect. They also govern our everyday functioning, down to the most mundane details. Our concepts structure what we perceive, how we get around in the world, and how we relate to other people. Our conceptual system thus plays a central role in defining our everyday realities." Lakoff and Johnson, *Metaphors We Live By*.

2. Nedelsky, *Private Property and the Limits of American Constitutionalism*. Parts of my argument may also be found in chapter 3.

3. Lord Camden, cited in Dworetz, *Unvarnished Doctrine*, 79.

4. The reference to *democracy* is an anachronistic usage. That term was used disparagingly by almost all the leading Framers. They used the term *republic*. I use *democracy* here because it captures the basic issues more easily for the modern reader.

5. James Madison articulated this important insight in *The Federalist*, No. 10. The phrase "tyranny of the majority" was coined by Alexis de Tocqueville in *Democracy in America*.

6. *Framers* is the term conventionally used for the members of the Convention of 1787 in which the U.S. Constitution was written.

7. One hundred fifty years after the Convention of 1787, *West Coast Hotel Co. v. Parrish*, 300 U.S. 379 (1937), signaled the end of the era beginning with *Lochner v. New York*, 198 U.S. 45 (1905), in which the U.S. Supreme Court had struck down social welfare legislation in the name of property and contract. But the Framer's basic paradigm of rights as limits has endured even though property no longer holds a central place. For an elaboration of the *Lochner* era, see chapter 3, notes 37 and 38. For a discussion of the impact of the property paradigm on American constitutionalism, see Nedelsky, *Private Property and the Limits of American Constitutionalism*.

8. See works cited in note 2 and Nedelsky, "Economic Liberties and the Foundations of American Constitutionalism," 220–243.

9. Of course, when the inequality of property is a given, problems of power and domination come to shape other rights, such as freedom of speech. See the debates over campaign finance, for example, as well as cases addressing the issue, such as *Harper v. Canada (Attorney General)*, [2004] 1 S.C.R. 827, and *McConnell v. Federal Election* Commission, 540 U.S. 93 (2003). For an analysis of campaign finance and free speech using a relational approach to autonomy see Susan H. Williams, *Truth, Autonomy, and Speech*.

10. The Constitution did contain some important prohibitions, particularly on state governments. The most direct efforts to protect property through prohibitions are found in Article 1, Section 10: "No State shall…coin Money; emit Bills of Credit; make any Thing but Gold and Silver Coin a Tender in Payment of Debts."

And Section 9 contains prohibitions on the federal government, the most famous of which refers to the suspension of the writ of habeas corpus. My point here is that specific prohibitions were not the primary means by which the Framers sought to secure individual rights.

11. Of course, the Bill of Rights was not included during the 1787 Constitution. It was added as a series of amendments in 1789. And the Bill of Rights had a purpose and rationale different from the rest of the Constitution. It was aimed at the Anti-Federalists' fear of tyrannical rule, not the Federalists' fear of the people. Nevertheless, it fit quite comfortably within the Federalist conceptual framework: it defined rights as limits to the legitimate authority of government. The irony is that the Bill of Rights has taken on the significance it has in our system because of the establishment of judicial review, the final consolidation of the Federalist conception of constitutional government. Herbert Storing offers an account of the Federalist and Anti-Federalist origins of the American Constitution and Bill of Rights in his commentary in *The Complete Anti-Federalist*. For Storing's discussion of the Anti-Federalist objections to judicial review, see his "The Aristocratic Tendency of the Constitution."

12. Property was once again a central focus. It was crucial to the justification and articulation of the powers of judicial review. By drawing on the ostensibly clear contours of common law property rights, the Court could declare its boundary-setting functions to be inherently legal rather than political, that is, dictated by the rule of law rather than involving matters of collective choice.

13. This phrase is from Keller, *From a Broken Web*.

14. Many readers will also recognize the status accorded to the vision of selves as separate, as bounded off from one another, as the subject of Michael Sandel's critique of John Rawls and liberalism. See Sandel, *Liberalism and the Limits of Justice*.

15. Reich, "New Property," 733.

16. Tribe, *American Constitutional Law*, 1305.

17. Ibid. Tribe elaborates: "The very idea of a fundamental right of personhood rests on the conviction that, even though one's identity is constantly and profoundly shaped by the rewards and penalties, the exhortations and scarcities and constraints of one's social environment, the 'personhood' resulting from this process is sufficiently "one's own" to be deemed fundamental in confrontation with the one entity that retains a monopoly over legitimate violence- the government. Thus active coercion by government to alter a person's being, or deliberate neglect by government which permits a being to suffer, are conceived as qualitatively different from the passive, incremental coercion that shapes all of life and for which no one bears precise responsibility" (1305–1306). Of course, I agree with Tribe's objective of protecting people from governmental coercion or neglect that does violence to people's selfhood or undermines their (relational) autonomy. I doubt, however, that the key distinction is between "active" and "incremental coercion" because such incremental coercion is often the result of structures of relationships, which while pervasive and not "deliberate," are significantly shaped by law. And, of course, I do not think that boundary imagery helps us think through this problem.

18. Ibid., 1312.

19. Post, "Social Foundations of Privacy," 970–72. Post argues that the privacy tort transcends the debate over whether we should think of the self as essentially independent and autonomous or as embedded in social norms, "for the tort presides over precisely those social norms which enable an autonomous self to emerge.... This mysterious fusion of civility and autonomy lies at the heart of the privacy tort" (974). This is, I think, in important ways the right sort of inquiry: how do our social structures foster or undermine autonomy? The further question is, though, whether our social structures and conceptions of boundary can encompass an adequate conception of autonomy. Post cites Edward Shils as capturing this fusion in his reference to "the 'social space' around an individual. He possesses [it] ... by virtue of the charisma which is inherent in his existence as an individual soul—as we say nowadays, in his individuality—and which is inherent in his membership in the civil community" (974n989). It is striking that the "social space" allocated to women has been very different from that of men. As Adrienne Rich reminds us, even going to the bathroom alone, surely one of the most basic instances of Western conceptions of privacy, is something many mothers of young children have to forego. Rich, *Of Woman Born*. Shils is right in the sense that the social space allotted to women does reflect both their peripheral membership in the community and the sense in which they are not treated as having full human individuality. But what is missing is a sensitivity to the notion that, since privacy will mean something different for women, if it is treated as an enclosed social space that is an index of their value and their membership both will be diminished in comparison to that of men.

20. Lakoff and Johnson, *Metaphors We Live By*. Indeed, their arguments have been extremely useful to me in providing a metaphoric base for my argument here.

21. See chapter 3, note 19, on the ways in which the legal and social reality of property is not actually as isolating as suggested by this image of the individual surrounded by the safe walls of property. This enduring image is part of the individualistic myth of property.

22. This problem does not disappear, but it is not the characteristic problem of the modern administrative state.

23. Dworkin, *Intercourse*, 137.

24. Ibid., 122.

25. Ibid., 123.

26. See, for example, Jane Adams, *Boundary Issues*; Whitfield, *Boundaries and Relationships*; and Katherine, *Boundaries*.

27. For a very different and interesting treatment of boundaries in legal discourse, see West, "Jurisprudence and Gender." West seems to think that boundary imagery *is* appropriate for men. I think she also tacitly accepts it for women when focusing on the nature of the threats they face, namely, invasion in the form of both intercourse and pregnancy.

28. Of course, the construction of genitals as "intimate" is not simply a physical matter.

29. I think men can also experience intercourse in ways similar to the middle ground of unease and distress. They may consent but feel used for purposes of reproduction, for example, when women are trying to get pregnant and want sex according to their ovulation cycle. Men can experience a painful disjuncture between the physical intimacy of intercourse belied by the lack of emotional intimacy, when they feel women's desire for use or outcome, not connection. Here, too, the sense of violation is tied to the nature of the physical connection in intercourse. Of course, actual rape poses horrors for men that also have to do with the physical nature of penetration.

30. Post, "Social Foundations of Privacy," 974.

31. Briggs, *Your Child's Self-Esteem*, 134.

32. I selected this book because, in general, l liked its tone and stance toward children. It was thus a source of boundary metaphor that inspired at least initial trust. It is worth noting that the book was written before most of the feminist work on parenting the separative self. But it is also the case that references to separation and the age of separation can still be found in virtually all parent guidebooks.

33. Briggs, *Your Child's Self-Esteem*, 124–125.

34. Ibid., 129–130.

35. Starhawk, *Spiral Dance, Dreaming the Dark*, and *Truth or Dare*.

36. In fact, Starhawk is drawing on the same psychological discourse that the child-development literature uses.

37. Starhawk, *Truth or Dare*, 148.

38. Ibid., 141.

39. Ibid., 148–149.

40. Ibid., 156.

41. Of course arbitrariness, inconsistency, and unpredictability in the behavior of those in power is antithetical to autonomy, whether for children or adults in relations of dependency. So, again, it is not that "clear, consistent rules" is completely misleading as a guideline, just suboptimal.

One could play out another variation on the theme of boundaries and "safe space" for children: Should one try to provide them with a physical environment that presents as few prohibitions as possible or a set of clearly delineated boundaries they are not to cross?

I should say that I do not think all spatial metaphors imply boundaries. We only assume they do.

42. For example, referring to a particular group she says, "We might have resolved our conflicts more effectively had we understood that they were about the group's boundaries, and that our real needs conflicted. Some of us strongly identified with the need to keep the group open; others identified with the need to create intimacy and trust. . . . We could have more consciously valued that tension." Starhawk, *Truth or Dare*, 152.

43. The claim "I have a right" often has that quality; it may invite action but not open conversation.

44. Ibid., 148.

45. Starhawk, *Truth or Dare*, 152.

46. Hale, "Coercion and Distribution in a Supposedly Non-Coercive State."

47. In large-scale societies, the state is the primary form of collective power that defines and enforces property rights. In small-scale societies without formal state structure, there can be collective norms that recognize, respect, and enforce property relations. Even in large-scale societies there can be efforts to create "property" through nonstate enforcement mechanisms, such as private armies and organized crime.

48. One could, of course, continue to debate the necessity of inequality as an incentive in markets, whether the laws structuring the market enable it to capture the true costs of production (such as environmental damage), the capacity of the market system to foster innovation, and the virtues of the distribution of power generated by the laws of property and contract that define the market.

49. The constitutions of both Canada and the United States protect citizens against unreasonable search and seizure: U.S. Constitution, Fourth Amendment; *Canadian Charter of Rights and Freedoms*, Part I of the Constitution Act, 1982, being Schedule B to the Canada Act 1982 (U.K.), 1982, chap. 11, sec. 8. In Canada, the Supreme Court has held that a search is "reasonable" only if (a) the search is authorized by law; (b) the law itself is reasonable; and (c) the manner in which the search is carried out is reasonable. *R. v. S.A.B.*, [2003] 2 S.C.R. 678 at para. 36. The Court has recognized that some searches and seizures "can involve significant intrusions on an individual's privacy and human dignity" (at para. 40, referring to "The taking of bodily samples") and emphasized that the "privacy" interests protected by section 8 include "territorial or spacial aspects, aspects related to the person, and aspects that arise in the informational context" (at para. 40).

50. For example, regard for a particular space of time as "private" may require an understanding of why it is important to the person claiming it. (I apply this same point in the legal context in the text above.) A person might best claim uninterrupted time for writing down dreams or journal reflections by being willing to explain to family members why it is important to her. That is, an offer of intimacy may lead to the attention, understanding, and respect that will then yield the desired privacy. The same might be true with respect to the private nature of physical notebooks in which this writing is done. The demand of a right to privacy may be an effort to claim respect and attention to needs without building the relationship that would sustain them. Perhaps that is part of what people want rights for. But in both public and private domains I think such claims are likely to be fragile. Rights must be understood and enforced in ways that sustain the relationships that can actually give life to the values people care about. Of course, the respect strangers claim from one another is different from that of family members.

51. Structurally, both Canadian and American jurisprudence are well suited to such analysis since privacy is not an explicitly listed right in either constitution.

52. For related arguments that privacy is best understood as protecting the conditions of self-presentation—which is not about social withdrawal but precisely social interaction, see Austin, "Privacy and Private Law."

53. Lakoff and Johnson, *Metaphors We Live By*.

54. Keller, *From a Broken Web*, 234. Of course she is also using in–out metaphors but for the purpose of merging them. When we leave conventional prose and become more poetic, it is easier to avoid the conventional metaphoric structure—and to begin to create a new one. For example, she also says, "If it is true, that 'everything is in a certain sense everywhere,' then bodies need not obey the conventions of fixed time and simple space. To the contrary: 'We have come to forget the feel of our own skin. Removed from our skin, we remain distant. You and I, apart.'" Ibid., 233–234, quoting Irigaray, *This Sex Which Is Not One*, 217.

55. Lakoff and Johnson, *Metaphors We Live By*, 29.

56. Griffin, *Pornography and Silence*; quoted in Keller, *From a Broken Web*, 155.

57. Lakoff and Johnson, *Metaphors We Live By*, 29. This bold assertion of "our" experience reminds me of a conversation I once had with a student in class. I asked the class why they thought legal and political theory continued to take the separate individual as its starting point when we had such good information about (at least) the social dimension of language and knowledge. A student answered that he thought it was because when we look inside ourselves, it is our singularity that most immediately and powerfully strikes us. I was at the time eight months pregnant. I certainly did not experience myself as essentially singular. When I first wrote this chapter, my first child was two and I still did not think that singularity could capture my sense of my essence (although Michael was only part of the reason for that). I think the intense bond to young children may be one of the sharpest experiences of connection, of nonsingularity. But a deep sense of interconnection that is in tension with a primary experience of bounded singularity can come from many sources.

I think it only fair to add that whatever subtle sexism inheres in images of the "separative self," the authors show no overt signs of it. Indeed, George Lakoff's *Women, Fire, and Dangerous Things* has one of the most illuminating discussions of rape that I have read.

58. Whitehead, *Process and Reality*; quoted in Keller, *From a Broken Web*, 155.

59. Lakoff, *Women, Fire, and Dangerous Things*, 271.

60. Of course many feminists make essentialist claims about the body, too. What is striking, of course, is that the "unmediated" messages they get from their bodies are radically different from those of Lakoff and Johnson and sometimes from those of other feminists. All in all, I think we should be wary of essentialist claims of any variety. The connections between body, mind, and experience are more complex than essentialist claims allow for, even very interesting ones like those Lakoff and Johnson propose. Nevertheless, I would make a concession to the way they treat bodily experience: although bodily experience is, like everything else in life, mediated by culture (and by language once language is acquired), it may be simultaneously true that bodily experience seems primal and foundational and thus underlies metaphoric structure even as it is itself shaped by such structures. I think some sense of this reciprocal relation rather than an insistence on unmediated bodily experience as foundational will prove most fruitful. But thanks to conversations with Tobold Rollo (doctoral candidate, University of Toronto) I would no longer deny this more qualified understanding of the body as part of what generates metaphor.

61. Lakoff and Johnson direct our attention to this important issue of coherence: "So it seems that our values are not independent but must form a coherent system with the metaphorical concepts we live by." Lakoff and Johnson, *Metaphors We Live By*, 22.

62. Keller, *From a Broken Web*, 1.

63. Ibid., 2.

64. Ibid.

65. Ibid., 3.

66. Lewis, *Surprised by Joy*; quoted in Keller, *From a Broken Web*, 1.

67. See particularly chapter 3 of Keller, *From a Broken Web*.

68. Ibid., 96.

69. Griffin, *Pornography and Silence*; quoted in Keller, *From a Broken Web*, 155.

70. Keller, *From a Broken Web*, 160–161. Keller also offers an illuminating quote from Mary Daly, *Gyn/Ecology: The Metaethics of Radical Feminism* (1978), 160:

> The mindbinders and those who remain mindbound do not see the patterns of the cosmic tapestries, nor do they hear the labyrinthine symphony. For their thinking has been crippled and tied to linear tracks....Since they do not understand that creativity means seeing the interconnectedness between seemingly disparate phenomena, the mindbound accuse Hags of "lumping things together." Their perception is a complete reversal.
>
> It is also worth noting that at one level Keller agrees with Johnson: "For it is a self conceived as separate that has after all projected its grid of fragmentation upon the world." Keller, *From a Broken Web*, 161. Compare Lakoff and Johnson: "Each of us is a container, with (bounding surface and an in-out orientation. We project our own in-out orientation onto other physical objects." Lakoff and Johnson, *Metaphors We Live By*, 29. They differ of course in the status they accord to the experience of separateness.

71. Keller, *From a Broken Web*, 163.

72. Ibid., 194.

73. Dinnerstein, *The Mermaid and the Minotaur*; Benjamin, "The Bonds of Love." Keller offers an interesting critique of Dinnerstein as aiming at making a separative self available for women too; see chapter 3 of Keller, *From a Broken Web*.

74. Keller, *From a Broken Web*, 200. I discuss these connections more fully in chapter 7, section III.

75. The *Federalist Papers*, for example, include references to the American people as having a "manly spirit" (No. 14 and 57) and the elected Convention in several states as having a "manly confidence" (No. 40). The Declaration of Independence echoes this gendered language, listing among the colonists' many complaints against the king that he had "dissolved Representative Houses repeatedly, for opposing with manly firmness his invasions on the rights of the people."

76. Estella Lauter, *Women as Mythmakers: Poetry and Visual Art by Twentieth-Century Women* (1984).

77. Ibid., 220. See also Helen Vendler on Jorie Graham in Vendler, *The Given and the Made*, and Lorde, "Poetry Is Not a Luxury," which help explain why we might look for genuinely new conceptions of the relationship between the individual and the collective (as well as the body and

the spirit) in the language of poetry rather than of prose. My thanks to Donna Freireich for introducing me to Vendler's work.

78. To explain what she sees in the art she presents, Lauter offers a series of boundary-dissolving metaphors from the philosopher Hilda Hein:

> Sexual intercourse, for example, is experienced by many women as an "active and mutual engulfment" wherein there is neither a loss nor a triumph of self, but a commingling and redistribution of self and reality. Similarly, "mother and child mutually shape each other not merely through the period of their direct physical attachment, but…throughout their lives." "Imagine knowing as an act of love…a giving of self to the subject matter, rather than an 'objective' standing at a distance. As one allows the known to suffuse one's being, one takes it in, envelops and is enveloped by it."

Lauter, *Women as Mythmakers*, 221.

79. Ibid., 223.

80. There is generally too little concern, however, about what it takes to foster or develop the capacity.

81. See, for example, Catherine MacKinnon's discussions of pornography in her *Feminism Unmodified*, though I should note that MacKinnon argues that pornography is not essentially speech. See also Justice Dickson's decision in *R. v. Keegstra*, [1990] 3 S.C.R. 697, where he reflects (at para. 97): "I am very reluctant to attach anything but the highest importance to expression relevant to political matters. But given the unparalleled vigour with which hate propaganda repudiates and undermines democratic values, and in particular its condemnation of the view that all citizens need be treated with equal respect and dignity so as to make participation in the political process meaningful, I am unable to see the protection of such expression as integral to the democratic ideal so central to the [rationale for protecting freedom of expression]."

82. As I noted in chapter 1, section III.C, Joseph Raz contends that the "primary purpose" of freedom of speech "has been to provide a collective good, to protect the democratic character of the society." Raz, *The Morality of Freedom*, 254.

83. Expressions of concern over expanding state power were pervasive in the debates leading up to the 2010 health care reforms in the United States. The American Enterprise Institute (AEI), a prominent conservative think tank explained that "Americans…will not tolerate a top-down health reform that further centralizes power and decision making in Washington. They distrust the promises of lower costs and more secure coverage, and they fear losing what they have now." Antos and Miller, "A Better Prescription," 23. AEI proposed that a decentralized market would better respond to health care needs since "Mandates, regulations, and other tools of government enforcement might aim to produce desirable responses, but they breed resistance and evasion that reduce our success in meeting social objectives and raise the cost of health care. There is a tendency to add more layers of regulation over time to seal off avenues of escape as affected individuals and firms react to reduce the adverse consequences they would incur as a result of the initial policies" (15).

84. Lauter, *Women as Mythmakers*, 218.

85. An obvious example is the "right" to use property and purchase services (such as airplane travel) in disregard of their environmental impact. I return to the question of changes in norms of

responsibility in my "Closing Reflections." I would note here, too, that the American health care debate has shown that it is not just those in positions of privilege who have these fears.

86. I think this is finally the place to say a brief word about communitarians. There is of course considerable diversity among those who might be so labeled, but I think it is fair to say that in general their work is characterized by mediating rather than combining antinomies. My own formulation of the "tension between the individual and the collective" also has some of this quality. It is an effort to take seriously the social dimensions of human beings; but this formulation does not succeed in capturing the unity, rather than the complementarity, of the individual and the social dimensions of human beings. I take the projects of the feminist theorists I have been discussing to be both more radical in their aspirations and more successful in them.

CHAPTER 3

1. See, for example, MacKenzie and Stoljar, *Relational Autonomy*.

2. The broad form of liberalism I refer to in this chapter is Anglo-American, which, of course, includes many variants, some of which are more individualistic than others.

3. Among the many relevant discussions of feminist theory and methodology are: Walker, *Moral Understandings*; Weir, *Sacrificial Logics*; Wendell, *Rejected Body*; Griffiths, *Feminisms and the Self*; Held, *Feminist Morality*; Meyers, *Feminists Rethink the Self*, *Subjection and Subjectivity*, and *Self, Society, and Personal Choice*; Flax, *Disputed Subjects*; Tronto, *Moral Boundaries*; Benhabib, *Situating the Self*; Minow, *Making All the Difference*; Code, *What Can She Know?*; Young, *Justice and the Politics of Difference* and *Throwing Like a Girl and Other Essays*; Butler, *Gender Trouble*; Hoagland, *Lesbian Ethics*; Spelman, *Inessential Woman*; hooks, *Feminist Theory*; Jaggar, *Feminist Politics and Human Nature*; Code et al., *Feminist Perspectives*; Harding, *Feminism and Methodology*; Gilligan, *In a Different Voice*; MacKinnon, "Feminism, Marxism, Method, and the State"; Scales, "Emergence of Feminist Jurisprudence"; and Friedman, *What Are Friends For?*

4. Among the best known critical studies of liberal individualism are: Taylor, "Politics of Recognition" and *Philosophy and the Human Sciences*, particularly chapter 7, "Atomism"; Sandel, *Liberalism and Its Critics* and *Liberalism and the Limits of Justice*; MacIntyre, *After Virtue*; and Walzer, *Spheres of Justice*. For attempts to reconstruct liberalism in response to the communitarian critique see Kymlicka, *Multicultural Citizenship* and *Liberalism, Community, and Culture*; and Rawls, *The Law of Peoples* and *Political Liberalism*.

5. See the list in note 3. For examples of feminist arguments, MacKenzie and Stoljar, *Relational Autonomy*, offers an excellent collection of essays on this issue. Koggel, *Perspectives on Equality*, offers a detailed critique of liberal individualism and its implications for equality. Kittay, *Love's Labor* (using Rawls as exemplar), provides a compelling critique of the failure of liberal individualism to take the need for care into account in constructing a theory of justice. Of course, liberal theorists are not always (perhaps not generally) persuaded. Will Kymlicka provides a helpful overview of a number of these criticisms in *Liberalism, Community, and Culture* (chaps. 4–6), though he ultimately concludes that these critiques "contain important mistakes" (2). In Kymlicka's view, "The individualism that underlies liberalism isn't valued at the expense of our social nature or our shared community" (2–3).

6. Charles Taylor provides a particularly compelling statement of the importance of this vision in the origins and enduring power of liberal thought in his *Justice after Virtue*. See also chapter 7, "Atomism," in his *Philosophy and the Human Sciences*.

7. The parallel with old theological debates about the freedom of man and the omnipotence of God is really quite striking. Taylor comments on the relevance of these debates to the emergence of liberalism in *Justice after Virtue*. I touch on the implications of autonomy as free will in chapter 7, section II.

8. de Beauvoir, *The Second Sex*, 69, 139–145.

9. The fact that contemporary liberal theorists know all about "social conditioning" doesn't always change the structure of their concepts. It may mean that they, too, face similar dilemmas but do not choose to make them central to their theoretical inquiries. I develop the idea of self-creation in chapter 4, section III.

10. The implications of women's experience of oppressive relationships for the larger community is explored in chapter 5.

11. See, for example, Weiss and Friedman, *Feminism and Community*.

12. Grace Clement, for example, explains that "feminine advocates of the ethic of care argue that autonomy is an individualist value that the ethic of care rejects in favor of relational values." Clement, *Care, Autonomy, and Justice*, 7. Clement elaborates: "Thus autonomy is a central value for an ethic of justice while it is generally regarded as illusory or a negative value by advocates of the ethic of care" (16). Although she does not cite any specific advocates of these positions, Clement asserts, "Many feminists who reject the ethic of care do so because they believe it undermines some notion of autonomy. . . . Similarly, those who criticise the notion of autonomy often do so because they believe it is inconsistent with an ethic of care. For instance, whereas autonomy is thought to be an individualistic notion, the ethic of care is based on the recognition that human beings are socially constituted" (21). Clement herself advocates a "non individualistic account of autonomy" (22), explaining that, "autonomy (properly defined) serves as a criterion for an adequate ethic of care" (21).

13. Sarah Lucia Hoagland, for example, prefers the notion term "autokoenonony," meaning "a self in community who is one among many." Hoagland, *Lesbian Ethics*, 12. Hoagland explains her terminology saying, "I take from the greek [*sic*] 'auto' ("self") and 'Koinonia' ('community, or any group whose members have something in common')" (145).

14. The word "autonomy" is derived from the Greek *autonomia*; *auto-* meaning "self" and *nomos* meaning "law." The *Oxford English Dictionary* (2nd ed., 1989) defines "autonomy" as "the having or making of one's own laws."

15. My colleague Audrey Macklin reminded me that the phrase "finding the law" has traditionally been used in a very different context in Anglo-American law. It was conventionally contrasted with "making the law," for the purpose of minimizing the creative role of common law judges. Although the law they develop is in fact made by judges rather than legislators, the phrase "finding the law" was intended to convey the idea that judges were only uncovering the underlying principles of the common law, or their implications, when they made their decisions. The phrase implied that judges were not imposing their own will, interests, or ideas.

16. Indeed, it may be that the idea of one's own law, as opposed to one's own wishes, presupposes some transcendent, spiritual order of which we are a part. Such a notion need not, of course, be anything like Kant's categorical imperative with its exclusive reliance on man's rationality. See Kant, *Groundwork of the Metaphysic of Morals*. This theme will be picked up in chapter 7, section II.

17. A passage in Ursula K. Le Guin's *The Beginning Place* expresses this connection: "There was no boundary. It was all his country. But this time, this was far enough: he would go no further

now. Part of the pleasure of being here was that he could listen for and obey such impulses and commands coming from within him, undistorted by external pressures and compulsions. In that obedience, for the first time since early childhood, he sensed the headiness of freedom, the calmness of power" (27).

Of course this connection is played out in the political realm as well and entails the same paradox: in a democracy, limited government means self-limiting government. The people must limit themselves. The fictions of constitutionalism try to obscure the paradox: a constitution spells out the limits the people have placed on themselves; those limits once set need not be reconsidered (except in the exceptional circumstances of amendments). The fiction works particularly nicely in the United States, where the Constitution was written so long ago. The reality, of course, is that the limits must be constantly reinterpreted. The "people," in the form of their representatives in the judiciary, must constantly set and reset the limits that they will treat as clear, fixed, and unquestioned. Within these self-defined limits, the collective finds its own law, which is an essential element of collective freedom. I discuss the paradox of self-limiting government more fully in Nedelsky, "American Constitutionalism and the Paradox of Private Property" and *Private Property and the Limits of American Constitutionalism*. I will also discuss this theme further on in chapter 6.

18. I am not suggesting that everything that contributes to our apprehension of "our own law" must be mediated through language. Some forms of meditation are intended to foster a capacity to discern meaning and purpose, or the nature of reality, in ways that are closely linked to finding one's own law. And part of the purpose of meditative practices is to move beyond the constraints of language. It is possible that some of the approaches to meditation and its relation to autonomy do not fit within my conception of the social dimension of autonomy. By and large, however, I think the process of meditation does fit even though it is individual and often private in its exercise, because it involves training, learning from tradition, often from a teacher. But I am less sure about the content. I think in some teachings the aspiration is toward a comprehension of a universal truth that is not mediated by language or other social dimensions of life. The aspiration may never by quite achieved (for most people) and thus may always be understood and experienced in ways that are so mediated. But if the ultimate comprehension is not, then "the content" does not have the socially mediated nature I am pointing to. In the Buddhist tradition, however, one of the central dimensions of the wisdom or insight one aspires to is the interconnection among all things. It thus has what I would call a relational content even if the aspiration is to transcend the mediation of transitory phenomena, such as language. And, in any case, the capacity to apprehend this ultimate wisdom and to live by it will be enabled by social relations, broadly understood. More particularly, many Buddhist traditions emphasize the importance of the Sangha, the community of practitioners.

19. There is an interesting corroboration of my view of property-based independence as isolation in J. G. A. Pocock's analyses of the relationship between property and autonomy in seventeenth-century liberal thought: "The point about freehold in this context is that it involves its proprietor as little as possible in dependence upon or *even in relations with other people* and so leaves him free for the full austerity of citizenship in the classical sense" (emphasis added). Pocock, *Politics, Language, and Time*, 91.

Ironically, the legal and social reality of property is not actually what is suggested by this image of the splendid isolation of the freeholder secure in his property rights against both the state and fellow citizens. Modern property in particular is routinely embedded in complex networks of relations, from family inheritance and loans to bank mortgages to spousal rights to property upon divorce. Even in the seventeenth and eighteenth centuries property was closely tied to inheritance, relations among sons, marriages arranged with property in mind, etc. It matters both that the image of property as the secure source of independence has remained powerful for so long and that it has never actually been accurate. My thanks to Joseph Singer for reminding me of these modern relational dimensions of property.

20. For a brilliant discussion of the Western conception of the separate self, see Keller, *From a Broken Web*. She also points to another connection between feminism and the reconception of autonomy: men's fear of women is tied to their fear of the collective (1, quoting C. S. Lewis, *Surprised by Joy*). See my discussion of this connection in chapter 2, section VI. Keller makes a persuasive and sweeping case about Western culture. My more specific claims are, however, limited to the Anglo-American tradition and, in some sections, to the United States as a particularly stark version of that tradition.

21. See below for a discussion of the public/private dichotomy.

22. I originally used the term "citizen" here. In this context "citizen" captures a great deal of what matters to my argument: the sense of rights and capacities of participation, of active engagement. On the other hand, the issues I address apply to many people who are not citizens. Immigrants and refugees have many encounters with bureaucracy and are particularly vulnerable to structures that are in no way designed to respect or enhance their autonomy. In Canada, some of the most important administrative law cases have involved the rights of noncitizens (for example, *Baker v. Canada (Ministry of Citizenship and Immigration)*, [1999] 2 S.C.R. 817).

After much debate with both myself and colleagues, I have decided against using the term "citizen" when what I really mean is a member of society or of some community. The problem is that legal citizenship is, in fact, an inherently exclusionary category such that real people are excluded from both participation and protection. For most of my claims about protecting people from arbitrary state action or enabling them to participate in the creation of norms that affect them, whether they meet current criteria for legal citizenship is not the key issue. Were I to use the term "citizen" as a stand-in for the more ambiguous notion of protected-and-participatory-membership, I would be tacitly excluding people I do not mean to exclude.

The choice of term is made more difficult than the statement above suggests because there is such a huge range of ways citizen is currently used. Many people do not mean legal citizenship when they use the term but, rather, something like social citizenship (see Macklin quote below). I thought about whether the fact of this diverse usage would justify my use of citizen in this chapter (when I don't mean legal citizen), but in the end I thought to do so would tacitly obscure the actual exclusion that goes on via the category of legal citizenship. I thank Sean Rehaag for forcefully arguing this point.

Audrey Macklin nicely summarizes the ways "citizen" is used:

> Citizenship as an analytic category is remarkably capacious, as if self-consciously resisting the exclusionary impulses that historical practices of citizenship cannot. Scholarship in this field is hospitable to an array of descriptive, critical and normative projects across a range of academic disciplines. Citizenship describes status, rights, practices and performances. It applies at the level of the state (national citizenship), below the state (urban citizenship), across states (supra-national citizenship), between states (transnational citizenship), beyond states (cosmopolitan and global citizenship),

and in deterritorialized socio-political spaces (the market, terrorist networks, the internet).... By legal citizenship, I refer to the formal status of membership in a state, or nationality as it is understood in international law.... For present purposes, social citizenship encompasses the more voluminous package of rights, responsibilities, entitlements, duties, practices and attachments that define membership in a polity, and situate individuals within that community. Although it is conventional to dismiss legal citizenship as (merely) formal, in contrast to the more substantive character of social citizenship, these designations are potentially misleading. The rights usually reserved to legal citizens, especially the unconditional right of entry and residence, remain crucial in an era where lawful access to the territory of a state (rather than citizenship per se) is the pre-requisite to the exercise and enjoyment of most rights, entitlements and opportunities available inside the state.

Macklin, "Who Is the Citizen's Other?" 334.

In Joseph Carens's terms, "unitary conception[s] of citizenship" are challenged by a modern political context in which "[i]nstead of unique, exclusive, compartmentalized versions of membership, we find multiple memberships and over-lapping identities along three dimensions of citizenship: the legal, the psychological, and the political." Carens, *Culture, Citizenship, and Community*, 19.

Thus for a variety of reasons, the term "citizen" is contested and sometimes contentious. So unless I actually mean legal citizenship, I will use a phrase like "member of society" or "members" or just "people," as I have done above. The term "member" can capture the fact of a variety of forms of membership—all of which can raise the sort of issues I discuss in this chapter. Unlike using the term "citizen" to stand for a variety of forms of membership, "member of society" does not obscure the actual exclusion of legal citizenship.

23. Canadian French language jurisprudence sometimes refers to "les administrés," those who are administered, capturing the sense of passive subjects of bureaucratic decision making. Leckey, *Contextual Subjects*, 157.

24. This focus on American political thought provides specificity in looking at how the problem of autonomy fits within a larger framework of political theory. The American treatment of autonomy is particularly focused on boundaries (as we shall see later), but it is not unique. On the contrary, I think it helps us understand a problem characteristic of all liberal thought.

25. In the course of my discussion I will use both the terms "state power" and "collective power." I am addressing the broad problem of the tension between individual autonomy and the power of the collective. In our political system that power is ordinarily exercised by the state, and thus in most contexts it is appropriate to refer to state or governmental power, but part of my argument is that the tension will endure however collective power is organized. The analysis therefore should be relevant both to alternative political systems and to the nongovernmental power exercised by such "private" entities as corporations. (I am placing "private" in quotes because corporations are granted much of their power through legislation.)

26. The legislative and bureaucratic "models" of democratic participation are in some ways in tension with one another. If the legislature managed to make all policy decisions, if it were possible to formulate rules that neutral, efficient bureaucrats could apply mechanically (i.e., without significant degrees of discretion), people would be spared the sense of being subject to arbitrary control. But they would also have little scope for participation in the decisions on their own cases.

In any case, in the modern state such a level of legislative detail would be impossible. That vision of ensuring people's autonomy through democratic decision making at the legislative level is unworkable.

27. The example of airwaves, of course, points to the complexity of governmental control. The government has assumed a much larger role in regulating radio and television than the written media, on the grounds of regulating a finite public resource. One need not approve of all the forms such regulation has taken in order to see that public control can take a wide range of forms.

28. The arguments in this section are spelled out more fully in Nedelsky, *Private Property and the Limits of American Constitutionalism*.

29. See chapter 2, note 11.

30. See Wood, *Creation of the American Republic, 1776–1787*.

31. Madison, Federalist No. 10.

32. The term "civil rights" is also used in this sense in Section 92 (13) of the Canadian Constitution Act, 1867 (British North America Act) in the reference to property and civil rights. This formulation dates from the Constitution Act, 1791.

33. Those who supported the new constitution proposed in 1787 came to be known as the Federalists, with their opponents stuck with the name Anti-Federalists. Leading Federalists included James Madison, Alexander Hamilton, and John Jay (authors of *The Federalist Papers*, the now famous set of essays advocating the adoption of the new constitution) as well as Gouverneur Morris and James Wilson. See Nedelsky, *Private Property and the Limits of American Constitutionalism*, and Wood, *Creation of the American Republic, 1776–1787*.

34. The Anti-Federalists did treat political participation in this way. See Nedelsky, "Review: Confining Democratic Politics."

35. See Nedelsky, *Private Property and the Limits of American Constitutionalism*, for an elaboration of this argument.

36. Friedrich A. Hayek offers a particularly clear statement of (and argument for) these contrasts in our tradition in his *Law, Legislation, and Liberty*.

37. Perhaps the most notorious example of this privileging of property rights over other values was the U.S. Supreme Court decision in *Lochner v. New York*, 198 U.S. 45 (1905), where the Court struck down legislation limiting the number of hours that bakers could legally be employed to work. As I have previously argued, *Lochner* and the decisions following its precedent exemplify a judicial emphasis on "the rights of property as the central boundary to state power, a suspicion of popular efforts to use democratic power to threaten those rights, and contract as a focus for protecting them." Nedelsky, *Private Property and the Limits of American Constitutionalism*, 228. The specter of democratic majorities using their legislative power to threaten contractual freedom (and thus undermine property rights) is clear in the Court's assertion that "[i]f...a proper case is made out in which to deny the right of an individual...to make contracts...there would seem to be no length to which legislation of this nature might not go." *Lochner*, 198 U.S. at 58.

38. The approach established in *Lochner*, described above in note 37, was followed by the American courts throughout the *Lochner* era, which came to an end with the 1937 decision *West Coast Hotel Co. v. Parrish*, 300 U.S. 379, where the Court upheld a Washington state law that established a mandatory minimum wage for women. The shift away from the *Lochner* Court's absolute prioritization of contractual freedom and property interests was evident in the Court's assertion that "The community may direct its law-making power to correct the abuse which

springs from [unconscionable employers'] selfish disregard of the public interest." *West Coast Hotel Co.*, 300 U.S. at 399–400.

39. Lowi, *End of Liberalism*, and Dahl and Lindblom, *Politics, Economics, and Welfare*, offer graphic illustrations of the inaptness of similar traditional categories.

40. The following argument is a condensed version of the sort advanced by such legal realists as Robert Hale. See Hale, "Coercion and Distribution in a Supposedly Non-Coercive State."

41. Friedrich Hayek endorses this conception of the market in chapters 1 and 2 of Hayek and Bartley, *Fatal Conceit*. The classic argument against government regulation of the market can be found in Friedman and Friedman, *Capitalism and Freedom*.

42. There can, of course, be markets where there is no legal system like those associated with the liberal democratic state. Custom alone may define both rules and sanctions. Even in our society there are areas of commercial transaction governed largely not by law, but by agreement among parties with adequate enforcement power of their own. I leave aside for the moment whether these customary norms constitute a form of collective power radically different from that exercised through legislation. But, in any case, in our system the market consists essentially of legal rules and is in that sense a creature of the state.

43. Hayek, *Law, Legislation, and Liberty*. See chapter 7, note 69 for a discussion of how legislation at times tries to codify common law; see chapter 4, note 54 for an example of codification of the common law defense of insanity in the Canadian context.

44. Hayek, *Law, Legislation, and Liberty*.

45. Horwitz, *Transformation of American Law, 1780–1860*, provides the clearest evidence of this. Even critics who challenge many of Horwitz's claims do not present a picture of the common law as having the natural and undirected quality which is a central part of Hayek's picture.

46. Nedelsky, "Judgment, Diversity, and Relational Autonomy."

47. I use this pronoun advisedly given the limited availability of ownership to women.

48. The importance of property has never been simple. Even in 1787 many of the Framers derived an important part of their income from complicated transactions in bonds and speculative ventures in joint stock companies. Certainly not all of these men shared Jefferson's vision of an agrarian republic. But they did see a close connection between widespread, small-scale ownership of property and political independence, and they feared the day when wage labor would sever that connection. Important dimensions of the connection have now disappeared, leaving behind, perhaps, residual dreams of home ownership as the last widely available form of autonomy sustained and protected by property. The receding reality of the property–autonomy nexus is not the same as the advantages and insulation that wealth continues to provide. The advantages and even power of wealth are not necessarily autonomy enhancing, even though wealth can shield one from the power and control of others.

49. There is, of course, the related but distinct question of whether some form of property is essential for autonomy. If property is so broadly defined that it means the concrete expression of autonomous action, then, practically tautologically, autonomy requires property. Such a definition leaves entirely open the practices of use, possession, alienation, and advantage that we associate with property. Margaret Radin has tried to distinguish between those dimensions of conventional property essential for what she calls personhood and those unsuitable to and even destructive of that value (which, I think, includes, but is not synonymous with autonomy). See Radin, *Contested Commodities*. The extent of my claim here is that the current meaning of property no longer stands in any clear or necessary relation to autonomy.

50. The problem of boundaries does not disappear. Part of the task of ensuring the good society is to redefine the relation between citizen and state, individual and collective. That task includes identifying those realms which should be considered private or beyond the scope of collective control. My point is that the definition of such boundaries cannot be the only basis for autonomy in a society that recognizes individual responsibility to the collective and collective responsibility for social and individual welfare. See "Closing Reflections," section V for the ways the relational approach disrupts categories of public and private.

51. At least one study has concluded that "Compared with Canadians, US residents are one third less likely to have a regular medical doctor, one fourth more likely to have unmet health care needs, and are more than twice as likely to forgo needed medicines.... Health disparities on the basis of race, income and immigrant status are present in both countries, but appear to be more pronounced in the United States." Lasser, Himmelstein, and Woolhandler, "Access to Care, Health Status, and Health Disparities in the United States and Canada," 6.

The Canadian system, however, has attracted criticism both on the basis of its quality and its accessibility. In particular, the length of time patients must at times wait for care has been noted, often by those who advocate a more privatized health care system. See, for example, Esmail, Hazel, and Walker, *Waiting Your Turn*, annual reports for 2006, 2007, and 2008; Wait Times Alliance, "Unfinished Business"; Canadian Institute for Health Information, "Waiting for Health Care in Canada." Even the Supreme Court of Canada, in the famous *Chaoulli* decision, declared Quebec's prohibition on private health insurance for certain medical treatments to constitute a violation of constitutional rights, as it risked patients' health and life to be forced to wait for publicly funded medical care. *Chaoulli v. Quebec (Attorney General)*, 2005 SCC 35, [2005] 1 S.C.R. 791. In terms of accessibility, two trends have been noted that detract from the idealized image of universally accessible health care for all Canadians. The first is the increased reliance on private health care by wealthier Canadians, both by traveling to the United States for medical treatment and by the increased use of private medical services within Canada. See, for example, Katz, Verrilli, and Barer, "Canadians' Use of U.S. Medical Services"; Katz et al., "Phantoms in the Snow"; Canadian Institute for Health Information, "Health Care in Canada 2008"; Steinbrook, "Private Health Care in Canada"; and Mehra, "Eroding Public Medicare." The second trend is that vast discrepancies in the quality and availability of care have been noted between wealthier urban communities and poorer rural communities, with Aboriginal Canadians receiving particularly poor care. One comparative study notes that aboriginal Canadians suffer from higher infant mortality and lower life expectancies than do Native Americans. Trovato, "Aboriginal Mortality in Canada, the United States and New Zealand." For discussions of rural and aboriginal health care in Canada, see Romanow, *Building on Values*, 159–170 and 211–231; and Kirby and LeBreton, *Health of Canadians*, 57–74 and 137–146.

Of course, both Canadian and (particularly) American health care systems are in processes of transition, so that these findings may shift.

52. In her comparative assessment of health care systems published in 1999, Carolyn Tuohy argues that, in Canada, the "accommodation between the profession and the state allowed the profession broad clinical autonomy and influence over the system as a whole.... This accommodation, however, was premised on generous levels of public funding. Leaving the levers of decision making in the hands of physicians, in a system of independent fee-for-service practice, yielded levels of spending that by the end of the 1980s were second (albeit a distant second) only to the United States." The system of decision making that was in place in the late 1990s, Tuohy notes, "continued to accord a central role to the clinical judgment of individual physicians in

establishing health care priorities." Tuohy, *Accidental Logics*, 247, 249. She concludes that individual doctors' decisions play a very significant role in the delivery of care in Canada, where "the pattern of care provided was... the aggregate of decisions made by individual physicians sub-ject only to norms enforced by collegial bodies at the hospital and provincial level." In the United States, by contrast, "The most dramatic change in the structural balance in the American health care arena was the decline of the influence of the medical profession in the private market-ori-ented system, and the rise of for-profit financial interests" (244). As a result, she contends that "managed care entities became more and more involved in clinical decision making" (249).

American physicians' unhappiness with their decreased autonomy is well documented. See, for example, the findings that "traditional core professional values and autonomy are the most impor-tant determinants of career satisfaction" and that "managed care appears to exert its effect on satisfaction through its impact on professional autonomy, not through income reduction." Stoddard et al., "Managed Care, Professional Autonomy, and Income," 675–684.

My point, of course, is not that physician autonomy is necessarily a good measure of an optimal health care system. It is rather to show that there can be no simple association between private/ market systems and autonomy, on the one hand, and public, state-funded systems and loss of autonomy, on the other hand.

53. The child rearing model is helpful here: parents are both a source of a child's autonomy and a potential threat to it. It is easy to see that the powerful relationship of dependency children have with their parents is a necessary foundation for the child's autonomy. But the relationship can also be structured in ways that undermine autonomy, that maintain dependence. It is probably the case that all relationships necessary for autonomy can easily be perverted to undermine it.

54. In our current discourse it is difficult to avoid such misleading language. The concept of "self-determination," which I described as central to autonomy, carries the tension implicit in the problem itself. Few people in our culture believe that people are truly self-determining. It is com-monly accepted that people are shaped to a great extent by their culture and genetic makeup. Yet self-determination remains an important value and aspiration. The new conception of autonomy must give force to the aspiration while incorporating a recognition of interdependence.

55. Bruno Bettelheim offers a brief but fascinating discussion of the kinds of relations that foster autonomy. In his account they are direct and personal rather than large-scale, anonymous, or abstract. If his views are correct, we can both understand something about why autonomy has been associated with the private sphere and see that the relevant characteristics are possible in spheres not conventionally considered private. Bettelheim offers as examples the relation to par-ents and to teachers. Bettelheim, *Informed Heart*, 95–97. For a recent reevaluation of Bettelheim's work, especially the modern dilemma of maintaining individual autonomy and integrity while living in a depersonalized, mass society, see Marcus, *Autonomy in the Extreme Situation*.

56. See, for example, Horwitz, *Transformation of American Law, 1780–1860*, and Scheiber, "Property Law, Expropriation, and Resource Allocation by Government."

57. This argument is elaborated in Nedelsky, *Private Property and the Limits of American Constitutionalism*.

58. This is true even though the power of the state alone would not be sufficient without a widespread sense of the legitimacy of property. In both the United States and Canada, these two dimensions of the system of property support one another.

59. I believe it was Elizabeth Mensch from the University of Buffalo Law School who pointed out to me that those who are in frequent conflict with the law, for theft or vandalism, may have a

very clear sense of the role of the state in property rights. In addition, some of those who deal with such property as stocks and securities may be conscious of the central role of state regulation. But for most people, even home ownership (which requires registration) provides only intermittent and fleeting reminders of the role of the state.

60. The link between home "ownership" and autonomy is a complicated social phenomenon. As Robert Leckey pointed out to me, the residential mortgage is one of the only "good," that is, ostensibly autonomy-enhancing, forms of debt for the ordinary consumer. The indebted "home-owner" is seen as freer, more autonomous than a fully solvent tenant. I would add that this may be in part because the law permits landlords much more control over the use of their property than it permits the banks that hold the mortgage. This is, presumably, one of the ways the law promotes the link between property ownership and autonomy.

61. It is important to avoid a misunderstanding about the "mere subjectivity" of feelings. In my view, feelings have two dimensions not commonly associated with the word: One, there is a truth about feelings. One can be right or wrong about them. Thus while they are subjective in the sense that only the person having the feeling can know whether she feels something, her true feelings are not simply whatever impression, or experience, or sensation she has at the moment. A person must inquire internally to determine her true feelings. They may be hard to discern, there may be confusion, but there is in the end a right answer to what she really feels. Two, the related point is that feelings are, at least in our culture, not always immediately ascertainable. There is a commonplace association between the word "feeling" and something like the experience of a pin-prick. One feels pain. No inquiry is necessary. The experience is immediate and obvious. The perception is instantaneous and (under normal circumstances, excluding states of hypnosis or delusion) infallible. But this association is misleading. Even a feeling like anger is by no means always obvious. No. Even though no one can know for sure what someone else is feeling, the "feeler" can be mistaken. A particularly common form of this "mistake" is to be angry without realizing it. In our culture most people seem to need to learn to recognize the signs by which one can tell the truth of a feeling. I think a particular form of judgment is called for in reflecting on what one is "really" feeling and whether that feeling is a good guide to action.

62. This notion of autonomy has the (apparent) virtue of being measurable, as was pointed out to me by someone advocating it.

63. Of course such constraints are often backed by real sanctions, including disapproval, exclusion, withholding of financial resources. But my point is that the experience of the constraint often far exceeds the cost of the sanctions. Sometimes these constraints can be so serious, particularly when the threat of violence is involved (say for a woman breaching familial sexual norms), that the case would no longer fit as an example of internally imposed constraint.

64. See, for example, Govier, "Self-Trust, Autonomy, and Self-Esteem."

65. In the original article version of this chapter I wrote that "focusing on the feelings of autonomy defines as authoritative the voices of those whose autonomy is at issue. Their autonomy is then not a question that can be settled for them by others. The focus on feeling or internal experience defines whose perspective is taken seriously, and by turning our attention in the right direction it enhances our ability to learn what fosters and constitutes autonomy." Nedelsky, "Reconceiving Autonomy," 25. Because I believe that people can hold powerful and destructive illusions about their autonomy (as I discuss at the end of this section), I am no longer willing to simply say that one's feelings of autonomy are authoritative. I do still believe that is essential to inquire into people's experiences of autonomy, or the lack of it, when they interact with institu-

tions. Listening to people's experiences does enhance our ability to learn what fosters and constitutes autonomy.

66. For example, the much-vaunted freedom of mainstream North American life seems to many Native Americans to entail patterns of work with such extreme regimentation as to be incompatible with freedom or autonomy. (Brian Slattery of Osgoode Hall Law School provided me with this example from his work with Native peoples.) Of course, this observation leaves open the question whether the participants in the mainstream patterns of life actually experience their lives as autonomous. Recognizing these variations is one of the virtues of a relational approach because it avoids the mistake of thinking that there is only one structure of relationships (e.g., those associated with private property) that could promote autonomy.

67. Bettelheim, *Informed Heart*, 45.

68. In the discussion above, there is a fine line between a belief that one is autonomous and the subjective experience of autonomy. For example, the people of relative privilege whom I describe as feeling autonomous may believe they are independent; they may also feel independent and feel proud of being so. Some of them may also believe, and thus feel (perhaps in varying degrees), that they are in control of their lives. These beliefs and feelings may be interpreted as meaning that the person has the valued characteristic of autonomy: he is what the dominant mythology depicts as the model citizen and participant in the market, the autonomous actor, independent and in control of his life. I have argued here that the basic reality of human life is interdependence and dependence, not independence, and that the essence of autonomy is not independence. In chapter 7, section III I argue that control is also not useful language for autonomy because control is not a respectful relationship with other human beings. So what does this mean if a person (call him Fred) has false beliefs about his independence and control that translate into feelings of both as well as into a belief that he is autonomous? Does that amount to a subjective experience of autonomy? I think it is likely that the subjective experience of such a person is different from the subjective experience of the person (call her Mary) who recognizes her interdependence and has been able to define for herself (always in the social context of language and relationship) the guiding principles of her life and live according to them. One might want to say that Mary's is the true subjective experience of autonomy, whereas Fred wrongly believes that his experience is that of autonomy. For my purposes here, I do not think I have to resolve this question: if people hold false beliefs about autonomy, can the experiences based on those beliefs be genuine feelings of autonomy? When I said that people could feel autonomous and not be so, I meant they could have feelings like Fred's that they interpret as autonomy. It is the attachment to such feelings and their underlying false beliefs that matters for the point about resistance to change.

69. 397 U.S. 254 (1970).

70. I do not mean to suggest anywhere in this chapter that a bureaucratic state is inevitable. And it seems quite possible that, ultimately, bureaucracy is incompatible with autonomy. Kathy Ferguson certainly thinks so. She has argued very persuasively that whenever people are being "managed" by others, something is wrong. The main point of her book *The Feminist Case against Bureaucracy* (1984) is the claim that there are viable and vastly preferable alternatives to bureaucracy. But as I noted at the outset, the hope is to find in our present practices clues to better solutions to the general problem that arises when there is collective control and provision of services and the application of collective decisions to individuals—currently carried out by administrative bodies. Only a very small community could avoid these issues. There may well be better alterna-

tives to bureaucracy, but I think it is worthwhile trying to make progress on the question of autonomy in the face of bureaucratic power.

71. *Goldberg* is a constitutional law case because the claims for the requirements of due process proceed from the Fourteenth Amendment to the Constitution, which guarantees that no state shall "deprive any person of life, liberty, or property, without due process of law." In the United States, the "due process revolution" and retrenchment thus took place on these constitutional terms. I describe them as part of administrative law because the procedural requirements for U.S. administrative bodies (such as social assistance agencies or health and safety agencies) were heavily governed by constitutional issues as well as statutes. In Canada, much of the law governing similar procedural requirements developed through the common law approach to administrative tribunals, which in Canada is called administrative law. As in the United States, there are also statutes that govern procedural requirements, and the *Charter* now also plays a role in the jurisprudence of procedure in administrative bodies. See note 88 for further comments on differences between American and Canadian administrative law.

72. The phrase and the idea come from Reich, "New Property."

73. In Canada, such claims might come through the *Charter.*

74. In terms of substantive outcomes, the provision of education for handicapped children, Handler considers the law largely a success. It is specifically with regard to the relationship between the clients and the official decision makers that there is a striking disparity between the admirable intentions and language of the law and its actual effects. See Handler, *Conditions of Discretion*, chap. 5.

75. There is, of course, an unusual quality to these decisions since their actual subject, the child, is often not a participant (although the Madison plan that Handler studies calls for them to be when appropriate). The more general problem of structuring autonomous dependence, when the subject of the decision must also be able to participate in the decision, is thus not the problem Handler addresses. There is some question whether he adequately considers the *children's* autonomy in his analysis. See Minow, "Part of the Solution, Part of the Problem."

76. Handler, *Conditions of Discretion*, chap. 4. Handler notes that his is a case study based on interviews with the full range of system participants, conducted during the 1983 school year. The data, he says, are not systematic.

77. Ibid., 66.

78. Ibid., 67.

79. Ibid., 68.

80. Reich, "New Property."

81. Handler, *Conditions of Discretion*, 79.

82. The quote he uses to open the chapter on Madison reads: "Our family has never been criticized, they've never said, 'you're failing him.' They've encouraged us to allow him to do more and try more, and not to be afraid. They've convinced us he can do more than we think he can do." Ibid. One can see that the relationship has been helpful, supportive, and respectful, but to me it does not quite convey the sense of fully equal partnership.

83. Handler also treats the failures of due process as a conceptual failure.

84. 400 U.S. 309 (1971).

85. *Wyman,* 400 U.S. at 328.

86. These developments began with *Board of Regents v. Roth*, 408 U.S. 564 (1972), in which the Court held that a one-year position at a state university did not constitute a property interest and therefore did not bring with it an entitlement to due process.

87. Another critique of Reich's property metaphor is Bussiere, "'New Property' Theory of Welfare Rights," 1–9.

88. At the constitutional level, both Canadian and American procedural fairness guarantees are activated only where certain rights are engaged. In the United States, the due process clauses of the Fourteenth and Fifteenth Amendments apply where "life, liberty, or property" is at stake. In Canada, Section 7 of the *Charter of Rights and Freedoms* guarantees that the "principles of fundamental justice" apply where "life, liberty, and security of the person" are at stake; at the quasi-constitutional level, Section 1(a) of the *Canadian Bill of Rights* (S.C. 1960, chap. 44) provides for due process where "life, liberty, security of the person and enjoyment of property" are at stake. For nonconstitutional administrative law, having a particular protected right at stake is necessary in the United States. Canadian administrative law, by contrast, has retained the common law doctrine of the duty of fairness, which has no such requirement. Jack Beermann explains that, "Although administrative law in the United States has its roots in the common law, its reach and substance today are governed largely by legislative enactment in a very positivist fashion." Beermann, "Reach of Administrative Law in the United States," 172. Beermann specifies that, "In all cases raising a due process claim that the government has not employed fair procedures, there is a threshold requirement that the plaintiff establish that he or she has a protected interest, usually either property or liberty, at stake. The existence of a protected interest, except when constitutionally-defined liberty is involved, is determined by looking to an external source of law, such as the statute governing the benefits programme or regulating the government employment. The existence of a protected interest in such cases involves the purely positive law question of whether governing law creates an entitlement to the benefit or employment" (184).

The continued application of the common law in Canada, however, means that procedural fairness guarantees do not depend on the engagement of predetermined rights. As one recent textbook on Canadian administrative law explains, unless explicitly barred by statute, "the duty of fairness applies to any decision that affects an individual's *rights*, *interests*, or *privileges*. There is little real dispute about the meaning of these terms. They are sufficiently broad to cover most decisions that affect or have the potential to affect an individual in important ways. [Thus fairness has been required in contexts as diverse as prison disciplinary proceedings, dismissal from statutory office, and deportation]." Flood and Sossin, *Administrative Law in Context*, 119. [(Note that, while in the United States procedural due process has been found to attach in all three of these contexts, these findings have been predicated on the establishment of either a statutory procedural right or a "life liberty or property" interest.)] In another textbook, David Mullan provides a helpful overview of the development of the Canadian common law of procedural fairness, illustrating the evolution of the applicability of the duty. Mullan, *Administrative Law*, 156–171. He notes that, while the common law once required that the decision at issue involve the determination of an individual's rights, the Court's decision in *Nicholson v. Haldimand-Norfolk Reg. Police Commrs.*, [1979] 1 S.C.R. 311) changed this requirement "from 'determines' to 'affects,' and embraced 'interests and privileges' as well as rights" (168). Moreover, unlike the American context, in which such interests must be created by statute, common law procedural fairness is presumed to apply in Canada unless the legislature explicitly excludes it: "[C]ourts have always required clear statutory direction in order to limit or oust procedural protection....Courts presume that the legislature intended procedural protection to apply....On this approach, the courts acknowledge the supremacy of the legislature and at the same time confer quasi-constitutional protection upon the common-law duty of fairness." Flood and Sossin, *Administrative Law in Context*, 121.

89. Mashaw, "'Rights' in the Federal Administrative State."

90. [1985] 1 S.C.R. 177.

91. Three of the justices also held that the protections of Section 7 of the *Canadian Charter of Rights and Freedoms*—"the right to life, liberty and security of the person and the right not to be deprived thereof except in accordance with the principles of fundamental justice"—applied not only to citizens but to every person physically present in Canada. I should note that the bases for the decisions in this case varied: for three of the justices it was Section 7 of the *Charter*; for three it was Section 2(e) of the 1960 *Canadian Bill of Rights*.

92. [1985] 2 S.C.R. 643.

93. The legal issue at stake was the duty of fairness.

94. *Cardinal* at para. 21.

95. *Cardinal* at para. 23.

96. [1999] 2 S.C.R. 817.

97. Mavis Baker was a Jamaican citizen who had been working illegally as a live-in domestic worker for eleven years. While in Canada, she had four children—all Canadian citizens by birth. In 1992, Baker was ordered deported, and she sought an exemption on the basis of humanitarian and compassionate considerations (as provided by the *Immigration Act*). Baker submitted evidence that her own health (as a diagnosed schizophrenic) and the well-being of her children depended on her ability to continue to reside in Canada. Her application was denied without reasons. When Baker requested reasons, she was provided with an immigration officer's cursory notes, which had formed the basis of the decision. (See note 113 for a discussion of these notes.) The Supreme Court's decision in this case was important for many reasons: it revised the test for determining what procedural fairness requires in a given case; expanded the procedural fairness owed to individuals applying for humanitarian and compassionate relief; found that the evidence before the Court supported a reasonable apprehension that the immigration officer was biased (see note 113 and para. 48 of the *Baker* decision); and held that administrative discretion must be informed by the values embodied in Canada's international obligations, including a commitment to the best interests of children.

98. See, for example, Dyzenhaus and Fox-Decent, "Rethinking the Process/Substance Distinction: *Baker v. Canada*."

99. *Baker*, per Justice L'Heureux-Dubé at para. 22.

100. Julie Anne White makes a compelling argument about the changes that would be necessary (not in the context of the contributions of administrative law): "A democratic politics of care...assumes that equal membership in a democratic community requires an egalitarian distribution of the work of caretaking. What does this mean in practice? It means moving away from an institutionalized class of providers and an alternative class of recipients. The fluidity of these positions is critical to avoiding the institutionalization of paternalistic care. Being in need is recognized as a social position rather than a character trait.... The alternative to paternalistic care becomes more mutual relationships of caretaking." White, *Democracy, Justice, and the Welfare State*, 164. White also notes the relationship between institutionalized classes and the understanding of dependence: "The authority of providers in the current processes of care is legitimated by reference to the dependency of their clients. Once dependency is normalized, we open up the possibility for democratizing authority" (157).

Her argument indirectly points to the difficulty of finding appropriate terms to characterize the subjects of bureaucratic decision making. "Recipient" may not have the pejorative connotation of "welfare mother," but it nonetheless runs the risk of reinforcing the idea of "an institution-alized class of providers and an alternative class of recipients."

101. *Baker*, per Justice L'Heureux-Dubé at 850, para. 47. Thanks to Robert Leckey for noting the relevance of this section of the decision to my argument.

102. Her approach thus also responds to the once powerful objection to the administrative state as involving discretion that is an intrinsic threat to individual liberty and autonomy.

103. Cartier, "Administrative Discretion as Dialogue."

104. Ibid.

105. Ibid.

106. I put "facts" in quotes to highlight the way facts require interpretation and construction just as much as rules of law do.

107. Cartier, "Reconceiving Discretion," 272, quoting Allan, "Fairness, Equality, Rationality," 19, and Handler, "Dependent People, the State, and the Modern/Postmodern Search for the Dialogic Community," 1066.

108. To be fair, it is not clear that Cartier intends her argument to apply directly to the front-line workers. But in my view, that is the ultimate—and valuable—implication of her argument.

109. Cartier, of course, does not make this mistake, as her focus on substance as well as procedure indicates. Note the correspondence to the argument that autonomy is the value at stake in assessing bureaucratic decision making, independent of or in addition to whatever interests (such as property or personal security) are at stake. This perspective is evident in Justice LeDain's sweeping statement in *Cardinal* (discussed in section IV.D) that "the right to a fair hearing must be regarded as an independent *unqualified right* which finds its essential justification in the sense of procedural justice which *any person affected by an administrative decision is entitled to have*" (emphasis added).

110. In presidential systems, the same issues might arise in terms of adequacy of participation in the election of the executive, given that some bureaucratic functions flow from the executive.

111. I put this in the plural since the answer will vary depending on the kind of administrative decisions at stake.

112. The protection of property rights was also important in the development of Canadian administrative law. See, for example, Leckey, *Contextual Subjects*.

113. The *Baker* decision discussed above provides another such example. In that case, the immigration officer, whose notes formed the basis of the decision to deny Baker's application on humanitarian and compassionate grounds, were found by the Court to give rise to a reasonable apprehension of bias: "His notes, and the manner in which they are written, do not disclose the existence of an open mind or a weighing of the particular circumstances of the case free from ste-reotypes" (at para. 48). The officer's notes, transcribed below, read:

> PC is unemployed—on Welfare. No income shown—no assets. Has four Cdn.-born children—four other children in Jamaica—HAS A TOTAL OF EIGHT CHILDREN
>   Says only two children are in her "direct custody." (No info on who has ghe [*sic*] other two).
>   There is nothing for her in Jamaica—hasn't been there in a long time—no longer close to her children there—no jobs there—she has no skills other than as a domestic—chil-dren would suffer—can't take them with her and can't leave them with anyone here. Says

has suffered from a mental disorder since '81—is now an outpatient and is improving. If sent back will have a relapse.

Letter from Children's Aid—they say PC has been diagnosed as a paranoid schizophrenic.—children would suffer if returned—

Letter of Aug.'93 from psychiatrist from Ont. Govm't.

Says PC had post-partum psychosis and had a brief episode of psychosis in Jam. when was 25 yrs. old. Is now an out-patient and is doing relatively well—deportation would be an extremely stressful experience.

Lawyer says PS [*sic*] is sole caregiver and single parent of two Cdn born children. Pc's mental condition would suffer a setback if she is deported etc.

This case is a catastrophy [*sic*]. It is also an indictment of our "system" that the client came as a visitor in Aug.'81, was not ordered deported until Dec.'92 and in APRIL'94 IS STILL HERE!

The PC is a paranoid schizophrenic and on welfare. She has no qualifications other than as a domestic. She has FOUR CHILDREN IN JAMAICA AND ANOTHER FOUR BORN HERE. She will, of course, be a tremendous strain on our social welfare systems for (probably) the rest of her life. There are no H&C factors other than her FOUR CANADIAN-BORN CHILDREN. Do we let her stay because of that? I am of the opinion that Canada can no longer afford this type of generosity. However, because of the circumstances involved, there is a potential for adverse publicity. I recommend refusal but you may wish to clear this with someone at Region.

There is also a potential for violence—see charge of "assault with a weapon."

114. Democratic decision making is not the only way collective power can threaten individual autonomy. The power wielded by corporations is, again, an obvious example. For example, this can take the form of workplace practices that undermine employees' autonomy.

115. For a thoughtful and imaginative effort at reenvisioning relationships in the administrative context see Sossin, "An Intimate Approach to Fairness, Impartiality and Reasonableness in Administrative Law."

116. Janet Mosher et al.'s report "Walking on Eggshells" notes complaints about constant sur-veillance, intricate and opaque rules that seemingly govern every aspect of life on welfare, control over and inaccessibility of information, and demeaning and humiliating treatment (v, ix). The authors report that "In our interviews with women, when asked what needed to change in the welfare system, the most common response was the way they were treated by welfare workers.…Many noted that the responses they experienced from particular workers were responses required by or encouraged by the dictates and culture of the welfare system" (ix–x).

117. See Joseph Raz on the importance of meaningful choices for autonomy. Raz, *Morality of Freedom*, 205, 373.

118. Law Commission of Canada, "Minister's Reference on Institutional Child Abuse." (The term "total institution" comes from Goffman, *Asylums*). Other examples they point to include schools for the deaf. Another example brought to my attention by Julie Maclean is refugee camps.

119. See, for example, Mosher et al., "Walking on Eggshells," 6–8, 27–40.

120. See Handler, *Poverty of Welfare Reform*, and Handler and Hasenfeld, *We the Poor People*.

121. *Falkiner v. Ontario (Minister of Community and Social Services)*, (2002), 212 D.L.R. (4th) 633. After this decision, the Ontario Liberal party defeated the then-governing Progressive Conservatives and did not pursue an appeal of this ruling to the Supreme Court of Canada. See also *R. v. Rehberg* (1993), 127 N.S.R. (2d) 331 (N.S.S.C.).

122. Even the guarantee of a small regular income will not meet the basic needs of what are often called "hard-to-serve" populations. For example, in the context of welfare regimes, Alan Weil and Kenneth Finegold explain, "Providing child care or transportation to a recipient with a substance abuse problem may not help until the larger problem of the substance abuse is addressed. Efforts to help a recipient increase literacy or job-related skills may fail because nothing is being done to address an undiagnosed severe learning disability." Weil and Finegold, *Welfare Reform*, 166.

Toronto's Strachan House (which won the 1999 Governor General's Award for Excellence in Architecture) provides a good example of how the particular needs of hard-to-serve populations might be accommodated. Strachan House was designed by Levitt Goodman Architects to respond to the specific needs of chronically homeless women and men. Robert Kronenburg, Joseph Lim, and Wong Yunn Chii explain that "Significant in the design and construction process was the consultation and active involvement of the future residents of the house.... This process of consultation helped define the social and political framework within which a group of men and women, living solitary lives excluded from society, could imagine how to come inside and live together in a communal setting." Lim, Wong Yunn Chii, and Kronenburg, *Transportable Environments*, 46. For a detailed account of the concerns expressed in these consultations, and the creative ways that Levitt Goodman Architects incorporated them into the design of Strachan House, see Bridgman, "Architecture of Homelessness and Utopian Pragmatics."

123. It seems likely that only a complete overhaul could render prisons remotely compatible with the autonomy, dignity, and democratic rights of those subject to them.

124. MacAdam, Swift, and Balmer, *Lives Still in the Balance*.

125. Nancy Fraser has charted the history of shelters for women who have been battered by their partners. A movement that began with women who previously had been battered setting up shelters for those currently in need, came gradually to be taken over by people with "expertise." Thus a hierarchy was created between staff and clients that had not existed in the beginning. Fraser, "Talking about Needs," 308–309.

126. See Sossin, "An Intimate Approach to Fairness, Impartiality and Reasonableness in Administrative Law."

127. For example, White, *Democracy, Justice, and the Welfare State*.

CHAPTER 4

1. Sometimes the terms "agency" and "autonomy" are used interchangeably. Susan Sherwin offers a helpful distinction, describing agency as the making of a choice and autonomy as self-governance. She argues that we need a relational conception of autonomy in order to "distinguish genuinely autonomous behavior from acts of merely rational agency." Sherwin, *Politics of Women's Health*, 33.

2. I use the term "affective" despite its relative unfamiliarity because the word "emotional" has strong connotations that mean something other than the capacity for emotion.

3. George Lakoff and Mark Johnson offered the important insight that "metaphor is pervasive in everyday life, not just in language but in thought and action. Our ordinary conceptual

system, in terms of which we both think and act, is fundamentally metaphorical in nature. The concepts that govern our thought are not just matters of the intellect. They also govern our everyday functioning, down to the most mundane details. Our concepts structure what we perceive, how we get around in the world, and how we relate to other people. Our conceptual system thus plays a central role in defining our everyday realities." Lakoff and Johnson, *Metaphors We Live By*.

4. I elaborate the argument with respect to control in chapter 7, section III.

5. I will not try to address the question of whether the exclusion generated by the dominant picture of the abstracted self in the language of rights has been part of the "purpose" of the abstraction. Nor will I try to account for the actual history of abstraction in the liberal concept of self.

6. I discuss this issue in Nedelsky, "Challenges of Multiplicity," 1591–1609.

7. The need for such justification stands even when one believes, as I do, that equality *frequently* requires different treatment for differently situated groups and individuals. Accommodation for the differently abled, maternity leave, and affirmative action are obvious examples. The need for justification persists because it remains the case that different treatment— such as gendered division of household work and childcare, with its implications for leisure time, access to the labor force, and civic participation—is still a source of inequality throughout the world. The requirement for justification does logically presuppose sameness as the starting point. But I think this need not be harmful as long as a cogent argument for the way difference advances equality is all that is required to overcome the presumption.

8. See particularly Young, "Impartiality and the Civic Public."

9. See, for example, Benhabib, "Judith Shklar's Dystopic Liberalism"; Shklar, "Liberalism of Fear"; Handler, *Conditions of Discretion*, 248.

10. Kant, for example, thought his arguments about reason applied to all reasoning beings, including angels. Kant, *Groundwork of the Metaphysic of Morals*.

11. I think people whose bodily abilities (and sometimes appearance) do not conform to the norm of the "able-bodied" have a much more constant sense of their embodiment. In a conversation I had, a person with asthma identified with the examples below of feeling the "otherness" of the asthma, reflected in language of "battling" her asthma and winning or losing. A woman who has been legally blind from birth said she experienced her limited sight as a much more integrated part of herself and experienced the problems it caused as the result of society's failures of accommodation.

12. Hannah Arendt also makes the important argument that our cognitive capacity for judgment also requires our social nature; we depend on our interactions with others for it to function. Arendt and Beiner, *Lectures on Kant's Political Philosophy*.

13. See, for example, Little, "Seeing and Caring"; Minow, "Feminist Reason," 47; Jaggar, "Love and Knowledge"; Nedelsky, "Embodied Diversity and the Challenges to Law"; Hall, *Trouble with Passion*; and Kinston and Ferry, *Bringing the Passions Back In*.

14. Not surprisingly there is no simple consensus on these issues among psychologists and neuroscientists. For a review of the literature, critiques, and response by Damasio see: Dunn, Dalgleish, and Lawrence, "Somatic Marker Hypothesis"; Pham, "Emotion and Rationality"; Bechara et al., "Iowa Gambling Task and the Somatic Marker Hypothesis."

15. Damasio, *Descartes' Error*, 208–212.

16. Ibid., 211.

17. Ibid., 173.

18. Ibid., 172.

19. Ibid.

20. Ibid., 38.

21. Ibid., 175.

22. Nedelsky, "Embodied Diversity and the Challenges to Law." In particular, I argue that "the sources of affective somatic markers—the gut feelings that are the starting points of decision making—are the product of experience, education and culture." I further suggest that, "the incompleteness of our perspectives can be remedied by extensive exposure to diversity" and that "affect can be educated as well as transcended through reflection" (241–242, 248).

23. Kompridis, *Critique and Disclosure*, 199–209.

24. Lakoff and Johnson, *Metaphors We Live By*. See chapter 2, note 1.

25. When the subject is not individual autonomy, but the rights of peoples under international law, I think the phrase "self-determination" works better. See Young, "Two Concepts of Self-Determination."

26. Benhabib, "Subjectivity, Historiography, and Politics," and Butler, "For a Careful Reading," in Benhabib et al., *Feminist Contentions*.

27. Benhabib et al., *Feminist Contentions*, 113.

28. Ibid., 137.

29. See, for example, Abrams, "Constitution of Women," 863–864; Schneider, "Describing and Changing"; Walker, "Response to Elizabeth M/Schneider's 'Describing and Changing.'"

30. Bad behavior may not even be a necessary condition for incarceration: social scientists argue that racism and class bias often play a part in wrongful convictions. See Maidment, *When Justice Is a Game*. An infamous Canadian example is the wrongful conviction of Donald Marshall Jr., a Mi'kmaq who spent eleven years in prison for a murder he did not commit. Marshall's case was the subject of a public inquiry, which determined that racism had played a significant role in his conviction. Royal Commission on the Donald Marshall Jr. Prosecution, "Digest of Findings and Recommendations."

31. Melissa Harris-Lacewell emphasized this point in response to President Obama's famous March 2008 "race speech" wherein he urged African Americans to take "full responsibility for [our] own lives—by demanding more from our fathers and spending more time with our children." Obama, "A More Perfect Union." Harris-Lacewell contends that "Barack's analysis fell into an easy claim that if we just 'live right' everything will be 'alright.'" She elaborates, "It is just false to believe that bad behavior leads to bad outcomes. Anyone who has spent time with the wealthy, white and privileged knows that bad habits, deviant behavior and criminal activities are standard practice. This is true for the Ivy-League kids cooking up Robitussin in their dorm rooms and for the CEOs earning millions off the backs of international child labor. All you have to do is turn on Access Hollywood to see that addiction, child neglect and out-of-wedlock births are perfectly acceptable as long as wealth and privilege are providing a safety net." Harris-Lacewell, "Obama's Cosby Moment Response," cited in Hill, "Down from the Tower—Obama's Popeyes Speech."

32. Borrows, *Drawing Out Law*.

33. See ibid., 22.

34. The distinction between autonomy and agency are elaborated above, in note 1. See Sherwin, *Politics of Women's Health*, 3.

35. Hoagland, *Lesbian Ethics*.

36. The capacities of these other forms are also relational in nature (see brief discussion in chapter 1, section II). Naturally, the claim that the capacity for creative interaction can be observed includes the recognition that the observation involves attention and interpretation.

37. Indeed, if it is a daily struggle to respond to one internalized demand after the next, one's autonomy may equally be impaired. This raises the issue of the link between consciousness and autonomy, which I discuss in chapter 3, section III.A and chapter 7, section II.

38. There are also interesting suggestions that letting go of the effort to control actually makes it more likely that the sense of being out of control will recede. Again, the struggle for control is not autonomy enhancing.

39. Keller, *From a Broken Web.*

40. Benhabib, *Situating the Self,* 69.

41. Lorde, "Uses of the Erotic," 56–57; emphasis added. Lorde defines the erotic this way: "The very word *erotic* comes from the Greek word *eros,* the personification of love in all its aspects— born of Chaos, and personifying creative power and harmony. When I speak of the erotic, then, I speak of it as an assertion of the lifeforce of women; of that creative energy empowered, the knowledge and use of which we are now reclaiming in our language, our history, our dancing, our loving, our work, our lives" (55). In my view, the capacity for creative interaction is equally shared by men and women.

42. Ibid., 57. She elaborates: "This is one reason why the erotic is so feared, and so often relegated to the bedroom alone, when it is recognized at all. For once we begin to feel deeply all aspects of our lives, we begin to demand from ourselves and from our life-pursuits that they feel in accordance with that joy which we know ourselves to be capable of. Our erotic knowledge empowers us, becomes a lens through which we scrutinize all aspects of our existence, forcing us to evaluate those aspects honestly in terms of the relative meaning within our lives. And this is a grave responsibility, projected from within each of us, not to settle for the convenient, the shoddy, the conventionally expected, nor the merely safe" (57).

43. I discuss these issues in chapter 7, section II.

44. See Young, "Impartiality and the Civic Public."

45. See note 85 on this term.

46. Raz, *Ethics in the Public Domain,* 33.

47. This was Neil MacCormick's response to my question about why he was assuming autonomy. Legal Theory Workshop, Faculty of Law, University of Toronto [date unknown].

48. The link between autonomy and responsibility is part of the reason for the "mental element" in criminal law. As Justice Wilson explained in *Reference re Section 94(2) of the Motor Vehicle Act,* [1985] 2 S.C.R. 486, "In the earliest beginnings of criminal liability the mental state of the wrongdoer was not considered at all; it was enough that he had done the fell deed. At a later stage the accused's state of mind was considered for two distinct purposes, namely (1) to determine whether his conduct was voluntary or involuntary; and (2) to determine whether he realized what the consequences of his conduct might be. But the first purpose was viewed as the key one. It was considerably later in the development of the law of criminal responsibility that the emphasis changed and an appreciation of the consequences of his act became the central focus. The movement towards the concept of the "guilty mind" was not, however, a sudden or dramatic one" (para. 112; citations omitted).

Justice Wilson was engaged in this inquiry because of a *Charter* challenge that an absolute liability offense with a mandatory jail sentence violated Section 7, which guarantees that no one will be deprived of life, liberty, and security of the person except in accordance with the principles of fundamental justice. *Canadian Charter of Rights and Freedoms*, Part I of the *Constitution Act, 1982*, being Schedule B to the *Canada Act 1982* (U.K.), 1982, chap. 11, sec. 7. As Justice Wilson put it, "Because of the absolute liability nature of the offence created by s. 94(2) of the *Motor Vehicle Act* a person can be convicted under the section even although he was unaware at the time he was driving that his licence was suspended and was unable to find this out despite the exercise of due diligence" (para. 128). She concluded, "I believe that a mandatory term of imprisonment for an offence committed unknowingly and unwittingly and after the exercise of due diligence is grossly excessive and inhumane....I believe, therefore, that such a sanction offends the principles of fundamental justice embodied in our penal system" (para. 130).

Justice Lamer put the point this way, "It has from time immemorial been part of our system of laws that the innocent not be punished. This principle has long been recognized as an essential element of a system for the administration of justice which is founded upon a belief in the dignity and worth of the human person and on the rule of law" (para. 69). He concluded, "A law that has the potential to convict a person who has not really done anything wrong offends the principles of fundamental justice and, if imprisonment is available as a penalty, such a law then violates a person's right to liberty under s. 7 of the *Charter of Rights and Freedoms.* In other words, absolute liability and imprisonment cannot be combined" (paras. 2–3).

49. See note 1 and Sherwin, *Politics of Women's Health*, 33.

50. Different jurisdictions handle the issue of provocation differently, relying on the principle either as a partial defense or as a mitigating circumstance in sentencing. Caroline Forell provides a helpful overview of the law of provocation in Canada, the United States, and Australia in "Gender Equality, Social Values and Provocation Law in the United States, Canada and Australia." Forell notes that provocation is generally available as a partial defense, for example reducing a charge of murder to manslaughter, in jurisdictions with mandatory minimum sentences for murder that prevent judges or juries from taking full account of the circumstances of a crime at sentencing. In Canada, where murder convictions carry a mandatory minimum sentence, provocation is liberally construed, omitting the traditional requirement that there has been no cooling-off period and using the broad term "heat of passion" to capture a range of circumstances beyond the traditional categories of provocation. She notes by way of contrast that two Australian jurisdictions, Tasmania and Victoria—both of which favor flexible sentencing over mandatory minimums for murder—have abolished the defense of provocation. Similarly, the notions of necessity and duress can play complex mitigating roles, handled differently in different jurisdictions.

51. My thanks to Diane Pothier for this example.

52. See chapter 1, Section II.B for a brief discussion of examples of debates surrounding legislation outlawing prostitution or prohibiting a woman from contracting to carry a child for another.

53. I am indebted to the work of Nicola Lacey (as well as to her comments on a draft of this chapter) for a more nuanced framework for this somewhat simplified version of the conceptions of autonomy and responsibility underlying the common law. First, I want to share her observation that although from a theoretical perspective autonomy has the on/off quality I attribute to it (with the exemptions and exceptions articulated through various defenses), in practice the criminal law has a wide variety of ways of responding to a continuum of autonomy. The different degrees of homicide, such as murder and manslaughter, together with the factors that can be

taken into account in sentencing, allow for a much more nuanced practical engagement with a continuum of autonomy than an account of the theory of responsibility (and autonomy) might suggest. I would add that in other areas of the law, such as contract, the twentieth century brought a range of concepts, such as duress, unconscionablity, and unjustifiable enrichment, that can allow for the recognition of constraint on autonomy, including a recognition of the role of power relations.

A broader, but related, point is that I think Lacey would argue that the way the criminal law assigns responsibility *is* vastly more complicated than the picture of autonomy-based responsibility I have sketched here. She develops this argument in "In Search of the Responsible Subject." In Lacey's terms, this is a capacity-based principle of responsibility: "The dominant argument is that individuals' criminal responsibility is at root based upon their capacities and opportunities: capacities of cognition or understanding: it is only fair to punish someone who has the capacity to understand why they are doing; and capacities of volition or will: it is only justifiable to punish someone who has the capacity or in some versions, the fair opportunity to act otherwise than they did" (353). I think that she would agree with me in my description of the dominant understanding of the autonomy–responsibility link and thus the normal assumption of autonomy. And she would agree also that this "principle of responsibility" fits within a larger framework of liberal thought. But she adds a variety of important caveats.

First, this conception of criminal responsibility does not map onto enlightenment thought in a simple way. It took a long time for this conception to evolve from what she calls a character-based approach to responsibility, so that it did not become firmly established in England until the late nineteenth or the early twentieth century—long after the philosophy of the Enlightenment. Moreover, she thinks this character approach still has some "resonance in Modern Anglo-American law" (357). She has also shown that the actual practices of criminal law do not consistently rely on the capacity model (with its tight link between autonomy and responsibility), despite the widely shared assumption that this is the foundation of criminal law: "one needs to step outside the boundaries of legal doctrine to throw further light on the significance of the fact that the responsibility principle is so extravagantly honoured while being so regularly breached....An example would be data on patterns of criminal enforcement, which show that crimes with no responsibility requirement or a partial responsibility requirement are empirically dominant—i.e. they are over-represented in enforcement practice relative to their numbers on the statute book" (355–356).

In addition, she shows in another article that alternatives to the capacity-based responsibility principle are currently being proposed. She discusses what she calls the "reasons-based" view. On this view, "exemptions such as insanity and diminished responsibility mark out subjects who are beyond the purview of criminal law's proscriptions....In contrast, defences such as duress, self-defence or (perhaps) provocation mark out subjects who have—according to different versions of the theory—acted on reasons which are approved as within the range which would be expected of a normal, socially responsible person, or acted in a way which manifests no disposition to resist or violate the norms or values protected by the criminal law." Lacey, "Partial Defences to Murder," 18n26.

Perhaps most important for my project here, Lacey thinks that the more complex or "oblique" relationship she traces between philosophical and legal conceptions of responsibility "makes it conceivable that multiple and philosophically inconsistent conceptions of responsibility may operate within legal practices of attribution without any necessary illogicality or incoherence in these distinctive practices. My [Lacey's] intellectual starting point is, therefore, skeptical about the propriety of an a priori unitary approach to theorizing criminal responsibility." Lacey, "In Search of the Responsible Subject."

I think my analysis in this chapter is consistent with Lacey's important arguments. The "battered women" cases I discuss below show an inconsistency of analysis, but my point is not about failure of consistency as such. My point, rather, is the importance of attending to the full range of relational factors that can make killing the battering partner "reasonable" under the circumstances. What matters here in Lacey's argument is, first, acknowledging that the links between dominant conceptions of self as a rational agent and notions of legal responsibility (and its presumed autonomy) are more complex and incomplete than my summary might suggest. Second, I do not think that in calling for the routine use of a relational approach that I am calling for an a priori unity. I think a relational framework is consistent with a variety of approaches (for example, the "reasons-based" view she discusses). The self-consciousness that I think the relational approach encourages will help make clearer the range of presumptions and tacit theories at work in legal decision making.

54. Section 16(1) of the Canadian Criminal Code states that "No person is criminally responsible for an act committed or an omission made while suffering from a mental disorder that rendered the person incapable of appreciating the nature and quality of the act or omission or of knowing that it was wrong." *Canadian Criminal Code*, R.S.C., 1985, chap. C-46, sec. 16(1). This formulation is effectively a codification of the common law definition of insanity, known as the M'Naghten Rules after the case in which they were first articulated (*M'Naghten's Case* 1843 10 C & F 200). The United States Insanity Defense Reform Act of 1984 codified a similar defense applicable in federal courts but specified that the underlying mental defect must be "severe": an accused person will be found not guilty under this provision only if "the defendant, as a result of a severe mental disease or defect, was unable to appreciate the nature and quality or the wrongfulness of his acts." Title 18, U.S. Code, Section 17. While in Canada the defendant bears the burden of establishing the elements of a defense of mental disorder on a balance of probabilities (*Canadian Criminal Code*, Section 16(2)), the American federal rule requires "clear and convincing evidence." Prior to the enactment of the Insanity Defense Reform Act, U.S. jurisdictions had adopted increasingly permissive insanity defenses; the act was enacted as part of a wave of insanity defense law reform at the state and federal level following John Hinckley Jr.'s successful employment of the insanity defense in his trial for the attempted assassination of President Ronald Reagan. R. D. MacKay notes that "Never in the history of the insanity defence has there been so much legislative change in such a brief period of time as in the United States since the Hinckley verdict....the M'Naghten Rules...are once again viewed as an appropriate test of legal insanity....The United States has moved back toward a more punitive approach in relation to the insanity defence." Mackay, *Mental Condition Defences in the Criminal Law*. For a review of these changes at the state and federal level in the United States, see pages 113–131.

55. In Canada, the provocation defense can reduce a charge from murder to manslaughter. George Mousourakis explains that, "Unlike other defences based upon the idea of moral or normative involuntariness, loss of self-control as a result of provocation falls short of totally excluding moral and legal culpability. Giving way to anger—justified though such anger may be—or allowing one's reasoning ability (and hence her freedom to choose) to be overcome by passion furnishes sufficient grounds for holding the provoked agent partially responsible for her wrongdoing....The agent remains morally and legally responsible for the lesser crime of manslaughter because, as a

"normal" person, she is assumed capable of resisting her impulse to kill the provoker.... This is precisely what justifies the provoked killer's being held, to some extent, morally and legally responsible for her actions." Mousourakis, "Reason, Passion and Self Control," para. 1. Interestingly, provocation did constitute a full defense at common law in some jurisdictions under certain circumstances. See note 71 on the defense of provocation for men who find their wives having sexual relations with another man.

56. White-Mair, "Experts and Ordinary Men," 406.

57. The Canadian Supreme Court explicitly recognized this problem in *R. v. Malott*, [1998] 1 S.C.R. 123, at para. 39–40.

58. See *Canadian Criminal Code*, R.S.C. 1985, chap. C-46, secs. 34–37.

59. [1990] 1 S.C.R. 852.

60. Stark, *Coercive Control*, 115.

61. Justice Wilson also makes this point in *Lavallee* at para. 58.

62. See Mahoney, "Legal Images of Battered Women."

63. Ibid., 81.

64. *Lavallee* at para. 3.

65. Mahoney comments on one judicial opinion: "This court received a sophisticated explanation of the impact battering has on women. Yet, as the court in turn explains the woman's situation, the objective difficulties of leaving and subjective fear and helplessness are both present, but seem unrelated." Mahoney, "Legal Images of Battered Women, 80.

66. *Malott* at para. 43.

67. An American judge, in dissent, offers an example of the recognition of such failure: "Mrs. Norman didn't leave because she believed, fully believed that escape was impossible. There was no place to go.... [S]he had left before; he had come and gotten her. She had gone to the Department of Social Services. He had come and gotten her. The law, she believed the law could not protect her, no one could protect her, and I must admit, looking over the records, that there was nothing done that would contradict that belief." *State v. Norman*, 378 S.E.2d 8, 17 (Martin J., dissenting), quoted in Mahoney, "Legal Images of Battered Women," 92.

68. There has been a long, troubling history of police failure to take seriously intimate partner violence (often referred to as domestic violence), as though violence in the home is somehow a distinct, lesser form of violence. Nevertheless, I want to be clear that I do not think that the persistence of wife assault is simply a police failure. (The same goes for the practice of battering intimate partners that occurs between same-sex couples: see chapter 5, note 15.) I doubt whether police can effectively prevent any kind of behavior without widespread social support for its prevention.

69. Mahoney, "Legal Images of Battered Women.

70. My gratitude to Martha Shaffer for helping me revise my view.

71. Cynthia Lee explains that the "husband's observation of his wife having sexual relations with another man was the only category of legally adequate provocation at common law that explicitly applied to male defendants (husbands who killed their wives)." Lee, *Murder and the Reasonable Man*, 20. In recent years, legislatures have attempted to mitigate the gender bias inherent in the traditional provocation defense, including a revision to the Texas penal code that eliminated "heat of passion" even as a partial defense to murder. Lee notes, however, that despite these legislative changes, judges and juries in some jurisdictions continue to show lenience in cases where men kill unfaithful wives (42–43).

72. Hartog, *Man and Wife in America*, 220–222.

73. Lacey, *Women, Crime, and Character*, 18–19.

74. Lee, *Murder and the Reasonable Man*, 20.

75. See note 71.

76. Troubling stereotypes have often informed judicial attempts to recognize the role of culture in the context of what I referred to as wronged husbands who kill or abuse their wives. Sirma Bilge provides a shocking survey of a number of these cases in her broader discussion of the invocation and application of "cultural defenses" to violent crime. In one such "wronged husband" case, for example, a Chinese immigrant relied on "cultural evidence" to have a murder charge reduced to manslaughter after attacking and killing his supposedly unfaithful wife with a hammer. Bilge explains that, relying on generalized, monolithic representation of Chinese culture presented to the court through the testimony of a white, male anthropologist, the court accepted "culture" as a relevant factor in reducing the charge to manslaughter; In the view of the trial judge, the defendant's autonomy was constrained by "cultural" factors, such that he was "driven to violence by traditional Chinese values about adultery and loss of manhood." Bilge, "Behind the 'Culture' Lens." The offender was sentenced to five years of probation for the killing.

77. David Dyzenhaus, for example, has described the idea that "government is subject to the constraints of principles such as fairness, reasonableness, and equality of treatment" as being among those "principles which make sense of the idea of government under the rule of law." Dyzenhaus, "'With the Benefit of Hindsight,'" 79.

78. Part of the problem is that it may seem that any increase in the scope of judges' discretion will invite in "discriminatory background assumptions." Moran, *Rethinking the Reasonable Person*, 300. But I think the issue is rather the desirability of disrupting well-entrenched, and thus stable and predictable, norms of exercising discretion, which are not optimal for attending to the issues a relational approach calls for. Such disruption then calls for doing the work of building new norms guided by commitments both to equality and a relational approach. See note 80.

79. Backhouse and Osgoode Society for Canadian Legal History, *Colour-Coded*; Moran, *Rethinking the Reasonable Person*.

80. Mayo Moran identifies such a double standard in a line of "allurement" cases wherein negligence defendants remain fully liable, despite any carelessness on the part of a child plaintiff, where the plaintiff was "enticed or allured into a dangerous situation." Moran, *Rethinking the Reasonable*, 96. Moran's survey of the sixty-four allurement cases in the Canadian Abridgment (only fourteen of which involved female plaintiffs) suggests that "boys are often exonerated in situations that they knew to be dangerous on the basis that they reasonably yielded to temptation," whereas "the claims of playing girls are routinely rejected even when the girl's behaviour does not seem nearly as dangerous as that of her male counterpart" (101).

Among the examples canvassed in support of this view, she contrasts the lenient judicial treatment of a boy plaintiff in *Gough v. National Coal Board*, [1953] 2 All ER 1283, 1295 (CA), with the less forgiving treatment of a girl plaintiff in *O'Connell v. Town of Chatham* (1949), 24 MPR 36 (NCBA). In the *Gough* case a six-and-a-half-year-old boy was injured after catching a ride on a tram and jumping off. Despite repeated warnings as to the danger of these trams, and despite the boy's own acknowledgment that he knew the activity to be dangerous, the plaintiff was not precluded from recovering for negligence from the Coal Board. *O'Connell*, on the other hand, concerned an eight-year-old girl who was injured while coasting on a street where the town had erected barricades and lights for the precise purpose of protecting children who were known to commonly engage in this pastime. Moran acknowledges the hazards of comparing the outcomes of these cases, since no two factual scenarios are identical; she emphasizes instead the court's language and attitude toward the two plaintiffs. While the girl's allurement argument was blithely rejected on the basis that "there was no hidden danger and therefore no trap," the boy was found to have been "allured" since the judge could think of "few things more likely to tempt small boys than a slow moving set of trams on which a boy can get for a little distance a pleasant and unusual ride. From time immemorial boys have always been anxious to get rides, and it has always been a very real allurement to them." Moran, *Rethinking the Reasonable Person*, 112, 103. As Moran's survey of the cases highlights, the judge's descriptions of childhood in cases of boy plaintiffs are replete with romantic references to boyhood mischief while cases involving girl plaintiffs consistently rely on a "pale thin vision" of girlhood characterized by timidity and caution (128).

81. See Moran, *Rethinking the Reasonable Person*, chap. 8, for a discussion of the various ways of infusing norms of equality into the law in areas where "discriminatory background understandings" (300) may shape judges exercise of their discretion. See also my discussion in chapter 5, sections V and VII.

82. A rare exception: Peter Singer holds that human fetuses are no more morally significant than nonhuman animals, and since (unlike nonhuman animals) fetuses lack the capacity for self-awareness, rational thought, and emotion, they thus are not "persons" in the sense necessary to require moral consideration Singer, *Practical Ethics*, 149–169. Singer extends this same reasoning to infant humans (169–174).

83. One might say that the empirical enters in to the extent that there must be substantive agreement about what counts as a human being. Ordinarily people do not have difficulty recognizing or agreeing on what creatures count as human beings. Of course, there important exceptions at the margins: when human life begins or death occurs.

84. What would count as an explicit rejection of equal moral worth would be an argument that some group, such as men or members of an aristocracy or "white" people, are intrinsically more valuable than women or nonaristocrats or racialized groups. In contemporary North America, one rarely encounters overt arguments of this kind. Historically, some forms of racism have claimed that the racialized people are not fully human. As a practical matter, arguments for inclusion in humanness or equal moral worth may have taken the form of empirical claims of sameness of relevant characteristics, such as reason. (Today, one can see similar substantive arguments on behalf of some of the great apes—they are sufficiently similar to us in their intellectual and social nature to be entitled to certain rights. See note 97. I will return in the coda to this chapter to the ways in which the empirical claims of humanness turn out to introduce another dimension of exclusion.) But that does not mean that there is some invariant substantive, empirical essence of humanness that can ground a constant equal moral worth across all human beings. Again, in practical terms the one contemporary example I can think of that formally denies equal moral worth is the practice within some American jurisdictions of allowing an assessment of the value of the victim to determine whether the death penalty is appropriate. For the purposes of such legal responsibility and sanction no life should be treated as more valuable than another.

85. "Racialism" is described by Michael MacDonald as "a term with two more-or-less distinct meanings in South African usage. In the first meaning, it is used, much as Americans use the word 'racism,' to denote racially motivated bigotry, inequality and oppression. But in the second meaning, 'racialism' is not necessarily coterminous with 'racism.' The word 'racialism' insinuates race as a defining human attribute, a central axis of human society and political organization, a

fulcrum of political representation and participation." MacDonald, *Why Race Matters in South Africa*, 93. Macdonald elaborates, "If racialism may mean either racism or racially organized political participation, the negation—the 'non'—multiplies the possibilities" (93). The most "uncompromising definition" of nonracialism, according to Macdonald, is expressed in the works of Neville Alexander, whom he quotes as asserting that "ethnic groups do not exist," casting "race" as a harmful social construction (93). Macdonald provides a comprehensive survey of the history of this highly contested term, noting that, even after the ANC "adopted, propagated, and carried 'non-racialism' to its current perch," they did not "substitute one fixed definition of 'non-racialism' …In its hands, the term's meaning became layered" (96).

86. In addition to guaranteeing women's equality rights (Section 9), the South African Constitution aims to protect cultural diversity (Sections 30 and 31) and contains explicit recognition of the continued force of indigenous 'customary law' (Sections 39(3), 211, and 212). In the context of these competing values, the courts have heard a number of challenges to customary inheritance laws that severely restricted women's rights to inherit property; as Justice Langa explained, "The exclusion of women from heirship and consequently from being able to inherit property was in keeping with a system dominated by a deeply embedded patriarchy which reserved for women a position of subservience and subordination and in which they were regarded as perpetual minors under the tutelage of the fathers, husbands, or the head of the extended family." *Bhe and Others v Khayelitsha Magistrate and Others* (CCT 49/03) [2004] ZACC 17; 2005 (1) SA 580 (CC); 2005 (1) BCLR 1 (CC) (15 October 2004), para. 78. (These rules were also challenged on the basis that they infringed the more general constitutional right to "human dignity" (sec. 10) and that they discriminated against younger siblings and children born out of wedlock.)

In *Mthembu v Letsela and Another* 1997 (2) SA 936 (T) (which was decided under South Africa's Interim Constitution but dealt with similar constitutional principles), Justice Le Roux upheld this customary law of "male primogeniture" on the basis that the attendant duty to "support" the deceased's family made it "difficult to equate this form of differentiation between men and women with the concept of 'unfair discrimination'" (at 945H-946C). The Supreme Court of Appeal declined to answer the constitutional question in *Mthembu*, holding that the interim constitution was inapplicable to that case since the deceased had died before the interim constitution took effect; after the final constitution took effect, however, the Constitutional Court was compelled to rule on the validity of male primogeniture. In the *Bhe* decision, the Court was unanimous in their view that this customary law of inheritance violated women's equality rights, with the majority affirming "It is a form of discrimination that entrenches past patterns of disadvantage among a vulnerable group, exacerbated by old notions of patriarchy and male domination incompatible with the guarantee of equality under this constitutional order" (91). Notably, however, both Justice Langa's majority decision and Justice Ngcobo's opinion (dissenting on the remedy) were careful to affirm that the courts should be sensitive to the specific cultural context when applying constitutional equality rights to customary law. Justice Langa restrains the scope of the decision, warning that it does not consider "the constitutionality of the rule of male primogeniture in other contexts within customary law, such as the rules which govern status and traditional leaders" (94). Justice Ngcobo objects to the majority's position that the customary law should be struck, urging that "The respect for our diversity and the right of communities to live and be governed by indigenous law must be balanced against the need to protect the vulnerable members of the family" (238) and preferring that the customary rule be retained but "developed so as to bring it in line with our Bill of Rights" (222).

87. There may also be arguments other than those of equality that would reject gendered divisions of labor, such as child care. As I noted in chapter 1, section IV.B, such divisions lead to political leadership by men who do not have the necessary knowledge and experience to make good public policy.

88. See Nedelsky, "Communities of Judgment and Human Rights."

89. Other contemporary examples of violence most people do not "see" as rights violations that attract their concern are violence in prisons and conditions in nursing homes. And as I noted in earlier chapters, although people in North America now routinely see homeless people on the street, they often do not see the problem as connected to them. I would make the same argument about what people "know." Most people know about poverty and hunger among children in their own country, they know about preventable deaths from poverty around the world, and they know about cruelty in the production of meat. But they are able to know and not *really* know, not think about, much less act upon, the information they have. As I discuss in "Closing Reflections," I think one of the consequences (and contributions) of the approach I am advocating here is that it would shift what we see and how we know.

90. Of course, there are a few scholars, lawyers, and activists—like Thomas Pogge, Martha Jackman, and Bruce Porter—who have devoted their work to show that poverty is a rights violation. See, for example, Pogge, *Politics as Usual* and *World Poverty and Human Rights*; Porter and Jackman, "Justiciability of Social and Economic Rights in Canada"; and Foscarinis et al., "Human Right to Adequate Housing."

91. As I noted in note 10, Kant thought his arguments about reason applied to all reasoning beings, including angels.

92. This quote comes from Grear, "Vulnerability, Freedom, Law and the Body." Elsewhere she elaborates:

> [e]mbodied vulnerability provides the beginning of a human rights universal (a 'concrete' universal) that moves decisively away from the abstract philosophical version of universalism so frequently criticised. A focus on human embodiment, its commonalities (both universal and culturally mediated) and its incessant reflection of the irreducible uniqueness of every human being, provides a potent critique of legal quasi-disembodiment and its associated ideological tilt towards the legal privileging of the white, western male and his morphology. Embodiment, conceptualised in such a way as to avoid a return to biological essentialism, holds out the hope for an ethical reinvigoration of the human rights ideal, one with a radically inclusive potential.

Grear, "Challenging Corporate 'Humanity,'" 540.

93. Martha Nussbaum comments and includes a quote from Kant's lecture on ethics, "Kant denies that we have any duties directly toward animals.... Animals have no self-consciousness. Therefore they 'are merely as a means to an end. That end is man.... Our duties toward animals are merely indirect duties toward humanity.'" Nussbaum, *Frontiers of Justice*, 329.

94. Consider Nussbaum again: "For Kant, only humanity and rationality are worthy of respect and wonder; the rest of nature is just a set of tools. The capabilities approach judges, instead, with the biologist Aristotle, that there is something wonderful and wonder-inspiring in all complex forms of life in nature." Nussbaum, *Frontiers of Justice*, 347. She focuses on animals. I ask why only complex forms of life should inspire wonder. And John Borrows invites Canadian courts to take

seriously the Anishinabek belief that the Earth is a living being, not something inanimate. Borrows, "Living Law on a Living Earth."

95. See Borrows, "Living Law on a Living Earth," and Simpson, "Looking after Gdoo-Naaganinaa."

96. Gilligan, *In a Different Voice*.

97. The Great Ape Project (www.greatapeproject.org) uses both cognitive similarity and social behavior to distinguish three kinds of apes that they think should be recognized as entitled to certain kinds of rights. I am sympathetic to their project in the sense that they make a compelling case against the unjustified cruelty these animals are subjected to, particularly the use of Chimpanzees in biomedical research. Roger Fouts (with Stephen Tukel Mills) makes a strong case that the trauma Chimpanzees are subject to casts doubt on the quality of the information the research can provide. Fouts and Mills, *Next of Kin*. But singling out a few species will not solve the larger problem. They recognize this but respond, "Let us take the first step now!"

98. The Earth Charter (Benchmark Draft II, April 1999) puts this point affirmatively and more broadly: "Humanity is part of a vast evolving universe. Earth, our home, is alive with a unique community of life.... We can treat Earth with respect, rejecting the idea that nature is merely a collection of resources to be used. We can realize that our social, economic, environmental, and spiritual problems are interconnected and cooperate in developing integrated strategies to address them.... The spirit of human solidarity and kinship with all life will be strengthened if we live with reverence for the sources of our being, gratitude for the gift of life, and humility regarding the human place in the larger scheme of things."

99. Rawls, *Theory of Justice*. See also Nussbaum, *Frontiers of Justice*.

100. The Great Ape Project pamphlet opens with the heading "Equality beyond the Species Barrier."

101. See Nussbaum, *Frontiers of Justice*.

CHAPTER 5

1. Cited in Johnson, *Measuring Violence against Women*, 8.

2. I had the good fortune to be thinking about the original version of this chapter while visiting the University of Chicago Law School. I would particularly like to thank the following for giving me the benefit of their responses: Carolyn M. Burns, Richard Epstein, Elena Kagan (who has since become an associate justice of the U.S. Supreme Court), Larry Lessig, Tracey Meares, Martha Nussbaum, and Stephen Shulhoffer. I also received particularly excellent questions and comments from Owen Fiss and his feminist theory class at Yale Law School. And I would like to thank the participants of the September 1993 NOMOS Meeting of the American Society of Political and Legal Philosophy held during the Annual meeting of the American Political Science Association, where the first draft of this essay was presented and discussed. More recently, George Kateb kindly took the time to discuss his thoughts on this chapter. I have tried to respond to some of his questions with additional elaboration.

3. For the purposes of this chapter, I believe it makes sense to focus on this particular failure. But while I was teaching in Chicago it was forcefully brought home to me that this is not the only such failure. In the United States, the state has failed perhaps even more dramatically to protect young black men from violence, and it might be said that there is a background of violence that pervades the lives of Native peoples in North America. The class of those for whom the liberal

state has succeeded in providing routine security from violence (which of course does not mean perfect security) begins to look suspiciously small. See further details in notes 9 and 128.

4. This chapter focuses on the issue of violence against women, only briefly returning to children at the end. Although I think the violence against women and children are closely linked, both issues were too much to take on in one discussion.

5. This argument is elaborated in chapter 2.

6. See, for example, Nedelsky, "Practical Possibilities of Feminist Theory"; Minow, *Making All the Difference.*

7. This is George Kateb's description of Shklar's argument in "Judith Shklar (1928–1992)."

8. This issue of "private violence" also characterizes wife assault, which is an even more widespread source of violence against women. The American Uniform Crime Reports reveal Intimate Partner Violence (IPV) to be the leading cause of injury to women between the ages of fifteen and forty-four—more than car accidents, muggings, and rapes combined. Stark, "Framing and Reframing Battered Women."

Stark reports also that homicide, almost always by an abusive partner, is the leading cause of death for black women under forty (273). This statistic is based on medical records at the Yale–New Haven Hospital between 1978 and 1983. I am grateful to Christina Kobi for providing me with this information from her unpublished paper, "Criminal Justice Response to Domestic Violence: A Feminist Perspective."

I discuss intimate partner violence in chapters 4 and 8.

9. As I discuss in chapter 1, feminists have an advantage in avoiding one of the pitfalls of challenges to liberal individualism: women's experience of relationships as oppressive as well as essential has the virtue of making us less likely to be romantic about the virtues of community as such. See chapter 1, section I.D.iii.

10. With some self-consciousness, I originally used the grandiose title "Relational Feminism Confronts the Problem of Evil." I think the essay still shows some of this broad aspiration to see if my relational approach can deal with the darkest parts of human interaction. I changed the title because the term "evil" is so complex, even contentious. What I actually address here is just one dimension of violence, but my driving concern remains the challenge of showing that the relational approach is equipped to take on the pain, fear, and violence that are part of the human condition. These phenomena are as much the result of structures of relations as autonomy, dignity, or security. I do not directly take up a relational account of malevolence or the desire to harm others, which is normally part of what is meant by evil.

11. In Fiscal Year 2005, U.S. Child Protective Services received approximately 3.3 million official referrals alleging the maltreatment of some six million children. U.S. Department of Health and Human Services, Administration for Children, Youth, and Families, "Child Maltreatment 2006." Note that this figure includes only reported cases. In Canada, the Canadian Incidence Study of Reported Child Abuse and Neglect reported that 217,319 investigations of maltreatment were conducted in 2003. Trocmé et al., "Canadian Incidence Study of Reported Child Abuse and Neglect—2003: Major Findings," 1. This Canadian study is similarly limited to reports investigated by child welfare services and does not include reports that were screened out, cases that were investigated by the police instead of child welfare services, or cases that were never reported. For statistics on the impact of domestic violence on women, see note 58.

According to one study, child abuse, like violence against women, may often be a means of expressing and enforcing male dominance. The authors rely upon an empirical study of child abuse in the homes of self-identified battered women in finding "a positive bivariate relationship between husband dominance...[in the marital relationship] and spousal child abuse." In their view, this finding supports a conclusion that child abuse is one of "a variety of oppressive strategies, including wife beating...marital rape, psychological abuse, punitive economic deprivation, and coerced social isolation" deployed by men in order to secure their position of dominance in the family. Bowker, Arbitell, and McFerron, "On the Relationship between Wife Beating and Child Abuse," 166.

    12. Perhaps the best known articulation of this idea is found in Susan Brownmiller's *Against Our Will: Men, Women, and Rape* (1975). According to Brownmiller, rape "is nothing more or less than a conscious process of intimidation by which *all men* keep *all women* in a state of fear" (15). There is, however, an important nuance and puzzle here. What most women fear, what controls their daily activities, is fear of stranger rape. Rennison and Welchans, "Intimate Partner Violence." And what they think will protect them is "having a man." The irony, of course, is that the vast majority of rapes are by men their victims know. According to the American National Violence against Women Survey, stranger rapes were reported by only 16.7 percent of women who reported being raped as adults. The majority (61.9 percent) were raped by a current or former intimate partner, and the remainder were raped by acquaintances or relatives. Tjaden and Thoennes, "Extent, Nature, and Consequences of Intimate Partner Violence," 43. The protection these women seek, then, is often the real source of the danger. Thus the pervasive fear is in some ways misguided. Elizabeth Stanko refers to this phenomenon as "the myth of the safe home" and attributes its resilience in part to the fact that "the feminist argument that the home may be a dangerous place for women confronts deeply ingrained and hostile beliefs that support the ideology of the home as man's haven." Stanko, "Fear of Crime and the Myth of the Safe Home," 86. If women's fears were more realistic, they probably would not function in the same way to foster women's dependence on men. The basic terror of vulnerability to rape would, however, still reinforce the power relations.

    13. Griffin, *A Chorus of Stones*.

    14. See Keller, *From a Broken Web*, for a rich, complex, and illuminating argument about the connections between the conception of the self and patriarchal traditions of theology, mythology, psychology, science, and philosophy. She does not address the question of rights.

    15. I do not mean to suggest that women do not commit violence against men, children, or other women. In fact, where the severity of violence is not taken into consideration, rates of intimate partner violence perpetuated by men and women are often found to be roughly equivalent. It is the severity of violence by men against women and the impact that this violence has on women's sense of autonomy that merit special consideration. A recent Statistics Canada report found that, "in 2004, twice as many women than men were beaten by their partners, and four times as many were choked....16% of women who were victimized by a spouse were sexually assaulted, and twice as many female as male victims of spousal assault reported chronic, ongoing assaults....This finding suggests that despite similar prevalence rates reported by women and men...assaults on women are more serious." Johnson, *Measuring Violence against Women*, 19. Moreover, violence perpetrated by men against women has a qualitatively different impact on victims. This same Statistics Canada report explained that "[m]en's and boys' experiences of violence are different than women's and girls' in important ways....[W]omen are in greater danger of experiencing violence from intimate partners in their own homes. Women are also at greater risk of sexual violence. The fear of violence is more pervasive for women and can prevent them

from taking part as full citizens in their communities" (8). The difference in severity and impact of domestic violence on women as opposed to men also holds true in the United States, where one Department of Justice study found that "in recent years, an intimate partner killed approximately 33% of female murder victims and 4% of male murder victims." Rennison and Welchans, "Intimate Partner Violence," 2.

We may be just beginning to understand the ways in which violence in intimate partnerships occurs in same-sex relationships and, thus, the extent to which the patterns of that violence are similar to the prevalent violence of men against their female intimate partners. See Peterman and Dixon, "Intimate Partner Abuse between Same-Sex Partners"; Elliott, "Shattering Illusions"; and Island and Letellier, *Men Who Beat the Men Who Love Them*.

16. See the description of the dark underside of twentieth-century American farm life in Jane Smiley's novel *A Thousand Acres* (1991).

17. See particularly Woodman, *Pregnant Virgin* and *Ravaged Bridegroom*.

I have a continuing unease with the use of the terms "masculine" and "feminine" even in Woodman's fully feminist, consistently enlightening reflections. For my brief purposes here, however, I think it is enough to say that "the feminine" does not refer to gender and that I always find that Woodman's insights are compelling even if I wish for slightly different language.

18. While I have found her approach extremely helpful, I do not think a reader need accept Jungian psychology to accept my argument.

19. See also Dinnerstein, *Mermaid and the Minotaur*, who, for all the problems of her universalizing language, has important insights on the mutuality of destructive gender roles.

20. Woodman, *Addiction to Perfection*, 132. The passage quoted continues, "D. M. Thomas's novel *The White Hotel* (1981) makes vividly clear the contemporary fate of the feminine." The apt metaphor of the "rape of the earth" is another instance of the iconic significance of rape—and of the violence toward the feminine.

21. See Starhawk, *Truth or Dare*, for an example of a feminist approach to power.

22. Johnson, *Ecstasy*, 18–20. Johnson also sees links to the destructive quality of gendered roles.

There are also important links here to Catherine MacKinnon's persuasive arguments about the eroticization of dominance and violence. MacKinnon, *Feminism Unmodified*.

23. Martha Nussbaum and Amartya Sen's "human capabilities" approach urges us to focus on the question "what are the people of the country in question actually able to do and be?" Nussbaum, *Women and Human Development*, 5. While I am at times troubled by the Rawlsian dimensions of some of Nussbaum's later work, I find the Aristotelian aspects of her work (i.e., the focus on goals and goods as realized in activity) to be useful. David Crocker explains that under a capabilities analysis, "rights…are defined as basic not because they are indispensable to the fulfillment of any other right but because they are a way of formulating the urgency of minimal levels of eminently valuable human (actual and possible) functionings." Crocker, "Functioning and Capability, 186.

24. Noddings, *Women and Evil*, 1.

25. "When I use the word *shadow*, I will refer not to an element in the realm of archetypes, but rather to a set of desires, inclinations, and behaviors that are observable in human experience…those of which the individual is unaware are part of his or her shadow. Similarly, a group, institution, nation, or culture may have a shadow. Sometimes the traits belonging to the shadow are vehemently denied, even despised, and then we may predict projection." Ibid., 75.

26. Helen Hardacre's contribution to Martin E. Marty and Scott Appleby's comprehensive study of religious fundamentalisms describes this projection of male fault onto the female "other": "Female sexuality tends to be seen as hindering male spiritual perfection.... Female sexuality is in some contexts viewed as dangerous: polluting, liable to bewitch men, causing them to lose all dignity, reason and self-respect, and thus leading to the ruin of the family and the downfall of the nation." Hardacre, "Impact of Fundamentalisms on Women, the Family, and Interpersonal Relations," 144.

27. Noddings, *Women and Evil*, 120.

28. Ibid., 211.

29. This is just one of the many ways in which I do not purport to address all the different forms that violence takes.

30. The idea of universal, equal rights applies only to other full humans. The concept itself thus is little, if any, impediment to mistreating those we do not think of as human or as so inferior that they are not entitled to equal rights. It is always useful to remember that the stirring invocations of universal rights in the American Declaration of Independence were written by a slaveholder.

31. "We have also found it useful to distinguish among natural, cultural, and moral forms of evil. The pain of illness and death are natural evils; poverty, racism, war, and sexism are cultural evils; the deliberate infliction of physical or psychic pain—unless we can show convincingly that it is necessary for a desirable state in the one undergoing pain—is moral evil." Noddings, *Women and Evil*, 120–121.

32. This is one of many points where the use of the language of "we" and "us" is complicated. While, as I noted earlier, I try to avoid presumptions about who "we" are, to shift the language here to "'peoples' insulation from the pain of poverty" perpetuates a version of the distancing I am discussing. For the overwhelming majority of my readers, theirs is the experience of privilege, not homelessness. The language of we and us highlights this.

33. As I noted above, I assume the readers of this essay are neither homeless nor impoverished (beyond the temporary constraints of being a student). I would be glad if the assumption proved incorrect, if my readership were wider than I expect.

34. This argument is elaborated in the following chapter, "Reconceiving Rights and Constitutionalism."

35. Noddings, *Women and Evil*, 210.

36. For Noddings, the "steady control" is internal; for traditional liberalism, it is provided by the state. My preferred language would be "self-conscious judgment" rather than "steady control." As we will see in chapter 7, I think the language of control is not optimal for a relational approach.

37. Kateb, "Judith Shklar (1928–1992)."

38. Although Kateb discusses Shklar in relation to constitutionalism, Shklar herself actually talks more about liberalism, and it is more the traditions of liberalism than constitutionalism that I want to take on here. Someone once said that my objective was to have constitutionalism without liberalism. In fact, I want to revise some of the basic terms of liberalism and to transform our understanding of constitutionalism in corresponding ways. The idea of boundaries (to the legitimate authority of the state) is as essential to the American conception of constitutionalism as it is to the dominant conception of rights (as the content of the boundaries). For more on liberalism, see chapter 1; for more on constitutionalism, see chapter 6.

39. Shklar, *Ordinary Vices*.

40. Shklar, "Liberalism of Fear."

41. Ibid., 29.

42. Shklar, *Ordinary Vices*, 235.

43. Ibid., 237.

44. Ibid., 241–242.

45. The United States is clearly her paradigmatic liberal society.

46. Which is not, of course, to say that there are not forms of violence and terror to which women are subjected elsewhere and from which women in North America are relatively well protected. To say that there are worse horrors elsewhere, however, is not to deny the claim that North American liberal society fails to provide some of its weakest and most powerless members with the security from fear that Shklar treats as fundamental.

47. Sidel, *Women and Children Last*; Buvinić, "Women in Poverty."

48. Herman, *Trauma and Recovery*, 33.

49. Ibid., 32.

50. Terr, *Too Scared to Cry*, 37; recall that for Shklar, the "evil is cruelty and the fear it inspires, and the very fear of fear itself." Shklar, "Liberalism of Fear," 29.

51. Herman, *Trauma and Recovery*, 50.

52. She also sees it as part of a broader pattern of violence that affects men as well: "Combat and rape, the public and private forms of organized social violence, are primarily experiences of adolescence and early adult life.... The period of greatest psychological vulnerability is also in reality the period of greatest traumatic exposure, for both young men and women. Rape and combat might thus be considered complementary social rites of initiation into the coercive violence at the foundation of adult society. They are the paradigmatic forms of trauma for women and men respectively." Ibid., 51. (There are strong echoes here of Susan Griffin.) But the fact that men in our culture are subjected to the horrors of war, long sanctioned as inevitable, and that there are links between these different, routine forms of violence does not mean that the absence of basic security for women and children does not pose a special challenge to the claims of liberalism.

53. The standard estimate in Canada is that less than one in ten people who have been sexually assaulted report the assault to the police. (This general estimate includes men and women but does not include children because they are not included in the victimization surveys.) Brennan and Taylor-Butts, "Sexual Assault in Canada: 2004 and 2007." In the United States, an often cited estimate is 16 percent of rapes are reported. Kilpatrick and McCauley, "Understanding National Rape Statistics," 2. These estimates are based on what are called victimization surveys, usually conducted by telephone interviews. For an excellent survey of the different kinds of data available on rape in the United States, see Kilpatrick and McCauley, "Understanding National Rape Statistics." For Canada, see report above as well as Johnson, *Measuring Violence against Women*, which found that 36 percent of female victims of spousal violence reported these crimes to the police in 2004 (14).

54. See Kilpatrick and McCauley, "Understanding National Rape Statistics." They also note that a 2006 New Hampshire study found that 19.5 percent of women reported a rape experience during their lifetime (11).

55. The Violence against Women Survey (VAWS) conducted by Statistics Canada was a special one-time survey funded by the (then) federal department of Health and Welfare.

56. In the *Canadian Criminal Code*, sexual assault is subsumed under the general category of assault rather than included as a separate crime. It therefore includes all acts of sexual touching

performed without consent. See *Canadian Criminal Code*, R.S.C., chap. C-34, sec. 244; 1974–75–76, chap. 93, sec. 21; 1980–81–82–83, chap. 125, sec. 19, sec. 265.

57. See Johnson, *Measuring Violence against Women*, 24. This report also finds that the "percentage of women who reported being sexually assaulted in the previous 12-month period was 3% in both 1999 and 2004" (24). Previous twelve-month rates in the major U.S. studies (of rape only, defined in terms of penetration) ranged from 0.71 percent to 0.9 percent. Kilpatrick and McCauley, "Understanding National Rape Statistics." It is worth noting, in light of Herman's comment about the vulnerability of young women, that in Canada in 2004, for women under the age of twenty-five, the one-year rates were 25.6 percent for sexual assault and 9 percent for criminal harassment or stalking. Johnson, *Measuring Violence against Women*.

58. The Women's Safety Project reported the "Highlights of the Findings" as follows:

SEXUAL ABUSE OF GIRLS (16 AND UNDER)
54% had experienced some unwanted or intrusive sexual experience.
24% of the cases were forced or attempted forced sexual intercourse.
17% reported at least one experience of incest.
34% had been sexually abused by a non-relative.
43% reported at least one experience of incest and/or extrafamilial sexual abuse.
96% of perpetrators of family-related child sexual abuse were men.

[This last statistic has remained the same for fifteen years. See Canadian Centre for Justice Statistics, "Family Violence in Canada," 35.]

SEXUAL ABUSE OF WOMEN (16 AND OLDER)
51% have been victims of rape or attempted rape.
40% reported at least one experience of rape.
31% reported at least one experience of attempted rape.
2/3 of women have experienced a legally recognized form of sexual assault, according to *Canadian Criminal Code* definitions. [See note 62.]
81% of rapes or attempted rapes were perpetrated by men who were known to the women.
PHYSICAL ASSAULT IN INTIMATE RELATIONSHIPS
27% experienced physical assault in an intimate relationship.
25% of cases involved partners threatening to kill them.
50% reporting physical assault also experienced sexual assault in the same relationship.
36% feared being killed by their male intimate.

Found in Bressette et al., *Changing the Landscape*, 9. All of the physical assaults on women were perpetrated by male intimate partners. It is important to point out that research methods for this study were "designed to overcome many of the usual limitations of studies on violence against women: subjects were randomly selected, the study took place in a centre with a diverse population and the large sample of 420 women was designed to yield more accurate statistics. In-depth interviews were conducted on a one-to-one basis by trained interviewers, and safety plans for the women interviewed were put in place. In addition, the project authors...brought with them an extensive knowledge of the topic" (8).

59. Bressette et al., *Changing the Landscape*, 10.

60. Health Canada offers another measure of the impact of violence against women: "Violence is a major factor in women's health and well-being. The measurable health-related costs of violence against women in Canada exceed $1.5 billion a year. These costs include short-term medical and dental treatment for injuries, long-term physical and psychological care, lost time at work, and use of transition homes and crisis centres." Health Canada, "Violence against Women."

Ignoring violence as a factor in women's health and well-being not only leads to misdiagnosis and inadequate treatment, it also disregards the full extent of the personal and social consequences of violence. "Women will not be free from violence until they achieve equality with men, and equality cannot be achieved until violence and the threat of violence are eliminated from women's lives." Ibid.

61. There is some reason for optimism about public opinion on violence against women. A recent survey conducted in New Brunswick, Canada, found that the "public reports high levels of concern about each of child abuse (91 per cent), elder abuse (89 per cent), and violence against women (86 per cent). In 2002, a gap was observed between men and women on these measures. This gap has been filled, as there are currently no significant attitudinal differences between the genders. Women, however, are twice as likely as men (15 per cent versus eight per cent, respectively) to perceive an increase in the amount of violence against women." Harris/Decima, "Attitudinal Survey on Violence against Women," iii. The study also showed concern about dating violence (in total, 79 percent reported being very/somewhat concerned). There are no gender differences on this measure (10).

The study also showed that considerable variations remain in the types of violence the public perceives as criminal: "Up from 65 per cent in 2002, three-quarters of those surveyed (73 per cent) believe it is a crime for a husband to force his wife to have sex with him against her will. Six-in-10 (58 per cent, up from 52 per cent) regard it as a crime for a 20-year-old man to slap his girlfriend around because she flirted with another man in a public place. If a husband were to slap his wife on the face after a dispute that was started when the wife complained that he doesn't make enough money for the household—47 per cent (up from 41 per cent) would see this as a crime, and 37 per cent (consistent with 38 per cent) as a serious incident, but not a crime. The least serious of the four scenarios was perceived to be a father slapping his six-year-old daughter on the face because she broke a vase she was forbidden to touch. Over one-quarter (28 per cent) of all those surveyed (up from 21 per cent) would consider the latter situation a crime, while four-in-10 (39 per cent) would consider this a serious incident, but not a crime" (18). While these trends are moving in the right direction, it is sobering to find that 40 percent of the respondents thought it was not a crime for a young man to "slap his girl friend around" (18–19).

62. The popular press is full of warnings to women not to leave their drinks unattended, etc. See, for example, Danylewich, *Fearless*, 33. For additional commentary, see Lawson, "Surrendering the Night!" which argues that women's entire lives are dictated by caution in our conduct, behavior, actions, and inactions, yet there is no evidence to suggest that sexual assault is on the decline. The question thus becomes, why uphold the myth that lists of do's and dont's restricting women's behavior will cease to make them targets for rape? Ibid.

I should note here that there has been a decline in the reporting of sexual assault to police in Canada:

> The statistics for reported sexual assaults show a steady increase starting in 1983 and a decline beginning in 1993. Overall sexual assault rates are driven by level I sexual assaults

since they account for over 90% of all incidents reported to the police [see below]. It is unknown to what extent these data reflect actual trends in changing levels of sexual violence in Canadian society, or changes in the willingness of sexual assault victims to bring these to the attention of the police. According to the 2004 GSS, just 8% of sexual assault victims reported the crime to the police.

Johnson, *Measuring Violence against Women*.
As we have seen, however, other sources (such as Lawson, "Surrender the Night!" referenced above) suggest that the actual incidence of assault has not declined.
The *Criminal Code* definition of sexual assault encompasses conduct ranging from unwanted sexual touching to sexual violence resulting in serious physical injury to the victim. Correspondingly, an offense is assigned to one of three levels according to the seriousness of the offence or the degree of physical injury sustained by the victim:

- a level I sexual assault involves minor physical injuries or no injuries to the victim;
- a level II sexual assault involves the use of a weapon or threats, or results in bodily harm;
- a level III sexual assault (aggravated sexual assault) results in wounding, maiming, disfiguring or endangering the life of the victim.

63. I once made a similar, even more sweeping statement in class: "all women live in fear." An undergraduate woman raised her hand and announced that she wasn't afraid because she didn't have a boyfriend. This provocative remark was intended to point out that most sexual assaults are perpetrated by men who know the woman they are attacking. According to the Violence Policy Center, "Of females killed with a firearm, almost two-thirds were killed by their intimate partners. The number of females shot and killed by their husband or intimate partner...was more than three times higher than the total number murdered by male strangers using all weapons combined...in single victim/single offender incidents in 2002." Violence Policy Center, "When Men Murder Women," 9. The very men to whom women look for protection from the "dark, male stranger" are thus a more common source of danger than the stranger. The student also asserted that her fearlessness took the form of walking the streets of Toronto at any time and place that suited her. She was the first and only woman I have ever met who claims this sort of immunity from fear. I think my point about the prevalence of fear holds, but I now make it in slightly less sweeping terms.
The New Brunswick study cited above at note 61 suggests that there is a growing awareness that the primary threat of violence against women comes from people they know rather than strangers: A woman's partner (59 percent current partner, 22 percent previous partner) is generally perceived as perpetrating the most acts of violence against women. Harris/Decima, "Attitudinal Survey on Violence against Women," 13
Living in the relatively safe city of Toronto, I experience far less daily intrusion into my life plans than I did while living in Hyde Park in Chicago. Like most women, I make accommodations to the fear I feel so routinely that I generally am scarcely conscious of the fear that lies behind the accommodations. For example, I consider my office in a large university building to be inaccessible to me late at night, whereas my male partner feels comfortable going there at 4:00 a.m. What brought home to me most clearly the way some level of fear pervades my life was hearing about the Michigan Womyn's Music Festival, which takes place on a vast area of land on which no

men are allowed—not even male infants. Although I found it troubling that male infants are part of the exclusion, for the first time I could imagine what it would be like to spend entire days and nights without the fear of being assaulted by a man. I found the idea of being able to walk alone through the woods without anxiety exhilarating—and as a result became more conscious of how such freedom from fear ordinarily feels impossible to me.

64. The New Brunswick study (at note 61) found that men are more likely than women (21 percent versus 14 percent, respectively) to say that they are not at all concerned about their own and their family's safety. I find the 14 percent figure high and would like to know if that means they make no accommodation to protect themselves. The comparative figure for men is hard to assess because it would include concern about the women in their families.

65. Rape, Abuse, and Incest National Network (RAINN), "How Often Does Sexual Assault Occur?" online <http://www.rainn.org/get-information/statistics/frequency-of-sexual-assault>.

66. I address the complications of group membership later. Of course, not every rapist holds a more powerful position in society, on every measure, than his victim.

67. Shklar, "Liberalism of Fear," 29.

68. Subtle revisions of this statement might be necessary when we have a full account of the frequency of the sexual abuse perpetrated on children by those in power over them in institutions such as orphanages, residential schools, and juvenile correctional institutions.

69. Cover, "Origins of Judicial Activism in the Protection of Minorities," 1303–1304.

70. It is probably always the case that violence and fear are necessary to keep a group subordinated. Women were once thought of as an exception, but we can now see that they are not.

71. Cover, "Origins of Judicial Activism in the Protection of Minorities," 1303.

72. Ibid. Courts generally protect constitutional rights exclusively against "state action" as opposed to the actions of private individuals (although where the line between private and public action is drawn varies between jurisdictions). (See, for example, the Canadian case *RWDSU v. Dolphin Delivery Ltd.,* [1986] 2 S.C.R. 573, and the American case *Shelley v. Kraemer,* 334 U.S. 1 (1948).) This approach has sparked extensive debate, not only as to the appropriate place to draw the line between "public" and "private" but also as to whether the distinction between these spheres is even coherent. Mark Tushnet explains that "the people or corporations exercising 'private' power are actually exercising power conferred on them by laws regulating market behaviour. Thus, the government is *always* somehow implicated in private decisions." Tushnet, "Issue of State Action/Horizontal Effect in Comparative Constitutional Law," 79. As Allan Hutchinson and Andrew Petter argue in their forceful critique of the leading Canadian case on this topic, "Distinctions like those developed in *Dolphin* provide formal paraphernalia behind which private power thrives relatively unchecked and substantive issues are arbitrarily and unjustly resolved." Hutchinson and Petter, "Private Rights/Public Wrongs," 297. Those conversant in feminist theory will undoubtedly note the parallel between this commentary and the feminist critique of the "public/private divide." Susan B. Boyd introduces *Challenging the Public/Private Divide* with Nicola Lacey's powerful articulation of this critique. As Lacey explains, "the ideology of the public/private dichotomy allows government to clean its hands of any *responsibility* for the state of the 'private' world and *depoliticizes* the disadvantages which inevitably spill over the alleged divide by affecting the position of the 'privately' disadvantaged in the 'public' world." Boyd, "Challenging the Public/Private Divide," 3.

73. Cover, "Origins of Judicial Activism in the Protection of Minorities," 1307. Cover is referring here to *Grovey v. Townsend,* 295 U.S. 45 (1935), a decision that upheld a rule excluding black

citizens from voting in the Texas Democratic primary, even though two similar exclusions had previously been found to constitute unconstitutional violations of the equal protection clause. (The exclusion of black citizens from the Texas Democratic primaries was a de facto exclusion from voting since, at the time, the Democratic party was "the only effective political organization in Texas," such that "the Democratic primary was in fact, if not in law, the real election machinery in Texas." Hine, *Black Victory*, 69. The rule in *Grovey* was upheld on the basis that it was the product of a party convention decision, placing it beyond the sphere of "state action" that is subject to constitutional law. In the previous cases where "white primaries" had been found unconstitutional, the restrictions were enacted by the state legislature (*Nixon v. Herndon*, 273 U.S. 536 (1927)) or by the party's executive committee, which had been created by statute (*Nixon v. Condon*, 286 U.S. 73 (1932)).

74. Cover, "Origins of Judicial Activism in the Protection of Minorities," 1308–1309.

75. Ibid., 1309.

76. Reva Siegel explores the rhetorical utility of the language of "privacy" in maintaining the de facto permissibility of spousal abuse even after the common law courts abandoned the "doctrine of chastisement" that permitted a husband to use "a whip or rattan, no bigger than [their] thumb, in order to enforce the salutary restraints of domestic discipline." Siegel, " 'Rule of Love'," 2152. Siegel explains that, "instead of reasoning about marriage in the older hierarchy-based norms of the common law, jurists began to justify the regulation of domestic violence in the language of privacy and love.... Once translated from an antiquated to a more contemporary gender idiom, the state's justification for treating wife beating differently from other kinds of assault seemed reasonable in ways the law of chastisement did not" (2120). For Siegel, this is an example of "preservation through transformation" whereby an underlying status regime is maintained in the face of contestation by modernizing its "rule structure and rationale" (2119).

77. Cover, "Origins of Judicial Activism in the Protection of Minorities," 1316.

78. Ibid. I have not tried to present Cover's central and fascinating argument about the importance for this process of the famous Footnote Four in *United States v. Carolene Products*, 304 U.S. 144, 152n4 (1938).

79. Herman, *Trauma and Recovery*, 53.

80. Ibid., 41.

81. Ibid., 61 and 51.

82. "The problem," Lundy Langston puts succinctly, "is that women can be invaded without being penetrated." Langston, "No Penetration—And It's Still Rape," 33.

Richard Posner describes the common law definition of rape as "sexual intercourse by a man with a woman, not his wife, by force and against her will," explaining that, "Sexual assaults that did not involve intercourse were treated under the assault and battery provisions of the criminal law rather than as a separate offense of sexual battery." Posner and Silbaug, *Guide to America's Sex Laws*, 5. Frances P. Bernat explains that two waves of reform (the first in the 1970s, the second in the 1980s) produced important changes to this understanding of rape. Bernat, "Rape Law Reform," 85. In his account of the statutory regime that has supplanted this common law definition, Posner explains, "Sexual assaults that do not involve intercourse are now usually treated in the same code section as rape, but in most cases with less severe punishment." Posner and Silbaug, *Guide to America's Sex Laws*, 6. Some states, however, have not departed significantly from this common law definition, choosing not to define rape at all or doing so only very briefly. For a state-by-state overview of contemporary American rape and sexual assault provisions, see ibid., 7–34.

In using the term "sexual intercourse," Posner is modernizing the original common law language of "carnal knowledge." Bernat explains that "the carnal knowledge element in common law rape defined the prohibited sex act as . . . sexual penetration between the male sex organ and female vagina." Any penetration, "be it ever so slight," was included in this definition; "the vagina did not have to be completely entered or the hymen ruptured." Langston, "No Penetration—And It's Still Rape," 3. In addition, "it was not necessary to prove that the sex act resulted in ejaculation." Bernat, "Rape Law Reform," 86. The common law crime of rape did not proscribe forced oral or anal sex or acts committed with an object (86). Rosemarie Tong, citing Susan Brownmiller, explains that, "according to standard feminist analysis, the law's customary preoccupation with penetration is a reflection of man's persistent desire to maintain exclusive control over woman's vagina so that his need to be 'sole physical instrument governing impregnation, progeny, and inheritance rights' is met. The rapist either robs the father of his daughter's virginity before this valuable 'commodity' reaches the matrimonial market, or he robs the husband of certitude with respect to the fatherhood of his progeny, in addition to damaging or stigmatizing his prized possession." *Women, Sex, and the Law*, 92.

83. Herman, *Trauma and Recovery*, 51.

84. Ibid., 53.

85. Ibid., 65.

86. Ibid., 62.

87. Ibid., 70.

88. Ibid., 67.

89. Brison, *Aftermath*, 73.

90. Ibid., 68.

91. Herman's compelling comment reveals the serious constraint on women's freedom that fear and violence entail: "Most women do not in fact recognize the degree of male hostility toward them, preferring to view the relations of the sexes as more benign than they are in fact. Similarly, women like to believe that they have greater freedom and higher status than they do in reality. A woman is especially vulnerable to rape when acting as though she were free—that is, when she is not observing conventional restrictions on dress, physical mobility, and social initiative. Women who act as though they were free are often described as 'loose,' meaning not only 'unbound' but also sexually provocative." Herman, *Trauma and Recovery*, 69.

92. It is important to remember that I have not begun to catalog the full range of fears, from economic dependency to a deep sense of inadequacy, that characterize so many women's lives. Indeed, as I read the descriptions of the consequences of trauma, I thought they sounded on a continuum with what many women seem to experience—especially the role of fear in their lives. Now this might turn out to be because such a huge percentage of women have suffered some kind of trauma, whether of child abuse or adult sexual violation. But I think it is more likely that there is something abusive about the role of women (extraordinarily diverse as the forms of the role are) in our society that itself generates a kind of pathology. I also have not discussed the special fear and pain of poverty that afflicts women disproportionately.

93. See the quote from Health Canada with which I began this chapter: "Women will not be free from violence until they achieve equality with men, and equality cannot be achieved until violence and the threat of violence are eliminated from women's lives." Health Canada, *Violence against Women*.

There are also close parallels here with the issue of wife assault.

94. MacKinnon, *Feminism Unmodified*, 6–7.

95. Jane Doe, famed for suing the Toronto Police for failing to warn her of a rapist known to target women of her description, described her experience at her rapist's trial: "I will never forget the final question put to me in defence of the man who had raped me.... Despite everything we know about the violent nature of rape, he asked if my rape had been violent. When I did not answer, could not answer, the judge instructed me that because I had not been cut or stabbed with the rapist's knife, because he hadn't beaten or mutilated or (most decisive of all) killed me, I must answer that my rape had not been violent." Jane Doe, *Story of Jane Doe*, 72.

96. In 1992, a Texas grand jury refused to indict an accused rapist even though he admitted to entering the complainant's apartment, uninvited and drunk, and approaching her with a knife he had taken from her kitchen. The woman had begged her attacker to wear a condom, and one grand juror reflected that the "woman's act of self-protection might have implied her consent." Da Luz and Weckerly, "Texas 'Condom-Rape' Case," 97. Carla M. da Luz and Pamela Weckerly note that, "Although this case seems unusual, it is not an anomaly." They point, for example, to a Long Island appellate court's decision to overturn a rape conviction; one of the judges, skeptical of the jury's findings of fact, reflected, "Who ever heard of a rapist that uses a condom?" (97).

97. Of course, this kind of description invites the notion of a continuum of coerced sex, of which rape forms one end. But to note this does not mean that we cannot distinguish rape from a boyfriend's emotional blackmail or a wife's tolerance of sex she does not want for fear of losing her husband.

98. In a conversation about these issues, Mary Ann Case of the University of Chicago Law School suggested that the norm should be attention to the *satisfaction* of desire. One might note here that Martha Nussbaum lists "having opportunities for sexual satisfaction" as among the basic human capabilities states and societies should enable. Nussbaum, *Women and Human Development*, 78.

99. This is not to say that the communication must be in words. There are many such nuances that I will not fully explore here.

100. *An Act to Amend the Criminal Code (Sexual Assault)*, S.C. 1992, chap. 38. In my reading of the preamble, I do not wish to sound overly naive. I am sure that many preambles express lofty sentiments that are either routinely ignored in interpretation or actually contradicted by the language of the statute. Nevertheless, in this context, I think these positive interpretations are potentially important in the statute's capacity to shift the relations of power around one of the most important uses of violence to express and maintain male dominance.

101. Herman, *Trauma and Recovery*, 72.

102. *Canadian Criminal Code*, R.S.C., chap. C-34, sec. 273.2(e).

103. Herman, *Trauma and Recovery*, 53.

104. Scheppele, "Just the Facts, Ma'am," 161–168, esp. 163–164. See also note 106.

105. *Canadian Criminal Code*, R.S.C., 1985, chap. C-46, sec. 273.2.

106. In *R. v. Ewanchuk*, [1999] 1 S.C.R. 33, Justice Major, writing for the majority of the Supreme Court of Canada, explained that under Section 273(2), "An accused cannot say that he thought 'no meant yes'.... Common sense should dictate that, once the complainant has expressed her unwillingness to engage in sexual contact, the accused should make certain that she has truly changed her mind before proceeding with further intimacies. The accused cannot rely on the mere lapse of time or the complainant's silence or equivocal conduct to indicate that there has been a change of heart and that consent now exists, nor can he engage in further sexual touching

to 'test the waters'. Continuing sexual contact after someone has said 'No' is, at a minimum, reckless conduct which is not excusable." *Ewanchuk* 1999 at paras. 51–52. What was "common sense" to Justice Major, however, was, to Justice McClung (speaking for the majority of the Alberta Court of Appeal), mere "sloganeering such as 'No means No!' 'Zero Tolerance!' and 'Take back the night!' which, while they marshal desired social ideals, are no safe substitute for the orderly and objective judicial application of Canada's criminal statutes." *R. v. Ewanchuk*, (1998), 57 Alta. L.R. (3d) 235, 13 C.R. (5th) 324, [1998] A.J. No. 150 (QL) at para. 12.

Ewanchuk had been charged with sexual assault after making sexual advances toward a young woman he had invited back to his trailer for a job interview. On three separate occasions the complainant said "no"; each time the complainant said "no," the accused desisted briefly but then escalated the level of sexual contact. Although Justice McClung agreed with the trial court's finding that the complainant was afraid of Ewanchuk (indeed, that Ewanchuk himself had repeatedly told the accused not to be afraid), he concluded that "the sum of the evidence indicates that Ewanchuk's advances to the complainant were far less criminal than hormonal. In a less litigious age going too far in the boyfriend's car was better dealt with on site—a well-chosen expletive, a slap in the face or, if necessary, a well-directed knee. What this accused tried to initiate hardly qualifies him for the lasting stigma of a conviction for sexual assault and Alberta's current bullet-train removal to the penitentiary for prolonged shrift." *Ewanchuk* 1998 at para. 21.

Justice L'Heureux-Dubé joined the majority in overturning the Alberta court's ruling. She also wrote a concurring judgment admonishing McClung for reinforcing myths (*Ewanchuk* 1999 at para. 89), minimizing the reality of sexual aggression against women (at para. 91), and relying upon stereotypes (at para. 93). In his now infamous reaction to L'Heureux-Dubé's outspoken opinion, McClung published a letter in the *National Post* reflecting that "the personal convictions of the judge, delivered again from her judicial chair, could provide a plausible explanation for the disparate (and growing) number of male suicides being reported in the Province of Quebec." He later apologized, claiming not to have known that L'Heureux-Dubé's own husband had committed suicide. Rennison and Welchans, *Intimate Partner Violence*.

107. In Canadian constitutional discrimination analysis, such systemic subordination is often referred to as "historical" or "pre-existing disadvantage." The inquiry into whether a claimant has suffered from discrimination has included a consideration of such disadvantage under every legal "test" that the Supreme Court of Canada has employed in interpreting the constitutional equality guarantee. See *Andrews v. Law Society of British Columbia*, [1989] 1 S.C.R. 143; *Law v. Canada (Minister of Employment and Immigration)*, [1999] 1 S.C.R. 497; *R. v. Kapp*, 2008 SCC 41, [2008] 2 S.C.R. 483.

108. See, for example, Don Stuart's comments in note 113.

109. Douglas N. Husak identifies the most frequently cited examples of strict and absolute liability offenses as being "(1) traffic violations, such as speeding; (2) public welfare offenses, such as selling adulterated food; and (3) "morals" offenses involving sexual behavior and the corruption of minors, such as statutory rape." Husak, "Varieties of Strict Liability," 192.

110. For an example of an argument opposing affirmative action on the basis that it is not neutral, see Eastland, "Case against Affirmative Action." As an example of a justification for a departure from neutrality, Steven M. Young cites affirmative action as another important example of the ways that the state has foregone strict concerns about "neutrality" in order to foster more substantive equality. Young, "Beyond Neutrality," 153. Discussing the work of Andrew Kernohan, Young elaborates his central concern about "neutrality": "In a society permeated by *false*

beliefs … that convey to individuals the sense that they are in some way inferior to others due to natural characteristics…. The only means of ensuring that such individuals have an equal chance of living the best lives possible is to try to transform the cultural environment to eliminate the false, pernicious, inegalitarian beliefs…. [N]on-neutral efforts to transform an oppressive cultural environment may be the best means of ensuring the liberal ideal of the moral equality of persons" (153).

111. Of course, in practice, laws often have a differential impact on particular groups. For example, narcotics laws are notorious for their disparate impact on minorities. See Schwartz, "Gender Differences in Drunk Driving Prevalence Rates and Trends; Radosh, "War on Drugs."

112. In a related point, Justice L'Heureux-Dubé and Justice McLachlin (now chief justice of the Supreme Court of Canada) said that "while judges can never be neutral, in the sense of purely objective, they can and must strive for impartiality." *R. v. S. (R.D.)*, [1997] 3 S.C.R. 484 at para. 29.

113. I heard this reaction when presenting these arguments in the United States. Similar concerns were also raised when the *Canadian Criminal Code* sexual assault provisions were amended to include a more objective fault element. Under the new provisions, defendants could no longer raise the defense of "mistaken belief in consent," where the mistake arose from self-induced intoxication, recklessness or wilful blindness, or failure to take reasonable steps to ascertain consent. (For a review of the political history of this provision, see notes 131 and 132.) Don Stuart believed that in passing this legislation "Parliament has gone too far respecting … the manner in which it has criminalized unreasonable behaviour." Stuart, "Pendulum Has Been Pushed Too Far," 356. In Stuart's view, "Surely there is a qualitative distinction between a man who deliberately rapes a woman knowing that she is not consenting, and one who engages in sexual intercourse where it was, in the circumstances, unreasonable for him to have understood that the woman was consenting" (353). The provision in question withstood constitutional challenge on these grounds. *R. v. Darrach*, 2000 SCC 46, [2000] 2 S.C.R. 443.

114. See Herman, *Trauma and Recovery*, chap. 1, "A Forgotten History," on the discovery and subsequent repudiation of childhood sexual abuse as the cause of hysteria.

115. MacKinnon, *Feminism Unmodified*.

116. I base this assessment on the number of government-funded studies of the incidence of rape, changes in the law, and references to training programs for police. For example, a Statistics Canada report notes: "While a notable increase in police-reported sexual offences did follow the 1983 changes to the *Criminal Code*, research has found that these legislative amendments alone were insufficient to explain the increase, and that other social change during this time period also contributed to the rise. Among these social changes, were improvements to the social, economic and political status of women; a heightened focus on victims of crime and a growth in victim's services such as sexual assault centres; as well as special training of police officers and hospitals staff to respond to victims of sexual assault and gather evidence to be used at trial." Brennan and Taylor-Butts, "Sexual Assault in Canada: 2004 and 2007," 10 (sources omitted). They conclude, "Victimization data suggest that the rates of sexual assault remained stable in recent years. However, police-reported data reveal a steady decline in offences coming to the attention of law enforcement for more than a decade" (6).

117. As I noted earlier, all estimates of incidence are fraught with difficulty. The low levels of reporting to police give rise to the need to rely on victimization studies. These studies, in turn, use different methodologies so that tracking change (and comparison across countries) is difficult. Nevertheless, I think one can conclude that the major studies do not show clear

change. A careful comparison of five large-scale studies in the United States between 1989 and 2007 concludes that "the burden of forcible rape on women in the U.S. appears to have increased since the NWS [National Women's Study] was completed in the early 1990's" (11). See note 116 above for the conclusion by Statistics Canada that "rates of sexual assault remained stable in recent years."

118. See Law Commission of Canada, "Restoring Dignity," on the kinds of factors that fostered child abuse in residential institutions, including residential schools for Aboriginal children, schools for the deaf and blind, training schools, and long-term mental health care facilities.

119. One in every ten children in Canada lives in poverty; for First Nations children, the statistic is one in four. Family Service Toronto, "2009 Report Card on Child and Family Poverty in Canada," 2.

120. A 2009 study from the Canadian Centre for Justice Statistics notes that the rate of police-reported child abuse in Canada for the reporting year (2007) was 833 per 100,000; the highest rate of abuse occurred in adolescents between the ages of twelve and seventeen, a rate four times that of the under-twelve category. Canadian Centre for Justice Statistics, "Family Violence in Canada," 32. The rate of sexual assault among children and youth was more than five times higher than that for adults, and physical assault among adolescents between the ages of twelve and seventeen was twice the rate of adults (32). Police-reported physical assault by a family member was highest among teenage girls (33). Four in ten child victims of family violence experienced physical injuries, and perpetrators of family violence were overwhelmingly male (in 96% of sexual assaults and in 71% of physical assaults) (35).

121. See Macy, "Taking Heart."

122. Justice McClung's infamous decision in *Ewanchuk* 1998 (described in more detail in note 106 above) asserted that "it must be pointed out that the complainant did not present herself to Ewanchuk or enter his trailer in a bonnet and crinolines. She told Ewanchuk that she was the mother of a six-month old baby and that, along with her boyfriend, she shared an apartment with another couple. (I must point out these aspects of the trial record, but with no intention of denigrating her or lessening the legal protection to which she was entitled)" (at para. 4). In overturning McClung's decision, L'Heureux-Dubé's concurring judgment for the Supreme Court of Canada dismissed McClung's bracketed caveat, explaining that "[e]ven though McClung J.A. asserted that he had no intention of denigrating the complainant, one might wonder why he felt necessary to point out these aspects of the trial record.... These comments made by an appellate judge help reinforce the myth that under such circumstances, either the complainant is less worthy of belief, she invited the sexual assault, or her sexual experience signals probable consent to further sexual activity. Based on those attributed assumptions, the implication is that if the complainant articulates her lack of consent by saying "no," she really does not mean it and even if she does, her refusal cannot be taken as seriously as if she were a girl of 'good' moral character." *Ewanchuk* 1999 at para. 89.

123. For a discussion of the code's development and its origins in student activism, see Herman, "Demands from the Women of Antioch." The full text of the code is included as an appendix to her book.

124. Mark Cowling explains that "the code was widely felt to impose artificial requirements on an intimate area of life in a mechanical fashion. There is a popular image of Antioch students setting off for dates with a pile of consent forms, a lawyer, and a breathalyser." Cowling, "Rape, Communicative Sexuality and Sex Education," 20.

125. Kristine Herman described Dr. Ruth Westheimer's discussion of the Antioch policy on *Eye to Eye with Connie Chung*: "Dr. Ruth chose to focus not on rape or sexual assault at all, but instead on the way the policy might affect a man's ability to maintain an erection if he is expected to be verbal during a sexual encounter." Herman, "Demands of the Women of Antioch," 132. It is notable that men and women students appeared to have had different reactions to the code. A *New York Times* article written shortly after the policy was enacted reported that "the boys were appalled. 'If I have to ask those questions I won't get what I want,' blurted one young man.... The girls, for their part, were trying on the idea that they could have sex if they wanted and refuse if they did not.... The prevailing sentiment on campus is the one articulated by Ms. Duggins, a transfer student, who said she 'didn't ever stick up' for herself—until she got to Antioch. 'It was easier to just do it and get it over with then say no, no no," [*sic*] Ms. Duggins, the hall adviser, said. 'Now I don't feel like I have to capitulate. Now if I say no and a man doesn't listen, it's wrong. And I have some big clout behind me.'" Gross, "Combating Rape on Campus in a Class on Sexual Consent."

126. Dworkin, *Taking Rights Seriously*, 273.

127. I do not mean to suggest that American state power is consistently marshaled to provide blacks with equal protection against violence. For example, there continue to be various forms of de facto tolerance of black-on-black violence. A recent American Bureau of Justice Statistics Special Report found that, although blacks represented only 13 percent of the American population, nearly half of all homicide victims were black. Harrell, *Black Victims of Violent Crime*, 1. With respect to prison violence, the causal relationship between victimization and "failure to protect" is borne out by studies showing that prison overcrowding (a factor entirely within the state's control and entirely beyond the control of inmates) is the most significant determinant of prison assault rates. Gaes and McGuire, "Prison Violence."

128. The issue of state protection against "private" violence is also central to the issue of intimate partner violence. See Siegel, "'Rule of Love,'" discussed in note 76 above.

129. The Drug-Induced Rape Prevention and Punishment Act of 1996, 21 U.S.C. sec. 841(b) (7), provides criminal penalties of up to twenty years of imprisonment for any person who distributes a controlled substance to a person with the intent to commit a crime of violence, including rape, without that person's (the victim's) knowledge. This act indicates that the lack of knowledge about the controlled substance on the part of the victim negates the victim's ability to consent.

130. See note 62 above.

131. In *R. v. Seaboyer; R. v. Gayme*, [1991] 2 S.C.R. 577, two defendants charged with sexual assault launched a constitutional challenge against provisions of the *Canadian Criminal Code* that restricted the admissibility of evidence regarding the complainants' past sexual history (sec. 276) or reputation (sec. 277), known popularly as the rape shield laws. In a 7–2 decision (with only Justices L'Heureux-Dubé and Gonthier dissenting), the majority found that Section 276 (regarding past sexual history) did violate the defendants' rights to "full answer and defense" under Sections 7 and 11(d) of the *Charter* and struck the legislation. Many feminists and other equality-seeking groups viewed this decision as a perversion of the *Charter*'s promise, seeing it either as part of a new "trend of disturbing significance [that] men began to use the *Charter*...to protest against the few protections women enjoyed in law" (Razack, "Women's Legal Education and Action Fund," 323) or as a continuation of the Court's "historical undermining of women's equality rights" (Del Bove and Stermac, "Psychological Evidence in Sexual Assault Court Cases," 120). As Martha Shaffer presciently reflected shortly after the decision was rendered, *Seaboyer*

may in fact have been "a blessing in disguise" by putting "the ball…in parliament's court," thus allowing feminists to weigh in on the drafting of the more robust provision that came to replace Section 276 (see note 132). Shaffer, "*R. v. Seaboyer and Gayme*," 211.

132. These consultations were originally limited to a small number of elite organizations: the Women's Legal Education and Action Fund (LEAF), the National Association of Women and the Law, the National Action Committee on the Status of Women, and the Canadian Bar Association. These organizations responded to Justice Minister Kim Campbell's subsequent indication that she would pursue only minor amendments by exerting pressure on Campbell to "slow down and expand the consultation process." McIntyre, "Feminist Movement in Law," 75. The ensuing series of consultations with frontline workers and women's groups across the country was "one of the relatively rare cases during the Conservative regime that the consultations were open and constructive and, as the litigation director of LEAF stated, 'it is clear that Justice Minister Campbell listened to the input from women's organizations.'" Phillips, "Legal as Political Strategies in the Canadian Women's Movement," 385. The resultant legislation not only filled in gaps left by the *Seaboyer* decision, it also provided for procedural protections for victims (including publication bans on admissibility hearings), the *Code*'s first definition of consent, and the controversial requirement that the defense of mistaken belief in consent be based on the defendant having taken "reasonable steps" to ascertain consent. For a more fulsome discussion of these changes, see Weiser, "Sexual Assault Legislation," 217–222. See also note 113 on objections to the changes.

133. One statistical study concluded that unwillingly unemployed men are nearly 50 percent more likely to be violent toward their female partners. In examining the relationship between violence and occupational gender roles, the study concluded that in the three categories of "men in female-dominated occupations, unwillingly unemployed men, and men earning disproportionately small percentage of the couple's income, compensatory violence may be used to protect men's gendered identities." Melzer, "Gender, Work, and Intimate Partner Violence," 830.

134. See notes 106 and 122 for a discussion of one Alberta Court of Appeal decision that maintained that "it must be pointed out that the complainant did not present herself to [the defendant] or enter his trailer in a bonnet and crinolines." *Ewanchuk* 1998 at para. 4. The provocative dress for which the complainant was implicitly criticized here consisted of shorts and a T-shirt. (This is also what the defendant wore, though the court did not seem to see this as undermining his credibility.) Although the complainant was never undressed throughout the events in question, the trial court judge also felt it necessary to explain (and the appellate court felt it necessary to repeat) that "[u]nderneath her shorts and T-shirt [the complainant] wore a brassiere and panties." *Ewanchuk* 1998 at para. 2.

135. I think it is fair to use this generalization of men as the dominant group in this context despite the reality that racialized men can be subordinate not only to "white" men but also to "white" women. Unfortunately, whenever one uses the criminal justice system, the problem of systemic racism arises. Williams, "Racism in Justice." There is some evidence that judges are less willing to protect black women against acquaintance rape by black men. I also had a concern that judges might credit claims of acquaintance rape more readily when the victim is white and the accused is black. But at least one American study suggests that concern is not valid: Cassia Spohn and Jeffrey Spears concluded that when whites are victims, the victim/offender relationship has no impact on outcome measures, regardless of the racial status of the perpetrator. Spohn and Spears, "Effect of Offender and Victim Characteristics on Sexual Assault Case Processing Decisions," 655. On the other hand, in cases involving black victims, the relationship

is important in the expected direction. That is, blacks charged with assaulting black acquaintances were significantly more likely to have their charges dismissed and were less likely to be incarcerated and received shorter sentences than blacks charged with assaulting black strangers.

136. Shklar, "Liberalism of Fear," 29.

CHAPTER 6

1. I discuss the puzzle of constitutionalism in Nedelsky, "Puzzle and Demands of Modern Constitutionalism."

2. For American examples, see Tushnet, "Against Judicial Review"; Waldron, "Core of the Case against Judicial Review." This issue used to be a significant part of Canadian critical legal studies in the early years of the *Charter*. For example, some of the objections to the Alternative Social Charter I discuss at the end of this chapter were framed in the context of suspicion of all forms of judicial review. See Bakan and Schneiderman, *Social Justice and the Constitution.* For related Canadian critical perspectives see Petter, *Politics of the Charter,* and Bakan, *Just Words.*

While this argument is no longer a major issue on the Left, it remains an ongoing concern on the Right. See, for example, the work of political scientists Ted Morton and Rainer Knopf.

3. Dworkin, *Taking Rights Seriously.*

4. As discussed below in section III.C, Section 1 of the *Canadian Charter of Rights and Freedoms* reads:

1. The *Canadian Charter of Rights and Freedoms* guarantees the rights and freedoms set out in it subject only to such reasonable limits prescribed by law as can be demonstrably justified in a free and democratic society.

Canadian Charter of Rights and Freedoms, Part I of the *Constitution Act, 1982,* being Schedule B to the *Canada Act 1982* (U.K.), 1982, chap. 11, sec. 1.

Section 36 of the South African Constitution's Bill of Rights reads as follows:

1. The rights in the Bill of Rights may be limited only in terms of law of general application to the extent that the limitation is reasonable and justifiable in an open and democratic society based on human dignity, equality and freedom, taking into account all relevant factors, including
   a. the nature of the right;
   b. the importance of the purpose of the limitation;
   c. the nature and extent of the limitation;
   d. the relation between the limitation and its purpose; and
   e. less restrictive means to achieve the purpose.
2. Except as provided in subsection (1) or in any other provision of the Constitution, no law may limit any right entrenched in the Bill of Rights.

Constitution of the Republic of South Africa, Schedule No. 108 of 1996, Chapter 2—Bill of Rights, sec. 36.

5. In some versions of proportionality, the claim of a violation of a specific right is no longer crucial. See Kumm, "What Do You Have in Virtue of Having a Constitutional Right?" and "Democracy Is Not Enough." What matters is that a person's interest has been harmed by governmental action in an arbitrary or unjustified (i.e., not proportional to the interest advanced) way. But in this chapter, I continue to use the language of rights because they remain central to many forms of constitutionalism as well as to other legal and political projects.

6. Of course, in practice, rights are defined, debated, and protected through many institutional means.

7. See White, *Living Speech*, 73, 100, 112–114.

8. The widespread belief that rights should act as trumps is distinct from the actual effects of striking down a law, which are much more complicated.

9. I discuss the ways in which alleged conflicts between universal human rights and local custom are best understood in terms of competing communities of judgment in Nedelsky, "Communities of Judgment and Human Rights."

10. In fact, however, it is only when rights are rooted in politics, when people have built deep support for them in the community, that rights can do their work. This is becoming increasingly clear in the international context, where the presence of rights in constitutional documents and even in elite understandings does not give actual effect to those rights when there is no grassroots support for them. Even in domestic constitutional contexts courts do not uphold rights against widespread popular opposition (for example, the internment of citizens of Japanese heritage in both Canada and the United States during the Second World War). And even *Brown v. Board of Education of Topeka*, 347 U.S. 483 (1954), perhaps the most vaunted example of rights enforced against (southern) majoritarian oppression, is best seen as a turning point in a long and carefully crafted political and legal campaign for change. See Rosenberg, *Hollow Hope*.

Michael Klarman makes a similar argument, tracing the role of political and social change in judicial decision making, including the *Brown* decision. In Klarman's view, "because constitutional law is generally quite indeterminate, constitutional interpretation almost inevitably reflects the broader social and political context of the times.... Once racial attitudes had changed ... the justices reconsidered the meaning of the Constitution." Klarman, *From Jim Crow to Civil Rights*, 5–6. Thus, Klarman posits, "the justices did not protect women under the Equal Protection Clause until after the women's movement, and they did not invalidate racial segregation until after public opinion on race had changed dramatically" (6).

11. For a discussion of wider uses of the term constitutionalism see Neil Walker, "Post-Constituent Constitutionalism?"

12. Bradley and Petro, *Truth Claims*.

13. Formally the *Convention for the Protection of Human Rights and Fundamental Freedoms*, CETS No. 5, November 4, 1950.

14. *Treaty on European Union*, February 7, 1992, O.J. C 224/1 (1992), [1992] 1 C.M.L.R. 719, 31 I.L.M. 247.

15. Schor, "Mapping Comparative Judicial Review."

16. Trindade, "Inter-American Court of Human Rights at a Crossroads."

17. In 1986, the Assembly of Heads of State and Government of the Organization of African Unity passed the *African Charter on Human and Peoples' Rights:* online <http://www.achpr.org/english/_info/charter_en.html>.

18. Consider, for example, Costas Douzinas's important argument about the way American foreign policy has been built around the destructive ideological use of rights. Douzinas, *Human Rights and Empire*. That is not one of the issues I take up here.

19. *Universal Declaration of Human Rights*, GA Res 217(III), UN GAOR, 3d sess., supp. no. 13, UN Doc. a/810 (1948), 71.

20. *United Nations Declaration on the Rights of Indigenous Peoples*, GA Res. 61/295, UN GAOR, 61st sess. (2007).

21. Stephen Waddams explains that the phrase "common law" has "a variety of meanings, according to the subject with which it is contrasted. Waddams, *Introduction to the Study of Law*, 75. In this case, I refer to "common law countries", or jurisdictions within the common law legal tradition, as opposed to jurisdictions governed by civil (also known as Roman) law. While civil law is generally based on codification, common law "is a system of law based primarily on judicial decisions" (75). Waddams explains that "the principle of reliance on decided cases is called the principle of *stare decisis* (to stand by what has been decided)" and elaborates that "the principle that like cases should be decided alike leads inevitably to records of past cases and an attempt to compare past cases with that to be currently decided" (79). See chapter 1, note 126, for a description of the other meanings of "common law."

22. For relational approaches, see also Minow, *Making All the Difference*; Singer, "Reliance Interest in Property" and *Entitlement*; Koggel, *Perspectives on Equality*.

23. In the corporate context, the law clearly operates to structure relationships and prioritize the responsibilities that different actors owe to one another. Depending on the structure, the values now associated with the term "corporate social responsibility" can be fostered or undermined. The traditional "property model" of the corporation understood shareholders to be the "owners" of a corporation, such that directors' responsibility must primarily be to the shareholders, even at the expense of other stakeholders, such as employees, creditors, or the broader community. For a discussion of the "property model" and the "social entity model" addressed below, see Allen, "Our Schizophrenic Conception of the Business Corporation." The property model drives the court's reasoning in the classic American case *Dodge v. Ford Motor Co.*, 204 Mich. 459, 170 N.W. 668 (Mich. 1919). In that case, two minority shareholders sued Ford Motor Co. for its decision to reinvest profits rather than pay dividends to Ford shareholders. Central to this dispute were public statements by Henry Ford that, "My ambition is to employ still more men; to spread the benefits of this industrial system to the greatest possible number, to help them build up their lives and their homes." *Dodge v. Ford Motor Co.*, 204 Mich. at 505. The minority shareholders argued that it was impermissible for majority shareholders to direct the corporation's energies toward humanitarian or charitable ends (in the shareholders' view, transforming the corporation into "a semi-eleemosynary institution" and not "a business institution"). The court in that case was clear that "it is not within the lawful powers of a board of directors to shape and conduct the affairs of a corporation for the merely incidental benefit of shareholders and for the primary purpose of benefiting others" (at 507).

The more modern "social entity" view of the corporation may work to change the substance of the law's role in structuring the relationships among stakeholders. According to this view, the role of the corporation within the broader community may give rise to legal and moral obligations to respect the environment, their employees, and the well-being of the communities in which they operate. While corporate law continues to emphasize that director duties are to the corporation, this is now understood to mean more than simply the shareholders. Delaware law, for example, now allows for "reasonable" donations to charitable causes and public welfare. Title 8, Section 122(9) of the Delaware Code; *Theodora Holding Corp v. Henderson*, 257 A.2d 398 (Del. Ch. 1969).

The Canadian Supreme Court has reconsidered what it means to act in the best interest of the corporation, concluding, "We accept as an accurate statement of law that in determining whether they are acting with a view to the best interests of the corporation it may be legitimate, given all the circumstances of a given case, for the board of directors to consider, inter alia, the interests of shareholders, employees, suppliers, creditors, consumers, governments and the environment." *Peoples Department Stores Inc. (Trustee of) v. Wise*, [2004] 3 S.C.R. 461, 2004 SCC 68, at para. 42.

24. It may even be possible to assess whether those who experienced a sense of dislocation from the split between their worldview and that now expressed in the law also experience an increased marginalization in society. But it will probably be impossible to tell whether some groups would experience some such marginalization regardless of the legal mechanism for achieving equality for homosexuals. For example, the Interfaith Coalition on Marriage and Family's factum in the Supreme Court of Canada case *Reference re. Same-Sex Marriage* argues that a change in the legal status of marriage would lead to normative changes in the background understanding of such concepts as reasonableness, public interest, and what is necessary in a free and democratic society among institutions, such as the judiciary and professional governing bodies, which would marginalize members of religious communities whose beliefs prohibit same-sex marriages: "The communities represented by the Interfaith Coalition are at risk of losing the ability to fully participate in public life in Canada." *Reference re Same-Sex Marriage* [2004] 3 S.C.R. 698, 2004 SCC 79 (Factum of the Intervener, The Interfaith Coalition on Marriage and Family, at paras. 32–33).

25. For a discussion of property rights from a relational perspective see Singer, "Reliance Interest in Property." My conversations with Joe Singer were helpful to me in writing the original version of this chapter. In a fine example of the best of academic relationships, Joe then used that essay in his book *Entitlement: The Paradoxes of Property* (2000), which in turn was helpful to me in writing this one.

26. *M'Alister (or Donoghue) v. Stevenson*, [1932] A.C. 562 (H.L.).

27. In some cases where one person has made statements which another has relied upon in making their plans and financial commitments, courts will say that the first person is responsible for that reliance even though the statements were not part of a formal contract. See, for example, Section 90 of the American Law Institute's Restatement of Contracts.

28. For example, the New Jersey Supreme Court found that it was not within the property rights of a farmer to prohibit doctors and lawyers from entering his land to visit the migrant workers living on his property. Such an interpretation of property rights would isolate the workers, deny them the ordinary forms of relationship consistent with dignity: "[W]e find it unthinkable that the farmer-employer can assert a right to isolate the worker in any respect significant for the worker's well being.... [T]he employer may not deny the worker his privacy or interfere with his opportunity to live with dignity and to enjoy associations customary among our citizens." *State v. Shack*, 277 A.2d 369, 374–375 (N.J. 1971), quoted in Singer, "Normative Methods for Lawyers," 964. Singer also provides other detailed examples of relational analyses of property rights.

29. See chapter 3, notes 37 and 38, for discussion of the U.S. case *Lochner v. New York*, 198 U.S. 45 (1905), and the judicial era it ushered in.

30. As I have argued elsewhere, the Constitution of 1787 did not focus primarily on rights as limits in the sense we now understand as requiring judicial review. Judicial review was not mentioned. The Constitution of 1787 was designed to structure the institutions so as to ensure that the sort of men who knew how to govern, including how to respect rights, would be the ones in office. See Nedelsky, *Private Property and the Limits of American Constitutionalism*.

31. The Framers were even sure that although there was no consensus on what constituted the violation of rights such as property, *they* knew what property rights really were and what kind of legislation would violate them. For example, James Madison tried to get his countrymen to see that depreciating currency constituted theft in the same way as stealing a horse. See Nedelsky, *Private Property and the Limits of American Constitutionalism*.

32. Throughout the common law world, for example, married women held the status of *feme covert* (literally "covered [i.e., protected] woman"), meaning all rights to property transferred to their husbands upon marriage. This doctrine was done away with in the United Kingdom through the *Married Women's Property Act, 1886* (U.K.), 45 & 46 Vict. Various campaigns throughout the United States to eliminate the *feme covert* doctrine took place throughout the nineteenth century, and it was not until 1900 that all states allowed married women to own property. For a detailed look at the normative reasoning behind the coverture doctrine, see Cogan, "Look Within," in particular the section on women's suffrage (beginning at 485). In 1873, the U.S. Supreme Court affirmed the decision to deny women admission to the Illinois state bar, justifying the *feme covert* status by noting that "the civil law, as well as nature herself, has always recognized a wide difference in the respective spheres and destinies of man and woman. Man is, or should be, woman's protector and defender. The natural and proper timidity and delicacy which belongs to the female sex evidently unfits it for many of the occupations of civil life." *Bradwell v. Illinois*, 83 U.S. (16 Wall.) 130, 21 L. Ed. 442 (U.S.S.C. 1873). In Canada, it took until 1930 for the Privy Council to decide that women were to be considered persons and therefore eligible to sit as members in the Canadian Senate. *Edwards v. A.G. Canada*, [1930] 1 D.L.R. 98 (P.C.). This came only two years after Canada's Supreme Court affirmed the view that women were not qualified—that is, incapable—to hold office. *Reference re Meaning of the Word "Persons" in Section 24 of the British North America Act, 1867*, [1928] S.C.R. 276.

33. Consider, for example, the U.S. Supreme Court's unwillingness to allow state legislatures to interfere with contractual freedom in order to limit the working hours of bakery employees to sixty hours per week in *Lochner v. New York*, 198 U.S. 45 (1905) (see chapter 3, notes 37 and 38). It is now a fundamental premise of labor law that the employer–employee relationship is characterized by inequality of bargaining power and therefore must be regulated in some manner. For example, the regulation of minimum wage and maximum hours is now routine throughout North America. For a Canadian perspective see Langille and Davidov, "Beyond Employees and Independent Contractors."

34. To leave aside the complexities of cabinet and administrative bodies.

35. See Nedelsky, "Judicial Conservatism in an Age of Innovation"; Horwitz, *Transformation of American Law, 1870–1960*.

36. For example, *Belvidere Tp. v. Heinze*, 241 Mich.App. 324, 615 N.W.2d 250 (Mich. App. 2000).

37. Singer, *Entitlement*, 56–58.

38. One workshop participant suggested that this formulation rested on a mistake: confusing the question of limits on democracy with the process of determining or enforcing those limits.

To the participant, the content of the rights that should serve as limits is given by a theory of rights, derived, I assume, from human nature or the nature of agency or freedom. My point, however, is that we cannot rely on such theoretically derived conceptions to justify limits on democracy. At the least, as I noted in the text above, the legal meaning of such rights must be determined, and the legitimacy of the process of that determination is inseparable from the legitimacy of treating rights as limits. And, in my terms, that process will inevitably be a collective determination and thus choice. More broadly, the historical shifts in meaning and the diversity of constitutionalized rights in different democracies make it difficult to believe that we can rely on a transcendent, universal, immutable source for the content of rights.

Bruce A. Ackerman, in *We the People* (1991), argues that the American Constitution is structured in a way that treats "the people," rather than some transcendent meaning, as the source of rights. Here he contrasts the American Constitution with the German Constitution. I elaborate this point in Nedelsky, "Puzzle and Demands of Modern Constitutionalism," 501.

39. My thanks to Laura Underkuffler for first alerting me to the need for this clarification in her review of my *Private Property and the Limits of American Constitutionalism*. Underkuffler, "Perfidy of Property."

40. Zerilli, *Feminism and the Abyss of Freedom*. See also chapter 1, note 37 for an explanation of the term "relations of freedom."

41. Larry Rasmussen has grappled with how to work environmental concerns into a language of rights that emerged from a tradition which is "anthropocentric without qualification." Rasmussen, "Human Environmental Rights and/or Biotic Rights," 37. He suggests two possibilities: "*Human environmental rights* are an extension of the moral framework and discourse that has grounded human rights; *biotic rights* reside in a different framework with a different rationale" (36n1). He argues that traditional human rights theory poses special challenges to his project since "Human rights are not integrally related to the moral standing of other species," and (citing Thomas Berry) "it considers humans a species essentially non-relational and self-encased" (38; citations omitted). Despite these problems, and his acknowledgment that "[not] everything that is ethically desirable should find its way into the domain of rights and law," he does "wave a banner for a new generation of rights, the rights of nature" (48). He does so because, in his view, "simple respect for nature and innumerable voluntary actions, or even laws, regulations, and negotiated treaties, will fall short of the necessary protection" (38).

42. The Supreme Court of Canada has held that the *Charter* will require heightened procedural protections in some circumstances of state interference with the parent–child relationship. In *New Brunswick (Minister of Health and Community Services) v. G. (J.)*, [1999] 3 S.C.R. 46, the majority of the Court held that in some cases indigent parents have a constitutional right to be provided with state-funded counsel in proceedings where the government seeks to suspend their custody of their children. The judgment focused on the rights of the parents, emphasizing "the obvious distress arising from the loss of companionship of the child," the "gross intrusion into a private and intimate sphere" associated with inspection and review, and the "stigma and distress resulting from a loss of parental status" (at para. 61).

For a discussion of the American context, see Mary Shanley's work on the government policies in the United States that do violence to the bonds between parent and child. Shanley, "Right to a Parent-Child Relationship." Two of her examples are deportation of "illegal aliens" whose children have been born in the United States (the same thing can happen in Canada) and prison policies that make no effort to sustain parent–child bonds. The Canadian province of British

Columbia recently canceled a program that had allowed nursing mothers to keep their children with them. Theodore, "BC Says No to Allowing Babies in Jail." Part of the problem Shanley points to is that the importance of this bond for both parent and child is not adequately recognized in American law and policy. She asks whether there ought to be something like a right to relationship that could be used to weigh in against such policies. Whether inherent right is the best way to capture this value or not, the value of the bond is not currently recognized in these terms. So at the moment, this would be a clear case where there should be an assessment of the law in terms of this value. This would involve a consideration of how government policies structure parent–child relationships and whether such structures enhance or undermine these relationships. Shanley, "Right to a Parent-Child Relationship."

43. In the disputes over the nature of the harm caused by residential schools (which Aboriginal children were forced to attend in both the United States and Canada), the Canadian Federal government strenuously resisted the legal recognition of loss of language and cultural identity [and integrity]. See *Blackwater v. Plint*, 2005 SCC 58, [2005] 3 S.C.R. 3; *Cloud v. Attorney General of Ontario* (2004), 73 O.R. (3d) 401 (2004), 247 D.L.R. (4th) 667. (The United Church initially joined in this resistance but then recognized that this stance of legal defense was inconsistent with their actual views on the harm and hope for reconciliation. The United Church has an excellent selection of documents on its website that track the decisions and positions of the church on this issue: <http://www.united-church.ca/aboriginal/schools/>.) The plaintiffs argued that the exclusive focus on the individual harms of physical and sexual abuse could not capture the nature of the harm done by the schools. One might also argue here that part of what is at stake in both the legal and political efforts at redress for the residential schools is the importance for Canadian society and its future relations with Aboriginal peoples that there be public acknowledgement of the harms done. After a long process, apologies were offered by the federal government, the United Church of Canada, the Catholic church, the Anglican church, and provincial governments. The Truth and Reconciliation Commission of Canada was established in September 2007. The mandate for The Truth and Reconciliation Commission of Canada is found in Schedule N of the Indian Residential Schools Settlement Agreement: online <http://www.residentialschool-settlement.ca/English.html>.

44. Smith, *Civic Ideals*.

45. Of course, as part of ongoing conversations about what those core values should be, in some cultures people will have recourse to philosophical argument. And some will arrive at convictions about the truth of their conception of those values on the basis of those arguments. Some will express that conviction in the language of inherent rights. But this conviction of truth cannot itself have legal or political weight. It will, however, matter if those convictions are widely taken up by the society and incorporated into the society's jurisprudence.

46. See, for example, the discussion of rule of law as "a principle of profound constitutional and political significance" in *Reference re Secession of Quebec*, [1998] 2 S.C.R. 217; 161 D.L.R. (4th) 385 (S.C.C.) at paras. 70–78.

47. Monahan draws on Ely but thinks Ely is wrong descriptively about the United States. Ely, *Democracy and Distrust*; Monahan, *Politics and the Constitution*.

48. See note 2 above for the more general critique of judicial review as undemocratic.

49. Of course it is possible to work back from democracy, asking what all the preconditions are for democratic participation and from that process generate a very wide range of values, including autonomy. But I think such a process distorts our understanding of the genuine diversity of values

that in fact are necessary for an optimal society or for the possibility of pursuing a full and good life. It has always struck me as particularly implausible to believe that the value of freedom of religion could be derived from even the most all-encompassing conception of the conditions for democracy. Here I think the distortion involved in such derivation is obvious. Some form of freedom of religion *is* necessary for democracy, but that does not exhaust or even distinctively capture its value in human life.

50. Unless one wants to make the strong claim that even though in principle it would be legitimate to protect those values, there is no institutional mechanism of doing so that could be legitimate.

51. Note that the sources of collective power might include large-scale corporations, but here I will just focus on the government.

52. *Canadian Charter of Rights and Freedoms*, Part I of the *Constitution Act, 1982*, being Schedule B to the *Canada Act 1982* (U.K.), 1982, chap. 11.

53. Section 33, the so-called override provision or notwithstanding clause, allows legislatures to expressly state that a piece of legislation shall operate notwithstanding provisions in Section 2 (fundamental freedoms of conscience, expression, assembly, and association) or sections 7–15 ("legal rights" and "equality rights.") Such legislation has effect for five years and may then be reenacted.

I should note that Section 33 has not been effective in promoting such dialogue. I think its capacity to do so was undermined by Liberal electioneering rhetoric in 2006, suggesting that the willingness to use the override amounted to a failure to respect the *Charter* and civil rights.

Mark Tushnet has rightly noted that the wording is not optimal for a dialogical interpretation. Tushnet, "Judicial Activism or Restraint in a Section 33 World." It suggests not a different interpretation of the rights listed in the *Charter* (or their underlying values) but a willingness to pass a law even though it violates those rights. It can, however, reasonably be interpreted as authorizing legislatures to pass a law notwithstanding the Supreme Court's *current interpretation* of the *Charter*. In practice, I think that has in fact been what has been at stake in debates about the use of the override.

54. On the limitations clause, see Roach, *Supreme Court on Trial*, and Hiebert, *Charter Conflicts*. For a good overview of Section 33, see Kahana, "Understanding the Notwithstanding Mechanism."

55. The relationship between the courts and the legislature in this ongoing debate over rights and limits was explored in the seminal article by Peter W. Hogg and Allison A. Bushell, "The *Charter* Dialogue between Courts and Legislatures (or Perhaps the *Charter of Rights* Isn't Such a Bad Thing after All)" (1997), which has since attracted substantial academic discussion and subsequent replies by the authors. See Hogg, Bushell Thornton, and Wright, "A Reply on '*Charter* Dialogue Revisited'" (2007), which argues that "the structure of the *Charter* (and especially Section 1) generally leaves room for the competent legislative body to respond to a court decision striking down a law on *Charter* grounds by enacting a new law that accomplishes the legislative purpose by other means" (193–194). According to Hogg, Bushell Thornton, and Wright, the result of these responses—or "legislative sequels"—was that "the legislative body typically had the last word" (194).

These authors are focusing, as most scholars who invoke dialogue in this context do, on the institutional exchange between courts and legislatures. I have in mind a broader issue of dialogue that would also include public deliberation on the meaning of rights.

56. Freedom of speech in the United States is a particularly clear case of the problems with treating rights as trumps. The constitutional prohibition is presented in especially absolute language: "Congress shall make no law abridging the freedom of speech, or of the press" (First Amendment). In practice, however, "speech" covers such a broad range of human conduct that the notion that "the boundaries of the First Amendment are delineated by the ordinary language meaning of the word 'speech' is simply implausible." Schauer, "Boundaries of the First Amendment." In Canada, although "the textual guarantee of the freedom of speech does not differ significantly from … the First Amendment," Section 1 of the *Charter* (which allows the law to place reasonable limits on rights so long as they are demonstrably justifiable in a free and democratic society) makes the values that restrain freedom of speech explicit by "directly invit[ing] judicial balancing of rights against other social interests." Krotoszynsk, *First Amendment in Cross-Cultural Perspective*, 28.

Frederick Schauer's inquiry into the "boundaries" of the First Amendment reveals that, with no provision akin to Section 1 of the *Charter*, the U.S. Supreme Court has often restrained the scope of the right by presuming some speech not to be "speech." Schauer helpfully canvasses the history of American free speech jurisprudence, showing how such expressive forms as defamation, obscenity, commercial advertising, and "fighting words" have each been characterized at times as being simply beyond the sphere of "speech" protected by the Constitution. (To this list, Schauer adds antitrust law, securities regulation, the law of criminal solicitation, and many laws of evidence.) Schauer, "Boundaries of the First Amendment," 1767–1768.

57. See, for example, Razack, "Cold Game of Equality Staring"; Tushnet, "Critique of Rights"; Gordon, "Some Critical Theories of Law and Their Critics."

58. See, for example, Glendon, *Rights Talk*; Bahm, "Rights and Duties"; Willard and Jennings, *Perversion of Autonomy*; Smoke, *Bill of Rights and Responsibilities*; Etzioni, *Rights and the Common Good* and *New Golden Rule*; Ackerman, "Tort Law and Communitarianism."

59. See Lessard, "Equality and Access to Justice in the Work of Bertha Wilson"; Bakan, *Just Words*; Frazer and Lacey, *Politics of Community*.

60. Consider, for example, Mary Ellen Turpel's critique of the individualistic rights paradigm originating in the (European) philosophies of Hobbes and Locke as being culturally insensitive to Aboriginal peoples' conceptions of rights and legality. Turpel, "Aboriginal Peoples and the Canadian Charter." See also Turner, *This Is Not a Peace Pipe*.

61. The South African incorporation of the African concept of *ubuntu* into their constitutional jurisprudence is an interesting counterweight to that tradition. See *S. v. Makwanyane and Another* (CCT3/94) [1995] ZACC 3; 1995 (6) BCLR 665; 1995 (3) SA 391; [1996] 2 CHRLD 164; 1995 (2) SACR 1 (6 June 1995) and *Bhe and Others v.Khayelitsha Magistrate and Others* (CCT 49/03) [2004] ZACC 17; 2005 (1) SA 580 (CC); 2005 (1) BCLR 1 (CC) (15 October 2004).

62. See Koggel, *Perspectives on Equality*; Gabel, "Phenomenology of Right Consciousness and the Pact of the Withdrawn Selves."

63. See Kittay, *Love's Labor*, for an excellent analysis of the relationship between those dependent on care and those who provide that care (overwhelmingly women) and the ways in which this relationship does not fit with an individualistic conception of justice or rights.

64. For arguments about taxation as a violation of property rights, see Epstein, *Takings*.

65. For example, in *State v. Shack* (see note 28 above), the court considered the interest in allowing the farmer to control how his land was used (including the exclusion of medical professionals who sought to enter to provide care for migrant workers living on his property) and the

way the values of dignity and privacy would be affected by the scope of the property right. Singer, "Normative Methods for Lawyers."

66. See, for example, Rosenberg, *Hollow Hope.*

67. For current examples of efforts to locate responsibility for rights and core values outside courts see Eskridge and Ferejohn, "Super-Statutes" and other essays in that volume.

68. Gabel, "Phenomenology of Right Consciousness and the Pact of the Withdrawn Selves," offers an excellent, thoughtful statement of this perspective.

69. See also chapter 1, section I.B.

70. This seems an appropriate place for a note of response to the allegation that my theory of "rights as relationship" is consequentialist and that I must therefore enter into the debate over deontological versus consequentialist theories of rights. A series of questions at the Legal Theory workshop at Columbia helped me to see why this debate is peripheral to my concerns here. The division between consequentialist and deontological theories is premised on the possibility of a useful conception of human beings whose nature can be understood in abstraction from any of the relations of which they are a part. Once one rejects this premise, the sharp distinction between rights defined on the basis of human nature versus rights defined in terms of the desirability of the relationships they foster simply dissolves. Since there is no freestanding human nature comprehensible in abstraction from all relationship, from which one could derive a theory of rights, the focus on relationship does not constitute a failure to respect the essential claims of humanness. The focus on relationship *is* a focus on the nature of humanness and what makes it possible for humans to thrive; a relational approach is not a willingness to sacrifice the requirements of humanness to a calculation of the benefits of outcomes.

Often the concern underlying the danger of such a sacrifice is that the benefits (consequences) to many will be calculated to outweigh the entitlement of an individual; to put it the other way around, some believe that a consequentialist approach would be unable to resist claims of benefits to many and thus would fail to provide adequate protection to individuals when such protection would harm many. I believe that a long-term relational approach need not fall prey to this problem. More generally, the concern is that some notion (inevitably shifting and contested and thus unreliable) of the public good might be the focus of consequentialist calculations, undermining the reliable rights derived from the very nature of human beings—a nature, such as rationality, that can be seen as constant, context-free, and thus reliable as the abstract foundation for rights. But, as I noted above, if the very nature of human beings is relational, then an attention to this is not a deviation from the heart of what rights are about.

71. Williams, *Alchemy of Race and Rights.*

72. There are still some unresolved problems here. We need to figure out both the scope for withdrawal that is optimal and the ways of structuring choice about entering relationships. These are complicated problems once one starts from a framework that treats relationships as primary and in many cases given rather than chosen.

73. For a discussion of the debate over whether to include property in the *Charter*, see Augustine, "Protection of the Right to Property under the Canadian Charter of Rights and Freedoms," esp. 66–68. Augustine cites concern about an "excessively wide definition of the term 'property'" as a determinative factor against its inclusion (67). Augustine also notes that the New Democratic Party, Canada's social democrat party, strongly opposed inclusion of property protections. Omitting property was part of the deal to ensure New Democrat support for the *Charter* in Parliament (67–68).

74. In 1983, the Progressive Conservatives, at the time the official opposition party, introduced a nonconfidence motion to amend Section 7 of the *Charter* to include protection of property. The bill was defeated. The issue came up again in Parliament in 1987, when a motion was passed supporting the principle of property protection in the *Charter*, though not proposing a specific amendment. The motion reads as follows: "That in the opinion of this House, the *Constitution Act, 1982* should be amended in order to recognize the right to enjoyment of property, and the right not to be deprived thereof, except in accordance with the principles of fundamental justice, and in keeping with the tradition of the usual federal-provincial consultative process." Johansen, "Property Rights and the Constitution." There were provincial attempts to amend the *Charter* as well, the most notable being Resolution 34 of the British Columbia legislature in 1982. This private member's bill, brought forward by the Hon. Garde Gardom, read: "Be it resolved that, as the Constitution Act, 1982, provides that an amendment to the constitution of Canada may be initiated by the Legislative Assembly of a province, we the members of the Legislative Assembly of the Province of British Columbia hereby authorize the Governor-General to issue a proclamation under the Great Seal of Canada to amend section 7 of the *Canadian Charter of Rights and Freedoms* so that it reads as follows: '7. Everyone has the right to life, liberty, security of the person and enjoyment of property and the right not to be deprived thereof except in accordance with the principles of fundamental justice, and urge that the Legislative Assemblies of all other provinces and the Senate and the House of Commons pass similar resolutions.'" Hansard, B.C. Legislative Assembly, 4th Sess., 32nd Parliament, 1982.

75. See Nedelsky, "Should Property Be Constitutionalized?" The main issues of the debate revolved around distribution and the legitimacy of acquisition of property. In the article, I think I was expressing a widely shared view that, "[a]ny effort to provide protection for property in the new South African constitution has to recognize that the meaning of such protection cannot simply be protection for the current distribution" (418).

76. Equality, in turn, is sometimes linked to dignity. With or without this link, my point here is that a core idea of equality is foundational for modern constitutionalism. For example, in a leading Canadian case on equality—*Law v. Canada (Minister of Employment and Immigration)*, [1999] 1 S.C.R. 497—Justice Iacobucci, writing for the majority, tied equality to basic human dignity in a constitutional framework: "It may be said that the purpose of s. 15(1) [equality guarantee] is to prevent the violation of essential human dignity and freedom...and to promote a society in which all persons enjoy equal recognition at law as human beings or as members of Canadian society, equally capable and equally deserving of concern, respect and consideration" (at para.51). The German Basic Law also links equality to human dignity as fundamental and foundational. As noted by Gerhard Robbers, such fundamental rights are "the centre and axis on which all legal thinking turns." Robbers, *Introduction to German Law*, 47.

77. Of course, many constitutions include some rights that are expressly *not* available to all members of society. In Canada, for example, Section 23 of the *Charter* specifies a subset of citizens who are provided with constitutionally protected minority language education rights; Section 25 provides special protections for Aboriginal peoples; Section 3 provides the right to vote only to citizens; and Section 6 provides mobility rights only to citizens and permanent residents. While some rights are explicitly provided for "everyone" (including, notably, the "fundamental freedoms" protected in Section 2), many are not. In Canada, some of these more narrowly available rights (particularly for official language minorities and Aboriginal peoples), reflect the view that

different communities may require different rights in order to participate fully in Canadian society.

78. Young, "Impartiality and the Civic Public."

79. Of course, other fundamental rights, such as freedom of speech and freedom of religion, also have been seen as threatening equality. See, for example, Sunstein, "Sex Equality versus Religion," 209–220, and Youm, "First Amendment Law."

80. *Canadian Charter of Rights and Freedoms*, Part I of the *Constitution Act, 1982*, being Schedule B to the *Canada Act 1982* (U.K.), 1982, chap. 11, sec. 7. There is also a protection against seizure of evidence that serves to define some of the contours of relations with the state with respect to material possessions (sec. 8).

81. See, for example, Gutmann and Thompson, *Why Deliberative Democracy?*

82. See, for example, Cover, "Origins of Judicial Activism in the Protection of Minorities."

83. There are important complications when someone is renting out a room in her home. Exceptions are carved out for these cases in both the United States and Canada. See Singer, "Reliance Interest in Property" and *Entitlement*, 44. In Canada, the Ontario *Human Rights Code*, R.S.O. 1990, chap. H.19, sec. 21 (1) provides:

> The right under section 2 to equal treatment with respect to the occupancy of residential accommodation without discrimination is not infringed by discrimination where the residential accommodation is in a dwelling in which the owner or his or her family reside if the occupant or occupants of the residential accommodation are required to share a bathroom or kitchen facility with the owner or family of the owner.

84. *Reference re Same-Sex Marriage*, [2004] 3 S.C.R. 698, 2004 SCC 79. Some American state courts have reached similar findings: *Goodridge v. Department of Public Health*, 440 Mass. 309, 798 N.E.2d 941 (2003); *Varnum v. Brien*, 763 N.W.2d 862 (Iowa 2009); *Kerrigan v. Commissioner of Public Health*, 289 Conn. 135, 957 A.2d 407 (2008); *Baker v. Vermont*, 744 A.2d 864 (Vt. 1999); *In re Marriage Cases*, 43 Cal. 4th 757, 183 P.3d 384, 76 Cal. Rptr. 3d 683 (2008). In 2008, a voter measure called Proposition 8 overturned the court's decision in *In re Marriage Cases*, legislating that "only marriage between a man and a woman is valid or recognized in California". Proposition 8 was itself overturned by a district court in *Perry v. Schwarzenegger*, No. 09-2292 VRW, 2010 WL 3025614 (N.D. Cal. Aug. 4, 2010), on the basis that it violated the equal protection and due process clauses of the federal Constitution. California's governor and attorney general have declined to appeal this decision, but the ruling has been stayed pending the outcome of proceedings before the California Superior Court regarding whether or not a group called "Yes on 8" has legal standing to appeal the decision. Keen, "Fourth Question Erupts on Prop. 8."

85. *Andrews v. Law Society British Columbia*, [1989] 1 S.C.R. 143. As Peter Hogg puts it, "In the *Andrews* case, McIntyre J., in the course of defining discrimination, used the phrase 'whether intentional or not' (174)....It follows that it is not necessary to show that the *purpose* of the challenged law was to impose a disadvantage on a person by reason of his or her race, national or ethnic origins, etc. It is enough to show that the *effect* of the law is to impose a disadvantage on a person by reference to one of the listed or analogous characteristics.... [*Andrews* also makes clear] that Section 15 prohibits not only direct discrimination but also systemic discrimination. Systemic discrimination is caused by a law that does not expressly employ any of the categories prohibited by s. 15, if the law nevertheless has a disproportionate adverse effect on persons defined by any of

the prohibited categories.... Systemic discrimination may be unintended." Hogg, *Constitutional Law of Canada*, 971–972.

86. See, for example, Constance Backhouse's discussion of the role of law in constructing and sustaining racism in Canada: "It is essential to recognize that racism is located in the systems and structures that girded the legal system of Canada's past. Racism is not primarily manifest in isolated, idiosyncratic, and haphazard acts by individual actors who, from time to time, consciously intended to assert hierarchy over others. The roots of racialization run far deeper than individualized, intentional activities." Backhouse and Osgoode Society for Canadian Legal History, *Colour-Coded*, 15.

87. The Canadian Supreme Court has said that equality is a lens through which all legal interpretation should take place but stops short of saying that private law rulings in cases between private parties can be directly challenged on *Charter* grounds. See Weinrib and Weinrib, "Constitutional Values and Private Law in Canada." With respect to the United States, Frank Michelman says that "under our prevailing canons of separations of powers and divisions of institutional labor, the work [of applying constitutional rights to private parties] perhaps cannot mainly be done by courts, but only legislatures." Michelman, "Rawls on Constitutionalism and Constitutional Law," 419.

South Africa's Constitution specifically mandates the application of the constitutional rights to private law. The Bill of Rights under the South African Constitution states at Section 8:

1. The Bill of Rights applies to all law, and binds the legislature, the executive, the judiciary and all organs of state.
2. A provision of the Bill of Rights binds a natural or a juristic person if, and to the extent that, it is applicable, taking into account the nature of the right and the nature of any duty imposed by the right.
3. When applying a provision of the Bill of Rights to a natural or juristic person in terms of subsection (2), a court
   a. in order to give effect to a right in the Bill, must apply, or if necessary develop, the common law to the extent that legislation does not give effect to that right; and
   b. may develop rules of the common law to limit the right, provided that the limitation is in accordance with section 36(1).
4. A juristic person is entitled to the rights in the Bill of Rights to the extent required by the nature of the rights and the nature of that juristic person.

Constitution of the Republic of South Africa, Schedule No. 108 of 1996, Chapter 2—Bill of Rights, sec. 8. Notably this section explicitly mentions common law but does not mention customary law, another important source of often uncodified private law in South Africa. Nonetheless, the courts have applied the Bill of Rights directly to customary law. See, for example, *Bhe and Others v.Khayelitsha Magistrate and Others* (CCT 49/03) [2004] ZACC 17; 2005 (1) SA 580 (CC); 2005 (1) BCLR 1 (CC) (15 October 2004) at para. 93.

88. *Canadian Charter of Rights and Freedoms*, Part I of the *Constitution Act, 1982*, being Schedule B to the *Canada Act 1982* (U.K.), 1982, chap. 11 (1982). Subsection 15(2) was included in the Canadian *Charter* in order to avoid the "formal equality" of American Constitutional jurisprudence. Section 15(2) has been referred to as an "Anti-Bakke" provision on the basis that it constitutes a response to the U.S. Supreme Court's decision in *Regents of the University of*

California v. Bakke, 438 U.S. 912 (1978), where an affirmative action program aimed at economically disadvantaged minority medical school applicants was struck down as a violation the constitutional equal protection guarantee. Eisen, "Rethinking Affirmative Action Analysis in the Wake of *Kapp*," 21–24.

89. [1989] 1 S.C.R. 143.

90. *R. v. Kapp*, 2008 SCC 41, [2008] 2 S.C.R. 483, at para 17.

91. *M. v. H.*, [1999] 2 S.C.R. 3, per Justice Cory, at para. 48, quoting Justice Iacobucci in *Law* at para. 39. Although this citation refers to the test for discrimination articulated in *Law*, this specific part of the test has not been changed by *Kapp*.

92. There have, however, been cases aimed at resisting legislation aimed at advancing equality. See Fudge, "Effect of Entrenching a Bill of Rights upon Political Discourse" and "What Do We Mean by Law and Social Transformation?" 57–58.

93. [1999] 2 S.C.R. 3.

94. *M. v. H.*, per Justice Cory at para. 64, citing *Egan v. Canada*, [1995] 2 S.C.R. 513 at para. 175 (per Justice Cory) and at para. 89 (per Justice L'Heureux-Dubé).

95. *M. v. H.* at para. 72.

96. Ibid., at para. 73.

97. *R. v. S. (R.D.)*, [1997] 3 S.C.R. 484. The relevant legal standard is not actual bias, but the reasonable apprehension of bias.

98. *R. v. S (R.D.)* at paras. 46–47.

99. The current leading equality case, *Kapp*, is particularly welcoming to governmental efforts to ameliorate disadvantage. Jess Eisen has argued that *Kapp* offers too uncritical an acceptance of any law with an ameliorative purpose. Her argument might be seen as example of using a full relational approach to reflect on the many forms of disadvantage that exist within Canadian society as well as a recognition that the relevance of historical disadvantage should itself shift as relations of equality shift. Eisen, "Rethinking Affirmative Action Analysis in the Wake of *Kapp*."

100. See volume 18, number 1 of *Canadian Journal of Women and the Law* (2006), containing the first six "judgments" of the Women's Court of Canada. The Women's Court is a feminist legal project bringing together academics, activists, and litigators in order to literally rewrite *Canadian Charter of Rights and Freedoms* equality jurisprudence. The Women's Court operates as a virtual court and "reconsiders" leading equality decisions, rendering alternative judgments as a means of articulating fresh conceptions of substantive equality (online: <http://womenscourt.ca/>). Some of the critiques of Canadian equality jurisprudence were in explicitly relational terms.

101. *Personnel Administrator of Massachusetts v. Feeney*, 442 U.S. 256, 272 (1979); *Washington v. Davis*, 426 U.S. 229, 239 (1976).

102. Justice Kennedy in *Ricci v. DeStafano*, 129 S. Ct. 2658 (2009).

103. Justice Kennedy's opening in *Ricci v. DeStefano*:

> In 2003, 118 New Haven firefighters took examinations to qualify for promotion to the rank of lieutenant or captain. Promotion examinations in New Haven (or City) were infrequent, so the stakes were high. The results would determine which firefighters would be considered for promotions during the next two years, and the order in which they would be considered. Many firefighters studied for months, at considerable personal and financial cost.

When the examination results showed that white candidates had outperformed minority candidates, the mayor and other local politicians opened a public debate that turned rancorous. Some firefighters argued the tests should be discarded because the results showed the tests to be discriminatory. They threatened a discrimination lawsuit if the City made promotions based on the tests. Other firefighters said the exams were neutral and fair. And they, in turn, threatened a discrimination lawsuit if the City, relying on the statistical racial disparity, ignored the test results and denied promotions to the candidates who had performed well. In the end the City took the side of those who protested the test results. It threw out the examinations.

Certain white and Hispanic firefighters who likely would have been promoted based on their good test performance sued the City and some of its officials. Theirs is the suit now before us.

104. The stance within current jurisprudence toward claims of historical disadvantage is elaborated by Justice Kennedy in the case *Ricci v. DeStefano*, 129 S. Ct. 2658 (2009) 2675: "The Court has held that certain government actions to remedy past racial discrimination—actions that are themselves based on race—are constitutional only where there is a 'strong basis in evidence' that the remedial actions were necessary" (citations removed). Kennedy relies in part on *Richmond v. J.A. Croson Co.*, 488 U. S. 469 (1989) 499, wherein the court observed that "an amorphous claim that there has been past discrimination…cannot justify the use of an unyielding racial quota."

105. "At that time, municipal fire departments across the country, including New Haven's, pervasively discriminated against minorities. The extension of Title VII to cover jobs in firefighting effected no overnight change. It took decades of persistent effort, advanced by Title VII litigation, to open firefighting posts to members of racial minorities." Judge Ginsberg's dissent in *Ricci v. DeStefano* at 1.

106. "Standing on an equal footing, these twin pillars of Title VII [disparate treatment and disparate impact] advance the same objectives: ending workplace discrimination and promoting genuinely equal opportunity. Yet the Court today sets at odds the statute's core directives. When an employer changes an employment practice in an effort to comply with Title VII's disparate-impact provision, the Court reasons, it acts "because of race"—something Title VII's disparate-treatment provision, see §2000e-2(a)(1), generally forbids. This characterization of an employer's compliance-directed action shows little attention to Congress' design or to the *Griggs* line of cases Congress recognized as path marking." Judge Ginsberg's dissent in *Ricci v. DeStefano* at 18 (citations removed).

107. Ibid., at 7 (citations removed). I am not claiming that Ginsberg consistently uses a relational approach, merely that one can see the ways relational dimensions of this opinion distinguish it from Kennedy's.

108. See volume 1, no. 18 of *Canadian Journal of Women and the Law* (2006).

109. The Supreme Court of Canada was confronted with this question in *Gosselin v. Québec (Attorney General)*, [2002] 4 S.C.R. 429, 2002 SCC 84, where inadequate levels of social assistance were argued to engage the "security of the person" protected by Section 7 of the *Charter*. While the majority of the Court declined to answer this question of whether economic interests could ever be protected, Justice Louise Arbour (with Justice Claire L'Heureux Dubé concurring in a separate decision) was emphatic that economic interests were not necessarily equivalent to

"property rights," and may thus be protected by the *Charter* despite the purposeful omission of "property" from the list of protected Section 7 interests. (See note 74 above for a discussion of the omission of "property" from Section 7.) In Justice Arbour's view, "the rights at issue here are so intimately intertwined with considerations related to one's basic health (and hence 'security of the person')—and, at the limit, even of one's survival (and hence 'life')—that they can readily be accommodated under the s. 7 rights of 'life, liberty and security of the person' without the need to constitutionalize 'property' rights or interests.... Their only kinship to the economic 'property' rights that are *ipso facto* excluded from s. 7 is that they involve some economic value.... What is truly significant, from the standpoint of inclusion under the rubric of s. 7 rights, is not...whether a right can be expressed in terms of its economic value, but as Dickson, Robert George Brian suggests, whether it 'fall[s]' within "security of the person"' or one of the other enumerated rights in that section.... [I]t is because the right to a minimum level of social assistance is clearly connected to 'security of the person' and 'life' that it distinguishes itself from corporate-commercial rights in being a candidate for s. 7 inclusion" (paras. 311–312).

The decision in *Gosselin* has received critical academic attention; see, for example, the Women's Court of Canada's rewritten version of the case, in which the authors argue that Section 7 of the *Charter* is engaged by poverty. Brodsky et al., "*Gosselin v. Quebec (Attorney General).*" See note 100 for a description of the Women's Court project.

110. (1988), 53 D.L.R. (4th) 171, [1989] 2 W.W.R. 1 (B.C.C.A.), reversing *Wilson v. Medical Services Commission of B.C.* (1987), 36 D.L.R. (4th) 31, [1987] W.W.R. 48 (B.C.S.C.), leave to appeal to Supreme Court of Canada, refused November 3, 1988.

111. The case was actually decided on the restrictions on "free movement," the court rejecting economic liberty as the basis for the doctors' claims.

112. I actually remember being promptly escorted out of a suburban shopping mall by security guards who said we had no right to enact our anti-Vietnam war skit in that privately owned, public space. The streets of downtown Chicago were fair game, even if we gathered crowds that impeded pedestrian traffic. The police came but just observed. Of course, in many places far more people gather and shop in shopping malls than on downtown streets, so the constraint on public exchange of ideas is significant.

113. *Harrison v. Carswell*, [1976] 2 S.C.R. 200, Justice Laskin's dissent in Canada. There is also some variation of the rules respecting labor picketing. In the United States, Justice Thurgood Marshall dissented in *Hudgens v. NLRB*, 424 U.S. 507 (1976).

114. The discussion below draws on the article "Constitutional Dialogue," which I coauthored with Craig Scott.

115. See ibid. I have appended a copy of the Alternative Social Charter (hereinafter ASC) at the end of this chapter.

116. The editors opened their introduction to the book from which this summary is taken, as follows: "In the fall of 1990, the New Democratic Party, the official political voice of the left in Canada, was elected in Ontario. Soon after, in the spring of 1991, the idea of entrenching a charter of social rights in the Constitution was raised in the Ontario legislature; this was followed by release of a series of discussion papers on the idea in the fall of 1991. Also, in the fall of 1991 there were electoral victories for the NDP in Saskatchewan and British Columbia, and this ensured the party a powerful presence in ongoing constitutional negotiations. The idea of a constitutional charter of social rights now had some prospect of becoming a reality." Bakan and Schneiderman, *Social Justice and the Constitution.*

117. One might say that because the rights of health care, food, clothing, and child care are, like property, second-order values, that is, means to the end of achieving equality and the other basic values outlined in the *Charter,* it is appropriate for the Social Charter to be a separate document rather than integrated into the *Charter.* There was some disagreement on this among those proposing this form of the Social Charter. In the proposed form, it was a separate document, with a provision that the *Charter* be interpreted in ways consistent with the Social Charter. I think health care and food are primary values, although traditional rights discourse has treated them quite differently from liberty or equality—presumably in part because they are more readily seen as "positive" rights rather than negative liberties. The meaning of equality needs to be interpreted in light of such social rights and vice-versa, all of which requires relational analysis.

118. ASC, secs. 1 and 5.

119. ASC, sec. 9(4).

120. ASC, sec. 9(5).

121. ASC, sec. 10(2).

122. ASC, sec. 10(5)(a).

123. ASC, sec. 10(5)(b).

124. ASC, sec. 10(7).

125. ASC, sec. 10(6)(a).

126. ASC, sec. 10(7).

127. Of course, how costly it would be would depend on the political culture of the country. The ASC was designed to build on a high level of respect for judicial rulings about rights violations.

128. ASC, sec. 10(8); emphasis added. Both the council and the tribunal would pose challenging problems to any reviewing court. They maximize the crossover between policy maker and adjudicator that characterize many administrative tribunals.

129. Douzinas, *Human Rights and Empire.*

CHAPTER 7

1. In chapter 4 I discuss autonomy as a component of the capacity for creative interaction.

2. The term "bodymind" is used to evoke a unity of "mind" and "body." The term has been most commonly employed in new age and popular psychology literature, but it has also found support in medical and academic circles (see Read and Stoll, "Healthy Behavior," 145–161). Don Read and Walt Stoll observe that, "it has only been recently that bodymind has been included in the scientific research as a holistic entity," despite the fact that "these newly discovered (by our Western scientific method) mechanisms and interactions have been applied empirically for the last ten thousand years" (151). For a discussion of the role of bodymind in Japanese Buddhist traditions see Shaner, *Bodymind Experience in Japanese Buddhism.*

3. Arendt and Beiner, *Lectures on Kant's Political Philosophy,* 22.

4. Wendell, "Feminism, Disability, and Transcendence of the Body" and "Toward a Feminist Theory of Disability."

5. I discussed this in chapter 4, section IV. In note 40, below, I will return to how Sarah Hoagland helps us think differently about this core moral problem.

6. Juhan, *Job's Body,* 279.

7. Ibid.

8. Ibid.

9. Twenty years later I discovered (equally belatedly) that there was a readily available plant substance (GLA, found in evening primrose oil) that virtually eliminated the mood changes (as well as discomfort).

10. For more on the body–mind connection, see Pert, *Molecules of Emotion*; Damasio, *Descartes' Error*; Littrell, "Mind-Body Connection," 17–37; Pally, "Emotional Processing"; Esch and Stefano, "Neurobiology of Love"; Leonard and Myint, "Psychoneuroimmunology of Depression."

11. Juhan, *Job's Body*, 298.

12. See, for example, Melissa Harris-Lacewell's comments on "bad behaviour" in response to President Obama's "race speech," cited in chapter 4, note 31. In some instances, one might also be persuaded that the choice of crime was, in fact, a rational assessment of the options and risks. See Pollack, "Focus Group Methodology in Research with Incarcerated Women" and "Anti-Oppressive Social Work Practice with Women in Prison."

13. I use Juhan's book because I find it offers an interesting example of using the mind–body connection to make an argument for responsibility for one's health. Its new age tone is part of what is interesting to me because this popular genre of literature consistently emphasizes such responsibility and often shares both the strengths and limitations of Juhan's argument.

14. Juhan, *Job's Body*, 3.

15. Ibid., 17.

16. Ibid., 17–18.

17. Ibid. 19; emphasis added.

18. From "Just as the Winged Energy of Delight" by Rainer Maria Rilke, *Selected Poems of Rainer Maria Rilke* 1981), 175; cited in Juhan, *Job's Body*, 19.

19. Susan Sontag wrote, "The speculations of the ancient world made disease most often an instrument of divine wrath. Judgment was meted out to a community…or to a single person.… The diseases around which modern fantasies have gathered—TB, cancer—are viewed as forms of self-judgment, of self-betrayal." Sontag, *Illness as Metaphor*, 39–40. Another example: "Thinking of syphilis as a punishment for an individual's transgression was for a long time, virtually until the disease became easily curable, not really distinct from regarding it as retribution for the licentiousness of a community—as with AIDS now, in the rich industrialized countries" (134).

The biblical story of Job actually sends a complicated message. It includes a number of characters who suggest that Job's suffering must have been caused by sin, even though God is clear that "he is blameless and upright, a man who fears God and shuns evil. And he still maintains his integrity, though [Satan] incited me against him to ruin him *without any reason*." (Job 2:3, New International Version); emphasis added. Nonetheless, Elihu, echoing sentiments also expressed by Eliphaz, Bildad, and Zophar, insists that Job's suffering is evidence that God "repays a man for what he has done; he brings upon him what his conduct deserves" (34:11).

20. Wendell, "Feminism, Disability, and Transcendence of the Body," 118.

21. Ibid., 120.

22. Ibid.

23. Ibid.

24. Ibid.

25. Ibid., 118.

26. Ibid., 121.

27. Ibid., 120.

28. I remind readers here of my discussion in the introduction about my use of the term "we." Although there are dangers of unwarranted assumptions of inclusion or sameness, the alternatives have a distancing quality. I want the reader to hear the claims about "our" relationships to our bodies as an invitation to reflect whether the claim is true for her. The language of "people" and "their" bodies invites an all too easy assumption that the claim is true of others but not of oneself.

29. Wendell, "Toward a Feminist Theory of Disability," 121.

30. Ibid.; emphasis added.

31. Kabat-Zinn, "Meditations," 123.

32. Ibid., 126.

33. McKee, "Bodily Suffering and Women with Disabilities."

34. Ibid.

35. My doctor only advised rest. The naturopath treated me for an intestinal yeast infection and provided various mysterious pills to reinvigorate my body.

36. A few years after the initial onset in 1994, another naturopath put me on a strict diet of no sugar, wheat, alcohol, caffeine (except green tea), or dairy (except plain yogurt). It made a huge difference and I continue to follow it, though no longer so strictly.

37. In retrospect, I think I should not have made that accommodation. Working at a research university where research is often valued more than teaching, and is in any case at least half of the job, I should not have given up my research time in order to be able to meet my teaching commitments. A more appropriate accommodation would have been to reduce both my teaching and my research commitments. But to have asked for that would have required a great deal more confidence in the legitimacy of my illness—and thus entitlement to accommodation—than I felt. And, of course, such a request would have required a lot more time and energy for institutional engagement than simply absorbing the loss of research time.

38. I do not see this consciousness as the same thing as the philosophers' arguments about the importance of deliberation and reflection. I take their understanding to have a more intellectual dimension than my understanding of consciousness, which can be fostered by such exercises as meditation that are not simply intellectual in nature.

39. For some, a degree of this spark exists in everything, rocks and electrons as well as plants and animals. One could interpret Alfred North Whitehead as holding this view. See Whitehead, *Process and Reality*.

40. Sarah Hoagland offers an extremely interesting and innovative account of agency (or autonomy) in the context of inevitably limiting circumstances. She also urges her chosen audience (lesbians) to shift their focus from accountability to intelligibility. The focus on accountability and blame does great harm, she persuasively argues. We should instead try to understand why things have happened, why people see things differently rather than trying to assign blame. See Hoagland, *Lesbian Ethics*, chap. 5.

41. Here I mean postpone until the end of the chapter. I will also address the question in chapter 8, "Restructuring Relations," and I discussed it in chapter 4.

42. Benjamin, *Bonds of Love*, "The Bonds of Love: Rational Violence and Erotic Domination," and *Shadow of the Other*.

43. In the following discussion I make clear that "gender" must be understood in the context of the ways "gendering" happens differently in the context of other systems of hierarchy, such as racialization and class.

44. See Benjamin, *Shadow of the Other*, xii, and Nedelsky, "Challenges of Multiplicity."

45. Personal communication, e-mail, December 4, 2007.

46. Stern, *Interpersonal World of the Infant.*

47. Benjamin critiques the contention that the struggle for absolute recognition between two selves must result in the stronger making the other its slave. In her estimation, this viewpoint "would imply that submission is simply the hard lot of the weak. And indeed, the question of why the oppressed submit is never fully explained. Yet the question of submission is implicitly raised by Hegel and Freud, who see that the slave must grant power of recognition to the master." Benjamin, *Bonds of Love*, 54.

48. This is Sara Ruddick's term in *Maternal Thinking: Toward a Politics of Peace* (1989).

49. I think this diffuse influence is important despite the quite limited role psychoanalytic theory now plays in academic training of either psychologists or psychiatrists and the very small number of people treated by psychoanalysts.

50. Spelman, *Inessential Woman.*

51. Benjamin disagrees with some dimension of Chodorow's view that reorganizing parenting will not in itself dismantle gender polarity. Although she concedes that such reorganization would require broader changes that would challenge structures of social organization, such as the public/private dichotomy, she insists that "this still casts the problem in terms of the relationship between family and social organization. In my view it is equally important to grasp the deep structure of gender as a binary opposition which is common to psychic and cultural representations." Benjamin, *Bonds of Love*, 218.

52. Spelman, *Inessential Woman*; Nedelsky, "Challenges of Multiplicity." Spelman also takes up the issue of class: the story of the autonomous man out in the work world and the woman at home with the children has only ever been true of a subset of upper- and middle-class families. Benjamin does comment on the changing dynamics of gendered parenting practices, noting that we will have to wait to see what changes that brings.

53. Ann Jones, whom I discuss in chapter 8, suggests that violence against women may serve to channel men's rage against destructive work environments, humiliations, and sense of powerlessness. The violence against women may be culturally tolerated because it diverts challenges to the structures of power that actually generate the rage. Jones, *Next Time, She'll Be Dead*. See also bell hooks, "Violence in Intimate Relationships." For an example of this in relation to abused immigrant women, see chapter 8, note 18.

54. Benjamin also does not talk much about the forms of control that come to characterize many women's ways of coping with threatened and thwarted autonomy.

55. I think this is so even when one recognizes, as Elizabeth V. Spelman shows, that "gender" and the relations between men and women cannot be understood without the complexities of class, race, and other forms of hierarchy with which gender intersects. Nedelsky, "Challenges of Multiplicity."

56. Holocaust scholars, for example, are now challenging the once widely held view that Jewish concentration camp inmates failed to resist their oppressors, passively submitting like "lambs to slaughter." See generally Bettleheim, *Surviving and Other Essays*, and Hilberg, *Destruction of the European Jews*. Many of these scholars have shifted the terms of this "resistance" discourse, not only by focusing on instances of forceful resistance (see Plotkin and Ritvo, *Sisters in Sorrow*, 275),

but also by redefining "resistance" to include acts of autonomy and "spiritual resistance" that subverted the "total system" that the Nazis sought to create. As James Cargas explains, "Daily expressions of human dignity, solidarity, and creativity enabled the victims to remain human beings in the most extreme circumstances.... The victims' attitude showed that determinism of the environment can never be total." Cargas, *Problems Unique to the Holocaust*, 73. Such covert forms of resistance have been found to include activities ranging from smuggling food to fellow prisoners to the maintenance of a sense of inner freedom and autonomy. See Langbein, *People in Auschwitz*, 242; Pawelczynska, *Values and Violence in Auschwitz*, 27–128, 133, respectively. Others have argued that survival itself, maintaining one's capacity to bear witness, should be understood as a mode of resistance and subversion. See Des Pres, *Survivor*, 31–35. The role of "community" in many of these forms of resistance illuminates the deeply relational nature of the autonomy expressed through these acts of defiance. Many of these accounts center on interactions within families and communities, working together in order to help each other survive, and inmates showing kindness to one another (132, 137).

57. For a related discussion of fear, which also connects to issues of autonomy, see chapters 2 and 5.

58. Pert, *Molecules of Emotion*.

59. See Young, "Impartiality and the Civic Public." Benjamin also discusses the role of reason in the dominant psychoanalytic framework. Benjamin, "Bonds of Love: Rational Violence and Erotic Domination," 149–150. See also Nedelsky, "Embodied Diversity and the Challenges to Law."

60. Of course, some people just ignore and neglect their bodies—until they scream in pain and a doctor is called in to take control of them. Or until that encounter with pain and control leads to a more mutual relationship.

61. See chapter 1, especially section IV.D.

62. Remember my discussion of the illusion of autonomy in chapter 3, section III.

63. Given that judges and legislators are generally among those who are on top, is it reasonable to believe that they will participate in such a transformation? This goes to the broad question of whether the elite's commitment to equality can be a serious impetus for change. As I have noted in chapter 1, section III, my reading of legal history reveals the complicity of the law both in sustaining hierarchy and privilege *and* in advancing equality.

64. The popularity of *Dilbert* cartoons about life in corporate cubicles is an indication that the frustration of being controlled (by idiots) and having no control over one's work life is not just the characteristic of work on the assembly line.

65. See the discussion of the *Lochner* era in chapter 3, notes 37–38.

66. Linda Mulcahy explains that the emergence of monopolies in modern capitalist economies tends to "dilute key concepts such as choice and consent in contract and undermine the importance of pre-contractual negotiations. The legal result of this has been the mass produced standard form of contract presented on 'take-it-or-leave-it' terms by those who are powerful in the market." Mulcahy, *Contract Law in Perspective*, 30. As the emergence of powerful commercial parties made consumers increasingly vulnerable to abusive contractual terms (particularly "exemption clauses" excluding vendors from liability), the judiciary struggled to protect weaker parties without running afoul of the existing law of contracts. As Lord Denning poignantly reflected in 1985,

None of you nowadays will remember the trouble we had—when I was called to the bar—with exemption clauses.... It was a bleak winter for our law of contract.... Faced with this abuse of power—by the strong against the weak—by the use of the small print of the conditions—the judges did what they could to put a curb upon it. They still had before them the idol, "freedom of contract." They still knelt down and worshipped it, but they concealed under their cloaks a secret weapon. They used it to stab the idol in the back. This weapon was called "the true construction of contract"....In case after case, they said that the words were not strong enough to give the big concern exemption from liability; or that in the circumstances the big concern was not entitled to rely on the exemption clause.

George Mitchell (Chesterhall) Ltd. v.Finney Lock Seeds Ltd., [1983], QB 284, 297; [1983] 2 AC 803, cited in Mulcahy, *Contract Law in Perspective*, 175. As Mulcahy explains, however, these judges had "no general power to strike down unreasonable exclusion clauses as being, for example, against public policy and therefore void. They felt that the concept of freedom of contract overrode such an approach" (180). Legislation was thus required to provide such constraints on "freedom of contract." Now, consumer protection statutes govern a vast range of commercial transactions, as governments seek to protect vulnerable consumers against oppressive exclusionary clauses. For an extensive overview of consumer protection laws governing such clauses in over thirty jurisdictions (including Canada, the United States, and England and Wales), see Kurer et al., *Warranties and Disclaimers*.

67. In *Moge v. Moge*, [1992] 3 S.C.R. 813, the Supreme Court of Canada established that an approach to termination of spousal support that focused solely on the goal of "self-sufficiency" was inappropriate under the *Divorce Act* and that courts should rather "be alert to a wide variety of factors and decisions made in the family interest during the marriage which have the effect of disadvantaging one spouse or benefitting the other upon its dissolution" (870). Writing for the majority, Justice L'Heureux Dubé emphasized the role of child rearing in shaping women's "choices" to forego advancements in their own careers and education, observing that the "most significant economic consequence of marriage or marriage breakdown...usually arises from the birth of children. This generally requires that the wife cut back on her paid labour force participation in order to care for the children, an arrangement which jeopardizes her ability to ensure her own income security and independent economic well-being" (867). Justice L'Heureux Dubé notes also that, even following divorce, custodial parents (who are overwhelmingly women) face further restraints on the "choices" that might increase their earning potential: "The diminished earning capacity with which an ex-wife enters the labor force after years of reduced or non-participation will be even more difficult to overcome when economic choice is reduced, unlike that of her ex-husband, due to the necessity of remaining within proximity to schools, not working late, remaining at home when the child is ill, etc. The other spouse encounters none of these impediments and is generally free to live virtually wherever he wants and work whenever he wants" (863–864).

Justice McLachlin's concurring judgment went on to explicitly refute the argument that Mrs. Moge's economic hardships were not sufficently "caused" by the divorce to merit ongoing support. She explains, "It was said that Mrs. Moge voluntarily elected to be the primary homemaker and caregiver; that it was her choice and not the marriage that caused the resultant economic disadvantage. Similarly, it was suggested that her present need and lack of self-sufficiency was not the product of the marriage but of her failure to choose to upgrade her education so she could earn more money" (881). McLachlin responds, "Mrs. Moge in keeping with the prevailing social expectation of the times, accepted primary responsibility for the home and the children and confined her extra activities to supplementing the family income rather than to getting a better education or to furthering her career. That was the actual domestic arrangement which prevailed. What Mrs. Moge might have done in a different arrangement with different social and domestic expectations is irrelevant" (881). Listing a number of emotional, practical, and psychological factors that might contribute to women's capacity to support themselves following a divorce, McLachlin concludes, "In short, the whole context of her conduct must be considered. It is not enough to say in the abstract that the ex-spouse should have done more or be doing more, and argue from this that it is her inaction rather than the breakup of the marriage which is the cause of her economic hardship. One must look at the actual social and personal reality of the situation in which she finds herself and judge the matter fairly from that perspective" (882).

68. As discussed in chapter 1, note 115 and accompanying text, a long line of cases referred to as the "surety wives" cases have grappled with the question of when, and to what extent, lenders should be obliged to inquire into the whether a wife, acting as a surety for her husband, is freely giving her consent to the transaction. For a thorough canvass of these cases in the U.K. context, see Pawlowski and Brown, *Undue Influence in the Family Home*. For a sociolegal inquiry into the underlying social and gender dynamics of these transactions, see Fehlberg, *Sexually Transmitted Debt*.

69. Nedelsky, "Challenges of Multiplicity."

70. At times, legislation aims at codifying common law; in such cases, the jurisprudence developed at common law is generally imported into the interpretation of these statutes, and the statutes themselves employ terms that are intended to be interpreted according to common law. Referring to the importation of common law jurisprudence and methodology into the application of statutory codes, A. W. B. Simpson argues that "judges shrink from identifying the law with the text of the statute, which they rapidly encrust with interpretation." Simpson, "Common Law and Legal Theory," 381. In the United States, The National Conference of Commissioners on Uniform State Law has made efforts to create uniformity in such codification through the promulgation of such "uniform laws" as the Uniform Commercial Code, which they have recommended to the states for adoption; state legislatures may then chose to adopt these uniform laws, in whole or in part. For a discussion of the American debates surrounding the increased reliance on codification in place of common law, and a study of codification in the contexts of the Uniform Commercial Code, Federal Rules of Civil Procedure, Sentencing Guidelines, and Common Law Crime, see Scott, *Dismantling American Common Law*, esp. chaps. 2 and 3. Another mode of codification, advanced by the American Law Institute, has taken the form of "Restatements of the Law" created with the goal of "promot[ing] clarification and simplification of the law." Although these restatements are nonbinding, legal research textbooks note that "[d]ue to their authoritativeness . . . , they are frequently cited by the courts and often accorded a recognition greater than that accorded to treatises." Putnam, *Legal Research, Analysis, and Writing*, 191.

Nonetheless, the "customary" nature of the common law means that such distillations are not "the law" itself, and common law theorists, such as A. W. B. Simpson, continue to argue that "the common law is more like a muddle than a system, and that it would be difficult to conceive of a less systematic body of law. The systematization of the common law—its reduction to a code of rules which satisfy accepted tests provided by other rules—is surely a programme, or an ideal, and not a description of the *status quo*." Simpson, "Common Law and Legal Theory," 38. In his leading textbook on the law of contracts, Stephen Waddams accounts for one failed attempt to codify the general law of contracts, explaining, "The attempt to impose on a highly developed and developing common law system a code sufficiently specific to implement useful changes and yet not so specific as to set up inflexibilities and anomalies in unforeseen cases, proves to be an almost impossible one." Waddams, *Law of Contracts*, 5, para. 5. For political critiques of the movement toward increased codification, see Scott, *Dismantling American Common Law*, and Feinman, *Un-Making Law*.

71. See, for example, Gaard, *Ecofeminism*; Warren, *Ecofeminism* and *Ecofeminist Philosophy*.

72. For an elaboration, see Nedelsky, "Dilemmas of Passion, Privilege and Isolation."

CHAPTER 8

1. Duncan Kennedy's phrase in , "Sexual Abuse, Sexy Dressing, and the Eroticization of Domination," 1390.

2. Jones, *Next Time, She'll Be Dead*.

3. Merry, "Rights Talk and the Experience of Law."

4. For U.S. statistics, see note 29 below. The most recent statistics on intimate partner violence for Canada as of this writing indicate that 7 percent of women (or 653,000) were assaulted by an intimate partner within the five years leading up to the survey year (2004), and 21 percent of women were assaulted by a former partner during the same period. Johnson, *Measuring Violence against Women*, 17–18. These numbers are actually a slight decrease from the previous survey year (1999), when the statistics were 8 percent and 28 percent, respectively. The report suggests several possible reasons for this decline, from pro-arrest and prosecution policies to increased training for police to improved economic situations for women who leave abusive relationships to increased availability and use of services for abused women (18). The rates of sexual assault by intimate partners remained constant between 1999 and 2004 while the rates of reporting to police declined (30).

In terms of severity, 81 percent of women abused by their partners experienced pushing, grabbing, or shoving; 36 percent experienced slapping; 19 percent were beaten; 19 percent were choked; 16 percent were sexually assaulted; 44 percent had something thrown at them; 23 percent were hit with something; and 11 percent were threatened or assaulted with a knife or gun (19). Furthermore, 44 percent of assaulted women were physically injured; 13 percent required medical attention, and 10 percent were hospitalized; 29 percent had to take time away from daily activities (33). Also, 21 percent of abused women experienced ten or more incidents of abuse (33). The psychological impacts of abuse on women victims include anger (37%), depression/anxiety (21%), lowered self-esteem (17%), difficulty sleeping (15%), hypervigilance (16%), and shame/guilt (12%) (32). Finally, 34 percent of abused women feared for their lives (33) and with good reason: one in five homicides in Canada involves the killing of an intimate partner (21).

Statistics in the area of intimate partner violence are difficult to obtain due to the way spousal relationships are often construed as private (16). Feelings of fear, depression, lowered self-esteem, and shame that often accompany abuse also serve as barriers to reporting. It is estimated that less than 10 percent of any sexual assaults are reported to police (16), and it is unlikely that the numbers are different in the context of intimate partner violence. These feelings also form barriers to escape for women victimized by their intimate partners.

The most common question with respect to abused women is "why doesn't she just leave?" This simple question has a very complicated response. Lenore Walker's famous theory, the "cycle of violence" (Walker, *Battered Woman Syndrome*, 91), holds that violence is part of a cyclical pattern in abusive relationships and that by the time violence starts to take place the victim has already formed a significant emotional attachment to the abuser. The first phase of the cycle typically begins after the relationship has already begun and consists of an escalation of tension within the relationship in the form of controlling or mean behavior and sometimes milder forms of physical aggression on the part of the abuser. The victim tries to placate the abuser and is sometimes successful in controlling his behavior (91). Phase two, the "acute battering incident," is an eruption of this tension in a violent act of physical and/or psychological hostility and aggression (94). The final phase, the "loving contrition" stage, involves the abuser attempting to reconcile with the victim and is characterized by apologies and displays of kindness and remorse toward the victim, or alternatively, simply an absence of tension (94–95). It should be noted that this third phase typically declines over time so that it is not always present to the same degree as earlier in the battering relationship (95–96). This cycle helps to explain some of the reasons why it is so difficult for women to leave their abusers: the battering incidents themselves are not always constant, and there are times when the abuser shows tenderness and care toward the victim; the victim often believes that the abuser wants to, and is capable of, changing—particularly early in the relationship; and the relationship has been established before the abuse begins. Another barrier to escape is often economic—abusers often control the victim's finances (82), typically as part of a larger program of social isolation, making it more difficult for the victim to help herself out of her situation and necessitating the use of help from family, friends, or community services. Combined with the common feelings of shame, depression, low self-esteem, guilt, and fear—often for her life—the picture becomes more clear as to why abused women find it so difficult to leave. (See also "learned helplessness/learned optimism" in Walker, *Battered Woman Syndrome*, chap. 4.)

5. See, for example, the range of accounts canvassed in the special issue "Ending Woman Abuse," *Canadian Woman Studies* 25, Winter 2006.

6. Tyagi, "Victimization, Adversity and Survival in the Lives of Women Offenders."

7. Graham, "This Trauma Is Not Vicarious," 19.

8. People (other than frontline workers directly working to assist women assaulted by their partners) may work on this issue in many ways, including as scholars, activists, politicians, journalists, police officers, judges, or teachers. All may suffer some version of the trauma of confronting violence.

9. Consider the rates of death by homicide among young black men in the United States or the routine violence of prisons in which Aboriginal peoples and blacks in Canada and blacks in the United States are disproportionably represented. See Wortley, "A Northern Taboo." A recent American Bureau of Justice Statistics Special Report found that, although blacks represented only 13 percent of the American population, nearly half of all homicide victims were black. Harrell, *Black Victims of Violent Crime*, 1. With respect to prison violence, the causal relationship between victimization and "failure to protect" is borne out by studies showing that prison overcrowding (a factor entirely within state control and entirely beyond the control of inmates) is the most significant determinant of prison assault rates. Gaes and McGuire, "Prison Violence."

10. Shamita Das Dasgupta argues that "American mainstream society still likes to believe that woman abuse is limited to minority ethnic communities, lower socio-economic strata, and individuals with dark skin colors. The impact of…public violence of imperialism, classism, and racism on battering in the private sphere of home and intimate relationships has unfortunately received little research." Dasgupta, "Women's Realities, 61.

11. Mason and Pellizzari, "Guidelines, Policies, Education and Coordination," 24n21.

12. Jones, *Next Time, She'll Be Dead*, 86–87.

13. Siegel, "'Rule of Love.'"

14. See, for example, Judith Resnik's argument that "violence against women is deemed a feature of private life, not public action and not commerce. Violence against women is seen as a regrettable, if under-regulated, feature of family life but not a problem central to the national juridical agenda." Resnik, "Reconstructing Equality," 406, discussing *United States v. Morrison,* 529 U.S. 598 (2000), on the federalism question of "what is truly national and what is truly local," violence against women not being truly national. She concludes, "Understanding violence against women as outside the purview of federal law stems from active efforts by judges, in conjunction with other political actors, to keep the concept of federal statutory rights and the work of federal judges from developing national norms of physical safety as part of dignitary rights of women and men in the United States" (416).

15. Jones, *Next Time, She'll Be Dead,* 161, 188–189.

16. One story that emerges frequently is the unwillingness of police to enforce temporary restraining orders that women have succeeded in getting from a court—usually at increased risk of violence. Robert Kane notes, "Because ROs [Restraining Orders] constrain police decision making, in theory, there should be no variation in patterns of arrest; all RO violators should be taken into immediate custody. In most of the studies [of police response to restraining orders]…however, the arrest rate for RO violations in domestic violence incidents is between 20% and 40%." Kane, "Police Responses to Restraining Orders in Domestic Violence Incidents," 562. These women do not stand in relation to the police as ordinary citizens threatened with criminal violence. The police may see them as women who are so locked into the abusive relationship that even though they call the police and seek restraining orders, they go back to their abusers again. The relationship comes to define them, and their troublesome and seemingly irrational behavior disentitles them to protection. Or the police may see them as troublemakers who are unreasonably resisting the authority of their husbands, who can be expected—when provoked—to exert that authority with occasional violence. Police officers' understanding of the appropriate relationship between husband and wife may override or define her legal entitlements. Prosecutors may also see women who have been assaulted by their partners through the lens of entanglement in an abusive relationship. The women may be seen as unreliable witnesses or "bad victims" who are violent themselves or who use "bad language" or alcohol. If prosecutors see them not as people demanding the legal protection to which they are entitled, but as unreliable, unpersuasive women who can't be counted upon to act rationally, then prosecutors might decide that it is a reasonable exercise of prosecutorial discretion to stay out of their sick relationships.

17. As we saw in chapter 4, section IV.A, the increasingly widespread acceptance of "the battered woman syndrome" has helped some women charged with murdering their violent partners and has led, I think, to a greater general understanding that being in such relationships is not the woman's fault. But while it might help both judges and the population at large over the initial hurdle of "why doesn't she just leave," the full answer to that question can only be found in the larger patterns of relations.

18. In light of the overwhelming practical obstacles facing women fleeing abuse, it seems unlikely that individual psychology can offer a full account of why some women don't leave. In Canada, for example, on April 17, 2002, 254 women attempting to flee abuse (many with their children) were turned away from shelters; 71 percent of those women were turned away because the shelters where they sought refuge were full. Statistics Canada, cited in Hodes, "Recognizing Economic, Social and Cultural Rights in Canada," 198. It seems disingenuous to suggest that if these women returned to their abusers to avoid homelessness (for themselves and their children)

that their decisions were the results of individual psychological problems. Despite the clear need for more shelter beds, moreover, the state's approach to such violence often reveals a failure to take shelter funding seriously. In 2005, the Alberta government released a statement pledging to increase funding for "family violence and bullying" programs by $9.5 million, a 7 percent increase over the previous year. Even with this increase (which was in fact proportional to an overall budget increase of 6%), one local feminist organization pointed out that the money allocated to fund shelter beds was exactly the same amount as that invested in "re-branding horse racing" to make it more appealing to young adults. Alberta Gaming Commission, cited in Lambert, "When Martha Met Goliath."

Caroline Hodes explains that another important structural problem lies in the fact that women are "rendered more vulnerable to violence, sexual exploitation and coercion under inadequate welfare schemes." Hodes, "Recognizing Economic, Social and Cultural Rights in Canada, 198. Ann Jones points out that in 1996 in the United States, when budget cuts suspended Aid to Families with Dependent Children, a full 60 percent of the poor women who had been receiving this aid were victims of domestic violence. Jones, *Next Time, She'll Be Dead*, 201. Even where the state offers these women financial support, the terms of many jurisdictions put women at risk by requiring them to seek support payments from their abusers as a precondition for welfare eligibility. Mosher et al., "Walking on Eggshells," vii. Mosher notes that, although the Ontario scheme provides for waivers of this requirement in cases involving domestic violence, women are rarely made aware of this option. As one woman pointedly explains, "It's crazy to have women track men down (for support), you're running from him for God's sake" (vii). Many abused women, moreover, experience poverty as a major obstacle to leaving. A group of eighteen women who participated in a weekly discussion group at a rural women's shelter in Ontario collaborated in writing a letter that posed the question "what happens to people like us?" Throughout the letter, poverty emerges as a central reason why these women "are being driven back to our abusers or to the shelter." "How do I get a job," the letter asks, "when I can't buy a uniform or work clothes, I don't have a phone for prospective employers to call me back, and I can't afford a babysitter?" The letter notes one battered woman's experience of having "to give up my kids so that I knew they would be fed." Anonymous, "Letter," 32.

Immigrant women, moreover, are often confronted with additional obstacles when seeking to flee abuse:

> [I]mmigrant women who experience IPV [intimate partner violence] face additional and intersecting legal, contextual and cultural barriers. Legal barriers relate to women's precarious immigration status. Women often are dependants of their spouse who may abuse their power and control by threatening with deportation and denied access to children, or to withdraw sponsorship of wife and extended family members. Contextual barriers relate to the immigrant experience and include lack of knowledge of services, lack of language-specific services or resources, lack of culturally appropriate services, racism, and fear of becoming involved with the Canadian legal system after experiences with repressive regimes. Cultural barriers relate to those shared beliefs, values, traditions and behaviours that influence understanding of normative male/female relations. Examples of these are patriarchal ideology, family values/filial piety, collectivism and religious beliefs, all of which shape understanding of how men and women should behave in response to IPV.

Hyman and Mason, "Perceptions of and Responses to Woman Abuse among Tamil Women in Toronto," 145–146.

These "cultural barriers" mean that the social networks of some immigrant women are unsupportive of the decision to leave an abusive partner. The Hyman and Mason study of Toronto Tamil women found participants to negatively judge women who flee their abusers. One woman reflected, "She is leaving because she wants to save herself but she is not considering her husband's respect.... Even if he does so much torturing and harassment, she needs to tolerate it" (148). Some women even expressly condoned violence in certain circumstances: "If I address my husband like 'engavada' ('come here,' using the familiar form) in a public place, I should be beaten by him. But at home if we are talking it's okay" (148). A respondent in a study of attitudes toward domestic violence among Nigerian Canadians noted that "most Nigerians are Christian...and according to their religious beliefs marriage is for better for worse. A woman leaving her marital relationship is conceived as violation of her religious faith and a sin against God." Nwosu, "Experience of Domestic Violence among Nigerian-Canadian Women in Toronto," 104. Another respondent in this study explained, "Your mum will even tell you, please, my daughter, don't leave, I don't want people to laugh at me. Don't bring shame to the family, my daughter, please endure the abuse.... Even if the man is killing you, don't leave.... It will be a disgrace for your family if you leave" (104).

19. Jones, *Next Time, She'll Be Dead*.

20. Ibid., 220; emphasis added. See note 4 for statistics suggesting a decline in rates of IPV in Canada between 1999 and 2004.

21. Ibid., citing Browne and Williams, "Exploring the Effect of Resource Availability and the Likelihood of Female-Perpetrated Homicides." "Brown and Williams report that between 1979 and 1984 the number of 'male partners' killed by women decreased by more that 25 percent." Jones, *Next Time, She'll Be Dead*, 277.

22. See, for example, note 18 on the obstacles facing immigrant women.

23. In many disadvantaged communities the state is seen as more of a threat than a source of protection. Stuart Henry and Mark Lanier point, for example, to "the belief, held by many blacks, that 'justice' means 'just us.'" Henry and Lanier, *What Is Crime?* 161. Joan Moore refers to one Anti-Defamation League poll that found "74 percent of African-Americans, compared with 49 percent of the total sample, felt that police treat black citizens less fairly than white citizens of the same class level." Moore, "Bearing the Burden," 80.

L. Ngozi Nwosu interviewed first-generation Nigerian immigrant women in Toronto and found that a number of factors contribute to their reluctance to seek judicial or social support to protect themselves from violence; many of these reasons relate to fear of the consequences that attend the involvement of state authority. Nwosu, "Experience of Domestic Violence among Nigerian-Canadian Women in Toronto." She identifies "a common belief among the respondents that once a man is reported to the police for spousal abuse, the record is indelible, and that this would create a significant barrier and impede a man from gaining employment opportunities.... Consequently the whole family suffers economic hardship because of the wife's report to the police" (104). Nwosu also found that respondents were reluctant to report violence to the authorities out of fear of losing their children; the Nigerian tradition favors the father's right to his children over the mothers, and women consequently fear losing custody of their children if they leave an abusive husband.

Aboriginal women, too, have reason to believe that the state is not a reliable source of protection from violence. An Amnesty International report points to the police's failure to act on reports of missing Aboriginal women; this same report presented the shocking finding that "the police had long been aware of white men sexually preying on Indigenous women and girls…but "did not feel that the practice necessitated any particular vigilance." Amnesty International (Canada), "Stolen Sisters," 1.

24. See the discussion in note 4 above regarding barriers to escaping IPV.

25. Jones, *Next Time, She'll Be Dead*.

26. Ibid., 214.

27. Ibid., 14.

28. In Sally Merry's study, which I will discuss shortly, none of the men defended their violence as appropriate. Of course, as she notes, the men her team interviewed may have thought that the researchers were connected to the mandatory training course in which they were enrolled. Merry, "Rights Talk and the Experience of Law, 348n317). But they were willing to characterize calling the police as betrayal and complain that the woman's reaction was excessive. Some of the responses seem to trivialize the violence and to treat it as properly a private matter (369).

29. A 2009 attitudinal survey conducted in New Brunswick revealed that there is still a long way to go in terms of raising awareness about IPV. Harris/Decima, "Attitudinal Survey on Violence against Women." Women were more likely than men, urbanites were more likely than rural dwellers, and respondents aged 25–64 were more likely than those sixty-five and older to recognize psychological and verbal abuse as forms of violence (14). Victims of IPV are perceived to come from lower income brackets (more men than women held this viewpoint) and cultural backgrounds that hold a "more traditional" view of gender roles (16). More troubling still: just 73 percent believe it is a crime for a husband to rape his wife, and only 58 percent believe it is a crime for a twenty-year-old man to slap his girlfriend around because she flirted with another man in a public place; 47 percent would think it a crime for a husband to slap his wife's face after she complained he was not making enough money for the household (18). The perceived causes of IPV are also highly problematic: 26 percent see it as a personality problem in the male abuser, 24 percent think IPV occurs as a result of stress, and 18 percent see the cause as addiction or substance abuse (26); 34 percent of men thought that women provoke IPV by nagging or criticizing her partner (26). Furthermore, 39 percent of respondents felt that IPV is a private matter (20). Relatedly, general attitudes about women also were troubling: 20 percent felt that a woman needed permission from her husband to visit friends/family, and 27 percent felt it was a woman's duty to obey her husband (20).

In terms of the actual decrease in incidence of IPV, it is—as always with violence against women—a complex matter to interpret the statistics. It does seem that the incidence is decreasing. As indicated in note 4, in Canada there appears to have been a decline from 12 percent of women who had been assaulted by a spousal partner in the preceding five years in 1993 to 7 percent in 2004. Johnson, *Measuring Violence against Women*.

In 2007, the United States the Department of Justice, citing the National Crime Victimization Survey reported that the rate of reported IPV had dropped by 50 percent between 1993 and 2001. See Sampson, "Problem of Domestic Violence," and Rennison, "Intimate Partner Violence, 1993–2001."

As always, there are variations in findings among different surveys using different methodologies. Patricia Tjaden and Nancy Thoennes found disparities in annual intimate partner victimization rates between the National Crime Victimization Survey (NCVS), the National Family Violence Survey, and the National Violence against Women (NVAW) survey. Tjaden and

Thoennes, "Full Report of the Prevalence, Incidence, and Consequences of Violence against Women." For example, annual intimate partner victimization rates generated by the NCVS (cited above) are substantially lower than those generated by the NVAW survey. A 1996 Bureau of Justice Statistics study that used NCVS and Federal Bureau of Investigation data—which combined data on intimate partner murder, rape, sexual assault and aggravated and simple assault—found that the annual rate of violent victimization by an intimate partner was 7.5 per 1,000 women twelve years of age and older, and 1.4 per 1,000 men twelve years of age and older. By comparison, the NVAW survey annual rate of physical assault by an intimate partner was 44.2 per 1,000 women eighteen years of age and older and 31.5 per 1,000 men eighteen years of age and older (29).

One explanation for this disparity is that researchers have attributed the low rate of intimate partner violence uncovered by the NCVS to the fact it is administered in the context of a crime survey. Because they reflect only violence perpetrated by intimates that victims label as criminal and report to interviewers, estimates of intimate partner violence generated from the NCVS are thought to underestimate the true amount of IPV.

30. To anticipate my argument in section III, if is often difficult to predict (or even measure) the connections between legal change and the transformation of relations. Sweden changed its law to make johns rather than prostitutes the target of arrest. Different studies make different findings about the impact of the law. The new law may increase the vulnerability of street prostitutes but also reduce trafficking. Assessing the net impact on the security of women in the sex trade remains difficult. For example, Gunilla Ekberg of the Swedish Ministry of Industry, Employment, and Communications claims Sweden's antiprostitution policy and the criminalization of johns helps to overcome trafficking. Ekburg, "Swedish Law That Prohibits the Purchase of Sexual Services." Phil Hubbard, Roger Matthews and Jane Scoular compare prohibition in Sweden, abolition in Britain, and legalization in the Netherlands to argue that these different laws produce similar effects with regard to street prostitution. Hubbard, Matthews, and Scoular, "Regulating Sex Work in the EU." They note that, "since passage of the Act, numerous consequences have become apparent. The situation on the street is described as more difficult for prostitutes due to greater policing, a drop in custom leading to lower prices, less choice of clients, a need for quicker transactions and greater risk-taking in client selection" (147). But they present similar findings with respect to trafficking: "Nonetheless, both police and prosecutors claim it deters traffickers, with numbers of trafficked women in Sweden estimated to be lower than for neighbouring countries (200–500 women are trafficked into Sweden each year, compared with an estimated 17,000 to Finland)" (147).

31. A "negative right" is usually thought to be a right against, or freedom from, interference by others (including limitations imposed by the state). Negative rights are usually contrasted with "positive rights," which are conceived as claims that the rights-holder be provided with certain benefits by others (usually the state), such as health care, voting rights, or a fair trial. Negative rights imply a duty on others not to act upon the rights-holder, while positive rights imply a duty on others to act in particular ways with respect to the rights-holder. As the comment above suggests, on a relational approach to rights it will be exceedingly rare that "non-action" will be sufficient for people to enjoy any right. There is always the background issue of how relations are structured and the role of the state in that structuring. See Hirschmann, *Subject of Liberty*, for a sophisticated discussion of the concepts of negative and positive liberty.

32. And, of course, some (such as libertarians) believe that the state action necessary for the kind of commitment I am talking about would itself violate rights of freedom and autonomy.

33. White, middle-class, professional women in New York City are probably also safer than young black men in Harlem, and white, middle-class, professional women in Toronto are probably also safer than young black men in Toronto. But the contrast is sharper as stated in the text.

34. Of course, there are debates within liberal theory about whether some forms are less contingent than others.

35. Merry, "Rights Talk and the Experience of Law."

36. Ibid., 254.

37. Ibid., 345.

38. Ibid., 353.

39. Ibid., 352.

40. Ibid., 356.

41. For example, Edwina Barvosa-Carter offers a compelling account of how Chicana women mediate conflicting roles and expectations in ways that can subtly shift those roles by the very ongoing acts of choice, vacillation, and compromise. Barvosa-Carter, "Mestiza Autonomy as Relational Autonomy."

42. Merry, "Rights Talk and the Experience of Law," 367.

43. Ibid., 357.

44. Ibid., 357–358.

45. Ibid., 358.

46. Of course, the concept of gender also exceeds the relationship between men and women.

47. For example, L.A. (Lisa) Lambert says that "the Alberta government's ideology appears to be that abusive relationships are not products of a patriarchal culture and system but simply relationships in which people don't know how to handle their anger." Lambert, "When Martha Met Goliath," 42. The evidence against the anger management analysis is that men who batter their partners are not generally or randomly violent. Abusive men target women who are their partners: "Violence is a chosen response with a chosen target. Men do not usually attack their bosses, friends, sisters or neighbours when they get stressed out, only their wives or girlfriends" (42). My question is whether the choice in the "chosen response" is understood in a thoroughly relational way (as a product of patriarchal culture which shapes and limits men as much as women) or whether it slips into a version of the individualistic psychology that Lambert is rejecting.

48. Jones, *Next Time, She'll Be Dead,* 259.

49. Ibid., 119–122.

50. Kuypers, *Man's Will to Hurt.*

51. Ibid., 41.

52. Ibid., 39.

53. Ibid., 38.

54. Ibid., 68.

55. Ibid., 88.

56. Kennedy, "Sexual Abuse, Sexy Dressing, and the Eroticization of Domination." As an example of the prevalence of sexual assault: 16 percent of women abused by their partners were sexually assaulted, 39 percent of Canadian women report experiencing at least one sexual assault since age sixteen, ranging from "violent sexual attacks" to unwanted sexual touching. Johnson, *Measuring Violence against Women,* 19, 24. This definition of sexual assault is consistent with the *Canadian Criminal Code,* R.S., 1985, chap. C-46, secs. 265(2), 271–273.

57. Kennedy, "Sexual Abuse, Sexy Dressing, and the Eroticization of Domination," 1320.

58. Ibid., 1324.

59. Ibid., 1338.

60. Mosher et al., "Walking on Eggshells," 44–45.

61. For a positive view of mandatory arrest policies see Ben-Ishai, "Autonomy-Fostering State." For a more negative view see Leisenring, "Controversies Surrounding Mandatory Arrest Policies and the Police Response to Intimate Partner Violence," 458: "Some researchers and battered women's advocates argue that mandatory arrest policies disempower women because they limit women's agency and ability to act in their own best interests, ignore their opinions, and revictimize them through forced submittal to state power."

62. Kennedy, "Sexual Abuse, Sexy Dressing, and the Eroticization of Domination," 1324.

63. Ibid., 1314.

64. Ibid., 1309–1310.

65. Ibid., 1323.

66. Ibid., 1309.

67. Ibid., 1326.

68. Ibid.

69. Ibid., 1327.

70. Ibid., 1328.

71. Ibid., 1312.

72. Ibid., 1336.

73. Ibid., 1337.

74. Ibid., 1314.

75. Ibid., 1387.

76. Ibid.

77. See Benjamin, *Bonds of Love*, and my discussion in chapter 7, section III.

78. Kennedy, "Sexual Abuse, Sexy Dressing, and the Eroticization of Domination," 1387.

79. Ibid., 1388, quoting Butler, *Gender Trouble*, 30.

80. Kennedy, "Sexual Abuse, Sexy Dressing, and the Eroticization of Domination," 1388, quoting "Metaphystical Feminism" in Morgan, *Going Too Far*, 290, 301; Kennedy's emphasis.

81. Kennedy, "Sexual Abuse, Sexy Dressing, and the Eroticization of Domination," 1393.

82. This phrase is from the quote above. Ibid., 1387.

83. Ibid., 1390.

84. Ibid., 1393.

85. Pamela Shime, personal conversation, March 20, 2009.

86. Kittay, *Love's Labor*.

87. Pamela Shime, personal conversation, March 20, 2009.

88. Kuypers, *Man's Will to Hurt*.

89. For example, he points to the "acts of violence done in the name of 'good,' 'aggressive,' and 'competitive' business…done by men." Kuypers, *Man's Will to Hurt*, 42. He cites evidence that physical harm done by corporate crime (in a corporate world dominated by men) "dwarfs that done by lone men acting violently on the street or at home. The interested reader is referred to *Power, Crime and Mystificaiton* by Steven Box (1983), who argues that 'if consumer and citizen avoidable death and injury were added to workers avoidably killed and injured, then the ratio between corporate criminal violence and "conventional" criminal violence would clearly put the former in an extremely unfavorable light'" (43).

90. I also want to note my sadness and ambivalence as I watched my eighteen-year old son learn one of the basic rituals of a violence-based patriarchy. Late at night, he regularly walked one of his female friends home the few blocks from our house, and when traveling part way home via public transit with a girl he paid attention to whether he should wait with her until her bus came or whether the area was safe enough for him to continue on home. I felt pleased that he was responsible and attentive. I felt dismayed this his young male responsibilities included learning to see women as potential victims, (bad) men as predators, and (good) men as protectors. He was learning to assume his role as protector. And he was doing it well and thoughtfully. I found it admirable and attractive. I found it sad and dismaying.

91. Halley, *Split Decisions*, 301–302.

92. Butler, *Undoing Gender*, 219.

93. Ibid., 219–220.

94. At one point Butler seems to hold out the hope of norms that are not normalizing. She talks about norms that will be useful in building a world in which "collective means are found to protect bodily vulnerability without precisely eradicating it." These norms "will have to work not through normalization or racial and ethnic assimilation, but through collective sites of continuous political labor" (231). I think it is more consistent with the rest of her argument to say that collectively we should strive to build institutions that foster open contestation, that invite democratic political labor to continuously shape and reshape norms, but that we should recognize that all norms will have some normalizing dimension to them. All we can do is be self-conscious about that and build habits, practices, relations, norms, and institutions that foster that self-consciousness and an ongoing openness to transformation. I will have more to say about this at the close of this chapter.

95. Ibid., 220.

96. Ibid., 221.

97. Ibid., 222.

98. Ibid.

99. Ibid., chap. 10.

100. For an excellent collection of essays about the complexities of consent see Hunter and Cowan, *Choice and Consent.*

101. Halley, *Split Decisions*, 237–234.

102. 523 U.S. 75 (1998).

103. Halley, *Split Decisions*, 290–291.

104. Ibid., 292.

105. Ibid., 295.

106. Halley emphasizes that this is an intellectual exercise: "I am not saying anything about the human being Joseph Oncale, or making any truth claims about what actually happened on the oil rig. Instead I want to show how his factual allegations can be read" (ibid.).

107. Ibid., 303.

108. Ibid., 296.

109. Ibid.

110. Ibid., 296–297.

111. Ibid., 297. The first possibility is that "Oncale performs a feminine man in order to signal his willingness to be mastered...; the other guys comply with a big display of masculinity." The second possibility is that Oncale "performs a perfectly masculine man but only one kind of mas-

culine man; it's the discrepancy between his masculinity and that performed by the other men involved that gets things going." The third is that the other men "perform a kind of femininity associated with power—for example, they become bitchy"; in this reading, Oncale could be a masculinized heterosexual partner ("henpecked or intensely phallic") or a lesbian partner ("butch or femme") or even "the bottom to the power on display—no gender at all." The fourth possibility is that "more than one of these is happening at the same time, or rather perhaps, they all flicker as the scene unfolds" (297–298).

112. Ibid., 300.

113. Ibid., 300–301.

114. Ibid., 299.

115. See note 111.

116. Halley, *Split Decisions*, 301.

117. Ibid., 302.

118. 855 S.W.2d 619 (Sup.Ct.Texas 1993).

119. Halley, *Split Decisions*, 349.

120. Ibid., 352.

121. Ibid., 353–354.

122. Ibid., 352.

123. It is important to remember that Halley says, "I disavow any suggestion that the resulting formulations [rereadings of "narrative bites we get" from the judicial opinions] describe the real human beings Sheila and William Twyman." Halley, *Split Decisions*, 348.

124. Ibid., 357.

125. I discuss this quote in the following pages: "Imagine further: *Twyman* as background family-law rule that husbands with enduring ineradicable desires for sex that their wives find humiliating must either stay married to those wives or, if they seek a divorce (which they might well want to do simply to remarry and have nonadulterous sex with women who do not find their desires humiliating), pay a heavy tax in shame, blame, and cash. Can feminism acknowledge that women emerge from the court's decision with new bargaining power in marriage and a new role as enforcers of marital propriety? And can feminism see how costly this bargaining endowment might be *to women,* who can tap into it only if they find the sex in question painful and humiliating? Can feminism read the case as male subordination and female domination—and *still* as bad for women?" Halley, *Split Decisions*, 356.

Of course, following the logic of Halley's argument, it is not really *women* who gain power over *men*—it is people who want only "normal" or "vanilla" sex who gain power over partners who want sex outside the bounds of what judges see as normal. But it not clear that judges would follow this logic, interpreting the power of enforcing marital propriety in the same way for men as for women or for people in same-sex relationships.

126. Khan, "Sadomasochism Once Removed," esp. chaps. 4 and 5; "Putting a Dominatrix in Her Place"; and "Not a Lust Story."

127. Khan, "Putting a Dominatrix in Her Place," 168–169. For example, in *R. v. Bedford* ([1998] O.J. No. 4033 (Ct. J. (Prov. Div.)) (QL); *R. v. Bedford* (2000), 184 D.L.R. (4th) 727, 143 C.C.C. (3d) 311), an Ontario case involving the prosecution of a professional dominatrix under the Canadian criminal code provisions prohibiting "common bawdy houses" (see *Canadian Criminal Code*, R.S.C., 1985, chap. C-46, sec. 210), the accused raised a defense of abuse of process

by police, who allegedly violated the accused's rights during the arrest by forcing strip searches on the accused and her staff, asking the women to demonstrate "boot-licking," ridiculing the sadomasochistic gear worn by the dominatrixes and their clients, demanding the accused call them "master," and using excessive physical force. Khan, "Putting a Dominatrix in Her Place," 168. The police actions were not considered by the court to be severe enough to violate the accused's rights; Khan argues that the police actions in this case functioned to reassert more traditional conceptions of "normal" gender and sexuality and that the judgments in this case indicate the court's unwillingness to disrupt "normal" gender roles and (hetero)sexual relations in which the male partner is "naturally" dominant and the female submissive (168–169). Khan points out that the accused and her clients were not legally permitted to engage in consensual degradation/humiliation, but it was considered by the court to be perfectly legal, and even "natural," for the police officers to demean and humiliate the accused against her will (169–170). See also further reference to Khan's work in section III.A of this chapter and at note 146 below.

The accused, Terri Jean Bedford, is now well known as the claimant in a successful constitutional challenge to Canada's prostitution laws. *Bedford v. Canada (Attorney General)*, 2010 ONSC 4264. In that decision, three provisions—communicating to solicit sex, running or working in a brothel, and living off income procured by sex work—were found to be inconsistent with the *Canadian Charter of Rights and Freedoms* and to be of no force or effect to the extent of these inconsistencies. At the time of this writing, the judgment has been stayed to permit appellate review. *Bedford v. Canada (Attorney General)*, 2010 ONCA 814.

128. To say this is not, of course, to adopt the view (usually associated with Catherine MacKinnon) that the essence of gender is the sexual oppression of women by men.

129. Judith Butler writes that "to assume a responsibility for a future is not to know its direction fully in advance, since the future, especially the future with and for others, requires a certain openness and unknowingness.... It may be that what is 'right' and what is 'good' consist in staying open to the tensions that beset the most fundamental categories we require, to know unknowingness at the core of what we know, and what we need." Butler, *Undoing Gender*, 226–227.

130. Halley, *Split Decisions*, 363.

131. Jane Mansbridge uses the examples of feminism to explore the way "everyday activists" ("ordinary people [without institutional involvement with politics] acting in the course of everyday life"; 340) take up ideas from more organized activists "to help create the change in everyday life that undermines the legitimacy of one normative order and replaces it with another." Mansbridge, "Cracking through Hegemonic Ideology," 345.

132. Halley, *Split Decisions*, 356 (emphasis added).

133. Khan, "Sadomasochism Once Removed," "A Woman's Right to Be Spanked," and "Not a Lust Story."

134. Halley says the judges in *Twyman* "use a strange temporal location—'the experience of having been raped'; 'the trauma of having been raped'—that locates the moment of injury in a perpetual present. Sheila is *always* undergoing the experience of having been raped, *always* suffering the trauma of having been raped. In much feminist rape discourse, this is exactly right. Once raped, always raped. Much contemporary feminist discourse repeatedly insists that the pain of rape extends into every future moment of a woman's life; it is a note played not on a piano, but on an organ." Halley, *Split Decisions*, 354.

135. Dorothy Allison offers a moving story of wanting her sexual desires to be accepted by her fellow lesbian feminists in *Skin: Talking about Sex, Class, and Literature* (1994). Even though she

suggests that these desires (unspecified but rejected with repulsion by those she otherwise feels as part of her community) are the result of her childhood sexual abuse, what she wants is acceptance of her desire as part of who she is, not therapy to change it.

136. There are also much stronger versions of the rejection of the legitimacy of any form or "unwantedness." In the 1990s I had a student in a class at the University of Chicago Law School who argued that any form of coercion, including "emotional blackmail," or other forms of pressure from a partner to engage in sex should be seen as illegitimate. Only mutually desired sex should be seen as legitimate. I cannot now remember whether she thought there should be legal recourse for what she saw as coercion. It is also worth noting that many forms of the discussion of legal engagement with sexual relations are built around the problematic (and heterosexist) assumption that sex is something men want and women provide. Mutual desire is not the underlying assumption.

137. And, of course, there is technical legislation, such as that governing copyright, zoning, pension funds, banks or scientific research, that is formally made in the democratic forum of the legislature but that usually finds little scope for public debate—despite its widespread implications. Of course, any of these issues can surface to claim public attention from time to time, but meanwhile other crucial legal issues remain outside the scope of common political conversation or media attention.

138. Title VII of the American Civil Rights Act of 1964 (often referred to simply as Title VII) prohibits employment discrimination on the basis of race, color, religion, sex, or national origin in establishments with at least fifteen employees. Judicial interpretation takes on an especially crucial role in Title VII jurisprudence since, as one leading resource explains, the statutory language is "almost deliberately vague." Specter and Spiegelman, "Employment Discrimination Action under Federal Civil Rights Acts," sec. 5. The Supreme Court and the courts of appeals also have tended to "write in rather broad terms in cases arising under Title VII," and this tendency has left judges with little guidance in interpreting the statute; as a result, "the art of counsel and the prejudices of the appellate courts play a far greater role in the disposition of Title VII litigation than one might ordinarily expect in litigation arising under federal law" (ibid.).

Amie L. Vanover canvasses the jurisprudence on two interpretive questions where the "prejudices of the appellate courts" define rights in ways that structure relationships: whether sexual harassment decisions should consider the type of work environment and whether "non-sexual" discrimination on the basis of sex can form the basis of a valid claim. Vanover, *"Williams v. General Motors Corporation."* Persistent divisions within the judiciary as to how these questions should be answered reveal differing conceptions of the way Title VII rights ought to structure work relationships. With respect to the work environment, Vanover summarizes the split as follows: "Some courts believe that if a woman chooses to enter or stay in a work environment that is known to be rough and sexually harassing, the woman does not have as strong of a claim under Title VII as a woman who chooses to work in an environment that is perceived to be wholesome and without sexual harassment. Other courts believe that work environments saturated with sexual harassment are exactly what Title VII was intended to eradicate and thus do not take the type of work environment into account when deciding if there is a claim under Title VII" (1569). She describes the second of these sites of interpretive contestation, explaining that to some courts "non-sex behavior can be harassing if the conduct is directed toward a plaintiff because of anti-female animus. Other courts, however, purport that only behavior that is sexual in nature can be considered sexually harassing. Some of these courts even require behavior that

is 'overtly sexual'" (1578). In both examples, the diverging judicial interpretations of Title VII
rights rely upon fundamentally different conceptions of what sorts of relationships are to be tolerated in the workplace.

139. Halley, *Split Decisions*, 20–21.

140. Jones, *Next Time, She'll Be Dead*, 220.

141. Ibid., 217.

142. Ibid., 216–217.

143. Ibid., 126, 128.

144. Ibid., 126.

145. It is possible that Jones would reject the introduction of this sort of evidentiary question,
which could in some cases require women to adduce evidence that they did not "want" to be
beaten. (Even if the law were to assume that women did not "want" to be beaten, at least some
women would bear the burden of proving this in cases where their batterers are able to adduce
some threshold level of evidence that the women *did* want it.) Jones would likely reject such an
approach on the basis that it would create further barriers to women reporting abuse (including
fear of embarrassing personal details being brought forward as "evidence" of their desire for violence or an exacerbated feeling of isolation and alienation from the justice system for considering
the possibility that they desired the abuse).

146. I should add, also, that although I am optimistic about the eventual possibility of making
the distinctions I draw above, there is reason to be doubtful about how this project would be
taken up by current judges. For example, consider Ummni Kahn's discussion of consent and sadomasochism in the Canadian Supreme Court case of *R. v. Jobidon*, [1991] 2 S.C.R. 714:

> The Supreme Court of Canada's decision in *R. v. Jobidon* is the leading precedent relied
> upon in cases where an accused raises consent to s/m activity as a defense to a charge of
> assault. In that case, the Court probed the limits of a consent defense within the con-
> text of a consensual fist fight. It ruled that while s. 265 of the Criminal Code defines
> assault as taking place "without the consent" of the other person, the common law has
> imposed limits on a consent defence. Ultimately, the Court was careful to narrow its
> finding to the circumstances of the case, stating: "The limitation demanded by s. 265 as
> it applies to the circumstances of this appeal is one which vitiates consent between
> adults intentionally to apply force causing serious hurt or non-trivial bodily harm to
> each other in the course of a fist fight or brawl" [at para. 127]. Despite this precise
> holding, Justice Gonthier's policy considerations wander beyond the issue of consent in
> fist fights. He states a concern, related to the issue of deterrence in the context of con-
> sensual force, that the recipient of the force "may find that he derives some form of
> pleasure from the activity" [at para. 116]. This pleasure is immediately pathologized by
> Justice Gonthier as he continues: "It is perhaps not inconceivable that this kind of per-
> version could arise in a domestic or marital setting where one or more of the family
> members are of frail or unstable mental health" [at para. 116]. If there is any doubt that
> Justice Gonthier is referencing sexual pleasure, he then quotes criminal law theorist
> George P. Fletcher, who states that "if someone is encouraged to inflict a sadomasoch-
> istic beating on a consenting victim, the experience of inflicting the beating might
> loosen the actor's inhibitions against sadism in general" [at para. 116]. Although Justice
> Gonthier is quick to differentiate the situation in the case at hand to what Fletcher is

describing, the fact that he cites the theorist with approval clearly indicates a condemnation of consensual s/m activity. Without any reference to medical opinion, Justice Gonthier imposes a pathologizing gaze to unequivocally define the experience of pleasure derived from pain as a perversion suffered by people with a "frail" or "unstable" mind. And once again, s/m is definitively mapped onto sadism. The satisfaction that a dominant partner derives from a sadomasochist encounter is defined as an enjoyment in hurting another, not an enjoyment in pleasuring another in an unusual way (i.e., through infliction of physical pain).

Khan, "Sadomasochism Once Removed," 365–366.

147. Jones, *Next Time, She'll Be Dead*, 106–107.

148. Comfort, *New Joy of Sex*, 92; cited in Jones, *Next Time, She'll Be Dead*, 108, 115.

149. Halley, *Split Decisions*, 301.

150. Jones, *Next Time, She'll Be Dead*, 115.

151. Ibid., 199, 204.

152. Ibid., 217.

153. Schechter and Mihaly, "Ending Violence against Women and Children in Massachusetts Families," 14.

154. Of course, it is possible that legislatures sometimes might be willing to pass laws because they know (at least tacitly) that they will be only selectively enforced.

155. Jones, *Next Time, She'll Be Dead*, 221.

156. For example, requiring women to name the father of their children and failing to inform them of existing exemptions from this requirement. Mosher et al., "Walking on Eggshells," 44–45.

157. Jones, *Next Time, She'll Be Dead*, 225.

158. Ibid., 227.

159. For an interesting discussion of this tendency see Carens-Nedelsky, "Truth Between."

160. Of course, serious libertarians would see this as part of the problem, but they, too, often underestimate the range of issues in which a complete absence of law is virtually inconceivable. Often they are relying on the Hayekian distinction between public law and private law (or common law in common law countries like the United States and Canada)—see chapter 3, notes 36 and 43, for a brief discussion of Hayek, *Law, Legislation, and Liberty*. Private law, such as property and contract, is thought to be freedom enhancing while public law is inherently coercive. I will return to this point in "Closing Reflections."

161. See chapter 3 for a discussion of the common law tradition.

162. As I have noted, some of the changes in gender norms necessary to end violence against women must be accomplished within families and communities in ways that may be supported by law but are not within its domain.

163. It is likely that the levels of direct state engagement would vary over time. Once patterns of opportunity—including practices of hiring and promotion—were well established, the laws against discrimination would exist but be rarely called upon and affirmative action mandates could be dispensed with. Discriminatory gender norms run so deep, however, that this process is likely to take a long time.

164. For example, debates among feminists about mandatory arrest in cases of intimate partner violence. See note 61.

486

CONCLUSION

1. Edmund Burke was famous for his admiration of traditional institutions and beliefs as the necessary foundation of society and more reliable than the ideas "reason" might come up with. His best-known work is *Reflections on the Revolution in France* (1790).

2. This is a quote from O'Donovan, "With Sense, Consent, or Just a Con," 63. Donovan herself rejects this as a description of the project in which she wants to engage.

3. Lacey, *Women, Crime, and Character*, 26.

4. Audre Lorde famously entitled an essay as "The Master's Tools Will Never Dismantle the Master's House."

5. Kapur, *Erotic Justice*, 20.

6. We have seen examples of the harm done through the imposition of "Structural Adjustments Programs." See, for example, Rittich, *Recharacterizing Restructuring*, 236; Babb, "Social Consequences of Structural Adjustment."

7. Mill, *On Liberty*.

8. This week of study of systemic injustice for first-year law students took place before the establishment of the Truth and Reconciliation Commission of Canada: online <http://www.trc.ca/websites/trcinstitution/index.php?p=3>. Part of the purpose of this commission was to bring public awareness to this shameful episode in Canadian history and to permit the voices of those harmed by the schools (descendents as well as residents) to be heard. Royal Commission on Aboriginal Peoples Canada, *Report of the Royal Commission on Aboriginal Peoples*, discusses the schools in Canada, known as "Indian Residential Schools," and Adams, *Education for Extinction*, gives a historical account of the U.S. version, "American Indian Boarding Schools."

9. My suggested answers were prisons and the current practices of commercial meat production. Pollution and the waste of resources are other likely candidates.

10. The intergenerational harm of those schools, the sometimes permanent loss of language, will carry on even after there are no more survivors living.

One might also include current social assistance (welfare) programs as examples of nonrespectful forms of conferring benefits (see chapter 3).

11. My thanks to Dawnis Kennedy for reminding me of this.

12. See Honig, *Emergency Politics*, chap. 2.

13. See note 1, above.

14. See Hutchings, "Feminist Perspectives on a Planetary Ethic." This stance is not characteristic of all versions of the ethic of care.

15. Both James Tully and Leslie Paul Thiele have important work on the issues of contingency and unpredictability. See Tully, "Public Philosophy and Civic Freedom," and Thiele, *Indra's Net and the Midas Touch*.

16. See examples mentioned in Nedelsky, "Communities of Judgment and Human Rights."

17. As opposed, for example, to the denial of harm by insisting that access to marriage for same-sex couples doesn't affect anyone but those who take advantage of it. Of course, arguments for the necessity of this access to full equality is essentially an argument that same-sex marriage *will* shift social relations within the entire society—thus affecting everyone.

18. This is not to suggest that every teacher behaved badly or even that every student had a bad experience.

19. Of course in particular contexts, some legal rights get better protection than others.

20. See Koggel, *Perspectives on Equality*.

21. See, for example, Schlegel, *Wisdom from a Rainforest*, on the importance of harmony for the Teduray people of the Philippines.

22. Lorde, "Master's Tools Will Never Dismantle the Master's House."

23. Dworkin, "Liberalism," 60.

24. Of course, individuals may be set free from jail and torture (say through the intervention of Amnesty International) and thus have certain rights vindicated. But I think it is fair to say that although Amnesty works by focusing on particular cases, its project is to transform norms and practices so that the right to be free from torture actually exists in the ordinary structures of relations.

25. Of course, the public/private dichotomy has been a long-standing subject of feminist critique. See chapter 5, note 72.

26. I discuss this briefly in chapter 6, section III.B.

27. I discuss this in chapter 6, note 87.

28. Judges often find themselves using concepts and frameworks of analysis that are in tension with one another. For example, what is a question of law and what is a matter of discretion remain standard categories in Canadian administrative law, despite the recognition of the inherent overlap of these terms in a leading case, *Baker v. Canada (Ministry of Citizenship and Immigration)*, [1999] 2 S.C.R. 817. In *R. v. Morgentaler*, [1988] 1 S.C.R. 30, the Canadian case that found the then existing law regulating abortion unconstitutional, Justice Wilson used both a relational analysis and an invocation of classic liberal boundary language. Sometimes these tensions are productive and ultimately lead to a new framework with greater coherence and explanatory power.

29. I have elaborated this issue in Nedelsky, *Private Property and the Limits of American Constitutionalism*.

30. I discuss the whole issue of public and private law and the scope of the state in Nedelsky, *Private Property and the Limits of American Constitutionalism*.

31. See chapter 2, note 83 for a discussion of these debates.

REFERENCES

JURISPRUDENCE
Canada

Andrews v. Law Society of British Columbia, [1989] 1 S.C.R. 143.

Baker v. Canada (Ministry of Citizenship and Immigration), [1999] 2 S.C.R. 817.

Bedford v. Canada (Attorney General), 2010 ONSC 4264.

Bedford v. Canada (Attorney General), 2010 ONCA 814.

Blackwater v. Plint, 2005 SCC 58, [2005] 3 S.C.R. 3.

Canadian Foundation for Children, Youth and the Law v. Canada, [2004] 1 S.C.R. 76.

Cardinal v. Director of Kent Institution, [1985] 2 S.C.R. 643.

Chaoulli v. Quebec (Attorney General), [2005] 1 S.C.R. 791, 2005 SCC 35.

Cloud v. Attorney General of Ontario (2004), 73 O.R. (3d) 401, 247 D.L.R. (4th) 667 (C.A.).

Edmonton Journal v. Alberta (Attorney General), [1989] 2 S.C.R. 1326, 64 D.L.R. (4th) 577.

Edwards v. A.G. Canada (1930), 1 D.L.R. 98 (P.C.).

Egan v. Canada, [1995] 2 S.C.R. 513.

Falkiner v. Ontario (Ministry of Community and Social Services) (2002), 212 D.L.R. (4th) 633 (Ont. C.A.).

Gosselin v. Québec (Attorney General), [2002] 4 S.C.R. 429, 2002 SCC 84.

Harper v. Canada (Attorney General), [2004] 1 S.C.R. 827.

Harrison v. Carswell, [1976] 2 S.C.R. 200.

Law v. Canada (Minister of Employment and Immigration), [1999] 1 S.C.R. 497.

M. v. H., [1999] 2 S.C.R. 3.

Moge v. Moge, [1992] 3 S.C.R. 813

New Brunswick (Minister of Health and Community Services) v. G. (J.), [1999] 3 S.C.R. 46.

Nicholson v. Haldimand-Norfolk Reg. Police Commrs., [1979] 1 S.C.R. 311.

O'Connell v. Town of Chatham (1949), 24 MPR 36 (NCBA).

Peoples Department Stores Inc. (Trustee of) v. Wise, [2004] 3 S.C.R. 461, 2004 SCC 68.

R. v. Antley (1963), 42 S.C.R. 384

R. v. Bedford ([1998] O.J. No. 4033 (Ct. J. (Prov. Div.))

R. v. Bedford (2000), 184 D.L.R. (4th) 727, 143 C.C.C. (3d) 311 (Ont. C.A.).

R. v. Darrach, [2000] 2 S.C.R. 443, 2000 SCC 46.

R. v. Ewanchuk, [1999] 1 S.C.R. 33.

R. v. Ewanchuk (1998), 57 Alta. L.R. (3d) 235, 13 C.R. (5th) 324, [1998] A.J. No. 150 (C.A.).

R. v. Jobidon, [1991] 2 S.C.R. 714.

R. v. Kapp, [2008] 2 S.C.R. 483, 2008 SCC 41.

R. v. Keegstra, [1990] 3 S.C.R. 697.

R. v. Laba, [1994] 3 S.C.R. 965, 94 C.C.C. (3rd) 385.

R. v. Lavallee, [1990] 1 S.C.R. 852.

R. v. Malott, [1998] 1 S.C.R. 123.

R. v. Morgentaler, [1988] 1 S.C.R. 30

R. v. Rehberg (1993), 127 N.S.R. (2d) 331 (N.S.S.C.).

R. v. S. (R.D.), [1997] 3 S.C.R. 484.

R. v. S.A.B., [2003] 2 S.C.R. 678.

R. v. Seaboyer; R. v. Gayme, [1991] 2 S.C.R. 577.

Reference re Meaning of the Word "Persons" in Section 24 of the British North America Act, 1867, [1928] S.C.R. 276.

Reference re Same-Sex Marriage, [2004] 3 S.C.R. 698, 2004 SCC 79.

Reference re Secession of Quebec, [1998] 2 S.C.R. 217; 161 D.L.R. (4th) 385.

Reference re Section 94(2) of the Motor Vehicle Act, [1985] 2 S.C.R. 486.

RWDSU v. Dolphin Delivery Ltd., [1986] 2 S.C.R. 573.

Singh v. Minister of Employment and Immigration, [1985] 1 S.C.R. 177.

Wilson v. Medical Services Commission (1988), 53 D.L.R. (4th) 171, [1989] 2 W.W.R. 1 (B.C.C.A.).

South Africa

Bhe and Others v Khayelitsha Magistrate and Others (CCT 49/03) [2004] ZACC 17; 2005 (1) SA 580 (CC); 2005 (1) BCLR 1 (CC) (15 Oct. 2004).

Mthembu v Letsela and Another 1997 (2) SA 936 (T).

S. v. Makwanyane and Another Constitutional Court (CCT3/94) [1995] ZACC 3; [1995] 6 BCLR 665; 1995 (3) SA 391; [1996] 2 CHRLD 164; 1995 (2) SACR 1 (6 June 1995).

United Kingdom

George Mitchell (Chesterhall) Ltd. v Finney Lock Seeds Ltd., [1983] QB 284; [1983] 2 AC 803.

Gough v. National Coal Board, [1953] 2 All ER 1283, 1295 (CA).

M'Alister (or Donoghue) v. Stevenson, [1932] A.C. 562 (H.L.).

M'Naghten's Case 1843 10 C & F 200.

Royal Bank of Scotland v. Etridge, [2001] UKHL 44.

United States

Baker v. Vermont, 744 A.2d 864 (Vt. 1999).

Belvidere Tp. v. Heinze, 241 Mich.App. 324, 615 N.W.2d 250 (2000).

Board of Regents v. Roth, 408 U.S. 564 (1972).

Bradwell v. Illinois, 83 U.S. (16 Wall.) 130, 21 L.Ed. 442 (1873).

Brown v. Board of Education of Topeka, 347 U.S. 483 (1954).

Dodge v. Ford Motor Co., 204 Mich. 459, 170 N.W. 668 (1919).

Goodridge v. Department of Public Health, 440 Mass. 309, 798 N.E.2d 941 (2003).

Goldberg v. Kelly, 397 U.S. 254 (1970).

Grovey v. Townsend, 295 U.S. 45 (1935).

Hudgens v. NLRB, 424 U.S. 507 (1976).

In re Marriage Cases, 43 Cal. 4th 757, 183 P.3d 384, 76 Cal. Rptr. 3d 683 (2008).

Kerrigan v. Commissioner of Public Health, 289 Conn. 135, 957 A.2d 407 (2008).

Lochner v. New York, 198 U.S. 45 (1905).

McConnell v. Federal Election Commission, 540 U.S. 93 (2003).

Nixon v. Condon, 286 U.S. 73 (1932).

Nixon v. Herndon, 273 U.S. 536 (1927).

Oncale v. Sundowner Offshore Services, Inc., 523 U.S. 75 (1998).

Perry v. Schwarzenegger, No. 09-2292 VRW, 2010 WL 3025614 (N.D. Cal. Aug. 4, 2010).

Personnel Administrator of Massachusetts v. Feeney, 442 U.S. 256, 272 (1979).

Regents of the University of California v. Bakke, 438 U.S. 912 (1978).

Ricci v. DeStefano, 129 S. Ct. 2658 (2009).

Richmond v. J.A. Croson Co., 488 U.S. 469 (1989).

Shelley v. Kraemer, 334 U.S. 1 (1948).

State v. Norman, 378 S.E.2d. 8, 324 N.C. 253 (1989).

State v. Shack, 277 A.2d 369 (N.J. 1971).

Theodora Holding Corp. v. Henderson, 257 A.2d 398 (Del.Ch. 1969).

Twyman v. Twyman, 855 S.W.2d 619 (Sup.Ct.Texas 1993).

United States v. Carolene Products, 304 U.S. 144, 152n4 (1938).

United States v. Morrison, 529 U.S. 598 (2000).

Varnum v. Brien, 763 N.W.2d 862 (Iowa Sup. 2009).

Washington v. Davis, 426 U.S. 229 (1976).

West Coast Hotel Co. v. Parrish, 300 U.S. 379 (1937).

Wyman v. James, 400 U.S. 309 (1971).

LEGISLATION
Canada

An Act to Amend the Criminal Code (Sexual Assault), S.C. 1992, chap. 38.

Canadian Bill of Rights, S.C. 1960, chap. 44.

Canadian Criminal Code, R.S.C., chap. C-34; 1974–75–76, chap. 93; 1980–81–82–83, chap. 125; 1985, chap. C-46.

Canadian Charter of Rights and Freedoms, Part I of the *Constitution Act, 1982*, being Schedule B to the *Canada Act* 1982 (U.K.), 1982, chap. 11.

South Africa

Constitution of the Republic of South Africa, Schedule No. 108 of 1996.

United Kingdom

Married Women's Property Act, 1886 (U.K.), 45 & 46 Vict.

United States

Constitution of the United States of America.
The Declaration of Independence.
The Drug-Induced Rape Prevention and Punishment Act of 1996 (Act), 21 U.S.C. § 841(b)(7).
Education for All Handicapped Children Act, P.L. 94–142.
Title 18—Crimes and Criminal Procedure, 18 U.S.C., pt. I, chap. 1, § 17.
United States Insanity Defense Reform Act of 1984.

Treaties, Conventions, Declarations

African Charter on Human and Peoples' Rights: online <http://www.achpr.org/english/_info/charter_en.html>.
Convention for the Protection of Human Rights and Fundamental Freedoms, CETS No. 005, November 4, 1950.
Treaty on European Union, February 7, 1992, O.J. C 224/1 (1992), [1992] 1 C.M.L.R. 719, 31 I.L.M. 247.
Universal Declaration of Human Rights, GA Res 217(III), UN GAOR, 3d sess., supp. no. 13, UN Doc. a/810 (1948), 71.
United Nations Declaration on the Rights of Indigenous Peoples, GA Res. 61/295, UN GAOR, 61st sess. (2007).

Secondary Sources

Abrams, Kathryn. 1996. "The Constitution of Women." *Alabama Law Review* 48(3):861–884.
———. 1998. "Choice, Dependence, and the Reinvigoration of the Traditional Family." *Indiana Law Journal* 73(2):517–534.
Ackerman, Bruce A. 1991. *We the People.* Cambridge, Mass.: Harvard University Press.
Ackerman, Robert M. 1995. "Tort Law and Communitarianism: Where Rights Meet Responsibilities." *Wake Forest Law Review* 30(4):55–82.
Adams, David Wallace. 1995. *Education for Extinction: American Indians and the Boarding School Experience 1875–1928.* Lawrence: University Press of Kansas.
Adams, Jane. 2005. *Boundary Issues: Using Boundary Intelligence to Get the Intimacy You Want and the Independence You Need in Life, Love, and Work.* Hoboken N.J.: John Wiley & Sons.
Allan, Trevor R. S. 1998. "Fairness, Equality, Rationality: Constitutional Theory and Judicial Review." In *The Golden Metwand and the Crooked Cord: Essays on Public Law in Honour of Sir William Wade QC*, ed. I. Hare and C. F. Forsyth. New York: Oxford University Press.
Allen, William T. 1992. "Our Schizophrenic Conception of the Business Corporation." *Cardozo Law Review* 14(2):621–681.

Allison, Dorothy. 1994. *Skin: Talking about Sex, Class, and Literature*. Ithaca, N.Y.: Firebrand Books.

Amnesty International (Canada). 2004. "Stolen Sisters: A Human Rights Response to Discrimination and Violence against Indigenous Women in Canada": online <http://www.amnesty.ca/campaigns/resources/amr2000304.pdf>.

Andersson, G. 1993. "Support and Relief: The Swedish Contact Person and Contact Family Program." *International Journal of Social Welfare* 2(2):54–62.

Anonymous. 2006. "Letter." *Canadian Woman Studies* 25(1/2):25.

Antos, Joseph, and Thomas P. Miller. 2010. "A Better Prescription: AEI Scholars on Realistic Health Reform." Washington, D.C.: American Enterprise Institute for Public Policy Research.

Arendt, Hannah. 1958. *The Human Condition: Second Edition*. Chicago: University of Chicago Press. Collectors' Edition 1969.

———. 2003. "Thinking and Moral Considerations." In *Responsibility and Judgment*, ed. J. Kohn. New York: Schocken Books.

Arendt, Hannah, and Ronald Beiner, eds. 1982. *Lectures on Kant's Political Philosophy*. Chicago: University of Chicago Press.

Augustine, Philip W. 1988. "Protection of the Right to Property under the Canadian Charter of Rights and Freedoms." *Ottawa Law Review* 18(1):55–82.

Austin, Lisa M. 2010. "Privacy and Private Law: The Dilemma of Justification." *McGill Law Journal* 55(2):165–210.

Babb, Sarah. 2005. "The Social Consequences of Structural Adjustment: Recent Evidence and Current Debates." *Annual Review of Sociology* 31:199–222.

Backhouse, Constance, and Osgoode Society for Canadian Legal History. 1999. *Colour-Coded: A Legal History of Racism in Canada, 1900–1950*. Toronto: Published for the Osgoode Society for Canadian Legal History by the University of Toronto Press.

Bahm, Archie J. 1983. "Rights and Duties: Restoring the Balance." *Ethics in Education* 3(1983):5.

Bakan, Joel. 1997. *Just Words: Constitutional Rights and Social Wrongs*. Toronto: University of Toronto Press.

Bakan, Joel, and David Schneiderman, eds. 1992. *Social Justice and the Constitution: Perspectives on a Social Union for Canada*. Ottawa: Carleton University Press.

Barclay, Linda. 2000. "Autonomy and the Social Self." In *Relational Autonomy: Feminist Perspectives on Autonomy, Agency, and the Social Self*, ed. C. Mackenzie and N. Stoljar. New York: Oxford University Press

Barvosa-Carter, Edwina. 2007. "Mestiza Autonomy as Relational Autonomy: Ambivalence and the Social Character of Free Will." *Journal of Political Philosophy* 15(1):1–21.

Bechara, A., H. Damasio, D. Tranel, and A. R. Damasio. 2005. "The Iowa Gambling Task and the Somatic Marker Hypothesis: Some Questions and Answers." *Trends in Cognitive Sciences* 9(4):159–162.

Beermann, Jack M. 1997. "The Reach of Administrative Law in the United States." In *The Province of Administrative Law*, ed. M. Taggart: Oxford: Hart.

Beiner, Ronald, and Jennifer Nedelsky, eds. 2001. *Judgment, Imagination and Politics: Themes from Kant and Arendt*. Lanham, Md.: Rowman & Littlefield.

Benhabib, Seyla. 1992. *Situating the Self: Gender, Community, and Postmodernism in Contemporary Ethics*. New York: Routledge.

———. 1996. "Judith Shklar's Dystopic Liberalism." In *Liberalism without Illusions: Essays on Liberal Theory and the Political Vision of Judith N. Shklar*, ed. J. Shklar and B. Yack. Chicago: University of Chicago Press.

Benhabib, Seyla, Judith Butler, Drucella Cornell, and Nancy Fraser, eds. 1995. *Feminist Contentions: A Philosophical Exchange*. New York: Routledge.

Ben-Ishai, Elizabeth. 2009. "The Autonomy-Fostering State: 'Coordinated Fragmentation' and Domestic Violence Services." *Journal of Political Philosophy* 17(3):307–331.

Benjamin, Jessica. 1980. "The Bonds of Love: Rational Violence and Erotic Domination." *Feminist Studies* 6(1):144–174; reprinted in *The Future of Difference*, ed. H. Eisenstein and A. Jardine. New York and Boston: Barnard College Women's Center and G. K. Hall.

———. 1988. *The Bonds of Love: Psychoanalysis, Feminism, and the Problem of Domination*: Pantheon Books.

———. 1998. *Shadow of the Other: Intersubjectivity and Gender in Psychoanalysis*. New York: Routledge.

Bennett, Jane. 2010. *Vibrant Matter: A Political Ecology of Things*. Durham, N.C.: Duke University Press.

Bernat, Frances P. 2002. "Rape Law Reform." In *Sexual Violence: Policies, Practices, and Challenges in the United States and Canada*, ed. J. F. Hodgson and D. S. Kelley. Westport, Conn.: Praeger.

Berry, Thomas. 1988. *The Dream of the Earth*. San Francisco: Sierra Club Books.

Bettelheim, Bruno. 1952. *Surviving and Other Essays*. New York: Alfred A. Knopf.

———. 1960. *The Informed Heart: Autonomy in a Mass Age*. Glencoe, Ill.: Free Press.

Bilge, Sirma. 2006. "Behind the 'Culture' Lens: Judicial Representations of Violence against Minority Women." *Canadian Woman Studies* 25(1/2):1–2.

Blauner, Bob. 2009. *Resisting McCarthyism: To Sign or Not to Sign California's Loyalty Oath*: Palo Alto, Calif.: Stanford University Press.

Borrows, John. 2001. "Indian Agency: Forming First Nations Law in Canada." *Political Legal Anthropology Review* 24(2):9–24.

———. 2002. *Recovering Canada: The Resurgence of Indigenous Law*. Toronto: University of Toronto Press.

———. 2008. "Living Law on a Living Earth: Aboriginal Religion, Law, and the Constitution." In *Law and Religious Pluralism in Canada*, ed. R. Moon. Vancouver: University of British Columbia Press.

———. 2010. *Drawing Out Law: A Spirits Guide*. Toronto: University of Toronto Press.

Bowker, Lee H., Michelle Arbitell, and J. Richard McFerron. 1988. "On the Relationship between Wife Beating and Child Abuse." In *Feminist Perspectives on Wife Abuse*, ed. K. Yllö and M. L. Bograd. Newbury Park, Calif.: Sage.

Boyd, Susan B. 1997. "Challenging the Public/Private Divide: An Overview." In *Challenging the Public/Private Divide: Feminism, Law, and Public Policy*, ed. S. B. Boyd. Toronto: University of Toronto Press.

Bradley, Mark, and Patrice Petro. 2002. *Truth Claims: Representation and Human Rights*. New Brunswick, N.J.: Rutgers University Press.

Brennan, Shannon, and Andrea Taylor-Butts. 2008. "Sexual Assault in Canada: 2004 and 2007." Ottawa: Canadian Centre for Justice Statistics (Statistics Canada).

Bressette, Shelly, Ellen Hamilton, Joan Jenkinson, Chantal Cholette, Sandra Harder, and Barbara Ladouceur. 1993. *Changing the Landscape: Ending* Violence—*Achieving Equality*. Final Report. Ottawa: Canadian Panel on Violence against Women.

Bridgman, Rae. 1998. "The Architecture of Homelessness and Utopian Pragmatics." *Utopian Studies* 9(1):50–67.

Briggs, Dorothy Corkille. 1975. *Your Child's Self-Esteem*. New York: Doubleday.

Brison, Susan J. 1997. "Outliving Oneself: Trauma, Memory, and Personal Identity." In *Feminists Rethink the Self*, ed. D. Meyers. Boulder, Colo.: Westview.

———. 2002. *Aftermath: Violence and the Remaking of a Self*. Princeton, N.J.: Princeton University Press.

Brodsky, Gwen, Rachel Cox, Shelagh Day, and M. Kate Stephenson. 2006. "*Gosselin v. Quebec (Attorney General)*: Women's Court of Canada [2006] 1 W. C. R. 193." *Canadian Journal of Women and the Law* 18(1):189–249.

Brown, Jorielle R., Hope M. Hill, and Sharon F. Lambert. 2005. "Traumatic Stress Symptoms in Women Exposed to Community and Partner Violence." *Journal of Interpersonal Violence* 20(11):1478–1494.

Brown, Wendy, and Janet Halley, eds. 2002. *Left Legalism, Left Critique*. Durham, NC: Duke University Press.

Browne, Angela, and Kirk R. Williams. 1989. "Exploring the Effect of Resource Availability and the Likelihood of Female-Perpetrated Homicides." *Law and Society Review* 23(1):75–94.

Brownmiller, Susan. 1975. *Against Our Will: Men, Women, and Rape*. New York: Simon & Schuster.

Bussiere, Elizabeth. 2004. "The 'New Property' Theory of Welfare Rights: Promises and Pitfalls." *The Good Society* 13(2):1–9.

Butler, Judith. 1990. *Gender Trouble: Feminism and the Subversion of Identity*. New York: Routledge.

———. 2004. *Undoing Gender*. New York: Routledge.

Buvinić, Mayra. Fall 1997. "Women in Poverty: A New Global Underclass." *Foreign Policy*, 38–53.

Canadian Centre for Justice Statistics. 2009. "Family Violence in Canada: A Statistical Profile." Ottawa: Canadian Centre for Justice Statistics (Statistics Canada).

Canadian Institute for Health Information. 2006. "Waiting for Health Care in Canada: What We Know and What We Don't Know." Ottawa: Canadian Institute for Health Information.

———. 2008. "Health Care in Canada 2008." Ottawa: Canadian Institute for Health Information.

Carens, Joseph H. 2000. *Culture, Citizenship, and Community*. New York: Oxford University Press.

Carens-Nedelsky, Michael. March 2007. "The Truth Between." *Diatribe Magazine*.

Cargas, James. 2003. *Problems Unique to the Holocaust*. Lexington: University Press of Kentucky.

Cartier, Geneviève. 2004. "Reconceiving Discretion: From Discretion as Power to Discretion as Dialogue." Ph.D. diss., University of Toronto.

———. 2005. "Administrative Discretion as Dialogue: A Response to John Willis (Or: From Theology to Secularization.)" *University of Toronto Law Journal* 55(3):629–656.

Clement, Grace. 1996. *Care, Autonomy, and Justice: Feminism and the Ethic of Care*. Boulder, Colo.: Westview.

Code, Lorraine. 1991. *What Can She Know? Feminist Theory and the Construction of Knowledge*. Ithaca, N.Y.: Cornell University Press.

Code, Lorraine, Sheila Mullett, Christine Overall, and Canadian Society for Women in Philosophy. 1988. *Feminist Perspectives: Philosophical Essays on Method and Morals*. Toronto: University of Toronto Press.

Cogan, Jacob Katz. 1997. "The Look Within: Property, Capacity, and Suffrage in Nineteenth-Century America." *Yale Law Journal* 107(2):473–498.

Comfort, Alex. 1991. *The New Joy of Sex: A Gourmet Guide to Lovemaking in the Nineties*. New York: Pocket Books.

Connolly, William. 2000. *Why I Am Not a Secularist*. Minneapolis: University of Minnesota Press.

Cornell, Drucilla. 1998. *At the Heart of Freedom: Feminism, Sex, and Equality*. Princeton, N.J.: Princeton University Press.

Cover, Robert M. 1982. "The Origins of Judicial Activism in the Protection of Minorities." *Yale Law Journal* 91(7):1287–1316.

Cowling, Mark. 2004. "Rape, Communicative Sexuality and Sex Education." In *Making Sense of Sexual Consent*, ed. M. Cowling and P. Reynolds. Aldershot, U.K.: Ashgate.

Craig, Carys J. 2007. "Reconstructing the Author-Self: Some Feminist Lessons for Copyright Law." *American University Journal of Gender, Social Policy & the Law* 15(2):207–268.

Crocker, David A. 1995. "Functioning and Capability: The Foundations of Sen's and Nussbaum's Development Ethic." In *Women, Culture, and Development: A Study of Human Capabilities*, ed. M. C. Nussbaum and J. Glover. New York: Oxford University Press.

Dahl, Robert Alan, and Charles Edward Lindblom. 1976. *Politics, Economics, and Welfare: Planning and Politico-Economic Systems Resolved into Basic Social Processes*. Chicago: University of Chicago Press.

da Luz, Carla M., and Pamela C. Weckerly. 1991. "The Texas 'Condom-Rape' Case: Caution Construed as Consent." *UCLA Women's Law Journal* 95(3):95–104.

Daly, Mary. 1978. *Gyn/Ecology: The Metaethics of Radical Feminism*. Boston: Beacon.

Damasio, Antonio R. 1994. *Descartes' Error: Emotion, Reason, and the Human Brain*. New York: Putnam.

Danylewich, Paul Henry. 2001. *Fearless: The Complete Personal Safety Guide for Women*. Toronto: University of Toronto Press.

Dasgupta, Shamita Das. 2005. "Women's Realities: Defining Violence against Women by Immigration, Race, and Class." In *Domestic Violence at the Margins: Readings on Race, Class, Gender, and Culture*, ed. N. J. Sokoloff and C. Pratt. New Brunswick, N.J: Rutgers University Press.

Davis, Madeline, and David Wallbridge. 1990. *Boundary and Space: An Introduction to the Work of D. W. Winnicott* New York: Brunner-Routledge.

Davis, Ronald. 2008. *Democratizing Pension Funds: Corporate Governance and Accountability*. Vancouver: University of British Columbia Press.

de Beauvoir, Simone. 1952. *The Second Sex*. Translated by H. M. Parshley. New York: Alfred A. Knopf.

Del Bove, Giannetta, and Lana Stermac. 2002. "Psychological Evidence in Sexual Assault Court Cases: The Use of Expert Testiomony and Third-Party Records by Trial Court Judges." In *Sexual Violence: Policies, Practices, and Challenges in the United States and Canada*, ed. J. F. Hodgson and D. S. Kelley. Westport, Conn.: Praeger.

Des Pres, Terrence. 1980. *The Survivor: An Anatomy of Life in the Death Camps*. New York: Oxford University Press.

Dinnerstein, Dorothy. 1976. *The Mermaid and the Minotaur: Sexual Arrangements and Human Malaise*. New York: Harper & Row.

Doe, Jane. 2003. *The Story of Jane Doe: A Book about Rape.* Toronto: Random House Canada.

Donnelly, Jennifer. 2004. *A Gathering Light.* London: Bloomsbury.

Douzinas, Costas. 2007. *Human Rights and Empire: The Political Philosophy of Cosmopolitanism.* London: Routledge-Cavendish.

Downie, Jocelyn, and Jennifer Llewellyn, eds. Forthcoming. *Being Relational: Reflections on Relational Theory and Health Law and Policy.* Vancouver: University of British Columbia Press.

Dunn, Barnaby D., Tim Dalgleish, and Andrew D. Lawrence. 2006. "The Somatic Marker Hypothesis: A Critical Evaluation." *Neuroscience and Biobehavioural Reviews* 30(2):239–271.

Dworetz, Steven M. 1990. *The Unvarnished Doctrine: Locke, Liberalism, and the American Revolution.* Durham, N.C.: Duke University Press.

Dworkin, Andrea. 1987. *Intercourse.* New York: Free Press.

Dworkin, Ronald. 1977. *Taking Rights Seriously.* London: Duckworth.

———. 1984. "Liberalism." In *Liberalism and Its Critics,* ed. M. J. Sandel. New York: New York University Press.

———. 1986. *Law's Empire.* Cambridge, Mass.: Harvard University Press.

Dyzenhaus, David. 2001. "'With the Benefit of Hindsight': Dilemmas of Legality in the Face of Injustice." In *Lethe's Law: Justice, Law, and Ethics in Reconciliation,* ed. E. A. Christodoulidis and S. Veitch. Oxford: Hart.

Dyzenhaus, David, and Evan Fox-Decent. 2001. "Rethinking the Process/Substance Distinction: *Baker v. Canada.*" *University of Toronto Law Journal* 51(3):193–242.

Eastland, Terry. 1992–1993. "The Case against Affirmative Action." *William and Mary Law Review* 34(1):33–51.

Easton, John. April 2003. "Survival of the Richest." *University of Chicago Magazine*: online <http://magazine.uchicago.edu/0304/features/survival.html>.

Ehrenreich, Barbara, and Arlie Russell Hochschild, eds. 2002. *Global Woman: Nannies, Maids, and Sex Workers in the New Economy.* New York: Henry Holt and Co.

Eisen, Jess. 2008. "Rethinking Affirmative Action Analysis in the Wake of *Kapp*: A Limitations-Interpretation Approach." *Journal of Law and Equality* 6(1):1–32.

Ekburg, Gunilla. 2004. "The Swedish Law That Prohibits the Purchase of Sexual Services: Best Practices for Prevention of Prostitution and Trafficking in Human Beings." *Violence against Women* 10(10):1187–1218.

Elliott, Pam. 1996. "Shattering Illusions: Same-Sex Domestic Violence." In *Violence in Gay and Lesbian Domestic Partnerships,* ed. C. M. Renzetti and C. H. Miley. New York: Harrington Park.

Ely, John Hart. 1980. *Democracy and Distrust: A Theory of Judicial Review.* Cambridge, Mass.: Harvard University Press.

Epstein, Richard Allen. 1985. *Takings: Private Property and the Power of Eminent Domain.* Cambridge, Mass.: Harvard University Press.

Esch, Tobias, and George B. Stefano. 2005. "The Neurobiology of Love." *Neuroendocrinology Letters* 26(3):175–192.

Eskridge, William N., and John Ferejohn. 2006. "Super-Statutes: The New American Constitutionalism." In *The Least Examined Branch: The Role of Legislatures in the Constitutional State,* ed. R. W. Bauman and T. Kahana. New York: Cambridge University Press.

Esmail, Nadeem, Maureen Hazel, and Michael A. Walker. October 2008. *Waiting Your Turn: Hospital Waiting Lists in Canada,* 2008 *Report.* 18th ed. Fraser Institute Studies in Health Care Policy: online <http://www.fraserinstitute.org/research-news/display.aspx?id=13587>.

Etzioni, Amitai. 1995. *Rights and the Common Good: The Communitarian Perspective*. New York: St. Martin's.

———. 1998. *The New Golden Rule: Community and Morality in a Democratic Society*. New York: Basic Books.

Family Service Toronto. 2009. "2009 Report Card on Child and Family Poverty in Canada: 1989–2009." Toronto: Family Service Toronto.

Fehlberg, Belinda. 1997. *Sexually Transmitted Debt: Surety Experience and English Law*. Oxford: Oxford University Press.

Feinman, Jay M. 2004. *Un-Making Law: The Conservative Campaign to Roll Back the Common Law*: Boston: Beacon.

Ferguson, Kathy E. 1984. *The Feminist Case against Bureaucracy*. Philadelphia: Temple University Press.

Fiss, Owen. 1996. *The Irony of Free Speech*. Cambridge, Mass.: Harvard University Press.

Flathman, Richard E. 2003. *Freedom and Its Conditions: Discipline, Autonomy, and Resistance*. New York: Routledge.

Flax, Jane. 1993. *Disputed Subjects: Essays on Psychoanalysis, Politics, and Philosophy*. New York: Routledge.

Flood, Colleen, and Lorne Sossin, eds. 2008. *Administrative Law in Context*. Toronto: Emond Montgomery.

Forell, Caroline A. 2006. "Gender Equality, Social Values and Provocation Law in the United States, Canada and Australia." *American University Journal of Gender, Social Policy and the Law* 41(1):27–69.

Foscarinis, Maria, Brad Paul, Bruce Porter, and Andrew Scherer. July–August 2004. "The Human Right to Adequate Housing: Making the Case in U.S. Advocacy." *Clearinghouse Review: Journal of Poverty Law and Policy*.

Fouts, Roger, with Stephen Tukel Mills. 2003. *Next of Kin: My Conversations with Chimpanzees*: New York: Quill.

Fraser, Nancy. 1989. "Talking About Needs: Interpretive Contests as Political Conflicts in Welfare-State Societies." *Ethics* 99(2):291–313.

———. 1994. "After the Family Wage: Gender Equity and the Welfare State." *Political Theory* 22(4):591–618.

Frazer, Elizabeth, and Nicola Lacey. 1993. *The Politics of Community: A Feminist Critique of the Liberal-Communitarian Debate*. Toronto: University of Toronto Press.

Friedman, Marilyn. 1993. *What Are Friends For? Feminist Perspectives on Personal Relationships and Moral Theory*. Ithaca, N.Y.: Cornell University Press.

———. 2000. "Autonomy, Social Disruption, and Women." In *Relational Autonomy: Feminist Perspectives on Autonomy, Agency, and the Social Self*, ed. C. Mackenzie and N. Stoljar. New York: Oxford University Press.

Friedman, Milton, and Rose D. Friedman. 1982. *Capitalism and Freedom*. Chicago: University of Chicago Press.

Fudge, Judy. 1989. "The Effect of Entrenching a Bill of Rights upon Political Discourse: Feminist Demands and Sexual Violence in Canada." *International Journal of the Sociology of Law* 17(4):445–463.

———. 1990. "What Do We Mean by Law and Social Transformation?" *Canadian Journal of Law and Society* 5:47–69.

Gaard, Greta, ed. 1993. *Ecofeminism: Women, Animals, Nature*. Philadelphia: Temple University Press.

Gabel, Peter. 1984. "The Phenomenology of Right Consciousness and the Pact of the Withdrawn Selves." *Texas Law Review* 62(8):156–1600.

Gaes, Gerald G., and William J. McGuire. 1985. "Prison Violence: The Contribution of Crowding versus Other Determinants of Prison Assault Rates." *Journal of Research in Crime and Delinquency* 22 (1):41–65.

Gilligan, Carol. 1982. *In a Different Voice: Psychological Theory and Women's Development*. Cambridge, Mass.: Harvard University Press.

Gilliom, John. 2001. *Overseers of the Poor: Surveillance, Resistance, and the Limits of Privacy*. Chicago: University of Chicago Press.

Glendon, Mary Ann. 1991. *Rights Talk: The Impoverishment of Political Discourse*. New York: Free Press.

Goffman, Erving. 1961. *Asylums: Essays on the Social Situation of Mental Patients and Other Inmates*. New York: Anchor Books.

Goodwin, Brian C. 1994. *How the Leopard Changed Its Spots: The Evolution of Complexity*. Princeton, N.J.: Princeton University Press.

Gordon, Robert. 1998. "Some Critical Theories of Law and Their Critics." In *The Politics of Law: A Progressive Critique*, ed. D. Kairys. New York: Basic Books.

Govier, Trudy. 1993 "Self-Trust, Autonomy, and Self-Esteem." *Hypatia* 8(1):99–120.

Graham, Erin. 2006. "This Trauma Is Not Vicarious." *Canadian Woman Studies* 25(1/2):17–19.

Grear, Anna M. 2007. "Challenging Corporate 'Humanity': Legal Disembodiment, Embodiment and Human Rights." *Human Rights Law Review* 7(3):511–543.

———. 2008. "Vulnerability, Freedom, Law and the Body." Paper presented at the conference "Human Rights without Freedom," held at Vanderbilt University, Nashville, Tennessee, October 23.

Griffin, Susan. 1981. *Pornography and Silence: Culture's Revenge against Nature*. New York: Harper & Row.

———. 1992. *A Chorus of Stones: The Private Life of War*. New York: Doubleday.

Griffiths, Morwenna. 1995. *Feminisms and the Self: The Web of Identity*. London: Routledge.

Gross, Jane. September 25, 1993. "Combating Rape on Campus in a Class on Sexual Consent." *New York Times*.

Gutmann, Amy, and Dennis Thompson. 2004. *Why Deliberative Democracy?* Princeton, N.J.: Princeton University Press.

Hale, Robert L. 1923. "Coercion and Distribution in a Supposedly Non-Coercive State." *Political Science Quarterly* 38(3):470–494.

Hall, Cheryl. 2005. *The Trouble with Passion: Political Theory beyond the Reign of Reason*. New York: Routledge.

Halley, Janet E. 2006. *Split Decisions: How and Why to Take a Break from Feminism*. Princeton, N.J.: Princeton University Press.

Hameed, Yavar, and Niiti Simmonds. 2007. "The *Charter*, Poverty Rights and the Space Between: Exploring Social Movements as a Forum for Advancing Social and Economic Rights in Canada." *National Journal of Constitutional Law* 23(1):181–213.

Handler, Joel. 1988. "Dependent People, the State, and the Modern/Postmodern Search for the Dialogic Community." *UCLA Law Review* 35(1987–1988):999–1114.

———. 1995. *The Poverty of Welfare Reform*. New Haven, Conn.: Yale University Press.

Handler, Joel F., and Yeheskel Hasenfeld. 1997. *We the Poor People: Work, Poverty, and Welfare*. New Haven, Conn.: Yale University Press.

Hardacre, Helen. 1993. "Impact of Fundamentalisms on Women, the Family, and Interpersonal Relations." In *Fundamentalisms and Society: Reclaiming the Sciences, the Family, and Education*, ed. M. E. Marty and R. S. Appleby. Chicago: University of Chicago Press.

Harding, Sandra G. 1987. *Feminism and Methodology: Social Science Issues*. Bloomington: Indiana University Press.

Harrell, Erika. August 2007. *Black Victims of Violent Crime*. Bureau of Justice Statistics Special Report. Washington, D.C.: U.S. Department of Justice.

Harris/Decima. July 14, 2009. "Attitudinal Survey on Violence against Women: Detailed Report Prepared for the Province of New Brunswick Executive Council Office—Women's Issues Branch": online <http://www.gnb.ca/0012/violence/PDF/AttitudinalSurvey-e.pdf>.

Harris-Lacewell, Melissa. 2008. "Obama's Cosby Moment Response." Posted at *The Root*, webzine edited by H. L. Gates for Washingtonpost. Newsweek Interactive.

Hartog, Hendrik. 2000. *Man and Wife in America: A History*. Cambridge, Mass.: Harvard University Press.

Hayek, Friedrich A. von. 1973. *Law, Legislation, and Liberty: A New Statement of the Liberal Principles of Justice and Political Economy*, vol. 1. Chicago: University of Chicago Press.

Hayek, Friedrich A. von, and William Warren Bartley. 1989. *The Fatal Conceit: The Errors of Socialism*. Chicago: University of Chicago Press.

Health Canada. March 1999. "Violence against Women." Fact sheet prepared for the Women's Health Bureau: online <http://www.hc-sc.gc.ca/hl-vs/pubs/women-femmes/violence-eng.php>.

Held, Virginia. 1993. *Feminist Morality: Transforming Culture, Society, and Politics*. Chicago: University of Chicago Press.

Henry, Stuart, and Mark M. Lanier. 2001. *What Is Crime? Controversies over the Nature of Crime and What to Do About It*. Lanham, Md.: Rowman & Littlefield.

Herman, Judith Lewis. 1992. *Trauma and Recovery*. New York: Basic Books.

Herman, Kristine. 2000. "Demands from the Women of Antioch." In *Just Sex: Students Rewrite the Rules on Sex, Violence, Activism, and Equality*, ed. J. Gold and S. Villari. Lanham, Md.: Rowman & Littlefield.

Hiebert, Janet. 2002. *Charter Conflicts: What Is Parliament's Role?* Montreal: McGill–Queen's University Press.

Hilberg, Raul. 1985. *The Destruction of the European Jews*. Abridged ed. New York: Holmes & Meier.

Hill, Marc Lamont. 2008. "Down from the Tower—Obama's Popeyes Speech." In *Marc Lamont Hill*. Philadelphia: Marc Lamont Hill.

Hine, Darlene Clark. 2003. *Black Victory: The Rise and Fall of the White Primary in Texas*. Columbia: University of Missouri Press.

Hirschmann, Nancy. 2003. *The Subject of Liberty: Toward a Feminist Theory of Freedom*. Princeton, N.J.: Princeton University Press.

Hoagland, Sarah Lucia. 1988. *Lesbian Ethics: Toward New Value*. Palo Alto, Calif.: Institute of Lesbian Studies.

Hodes, Caroline. 2006. "Recognizing Economic, Social, and Cultural Rights in Canada: One Step toward Eliminating Violence against Women in All Its Forms." *Canadian Woman Studies* 25(1/2):195–201.

Hogg, Peter W. 1997. *Constitutional Law of Canada*. 4th ed. Scarborough, Ont.: Carswell.

Hogg, Peter W., and Allison A. Bushell. 1997. "The *Charter* Dialogue between Courts and Legislatures (or Perhaps the *Charter of Rights* Isn't Such a Bad Thing after All)." *Osgoode Hall Law Journal* 35(1):75–124.

Hogg, Peter W., Allison A. Bushell Thornton, and Wade K. Wright. 2007. "A Reply on '*Charter* Dialogue Revisited.'" *Osgoode Hall Law Journal* 45(1):193–202.

Hohfeld, Wesley Newcomb. 1913. "Some Fundamental Legal Conceptions as Applied in Judicial Reasoning." *Yale Law Journal* 23(1):16–59.

Honig, Bonnie. 2009. *Emergency Politics: Paradox, Law, Democracy*. Princeton, N.J.: Princeton University Press.

hooks, bell. 1984. *Feminist Theory: From Margin to Center*. Boston: South End Press.

——. 1993. "Violence in Intimate Relationships." In *Gender Basics: Feminist Perspectives on Women and Men*, ed. A. Minas. Belmont, California: Wadsworth.

Horwitz, Morton J. 1977. *The Transformation of American Law, 1870–1960*. Cambridge, Mass.: Harvard University Press.

Hubbard, Phil, Roger Matthews, and Jane Scoular. 2008. "Regulating Sex Work in the EU: Prostitute Women and the New Spaces of Exclusion." *Gender, Place & Culture* 15(2):137–152.

Hunter, Rosemary, and Sharon Cowan, eds. 2007. *Choice and Consent: Feminist Engagements with Law and Subjectivity*. London: Routledge-Cavendish.

Husak, Douglas N. 1995. "Varieties of Strict Liability." *Canadian Journal of Law and Jurisprudence* 8:189–225.

Hutchings, Kimberly. 2007. "Feminist Perspectives on a Planetary Ethic." In *The Globalization of Ethics*, ed. W. M. Sullivan and W. Kymlicka: Cambridge University Press.

Hutchinson, Allan C., and Andrew Petter. 1988. "Private Rights/Public Wrongs: The Liberal Lie of the Charter." *University of Toronto Law Journal* 38(3):278–297.

Hyman, Ilene, and Robin Mason. 2006. "Perceptions of and Responses to Woman Abuse among Tamil Women in Toronto." *Canadian Woman Studies* 25(1/2):145–150.

Irigaray, Luce. 1985. *This Sex Which Is Not One*. Ithaca, N.Y.: Cornell University Press.

Island, David, and Patrick Letellier. 1991. *Men Who Beat the Men Who Love Them: Battered Gay Men and Domestic Violence*. New York: Harrington Park.

Jackson, Emily. 2001. *Regulating Reproduction: Law, Technology, and Autonomy*. Portland, Oreg: Hart.

Jaggar, Alison M. 1983. *Feminist Politics and Human Nature*. Totowa, N.J.: Rowman & Allanheld.

——. 1989. "Love and Knowledge: Emotion in Feminist Epistemology." *Inquiry* 32(2):151–176.

Jamieson, Beth Kiyoko. 2001. *Real Choice: Feminism, Freedom, and the Limits of Law*. University Park: Pennsylvania State University Press.

Johansen, David. October 1991. "Property Rights and the Constitution." BP-268E. Publishing and Depository Services, Law and Government Division, Government of Canada: online <http://dsp-psd.pwgsc.gc.ca/Collection-R/LoPBdP/BP/bp268-e.htm>.

Johnson, Harold. 2007. *Two Families: Treaties and Government*. Saskatoon, Sask.: Purich.

Johnson, Holly. 2006. *Measuring Violence against Women: Statistical Trends 2006*. Ottawa: Canadian Centre for Justice Statistics (Statistics Canada).

Johnson, Robert A. 1987. *Ecstasy: Understanding the Psychology of Joy*. San Francisco: Harper & Row.

Johnston, Darlene. Forthcoming. *Litigating Identity: The Challenge of Aboriginality*. Vancouver: University of British Columbia Press.

Jones, Ann. 2000. *Next Time, She'll Be Dead: Battering and How to Stop It*. Rev. and updated ed. Boston: Beacon.

Juhan, Deane. 1987. *Job's Body: A Handbook of Bodywork*. Barrytown, N.Y.: Station Hill.

Kabat-Zinn, Jon. 1993, "Meditation." In *Healing and the Mind*, ed. Bill D. Moyers, Betty S. Flowers, and David Grubin. New York: Doubleday.

———. 2005. *Coming to Our Senses: Healing Ourselves and the World through Mindfulness*. New York: Hyperion.

Kahana, Tsvi. 2002. "Understanding the Notwithstanding Mechanism." *University of Toronto Law Journal* 52(2):221–274.

Kane, Robert J. 2000. "Police Responses to Restraining Orders in Domestic Violence Incidents." *Criminal Justice and Behavior* 27(5):561–580.

Kant, Immanuel. 1964. *Groundwork of the Metaphysic of Morals*. Edited by H. J. Paton. New York: Harper & Row.

Kapur, Ratna. 2005. *Erotic Justice: Law and the New Politics of Postcolonialism*. London: GlassHouse.

Kateb, George. November 1992. "Judith Shklar (1928–1992)." *CSPT Newsletter* (Conference for the Study of Political Thought).

Katherine, Anne. 1991. *Boundaries: Where You End and I Begin*. New York: Simon & Schuster.

Katz, Steven J., Karen Cardiff, Marina Pascali, Morris L. Barer, and Robert G. Evans. 2002. "Phantoms in the Snow: Canadians' Use of Health Care Services in the United States." *Health Affairs* 21(3): 19–31.

Katz, Steven J., Diana Verrilli, and Morris L. Barer. 1998. "Canadians' Use of U.S. Medical Services." *Health Affairs* 17(1):225–235.

Keen, Lisa. April 18, 2011. "Fourth Question Erupts on Prop 8." *Bay Windows*.

Keller, Catherine. 1986. *From a Broken Web: Separation, Sexism, and Self*. Boston: Beacon.

Keller, Evelyn Fox. 1983. *A Feeling for the Organism: The Life and Work of Barbara Mcclintock* New York: W. H. Freeman and Co.

Kennedy, Dawnis (Minniwaanagogiizhigook). 2007. "Reconciliation without Respect? Section 35 and Indigenous Legal Orders." In *Indigenous Legal Traditions*, ed. Law Commission of Canada. Vancouver: University of British Columbia Press.

Kennedy, Duncan. 1992. "Sexual Abuse, Sexy Dressing, and the Eroticization of Domination." *New England Law Review* 26:1309–1393.

Khan, Ummni. 2008. "A Woman's Right to Be Spanked: Testing the Limits of Tolerance of S/M in the Socio-Legal Imaginary": online <http://works.bepress.com/ummni_khan/1>.

———. 2008 "Sadomasochism Once Removed: S/M in the Socio-Legal Imaginary." S.J.D. thesis, University of Toronto.

———. August 4, 2009. "Not a Lust Story: Judicial Imaginaries of Sexual Citizenship." *SSRN eLibrary*: online <http://ssrn.com/abstract=1444065>.

————. 2009. "Putting a Dominatrix in Her Place: The Representation and Regulation of Female Dom/Male Sub Sexuality." *Canadian Journal of Women and the Law* 21(1):143–175.

Kilpatrick, Dean, and Jeanna McCauley. September 2009. "Understanding National Rape Statistics." Harrisburg, Penn.: VAWnet: online <new.vawnet.org/Assoc_Files_VAWnet/AR_RapeStatistics.pdf>.

Kinston, Rebecca, and Leonard Ferry, eds. 2008. *Bringing the Passions Back In: The Emotions in Political Philosophy*. Vancouver: University of British Columbia Press.

Kirby, Michael J. L., and Marjory LeBreton. January 2002. "The Health of Aboriginal Canadians" and "Rural Health," chapters 5 and 10 of *The Health of Canadians—The Federal Role: Interim Report, Volume Two: Current Trends and Future Challenges*. Ottawa: Standing Senate Committee on Social Affairs, Science and Technology, Parliament of Canada.

Kittay, Eva Feder. 1999. *Love's Labor: Essays on Women, Equality, and Dependency*. New York: Routledge.

Klarman, Michael. 2004. *From Jim Crow to Civil Rights: The Supreme Court and the Struggle for Racial Equality*. New York: Oxford University Press.

Koggel, Christine M. 1998. *Perspectives on Equality: Constructing a Relational Theory*. Lanham, Md.: Rowman & Littlefield.

Kompridis, Nikolas. 2006. *Critique and Disclosure: Critical Theory between Past and Future*. Abridged ed. Cambridge, Mass.: MIT Press.

Krotoszynsk, Ronald J. 2009. *The First Amendment in Cross-Cultural Perspective: A Comparative Legal Analysis of the Freedom of Speech*. New York: New York University Press.

Kumm, Mattias December 15, 2006. "What Do You Have in Virtue of Having a Constitutional Right? On the Place and Limits of the Proportionality Requirement." New York University Public Law and Legal Theory Working Papers No. 46. New York: New York University.

————. March 2009. "Democracy Is Not Enough: Rights, Proportionality and the Point of Judicial Review." New York University Public Law and Legal Theory Working Papers No. 118. New York: New York University.

Kuokkanen, Rauna. 2007. *Reshaping the University: Responsibility, Indigenous Epistemes and the Logic of the Gift*. Vancouver: University of British Columbia Press.

Kurer, Martin, Stefano Codoni, Klaus Gunther, Forge Santiago Neves, and Lawrence Teh, eds. 2002. *Warranties and Disclaimers: Limitation of Liability in Consumer-Related Transactions*. London: Kluwer Law International.

Kuypers, Joseph A. 1992. *Man's Will to Hurt: Investigating the Causes, Supports and Varieties of His Violence*. Halifax, N.S.: Fernwood.

Kymlicka, Will. 1989. *Liberalism, Community, and Culture*. Oxford: Clarendon.

————. 1995. *Multicultural Citizenship: A Liberal Theory of Minority Rights*. Oxford: Clarendon.

Lacey, Nicola. 2000. "Partial Defences to Murder: Questions of Power and Principle in Imperfect and Less Imperfect Worlds." In *Rethinking English Homicide Law*, ed. A. Ashworth and B. Mitchell. Oxford: Oxford University Press.

————. 2001. "In Search of the Responsible Subject: History, Philosophy, and Social Sciences in Criminal Law Theory." *Modern Law Review* 64(3):350–371.

————. 2008. *Women, Crime, and Character: From Moll Flanders to Tess of the D'urbervilles* New York: Oxford University Press.

Lakoff, George. 1987. *Women, Fire, and Dangerous Things: What Categories Reveal about the Mind*. Chicago: University of Chicago Press.

Lakoff, George, and Mark Johnson. 1980. *Metaphors We Live By*. Chicago: University of Chicago Press.

Lambert, L. A. (Lisa). 2006. "When Martha Met Goliath: Feminists and the State in Alberta." *Canadian Woman Studies* 25(1/2):39–44.

Langbein, Hermann. 2004. *People in Auschwitz*: Chapel Hill: University of North Carolina Press.

Langille, Brian, and Guy Davidov. 1999. "Beyond Employees and Independent Contractors: A View from Canada." *Comparative Labor Law and Policy Journal* 21(1):7–46.

Langston, Lundy. 1998. "No Penetration—And It's Still Rape." *Pepperdine Law Review* 26(1):1–36.

Lasser, Karen E., David U. Himmelstein, and Steffie Woolhandler. 2006. "Access to Care, Health Status, and Health Disparities in the United States and Canada: Results of a Cross-National Population-Based Survey." *American Journal of Public Health* 96(7)1–8.

Lauter, Estella. 1984. *Women as Mythmakers: Poetry and Visual Art by Twentieth-Century Women*. Bloomington: Indiana University Press.

Law Commission of Canada. 1999. "Minister's Reference on Institutional Child Abuse: Discussion Paper." ed. Department of Justice. Ottawa: Law Commission of Canada.

———. 2000. "Restoring Dignity: Responding to Child Abuse in Canadian Institutions." Ottawa: Law Commission of Canada.

Lawson, Sheri. 2003. "Surrendering the Night! The Seduction of Victim Blaming in Drug and Alcohol Facilitated Sexual Assault Prevention Strategies." *Women against Violence: An Australian Feminist Journal* (13):33–38.

Leckey, Robert. 2008. *Contextual Subjects: Family, State, and Relational Theory*. Toronto: University of Toronto Press.

Lee, Cynthia. 2003. *Murder and the Reasonable Man: Passion and Fear in the Criminal Courtroom*. New York: New York University Press.

Le Guin, Ursula K. 1980. *The Beginning Place*. New York: Harper & Row.

Leisenring, Amy. 2008. "Controversies Surrounding Mandatory Arrest Policies and the Police Response to Intimate Partner Violence." *Sociology Compass* 2(2):451–466.

Leonard, B. E., and A. Myint. 2009. "The Psychoneuroimmunology of Depression." *Human Psychopharmacology* 24(3):165–175.

Lessard, Hester. 1992. "Equality and Access to Justice in the Work of Bertha Wilson." *Dalhousie Law Journal* 15(1):35–64.

Lewis, C. S. 1955. *Surprised by Joy: The Shape of My Early Life*. London: G. Bles.

Lim, Joseph, Wong Yunn Chii, and Robert Kronenburg, eds. 2003. *Transportable Environments*. Vol. 2. New York: Spon.

Little, Margaret Olivia. 1995. "Seeing and Caring: The Role of Affect in Feminist Moral Epistemology." *Hypatia* 10(3):117–137.

Littrell, J. 2008. "The Mind-Body Connection: Not Just a Theory Anymore." *Social Work in Health Care* 46(4):17–37.

Lorde, Audre. 1984. "The Master's Tools Will Never Dismantle the Master's House"; "Poetry Is Not a Luxury"; "The Uses of Anger: Women Responding to Racism"; and "Uses of the Erotic: The Erotic as Power." All in *Sister Outsider: Essays & Speeches by Audre Lorde. Berkeley*, Calif.: Crossing.

Lowi, Theodore J. 1979. *The End of Liberalism: The Second Republic of the United States*. 2d ed. New York: Norton.

Macaulay, Stewart. 1985. "An Empirical View of Contract." 1985 *Wisconsin Law Review* 465–482.

MacDonald, Michael. 2006. *Why Race Matters in South Africa*. Cambridge, Mass.: Harvard University Press.

MacIntyre, Alasdair C. 1981. *After Virtue: A Study in Moral Theory*. Notre Dame, Ind.: University of Notre Dame Press.

———. 1999. *Dependent Rational Animals: Why Human Beings Need the Virtues (the Paul Carus Lectures)*. Peru, Ill.: Open Court.

Mackay, R. D. 1995. *Mental Condition Defences in the Criminal Law*. Oxford: Clarendon.

Mackenzie, Catriona, and Natalie Stoljar, eds. 2000. *Relational Autonomy: Feminist Perspectives on Autonomy, Agency, and the Social Self*. New York: Oxford University Press.

MacKinnon, Catharine A. 1983. "Feminism, Marxism, Method, and the State: Toward Feminist Jurisprudence." *Signs* 8(4):635–658.

———. 1987. *Feminism Unmodified: Discourses on Life and Law*. Cambridge, Mass.: Harvard University Press.

Macklin, Audrey. 2007. "Who Is the Citizen's Other? Considering the Heft of Citizenship." *Theoretical Inquiries in Law* 8:333–366.

Macneil, Ian R. 1985. "Relational Contract: What We Do and Do Not Know." 1985 *Wisconsin Law Review* 483–525.

Macy, Joanna. 1988. "Taking Heart: Exercises for Social Activists." In *The Path of Compassion: Writings on Socially Engaged Buddhism*, ed. F. Eppsteiner. Berkeley, Calif.: Parallax.

Madison, James. November 22, 1787. "The Federalist No. 10: The Utility of the Union as a Safeguard against Domestic Faction and Insurrection (continued)." *Daily Advertiser*.

Mahoney, Martha R. 1991. "Legal Images of Battered Women: Redefining the Issue of Separation." *Michigan Law Review* 90(1):1–94.

Maidment, MaDonna. 2010. *When Justice Is a Game: Unravelling Wrongful Convictions in Canada*. Halifax, N.S.: Fernwood.

Mansbridge, Jane. 2005 "Cracking through Hegemonic Ideology: The Logic of Formal Justice." *Social Justice Research* 18(3):335–347.

Marcus, Paul. 1999. *Autonomy in the Extreme Situation: Bruno Bettelheim, the Nazi Concentration Camps, and the Mass Society*. Westport, Conn.: Praeger.

Mashaw, Jerry L. 1983. "'Rights' In the Federal Administrative State." *Yale Law Journal* 92(7):1129–1173.

Mason, Robin, and Rosana Pellizzari. 2006. "Guidelines, Policies, Education and Coordination: Better Practices for Addressing Violence against Women." *Canadian Woman Studies* 25(1/2):20–25.

McIntyre, Sheila. 2002. "Feminist Movement in Law: Beyond Privileged and Privileging Theory." In *Women's Legal Strategies in Canada*, ed. R. Jhappan. Toronto: University of Toronto Press.

McKee, Heather. [n.d.]. "Bodily Suffering and Women with Disabilities: A Feminist Theory of Disability." Unpublished manuscript. Available from the author.

McLeod, Carolyn. Forthcoming. "A Feminist Relational Perspective on Conscience." In *Being Relational: Reflections on Relational Theory and Health Law and Policy*, ed. J. Downie and J. Llewellyn. Vancouver: University of British Columbia Press.

Mehra, Natalie. October 6, 2008. "Eroding Public Medicare: Lessons and Consequences of for For-Profit Health Care across Canada." Toronto: Ontario Health Coalition.

Melzer, Scott A. 2002. "Gender, Work, and Intimate Violence: Men's Occupational Violence Spillover and Compensatory Violence." *Journal of Marriage and the Family* 64(4):820–832.

Merry, Sally Engle. 2003. "Rights Talk and the Experience of Law: Implementing Women's Human Rights to Protection from Violence." *Human Rights Quarterly* 25(2):343–381.

Meyers, Diana T. 1989. *Self, Society, and Personal Choice*. New York: Columbia University Press.

———. 1994. *Subjection and Subjectivity: Psychoanalytic Feminism and Moral Philosophy*. New York: Routledge.

———. 1997. *Feminists Rethink the Self*. Boulder, Colo.: Westview.

Michelman, Frank. 1988. "Law's Republic." *Yale Law Journal* 97(8):1493–1538.

———. 1999. *Brennan and Democracy*. Princeton, N.J.: Princeton University Press.

———. 2003. "Rawls on Constitutionalism and Constitutional Law." In *The Cambridge Companion to Rawls*, ed. S. Freedman. Cambridge: Cambridge University Press.

Mill, John Stuart. 1869. *On Liberty*. 4th ed. London: Longman, Roberts & Green.

Minow, Martha L. 1987. "Part of the Solution, Part of the Problem: Review of Joel Handler, *The Conditions of Discretion*." *UCLA Law Review* 34(3):981.

———. 1988. "Feminist Reason: Getting It and Losing It." *Journal of Legal Education* 38:47.

———. 1990. *Making All the Difference: Inclusion, Exclusion, and American Law*. Ithaca, N.Y.: Cornell University Press.

Monahan, Patrick. 1987. *Politics and the Constitution: The Charter, Federalism, and the Supreme Court of Canada*. Toronto: Carswell.

Monture, Patricia. 1999. *Journeying Forward: Dreaming First Nations Independence*. Halifax, N.S.: Fernwood.

Moore, Joan. 1996. "Bearing the Burden: How Incarceration Weakens Inner-City Communities." In *The Unintended Consequences of Incarceration*, compilation of papers commissioned for the conference "The Unintended Consequences of Incarceration," held at Arden House in Harriman, New York, in June 1995. New York: Vera Institute of Justice.

Moran, Mayo. 2003. *Rethinking the Reasonable Person: An Egalitarian Reconstruction of the Objective Standard*. Oxford: Oxford University Press.

Morgan, Robin. 1977. *Going Too Far: The Personal Chronicle of a Feminist*. New York: Random House.

Mosher, Janet, Patricia Evans, Margaret Little, Eileen Morrow, Jo-Anne Boulding, and Nancy VanderPlaats. April 5, 2004. "Walking on Eggshells: Abused Women's Experiences of Ontario's Welfare System." Final Report of Research Findings from the Woman and Abuse Welfare Research Project: online <www.yorku.ca/yorkweb/special/Welfare_Report_walking_on_eggshells_final_report.pdf>.

Mousourakis, George. 2007. "Reason, Passion and Self Control: Understanding the Moral Basis of the Provocation Defence." *Revue de droit de l'Université de Sherbrooke* 38:115–126.

Mulcahy, Linda. 2008. *Contract Law in Perspective*. 5th ed. New York: Routledge.

Mullan, David. 2001. *Administrative Law*. Toronto: Irwin Law.

Murray MacAdam, Jamie Swift, and Brice Balmer, eds. 2007. *Lives Still in the Balance: Ontario's Social Audit*. 2nd ed. Kitchener, Ont.: Interfaith Social Assistance Reform Coalition.

Napolean, Val. 2005. "Aboriginal Self Determination: Individual Self and Collective Selves." *Atlantis: A Women's Studies Journal* 29(2):31–46.

———. 2009. "Living Together: Gitksan Legal Reasoning as a Foundation for Consent." In *Challenges of Consent: Consent as the Foundation of Political Community in Indigenous/*

Non-Indigenous Contexts, ed. J. Webber and C. McLeod. Vancouver: University of British Columbia Press.

———. 2009. "Looking Beyond the Law—Questions about Indigenous Peoples' Tangible and Intangible Property." In *Protection of First Nations Cultural Heritage: Laws, Policy, and Reform*, ed. C. Bell and R. K. Paterson (companion volume to *First Nations Cultural Heritage and Law: Case Studies, Voices, and Perspectives*, ed. C. Bell and V. Napoleon). Vancouver: University of British Columbia Press.

Nedelsky, Jennifer. 1981. "Judicial Conservatism in an Age of Innovation: Comparative Perspectives on Canadian Nuisance Law, 1890–1930." In *Essays in Canadian Legal History*, ed. D. Flaherty. Toronto: University of Toronto Press.

———. 1982. "Review: Confining Democratic Politics: Anti-Federalists, Federalists, and the Constitution." *Harvard Law Review* 96(1):340–360.

———. 1988. "American Constitutionalism and the Paradox of Private Property." In *Constitutionalism and Democracy*, ed. J. Elster and R. Slagstad. Cambridge and Paris: Cambridge University Press and Maison des sciences de l'homme.

———. 1988. "Economic Liberties and the Foundations of American Constitutionalism: The Federalist Perspective." In *To Secure the Blessings of Liberty: First Principles of the Constitution*, ed. S. B. Thurow. Lanham, Md.: University Press of America.

———. 1989. "Reconceiving Autonomy: Sources, Thoughts, and Possibilities." *Yale Journal of Law and Feminism* 1:7–36.

———. 1990. *Private Property and the Limits of American Constitutionalism: The Madisonian Framework and Its Legacy*. Chicago: University of Chicago Press.

———. 1991. "The Challenges of Multiplicity." Review of Elizabeth V. Spelman, *Inessential Woman: Problems of Exclusion in Feminist Thought* (1988). *Michigan Law Review* 89(6):1591–1609.

———. 1993. "The Practical Possibilities of Feminist Theory." *Northwestern Law Review* 87(4):1286–1301.

———. 1993. "Property in Potential Life? A Relational Approach to Choosing Legal Categories." *Canadian Journal of Law and Jurisprudence* 6(2):343–365.

———. 1993. "Reconceiving Rights as Relationship." *Review of Constitutional Studies/Revue d' études constitutionnelles* 1:1–26.

———. 1994. "The Puzzle and Demands of Modern Constitutionalism." *Ethics* 105:500.

———. 1996. "Should Property Be Constitutionalized? A Relational and Comparative Approach." In *Property Law on the Threshold of the 21st Century: Proceedings of an International Colloquium "Property Law on the Threshold of the 21st Century," 28–30 August 1995, Maastricht*, ed. G. v. Maanen and A. J. Van der Walt. Apeldoorn, Netherlands: Maklu.

———. 1997. "Embodied Diversity and the Challenges to Law." *McGill Law Journal* 42(1):91–118.

———. 1999. "Dilemmas of Passion, Privilege and Isolation: Reflections on Mothering in a White, Middle Class Nuclear Family." In *Mother Troubles: Rethinking Contemporary Maternal Dilemmas*, ed. J. Hanigsberg and S. Ruddick. Boston: Beacon.

———. 2000. "Communities of Judgment and Human Rights." *Theoretical Inquires in Law* 1:245–282.

———. 2001. "Judgment, Diversity, and Relational Autonomy." In *Judgment, Imagination and Politics: Themes from Kant and Arendt*, ed. R. Beiner and J. Nedelsky. Lanham, Md.: Rowman & Littlefield.

———. 2010. "Feminist Constitutionalism: Through the Lens of Gendered Division of Household Labor." In *Feminist Constitutionalism*, ed. D. Barak Erez, B. Baines, and T. Kahana. Cambridge: Cambridge University Press.

———. Forthcoming. "Judgment and Autonomy: The Reciprocal Relation." In *Being Relational: Reflections on Relational Theory and Health Law and Policy*, ed. J. Downie and J. Llewellyn. Vancouver: University of British Columbia Press.

Nedelsky, Jennifer, and Craig Scott. 1992. "Constitutional Dialogue." In *Social Justice and the Constitution: Perspectives on a Social Union for Canada*, ed. J. Bakan, D. Schneiderman, and University of Alberta Centre for Constitutional Studies. Ottawa: Carleton University Press.

Noddings, Nel. 1989. *Women and Evil*. Berkeley: University of California Press.

Novick, Peter. 1999. *The Holocaust in American Life*. New York: Houghton Mifflin.

Nussbaum, Martha C. 2000. *Women and Human Development: The Capabilities Approach*. Cambridge: Cambridge University Press.

———. 2006. *Frontiers of Justice: Disability, Nationality, Species Membership*. Cambridge, Mass.: Harvard University Press.

Nwosu, L. Ngozi. 2006. "The Experience of Domestic Violence among Nigerian-Canadian Women in Toronto." *Canadian Woman Studies* 25(1/2):99–106.

Obama, Barack. March 18, 2008. "A More Perfect Union." Speech given at Constitution Center, Philadelphia.

O'Donovan, Katherine. 1997. "With Sense, Consent, or Just a Con." In *Sexing the Subject of Law*, ed. N. Naffine and R. J. Owens. North Ryde, N.S.W.: LBC Information Services.

Pally, Regina. 1998. "Emotional Processing: The Mind-Body Connection." *International Journal of Psychoanalysis* 79:349–362.

Pawelczynska, Anna. 1979. *Values and Violence in Auschwitz*. Los Angeles: University of California Press.

Pawlowski, Mark, and James Brown. 2001. *Undue Influence in the Family Home*. London: Cavendish.

Perry, Bruce D. 1996. "Neurodevelopmental Adaptations to Violence: How Children Survive the Intergenerational Vortex of Violence." In *Violence and Childhood Trauma: Understanding and Responding to the Effects of Violence on Young Children*. Cleveland, Ohio: Gund Foundation.

Perry, Bruce D., and Ishnella Azad. Aug 1999. "Posttraumatic Stress Disorders in Children and Adolescents." *Current Opinion in Pediatrics* 11(4):310–316.

Pert, Candace B. 1997. *Molecules of Emotion: The Science behind Mind-Body Medicine*. New York: Touchstone.

Peterman, Linda M., and Charlotte G. Dixon. 2003. "Intimate Partner Abuse between Same-Sex Partners: Implications for Counseling." *Journal of Counseling & Development* 81(1):40–47.

Petter, Andrew. 2010. *The Politics of the Charter: The Illusive Promise of Constitutional Rights*. Toronto: University of Toronto Press.

Pierce, Tamora. 2004. *The Song of the Lioness Quartet*. New York: Scholastic.

Pham, Michael Tuan. 2007. "Emotion and Rationality: A Critical Review and Interpretation of Empirical Evidence." *Review of General Psychology* 11(2):155.

Phillips, Susan D. 2002. "Legal as Political Strategies in the Canadian Women's Movement: Who's Speaking, Who's Listening?" In *Women's Legal Strategies in Canada*, ed. R. Jhappan. Toronto: University of Toronto Press.

Plotkin, Diane M., and Roger A. Ritvo. 1998. *Sisters in Sorrow: Voices of Care in the Holocaust*. College Station: Texas A & M University Press.

Pocock, J. G. A. 1971. *Politics, Language, and Time; Essays on Political Thought and History*. New York: Atheneum.

Pogge, Thomas. 2008. *World Poverty and Human Rights: Cosmopolitan Responsibilities and Reforms*. 2d ed. Cambridge: Polity.

———. 2009. *Politics as Usual: What Lies behind the Pro-Poor Rhetoric*. Cambridge: Polity.

Pollack, Shoshana. 2003. "Focus Group Methodology in Research with Incarcerated Women: Race, Power, and Collective Experience." *Affilia* 18(4):461–472.

———. 2004. "Anti-Oppressive Social Work Practice with Women in Prison: Discursive Reconstructions and Alternative Practices." *British Journal of Social Work* 34(5):693–707.

Porter, Bruce, and Martha Jackman. 2008. "Justiciability of Social and Economic Rights in Canada." In *Socio-Economic Rights Jurisprudence: Emerging Trends in Comparative International Law*, ed. M. Langford. Cambridge: Cambridge University Press.

Posner, Richard, and Katharine Silbaug. 1996. *A Guide to America's Sex Laws*. Chicago: University of Chicago Press.

Post, Robert C. 1989. "The Social Foundations of Privacy: Community and Self in the Common Law Tort." *California Law Review* 77(5):957–1010.

Putnam, William H. 2003. *Legal Research, Analysis, and Writing*. Clifton, N.Y.: Delmar.

Radin, Margaret Jane. 1996. *Contested Commodities: The Trouble with Trade in Sex, Children, Body Parts, and Other Things* Cambridge, Mass.: Harvard University Press.

Radosh, Polly F. 2008. "War on Drugs: Gender and Race Inequities in Crime Control Strategies." *Criminal Justice Studies* 21(2):167–178.

Rasmussen, Larry. 1999. "Human Environmental Rights and/or Biotic Rights." In *Religion and Human Rights*, ed. P. Juviler and C. Gustafson. New York: M. E. Sharpe.

Rawls, John. 1993. *Political Liberalism*. New York: Columbia University Press.

———. 1999. *The Law of Peoples: With "The Idea of Public Reason Revisited."* Cambridge, Mass.: Harvard University Press.

———. 1999. *Theory of Justice*. 2d ed. Oxford: Oxford University Press.

Raz, Joseph. 1986. *The Morality of Freedom*. Oxford: Clarendon.

———. 1994. *Ethics in the Public Domain: Essays in the Morality of Law and Politics*. Rev. ed. Oxford: Oxford University Press.

Razack, Sherene. 1992. "The Cold Game of Equality Staring." *Critical Criminology* 4(1):1–12.

———. 2002. "The Women's Legal Education and Action Fund." In *Law, Politics, and the Judicial Process in Canada*, ed. F. L. Morton. Calgary: University of Calgary Press.

Read, Don, and Walt Stoll. 2010. "Healthy Behavior: The Implications of a Holistic Paradigm Thinking through Bodymind Research." In *Philosophical Foundations of Health Education*, ed. J. M. Black, S. R. Furney and H. M. Graf. San Francisco: Jossey-Bass.

Reich, Charles A. 1964. "The New Property." *Yale Law Journal* 73(5):733–787.

Rennison, C. 2003. "Intimate Partner Violence, 1993–2001: Crime Data Brief." Washington, D.C.: Bureau of Justice Statistics, U.S. Department of Justice.

Rennison, Callie Marie, and Sarah Welchans. 2000. *Intimate Partner Violence*. Special Report. Washington, D.C.: Bureau of Justice Statistics, U.S. Department of Justice.

Resnik, Judith. 2002. "Reconstructing Equality: Of Justice, Justicia, and the Gender of Jurisdiction." *Yale Journal of Law and Feminism* 14:393–418.

Rich, Adrienne Cecile. 1986. *Of Woman Born: Motherhood as Experience and Institution*. 10th anniversary ed. New York: Norton.

Rilke, Rainer Maria. 1981. *Selected Poems of Rainer Maria Rilke*. Translated by Robert Bly. New York: Harper & Row.

Rittich, Kerry. 2002. *Recharacterizing Restructuring: Law, Distribution, and Gender in Market Reform*. Boston: Kluwer.

Roach, Kent. 2001. *The Supreme Court on Trial: Judicial Activism or Democratic Dialogue*. Toronto: Irwin Law.

Robbers, Gerhard. 1998. *An Introduction to German Law*. 1. Aufl. ed. Baden-Baden: Nomos.

Romanow, Roy J. November 2002. "Rural and Remote Communities" and "A New Approach to Aboriginal Health," chapters 7 and 10 of *Building on Values: The Future of Health Care in Canada—Final Report*. Ottawa: Commission on the Future of Health Care in Canada (Romanow Commission).

Römkens, Renée. 2001. "Law as Trojan Horse: Unintended Consequences of Right-Based Interventions to Support Battered Women." *Yale Journal of Law and Feminism* 13(2):265–290.

Rosenberg, Gerald N. 1993. *The Hollow Hope: Can Courts Bring about Social Change?* Chicago: University of Chicago.

Royal Commission on Aboriginal Peoples Canada. 1996. *Report of the Royal Commission on Aboriginal Peoples*: online <www.collectionscanada.gc.ca/webarchives/20071115053257/http://www.ainc-inac.gc.ca/ch/rcap/sg/sgmm_e.html>.

Royal Commission on the Donald Marshall Jr. Prosecution. 1989. "Digest of Findings and Recommendations." Halifax: Province of Nova Scotia.

Ruddick, Sara. 1989. *Maternal Thinking: Toward a Politics of Peace*. New York: Ballantine Books.

Sampson, Rana. 2007. "The Problem of Domestic Violence." Problem-Oriented Guides for Police, Problem-Specific Guides Series. Guide No. 45. Washington D.C.: Center for Problem-Oriented Policing.

Sandel, Michael J. 1982. *Liberalism and the Limits of Justice*. Cambridge: Cambridge University Press.

———. 1984. *Liberalism and Its Critics*. New York: New York University Press.

Scales, Ann C. 1986. "The Emergence of Feminist Jurisprudence: An Essay." *Yale Law Journal* 95(7):1373–1403.

Schauer, Frederick. 2004. "The Boundaries of the First Amendment: A Preliminary Exploration of Constitutional Salience." *Harvard Law Review* 117(6):1765–1809.

Schechter, Susan, and Lisa Klee Mihaly. November 1992. "Ending Violence against Women and Children in Massachusetts Families: Critical Steps for the Next Five Years." Boston: Massachusetts Coalition for Battered Women Service Groups.

Scheiber, Harry N. 1973. "Property Law, Expropriation, and Resource Allocation by Government: The United States, 1789–1910." *Journal of Economic History* 33(1):232–251.

Scheppele, Kim. 1992. "Just the Facts, Ma'am: Sexualized Violence, Evidentiary Habits, and the Revision of Truth." *New York Law School Law Review* 37:123–172.

Schlegel, Stuart A. 1998. *Wisdom from a Rainforest: The Spiritual Journey of an Anthropologist*. Athens: University of Georgia Press.

Schneider, Elizabeth M. 1986. "Describing and Changing: Women's Self-Defense Work and the Problem of Expert Testimony on Battering." *Women's Rights Law Reporter* 9:195–222.

Schor, Miguel. 2008. "Mapping Comparative Judicial Review." *Washington University Global Studies Law Review* 7:257–287.

Schwartz, Jennifer. 2008. "Gender Differences in Drunk Driving Prevalence Rates and Trends: A 20-Year Assessment Using Multiple Sources of Evidence." *Addictive Behaviours* 33(9):1217–1222.

Scott, Kyle. 2007. *Dismantling American Common Law: Liberty and Justice in Our Transformed Courts*. Lanham, Md.: Lexington Books.

Shaffer, Martha. 1992. "*R. v. Seaboyer and Gayme*: A Case Comment." *Canadian Journal of Women and the Law* 5:202.

Shaner, David Edward. 1985. *The Bodymind Experience in Japanese Buddhism: A Phenomenological Study of Kukai and Dogen*. Albany: State University of New York Press.

Shanley, Mary Lynn. 2009. "The Right to a Parent-Child Relationship." Paper presented at the 2009 Annual Meeting and Exhibition of the American Political Science Association, Toronto, September 3–6.

Sherwin, Susan. 1998. *The Politics of Women's Health: Exploring Agency and Autonomy*. Philadelphia: Temple University Press.

Shklar, Judith. 1984. *Ordinary Vices*. Cambridge, Mass.: Harvard University Press.

———. 1989. "The Liberalism of Fear." In *Liberalism and the Moral Life*, ed. N. L. Rosenblum. Cambridge, Mass.: Harvard University Press.

Sidel, Ruth. 1992. *Women and Children Last: The Plight of Poor Women in Affluent America*. New York: Penguin Books.

Siegel, Reva B. 1996. "'The Rule of Love': Wife Beating as Prerogative and Privacy." *Yale Law Journal* 105(8):2117–2207.

Simpson, A. W. B. 1987. "The Common Law and Legal Theory." In *Legal Theory and Legal History: Essays on the Common Law*, ed. A. W. B. Simpson. London: Hambledon.

Simpson, Leanne. Fall 2008. "Looking after Gdoo-Naaganinaa: Precolonial Nishhaabeg Diplomatic and Treaty Relationships." *Wicazo Sa Review* 23(2):29–42.

Singer, Joseph William. 1988. "The Reliance Interest in Property." *Stanford Law Review* 40(3):611–751.

———. 2000. *Entitlement: The Paradoxes of Property*. New Haven, Conn.: Yale University Press.

———. 2007. "Normative Methods for Lawyers." *UCLA Law Review* 56(2008–2009): 899–982.

Singer, Peter. 1993. *Practical Ethics*. 2d ed. Cambridge: Cambridge University Press.

Smiley, Jane. 1991. *A Thousand Acres*. New York: Knopf.

Smith, Rogers. 1997. *Civic Ideals: Conflicting Visions of Citizenship in U.S. History*. New Haven, Conn.: Yale University Press.

Smoke, Stephen. 1996. *The Bill of Rights and Responsibilities*. Los Angeles: General Publishing Group.

Sontag, Susan. 1978 and 1988. *Illness as Metaphor and Aids and Its Metaphors*. New York: Picador.

Sossin, Lorne. 2002. "An Intimate Approach to Fairness, Impartiality and Reasonableness in Administrative Law." *Queen's Law Journal* 27(2):809–858.

Specter, Russell, and Paul J. Spiegelman. 2008. "Employment Discrimination Action under Federal Civil Rights Acts." *American Jurisprudence Trials* 21:1–229.

Spelman, Elizabeth V. 1988. *Inessential Woman: Problems of Exclusion in Feminist Thought*. Boston: Beacon.

Spohn, Cassia, and Jeffrey Spears. 1996. "The Effect of Offender and Victim Characteristics on Sexual Assault Case Processing Decisions." *Justice Quarterly* 13(4):649–679.

Stanko, Elizabeth A. 1988. "Fear of Crime and the Myth of the Safe Home: A Feminist Critique of Criminology." In *Feminist Perspectives on Wife Abuse*, ed. K. Yllö and M. L. Bograd. Newbury Park, Calif.: Sage.

Starhawk. 1979. *The Spiral Dance: A Rebirth of the Ancient Religion of the Great Goddess*. San Francisco: Harper & Row.

———. 1982. *Dreaming the Dark: Magic, Sex, & Politics*. Boston: Beacon.

———. 1987. *Truth or Dare: Encounters with Power, Authority, and Mystery*. San Francisco: Harper & Row.

Stark, Evan. 1992. "Framing and Reframing Battered Women." In *Domestic Violence: The Changing Criminal Justice Response*, ed. E. S. Buzawa and C. G. Buzawa. Westport, Conn.: Auburn House.

———. 2007. *Coercive Control: How Men Entrap Women in Personal Life*. New York: Oxford University Press.

Steinbrook, Robert. 2006. "Private Health Care in Canada." *New England Journal of Medicine* 354(No. 16):1661–1664.

Stern, Daniel N. 1985. *The Interpersonal World of the Infant: A View from Psychoanalysis and Developmental Psychology*. New York: Basic Books.

Stoddard, J. J., J. L Hargraves, M. Reed, and A. Vratil. 2001. "Managed Care, Professional Autonomy, and Income." *Journal of General Internal Medicine* 16(10):675–684.

Storing, Herbert. 1981. "The Aristocratic Tendency of the Constitution." In *What the Anti-Federalists Were For: The Political Thought of the Opponents of the Constitution*. Chicago: University of Chicago Press.

———. 1995. "The Constitution and the Bill of Rights." In *Toward a More Perfect Union: Writings of Herbert J. Storing*, ed. J. M. Bessette. Washington, D.C.: American Enterprise Institute for Public Policy Research.

Stuart, Don. 1993. "The Pendulum Has Been Pushed Too Far: The Effects of Bill C-49." *University of New Brunswick Law Journal* 42:349–372.

Sugunasiri, Shalin M. 1999. "Contextualism: The Supreme Court's New Standard of Judicial Analysis and Accountability." *Dalhousie Law Journal* 22:126–184.

Sullivan, Sherry E. 1999. "The Changing Nature of Careers: A Review and Research Agenda." *Journal of Management* 25(3):457–484.

Sunstein, Cass R. 2001. "Sex Equality versus Religion." In *Designing Democracy: What Constitutions Do*. New York: Oxford University Press.

Taylor, Charles. 1985. *Philosophy and the Human Sciences*. Cambridge: Cambridge University Press.

———. 1987. *Justice after Virtue*. Toronto: Faculty of Law, University of Toronto.

———. 1994. "The Politics of Recognition." In *Multiculturalism and the Politics of Recognition*, ed. A. Guttman. Princeton, N.J.: Princeton University Press.

Terr, Lenore. 1990. *Too Scared to Cry: Psychic Trauma in Childhood*. New York: Harper & Row.

The Holy Bible, New International Version. Book of Job.

Theodore, Terri. August 14, 2008. "BC Says No to Allowing Babies in Jail": online <http://www.thestar.com/News/Canada/article/478147>.

Thiele, Leslie Paul. Forthcoming. *Indra's Net and the Midas Touch: Sustainable Living in a Connected World*. Cambridge, Mass.: MIT Press.

Tjaden, Patricia Godeke, and Nancy Thoennes. July 2000. "Extent, Nature, and Consequences of Intimate Partner Violence: Findings from the National Violence against Women Survey." Washington, D.C.: Office of Justice Programs, U.S. Department of Justice.

———. November 2000. "Full Report of the Prevalence, Incidence, and Consequences of Violence against Women: Findings from the National Violence against Women Survey." Washington, D.C.: Office of Justice Programs, U.S. Department of Justice.

Tocqueville, Alexis de. 2004. *Democracy in America*. Translated by Arthur Goldhammer. New York: Library of America.

Tong, Rosemarie. 1984. *Women, Sex, and the Law*. Totowa, N.J.: Rowman & Allanheld.

Tough, Paul. March 21, 2011. "The Poverty Clinic: Can a Stressful Childhood Make You a Sick Adult?" *New Yorker*.

Trainor, Catherine, and Karen Mihorean, eds. 2001. "Family Violence in Canada: A Statistical Profile 2001." 2001. Ottawa: Canadian Centre for Justice Statistics (Statistics Canada).

Tribe, Laurence H. 1988. *American Constitutional Law*. 2nd ed. Mineola, N.Y.: Foundation.

Trindade, Antonio Augusto Cançado. 2000. "The Inter-American Court of Human Rights at a Crossroads: Current Challenges and Its Emerging Case-Law on the Eve of the New Century." In *Protection Des Droits De L'homme: La Perspective Européenne—Mélanges À La Mémoire De Rolv Ryssdal*, ed. P. Mahoney, F. Matscher, H. Petzold, and L. Wildhaber. Köln/Berlin: C. Heymanns Verlag.

Trocmé, Nico, Barbara Fallon, Bruce MacLaurin, Joanne Daciuk, Caroline Felstiner, Tara Black, Lil Tonmyr, Cindy Blackstock, Ken Barter, Daniel Turcotte, and Richard Cloutier. 2005. "Canadian Incidence Study of Reported Child Abuse and Neglect—2003: Major Findings." Ottawa: Minister of Public Works and Government Services Canada.

Tronto, Joan C. 1993. *Moral Boundaries: A Political Argument for an Ethic of Care*. New York: Routledge.

Tully, James. July 2010 "Public Philosophy and Civic Freedom: A Guide to the Two Volumes" of *Public Philosophy in a New Key*: online <ebooks.cambridge.org/chapter.jsf?bid=CBO978051 1790737&cid=CBO9780511790737A008>.

Trovato, Frank. January 2001 "Aboriginal Mortality in Canada, the United States and New Zealand." *Journal of Biosocial Science* 33(1):67–86.

Tuohy, Carolyn. 1999. *Accidental Logics: The Dynamics of Change in the Health Care Arena in the United States, Britain, and Canada*. New York: Oxford University Press.

Turner, Dale A. 2006. *This Is Not a Peace Pipe: Towards a Critical Indigenous Philosophy*. Toronto: University of Toronto Press.

Turpel, Mary Ellen. 1989. "Aboriginal Peoples and the Canadian Charter: Interpretive Monopolies, Cultural Differences." *Canadian Human Rights Yearbook* 6:3–46.

Tushnet, Mark. 1993. "The Critique of Rights." *SMU Law Review* 47(1):23–36.

———. 2002. "Judicial Activism or Restraint in a Section 33 World." *University of Toronto Law Review* 52(1):89–100.

———. 2003. "The Issue of State Action/Horizontal Effect in Comparative Constitutional Law." *International Journal of Constitutional Law* 1(1):79–98.

———. March 26, 2009. "Against Judicial Review." Harvard Law School Public Law & Legal Theory Working Paper Series No. 09–20: online <http://ssrn.com/abstract=1368857>.

Tyagi, Smita Vir. 2006. "Victimization, Adversity and Survival in the Lives of Women Offenders: Implications for Social Policy and Correctional Practice." *Canadian Woman Studies* 25(1/2):133–138.

Underkuffler, Laura S. 1991. "The Perfidy of Property." *Texas Law Review* 70(1):293–316.

U.S. Department of Health and Human Services, Administration for Children, Youth, and Families. 2008. "Child Maltreatment 2006." Washington, D.C.: U.S. Government Printing Office.

Vanover, Amie L. 2000. "*Williams v. General Motors Corporation*: Giving Sexual Harassment Plaintiffs a Chance." *Ohio State Law Journal* 61:1559–1596.

Vendler, Helen. 1995. *The Given and the Made: Strategies of Poetic Redefinition*. Cambridge, Mass.: Harvard University Press.

Violence Policy Center. 2004. "When Men Murder Women: An Analysis of 2002 Homicide Data." Washington D.C.: Violence Policy Center.

Waddams, S. M. 2004. *Introduction to the Study of Law*. 6th ed. Toronto: Thomson Carswell.

———. 2005. *The Law of Contracts*. 5th ed. Toronto: Canada Law Book Inc.

Wahrman, Dror. 2004. *The Making of the Modern Self: Identity and Culture in Eighteenth-Century England*. New Haven, Conn.: Yale University Press.

Wait Times Alliance. June 18, 2009. "Unfinished Business: A Report Card on Wait Times in Canada." Wait Times Alliance: online <www.waittimealliance.ca/publications.htm>.

Waldron, Jeremy. 2006. "The Core of the Case against Judicial Review." *Yale Law Journal* 115(6):1346–1406.

Walker, Lenore E. 1986. "A Response to Elizabeth M/Schneider's 'Describing and Changing: Women's Self-Defense Work and the Problem of Expert Testimony on Battering.'" *Women's Rights Law Reporter* 9:223–225.

———. 2009. *The Battered Woman Syndrome*. 3rd ed. New York: Springer.

Walker, Margaret Urban. 1998. *Moral Understandings: A Feminist Study in Ethics*. New York: Routledge.

———. 2003. *Moral Contexts*. Lanham, Md.: Rowman & Littlefield.

Walker, Neil. 2007. "Post-Constituent Constitutionalism? The Case of the European Union." In *The Paradox of Constitutionalism: Constituent Power and Constitutional Form*, ed. M. Loughlin and N. Walker. Oxford: Oxford University Press.

Walzer, Michael. 1983. *Spheres of Justice: A Defense of Pluralism and Equality*. New York: Basic Books.

Warren, Karen, ed. 1997. *Ecofeminism: Women, Culture, Nature*. Bloomington: Indiana University Press.

———, ed. 2000. *Ecofeminist Philosophy: A Western Perspective on What It Is and Why It Matters*. Lanham, Md.: Rowman & Littlefield.

Weil, Alan, and Kenneth Finegold, eds. 2002. *Welfare Reform: The Next Act*. Washington, D.C.: Urban Institute Press.

Weinrib, Lorraine, and E. J. Weinrib. 2002. "Constitutional Values and Private Law in Canada." In *Constitutional Rights in Private Law*, ed. D. Bazak-Erez and D. Friedmann. Oxford: Hart.

Weir, Allison. 1996. *Sacrificial Logics: Feminist Theory and the Critique of Identity*. New York: Routledge.

———. 2005. "The Global Caregiver: Imagining Women's Liberation in the New Millennium." *Constellations* 12(3):308–330.

Weiser, Irit. 1993. "Sexual Assault Legislation: The Balancing Act." *University of New Brunswick Law Journal* 42:213–222.

Weiss, Penny A., and Marilyn Friedman, eds. 1995. *Feminism and Community*. Philadelphia: Temple University Press.

Wendell, Susan. 1989. "Toward a Feminist Theory of Disability." *Hypatia* 4(2):104–124.

———. 1993. "Feminism, Disability, and Transcendence of the Body." *Canadian Woman Studies* 13(4):116–122.

———. 1996. *The Rejected Body: Feminist Philosophical Reflections on Disability*. New York: Routledge.

West, Robin. 1988. "Jurisprudence and Gender." *University of Chicago Law Review* 55(1):1–72.

White, James Boyd. 2006. *Living Speech: Resisting the Empire of Force*. Princeton, N.J.: Princeton University Press.

White, Julie Ann. 2000. *Democracy, Justice, and the Welfare State: Reconstructing Public Care*. University Park: Pennsylvania State University Press.

White, Julie A., and Joan C. Tronto. December 2004. "Political Practices of Care: Needs and Rights." *Ratio Juris* 17(4):425–453.

Whitehead, Alfred North. 1929. *Process and Reality: An Essay in Cosmology*. Cambridge: Cambridge University Press.

White-Mair, Kimberley. 2000. "Experts and Ordinary Men: Locating *R. v. Lavallee*, Battered Women Syndrome, and the 'New' Psychiatric Expertise on Women within Canadian Legal History." *Canadian Journal of Women and the Law* 12(2):406–438.

Whitfield, Charles L. 1993. *Boundaries and Relationships: Knowing, Protecting, and Enjoying the Self*. Deerfield Beach, Fla.: Health Communications Inc.

Willard, Gaylin, and Bruce Jennings. 1996. *The Perversion of Autonomy: The Proper Uses of Coercion and Constraints in a Liberal Society*. New York: Free Press.

Williams, Patricia J. 1991. *The Alchemy of Race and Rights*. Cambridge, Mass.: Harvard University Press.

Williams, Susan. 2004. *Truth, Autonomy, and Speech: Feminist Theory and the First Amendment*. New York: New York University Press.

Williams, Toni. 2001. "Racism in Justice: The Report of the Commission on Systemic Racism in the Ontario Criminal Justice System." In *(Ab)Using Power: The Canadian Experience*, ed. S. C. Boyd, D. E. Chunn and R. Menzies. Halifax, N.S.: Fernwood.

Wingo, Ajume. 2006. "The Akan Philosophy of the Person." In *Stanford Encyclopedia of Philosophy* (fall 2008 ed.), ed. E. N. Zalta: online <http://plato.stanford.edu/archives/fall2008/entries/akan-person/>.

Winter, Steven L. 1990. "Indeterminacy and Incommensurability in Constitutional Law." *California Law Review* 78(6):1441–1541.

Wood, Gordon S. 1969. *The Creation of the American Republic, 1776–1787*. Chapel Hill: University of North Carolina Press (for the Omohundro Institute of Early American History and Culture, Williamsburg, Va.).

Woodman, Marion. 1982. *Addiction to Perfection: The Still Unravished Bride: A Psychological Study*. Toronto: Inner City Books.

———. 1985. *The Pregnant Virgin: A Process of Psychological Transformation*. Toronto: Inner City Books.

———. 1990. *The Ravaged Bridegroom: Masculinity in Women*. Toronto: Inner City Books.

Woolf, Virginia. 1929. *A Room of One's Own*. London: Harcourt.

Wortley, Scot. 1999. "A Northern Taboo: Research on Race, Crime, and Criminal Justice in Canada." *Canadian Journal of Criminology* 41(2):261–274.

Yeatman, Anna. 2000. "What Can Disability Tell Us about Participation?" In *Exploration on Law and Disability in Australia*, ed. M. Jones and L. A. B. Marks. Leichardt, N.S.W.: Foundation.

Yehuda, Rachel. 2002. "Post-Traumatic Stress Disorder." *New England Journal of Medicine* 346(2):108–114.

Youm, K. H. 2006. "First Amendment Law: Hate Speech, Equality, and Freedom of Expression." *Journal of Communication* 51(2):406–412.

Young, Iris M. 1988. "Impartiality and the Civic Public." In *Feminism as Critique: On the Politics of Gender*, ed. S. Benhabib and D. Cornell. Minneapolis: University of Minnesota Press.

———. 1990. *Justice and the Politics of Difference*. Princeton, N.J.: Princeton University Press.

———. 1990. *Throwing Like a Girl and Other Essays in Feminist Philosophy and Social Theory*. Bloomington: Indiana University Press.

———. 2002. "Two Concepts of Self-Determination." In *Human Rights: Concepts, Contests, Contingencies*, ed. A. Sarat and T. R. Kearns. Ann Arbor: University of Michigan Press.

Young, Steven M. 1999. "Beyond Neutrality." *University of Toronto Law Journal* 49:151–166.

Zerilli, Linda. 2005. *Feminism and the Abyss of Freedom*. Chicago: University of Chicago Press.

against women and children as systemic, 209–13

women killing battering partners, 175–83

women perpetuating, 432n15

against women with liberal state and relational feminism, 13, 15–16, 200–230

Violence against Women Survey (VAWS), 210, 435n55

Violence Policy Center, 438n63

von Braun, Werner, 203

voting, 439n73

Waddams, Stephen, 391n126, 450n21, 470n70

wage. *See* minimum wage

Waldron, Jeremy, 382n14

Walker, Lenore, 471n4

Walker, Margaret Urban, 42–44

Wallbridge, David, 47

we, as term, 381n1

wealth, 26

Weckerly, Pamela, 442n96

Weil, Alan, 418n122

Welchans, Sarah, 432n12

welfare

autonomy with problems of, 14, 66–67, 139–40, 415n100

Baker v. Canada and, 405n22, 416n113

children and, 431n11

controlling culture of, 417n116

dignity with, 140–41

hearings, 139–40

recipients and language of rights, 392n127

women's autonomy influenced by workability programs and, 386n46

Wendell, Susan, 279, 285–86, 289, 303

West Africa, 382n20

West Coast Hotel Co. v. Parrish, 395n7, 407n38

Westheimer, Ruth, 446n125

We the People (Ackerman), 452n38

White, Julie A., 394n159, 415n100

Whitehead, Alfred North, 111, 113, 466n39

whites, police treatment of, 475n23

The White Hotel (Thomas), 433n20

William, Bernard, 386n56

Williams, Patricia, 76, 251–52

Williams, Susan H., 395n9

Wilson, Bertha, 186, 393n144, 421n48, 487n28

Wilson, James, 407n33

Wilson v. Medical Services Commission, 263

Winnicott, D. W., 47, 48, 388n75

Winter, Steven, 32

witchcraft, 103, 205

wives

assault, 431n8

husbands killing, 184–86, 425n71, 426n76, 438n63

husbands' relationships with, 79–80, 469n67

surety, 390n115, 470n68

women, 408n48, 435n46, 437n60

abuse of immigrant, 473n18

autonomy influenced by workability programs and welfare, 386n46

battering and impact on, 425n65, 425n67

with caregiving, 29, 32, 86

care work for impoverished, 21

common law's *feme covert* and, 452n32

dangers of female sexuality with, 434n26

disenfranchisement and legal inequality of, 394n153

in dissociation, 383n13

equality for men and, 441n93

equality in South Africa for, 428n86

erotic as lifeforce of, 421n41

escaping abuse, 177–81, 473n18

fear and violence curtailing freedom of, 441n91

fear of stranger rape with, 432n12

fears of, 441n92

feelings of safety for white, 478n33

freedom for, 383n12

harm and sexual violence influencing, 23

homicide as leading cause of death in African American, 431n8

husband-wife relationships and, 79–80, 469n67

in India and interdependence on families, 29–30

IPV as leading cause of injury to, 431n8

killed with firearms, 438n63

language of rights with welfare and, 392n127

with law and responsibility for killing battering partners, 175–83

liberal state, relational feminism and violence against, 13, 15–16, 200–230

living in fear, 211–13, 438n63

minimum wage for, 407n38

myth of sexual assault as fault of, 437n62

oppressive relationships and, 403n10

as other, 122